FORD

CROWN VICTORIA/GRAND MARQUIS
1989-98 REPAIR MANUAL

CHILTON'S

CEO	Rick Van Dalen
President	Dean F. Morgantini
Vice President–Finance	Barry L. Beck
Vice President–Sales	Glenn D. Potere
Executive Editor	Kevin M. G. Maher, A.S.E.
Manager–Consumer Automotive	Richard Schwartz, A.S.E.
Manager–Professional Automotive	Richard J. Rivele
Manager–Marine/Recreation	James R. Marotta, A.S.E.
Production Specialist	Melinda Possinger
Project Managers	Tim Crain, A.S.E., Thomas A. Mellon, A.S.E., S.A.E., Eric Michael Mihalyi, A.S.E., S.T.S., S.A.E., Christine L. Sheeky, S.A.E., Richard T. Smith, Ron Webb
Schematics Editors	Christopher G. Ritchie, A.S.E., S.A.E., S.T.S., Stephanie A. Spunt
Editor	Eric Michael Mihalyi, A.S.E., S.A.E., S.T.S.

CHILTON *Automotive Books*

PUBLISHED BY **W. G. NICHOLS, INC.**

Manufactured in USA
© 2000 W. G. Nichols, Inc.
1025 Andrew Drive
West Chester, PA 19380
ISBN 0-8019-8960-4
Library of Congress Catalog Card No. 99-072310
2345678901 0987654321

Contents

Contents

SAFETY NOTICE

Proper service and repair procedures are vital to the safe, reliable operation of all motor vehicles, as well as the personal safety of those performing repairs. This manual outlines procedures for servicing and repairing vehicles using safe, effective methods. The procedures contain many NOTES, CAUTIONS and WARNINGS which should be followed, along with standard procedures to eliminate the possibility of personal injury or improper service which could damage the vehicle or compromise its safety.

It is important to note that repair procedures and techniques, tools and parts for servicing motor vehicles, as well as the skill and experience of the individual performing the work vary widely. It is not possible to anticipate all of the conceivable ways or conditions under which vehicles may be serviced, or to provide cautions as to all possible hazards that may result. Standard and accepted safety precautions and equipment should be used when handling toxic or flammable fluids, and safety goggles or other protection should be used during cutting, grinding, chiseling, prying, or any other process that can cause material removal or projectiles.

Some procedures require the use of tools specially designed for a specific purpose. Before substituting another tool or procedure, you must be completely satisfied that neither your personal safety, nor the performance of the vehicle will be endangered.

Although information in this manual is based on industry sources and is complete as possible at the time of publication, the possibility exists that some car manufacturers made later changes which could not be included here. While striving for total accuracy, Nichols Publishing cannot assume responsibility for any errors, changes or omissions that may occur in the compilation of this data.

PART NUMBERS

Part numbers listed in this reference are not recommendations by Nichols Publishing for any product brand name. They are references that can be used with interchange manuals and aftermarket supplier catalogs to locate each brand supplier's discrete part number.

SPECIAL TOOLS

Special tools are recommended by the vehicle manufacturer to perform their specific job. Use has been kept to a minimum, but where absolutely necessary, they are referred to in the text by the part number of the tool manufacturer. These tools can be purchased, under the appropriate part number, from your local dealer or regional distributor, or an equivalent tool can be purchased locally from a tool supplier or parts outlet. Before substituting any tool for the one recommended, read the SAFETY NOTICE at the top of this page.

ACKNOWLEDGMENTS

This publication contains material that is reproduced and distributed under a license from Ford Motor Company. No further reproduction or distribution of the Ford Motor Company material is allowed without the express written permission from Ford Motor Company.

Nichols Publishing would like to express thanks to all of the fine companies who participate in the production of our books:
- Hand tools supplied by Craftsman are used during all phases of our vehicle teardown and photography.
- Many of the fine specialty tools used in our procedures were provided courtesy of Lisle Corporation.
- Lincoln Automotive Products (1 Lincoln Way, St. Louis, MO 63120) has provided their industrial shop equipment, including jacks (engine, transmission and floor), engine stands, fluid and lubrication tools, as well as shop presses.
- Rotary Lifts (1-800-640-5438 or www.Rotary-Lift.com), the largest automobile lift manufacturer in the world, offering the biggest variety of surface and in-ground lifts available, has fulfilled our shop's lift needs.
- Much of our shop's electronic testing equipment was supplied by Universal Enterprises Inc. (UEI).
- Safety-Kleen Systems Inc. has provided parts cleaning stations and assistance with environmentally sound disposal of residual wastes.
- United Gilsonite Laboratories (UGL), manufacturer of Drylok® concrete floor paint, has provided materials and expertise for the coating and protection of our shop floor.

1

GENERAL INFORMATION AND MAINTENANCE

HOW TO USE THIS BOOK

Chilton's Total Car Care manual for 1989–98 Ford Crown Victoria and Mercury Grand Marquis is intended to help you learn more about the inner workings of your vehicle while saving you money on its upkeep and operation.

The beginning of the book will likely be referred to the most, since that is where you will find information for maintenance and tune-up. The other sections deal with the more complex systems of your vehicle. Operating systems from engine through brakes are covered to the extent that the average do-it-yourselfer becomes mechanically involved. This book will not explain such things as rebuilding a differential for the simple reason that the expertise required and the investment in special tools make this task uneconomical. It will, however, give you detailed instructions to help you change your own brake pads and shoes, replace spark plugs, and perform many more jobs that can save you money, give you personal satisfaction and help you avoid expensive problems.

A secondary purpose of this book is a reference for owners who want to understand their vehicle and/or their mechanics better. In this case, no tools at all are required.

Where to Begin

Before removing any bolts, read through the entire procedure. This will give you the overall view of what tools and supplies will be required. There is nothing more frustrating than having to walk to the bus stop on Monday morning because you were short one bolt on Sunday afternoon. So read ahead and plan ahead. Each operation should be approached logically and all procedures thoroughly understood before attempting any work.

All sections contain adjustments, maintenance, removal and installation procedures, and in some cases, repair or overhaul procedures. When repair is not considered practical, we tell you how to remove the part and then how to install the new or rebuilt replacement. In this way, you at least save labor costs. "Backyard" repair of some components is just not practical.

Avoiding Trouble

Many procedures in this book require you to "label and disconnect . . ." a group of lines, hoses or wires. Don't be lulled into thinking you can remember where everything goes—you won't. If you hook up vacuum or fuel lines incorrectly, the vehicle may run poorly, if at all. If you hook up electrical wiring incorrectly, you may instantly learn a very expensive lesson.

You don't need to know the official or engineering name for each hose or line. A piece of masking tape on the hose and a piece on its fitting will allow you to assign your own label such as the letter A or a short name. As long as you remember your own code, the lines can be reconnected by matching similar letters or names. Do remember that tape will dissolve in gasoline or other fluids; if a component is to be washed or cleaned, use another method of identification. A permanent felt-tipped marker or a metal scribe can be very handy for marking metal parts. Remove any tape or paper labels after assembly.

Maintenance or Repair?

It's necessary to mention the difference between maintenance and repair. Maintenance includes routine inspections, adjustments, and replacement of parts which show signs of normal wear. Maintenance compensates for wear or deterioration. Repair implies that something has broken or is not working. A need for repair is often caused by lack of maintenance. Example: draining and refilling the automatic transmission fluid is maintenance recommended by the manufacturer at specific mileage intervals. Failure to do this can shorten the life of the transmission, requiring very expensive repairs. While no maintenance program can prevent items from breaking or wearing out, a general rule can be stated: MAINTENANCE IS CHEAPER THAN REPAIR.

TOOLS AND EQUIPMENT

▶ **See Figures 1 thru 15**

Naturally, without the proper tools and equipment it is impossible to properly service your vehicle. It would also be virtually impossible to catalog every tool that you would need to perform all of the operations in this book. Of course, It would be unwise for the amateur to rush out and buy an expensive

Two basic mechanic's rules should be mentioned here. First, whenever the left side of the vehicle or engine is referred to, it is meant to specify the driver's side. Conversely, the right side of the vehicle means the passenger's side. Second, screws and bolts are removed by turning counterclockwise, and tightened by turning clockwise unless specifically noted.

Safety is always the most important rule. Constantly be aware of the dangers involved in working on an automobile and take the proper precautions. See the information in this section regarding SERVICING YOUR VEHICLE SAFELY and the SAFETY NOTICE on the acknowledgment page.

Avoiding the Most Common Mistakes

Pay attention to the instructions provided. There are 3 common mistakes in mechanical work:

1. Incorrect order of assembly, disassembly or adjustment. When taking something apart or putting it together, performing steps in the wrong order usually just costs you extra time; however, it CAN break something. Read the entire procedure before beginning disassembly. Perform everything in the order in which the instructions say you should, even if you can't immediately see a reason for it. When you're taking apart something that is very intricate, you might want to draw a picture of how it looks when assembled at one point in order to make sure you get everything back in its proper position. We will supply exploded views whenever possible. When making adjustments, perform them in the proper order. One adjustment possibly will affect another.

2. Overtorquing (or undertorquing). While it is more common for overtorquing to cause damage, undertorquing may allow a fastener to vibrate loose causing serious damage. Especially when dealing with aluminum parts, pay attention to torque specifications and utilize a torque wrench in assembly. If a torque figure is not available, remember that if you are using the right tool to perform the job, you will probably not have to strain yourself to get a fastener tight enough. The pitch of most threads is so slight that the tension you put on the wrench will be multiplied many times in actual force on what you are tightening. A good example of how critical torque is can be seen in the case of spark plug installation, especially where you are putting the plug into an aluminum cylinder head. Too little torque can fail to crush the gasket, causing leakage of combustion gases and consequent overheating of the plug and engine parts. Too much torque can damage the threads or distort the plug, changing the spark gap.

There are many commercial products available for ensuring that fasteners won't come loose, even if they are not torqued just right (a very common brand is Loctite®). If you're worried about getting something together tight enough to hold, but loose enough to avoid mechanical damage during assembly, one of these products might offer substantial insurance. Before choosing a threadlocking compound, read the label on the package and make sure the product is compatible with the materials, fluids, etc. involved.

3. Crossthreading. This occurs when a part such as a bolt is screwed into a nut or casting at the wrong angle and forced. Crossthreading is more likely to occur if access is difficult. It helps to clean and lubricate fasteners, then to start threading the bolt, spark plug, etc. with your fingers. If you encounter resistance, unscrew the part and start over again at a different angle until it can be inserted and turned several times without much effort. Keep in mind that many parts, especially spark plugs, have tapered threads, so that gentle turning will automatically bring the part you're threading to the proper angle. Don't put a wrench on the part until it's been tightened a couple of turns by hand. If you suddenly encounter resistance, and the part has not seated fully, don't force it. Pull it back out to make sure it's clean and threading properly.

Be sure to take your time and be patient, and always plan ahead. Allow yourself ample time to perform repairs and maintenance. You may find maintaining your car a satisfying and enjoyable experience.

set of tools on the theory that he/she may need one or more of them at some time.

The best approach is to proceed slowly, gathering a good quality set of those tools that are used most frequently. Don't be misled by the low cost of bargain tools. It is far better to spend a little more for better quality. Forged wrenches, 6 or 12-point sockets and fine tooth ratchets are by far preferable to their less expensive counterparts. As any good mechanic can tell you, there are few worse experiences than trying to work on a vehicle with bad tools. Your monetary savings will be far outweighed by frustration and mangled knuckles.

Begin accumulating those tools that are used most frequently: those associated with routine maintenance and tune-up. In addition to the normal assortment of screwdrivers and pliers, you should have the following tools:

• Wrenches/sockets and combination open end/box end wrenches in sizes from ⅛–¾ in. or 3–19mm, as well as a ¹³⁄₁₆ in. or ⅝ in. spark plug socket (depending on plug type).

➡ **If possible, buy various length socket drive extensions. Universal-joint and wobble extensions can be extremely useful, but be careful when using them, as they can change the amount of torque applied to the socket.**

• Jackstands for support.
• Oil filter wrench.

• Spout or funnel for pouring fluids.
• Grease gun for chassis lubrication (unless your vehicle is not equipped with any grease fittings—for details, please refer to information on Fluids and Lubricants, later in this section).
• Hydrometer for checking the battery (unless equipped with a sealed, maintenance-free battery).
• A container for draining oil and other fluids.
• Rags for wiping up the inevitable mess.

In addition to the above items there are several others that are not absolutely necessary, but handy to have around. These include Oil Dry• (or an equivalent oil absorbent gravel—such as cat litter) and the usual supply of lubricants, antifreeze and fluids, although these can be purchased as needed. This is a basic list for routine maintenance, but only your personal needs and desire can accurately determine your list of tools.

After performing a few projects on the vehicle, you'll be amazed at the other tools and non-tools on your workbench. Some useful household items are: a large turkey baster or siphon, empty coffee cans and ice trays (to store parts),

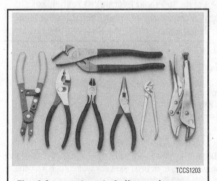

Fig. 1 All but the most basic procedures will require an assortment of ratchets and sockets

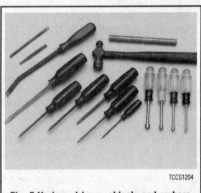

Fig. 2 In addition to ratchets, a good set of wrenches and hex keys will be necessary

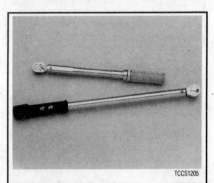

Fig. 3 A hydraulic floor jack and a set of jackstands are essential for lifting and supporting the vehicle

Fig. 4 An assortment of pliers, grippers and cutters will be handy for old rusted parts and stripped bolt heads

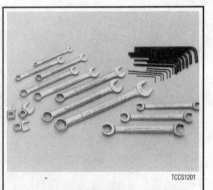

Fig. 5 Various drivers, chisels and prybars are great tools to have in your toolbox

Fig. 6 Many repairs will require the use of a torque wrench to assure the components are properly fastened

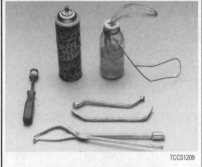

Fig. 7 Although not always necessary, using specialized brake tools will save time

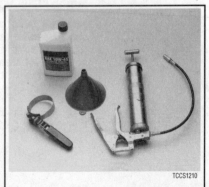

Fig. 8 A few inexpensive lubrication tools will make maintenance easier

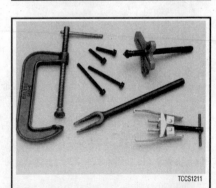

Fig. 9 Various pullers, clamps and separator tools are needed for many larger, more complicated repairs

Fig. 10 A variety of tools and gauges should be used for spark plug gapping and installation

Fig. 11 Inductive type timing light

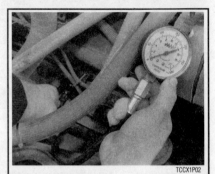

Fig. 12 A screw-in type compression gauge is recommended for compression testing

Fig. 13 A vacuum/pressure tester is necessary for many testing procedures

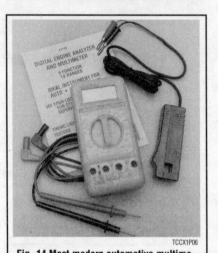

Fig. 14 Most modern automotive multimeters incorporate many helpful features

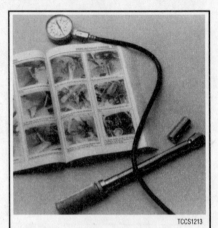

Fig. 15 Proper information is vital, so always have a Chilton Total Car Care manual handy

ball of twine, electrical tape for wiring, small rolls of colored tape for tagging lines or hoses, markers and pens, a note pad, golf tees (for plugging vacuum lines), metal coat hangers or a roll of mechanic's wire (to hold things out of the way), dental pick or similar long, pointed probe, a strong magnet, and a small mirror (to see into recesses and under manifolds).

A more advanced set of tools, suitable for tune-up work, can be drawn up easily. While the tools are slightly more sophisticated, they need not be outrageously expensive. There are several inexpensive tach/dwell meters on the market that are every bit as good for the average mechanic as a professional model. Just be sure that it goes to a least 1200–1500 rpm on the tach scale and that it works on 4, 6 and 8-cylinder engines. The key to these purchases is to make them with an eye towards adaptability and wide range. A basic list of tune-up tools could include:

- Tach/dwell meter.
- Spark plug wrench and gapping tool.
- Feeler gauges for valve adjustment.
- Timing light.

The choice of a timing light should be made carefully. A light which works on the DC current supplied by the vehicle's battery is the best choice; it should have a xenon tube for brightness. On any vehicle with an electronic ignition system, a timing light with an inductive pickup that clamps around the No. 1 spark plug cable is preferred.

In addition to these basic tools, there are several other tools and gauges you may find useful. These include:

- Compression gauge. The screw-in type is slower to use, but eliminates the possibility of a faulty reading due to escaping pressure.

- Manifold vacuum gauge.
- 12V test light.
- A combination volt/ohmmeter
- Induction Ammeter. This is used for determining whether or not there is current in a wire. These are handy for use if a wire is broken somewhere in a wiring harness.

As a final note, you will probably find a torque wrench necessary for all but the most basic work. The beam type models are perfectly adequate, although the newer click types (breakaway) are easier to use. The click type torque wrenches tend to be more expensive. Also keep in mind that all types of torque wrenches should be periodically checked and/or recalibrated. You will have to decide for yourself which better fits your pocketbook, and purpose.

Special Tools

Normally, the use of special factory tools is avoided for repair procedures, since these are not readily available for the do-it-yourself mechanic. When it is possible to perform the job with more commonly available tools, it will be pointed out, but occasionally, a special tool was designed to perform a specific function and should be used. Before substituting another tool, you should be convinced that neither your safety nor the performance of the vehicle will be compromised.

Special tools can usually be purchased from an automotive parts store or from your dealer. In some cases special tools may be available directly from the tool manufacturer.

IN A SPORT THAT DEMANDS NERVES BE MADE OF STEEL, YOU CAN IMAGINE HOW TOUGH THE TOOLS HAVE TO BE.

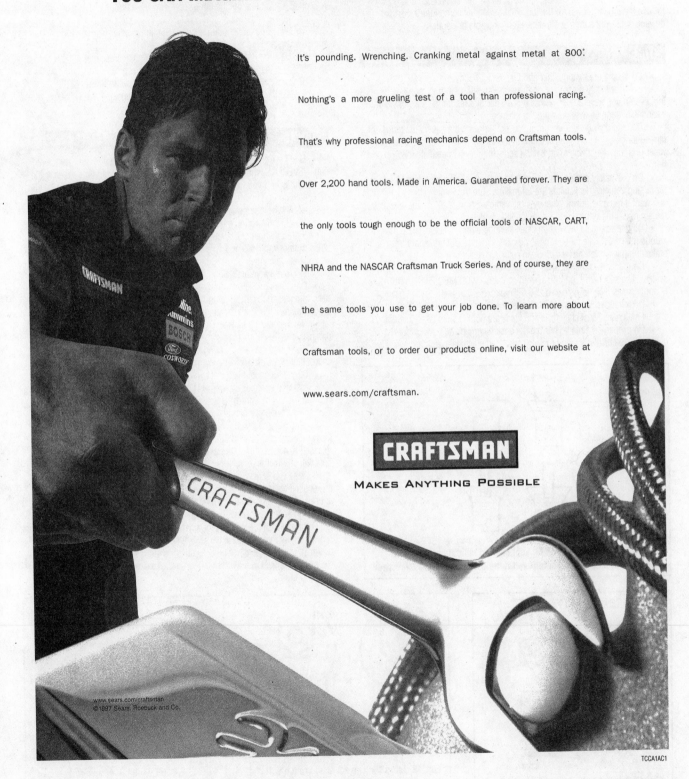

TCCA1AC1

SERVICING YOUR VEHICLE SAFELY

▶ **See Figures 16, 17, 18 and 19**

It is virtually impossible to anticipate all of the hazards involved with automotive maintenance and service, but care and common sense will prevent most accidents.

The rules of safety for mechanics range from "don't smoke around gasoline," to "use the proper tool(s) for the job." The trick to avoiding injuries is to develop safe work habits and to take every possible precaution.

Do's

- Do keep a fire extinguisher and first aid kit handy.
- Do wear safety glasses or goggles when cutting, drilling, grinding or prying, even if you have 20–20 vision. If you wear glasses for the sake of vision, wear safety goggles over your regular glasses.
- Do shield your eyes whenever you work around the battery. Batteries contain sulfuric acid. In case of contact with the eyes or skin, flush the area with water or a mixture of water and baking soda, then seek immediate medical attention.
- Do use safety stands (jackstands) for any undervehicle service. Jacks are for raising vehicles; jackstands are for making sure the vehicle stays raised until you want it to come down. Whenever the vehicle is raised, block the wheels remaining on the ground and set the parking brake.
- Do use adequate ventilation when working with any chemicals or hazardous materials. Like carbon monoxide, the asbestos dust resulting from some brake lining wear can be hazardous in sufficient quantities.
- Do disconnect the negative battery cable when working on the electrical system. The secondary ignition system contains EXTREMELY HIGH VOLTAGE. In some cases it can even exceed 50,000 volts.
- Do follow manufacturer's directions whenever working with potentially hazardous materials. Most chemicals and fluids are poisonous if taken internally.
- Do properly maintain your tools. Loose hammerheads, mushroomed punches and chisels, frayed or poorly grounded electrical cords, excessively worn screwdrivers, spread wrenches (open end), cracked sockets, slipping ratchets, or faulty droplight sockets can cause accidents.
- Likewise, keep your tools clean; a greasy wrench can slip off a bolt head, ruining the bolt and often harming your knuckles in the process.
- Do use the proper size and type of tool for the job at hand. Do select a wrench or socket that fits the nut or bolt. The wrench or socket should sit straight, not cocked.
- Do, when possible, pull on a wrench handle rather than push on it, and adjust your stance to prevent a fall.
- Do be sure that adjustable wrenches are tightly closed on the nut or bolt and pulled so that the force is on the side of the fixed jaw.
- Do strike squarely with a hammer; avoid glancing blows.
- Do set the parking brake and block the drive wheels if the work requires a running engine.

Don'ts

- Don't run the engine in a garage or anywhere else without proper ventilation—EVER! Carbon monoxide is poisonous; it takes a long time to leave the human body and you can build up a deadly supply of it in your system by simply breathing in a little every day. You may not realize you are slowly poisoning yourself. Always use power vents, windows, fans and/or open the garage door.
- Don't work around moving parts while wearing loose clothing. Short sleeves are much safer than long, loose sleeves. Hard-toed shoes with neoprene soles protect your toes and give a better grip on slippery surfaces. Jewelry such as watches, fancy belt buckles, beads or body adornment of any kind is not safe working around a vehicle. Long hair should be tied back under a hat or cap.
- Don't use pockets for toolboxes. A fall or bump can drive a screwdriver deep into your body. Even a rag hanging from your back pocket can wrap around a spinning shaft or fan.
- Don't smoke when working around gasoline, cleaning solvent or other flammable material.
- Don't smoke when working around the battery. When the battery is being charged, it gives off explosive hydrogen gas.
- Don't use gasoline to wash your hands; there are excellent soaps available. Gasoline contains dangerous additives which can enter the body through a cut or through your pores. Gasoline also removes all the natural oils from the skin so that bone dry hands will suck up oil and grease.
- Don't service the air conditioning system unless you are equipped with the necessary tools and training. When liquid or compressed gas refrigerant is released to atmospheric pressure it will absorb heat from whatever it contacts. This will chill or freeze anything it touches.
- Don't use screwdrivers for anything other than driving screws! A screwdriver used as an prying tool can snap when you least expect it, causing injuries. At the very least, you'll ruin a good screwdriver.
- Don't use an emergency jack (that little ratchet, scissors, or pantograph jack supplied with the vehicle) for anything other than changing a flat! These jacks are only intended for emergency use out on the road; they are NOT designed as a maintenance tool. If you are serious about maintaining your vehicle yourself, invest in a hydraulic floor jack of at least a 1½ ton capacity, and at least two sturdy jackstands.

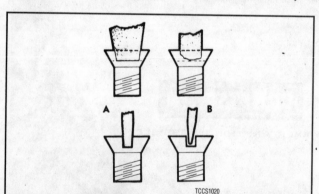

TCCS1020

Fig. 16 Screwdrivers should be kept in good condition to prevent injury or damage which could result if the blade slips from the screw

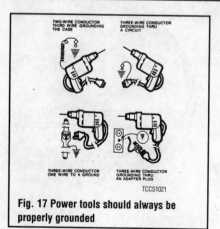

TCCS1021

Fig. 17 Power tools should always be properly grounded

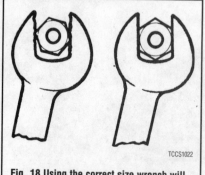

TCCS1022

Fig. 18 Using the correct size wrench will help prevent the possibility of rounding off a nut

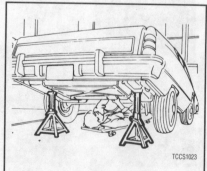

TCCS1023

Fig. 19 NEVER work under a vehicle unless it is supported using safety stands (jackstands)

FASTENERS, MEASUREMENTS AND CONVERSIONS

Bolts, Nuts and Other Threaded Retainers

▶ **See Figures 20, 21, 22 and 23**

Although there are a great variety of fasteners found in the modern car or truck, the most commonly used retainer is the threaded fastener (nuts, bolts, screws, studs, etc.). Most threaded retainers may be reused, provided that they are not damaged in use or during the repair. Some retainers (such as stretch bolts or torque prevailing nuts) are designed to deform when tightened or in use and should not be reinstalled.

Whenever possible, we will note any special retainers which should be replaced during a procedure. But you should always inspect the condition of a retainer when it is removed and replace any that show signs of damage. Check all threads for rust or corrosion which can increase the torque necessary to achieve the desired clamp load for which that fastener was originally selected. Additionally, be sure that the driver surface of the fastener has not been compromised by rounding or other damage. In some cases a driver surface may become only partially rounded, allowing the driver to catch in only one direction. In many of these occurrences, a fastener may be installed and tightened, but the driver would not be able to grip and loosen the fastener again. (This could lead to frustration down the line should that component ever need to be disassembled again).

If you must replace a fastener, whether due to design or damage, you must ALWAYS be sure to use the proper replacement. In all cases, a retainer of the same design, material and strength should be used. Markings on the heads of most bolts will help determine the proper strength of the fastener. The same material, thread and pitch must be selected to assure proper installation and safe operation of the vehicle afterwards.

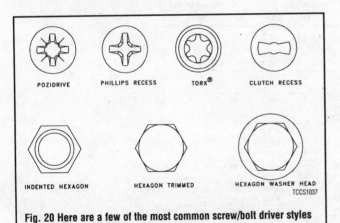

Fig. 20 Here are a few of the most common screw/bolt driver styles

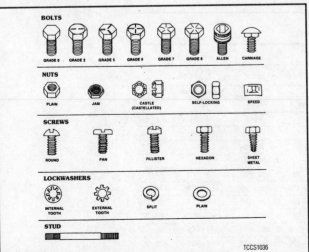

Fig. 21 There are many different types of threaded retainers found on vehicles

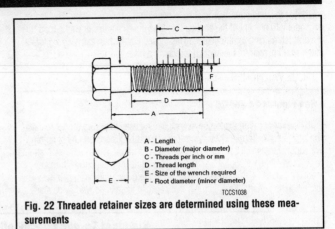

Fig. 22 Threaded retainer sizes are determined using these measurements

A - Length
B - Diameter (major diameter)
C - Threads per inch or mm
D - Thread length
E - Size of the wrench required
F - Root diameter (minor diameter)

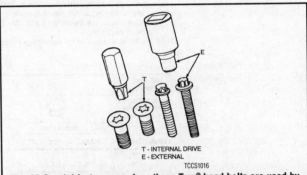

T - INTERNAL DRIVE
E - EXTERNAL

Fig. 23 Special fasteners such as these Torx® head bolts are used by manufacturers to discourage people from working on vehicles without the proper tools

Thread gauges are available to help measure a bolt or stud's thread. Most automotive and hardware stores keep gauges available to help you select the proper size. In a pinch, you can use another nut or bolt for a thread gauge. If the bolt you are replacing is not too badly damaged, you can select a match by finding another bolt which will thread in its place. If you find a nut which threads properly onto the damaged bolt, then use that nut to help select the replacement bolt. If however, the bolt you are replacing is so badly damaged (broken or drilled out) that its threads cannot be used as a gauge, you might start by looking for another bolt (from the same assembly or a similar location on your vehicle) which will thread into the damaged bolt's mounting. If so, the other bolt can be used to select a nut; the nut can then be used to select the replacement bolt.

In all cases, be absolutely sure you have selected the proper replacement. Don't be shy, you can always ask the store clerk for help.

❈❈ WARNING

Be aware that when you find a bolt with damaged threads, you may also find the nut or drilled hole it was threaded into has also been damaged. If this is the case, you may have to drill and tap the hole, replace the nut or otherwise repair the threads. NEVER try to force a replacement bolt to fit into the damaged threads.

Torque

Torque is defined as the measurement of resistance to turning or rotating. It tends to twist a body about an axis of rotation. A common example of this would be tightening a threaded retainer such as a nut, bolt or screw. Measuring torque is one of the most common ways to help assure that a threaded retainer has been properly fastened.

When tightening a threaded fastener, torque is applied in three distinct areas, the head, the bearing surface and the clamp load. About 50 percent of the measured torque is used in overcoming bearing friction. This is the friction between the bearing surface of the bolt head, screw head or nut face and the base material or washer (the surface on which the fastener is rotating). Approximately 40 percent of the applied torque is used in overcoming thread friction. This leaves only about 10 percent of the applied torque to develop a useful clamp load (the force which holds a joint together). This means that friction can account for as much as 90 percent of the applied torque on a fastener.

TORQUE WRENCHES

➧ See Figures 24 and 25

In most applications, a torque wrench can be used to assure proper installation of a fastener. Torque wrenches come in various designs and most automotive supply stores will carry a variety to suit your needs. A torque wrench should be used any time we supply a specific torque value for a fastener. A torque wrench can also be used if you are following the general guidelines in the accompanying charts. Keep in mind that because there is no worldwide stan-

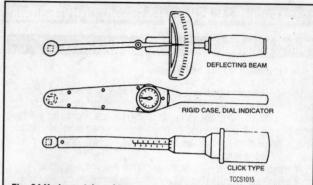

Fig. 24 Various styles of torque wrenches are usually available at your local automotive supply store

Standard Torque Specifications and Fastener Markings

In the absence of specific torques, the following chart can be used as a guide to the maximum safe torque of a particular size/grade of fastener.

- There is no torque difference for fine or coarse threads.
- Torque values are based on clean, dry threads. Reduce the value by 10% if threads are oiled prior to assembly.
- The torque required for aluminum components or fasteners is considerably less.

U.S. Bolts

SAE Grade Number	1 or 2			5			6 or 7		
Number of lines always 2 less than the grade number.									
Bolt Size	Maximum Torque			Maximum Torque			Maximum Torque		
(Inches)—(Thread)	Ft./Lbs.	Kgm	Nm	Ft./Lbs.	Kgm	Nm	Ft./Lbs.	Kgm	Nm
¼—20	5	0.7	6.8	8	1.1	10.8	10	1.4	13.5
—28	6	0.8	8.1	10	1.4	13.6			
5/16—18	11	1.5	14.9	17	2.3	23.0	19	2.6	25.8
—24	13	1.8	17.6	19	2.6	25.7			
⅜—16	18	2.5	24.4	31	4.3	42.0	34	4.7	46.0
—24	20	2.75	27.1	35	4.8	47.5			
7/16—14	28	3.8	37.0	49	6.8	66.4	55	7.6	74.5
—20	30	4.2	40.7	55	7.6	74.5			
½—13	39	5.4	52.8	75	10.4	101.7	85	11.75	115.2
—20	41	5.7	55.6	85	11.7	115.2			
9/16—12	51	7.0	69.2	110	15.2	149.1	120	16.6	162.7
—18	55	7.6	74.5	120	16.6	162.7			
⅝—11	83	11.5	112.5	150	20.7	203.3	167	23.0	226.5
—18	95	13.1	128.8	170	23.5	230.5			
¾—10	105	14.5	142.3	270	37.3	366.0	280	38.7	379.6
—16	115	15.9	155.9	295	40.8	400.0			
⅞—9	160	22.1	216.9	395	54.6	535.5	440	60.9	596.5
—14	175	24.2	237.2	435	60.1	589.7			
1—8	236	32.5	318.6	590	81.6	799.9	660	91.3	894.8
—14	250	34.6	338.9	660	91.3	849.8			

Metric Bolts

Relative Strength Marking	4.6, 4.8			8.8		
Bolt Markings						
Bolt Size	Maximum Torque			Maximum Torque		
Thread Size x Pitch (mm)	Ft./Lbs.	Kgm	Nm	Ft./Lbs.	Kgm	Nm
6 x 1.0	2–3	.2–.4	3–4	3–6	4–.8	5–8
8 x 1.25	6–8	.8–1	8–12	9–14	1.2–1.9	13–19
10 x 1.25	12–17	1.5–2.3	16–23	20–29	2.7–4.0	27–39
12 x 1.25	21–32	2.9–4.4	29–43	35–53	4.8–7.3	47–72
14 x 1.5	35–52	4.8–7.1	48–70	57–85	7.8–11.7	77–110
16 x 1.5	51–77	7.0–10.6	67–100	90–120	12.4–16.5	130–160
18 x 1.5	74–110	10.2–15.1	100–150	130–170	17.9–23.4	180–230
20 x 1.5	110–140	15.1–19.3	150–190	190–240	26.2–46.9	160–320
22 x 1.5	150–190	22.0–26.2	200–260	250–320	34.5–44.1	340–430
24 x 1.5	190–240	26.2–46.9	260–320	310–410	42.7–56.5	420–550

TCCS1098

Fig. 25 Standard and metric bolt torque specifications based on bolt strengths—WARNING: use only as a guide

dardization of fasteners, the charts are a general guideline and should be used with caution. Again, the general rule of "if you are using the right tool for the job, you should not have to strain to tighten a fastener" applies here.

Beam Type

▶ See Figure 26

The beam type torque wrench is one of the most popular types. It consists of a pointer attached to the head that runs the length of the flexible beam (shaft) to a scale located near the handle. As the wrench is pulled, the beam bends and the pointer indicates the torque using the scale.

Click (Breakaway) Type

▶ See Figure 27

Another popular design of torque wrench is the click type. To use the click type wrench you pre-adjust it to a torque setting. Once the torque is reached, the wrench has a reflex signaling feature that causes a momentary breakaway of the torque wrench body, sending an impulse to the operator's hand.

Pivot Head Type

▶ See Figures 27 and 28

Some torque wrenches (usually of the click type) may be equipped with a pivot head which can allow it to be used in areas of limited access. BUT, it must be used properly. To hold a pivot head wrench, grasp the handle lightly, and as you pull on the handle, it should be floated on the pivot point. If the handle comes in contact with the yoke extension during the process of pulling, there is a very good chance the torque readings will be inaccurate because this could alter the wrench loading point. The design of the handle is usually such as to make it inconvenient to deliberately misuse the wrench.

➡️It should be mentioned that the use of any U-joint, wobble or extension will have an effect on the torque readings, no matter what type of wrench you are using. For the most accurate readings, install the socket directly on the wrench driver. If necessary, straight extensions (which hold a socket directly under the wrench driver) will have the least effect on the torque reading. Avoid any extension that alters the length of the wrench from the handle to the head/driving point (such as a crow's foot). U-joint or wobble extensions can greatly affect the readings; avoid their use at all times.

Rigid Case (Direct Reading)

▶ See Figure 29

A rigid case or direct reading torque wrench is equipped with a dial indicator to show torque values. One advantage of these wrenches is that they can be held at any position on the wrench without affecting accuracy. These wrenches are often preferred because they tend to be compact, easy to read and have a great degree of accuracy.

TORQUE ANGLE METERS

▶ See Figure 30

Because the frictional characteristics of each fastener or threaded hole will vary, clamp loads which are based strictly on torque will vary as well. In most applications, this variance is not significant enough to cause worry. But, in certain applications, a manufacturer's engineers may determine that more precise clamp loads are necessary (such is the case with many aluminum cylinder heads). In these cases, a torque angle method of installation would be specified. When installing fasteners which are torque angle tightened, a predetermined seating torque and standard torque wrench are usually used first to remove any compliance from the joint. The fastener is then tightened the specified additional portion of a turn measured in degrees. A torque angle gauge (mechanical protractor) is used for these applications.

Standard and Metric Measurements

▶ See Figure 31

Throughout this manual, specifications are given to help you determine the condition of various components on your vehicle, or to assist you in their installation. Some of the most common measurements include length (in. or

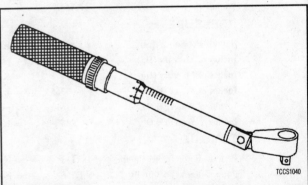

Fig. 27 A click type or breakaway torque wrench—note that this one has a pivoting head

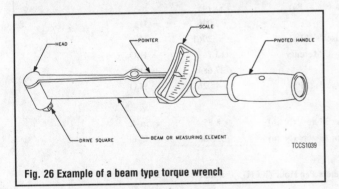

Fig. 26 Example of a beam type torque wrench

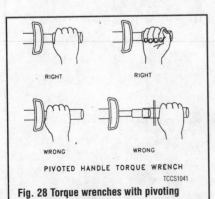

Fig. 28 Torque wrenches with pivoting heads must be grasped and used properly to prevent an incorrect reading

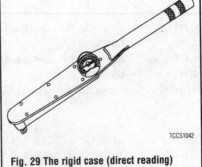

Fig. 29 The rigid case (direct reading) torque wrench uses a dial indicator to show torque

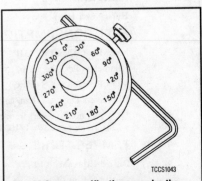

Fig. 30 Some specifications require the use of a torque angle meter (mechanical protractor)

cm/mm), torque (ft. lbs., inch lbs. or Nm) and pressure (psi, in. Hg, kPa or mm Hg). In most cases, we strive to provide the proper measurement as determined by the manufacturer's engineers.

Though, in some cases, that value may not be conveniently measured with what is available in your toolbox. Luckily, many of the measuring devices which are available today will have two scales so the Standard or Metric measurements may easily be taken. If any of the various measuring tools which are available to you do not contain the same scale as listed in the specifications, use the accompanying conversion factors to determine the proper value.

The conversion factor chart is used by taking the given specification and multiplying it by the necessary conversion factor. For instance, looking at the first line, if you have a measurement in inches such as "free-play should be 2 in." but your ruler reads only in millimeters, multiply 2 in. by the conversion factor of 25.4 to get the metric equivalent of 50.8mm. Likewise, if the specification was given only in a Metric measurement, for example in Newton Meters (Nm), then look at the center column first. If the measurement is 100 Nm, multiply it by the conversion factor of 0.738 to get 73.8 ft. lbs.

CONVERSION FACTORS

LENGTH–DISTANCE

Inches (in.)	x 25.4	= Millimeters (mm)	x .0394	= Inches
Feet (ft.)	x .305	= Meters (m)	x 3.281	= Feet
Miles	x 1.609	= Kilometers (km)	x .0621	= Miles

VOLUME

Cubic Inches (in3)	x 16.387	= Cubic Centimeters	x .061	= in3
IMP Pints (IMP pt.)	x .568	= Liters (L)	x 1.76	= IMP pt.
IMP Quarts (IMP qt.)	x 1.137	= Liters (L)	x .88	= IMP qt.
IMP Gallons (IMP gal.)	x 4.546	= Liters (L)	x .22	= IMP gal.
IMP Quarts (IMP qt.)	x 1.201	= US Quarts (US qt.)	x .833	= IMP qt.
IMP Gallons (IMP gal.)	x 1.201	= US Gallons (US gal.)	x .833	= IMP gal.
Fl. Ounces	x 29.573	= Milliliters	x .034	= Ounces
US Pints (US pt.)	x .473	= Liters (L)	x 2.113	= Pints
US Quarts (US qt.)	x .946	= Liters (L)	x 1.057	= Quarts
US Gallons (US gal.)	x 3.785	= Liters (L)	x .264	= Gallons

MASS–WEIGHT

Ounces (oz.)	x 28.35	= Grams (g)	x .035	= Ounces
Pounds (lb.)	x .454	= Kilograms (kg)	x 2.205	= Pounds

PRESSURE

Pounds Per Sq. In. (psi)	x 6.895	= Kilopascals (kPa)	x .145	= psi
Inches of Mercury (Hg)	x .4912	= psi	x 2.036	= Hg
Inches of Mercury (Hg)	x 3.377	= Kilopascals (kPa)	x .2961	= Hg
Inches of Water (H_2O)	x .07355	= Inches of Mercury	x 13.783	= H_2O
Inches of Water (H_2O)	x .03613	= psi	x 27.684	= H_2O
Inches of Water (H_2O)	x .248	= Kilopascals (kPa)	x 4.026	= H_2O

TORQUE

Pounds–Force Inches (in–lb)	x .113	= Newton Meters (N·m)	x 8.85	= in–lb
Pounds–Force Feet (ft–lb)	x 1.356	= Newton Meters (N·m)	x .738	= ft–lb

VELOCITY

Miles Per Hour (MPH)	x 1.609	= Kilometers Per Hour (KPH)	x .621	= MPH

POWER

Horsepower (Hp)	x .745	= Kilowatts	x 1.34	= Horsepower

FUEL CONSUMPTION*

Miles Per Gallon IMP (MPG)	x .354	= Kilometers Per Liter (Km/L)
Kilometers Per Liter (Km/L)	x 2.352	= IMP MPG
Miles Per Gallon US (MPG)	x .425	= Kilometers Per Liter (Km/L)
Kilometers Per Liter (Km/L)	x 2.352	= US MPG

*It is common to covert from miles per gallon (mpg) to liters/100 kilometers (1/100 km), where mpg (IMP) x 1/100 km = 282 and mpg (US) x 1/100 km = 235.

TEMPERATURE

Degree Fahrenheit (°F)	= (°C x 1.8) + 32
Degree Celsius (°C)	= (°F – 32) x .56

TCCS1044

Fig. 31 Standard and metric conversion factors chart

SERIAL NUMBER IDENTIFICATION

Vehicle

♦ See Figures 32, 33 and 34

The Vehicle Identification Number (VIN) is stamped on a metal plate that is fastened to the instrument panel adjacent to the windshield. It can be seen by looking through the lower corner of the windshield on the driver's side.

The VIN is a 17 digit combination of numbers and letters. The first 3 digits represent the world manufacturer identifier. Using the example in the figure, the number and letter combination 2FA signifies Ford Motor Company of Canada, Ltd. The 4th digit indicates the type of passenger restraint system; in the exam-

ple the letter C stands for active belts and a driver's side air bag. The 5th digit is a constant, the letter P signifying passenger car. The 6th and 7th digits indicate the body style, in this case 74 for a Crown Victoria LX. The 8th digit is the engine code: F for the 5.0L engine, G for the 5.8L engine or in this case W for the 4.6L engine. The 9th digit is a check digit for all vehicles. The 10th digit indicates the model year. The 11th digit is the assembly plant code, the letter X represents St. Thomas, Ontario, Canada. The 12th through 17th digits indicate the production sequence number.

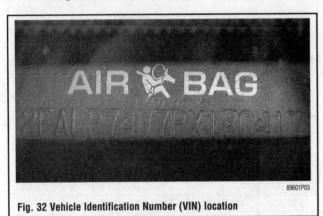

Fig. 32 Vehicle Identification Number (VIN) location

MFD. BY FORD MOTOR CO. OF CANADA LTD.
DATE: 05/93   GVWR: 5438LB/2466KG
FRONT GAWR: 2598LB   1178KG
REAR GAWR: 2865LB   1299KG
THIS VEHICLE CONFORMS TO ALL APPLICABLE FEDERAL MOTOR
VEHICLE SAFETY, BUMPER, AND THEFT PREVENTION STANDARDS
IN EFFECT ON THE DATE OF MANUFACTURE SHOWN ABOVE.
VIN: 2FALP74W7PX180417   F0104
TYPE: PASSENGER   R0295

YZ   16   DSO
EXTERIOR PAINT COLORS
BODY |VR |HLDG.| INT TRIM |TAPE |R |S |AX | TR
LX4   W   CH   H   Y   PJD33
           MADE IN CANADA   ▽F0EB-58Z04A10-BB

Fig. 33 The Vehicle Certification Label is typically located on the driver's door or the door jam

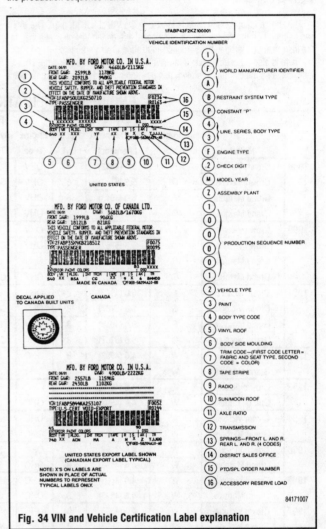

Fig. 34 VIN and Vehicle Certification Label explanation

VEHICLE IDENTIFICATION CHART

Engine Code						Model Year	
Code	Liters	Cu. In. (cc)	Cyl.	Fuel Sys.	Eng. Mfg.	Code	Year
F	5.0	302 (4943)	8	SFI	Ford	K	1989
G	5.8	351 (5767)	8	Carb.	Ford	L	1990
W	4.6	280 (4593)	8	SFI	Ford	M	1991
9	4.6	280 (4593)	8	NGV	Ford	N	1992
						P	1993
SFI - Sequential Fuel Injection						R	1994
Carb. - Carbureted						S	1995
NGV - Natural Gas Vehicle						T	1996
						V	1997
						W	1998

The Vehicle Certification Label is attached to the driver's door or the door jam. The upper half of the label contains the name of the manufacturer, month and year of manufacture, Gross Vehicle Weight Rating (GVWR), Gross Axle Weight Rating (GAWR), and the certification statement. The lower half of the label contains the VIN and a series of codes indicating exterior color, body type, interior trim type and color, radio type, sun roof type (if any), as well as axle, transmission, spring, district and special order codes.

Engine

▶ See Figure 35

The engine identification code is located in the VIN at the 8th digit. The VIN can be found on the Vehicle Certification Label and on the VIN plate attached to the instrument panel. See the Engine Identification chart for engine VIN codes.

There is also an engine code information label located on the engine. This label contains the engine calibration number, engine build date and engine plant

Fig. 35 Sample engine code information label

ENGINE IDENTIFICATION AND SPECIFICATIONS

Year	Model	Engine ID/VIN	Engine Displacement Liters (cc)	No. of Cyl.	Engine Type	Fuel System Type	Net Horsepower @ rpm	Net Torque @ rpm (ft. lbs.)	Bore x Stroke (in.)	Compression Ratio	Oil Pressure @ rpm
1989	Crown Victoria	F	5.0 (4943)	8	OHV	SFI	①	②	4.00 X 3.00	8.9:1	40-60@2000
	Crown Victoria	G	5.8 (5767)	8	OHV	Carb.	180@3600	285@2400	4.00 X 3.50	8.3:1	40-60@2000
	Grand Marquis	F	5.0 (4943)	8	OHV	SFI	①	②	4.00 X 3.00	8.9:1	40-60@2000
	Grand Marquis	G	5.8 (5767)	8	OHV	Carb.	180@3600	285@2400	4.00 X 3.50	8.3:1	40-60@2000
1990	Crown Victoria	F	5.0 (4943)	8	OHV	SFI	①	②	4.00 X 3.00	8.9:1	40-60@2000
	Crown Victoria	G	5.8 (5767)	8	OHV	Carb.	180@3600	285@2400	4.00 X 3.50	8.3:1	40-60@2000
	Grand Marquis	F	5.0 (4943)	8	OHV	SFI	①	②	4.00 X 3.00	8.9:1	40-60@2000
	Grand Marquis	G	5.8 (5767)	8	OHV	Carb.	180@3600	285@2400	4.00 X 3.50	8.3:1	40-60@2000
1991	Crown Victoria	F	5.0 (4943)	8	OHV	SFI	①	②	4.00 X 3.00	8.9:1	40-60@2000
	Crown Victoria	G	5.8 (5767)	8	OHV	Carb.	180@3600	285@2400	4.00 X 3.50	8.3:1	40-60@2000
	Grand Marquis	F	5.0 (4943)	8	OHV	SFI	①	②	4.00 X 3.00	8.9:1	40-60@2000
	Grand Marquis	G	5.8 (5767)	8	OHV	Carb.	180@3600	285@2400	4.00 X 3.50	8.3:1	40-60@2000
1992	Crown Victoria	W	4.6 (4593)	8	OHC	SFI	③	④	3.55 X 3.54	9.0:1	20-45@1500
	Grand Marquis	W	4.6 (4593)	8	OHC	SFI	③	④	3.55 X 3.54	9.0:1	20-45@1500
1993	Crown Victoria	W	4.6 (4593)	8	OHC	SFI	③	④	3.55 X 3.54	9.0:1	20-45@1500
	Grand Marquis	W	4.6 (4593)	8	OHC	SFI	③	④	3.55 X 3.54	9.0:1	20-45@1500
1994	Crown Victoria	W	4.6 (4593)	8	OHC	SFI	③	④	3.55 X 3.54	9.0:1	20-45@1500
	Grand Marquis	W	4.6 (4593)	8	OHC	SFI	③	④	3.55 X 3.54	9.0:1	20-45@1500
1995	Crown Victoria	W	4.6 (4593)	8	OHC	SFI	③	④	3.55 X 3.54	9.0:1	20-45@1500
	Grand Marquis	W	4.6 (4593)	8	OHC	SFI	③	④	3.55 X 3.54	9.0:1	20-45@1500
1996	Crown Victoria	W	4.6 (4593)	8	OHC	SFI	③	④	3.55 X 3.54	9.0:1	20-45@1500
	Grand Marquis	W	4.6 (4593)	8	OHC	SFI	③	④	3.55 X 3.54	9.0:1	20-45@1500
1997	Crown Victoria	W	4.6 (4593)	8	OHC	SFI	③	④	3.55 X 3.54	9.0:1	20-45@1500
	Crown Victoria	9	4.6 (4593)	8	OHC	NGV	175@4500	235@3500	3.55 X 3.54	9.0:1	20-45@1500
	Grand Marquis	W	4.6 (4593)	8	OHC	SFI	③	④	3.55 X 3.54	9.0:1	20-45@1500
	Grand Marquis	9	4.6 (4593)	8	OHC	NGV	175@4500	235@3500	3.55 X 3.54	9.0:1	20-45@1500
1998	Crown Victoria	W	4.6 (4593)	8	OHC	SFI	③	④	3.55 X 3.54	9.0:1	20-45@1500
	Crown Victoria	9	4.6 (4593)	8	OHC	NGV	175@4500	235@3500	3.55 X 3.54	9.0:1	20-45@1500
	Grand Marquis	W	4.6 (4593)	8	OHC	SFI	③	④	3.55 X 3.54	9.0:1	20-45@1500
	Grand Marquis	9	4.6 (4593)	8	OHC	NGV	175@4500	235@3500	3.55 X 3.54	9.0:1	20-45@1500

SFI - Sequential Fuel Injection
OHC - Overhead Camshaft
① Single exhaust: 150@3200
   Double exhaust: 160@3400
② Single exhaust: 270@2000
   Double exhaust: 280@2200
③ Single exhaust: 190@4200
   Double exhaust: 210@4600
④ Single exhaust: 260@3200
   Double exhaust: 270@3400

89601C02

code. On the 5.0L and 5.8L engines, the label is located on the side of the right rocker arm cover. On the 4.6L engine, the label is located on the front of the engine.

Transmission

▶ See Figures 36 and 37

The transmission identification code can be found in the space marked TR on the Vehicle Certification Label. There is also an identification tag located on the transmission case which contains the transmission model code, build date code, serial number and assembly part number prefix and suffix.

All 1989–92½ vehicles are equipped with a 4-speed Automatic Overdrive (AOD) transmission. Beginning in February 1992, an electronically controlled Automatic Overdrive (AODE) transmission replaced the AOD transmission.

Drive Axle

▶ See Figures 38 and 39

The drive axle identification code can be found in the space marked AX on the Vehicle Certification Label. There is also an identification tag located on the axle.

The plant code on the identification tag is the official service identifier. The plant code for a particular axle assembly will not be duplicated. As long as that particular axle assembly never undergoes an external design change, the plant code will not change. However, if an internal design change takes place in the same axle during the production life of the axle, and the change affects service parts interchangeability, a dash and numerical suffix is added to the plant code.

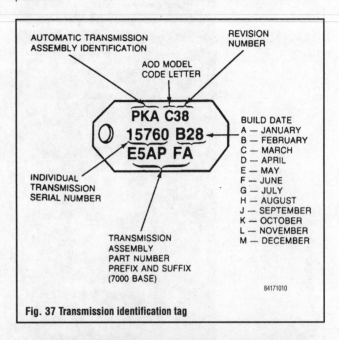

Fig. 37 Transmission identification tag

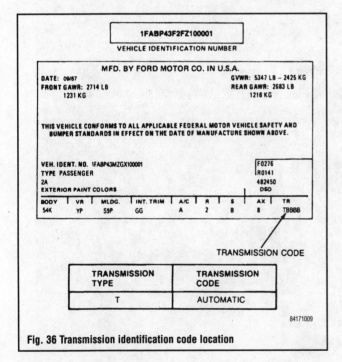

Fig. 36 Transmission identification code location

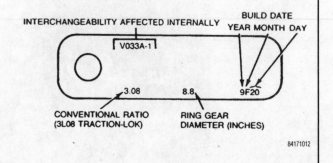

Fig. 38 Drive axle identification tag location

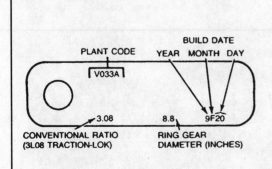

Fig. 39 Drive axle identification tags

ROUTINE MAINTENANCE AND TUNE-UP

UNDERHOOD MAINTENANCE COMPONENT LOCATIONS—4.6L ENGINE

1. Battery
2. Engine compartment fuse box
3. Drive belt
4. Spark plug wires
5. Spark plugs (4 on each side of the engine)
6. PCV valve
7. Coolant recovery tank
8. Automatic transmission oil dipstick
9. Brake master cylinder reservoir
10. Engine oil dipstick
11. Engine oil fill cap
12. Power steering fluid reservoir
13. Air cleaner assembly
14. Windshield washer fluid reservoir

89601P97

UNDERHOOD MAINTENANCE COMPONENT LOCATIONS—5.0L ENGINE

1. Battery
2. Spark plugs (4 on each side of the engine)
3. Drive belt
4. Engine oil fill cap
5. Automatic transmission oil dipstick
6. PCV valve
7. Spark plug wires
8. Distributor cap and rotor (under dust cover)
9. Engine oil dipstick
10. Brake master cylinder reservoir
11. Air cleaner assembly
12. Power steering fluid reservoir
13. Coolant recovery tank
14. Radiator cap

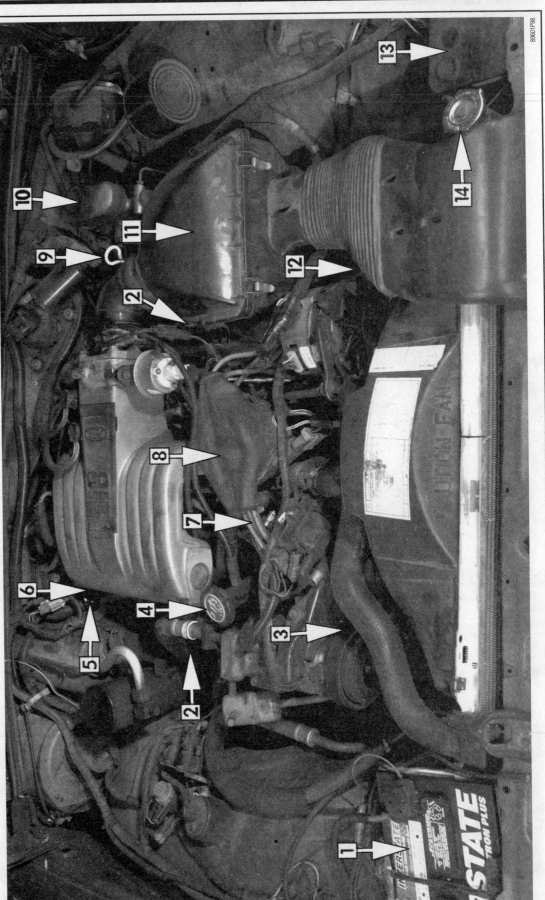

89601P98

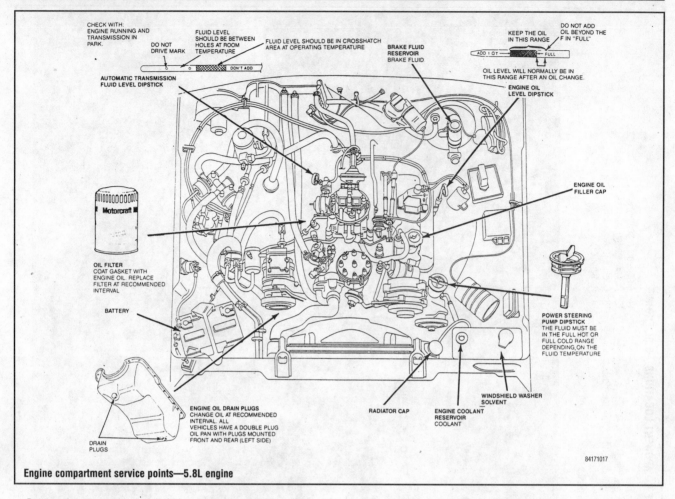

CHECK WITH:
ENGINE RUNNING AND
TRANSMISSION IN
PARK.

DO NOT
DRIVE MARK

FLUID LEVEL
SHOULD BE BETWEEN
HOLES AT ROOM
TEMPERATURE

FLUID LEVEL SHOULD BE IN CROSSHATCH
AREA AT OPERATING TEMPERATURE

BRAKE FLUID
RESERVOIR
BRAKE FLUID

KEEP THE OIL
IN THIS RANGE

DO NOT ADD
OIL BEYOND THE
F IN "FULL"

ADD 1 QT   FULL

OIL LEVEL WILL NORMALLY BE IN
THIS RANGE AFTER AN OIL CHANGE.

AUTOMATIC TRANSMISSION
FLUID LEVEL DIPSTICK

ENGINE OIL
LEVEL DIPSTICK

ENGINE OIL
FILLER CAP

Motorcraft

OIL FILTER
COAT GASKET WITH
ENGINE OIL. REPLACE
FILTER AT RECOMMENDED
INTERVAL

BATTERY

POWER STEERING
PUMP DIPSTICK
THE FLUID MUST BE
IN THE FULL HOT OR
FULL COLD RANGE
DEPENDING ON THE
FLUID TEMPERATURE

ENGINE OIL DRAIN PLUGS
CHANGE OIL AT RECOMMENDED
INTERVAL. ALL
VEHICLES HAVE A DOUBLE PLUG
OIL PAN WITH PLUGS MOUNTED
FRONT AND REAR (LEFT SIDE)

RADIATOR CAP

ENGINE COOLANT
RESERVOIR
COOLANT

WINDSHIELD WASHER
SOLVENT

DRAIN
PLUGS

84171017

Engine compartment service points—5.8L engine

Proper maintenance and tune-up is the key to long and trouble-free vehicle life, and the work can yield its own rewards. Studies have shown that a properly tuned and maintained vehicle can achieve better gas mileage than an out-of-tune vehicle. As a conscientious owner and driver, set aside a Saturday morning, say once a month, to check or replace items which could cause major problems later. Keep your own personal log to jot down which services you performed, how much the parts cost you, the date, and the exact odometer reading at the time. Keep all receipts for such items as engine oil and filters, so that they may be referred to in case of related problems or to determine operating expenses. As a do-it-yourselfer, these receipts are the only proof you have that the required maintenance was performed. In the event of a warranty problem, these receipts will be invaluable.

The literature provided with your vehicle when it was originally delivered includes the factory recommended maintenance schedule. If you no longer have this literature, replacement copies are usually available from the dealer. A main-

tenance schedule is provided later in this section, in case you do not have the factory literature.

Air Cleaner Element

REMOVAL & INSTALLATION

Except 5.8L Engine
▶ See Figures 40, 41, 42, 43 and 44

1. Release the spring clips retaining the air cleaner cover to the air cleaner tray.
2. Lift the cover and remove the air cleaner element.

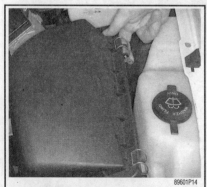

89601P14

Fig. 40 Releasing the spring clips to remove the air cleaner cover—4.6L engine

89601P15

Fig. 41 Lift the lid to access the spring clips and . . .

89601P16

Fig. 42 . . . remove the air cleaner element—4.6L engine

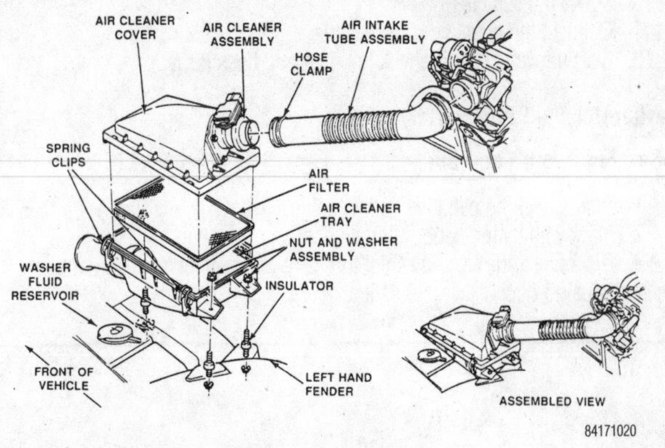

Fig. 43 Air cleaner assembly—5.0L engine

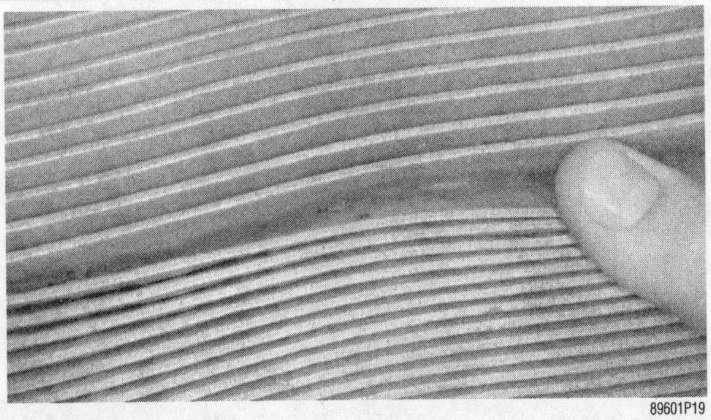

Fig. 44 Spread the air cleaner element to inspect it for dirt and contamination

To install:

3. Inspect the air cleaner, cover and tray for signs of dust or dirt leaking through holes in the filter element or past the sealing edges. Shine a light on the bottom (clean side) of the filter element and look through the filter at the light. If any holes can be seen, no matter how small, the filter must be replaced.

4. Wipe all the inside surfaces of the air cleaner tray and cover. Install the air cleaner element.

5. Place the air cleaner cover on the air cleaner tray and secure with the clips.

5.8L Engine

➧ See Figures 45 and 46

1. Remove the wing nut retaining the air cleaner cover.
2. Remove the air cleaner cover and remove the air cleaner element.

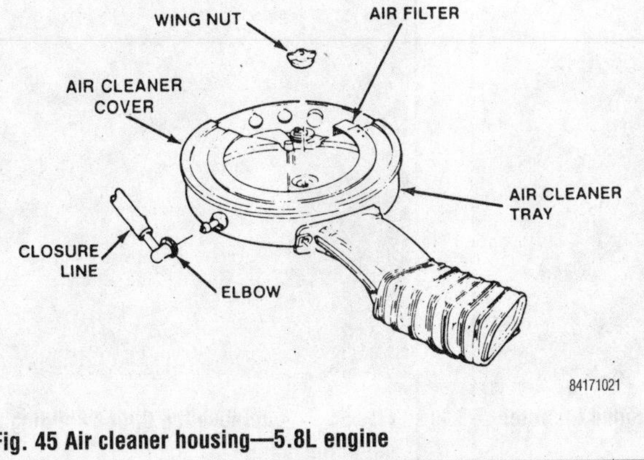

Fig. 45 Air cleaner housing—5.8L engine

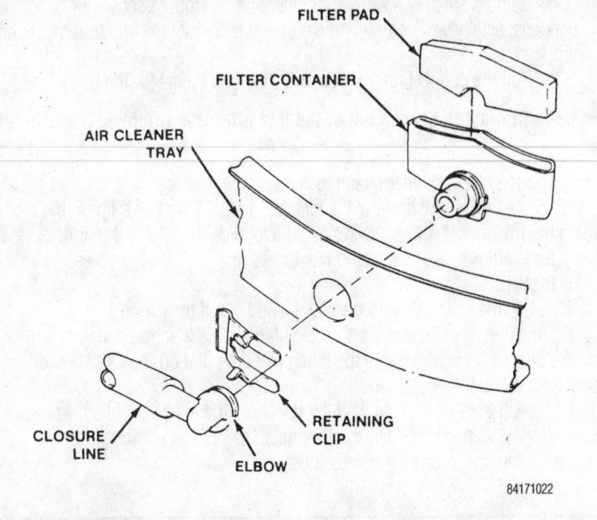

Fig. 46 Crankcase emission filter assembly—5.8L engine

3. If necessary, remove the retaining clip from the crankcase emission filter assembly and remove the assembly from the air cleaner tray. Remove the filter pad from the crankcase emission filter container and discard.

To install:

4. If removed, clean the crankcase emission filter container. Lightly oil a new filter pad with clean engine oil and install it in the container.

5. Inspect the air cleaner, cover and tray for signs of dust or dirt leaking through holes in the filter element or past the sealing edges. Shine a light on the clean side of the filter element and look through the filter at the light. If any holes can be seen, no matter how small, the filter must be replaced.

6. Wipe the inside surfaces of the air cleaner cover and tray.

7. If removed, install the crankcase emission filter assembly and secure with the retaining clip. Make sure the filter container is fully secured to the elbow; the retaining clip must engage the inner ring of the elbow, not between the rings.

8. Install the air cleaner element.

9. Install the air cleaner cover and secure with the wing nut.

Fuel Filter

REMOVAL & INSTALLATION

In-Line Fuel Filter

➧ See Figures 47 thru 54

➡The in-line fuel filter is located under the rear of the vehicle, along the frame rail.

✲✲ CAUTION

Observe all applicable safety precautions when working around fuel. Whenever servicing the fuel system, always work in a well ventilated area. Do not allow fuel spray or vapors to come in contact with a spark or open flame. Keep a dry chemical fire extinguisher near the work area. Always keep fuel in a container specifically designed for fuel storage; also, always properly seal fuel containers to avoid the possibility of fire or explosion.

1. Disconnect the negative battery cable.
2. Properly relieve the fuel system pressure, as outlined in Section 5.
3. Raise and safely support the vehicle securely on jackstands.
4. Remove the two push-connect fittings on the fuel lines. The fittings are removed in the following manner:
    a. Using a small screwdriver or other suitable tool, spread the clip legs outward so that the clip can clear the line.

b. Using a small screwdriver or other suitable tool (a cotter pin puller works especially well) pull up on the triangular end of the clip to remove the clip.

c. Pull the connection from the fuel filter and repeat for the other line.

➡**Fuel will most likely run out of the line after it is removed from the filter.**

5. Loosen the fuel filter retaining clamp.

6. Slide the fuel filter out of the clamp. The fuel filter has a lip on the side facing the filter outlet fitting, always be sure to slide the filter out from this side as the filter will not clear the clamp due to this lip.

To install:

7. Slide the new filter into the clamp and tighten the clamp.

8. Install new clips into the fuel line fittings. The triangular shaped end of the clip should be on the top of the fitting and the point on the clip should face away from the fuel filter.

9. Attach the fuel lines to the filter until an audible click is heard from the connection. Sometimes the click is very quiet, so test the fitting by gently pulling on the line to see if it comes loose.

10. Lower the vehicle
11. Connect the negative battery cable.
12. Start the vehicle and check the filter and lines for leaks.

Carburetor Fuel Inlet Filter

◆ **See Figures 55 and 56**

1. Disconnect the negative battery cable.
2. Remove the air cleaner filter element as detailed in this section.
3. Disconnect the fresh air inlet tube and hot air inlet tube from the air cleaner housing duct.

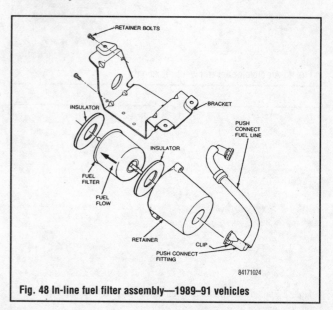

Fig. 48 In-line fuel filter assembly—1989–91 vehicles

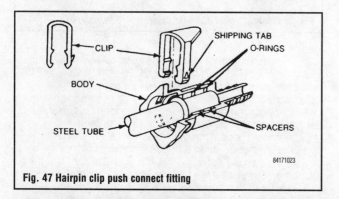

Fig. 47 Hairpin clip push connect fitting

Fig. 49 The fuel filter is located under the vehicle, along the frame rail on the passenger side—1992–98 vehicles

Fig. 50 Release the clips holding the fuel lines to the filter by gently prying them from the line. A cotter pin puller works very well for this

Fig. 51 After the clip's tangs are released, remove the clip from the line

Fig. 52 After the clip is removed, slide the line off of the filter

Fig. 53 Loosen the clamp around the filter and . . .

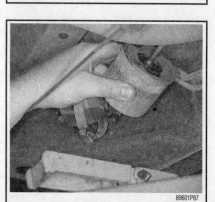

Fig. 54 . . . remove the filter by sliding it out of the clamp

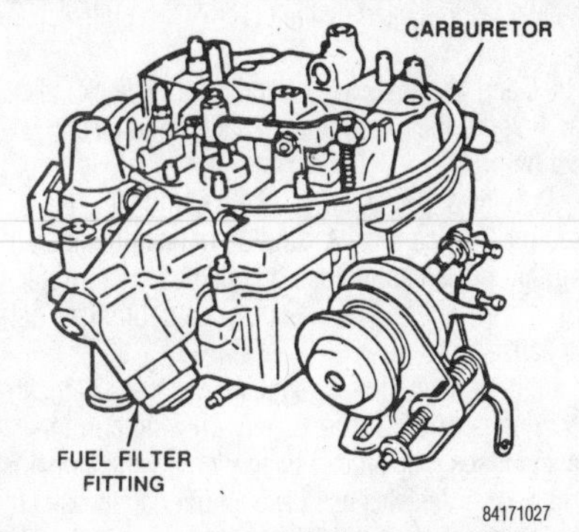

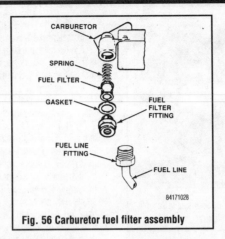

Fig. 55 Carburetor fuel filter fitting location

Fig. 56 Carburetor fuel filter assembly

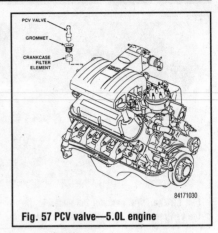

Fig. 57 PCV valve—5.0L engine

4. Disconnect the crankcase emission filter hose and the necessary vacuum hoses. Label the vacuum hoses prior to removal so they can be reinstalled in their proper locations. Remove the air cleaner housing.

5. Place a rag under the carburetor inlet fitting to catch fuel spillage.

6. Hold the carburetor inlet fitting with a backup wrench and unscrew the fuel line tube nut from the fitting.

7. Unscrew the fuel inlet fitting and remove the gasket, filter and spring. Discard the gasket and filter.

To install:

8. Install the spring, new filter and gasket.

9. Hand start the fuel inlet fitting into the carburetor. Tighten to 90–125 inch lbs. (10–14 Nm).

10. Apply clean engine oil to the fuel tube nut threads and tube flare. Hand start the fuel line tube nut into the fuel inlet fitting, approximately 2 threads.

11. Use a backup wrench on the fuel inlet fitting while tightening the fuel line tube nut to 15–18 ft. lbs. (20–24 Nm).

12. Start the engine and check for leaks. Install the air cleaner housing assembly.

PCV Valve

REMOVAL & INSTALLATION

▶ **See Figures 57, 58, 59, 60 and 61**

1. Remove the PCV valve from the grommet or elbow.

2. Disconnect the hose(s) from the PCV valve and remove it from the vehicle.

3. Check the PCV valve for deposits and clogging. If the valve rattles when shaken, it is okay. If the valve does not rattle, clean the valve with solvent until the plunger is free, or replace it.

4. Check the PCV hose(s) and the grommet or elbow for clogging and signs of wear or deterioration. Clean or replace parts, as necessary.

5. If necessary, on the 5.0L engine remove the grommet and remove the crankcase emission filter.

To install:

6. If removed, on the 5.0L engine install a new crankcase emission filter element and install the grommet.

7. Connect the PCV hose(s) to the PCV valve.

8. Install the PCV valve in the grommet or elbow.

Evaporative Canister

SERVICING

▶ **See Figure 62**

The evaporative canister requires no periodic servicing. However, a careful inspection of the canister and hoses should be made frequently. Replace damaged components as required.

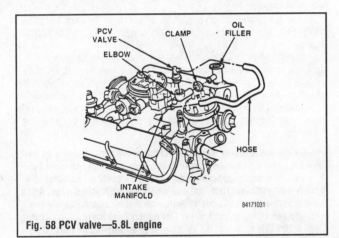

Fig. 58 PCV valve—5.8L engine

Fig. 59 The PCV valve is located in the passenger side valve cover—4.6L engine

Fig. 60 Grasp the valve and gently remove it from the grommet in the valve cover

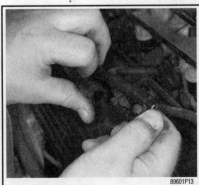

Fig. 61 Remove the valve from the hose by carefully twisting it out

Fig. 62 The EVAP canister is located in the front passenger side of the vehicle, near the radiator on models through 1997

The canister is located in the front passenger side of the vehicle, near the radiator on models through 1997. On 1998 models, the canister is located under the vehicle, near the fuel tank.

Battery

PRECAUTIONS

Always use caution when working on or near the battery. Never allow a tool to bridge the gap between the negative and positive battery terminals. Also, be careful not to allow a tool to provide a ground between the positive cable/terminal and any metal component on the vehicle. Either of these conditions will cause a short circuit, leading to sparks and possible personal injury.

Do not smoke, have an open flame or create sparks near a battery; the gases contained in the battery are very explosive and, if ignited, could cause severe injury or death.

All batteries, regardless of type, should be carefully secured by a battery hold-down device. If this is not done, the battery terminals or casing may crack from stress applied to the battery during vehicle operation. A battery which is not secured may allow acid to leak out, making it discharge faster; such leaking corrosive acid can also eat away at components under the hood.

Always visually inspect the battery case for cracks, leakage and corrosion. A white corrosive substance on the battery case or on nearby components would indicate a leaking or cracked battery. If the battery is cracked, it should be replaced immediately.

GENERAL MAINTENANCE

♦ See Figure 63

A battery that is not sealed must be checked periodically for electrolyte level. You cannot add water to a sealed maintenance-free battery (though not all maintenance-free batteries are sealed); however, a sealed battery must also be

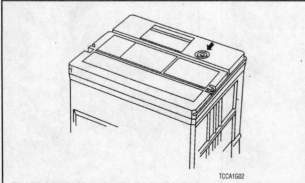

TCCA1G02

Fig. 63 A typical location for the built-in hydrometer on maintenance-free batteries

checked for proper electrolyte level, as indicated by the color of the built-in hydrometer "eye."

Always keep the battery cables and terminals free of corrosion. Check these components about once a year. Refer to the removal, installation and cleaning procedures outlined in this section.

Keep the top of the battery clean, as a film of dirt can help completely discharge a battery that is not used for long periods. A solution of baking soda and water may be used for cleaning, but be careful to flush this off with clear water. DO NOT let any of the solution into the filler holes. Baking soda neutralizes battery acid and will de-activate a battery cell.

Batteries in vehicles which are not operated on a regular basis can fall victim to parasitic loads (small current drains which are constantly drawing current from the battery). Normal parasitic loads may drain a battery on a vehicle that is in storage and not used for 6–8 weeks. Vehicles that have additional accessories such as a cellular phone, an alarm system or other devices that increase parasitic load may discharge a battery sooner. If the vehicle is to be stored for 6–8 weeks in a secure area and the alarm system, if present, is not necessary, the negative battery cable should be disconnected at the onset of storage to protect the battery charge.

Remember that constantly discharging and recharging will shorten battery life. Take care not to allow a battery to be needlessly discharged.

BATTERY FLUID

Check the battery electrolyte level at least once a month, or more often in hot weather or during periods of extended vehicle operation. On non-sealed batteries, the level can be checked either through the case on translucent batteries or by removing the cell caps on opaque-cased types. The electrolyte level in each cell should be kept filled to the split ring inside each cell, or the line marked on the outside of the case.

If the level is low, add only distilled water through the opening until the level is correct. Each cell is separate from the others, so each must be checked and filled individually. Distilled water should be used, because the chemicals and minerals found in most drinking water are harmful to the battery and could significantly shorten its life.

If water is added in freezing weather, the vehicle should be driven several miles to allow the water to mix with the electrolyte. Otherwise, the battery could freeze.

Although some maintenance-free batteries have removable cell caps for access to the electrolyte, the electrolyte condition and level on all sealed maintenance-free batteries must be checked using the built-in hydrometer "eye." The exact type of eye varies between battery manufacturers, but most apply a sticker to the battery itself explaining the possible readings. When in doubt, refer to the battery manufacturer's instructions to interpret battery condition using the built-in hydrometer.

➡**Although the readings from built-in hydrometers found in sealed batteries may vary, a green eye usually indicates a properly charged battery with sufficient fluid level. A dark eye is normally an indicator of a battery with sufficient fluid, but one which may be low in charge. And a light or yellow eye is usually an indication that electrolyte supply has dropped below the necessary level for battery (and hydrometer) operation. In this last case, sealed batteries with an insufficient electrolyte level must usually be discarded.**

Checking the Specific Gravity

♦ See Figures 64, 65 and 66

A hydrometer is required to check the specific gravity on all batteries that are not maintenance-free. On batteries that are maintenance-free, the specific gravity is checked by observing the built-in hydrometer "eye" on the top of the battery case. Check with your battery's manufacturer for proper interpretation of its built-in hydrometer readings.

✳✳ CAUTION

Battery electrolyte contains sulfuric acid. If you should splash any on your skin or in your eyes, flush the affected area with plenty of clear water. If it lands in your eyes, get medical help immediately.

The fluid (sulfuric acid solution) contained in the battery cells will tell you many things about the condition of the battery. Because the cell plates must be

Fig. 64 On non-maintenance-free batteries, the fluid level can be checked through the case on translucent models; the cell caps must be removed on other models

Fig. 65 If the fluid level is low, add only distilled water through the opening until the level is correct

Fig. 66 Check the specific gravity of the battery's electrolyte with a hydrometer

kept submerged below the fluid level in order to operate, maintaining the fluid level is extremely important. And, because the specific gravity of the acid is an indication of electrical charge, testing the fluid can be an aid in determining if the battery must be replaced. A battery in a vehicle with a properly operating charging system should require little maintenance, but careful, periodic inspection should reveal problems before they leave you stranded.

As stated earlier, the specific gravity of a battery's electrolyte level can be used as an indication of battery charge. At least once a year, check the specific gravity of the battery. It should be between 1.20 and 1.26 on the gravity scale. Most auto supply stores carry a variety of inexpensive battery testing hydrometers. These can be used on any non-sealed battery to test the specific gravity in each cell.

The battery testing hydrometer has a squeeze bulb at one end and a nozzle at the other. Battery electrolyte is sucked into the hydrometer until the float is lifted from its seat. The specific gravity is then read by noting the position of the float. If gravity is low in one or more cells, the battery should be slowly charged and checked again to see if the gravity has come up. Generally, if after charging, the specific gravity between any two cells varies more than 50 points (0.50), the battery should be replaced, as it can no longer produce sufficient voltage to guarantee proper operation.

CABLES

♦ **See Figures 67, 68, 69, 70 and 71**

Once a year (or as necessary), the battery terminals and the cable clamps should be cleaned. Loosen the clamps and remove the cables, negative cable first. On batteries with posts on top, the use of a puller specially made for this purpose is recommended. These are inexpensive and available in most auto parts stores. Side terminal battery cables are secured with a small bolt.

Clean the cable clamps and the battery terminal with a wire brush, until all corrosion, grease, etc., is removed and the metal is shiny. It is especially important to clean the inside of the clamp thoroughly (an old knife is useful here), since a small deposit of foreign material or oxidation there will prevent a sound electrical connection and inhibit either starting or charging. Special tools are available for cleaning these parts, one type for conventional top post batteries

and another type for side terminal batteries. It is also a good idea to apply some dielectric grease to the terminal, as this will aid in the prevention of corrosion.

After the clamps and terminals are clean, reinstall the cables, negative cable last; DO NOT hammer the clamps onto battery posts. Tighten the clamps securely, but do not distort them. Give the clamps and terminals a thin external coating of grease after installation, to retard corrosion.

Check the cables at the same time that the terminals are cleaned. If the cable insulation is cracked or broken, or if the ends are frayed, the cable should be replaced with a new cable of the same length and gauge.

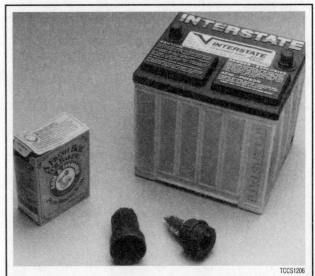

Fig. 67 Maintenance is performed with household items and with special tools like this post cleaner

Fig. 68 The underside of this special battery tool has a wire brush to clean post terminals

Fig. 69 Place the tool over the battery posts and twist to clean until the metal is shiny

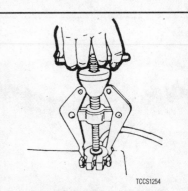

Fig. 70 A special tool is available to pull the clamp from the post

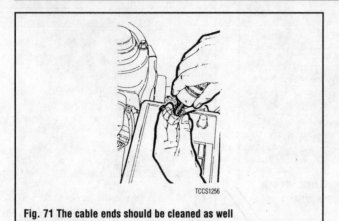

Fig. 71 The cable ends should be cleaned as well

CHARGING

A battery should be charged at a slow rate to keep the plates inside from getting too hot. However, if some maintenance-free batteries are allowed to discharge until they are almost "dead," they may have to be charged at a high rate to bring them back to "life." Always follow the charger manufacturer's instructions on charging the battery.

REPLACEMENT

When it becomes necessary to replace the battery, select one with an amperage rating equal to or greater than the battery originally installed. Deterioration and just plain aging of the battery cables, starter motor, and associated wires makes the battery's job harder in successive years. The slow increase in electrical resistance over time makes it prudent to install a new battery with a greater capacity than the old.

Belts

INSPECTION

▶ **See Figures 72, 73, 74, 75 and 76**

Inspect the belts for signs of glazing or cracking. A glazed belt will be perfectly smooth from slippage, while a good belt will have a slight texture of fabric visible. Cracks will usually start at the inner edge of the belt and run outward. All worn or damaged drive belts should be replaced immediately. It is best to replace all drive belts at one time, as a preventive maintenance measure, during this service operation.

ADJUSTMENT

▶ **See Figure 77**

Proper belt tension is important and should be checked periodically, where adjustment is possible. A loose belt will result in slippage, which may cause noise or improper accessory operation (alternator not charging, etc.). A belt that is too tight will overload the accessory bearings, shortening their life.

The alternator and air conditioner compressor drive belts on the 5.0L and 5.8L engines are adjustable. The serpentine drive belt on the 4.6L engine is kept in proper adjustment with an automatic tensioner; no adjustment is necessary or possible, however periodic checking of the belt tension will aid in determining whether or not belt replacement is necessary.

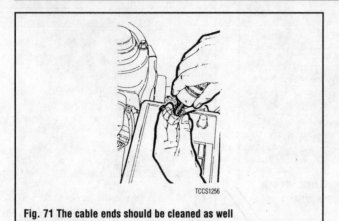

Fig. 72 There are typically 3 types of accessory drive belts found on vehicles today

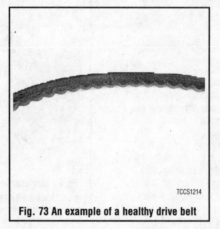

Fig. 73 An example of a healthy drive belt

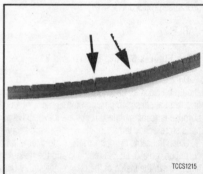

Fig. 74 Deep cracks in this belt will cause flex, building up heat that will eventually lead to belt failure

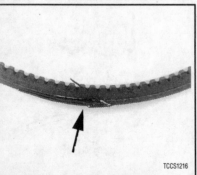

Fig. 75 The cover of this belt is worn, exposing the critical reinforcing cords to excessive wear

Fig. 76 Installing too wide a belt can result in serious belt wear and/or breakage

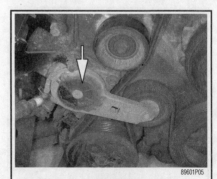

Fig. 77 The serpentine drive belt on the 4.6L engine is kept in proper adjustment with an automatic tensioner

5.0L and 5.8L Engines

ALTERNATOR BELT

▶ See Figures 78 and 79

1. Loosen the alternator pivot and adjustment bolts.
2. Position a suitable belt tension gauge at the point indicated in the figure. Install an open end wrench over the alternator adjustment boss, then apply tension to the belt, using the wrench.
3. Set the tension to 170 lbs. for a new belt, or to 140 lbs. on a used belt. While maintaining the tension, tighten the alternator adjustment bolt to 29 ft. lbs. (39 Nm).
4. Remove the belt tension gauge, start the engine and let it idle for 5 minutes.
5. Shut off the engine and install the tension gauge. Apply tension with the open end wrench and slowly loosen the adjustment bolt to allow belt tension to increase to the used belt specification, 140 lbs. Tighten the adjustment bolt to 29 ft. lbs. (39 Nm).
6. Tighten the pivot bolt to 50 ft. lbs. (68 Nm).

AIR CONDITIONER COMPRESSOR BELT

▶ See Figures 78 and 79

1. Loosen the idler pulley bracket adjustment and pivot bolts.
2. Position a suitable belt tension gauge at the point indicated in the figure.
3. Install a ½ in. breaker bar in the hole in the idler pulley bracket as shown in the figure. Apply tension to the belt using the breaker bar.

4. Set the tension to 170 lbs. for a new belt, or to 140 lbs. on a used belt. While maintaining the tension, tighten the adjustment bolt to 30 ft. lbs. (40 Nm).
5. Remove the belt tension gauge and the breaker bar. Start the engine and let it idle for 5 minutes.
6. Shut the engine off, then reinstall the belt tension gauge and breaker bar. Apply tension with the breaker bar and slowly loosen the adjustment bolt to allow belt tension to increase to the used belt specification, 140 lbs. Tighten the adjustment bolt to 30 ft. lbs. (40 Nm).
7. Tighten the pivot bolt to 50 ft. lbs. (68 Nm).

REMOVAL & INSTALLATION

The drive belt routing can be found on a label under the hood or in the engine compartment. If the label is missing, there are diagrams of all the engines covered in this manual. However, be sure to verify the belt routing on your engine matches one of these before removing the belt. If the routing does not match one of our diagrams, the belt could possibly be routed wrong. A good idea is to draw your own diagram of the belt routing prior to removing the old belt from the engine.

4.6L Engine

▶ See Figures 80, 81, 82 and 83

1. Disconnect the negative battery cable.

➡**The proper belt routing is included in this section, however, it is a good idea to make a simple drawing of the belt routing of your engine for installation reference before removing the belt.**

2. Rotate the drive belt tensioner to relieve the belt tension. The procedure is as follows:
   a. Use a ½ drive tool or a special belt removal tool to rotate the tensioner in the proper direction as directed by the rotation arrow on the tensioner.
   b. While holding the tensioner back, remove the belt from around one pulley.
3. Remove the belt from around the remaining pulleys.

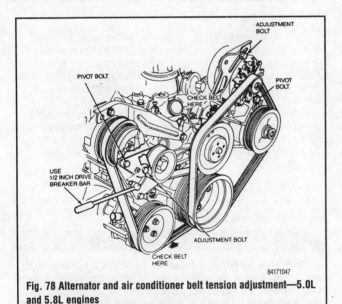

Fig. 78 Alternator and air conditioner belt tension adjustment—5.0L and 5.8L engines

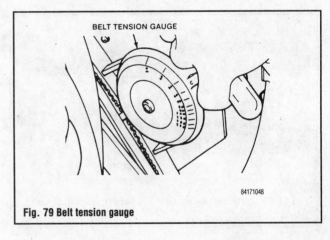

Fig. 79 Belt tension gauge

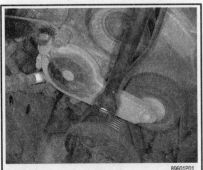

Fig. 80 Rotate the tensioner to release the tension and remove the drive belt from the engine

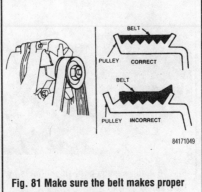

Fig. 81 Make sure the belt makes proper contact with the pulley grooves

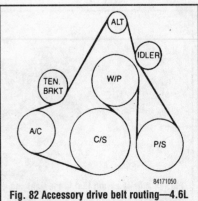

Fig. 82 Accessory drive belt routing—4.6L engine

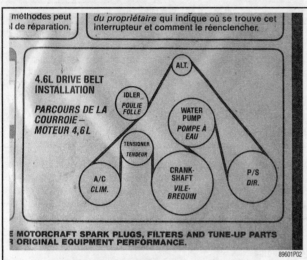

Fig. 83 Typically a label is affixed in the engine compartment that shows the proper routing of the drive belt

To install:

4. Position the belt around the pulleys in the proper routing with the exception of one pulley. It is easiest to keep the belt off of the easiest pulley to access. Hold the belt tight with your hands and using the proper tool for your engine, rotate the tensioner in the correct direction and place the belt around the final pulley.

5. Release the tensioner slowly until it sits firmly against the belt.

➡**If the tensioner does not touch the belt or the wear indicator marks are not within specification, the belt is routed incorrectly or the wrong belt has been installed.**

6. Connect the negative battery cable.

Fig. 84 The cracks developing along this hose are a result of age-related hardening

5.0L and 5.8L Engines

▶ See Figure 81

ALTERNATOR BELT

1. Loosen the alternator adjustment and pivot bolts.
2. Rotate the alternator towards the engine until the belt is slack enough to remove from the pulleys.

To install:

3. Install the belt over the pulleys. Make sure the ribs on the belt properly contact the grooves on the pulleys.
4. Adjust the belt tension as described earlier in this Section.

AIR CONDITIONER COMPRESSOR BELT

1. Remove the alternator belt.
2. Loosen the idler bracket adjustment and pivot bolts.
3. Rotate the idler bracket away from the belt until the belt is slack enough to remove from the pulleys.

To install:

4. Install the belt over the pulleys. Make sure the ribs on the belt properly contact the grooves on the pulleys.
5. Adjust the belt tension as described earlier in this Section.
6. Install the alternator belt and adjust the tension.

Hoses

INSPECTION

▶ See Figures 84, 85, 86 and 87

Upper and lower radiator hoses, along with the heater hoses, should be checked for deterioration, leaks and loose hose clamps at least every 15,000 miles (24,000 km). It is also wise to check the hoses periodically in early spring and at the beginning of the fall or winter when you are performing other maintenance. A quick visual inspection could discover a weakened hose which might have left you stranded if it had remained unrepaired.

Whenever you are checking the hoses, make sure the engine and cooling system are cold. Visually inspect for cracking, rotting or collapsed hoses, and replace as necessary. Run your hand along the length of the hose. If a weak or swollen spot is noted when squeezing the hose wall, the hose should be replaced.

REMOVAL & INSTALLATION

1. Remove the radiator pressure cap.

✳✳ CAUTION

Never remove the pressure cap while the engine is running, or personal injury from scalding hot coolant or steam may result. If possible, wait until the engine has cooled to remove the pressure cap. If this is not possible, wrap a thick cloth around the pressure cap and

Fig. 85 A hose clamp that is too tight can cause older hoses to separate and tear on either side of the clamp

Fig. 86 A soft spongy hose (identifiable by the swollen section) will eventually burst and should be replaced

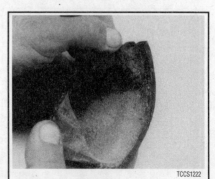

Fig. 87 Hoses are likely to deteriorate from the inside if the cooling system is not periodically flushed

turn it slowly to the stop. **Step back while the pressure is released from the cooling system. When you are sure all the pressure has been released, use the cloth to turn and remove the cap.**

2. Position a clean container under the radiator and/or engine draincock or plug, then open the drain and allow the cooling system to drain to an appropriate level. For some upper hoses, only a little coolant must be drained. To remove hoses positioned lower on the engine, such as a lower radiator hose, the entire cooling system must be emptied.

✳✳ CAUTION

When draining coolant, keep in mind that cats and dogs are attracted by ethylene glycol antifreeze, and are quite likely to drink any that is left in an uncovered container or in puddles on the ground. This will prove fatal in sufficient quantity. Always drain coolant into a sealable container. Coolant may be reused unless it is contaminated or several years old.

3. Loosen the hose clamps at each end of the hose requiring replacement. Clamps are usually either of the spring tension type (which require pliers to squeeze the tabs and loosen) or of the screw tension type (which require screw or hex drivers to loosen). Pull the clamps back on the hose away from the connection.

4. Twist, pull and slide the hose off the fitting, taking care not to damage the neck of the component from which the hose is being removed.

✳✳ WARNING

If the hose is stuck at the connection, do not try to insert a screwdriver or other sharp tool under the hose end in an effort to free it, as the connection and/or hose may become damaged. Heater connections especially may be easily damaged by such a procedure. If the hose is to be replaced, use a single-edged razor blade to make a slice along the portion of the hose which is stuck on the connection, perpendicular to the end of the hose. Do not cut deep so as to prevent damaging the connection. The hose can then be peeled from the connection and discarded.

5. Clean both hose mounting connections. Inspect the condition of the hose clamps and replace them, if necessary.

To install:

6. Dip the ends of the new hose into clean engine coolant to ease installation.

7. Slide the clamps over the replacement hose, then slide the hose ends over the connections into position.

8. Position and secure the clamps at least ¼ in. (6.35mm) from the ends of the hose. Make sure they are located beyond the raised bead of the connector.

9. Close the radiator or engine drains and properly refill the cooling system with the clean drained engine coolant or a suitable mixture of ethylene glycol coolant and water.

10. If available, install a pressure tester and check for leaks. If a pressure tester is not available, run the engine until normal operating temperature is reached (allowing the system to naturally pressurize), then check for leaks.

✳✳ CAUTION

If you are checking for leaks with the system at normal operating temperature, BE EXTREMELY CAREFUL not to touch any moving or hot engine parts. Once temperature has been reached, shut the engine OFF, and check for leaks around the hose fittings and connections which were removed earlier.

Spark Plugs

▶ See Figure 88

A typical spark plug consists of a metal shell surrounding a ceramic insulator. A metal electrode extends downward through the center of the insulator and protrudes a small distance. Located at the end of the plug and attached to the side of the outer metal shell is the side electrode. The side electrode bends in at a 90° angle so that its tip is just past and parallel to the tip of the center elec-

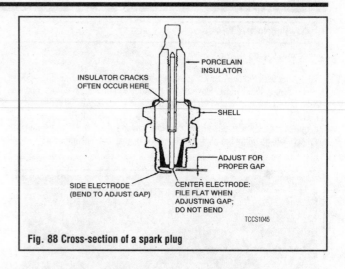

Fig. 88 Cross-section of a spark plug

trode. The distance between these two electrodes (measured in thousandths of an inch or hundredths of a millimeter) is called the spark plug gap.

The spark plug does not produce a spark, but instead provides a gap across which the current can arc. The coil produces anywhere from 20,000 to 50,000 volts (depending on the type and application) which travels through the wires to the spark plugs. The current passes along the center electrode and jumps the gap to the side electrode, and in doing so, ignites the air/fuel mixture in the combustion chamber.

SPARK PLUG HEAT RANGE

▶ See Figure 89

Spark plug heat range is the ability of the plug to dissipate heat. The longer the insulator (or the farther it extends into the engine), the hotter the plug will operate; the shorter the insulator (the closer the electrode is to the block's cooling passages) the cooler it will operate. A plug that absorbs little heat and remains too cool will quickly accumulate deposits of oil and carbon since it is not hot enough to burn them off. This leads to plug fouling and consequently to misfiring. A plug that absorbs too much heat will have no deposits but, due to the excessive heat, the electrodes will burn away quickly and might possibly lead to preignition or other ignition problems. Preignition takes place when plug tips get so hot that they glow sufficiently to ignite the air/fuel mixture before the actual spark occurs. This early ignition will usually cause a pinging during low speeds and heavy loads.

The general rule of thumb for choosing the correct heat range when picking a spark plug is: if most of your driving is long distance, high speed travel, use a colder plug; if most of your driving is stop and go, use a hotter plug. Original equipment plugs are generally a good compromise between the 2 styles and most people never have the need to change their plugs from the factory-recommended heat range.

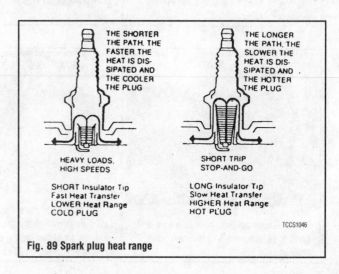

Fig. 89 Spark plug heat range

REMOVAL & INSTALLATION

♦ **See Figures 90 thru 97**

A set of spark plugs usually requires replacement after about 20,000–30,000 miles (32,000–48,000 km), depending on your style of driving. In normal operation plug gap increases about 0.001 in. (0.025mm) for every 2,500 miles (4,000km). As the gap increases, the plug's voltage requirement also increases. It requires a greater voltage to jump the wider gap and about two to three times as much voltage to fire the plug at high speeds than at idle. The improved air/fuel ratio control of modern fuel injection combined with the higher voltage output of modern ignition systems will often allow an engine to run significantly longer on a set of standard spark plugs, but keep in mind that efficiency will drop as the gap widens (along with fuel economy and power).

When you're removing spark plugs, work on one at a time. Don't start by removing the plug wires all at once, because, unless you number them, they may become mixed up. Take a minute before you begin and number the wires with tape.

1. Disconnect the negative battery cable, and if the vehicle has been run recently, allow the engine to thoroughly cool.

Fig. 90 Grasp and carefully twist the plug wire to release the retainer from the spark plug. If the plug wire is stubborn, a pair of special removal pliers is recommended to remove the wires from the plugs

Fig. 91 Carefully remove the plug wire from the cylinder head

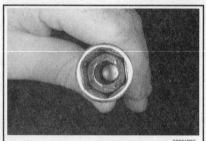

Fig. 92 A special spark plug socket with a rubber insert is needed to remove the spark plugs. Typically the spark plugs on engines covered by this manual require a ⅝ socket

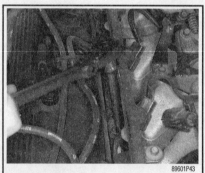

Fig. 93 Using a suitable drive tool and the special socket, loosen the spark plug and . . .

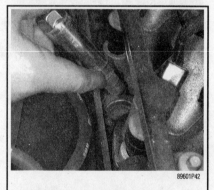

Fig. 94 . . . remove the spark plug from the engine

Fig. 95 Clean out the spark plug bore and threads before installing the new spark plug

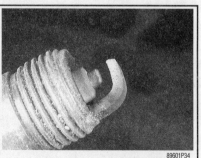

Fig. 96 An inspection of the old spark plugs will give a general idea of the condition of the motor; compare the spark plugs to the chart in this section

Fig. 97 A piece of fuel line or a small hose is useful in installing the spark plugs to avoid stripping the threads

2. Carefully twist the spark plug wire boot to loosen it, then pull upward and remove the boot from the plug. Be sure to pull on the boot and not on the wire, otherwise the connector located inside the boot may become separated.

3. Using compressed air, blow any water or debris from the spark plug well to assure that no harmful contaminants are allowed to enter the combustion chamber when the spark plug is removed. If compressed air is not available, use a rag or a brush to clean the area.

➡Remove the spark plugs when the engine is cold, if possible, to prevent damage to the threads. If removal of the plugs is difficult, apply a few drops of penetrating oil or silicone spray to the area around the base of the plug, and allow it a few minutes to work.

4. Using a spark plug socket that is equipped with a rubber insert to properly hold the plug, turn the spark plug counterclockwise to loosen and remove the spark plug from the bore.

✳✳ WARNING

Be sure not to use a flexible extension on the socket. Use of a flexible extension may allow a shear force to be applied to the plug. A shear force could break the plug off in the cylinder head, leading to costly and frustrating repairs.

To install:

5. Inspect the spark plug boot for tears or damage. If a damaged boot is found, the spark plug wire must be replaced.

6. Using a wire feeler gauge, check and adjust the spark plug gap. When using a gauge, the proper size should pass between the electrodes with a slight drag. The next larger size should not be able to pass while the next smaller size should pass freely.

7. Carefully thread the plug into the bore by hand. If resistance is felt before the plug is almost completely threaded, back the plug out and begin threading again. In small, hard to reach areas, an old spark plug wire and boot could be used as a threading tool. The boot will hold the plug while you twist the end of the wire and the wire is supple enough to twist before it would allow the plug to crossthread.

✳✳ WARNING

Do not use the spark plug socket to thread the plugs. Always carefully thread the plug by hand or using an old plug wire to prevent the possibility of crossthreading and damaging the cylinder head bore.

8. Carefully tighten the spark plug. If the plug you are installing is equipped with a crush washer, seat the plug, then tighten about ¼ turn to crush the washer. If you are installing a tapered seat plug, tighten the plug to specifications provided by the vehicle or plug manufacturer.

9. Apply a small amount of silicone dielectric compound to the end of the spark plug lead or inside the spark plug boot to prevent sticking, then install the boot to the spark plug and push until it clicks into place. The click may be felt or heard, then gently pull back on the boot to assure proper contact.

INSPECTION & GAPPING

▶ **See Figures 98, 99, 100, 101 and 102**

Check the plugs for deposits and wear. If they are not going to be replaced, clean the plugs thoroughly. Remember that any kind of deposit will decrease the efficiency of the plug. Plugs can be cleaned on a spark plug cleaning machine, which can sometimes be found in service stations, or you can do an acceptable job of cleaning with a stiff brush. If the plugs are cleaned, the electrodes must be filed flat. Use an ignition points file, not an emery board or the like, which will leave deposits. The electrodes must be filed perfectly flat with sharp edges; rounded edges reduce the spark plug voltage by as much as 50%.

Check spark plug gap before installation. The ground electrode (the L-shaped one connected to the body of the plug) must be parallel to the center electrode and the specified size wire gauge (please refer to the Tune-Up Specifications chart for details) must pass between the electrodes with a slight drag.

➡**NEVER adjust the gap on a used platinum type spark plug.**

Always check the gap on new plugs as they are not always set correctly at the factory. Do not use a flat feeler gauge when measuring the gap on a used plug, because the reading may be inaccurate. A round-wire type gapping tool is the best way to check the gap. The correct gauge should pass through the electrode gap with a slight drag. If you're in doubt, try one size smaller and one larger. The smaller gauge should go through easily, while the larger one shouldn't go through at all. Wire gapping tools usually have a bending tool attached. Use that to adjust the side electrode until the proper distance is obtained. Absolutely never attempt to bend the center electrode. Also, be careful not to bend the side electrode too far or too often as it may weaken and break off within the engine, requiring removal of the cylinder head to retrieve it.

TCCS1212

Fig. 98 A variety of tools and gauges are needed for spark plug service

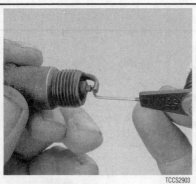

TCCS2903

Fig. 99 Checking the spark plug gap with a feeler gauge

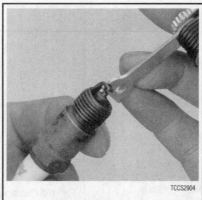

TCCS2904

Fig. 100 Adjusting the spark plug gap

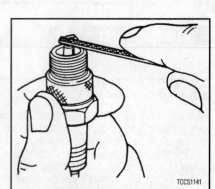

TCCS1141

Fig. 101 If the standard plug is in good condition, the electrode may be filed flat—WARNING: do not file platinum plugs

A normally worn spark plug should have light tan or gray deposits on the firing tip.

A carbon fouled plug, identified by soft, sooty, black deposits, may indicate an improperly tuned vehicle. Check the air cleaner, ignition components and engine control system.

This spark plug has been **left in the engine too long,** as evidenced by the extreme gap. Plugs with such an extreme gap can cause misfiring and stumbling accompanied by a noticeable lack of power.

An oil fouled spark plug indicates an engine with worn poston rings and/or bad valve seals allowing excessive oil to enter the chamber.

A physically damaged spark plug may be evidence of severe detonation in that cylinder. Watch that cylinder carefully between services, as a continued detonation will not only damage the plug, but could also damage the engine.

A bridged or almost bridged spark plug, identified by a build-up between the electrodes caused by excessive carbon or oil build-up on the plug.

TCCA1P40

Fig. 102 Inspect the spark plug to determine engine running conditions

Spark Plug Wires

TESTING

◗ **See Figures 103 and 104**

At every tune-up/inspection, visually check the spark plug cables for burns cuts, or breaks in the insulation. Check the boots and the nipples on the distributor cap and/or coil. Replace any damaged wiring.

Every 50,000 miles (80,000 km) or 60 months, the resistance of the wires should be checked with an ohmmeter. Wires with excessive resistance will cause misfiring, and may make the engine difficult to start in damp weather.

To check resistance, an ohmmeter should be used on each wire to test resistance between the end connectors. Remove and install/replace the wires in order, one-by-one.

Resistance on these wires should be 4,000–6,000 ohms per foot. To properly

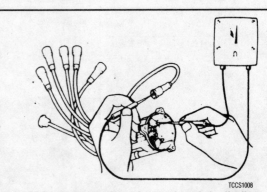
TCCS1008

Fig. 103 Checking plug wire resistance through the distributor cap with an ohmmeter

Fig. 104 Checking individual plug wire resistance with a digital ohmmeter

Fig. 105 Grasp the plug wire and carefully twist the wire to release the retainer from the spark plug

Fig. 106 If the plug wire is stubborn, a pair of special removal pliers is recommended to remove the wires from the plugs

measure this, remove the wires from the plugs and the coil pack. Do not pierce any ignition wire for any reason. Measure only from the two ends. Take the length and multiply it by 6,000 to achieve the maximum resistance allowable in each wire, resistance should not exceed this value. If resistance does exceed this value, replace the wire.

➡Whenever the high tension wires are removed from the plugs, coil, or distributor, silicone grease must be applied to the boot before reconnection. Coat the entire interior surface with Ford silicone grease D7AZ-19A331-A or its equivalent.

REMOVAL & INSTALLATION

▶ **See Figures 105 thru 110**

1. Remove the air cleaner inlet tube.
2. Label each spark plug wire and make a note of its routing.

Fig. 107 Carefully remove the plug wire from the cylinder head

➡Don't rely on wiring diagrams or sketches for spark plug wire routing. Improper arrangement of spark plug wires will induce voltage between wires, causing misfiring and surging. Be careful to arrange spark plug wires properly.

3. Starting with the longest wire, disconnect the spark plug wire from the spark plug and then from the coil pack (4.6L) or distributor cap (5.0/5.8L).
4. Disconnect the ignition wire from the coil pack by squeezing the locking tabs and twisting while pulling upward.

To install:

5. If replacing the spark plug wires, match the old wire with an appropriately sized wire in the new set.
6. Lubricate the boots and terminals with dielectric grease and install the wire on the coil pack. Make sure the wire snaps into place.
7. Route the wire in the exact path as the original and connect the wire to the spark plug.
8. Repeat the process for each remaining wire, working from the longest wire to the shortest.
9. Install the air cleaner inlet tube.

Distributor Cap and Rotor

REMOVAL & INSTALLATION

1. Disconnect the negative battery cable.
2. Label and disconnect the spark plug wires from the distributor cap.

➡Depending on the reason for removing the distributor cap, it may make more sense to leave the spark plug wires attached. This is handy if you are testing spark plug wires, or if removal is necessary to access other components, and wire length allows you to reposition the cap out of the way.

3. Detach the two spring clips that secure the cap to the distributor.
4. Remove the cap from the distributor.

Fig. 108 Remove the plug wires from the ignition coil by squeezing the retaining tabs and carefully lifting the wires up

Fig. 109 Disconnect the plug wire retaining clips from the wires and . . .

Fig. 110 . . . remove the plug wires from the engine

➡ **The rotor is press fit onto the distributor shaft.**

5. Pull the rotor straight up to remove.

To install:

6. Inspect the cap and rotor as described below.

7. Align the rotor locating boss on the distributor shaft and install by pressing into place.

8. Align the distributor cap on the distributor and secure the spring clips.

9. Connect the spark plug wires to their proper terminals.

10. Connect the negative battery cable.

INSPECTION

▶ **See Figures 111 and 112**

After removing the distributor cap and rotor, clean the components (both inside and outside of the cap) using soap and water. If compressed air is available, carefully dry the components (wearing safety goggles) or allow the parts to air dry. You can dry them with a clean, soft cloth, but don't leave any lint or moisture behind.

Once the cap and rotor have been thoroughly cleaned, check for cracks, carbon tracks, burns or other physical damage. Make sure the distributor cap's center button is free of damage. Check the cap terminals for dirt or corrosion. Always check the rotor blade and spring closely for damage. Replace any components where damage is found.

Ignition Timing

GENERAL INFORMATION

Ignition timing is the measurement, in degrees of crankshaft rotation, of the point at which the spark plugs fire in each of the cylinders. It is measured in degrees before or after Top Dead Center (TDC) of the compression stroke.

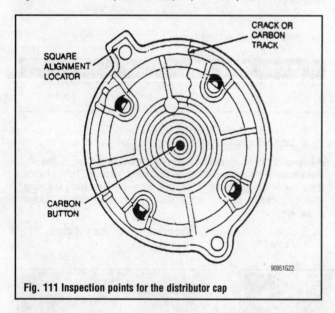

Fig. 111 Inspection points for the distributor cap

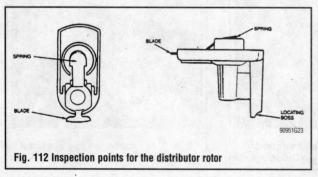

Fig. 112 Inspection points for the distributor rotor

Ideally, the air/fuel mixture in the cylinder will be ignited by the spark plug just as the piston passes TDC of the compression stroke. If this happens, the piston will be beginning the power stroke just as the compressed and ignited air/fuel mixture starts to expand. The expansion of the air/fuel mixture then forces the piston down on the power stroke and turns the crankshaft.

Because it takes a fraction of a second for the spark plug to ignite the mixture in the cylinder, the spark plug must fire a little before the piston reaches TDC. Otherwise, the mixture will not be completely ignited as the piston passes TDC and the full power of the explosion will not be used by the engine.

The timing measurement is given in degrees of crankshaft rotation before the piston reaches TDC (BTDC, or Before Top Dead Center). If the setting for the ignition timing is 10 BTDC, each spark plug must fire 10 degrees before each piston reaches TDC. This only holds true, however, when the engine is at idle speed.

As the engine speed increases, the pistons go faster. The spark plugs have to ignite the fuel even sooner if it is to be completely ignited when the piston reaches TDC.

With the Duraspark II ignition system, the distributor has a means to advance the timing of the spark as the engine speed increases. This is accomplished by centrifugal weights within the distributor and a vacuum diaphragm mounted on the side of the distributor. With the TFI-IV and EDIS ignition systems, ignition timing is calculated at all phases of vehicle operation by the ignition control module or the Powertrain Control Module (PCM).

If the ignition is set too far advanced (BTDC), the ignition and expansion of the fuel in the cylinder will occur too soon and tend to force the piston down while it is still traveling up. This causes engine ping. If the ignition spark is set too far retarded after TDC (ATDC), the piston will have already passed TDC and started on its way down when the fuel is ignited. This will cause the piston to be forced down for only a portion of its travel. This will result in poor engine performance and lack of power.

The ignition timing is checked with a timing light on 5.0L and 5.8L engines. This device is connected in series with the No. 1 spark plug. The current that fires the spark plug also causes the timing light to flash. The timing scale is located on the crankshaft pulley and a pointer is attached to the front timing cover. When the engine is running, the timing light is aimed at the mark on the crankshaft pulley and the scale. Timing adjustment is made at the distributor.

On the 4.6L engine, the base ignition timing is set at the factory to 10 degrees BTDC and is not adjustable.

INSPECTION & ADJUSTMENT

5.0L Engine

▶ **See Figure 113**

1. Locate the timing marks and pointer on the crankshaft pulley and the timing cover. Clean the marks so they will be visible with a timing light. Apply chalk or bright-colored paint, if necessary.

2. Place the transmission in **P** or **N**. The air conditioning and heater controls should be in the OFF position.

3. Connect a suitable tachometer and inductive timing light according to the manufacturer's instructions.

➡ **The tachometer can be connected to the ignition coil without removing the coil connector. Insert an alligator clip into the back of the connector, onto the dark green/yellow dotted wire. Do not let the clip accidentally ground to a metal surface as it may permanently damage the coil.**

4. Disconnect the single wire in-line SPOUT connector or remove the shorting bar from the double wire SPOUT connector.

5. Start the engine and allow it to warm up to operating temperature.

➡ **To set timing correctly, a remote starter should not be used. Use the ignition key only to start the vehicle. Disconnecting the start wire at the starter relay will cause the TFI module to revert to start mode timing after the vehicle is started. Reconnecting the start wire after the vehicle is running will not correct the timing.**

6. With the engine at the timing rpm specified, check the initial timing by aiming the timing light at the timing marks and pointer. Refer to the Vehicle Emission Control Information Label for specifications.

7. If the marks align, shut the engine **OFF** and proceed to Step 8. If the marks do not align, shut the engine **OFF** and loosen the distributor hold-down

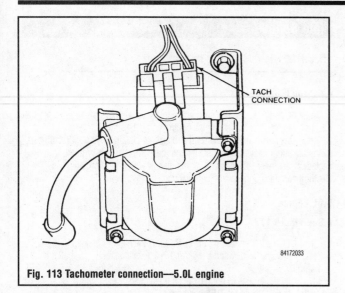

Fig. 113 Tachometer connection—5.0L engine

clamp bolt. Start the engine, aim the timing light and turn the distributor until the timing marks align. Shut off the engine and tighten the distributor hold-down clamp bolt to 17–25 ft. lbs. (23–34 Nm). Recheck the timing after the bolt has been tightened.

8. Reconnect the single wire in-line SPOUT connector or reinstall the shorting bar on the double wire SPOUT connector. Check the timing advance to verify the distributor is advancing beyond the initial setting.

9. Remove the inductive timing light and tachometer.

5.8L Engine

▶ **See Figure 114**

1. Locate the timing marks and pointer on the crankshaft pulley and the timing cover. Clean the marks so they will be visible with a timing light. Apply chalk or bright-colored paint, if necessary.

2. Place the transmission in **P** or **N**. The air conditioning and heater controls should be in the **OFF** position.

3. Disconnect the vacuum hoses from the distributor vacuum advance connection at the distributor and plug the hoses.

4. Connect a suitable inductive timing light and a tachometer according to the manufacturer's instructions.

➡ **The tachometer can be connected to the ignition coil without removing the coil connector. Insert an alligator clip into the TACH TEST cavity and connect the tachometer lead to the alligator clip.**

5. If equipped with a barometric pressure switch, detach it from the ignition module and place a jumper wire across the pins at the ignition module connector (yellow and black wires).

6. Start the engine and allow it to warm up to operating temperature.

7. With the engine at the timing rpm specified, check the initial timing by aiming the timing light at the timing marks and pointer. Refer to the Vehicle Emission Control Information Label for specifications.

8. If the marks align, proceed to Step 9. If the marks do not align, shut OFF the engine and loosen the distributor hold-down clamp bolt. Start the engine, aim the timing light and turn the distributor until the timing marks align. Shut OFF the engine and tighten the distributor hold-down clamp bolt to 17–25 ft. lbs. (23–34 Nm). Recheck the timing after the bolt has been tightened.

9. Remove the timing light and tachometer.

10. Unplug and reconnect the vacuum hoses. Remove the jumper wire from the ignition connector and reconnect, if applicable.

Valve Lash

ADJUSTMENT

4.6L Engine

The 4.6L engine requires no valve lash adjustment. Refer to Section 3 for information on the valvetrain on the 4.6L engine.

5.0L Engine

▶ **See Figures 115 and 116**

1. Disconnect the negative battery cable.

2. Remove the rocker arm covers. Refer to Section 3.

3. Disconnect the spark plug wire from the No. 1 cylinder spark plug. Remove the spark plug.

4. Place a finger over the spark plug hole. Turn the crankshaft in the normal direction of engine rotation, using a socket and ratchet or breaker bar on the crankshaft bolt. Turn the crankshaft until compression is felt with your finger, indicating the piston is approaching Top Dead Center (TDC) on the compression stroke.

5. Continue turning the crankshaft until the **0** mark on the crankshaft damper aligns with the pointer on the timing cover. The piston in No. 1 cylinder is now at TDC on the compression stroke.

6. With the crankshaft in the positions designated in Steps 8, 9 and 10, position lifter bleed down wrench tool T71P–6513–B or equivalent, on the rocker arm. Slowly apply pressure to bleed down the lifter until the plunger is completely bottomed. Hold the lifter in this position and check the available clearance between the rocker arm and the valve stem tip with a feeler gauge.

7. The clearance should be 0.071–0.171 in. If the clearance is less than specification, install a shorter pushrod. If the clearance is greater than specification, install a longer pushrod.

8. The following valves can be checked with the engine in position 1, No. 1 piston at TDC on the compression stroke:

   a. No. 1 intake—No. 1 exhaust
   b. No. 7 intake—No. 5 exhaust
   c. No. 8 intake—No. 4 exhaust

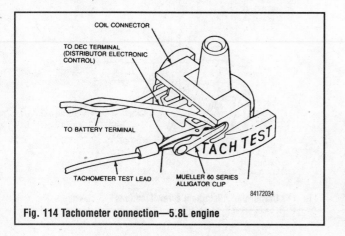

Fig. 114 Tachometer connection—5.8L engine

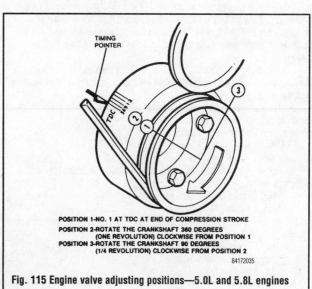

POSITION 1-NO. 1 AT TDC AT END OF COMPRESSION STROKE
POSITION 2-ROTATE THE CRANKSHAFT 360 DEGREES
(ONE REVOLUTION) CLOCKWISE FROM POSITION 1
POSITION 3-ROTATE THE CRANKSHAFT 90 DEGREES
(1/4 REVOLUTION) CLOCKWISE FROM POSITION 2

Fig. 115 Engine valve adjusting positions—5.0L and 5.8L engines

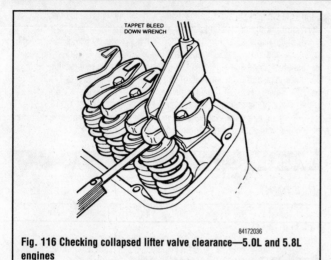

Fig. 116 Checking collapsed lifter valve clearance—5.0L and 5.8L engines

9. Rotate the crankshaft 360 degrees (1 revolution) from the 1st position and check the following valves:
   a. No. 5 intake—No. 2 exhaust
   b. No. 4 intake—No. 6 exhaust
10. Rotate the crankshaft 90 degrees (¼ revolution) from the 2nd position and check the following valves:
   a. No. 2 intake—No. 7 exhaust
   b. No. 3 intake—No. 3 exhaust
   c. No. 6 intake—No. 8 exhaust

5.8L Engine

▶ See Figures 115 and 116

1. Disconnect the negative battery cable.
2. Remove the rocker arm covers. Refer to Section 3.
3. Disconnect the spark plug wire from the No. 1 cylinder spark plug. Remove the spark plug.
4. Place a finger over the spark plug hole. Turn the crankshaft in the normal direction of engine rotation, using a socket and ratchet or breaker bar on the crankshaft bolt. Turn the crankshaft until compression is felt with your finger, indicating the piston is approaching Top Dead Center (TDC) on the compression stroke.
5. Continue turning the crankshaft until the **0** mark on the crankshaft damper aligns with the pointer on the timing cover. The piston in No. 1 cylinder is now at TDC on the compression stroke.
6. With the crankshaft in the positions designated in Steps 8, 9 and 10, position lifter bleed down wrench tool T71P–6513–B or equivalent, on the rocker arm. Slowly apply pressure to bleed down the lifter until the plunger is completely bottomed. Hold the lifter in this position and check the available clearance between the rocker arm and the valve stem tip with a feeler gauge.
7. The clearance should 0.092–0.192 in. If the clearance is less than specification, install a shorter pushrod. If the clearance is greater than specification, install a longer pushrod.
8. The following valves can be checked with the engine in position 1, No. 1 piston at TDC on the compression stroke:
   a. No. 1 intake—No. 1 exhaust
   b. No. 4 intake—No. 3 exhaust
   c. No. 8 intake—No. 7 exhaust
9. Rotate the crankshaft 360 degrees (1 revolution) from the 1st position and check the following valves:
   a. No. 3 intake—No. 2 exhaust
   b. No. 7 intake—No. 6 exhaust
10. Rotate the crankshaft 90 degrees (¼ revolution) from the 2nd position and check the following valves:
   a. No. 2 intake—No. 4 exhaust
   b. No. 5 intake—No. 5 exhaust
   c. No. 6 intake—No. 8 exhaust

Idle Speed

ADJUSTMENT

4.6L and 5.0L Engines

The 4.6L and 5.0L engines covered by this manual utilize a sophisticated fuel injection system in which an engine control computer utilizes information from various sensors to control idle speed and air/fuel mixtures. No periodic adjustments are either necessary or possible on these systems. If a problem is suspected, please refer to Sections 4 of this manual for more information on electronic engine controls and fuel injection.

5.8L Engine

▶ See Figure 117

1. Place the transmission in **N** or **P**. Apply the parking brake and block the wheels. If equipped with automatic brake release, disconnect the vacuum hose and plug it.
2. Bring the engine to normal operating temperature. Place the air conditioner/heater selector to the **OFF** position.
3. Disconnect the vacuum hose at the EGR valve and plug.
4. Place the fast idle adjustment on the second step of the fast idle cam. Check and/or adjust fast idle rpm to specification. Refer to the Vehicle Emission Control Information label.
5. Rev the engine momentarily and repeat Step 4. Remove the plug from the EGR vacuum hose and reconnect.
6. Disconnect and plug the vacuum hose at the throttle kicker and place the transmission in the idle setting position specified on the Vehicle Emission Control Information label. If adjustment is required, turn the curb idle speed screw and set the idle to the speed specified on the label.
7. Put the transmission in **N** or **P**, increase the engine speed momentarily and recheck.
8. Apply a slight pressure on top of the nylon nut located on the accelerator pump to take up the linkage clearance. Turn the nut on the accelerator pump rod clockwise until a clearance of 0.010 in. plus or minus 0.005 in. is obtained between the top of the accelerator pump and the pump lever.
9. Turn the accelerator pump rod 1 turn counterclockwise to set the lever lash preload. Remove the plug from the throttle kicker vacuum hose and reconnect.

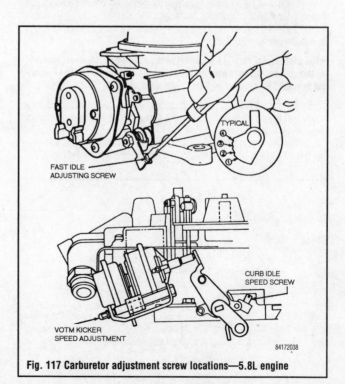

Fig. 117 Carburetor adjustment screw locations—5.8L engine

GASOLINE ENGINE TUNE-UP SPECIFICATIONS

Year	Engine ID/VIN	Engine Displacement Liters (cc)	Spark Plugs Gap (in.)	Ignition Timing (deg.) MT	Ignition Timing (deg.) AT	Fuel Pump (psi)	Idle Speed (rpm) MT	Idle Speed (rpm) AT	Valve Clearance In.	Valve Clearance Ex.
1989	F	5.0 (4993)	0.050 in.	-	10B	35-40 ①	-	②	HYD	HYD
	G	5.8 (5767)	0.044 in.	-	14B	③	-	②	HYD	HYD
1990	F	5.0 (4993)	0.050 in.	-	10B	35-40 ①	-	②	HYD	HYD
	G	5.8 (5767)	0.044 in.	-	14B	③	-	②	HYD	HYD
1991	F	5.0 (4993)	0.050 in.	-	10B	35-40 ①	-	②	HYD	HYD
	G	5.8 (5767)	0.044 in.	-	14B	③	-	②	HYD	HYD
1992	W	4.6 (4593)	0.054 in.	-	10B	35-40 ①	-	560	HYD	HYD
1993	W	4.6 (4593)	0.054 in.	-	10B	35-40 ①	-	560	HYD	HYD
1994	W	4.6 (4593)	0.054 in.	-	10B	35-40 ①	-	560	HYD	HYD
1995	W	4.6 (4593)	0.054 in.	-	10B	35-40 ①	-	560	HYD	HYD
1996	W	4.6 (4593)	0.054 in.	-	10B	35-40 ①	-	560	HYD	HYD
1997	W	4.6 (4593)	0.054 in.	-	10B	35-40 ①	-	560	HYD	HYD
	9	4.6 (4593)	0.054 in.	-	10B	35-40 ①	-	560	HYD	HYD
1998	W	4.6 (4593)	0.054 in.	-	10B	35-40 ①	-	560	HYD	HYD
	9	4.6 (4593)	0.054 in.	-	10B	35-40 ①	-	560	HYD	HYD

NOTE: The Vehicle Emission Control Information label often reflects specification changes made during production. The label figures must be used if they differ from those in this chart.

B - Before Top Dead Center

HYD - Hydraulic

① Fuel pressure with engine running, pressure regulator vacuum hose connected

② Refer to Vehicle Emission Control Information label

③ 6-8 psi, vehicle is carbureted and equipped with a mechanical fuel pump

89601C03

10. Disconnect and plug the vacuum hose at the Vacuum Operated Throttle Modulator (VOTM) kicker. Connect an external vacuum source providing a minimum of 10 in. Hg to the VOTM kicker. With the transmission in the specified position, check/adjust the VOTM kicker speed.

11. If adjustment is required, turn the VOTM kicker speed adjusting screw. Remove external vacuum source and reconnect VOTM kicker hose.

Air Conditioning System

SYSTEM SERVICE & REPAIR

➡ It is recommended that the A/C system be serviced by an EPA Section 609 certified automotive technician utilizing a refrigerant recovery/recycling machine.

The do-it-yourselfer should not service his/her own vehicle's A/C system for many reasons, including legal concerns, personal injury, environmental damage and cost. The following are some of the reasons why you may decide not to service your own vehicle's A/C system.

According to the U.S. Clean Air Act, it is a federal crime to service or repair (involving the refrigerant) a Motor Vehicle Air Conditioning (MVAC) system for money without being EPA certified. It is also illegal to vent R-12 and R-134a refrigerants into the atmosphere. Selling or distributing A/C system refrigerant (in a container which contains less than 20 pounds of refrigerant) to any person who is not EPA 609 certified is also not allowed by law.

State and/or local laws may be more strict than the federal regulations, so be sure to check with your state and/or local authorities for further information. For further federal information on the legality of servicing your A/C system, call the EPA Stratospheric Ozone Hotline.

➡ Federal law dictates that a fine of up to $25,000 may be levied on people convicted of venting refrigerant into the atmosphere. Additionally, the EPA may pay up to $10,000 for information or services leading to a criminal conviction of the violation of these laws.

When servicing an A/C system you run the risk of handling or coming in contact with refrigerant, which may result in skin or eye irritation or frostbite. Although low in toxicity (due to chemical stability), inhalation of concentrated refrigerant fumes is dangerous and can result in death; cases of fatal cardiac arrhythmia have been reported in people accidentally subjected to high levels of refrigerant. Some early symptoms include loss of concentration and drowsiness.

➡ Generally, the limit for exposure is lower for R-134a than it is for R-12. Exceptional care must be practiced when handling R-134a.

Also, refrigerants can decompose at high temperatures (near gas heaters or open flame), which may result in hydrofluoric acid, hydrochloric acid and phosgene (a fatal nerve gas).

R-12 refrigerant can damage the environment because it is a Chlorofluorocarbon (CFC), which has been proven to add to ozone layer depletion, leading to increasing levels of UV radiation. UV radiation has been linked with an increase in skin cancer, suppression of the human immune system, an increase in cataracts, damage to crops, damage to aquatic organisms, an increase in ground-level ozone, and increased global warming.

R-134a refrigerant is a greenhouse gas which, if allowed to vent into the atmosphere, will contribute to global warming (the Greenhouse Effect).

It is usually more economically feasible to have a certified MVAC automotive technician perform A/C system service on your vehicle. Some possible reasons for this are as follows:

• While it is illegal to service an A/C system without the proper equipment, the home mechanic would have to purchase an expensive refrigerant recovery/recycling machine to service his/her own vehicle.

• Since only a certified person may purchase refrigerant—according to the Clean Air Act, there are specific restrictions on selling or distributing A/C system refrigerant—it is legally impossible (unless certified) for the home mechanic to service his/her own vehicle. Procuring refrigerant in an illegal fashion exposes one to the risk of paying a $25,000 fine to the EPA.

R-12 Refrigerant Conversion

If your vehicle still uses R-12 refrigerant, one way to save A/C system costs down the road is to investigate the possibility of having your system converted to R-134a. The older R-12 systems can be easily converted to R-134a refrigerant by a certified automotive technician by installing a few new components and changing the system oil.

The cost of R-12 is steadily rising and will continue to increase, because it is no longer imported or manufactured in the United States. Therefore, it is often possible to have an R-12 system converted to R-134a and recharged for less than it would cost to just charge the system with R-12.

If you are interested in having your system converted, contact local automotive service stations for more details and information.

PREVENTIVE MAINTENANCE

▶ See Figures 118 and 119

Although the A/C system should not be serviced by the do-it-yourselfer, preventive maintenance can be practiced and A/C system inspections can be performed to help maintain the efficiency of the vehicle's A/C system. For preventive maintenance, perform the following:

• The easiest and most important preventive maintenance for your A/C system is to be sure that it is used on a regular basis. Running the system for five minutes each month (no matter what the season) will help ensure that the seals and all internal components remain lubricated.

➡ Some newer vehicles automatically operate the A/C system compressor whenever the windshield defroster is activated. When running, the compressor lubricates the A/C system components; therefore, the A/C system would not need to be operated each month.

• In order to prevent heater core freeze-up during A/C operation, it is necessary to maintain proper antifreeze protection. Use a hand-held coolant tester (hydrometer) to periodically check the condition of the antifreeze in your engine's cooling system.

➡ Antifreeze should not be used longer than the manufacturer specifies.

• For efficient operation of an air conditioned vehicle's cooling system, the radiator cap should have a holding pressure which meets manufacturer's specifications. A cap which fails to hold these pressures should be replaced.

• Any obstruction of or damage to the condenser configuration will restrict air flow which is essential to its efficient operation. It is, therefore, a good rule to keep this unit clean and in proper physical shape.

➡ Bug screens which are mounted in front of the condenser (unless they are original equipment) are regarded as obstructions.

• The condensation drain tube expels any water which accumulates on the bottom of the evaporator housing into the engine compartment. If this tube is obstructed, the air conditioning performance can be restricted and condensation buildup can spill over onto the vehicle's floor.

SYSTEM INSPECTION

▶ See Figure 120

Although the A/C system should not be serviced by the do-it-yourselfer, preventive maintenance can be practiced and A/C system inspections can be performed to help maintain the efficiency of the vehicle's A/C system. For A/C system inspection, perform the following:

The easiest and often most important check for the air conditioning system consists of a visual inspection of the system components. Visually inspect the air conditioning system for refrigerant leaks, damaged compressor clutch, abnormal compressor drive belt tension and/or condition, plugged evaporator drain tube, blocked condenser fins, disconnected or broken wires, blown fuses, corroded connections and poor insulation.

A refrigerant leak will usually appear as an oily residue at the leakage point in the system. The oily residue soon picks up dust or dirt particles from the surrounding air and appears greasy. Through time, this will build up and appear to be a heavy dirt impregnated grease.

For a thorough visual and operational inspection, check the following:

• Check the surface of the radiator and condenser for dirt, leaves or other material which might block air flow.

• Check for kinks in hoses and lines. Check the system for leaks.

• Make sure the drive belt is properly tensioned. When the air conditioning is operating, make sure the drive belt is free of noise or slippage.

• Make sure the blower motor operates at all appropriate positions, then check for distribution of the air from all outlets with the blower on **HIGH** or **MAX**.

➡ Keep in mind that under conditions of high humidity, air discharged from the A/C vents may not feel as cold as expected, even if the system is working properly. This is because vaporized moisture in humid air retains heat more effectively than dry air, thereby making humid air more difficult to cool.

• Make sure the air passage selection lever is operating correctly. Start the engine and warm it to normal operating temperature, then make sure the temperature selection lever is operating correctly.

Windshield Wipers

ELEMENT (REFILL) CARE & REPLACEMENT

▶ See Figures 121 thru 130

For maximum effectiveness and longest element life, the windshield and wiper blades should be kept clean. Dirt, tree sap, road tar and so on will cause streaking, smearing and blade deterioration if left on the glass. It is advisable to wash the windshield carefully with a commercial glass cleaner at least once a month. Wipe off the rubber blades with the wet rag afterwards. Do not attempt to move wipers across the windshield by hand; damage to the motor and drive mechanism will result.

To inspect and/or replace the wiper blade elements, place the wiper switch in the **LOW** speed position and the ignition switch in the **ACC** position. When the wiper blades are approximately vertical on the windshield, turn the ignition switch to **OFF**.

Examine the wiper blade elements. If they are found to be cracked, broken or torn, they should be replaced immediately. Replacement intervals will vary with usage, although ozone deterioration usually limits element life to about one year. If the wiper pattern is smeared or streaked, or if the blade chatters across the glass, the elements should be replaced. It is easiest and most sensible to replace the elements in pairs.

If your vehicle is equipped with aftermarket blades, there are several different types of refills and your vehicle might have any kind. Aftermarket blades and arms rarely use the exact same type blade or refill as the original equipment. Here are some typical aftermarket blades; not all may be available for your vehicle:

Fig. 118 A coolant tester can be used to determine the freezing and boiling levels of the coolant in your vehicle

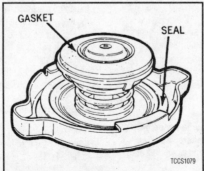

GASKET

SEAL

Fig. 119 To ensure efficient cooling system operation, inspect the radiator cap gasket and seal

Fig. 120 Periodically remove any debris from the condenser and radiator fins

The Anco® type uses a release button that is pushed down to allow the refill to slide out of the yoke jaws. The new refill slides back into the frame and locks in place.

Some Trico® refills are removed by locating where the metal backing strip or the refill is wider. Insert a small screwdriver blade between the frame and metal backing strip. Press down to release the refill from the retaining tab.

Other types of Trico® refills have two metal tabs which are unlocked by squeezing them together. The rubber filler can then be withdrawn from the frame jaws. A new refill is installed by inserting the refill into the front frame jaws and sliding it rearward to engage the remaining frame jaws. There are usually four jaws; be certain when installing that the refill is engaged in all of them. At the end of its travel, the tabs will lock into place on the front jaws of the wiper blade frame.

Another type of refill is made from polycarbonate. The refill has a simple locking device at one end which flexes downward out of the groove into which the jaws of the holder fit, allowing easy release. By sliding the new refill through all the jaws and pushing through the slight resistance when it reaches the end of its travel, the refill will lock into position.

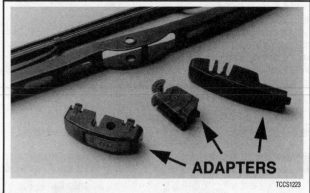

ADAPTERS

TCCS1223

Fig. 121 Bosch® wiper blade and fit kit

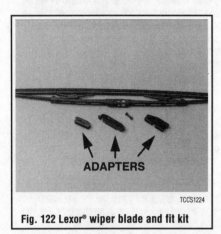

ADAPTERS

TCCS1224

Fig. 122 Lexor® wiper blade and fit kit

TCCS1225

Fig. 123 Pylon® wiper blade and adapter

TCCS1226

Fig. 124 Trico® wiper blade and fit kit

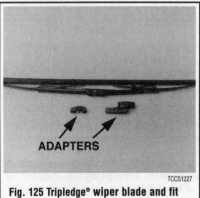

ADAPTERS

TCCS1227

Fig. 125 Tripledge® wiper blade and fit kit

TCCS1228

Fig. 126 To remove and install a Lexor® wiper blade refill, slip out the old insert and slide in a new one

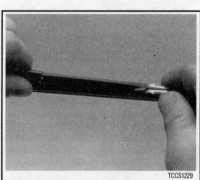

TCCS1229

Fig. 127 On Pylon® inserts, the clip at the end has to be removed prior to sliding the insert off

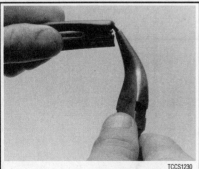

TCCS1230

Fig. 128 On Trico® wiper blades, the tab at the end of the blade must be turned up . . .

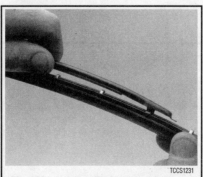

TCCS1231

Fig. 129 . . . then the insert can be removed. After installing the replacement insert, bend the tab back

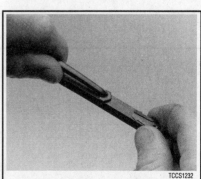

TCCS1232

Fig. 130 The Tripledge® wiper blade insert is removed and installed using a securing clip

To replace the Tridon® refill, it is necessary to remove the wiper blade. This refill has a plastic backing strip with a notch about 1 in. (25mm) from the end. Hold the blade (frame) on a hard surface so that the frame is tightly bowed. Grip the tip of the backing strip and pull up while twisting counterclockwise. The backing strip will snap out of the retaining tab. Do this for the remaining tabs until the refill is free of the blade. The length of these refills is molded into the end and they should be replaced with identical types.

Regardless of the type of refill used, be sure to follow the part manufacturer's instructions closely. Make sure that all of the frame jaws are engaged as the refill is pushed into place and locked. If the metal blade holder and frame are allowed to touch the glass during wiper operation, the glass will be scratched.

Tires and Wheels

Common sense and good driving habits will afford maximum tire life. Fast starts, sudden stops and hard cornering are hard on tires and will shorten their useful life span. Make sure that you don't overload the vehicle or run with incorrect pressure in the tires. Both of these practices will increase tread wear.

➡**For optimum tire life, keep the tires properly inflated, rotate them often and have the wheel alignment checked periodically.**

Inspect your tires frequently. Be especially careful to watch for bubbles in the tread or sidewall, deep cuts or underinflation. Replace any tires with bubbles in the sidewall. If cuts are so deep that they penetrate to the cords, discard the tire. Any cut in the sidewall of a radial tire renders it unsafe. Also look for uneven tread wear patterns that may indicate the front end is out of alignment or that the tires are out of balance.

TIRE ROTATION

▶ **See Figures 131 and 132**

Tires must be rotated periodically to equalize wear patterns that vary with a tire's position on the vehicle. Tires will also wear in an uneven way as the front steering/suspension system wears to the point where the alignment should be reset.

Rotating the tires will ensure maximum life for the tires as a set, so you will not have to discard a tire early due to wear on only part of the tread. Regular rotation is required to equalize wear.

When rotating "unidirectional tires," make sure that they always roll in the same direction. This means that a tire used on the left side of the vehicle must not be switched to the right side and vice-versa. Such tires should only be rotated front-to-rear or rear-to-front, while always remaining on the same side of the vehicle. These tires are marked on the sidewall as to the direction of rotation; observe the marks when reinstalling the tire(s).

Some styled or "mag" wheels may have different offsets front to rear. In these cases, the rear wheels must not be used up front and vice-versa. Furthermore, if these wheels are equipped with unidirectional tires, they cannot be rotated unless the tire is remounted for the proper direction of rotation.

➡**The compact or space-saver spare is strictly for emergency use. It must never be included in the tire rotation or placed on the vehicle for everyday use.**

TIRE DESIGN

▶ **See Figure 133**

For maximum satisfaction, tires should be used in sets of four. Mixing of different types (radial, bias-belted, fiberglass belted) must be avoided. In most cases, the vehicle manufacturer has designated a type of tire on which the vehicle will perform best. Your first choice when replacing tires should be to use the same type of tire that the manufacturer recommends.

When radial tires are used, tire sizes and wheel diameters should be selected to maintain ground clearance and tire load capacity equivalent to the original specified tire. Radial tires should always be used in sets of four.

❊❊ CAUTION

Radial tires should never be used on only the front axle.

When selecting tires, pay attention to the original size as marked on the tire. Most tires are described using an industry size code sometimes referred to as P-Metric. This allows the exact identification of the tire specifications, regardless of the manufacturer. If selecting a different tire size or brand, remember to check the installed tire for any sign of interference with the body or suspension while the vehicle is stopping, turning sharply or heavily loaded.

Snow Tires

Good radial tires can produce a big advantage in slippery weather, but in snow, a street radial tire does not have sufficient tread to provide traction and control. The small grooves of a street tire quickly pack with snow and the tire behaves like a billiard ball on a marble floor. The more open, chunky tread of a snow tire will self-clean as the tire turns, providing much better grip on snowy surfaces.

To satisfy municipalities requiring snow tires during weather emergencies, most snow tires carry either an M + S designation after the tire size stamped on the sidewall, or the designation "all-season." In general, no change in tire size is necessary when buying snow tires.

Most manufacturers strongly recommend the use of 4 snow tires on their vehicles for reasons of stability. If snow tires are fitted only to the drive wheels, the opposite end of the vehicle may become very unstable when braking or turning on slippery surfaces. This instability can lead to unpleasant endings if the driver can't counteract the slide in time.

Note that snow tires, whether 2 or 4, will affect vehicle handling in all non-snow situations. The stiffer, heavier snow tires will noticeably change the turning and braking characteristics of the vehicle. Once the snow tires are installed, you must re-learn the behavior of the vehicle and drive accordingly.

➡**Consider buying extra wheels on which to mount the snow tires. Once done, the "snow wheels" can be installed and removed as needed. This eliminates the potential damage to tires or wheels from seasonal removal and installation. Even if your vehicle has styled wheels, see if inexpensive steel wheels are available. Although the look of the vehicle will change, the expensive wheels will be protected from salt, curb hits and pothole damage.**

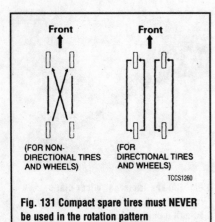

Fig. 131 Compact spare tires must NEVER be used in the rotation pattern

Fig. 132 Unidirectional tires are identifiable by sidewall arrows and/or the word "rotation"

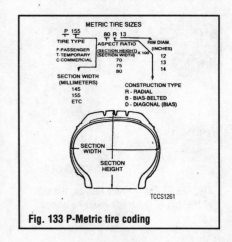

Fig. 133 P-Metric tire coding

TIRE STORAGE

If they are mounted on wheels, store the tires at proper inflation pressure. All tires should be kept in a cool, dry place. If they are stored in the garage or basement, do not let them stand on a concrete floor; set them on strips of wood, a mat or a large stack of newspaper. Keeping them away from direct moisture is of paramount importance. Tires should not be stored upright, but in a flat position.

INFLATION & INSPECTION

▶ **See Figures 134 thru 141**

The importance of proper tire inflation cannot be overemphasized. A tire employs air as part of its structure. It is designed around the supporting strength of the air at a specified pressure. For this reason, improper inflation drastically reduces the tire's ability to perform as intended. A tire will lose some

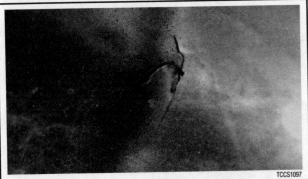

Fig. 134 Tires should be checked frequently for any sign of puncture or damage

air in day-to-day use; having to add a few pounds of air periodically is not necessarily a sign of a leaking tire.

Two items should be a permanent fixture in every glove compartment: an accurate tire pressure gauge and a tread depth gauge. Check the tire pressure (including the spare) regularly with a pocket type gauge. Too often, the gauge on the end of the air hose at your corner garage is not accurate because it suffers too much abuse. Always check tire pressure when the tires are cold, as pressure increases with temperature. If you must move the vehicle to check the tire inflation, do not drive more than a mile before checking. A cold tire is generally one that has not been driven for more than three hours.

A plate or sticker is normally provided somewhere in the vehicle (door post, hood, tailgate or trunk lid) which shows the proper pressure for the tires. Never counteract excessive pressure build-up by bleeding off air pressure (letting some air out). This will cause the tire to run hotter and wear quicker.

❊❊ CAUTION

Never exceed the maximum tire pressure embossed on the tire! This is the pressure to be used when the tire is at maximum loading, but it is rarely the correct pressure for everyday driving. Consult the owner's manual or the tire pressure sticker for the correct tire pressure.

Once you've maintained the correct tire pressures for several weeks, you'll be familiar with the vehicle's braking and handling personality. Slight adjustments in tire pressures can fine-tune these characteristics, but never change the cold pressure specification by more than 2 psi. A slightly softer tire pressure will give a softer ride but also yield lower fuel mileage. A slightly harder tire will give crisper dry road handling but can cause skidding on wet surfaces. Unless you're fully attuned to the vehicle, stick to the recommended inflation pressures.

All tires made since 1968 have built-in tread wear indicator bars that show up as ½ in. (13mm) wide smooth bands across the tire when ¹⁄₁₆ in. (1.5mm) of tread remains. The appearance of tread wear indicators means that the tires should be replaced. In fact, many states have laws prohibiting the use of tires with less than this amount of tread.

Fig. 135 Tires with deep cuts, or cuts which bulge, should be replaced immediately

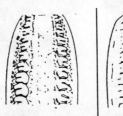

- DRIVE WHEEL HEAVY ACCELERATION
- OVERINFLATION

- HARD CORNERING
- UNDERINFLATION
- LACK OF ROTATION

Fig. 136 Examples of inflation-related tire wear patterns

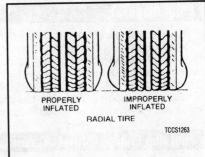

PROPERLY INFLATED   IMPROPERLY INFLATED

RADIAL TIRE

Fig. 137 Radial tires have a characteristic sidewall bulge; don't try to measure pressure by looking at the tire. Use a quality air pressure gauge

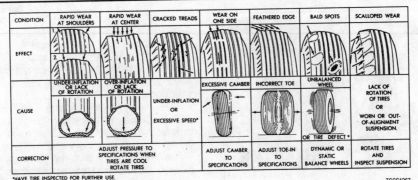

CONDITION	RAPID WEAR AT SHOULDERS	RAPID WEAR AT CENTER	CRACKED TREADS	WEAR ON ONE SIDE	FEATHERED EDGE	BALD SPOTS	SCALLOPED WEAR
EFFECT							
CAUSE	UNDER-INFLATION OR LACK OF ROTATION	OVER-INFLATION OR LACK OF ROTATION	UNDER-INFLATION OR EXCESSIVE SPEED*	EXCESSIVE CAMBER	INCORRECT TOE	UNBALANCED WHEEL OR TIRE DEFECT*	LACK OF ROTATION OF TIRES OR WORN OR OUT-OF-ALIGNMENT SUSPENSION*
CORRECTION		ADJUST PRESSURE TO SPECIFICATIONS WHEN TIRES ARE COOL ROTATE TIRES		ADJUST CAMBER TO SPECIFICATIONS	ADJUST TOE-IN TO SPECIFICATIONS	DYNAMIC OR STATIC BALANCE WHEELS	ROTATE TIRES AND INSPECT SUSPENSION

*HAVE TIRE INSPECTED FOR FURTHER USE.

TCCS1267

Fig. 138 Common tire wear patterns and causes

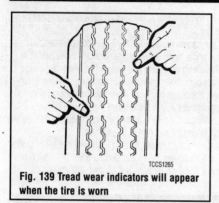

Fig. 139 Tread wear indicators will appear when the tire is worn

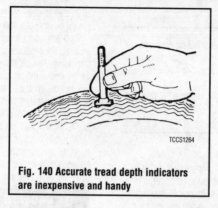

Fig. 140 Accurate tread depth indicators are inexpensive and handy

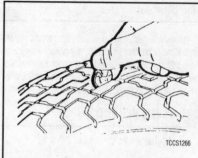

Fig. 141 A penny works well for a quick check of tread depth

You can check your own tread depth with an inexpensive gauge or by using a Lincoln head penny. Slip the Lincoln penny (with Lincoln's head upside-down) into several tread grooves. If you can see the top of Lincoln's head in 2 adjacent grooves, the tire has less than 1/16 in. (1.5mm) tread left and should be replaced. You can measure snow tires in the same manner by using the "tails" side of the Lincoln penny. If you can see the top of the Lincoln memorial, it's time to replace the snow tire(s).

CARE OF SPECIAL WHEELS

If you have invested money in magnesium, aluminum alloy or sport wheels, special precautions should be taken to make sure your investment is not wasted and that your special wheels look good for the life of the vehicle.

Special wheels are easily damaged and/or scratched. Occasionally check the rims for cracking, impact damage or air leaks. If any of these are found, replace the wheel. But in order to prevent this type of damage and the costly replacement of a special wheel, observe the following precautions:

• Use extra care not to damage the wheels during removal, installation, balancing, etc. After removal of the wheels from the vehicle, place them on a mat or other protective surface. If they are to be stored for any length of time, support them on strips of wood. Never store tires and wheels upright; the tread may develop flat spots.

• When driving, watch for hazards; it doesn't take much to crack a wheel.

• When washing, use a mild soap or non-abrasive dish detergent (keeping in mind that detergent tends to remove wax). Avoid cleansers with abrasives or the use of hard brushes. There are many cleaners and polishes for special wheels.

• If possible, remove the wheels during the winter. Salt and sand used for snow removal can severely damage the finish of a wheel.

• Make certain the recommended lug nut torque is never exceeded or the wheel may crack. Never use snow chains on special wheels; severe scratching will occur.

FLUIDS AND LUBRICANTS

Fluid Disposal

Used fluids such as engine oil, transmission fluid, antifreeze and brake fluid are hazardous wastes and must be disposed of properly. Before draining any fluids, consult with your local authorities; in many areas, waste oil, antifreeze, etc. is being accepted as a part of recycling programs. A number of service stations and auto parts stores are also accepting waste fluids for recycling.

Be sure of the recycling center's policies before draining any fluids, as many will not accept different fluids that have been mixed together.

Fuel and Engine Oil Recommendations

FUEL

▶ **See Figure 142**

Depending on the year produced, your vehicle may be equipped with a catalytic converter as a part of its emission control system, necessitating the use of unleaded gasoline. Using leaded fuel will damage the catalytic converter, resulting in poor vehicle performance and excessive exhaust emissions.

If your car is equipped with a converter, the engine is designed to use gasoline with a minimum octane rating of 87, which in most areas means regular unleaded gasoline. Always use a high quality fuel containing detergent additives, to keep fuel injectors and intake valves clean.

If the engine occasionally knocks lightly under acceleration, or when going up a hill, do not be concerned. However, if the engine knocks heavily under all driving conditions, or knocks lightly at cruising speeds, try switching to another brand or higher grade of gasoline. If knocking persists, the cause should be investigated or serious engine damage could result.

OIL

▶ **See Figure 143**

Always use a high quality detergent motor oil. To determine an oil's quality and viscosity, look for the American Petroleum Institute (API) symbol on the oil container label. The highest quality oil currently available carries the API Service rating "SG". Look for the letters "SG" alone or in combination with other letters such as "SG/CC" or "SG/CD". An oil rated "SC", "SD", "SE" or "SF" is not acceptable for use in your car's engine.

For maximum fuel economy, look for an oil that carries the words "Energy Conserving II" in the API symbol. This means that the oil contains friction reducing additives that help reduce the amount of fuel burned to overcome engine friction.

The Society of Automotive Engineers (SAE) viscosity rating indicates an oil's ability to flow at a given temperature. The number designation indicates the thickness or "weight" of the oil. An SAE 5 weight oil is a thin, light oil; it allows the engine to crank over easily even when it is very cold, and quickly provides lubrication for all parts of the engine. However, as the engine temperature increases, the 5 weight oil becomes too thin, resulting in metal-to-metal contact and damage to internal engine parts. A heavier SAE 50 weight oil can lubricate and protect internal engine parts even under extremely high operating temperatures, but would not be able to flow quickly enough to provide internal engine

Fig. 142 On some models, a release cable is located in the trunk in the event that the fuel door remote release is inoperative

Fig. 143 An example of the API Symbol

Fig. 144 Grasp the engine oil dipstick and . . .

Fig. 145 . . . pull the dipstick out of the tube

protection during cold weather start-up, one of the most critical periods for lubrication protection in an engine.

The answer to the temperature extremes problem is the multi-grade or multi-viscosity oil. Multi-viscosity oils carry multiple number designations, such as SAE 10W-40 or SAE 20W-50 (the "W" in the designation stands for winter). A 10W-40 oil has the flow characteristics of the thin 10 weight oil in cold weather, providing rapid lubrication and allowing easy engine cranking. When the engine warms up, the oil acts like a straight 40 weight oil, providing internal engine protection under higher temperatures.

Ford Motor Company recommends using either SAE 5W-30 or SAE 10W-30 oil. SAE 5W-30 should be used if you anticipate the ambient temperature in which you'll be driving to fall below 0°F (−18°C) but not go higher than 100°F (38°C) during the period before your next oil change. SAE 10W-30 should be used if you anticipate the temperature in which you'll be driving to be between 0°F (−18°C) and 100°F (38°C) and above, during the period before your next oil change.

Engine

OIL LEVEL CHECK

▶ **See Figures 144 thru 151**

❋❋ CAUTION

The EPA warns that prolonged contact with used engine oil may cause a number of skin disorders, including cancer! You should make every effort to minimize your exposure to used engine oil. Protective gloves should be worn when changing the oil. Wash your hands and any other exposed skin areas as soon as possible after exposure to used engine oil. Soap and water, or waterless hand cleaner should be used.

Fig. 146 Wipe the dipstick clean and replace it into the tube to inspect the oil level

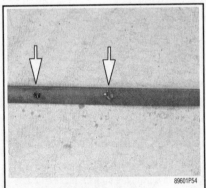

Fig. 147 Ensure that the oil level is between the MIN and MAX lines

Fig. 148 To remove the oil fill cap, grasp the cap and turn it counter-clockwise until . . .

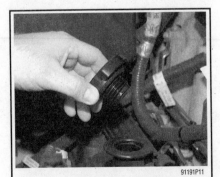

Fig. 149 . . . the cap unscrews from the valve cover. Be sure to place the oil cap in a safe place so as not to lose it

Fig. 150 Place a funnel directly into the oil fill port and . . .

Fig. 151 . . . pour oil into the engine

The engine oil dipstick is typically located on the driver's side of the vehicle, near the brake master cylinder.

Engine oil level should be checked every time you put fuel in the vehicle or are under the hood performing other maintenance.

1. Park the vehicle on a level surface.

2. The engine may be either hot or cold when checking oil level. However, if it is hot, wait a few minutes after the engine has been turned **OFF** to allow the oil to drain back into the crankcase. If the engine is cold, do not start it before checking the oil level.

3. Open the hood and locate the engine oil dipstick. Pull the dipstick from its tube, wipe it clean, and reinsert it. Make sure the dipstick is fully inserted.

4. Pull the dipstick from its tube again. Holding it horizontally, read the oil level. The oil should be between the MIN and MAX mark. If the oil is below the MIN mark, add oil of the proper viscosity through the capped opening of the valve cover.

5. Replace the dipstick, and check the level again after adding any oil. Be careful not to overfill the crankcase. Approximately one quart of oil will raise the level from the low mark to the high mark. Excess oil will generally be consumed at an accelerated rate even if no damage to the engine seals occurs.

OIL & FILTER CHANGE

▶ **See Figures 152 thru 159**

The oil and filter should be changed every 5,000 miles (8,000 km) under normal service and every 3,000 miles (5,000 km) under severe service.

✳✳ CAUTION

The EPA warns that prolonged contact with used engine oil may cause a number of skin disorders, including cancer! You should make every effort to minimize your exposure to used engine oil. Protective gloves should be worn when changing the oil. Wash your hands and any other exposed skin areas as soon as possible after exposure to used engine oil. Soap and water, or waterless hand cleaner should be used.

➡The engine oil and oil filter should be changed at the recommended intervals on the Maintenance Chart. Though some manufacturers have at times recommended changing the filter only at every other oil change, Chilton recommends that you always change the filter with the oil. The benefit of fresh oil is quickly lost if the old filter is clogged and unable to do its job. Also, leaving the old filter in place leaves a significant amount of dirty oil in the system.

➡Before beginning to change the engine oil and filter, it is necessary to turn the wheel all the way to the left to access the oil filter. The filter is blocked by the pitman arm, unless this is done. It should be done while the engine is still able to started, so that the power steering can be engaged, otherwise the wheel can be extremely hard to turn.

The oil should be changed more frequently if the vehicle is being operated in a very dusty area. Before draining the oil, make sure that the engine is at operating temperature. Hot oil will hold more impurities in suspension and will flow better, allowing the removal of more oil and dirt.

It is a good idea to warm the engine oil first so it will flow better. This can be accomplished by 15–20 miles of highway driving. Fluid which is warmed to normal operating temperature will flow faster, drain more completely and remove more contaminants from the engine.

1. Raise and support the vehicle safely on jackstands. Make sure the oil drain plug is at the lowest point on the oil pan. If not, you may have to raise the vehicle slightly higher on one jackstand (side) than the other.

2. Before you crawl under the vehicle, take a look at where you will be working and gather all the necessary tools, such as a few wrenches or a ratchet and strip of sockets, the drain pan, some clean rags and, if the oil filter is more accessible from underneath the vehicle, you will also want to grab a bottle of oil, the new filter and a filter wrench at this time.

3. Position the drain pan beneath the oil pan drain plug. Keep in mind that the fast flowing oil, which will spill out as you pull the plug from the pan, will flow with enough force that it could miss the pan. Position the drain pan accordingly and be ready to move the pan more directly beneath the plug as the oil flow lessens to a trickle.

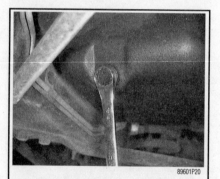

Fig. 152 Loosen the engine oil drain plug. Typically the oil drain plug requires a 16mm wrench

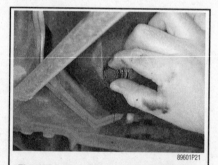

Fig. 153 Loosen the drain plug but do not remove it from the oil pan. Make sure to keep constant inward pressure on the drain plug because . . .

Fig. 154 . . . the oil drains out rather fast when the drain plug is removed

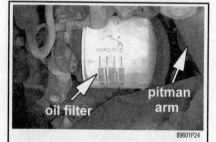

Fig. 155 The oil filter is located on the driver's side of the engine—4.6L engine. On most models, it is necessary to turn the steering wheel all the way to the left so that the filter can clear the pitman arm

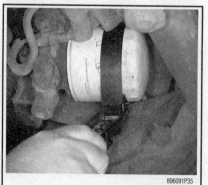

Fig. 156 Loosen the oil filter using a suitable oil filter wrench

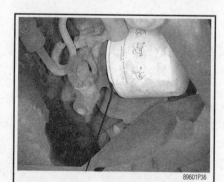

Fig. 157 After the filter is sufficiently loose, oil will typically flow out, so be sure to have a drain pan under the filter

Fig. 158 Unscrew the filter the rest of the way by hand and remove the filter from the engine

Fig. 159 Before installing a new oil filter, lightly coat the rubber gasket with clean oil

Fig. 160 Grasp the dipstick and . . .

➡Vehicles equipped with 5.0L or 5.8L engines, have 2 oil drain plugs on the oil pan; both must be removed. Typically the drain plug requires a 16mm wrench on the 4.6L engine and a ⅞ wrench on the 5.0/5.8L engines.

4. Loosen the drain plug with a wrench (or socket and driver), then carefully unscrew the plug with your fingers. Use a rag to shield your fingers from the heat. Push in on the plug as you unscrew it so you can feel when all of the screw threads are out of the hole (and so you will keep the oil from seeping past the threads until you are ready to remove the plug). You can then remove the plug quickly to avoid having hot oil run down your arm. This will also help assure that have the plug in your hand, not in the bottom of a pan of hot oil.

✳✳✳ CAUTION

Be careful of the oil; when at operating temperature, it is hot enough to cause a severe burn.

5. Allow the oil to drain until nothing but a few drops come out of the drain hole. Check the drain plug to make sure the threads and sealing surface are not damaged. Carefully thread the plug into position and tighten the drain plugs on 5.0L and 5.8L engines to 15–25 ft. lbs. (20–34 Nm) and 8–12 ft. lbs. (11–16 Nm) on the 4.6L engine. If a torque wrench is not available, snug the drain plug and give a slight additional turn. You don't want the plug to fall out (as you would quickly become stranded), but the pan threads are EASILY stripped from overtightening (and this can be time consuming and/or costly to fix).

6. To remove the filter, you may need an oil filter wrench since the filter may have been fitted too tightly and/or the heat from the engine may have made it even tighter. A filter wrench can be obtained at any auto parts store and is well-worth the investment. Loosen the filter with the filter wrench. With a rag wrapped around the filter, unscrew the filter from the boss on the side of the engine. Be careful of hot oil that will run down the side of the filter. Make sure that your drain pan is under the filter before you start to remove it from the engine; should some of the hot oil happen to get on you, there will be a place to dump the filter in a hurry and the filter will usually spill a good bit of dirty oil as it is removed.

7. Wipe the base of the mounting boss with a clean, dry cloth. When you install the new filter, smear a small amount of fresh oil on the gasket with your finger, just enough to coat the entire contact surface. When you tighten the filter, rotate it about a quarter-turn after it contacts the mounting boss (or follow any instructions which are provided on the filter or parts box).

✳✳✳ WARNING

Operating the engine without the proper amount and type of engine oil will result in severe engine damage.

8. Remove the jackstands and carefully lower the vehicle, then IMMEDIATELY refill the engine crankcase with the proper amount of oil. DO NOT WAIT TO DO THIS because if you forget and someone tries to start the vehicle, severe engine damage will occur.

9. Refill the engine crankcase slowly, checking the level often. You may notice that it usually takes less than the amount of oil listed in the capacity chart to refill the crankcase. But, that is only until the engine is run and the oil filter is

filled with oil. To make sure the proper level is obtained, run the engine to normal operating temperature, shut the engine OFF, allow the oil to drain back into the oil pan, and recheck the level. Top off the oil at this time to the fill mark.

➡If the vehicle is not resting on level ground, the oil level reading on the dipstick may be slightly off. Be sure to check the level only when the vehicle is sitting level.

10. Drain your used oil in a suitable container for recycling.

Automatic Transmission

FLUID RECOMMENDATIONS

Ford recommends using Motorcraft Mercon ATF (Automatic Transmission Fluid) XT-2-QDX or equivalent Mercon ATF fluid (Dexron Mercon III).

LEVEL CHECK

◆ See Figures 160 thru 166

The transmission dipstick is typically located near the back of the engine, towards the firewall.

1. Park the vehicle on a level surface.
2. The transmission should be at normal operating temperature when checking fluid level. To ensure the fluid is at normal operating temperature, drive the vehicle at least 10 miles.
3. With the selector lever in **P** and the parking brake applied, start the engine.
4. Open the hood and locate the transmission fluid dipstick. Pull the dipstick from its tube, wipe it clean, and reinsert it. Make sure the dipstick is fully inserted.

Fig. 161 . . . remove the dipstick from the tube

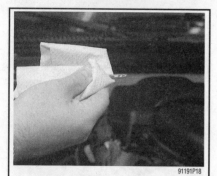

Fig. 162 Wipe the dipstick clean, reinsert the dipstick into the tube, then remove the dipstick again

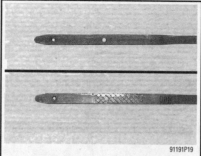

Fig. 163 The dipstick has two sides, the level should be checked on the side with the cross-hatches. If the level is in the cross-hatched area, do not add fluid

Fig. 164 Fluid is added directly into the dipstick tube

Fig. 165 Place a suitable funnel into the dipstick tube and . . .

Fig. 166 . . . pour the proper fluid into the transmission

Fig. 167 The transmission pan is held to the transmission case by retaining bolts. Typically the retaining bolts require a 10mm socket

5. Pull the dipstick from its tube again. Holding it horizontally, read the fluid level. The fluid should be between the MIN and MAX mark. If the fluid is below the MIN mark, add fluid through the dipstick tube.

6. Insert the dipstick, and check the level again after adding any fluid. Be careful not to overfill the transmission.

PAN & FILTER SERVICE

▶ **See Figures 167 thru 179**

The fluid should be changed according to the schedule in the Maintenance Intervals chart. If the car is normally used in severe service, such as stop and start driving, trailer towing, or the like, the interval should be halved. If the car is driven under especially nasty conditions, such as in heavy city traffic where the temperature normally reaches 90°F (32°C), or in very hilly or mountainous areas, or in police, taxi, or delivery service, the fluid should be changed according to the severe service schedule.

➡**To drain the automatic transmission fluid, the fluid pan must be removed.**

1. Raise and safely support the vehicle.

2. Place a drain pan underneath the transmission pan, then remove the pan attaching bolts except for the bolts on the four corners of the pan.

3. Loosen the four attaching bolts on the corners approximately four turns each, but do not remove them.

4. Very carefully pry the pan loose on one corner. You can use a small pry-bar for this if you work CAREFULLY. Do not distort the pan flange, or score the mating surface of the transmission case. You'll be very sorry later if you do. As the pan is pried loose, all of the fluid is going to come pouring out.

5. Carefully break the other corners loose until fluid is flowing steadily from the entire pan.

➡**If the drained fluid is discolored (brown or black), thick, or smells burnt, serious transmission troubles, probably due to overheating,**

Fig. 168 Remove all of the retaining bolts on the transmission pan except . . .

Fig. 169 . . . for the bolts on the four corners of the pan

Fig. 170 Slowly loosen the four corner bolts and lower the pan. As the pan is lowered fluid will begin to pour out

Fig. 171 After the fluid is drained out, remove the pan from the transmission

Fig. 172 Remove the transmission filter by gently pulling it out of the valve body

Fig. 173 Make sure that the O-ring on the filter nipple is removed from the valve body, typically it will stay on the filter nipple

Fig. 174 If you happen to find this piece in your transmission pan upon removal, don't panic, it is a dipstick tube plug that is knocked out on the assembly line while the vehicle is being built

Fig. 175 If the gasket is reusable as this one is, remove the transmission pan gasket from the pan and place it in a safe place

Fig. 176 Remove the transmission pan magnets from the pan and . . .

Fig. 177 . . . wipe the magnets clean before installing them back into the pan

Fig. 178 Thoroughly clean the mating surfaces of the pan and . . .

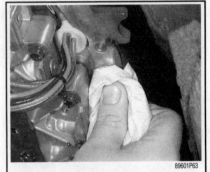

Fig. 179 . . . the transmission case before installing the gasket and pan onto the case

should be suspected. Your car's transmission should be inspected by a reliable transmission specialist to determine the problem.

6. After the fluid is done flowing, remove one corner bolt and attempt to drain any remaining fluid. Remove the remaining bolts and remove the pan and gasket.

➡**On some later models, the transmission pan gasket is reusable, do no throw it away.**

7. Clean the pan and the magnets with solvent and allow them to air dry. If you use a rag to wipe out the pan, you risk leaving bits of lint behind, which will clog the tiny hydraulic passages in the transmission.

8. Remove and discard the filter and the O-ring seal if applicable.

➡**On some models, the filter may be retained by bolts; on these, remove the bolts and the filter from the valve body.**

To install:

9. Install a new filter and O-ring, if applicable.

10. If the filter is retained by bolts, tighten the bolts to 80–120 inch lbs. (9–14 Nm).

➡**If removed from the pan, make sure the magnets are repositioned back into the pan.**

11. Position the gasket on the pan, then install the pan. Tighten the bolts evenly and in rotation to 10 ft. lbs. (13 Nm.). Do not overtighten.

12. Lower the vehicle.

13. Add the recommended automatic transmission fluid to the transmission through the dipstick tube. You will need a long necked funnel, or a funnel and tube to do this. A quick check of the capacities chart later in this Section will reveal the capacity of the transmission in your vehicle. On a first fill after removing the pan and filter, this number should cut into a ⅓ and checked on the dipstick before refilling.

14. With the transmission in **P**, put on the parking brake, block the front wheels, start the engine and let it idle. DO NOT RACE THE ENGINE. DO NOT MOVE THE LEVER THROUGH ITS RANGES.

15. With the lever in Park, check the fluid level. If it's OK, take the car out for a short drive, park on a level surface, and check the level again, as outlined earlier in this section. Add more fluid if necessary. Be careful not to overfill, which will cause foaming and fluid loss.

Drive Axle

FLUID RECOMMENDATIONS

SAE 90 weight hypoid gear oil is required. If equipped with Traction-Lok differential, the addition of friction modifier additive C8AZ–19B546–A or equivalent, is also required when draining and refilling.

LEVEL CHECK

▶ **See Figures 180, 181, 182, 183 and 184**

Checking the differential fluid level is generally unnecessary unless a leak is suspected.

1. Raise and safely support the vehicle on jackstands.
2. Remove the oil fill plug from the differential housing. The hex drive on a ⅜ in. drive ratchet, breaker bar or extension works well on some applications.
3. Insert a finger into the fill hole; be careful as the threads can be sharp. The oil level should be about ¼ in. below the bottom of the fill hole with the axle in normal running position.
4. If the oil level feels low, add oil through the fill hole. Most hypoid gear oil comes in squeeze bottles equipped with small fill nozzles, designed for this purpose.

5. When the oil level is correct, install the oil fill plug and tighten to 15–30 ft. lbs. (20–41 Nm).

DRAIN & REFILL

▶ **See Figures 185 thru 191**

The differential should be drained and refilled every 100,000 miles (160,000km) or if the axle has been submerged in water.

1. Raise and safely support the vehicle on jackstands.
2. Clean all dirt from the area of the differential cover.
3. Position a drain pan under the differential.
4. Remove all but 2 cover retaining bolts and allow the fluid to drain from the differential. Once the fluid has drained, remove the remaining bolts to free the cover.
5. Thoroughly clean the differential cover. Cover the differential carrier with a clean rag to prevent axle contamination, then clean all the old sealant from the machined surface of the differential housing.
6. Make sure the machined surfaces of the cover and differential are clean and free of oil. Apply a ¼ in. wide bead of silicone sealer around the circumference of the cover, going inside the bolt holes.
7. Install the cover with the retaining bolts. Tighten the bolts evenly, to 25–35 ft. lbs. (34–47 Nm) in a crisscross pattern.
8. Remove the oil fill plug and add the required amount of hypoid gear oil through the oil fill hole. Refer to the Capacities chart at the end of this section.

➡ **If equipped with Traction-Lok differential, 4 oz. of friction modifier additive C8AZ–19B546–A or equivalent, must be included in the refill.**

9. Install the oil fill plug and tighten to 15–30 ft. lbs. (20–41 Nm). Lower the vehicle.
10. Road test the vehicle to warm the fluid. Check for leaks.

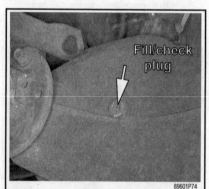

Fig. 180 The check/fill plug location—rear axle

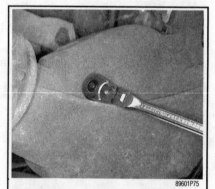

Fig. 181 Loosen the check/fill plug with a ⅜ drive tool . . .

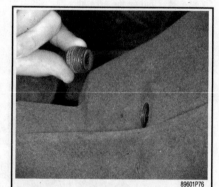

Fig. 182 . . . then remove the check/fill plug

Fig. 183 Check the fluid level by placing a finger into the hole—rear axle

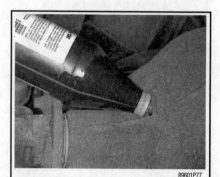

Fig. 184 Add the proper lubricant into the differential through the check/fill plug location

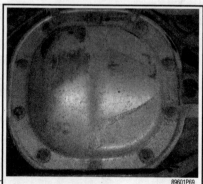

Fig. 185 Remove the axle cover retaining bolts

Fig. 186 After the cover bolts are removed, carefully pry the cover loose so that fluid begins to drain from the bottom

Fig. 187 After most of the fluid has drained out, remove the cover from the axle

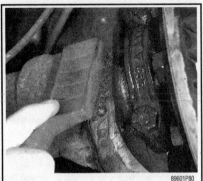

Fig. 188 Thoroughly clean the axle housing and . . .

Fig. 189 . . . cover mating surfaces using a brush or other suitable tool

Fig. 190 Wipe the cover mating surface using a cloth or other rag and a suitable solvent to remove any contaminants on the surface

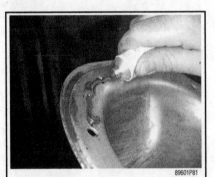

Fig. 191 Apply a bead of silicone to the cover mating surface before installing the cover onto the rear axle

Cooling System

FLUID RECOMMENDATIONS

A good quality ethylene glycol based or other aluminum compatible antifreeze is recommended for use in the vehicles covered by this Manual. It is best to add a 50/50 mix of antifreeze and distilled water to avoid diluting the coolant in the system.

LEVEL CHECK

▶ **See Figures 192, 193 and 194**

The coolant recovery tank is located on the right side of the engine compartment, on the top of the passenger side wheel well.

The proper coolant level is slightly above the **COLD FILL LEVEL** marking on the recovery tank when the engine is cold. Top off the cooling system using the recovery tank and its marking as a guideline.

➡**Never overfill the recovery tank.**

A coolant level that consistently drops is usually a sign of a small, hard to detect leak, although in the worst case it could be a sign of an internal engine leak. In most cases, you will be able to trace the leak to a loose fitting or damaged hose.

Evaporating ethylene glycol antifreeze will have a sweet smell and leave small, white (salt-like) deposits, which can be helpful in tracing a leak.

❋❋ CAUTION

Never open, service or drain the radiator or cooling system when hot; serious burns can occur from the steam and hot coolant. Also, when draining engine coolant, keep in mind that cats and dogs are

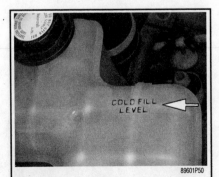

Fig. 192 The proper coolant level is slightly above the COLD FILL LEVEL marking on the recovery tank when the engine is cold

Fig. 193 Ensure that the engine is not hot, then loosen the recovery tank cap

Fig. 194 Carefully pour the proper ⁵⁰/₅₀ mixture of coolant and water directly into the recovery tank. If you do not use a funnel, it is easier if you hold the coolant bottle sideways

attracted to ethylene glycol antifreeze and could drink any that is left in an uncovered container or in puddles on the ground. This will prove fatal in sufficient quantities. Always drain coolant into a sealable container. Coolant should be reused unless it is contaminated or is several years old.

TESTING FOR LEAKS

▶ **See Figures 195, 196, 197, 198 and 199**

If a the fluid level of your cooling system is constantly low, the chances of a leak are probable. There are several ways to go about finding the source of your leak.

The first way should be a visual inspection. During the visual inspection, look around the entire engine area including the radiator and the heater hoses. The interior of the car should be inspected behind the glove box and passenger side floorboard area, and check the carpet for any signs of moisture. The smartest way to go about finding a leak visually is to first inspect any and all joints in the system such as where the radiator hoses connect to the radiator and the engine. Another thing to look for is white crusty stains that are signs of a leak where the coolant has already dried.

If a visual inspection cannot find the cause of your leak, a pressure test is a logical and extremely helpful way to find a leak. A pressure tester will be needed to perform this and if one is not available they can be purchased or even rented at many auto parts stores. The pressure tester usually has a standard size radiator cap adapter on the pressure port, however, other adapters are available based on the size of the vehicle's radiator neck or recovery tank depending on where the pressure tester connects. When pressurizing the cooling system, make sure you do not exceed the pressure rating of the system, which can be found on the top of the radiator cap. However, if you have and aftermarket or replacement cap that does not have the rating on it, 16psi is a standard to use, but some cars are higher. Overpressurizing the system can cause a rupture in a hose or worse, in the radiator or heater core and possibly cause an injury or a burn if the coolant is hot. Overpressurizing is normally controlled by the radiator cap which has a vent

valve in it which is opened when the system reaches it's maximum pressure rating. To pressure test the system, perform the following:

➡ **The pressure test should be performed with the engine OFF.**

1. Remove the radiator or recovery tank cap.
2. Using the proper adapter, insert it onto the opening and connect the pressure tester,
3. Begin pressurizing the system by pumping the pressure tester and watching the gauge, when the maximum pressure is reached, stop.
4. Watch the gauge slowly and see if the pressure on the gauge drops, if it does, a leak is definitely present.
5. If the pressure stayed somewhat stable, visually inspect the system for leaks. If the pressure dropped, repressurize the system and then visually inspect the system.
6. If no signs of a leak are noticed visually, pressurize the system to the maximum pressure rating of the system and leave the pressure tester connected for about 30 minutes. Return after 30 minutes and verify the pressure on the gauge, if the pressure dropped more than 20%, a leak definitely exists, if the pressure drop is less than 20%, the system is most likely okay.

Another way coolant is lost is by a internal engine leak, causing the oil to be contaminated or the coolant to be burned in the process of combustion and sent out the exhaust. To check for oil contamination, remove the dipstick and check the condition of the oil in the oil pan. If the oil is murky and has a white or beige "milkshake" look to it, the coolant is contaminating the oil through an internal leak and the engine must be torn down to find the leak. If the oil appears okay, the coolant can be burned and going out the tailpipe. A quick test for this is a cloud of white smoke appearing from the tailpipe, especially on start-up. On cold days, the white smoke will appear, this is due to condensation and the outside temperature, not a coolant leak. If the "smoke test" does not verify the situation, removing the spark plugs one at a time and checking the electrodes for a green or white tint can verify an internal coolant leak and iden-

Fig. 195 Remove the recovery tank cap to allow the pressure tester to be connected to the system

Fig. 196 This cooling system requires a threaded adapter for the recovery tank to allow the pressure tester to be connected

Fig. 197 Thread the adapter onto the recovery tank

Fig. 198 Pump the cooling system with pressure, making sure not to overpressurize the system or damage can occur

Fig. 199 Watch the gauge on the system and observe the pressure reading

tify which cylinder(s) is the culprit, aiding your search for the cause of the leak. If the spark plugs appear okay, another method is to use a gas analyzer or emissions tester, or one of several hand-held tools that most professional shops possess. This tools are used to check the cooling system for the presence of Hydrocarbons (HC's) in the coolant.

DRAIN & REFILL

▶ **See Figures 200, 201, 202 and 203**

Ensure that the engine is completely cool prior to starting this service.

✳✳ CAUTION

Never open, service or drain the radiator or cooling system when hot; serious burns can occur from the steam and hot coolant. Also, when draining engine coolant, keep in mind that cats and dogs are attracted to ethylene glycol antifreeze and could drink any that is left in an uncovered container or in puddles on the ground. This will prove fatal in sufficient quantities. Always drain coolant into a sealable container. Coolant should be reused unless it is contaminated or is several years old.

1. Remove the recovery tank or radiator cap.
2. Raise and support the vehicle.
3. Remove the front air deflector, if necessary.
4. Place a drain pan of sufficient capacity under the radiator and open the petcock (drain) on the radiator.

➡**Plastic petcocks bind easily. Before opening a plastic radiator petcock, spray it with some penetrating lubricant.**

5. Drain the cooling system completely.
6. Close the petcock.
7. Remove the drain pan.
8. If removed, install the air deflector.

9. Lower the vehicle.
10. Determine the capacity of the cooling system, then properly refill the system at the recovery tank or radiator opening with a 50/50 mixture of fresh coolant and distilled water until it reaches the **FULL COLD** line on the recovery tank or the radiator is full.
11. Leave the recovery tank or radiator cap off to aid in bleeding the system.
12. Start the engine and allow it to idle until the thermostat opens (the upper radiator hose will become hot). The coolant level should go down, this is normal as the system bleeds the air pockets out of the system.
13. Refill the system with coolant to the proper level.
14. Turn the engine **OFF** and check for leaks.

FLUSHING & CLEANING THE SYSTEM

▶ **See Figure 204**

1. Drain the cooling system completely as described earlier.
2. Close the petcock and fill the system with a cooling system flush (clean water may also be used, but is not as efficient).
3. Idle the engine until the upper radiator hose gets hot.
4. Allow the engine to cool completely and drain the system again.
5. Repeat this process until the drained water is clear and free of scale.
6. Flush the recovery tank with water and leave empty.

✳✳ CAUTION

Never open, service or drain the radiator or cooling system when hot; serious burns can occur from the steam and hot coolant. Also, when draining engine coolant, keep in mind that cats and dogs are attracted to ethylene glycol antifreeze and could drink any that is left in an uncovered container or in puddles on the ground. This will prove fatal in sufficient quantities. Always drain coolant into a sealable container. Coolant should be reused unless it is contaminated or is several years old.

7. Fill and bleed the cooling system as described earlier.

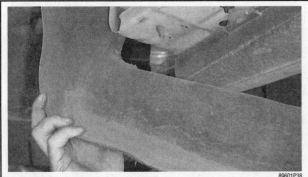

Fig. 200 On later models, it might be necessary to remove the air deflector

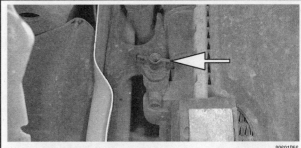

Fig. 201 The radiator petcock (drain) is typically located on the driver's side of the radiator, on the side tank. It is accessible from underneath the vehicle

Fig. 202 Make sure you have a drain pan in place before you open the drain because coolant will immediately begin to flow out

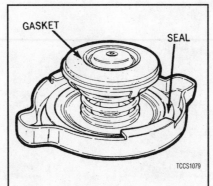

Fig. 203 Be sure the rubber gasket on the radiator cap has a tight seal

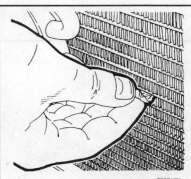

Fig. 204 Periodically remove all debris from the radiator fins

Brake Master Cylinder

The brake master cylinder reservoir is located under the hood, attached to the brake booster and firewall on the driver's side of the engine compartment.

FLUID RECOMMENDATIONS

> ※※ **CAUTION**
>
> Brake fluid contains polyglycol ethers and polyglycols. Avoid contact with the eyes and wash your hands thoroughly after handling brake fluid. If you do get brake fluid in your eyes, flush your eyes with clean, running water for 15 minutes. If eye irritation persists, or if you have taken brake fluid internally, IMMEDIATELY seek medical assistance.

> ※※ **WARNING**
>
> Clean, high quality brake fluid is essential to the safe and proper operation of the brake system. You should always buy the highest quality brake fluid that is available. If the brake fluid becomes contaminated, drain and flush the system, then refill the master cylinder with new fluid. Never reuse any brake fluid. Any brake fluid that is removed from the system should be discarded. Also, do not allow any brake fluid to come in contact with a painted surface; it will damage the paint.

When adding fluid to the system, ONLY use fresh DOT 3 brake fluid from a sealed container. DOT 3 brake fluid will absorb moisture when it is exposed to the atmosphere, which will lower its boiling point. A container that has been opened once, closed and placed on a shelf will allow enough moisture to enter over time to contaminate the fluid within. If your brake fluid is contaminated with water, you could boil the brake fluid under hard braking conditions and lose all or some braking ability. Don't take the risk, buy fresh brake fluid whenever you must add to the system.

Fig. 205 The brake fluid level should not be above the MAX line on the side of the reservoir

LEVEL CHECK

▶ See Figures 205, 206, 207 and 208

> ※※ **CAUTION**
>
> Brake fluid contains polyglycol ethers and polyglycols. Avoid contact with the eyes and wash your hands thoroughly after handling brake fluid. If you do get brake fluid in your eyes, flush your eyes with clean, running water for 15 minutes. If eye irritation persists, or if you have taken brake fluid internally, IMMEDIATELY seek medical assistance.

Observe the fluid level indicators on the master cylinder; the fluid level should be between the MIN and MAX lines.

Before removing the master cylinder reservoir cap, make sure the vehicle is resting on level ground and clean all dirt away from the top of the master cylinder. Unscrew the cap and fill the master cylinder until the level is between the MIN and MAX lines.

If the level of the brake fluid is less than half the volume of the reservoir, it is advised that you check the brake system for leaks. Leaks in a hydraulic brake system most commonly occur at the wheel cylinder and brake line junction points.

Power Steering Pump

FLUID RECOMMENDATIONS

Ford power steering fluid part number E6AZ–19582–AA or equivalent, or Type F automatic transmission fluid should be used.

LEVEL CHECK

▶ See Figures 209, 210 and 211

1. Run the engine until the fluid reaches a normal operating temperature of 165–175°F (74–79°C).
2. Turn the steering wheel all the way to the left and right, several times.
3. Shut the engine **OFF**.
4. On vehicles with the 4.6L engine, check the fluid level in the power steering fluid reservoir. The reservoir is translucent, enabling the fluid level to be checked without removing the reservoir cap. The fluid level should be between the MIN and MAX marks on the side of the reservoir.
5. On vehicles with 5.0L or 5.8L engines, wipe away any accumulated dirt or grease, then remove the dipstick from the power steering fluid reservoir. Wipe the dipstick with a clean cloth, reinsert it fully into the reservoir, then remove it. The fluid level should be within the FULL HOT range on the dipstick if the fluid is at normal operating temperature, within the FULL COLD range if it is not.
6. If the fluid level is low, add the specified fluid, being careful not to overfill. Be sure to wipe away any accumulated dirt or grease before removing the reservoir cap.

Fig. 206 Wipe the master cylinder reservoir clean before . . .

Fig. 207 . . . removing the reservoir cap

Fig. 208 Pour brake fluid from a sealed container directly into the reservoir

Fig. 209 The power steering pump reservoir is marked with MIN and MAX lines on the side. The fluid level should be between these marks

Fig. 210 Remove the reservoir cap and . . .

Fig. 211 . . . pour the proper fluid directly into the reservoir, but make sure not to overfill the reservoir

Chassis Greasing

▶ See Figures 212, 213, 214 and 215

Lubrication of steering and suspension parts requires the use of a pressure-type grease gun, in order to force the lubricant through the grease fitting. A premium long life chassis grease should be used.

There are grease fittings located on the inner and outer tie rod ends, pitman arm and lower ball joints on most models covered by this manual. In addition, some vehicles are equipped with grease fittings on the upper ball joints. These should be lubricated as indicated in the Maintenance Intervals chart in this section.

Wipe away any dirt or accumulated grease from the fitting. Attach the grease gun to the fitting and pump lubricant into the joint. Be careful not to pump in so much lubricant that the joint boot splits.

Use a brush to apply grease to the steering stop pads, located on the lower control arms.

In addition to the steering and suspension components, the cable guides, levers and linkage of the parking brake should be lubricated periodically, using a multi-purpose spray grease.

Body Lubrication and Maintenance

CAR WASHING

The car should be washed at regular intervals to remove dirt, dust, insects, and tar and other possibly damaging stains that can adhere to the paint and may cause damage. Proper exterior maintenance also helps in the resale value of the vehicle by maintaining its like-new appearance.

➡**It is particularly important to frequently wash the car in the wintertime to prevent corrosion, when salt has been used on the roads.**

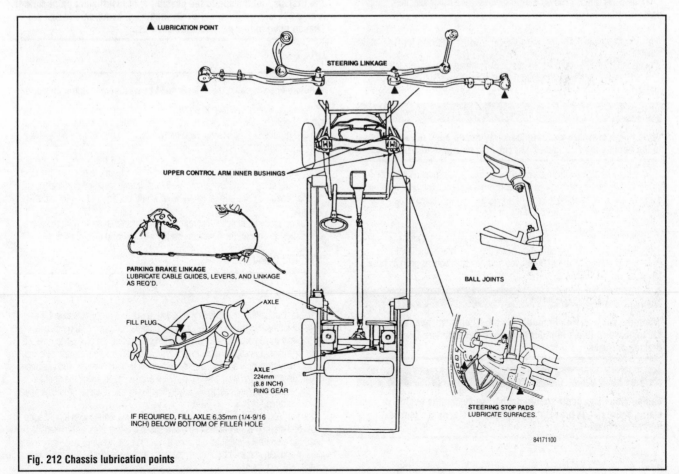

Fig. 212 Chassis lubrication points

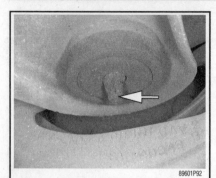

Fig. 213 Any greasable item will have a Zerk® fitting located on it such as this lower ball joint

Fig. 214 Wipe any road grime or old grease off of the fitting before inserting new grease

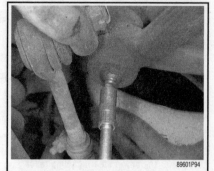

Fig. 215 Place the grease gun nozzle on the fitting and squeeze 2-3 pumps into the fitting

There are many precautions and tips on washing, including the following:
- When washing the car, do not expose it do direct sunlight.
- Use lukewarm water to soften the dirt before you wash with a sponge, and plenty of water, to avoid scratching.
- A detergent can be used to facilitate the softening of dirt and oil.
- A water-soluble grease solvent may be used in cases of sticky dirt. However, use a washplace with a drainage separator.
- Dry the car with a clean chamois and remember to clean the drain holes in the doors and rocker panels.
- If equipped with a power radio antenna, it must be dried after washing.

❊❊ CAUTION

Never clean the bumpers with gasoline or paint thinner, always use the same agent as used on the painted surfaces of the vehicle.

- Tar spots can be removed with tar remover or kerosene after the car has been washed.
- A stiff-bristle brush and lukewarm soapy water can be used to clean the wiper blades. Frequent cleaning considerably improves visibility when using the wipers.
- Wash off the dirt from the underside (wheel housings, fenders, etc.).
- In areas of high industrial fallout, more frequent washing is recommended.

❊❊ CAUTION

During high pressure washing the spray nozzle must never be closer to the vehicle than 13 inches (30 cm). Do not spray into the locks.

- When washing or steam cleaning the engine, avoid spraying water or steam directly on the electrical components or near the distributor or ignition components. After cleaning the engine, the spark plug wells should be inspected for water and blown dry if necessary.
- Special car washing detergent is the best to use. Liquid dishwashing detergent can remove wax and leave the car's paint unprotected and, in addition, some liquid detergents contains abrasives which can scratch the paint.
- Bird droppings should be removed from the paintwork as soon as possible, otherwise the finish may be permanently stained.

❊❊ WARNING

When the car is driven immediately after being washed, apply the brakes several times in order to remove any moisture from the braking surfaces.

❊❊ WARNING

Engine cleaning agents should not be used when the engine is warm, a fire risk is present as most engine cleaning agents are highly flammable.

Automatic car washing is a simple and quick way to clean your car, but it is worth remembering that it is not as thorough as when you yourself clean the car.

Keeping the underbody clean is vitally important, and some automatic washers do not contain equipment for washing the underside of the car.

When driving into an automatic was, make sure the following precautions have been taken:
- Make sure all windows are up, and no objects that you do not want to get wet are exposed.
- In some cases, rotating the side view mirrors in can help to avoid possible damage.
- If your car is equipped with a power antenna, lower it. If your vehicle has a solid mounted, non-power antenna, it is best to remove it, but this is not always practical. Inspect the surroundings to reduce the risk of possible damage, and check to see if the antenna can be manually lowered.

❊❊ WARNING

Most manufacturers do not recommend automatic car washing in the first six months due to the possibility of insufficient paint curing; a safe bet is to wait until after six months of ownership (when purchased new) to use an automatic car wash.

WAXING

➡**Before applying wax, the vehicle must be washed and thoroughly dried.**

Waxing a vehicle can help to preserve the appearance of your vehicle. A wide range of polymer-based car waxes are available today. These waxes are easy to use and produce a long-lasting, high gloss finish that protects the body and paint against oxidation, road dirt, and fading.

Sometimes, waxing a neglected vehicle, or one that has sustained chemical or natural element damage (such as acid rain) require more than waxing, and a light-duty compound can be applied. For severely damaged surfaces, it is best to consult a professional to see what would be required to repair the damage.

Waxing procedures differ according to manufacturer, type, and ingredients, so it is best to consult the directions on the wax and/or polish purchased.

INTERIOR CLEANING

Upholstery

Fabric can usually be cleaned with soapy water or a proper detergent. For more difficult spots caused by oil, ice cream, soda, etc., use a fabric cleaner available at most parts stores. Be sure when purchasing the cleaner to read the label to ensure it is safe to use on your type of fabric. A safe method of testing the cleaner is to apply a small amount to an area usually unseen, such as under a seat, or other areas. Wait a while, perhaps even a day to check the spot for fading, discoloring, etc., as some cleaners will only cause these problems after they have dried.

Leather upholstery requires special care, it can be cleaned with a mild soap and a soft cloth. It is recommended that a special leather cleaner be used to clean but also treat the leather surfaces in your vehicle. Leather surfaces can age quickly and can crack if not properly taken care of, so it is vital that the leather surfaces be maintained.

Floor Mats and Carpet

The floor mats and carpet should be vacuumed or brushed regularly. They can be cleaned with a mild soap and water. Special cleaners are available to clean the carpeted surfaces of your vehicle, but take care in choosing them, and again it is best to test them in a usually unseen spot.

Dashboard, Console, Door Panels, Etc.

The dashboard, console, door panels, and other plastic, vinyl, or wood surfaces can be cleaned using a mild soap and water. Caution must be taken to keep water out of electronic accessories and controls to avoid shorts or ruining the components. Again special cleaners are available to clean these surfaces, as with other cleaners care must taken in purchasing and using such cleaners.

There are protectants available which can treat the various surfaces in your car giving them a "shiny new look", however some of these protectants can cause more harm than good in the long run. The shine that is placed on your dashboard attracts sunlight accelerating the aging, fading and possibly even cracking the surfaces. These protectants also attract more dust to stick to the surfaces they treat, increasing the cleaning you must do to maintain the appearance of your vehicle. Personal discretion is advised here.

Wheel Bearings

REPACKING

1989–91 Vehicles

▶ **See Figures 216, 217, 218, 219 and 220**

1. Raise and support the vehicle safely on jackstands.
2. Remove the wheel and tire assembly and the disc brake caliper.

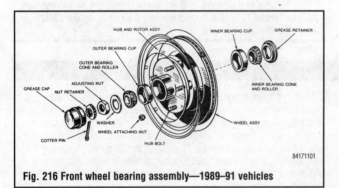

Fig. 216 Front wheel bearing assembly—1989–91 vehicles

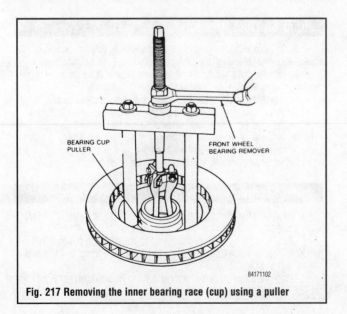

Fig. 217 Removing the inner bearing race (cup) using a puller

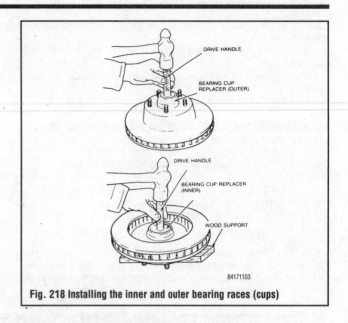

Fig. 218 Installing the inner and outer bearing races (cups)

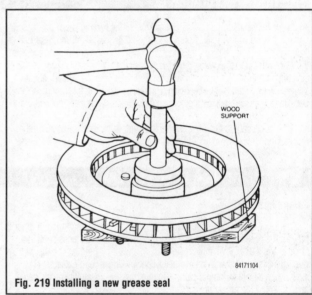

Fig. 219 Installing a new grease seal

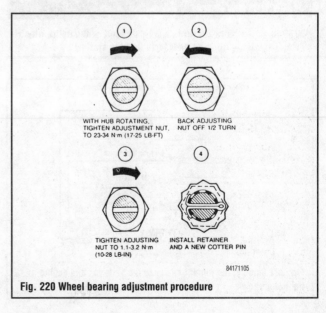

Fig. 220 Wheel bearing adjustment procedure

Suspend the caliper with a length of wire; do not let it hang from the brake hose.

3. Pry off the dust cap. Tap out and discard the cotter pin. Remove the nut retainer.

4. Being careful not to drop the outer bearing, pull off the brake disc and wheel hub assembly.

5. Remove the inner grease seal using a prybar. Remove the inner wheel bearing.

6. Clean the wheel bearings with solvent and inspect them for pits, scratches and excessive wear. Wipe all the old grease from the hub and inspect the bearing races (cups). If either bearings or races are damaged, the bearing races must be removed and the bearings and races replaced as an assembly.

7. If the bearings are to be replaced, drive out the races (cups) from the hub using a brass drift, or pull them from the hub using a puller.

8. Make sure the spindle, hub and bearing assemblies are clean prior to installation.

To install:

9. If the bearing races (cups) were removed, install new ones using a suitable bearing race installer. Pack the bearings with high-temperature wheel bearing grease using a bearing packer. If a packer is not available, work as much grease as possible between the rollers and cages using your hands.

10. Coat the inner surface of the hub and bearing races (cups) with grease.

11. Install the inner bearing in the hub. Using a seal installer, install a new grease seal into the hub. Lubricate the lip of the seal with grease.

12. Install the hub/disc assembly on the spindle, being careful not to damage the oil seal.

13. Install the outer bearing, washer and spindle nut. Install the caliper and the wheel and tire assembly. Adjust the bearings as follows:

a. Loosen the adjusting nut 3 turns and rock the wheel in and out a few times to release the brake pads from the rotor.

b. While rotating the wheel and hub assembly in a counterclockwise direction, tighten the adjusting nut to 17–25 ft. lbs. (23–34 Nm).

c. Back off the adjusting nut ½ turn, then retighten to 10–28 inch lbs. (1.1–3.2 Nm).

d. Install the nut retainer and a new cotter pin. Replace the grease cap.

14. Lower the vehicle. Before driving the vehicle, pump the brake pedal several times to restore normal brake pedal travel.

1992–98

The front wheel bearings are of a hub unit design and are pregreased, sealed and require no maintenance. The bearings are preset and cannot be adjusted. For bearing hub removal and installation, see Section 8.

TOWING THE VEHICLE

If your car needs to be towed, first make sure the parking brake is released and place the gearshift in **N**. Optimally it should be towed utilizing a flat bed or "roll back" tow truck by a professional. However the vehicle can be towed from the rear, with the rear wheels off the ground. When towed in this manner, the steering wheel must be clamped with the front wheels in the straight-ahead position, using a steering wheel clamping device designed for towing service use. Do not rely on the steering column lock to lock the wheels in the straight-ahead position.

If it is necessary to tow the car from the front, with the rear wheels on the ground, the transmission and differential must be working properly. When towed in this manner, do not exceed 35 mph or go farther than 50 miles, or transmission damage may result.

If the transmission or differential is inoperable, or the speed and distance requirement stated above cannot be maintained, use a dolly under the rear wheels.

❊❊ WARNING

If your vehicle is equipped with air suspension, the air suspension must be turned OFF. this is accomplished by flipping the switch located in the trunk to OFF.

JUMP STARTING A DEAD BATTERY

♦ **See Figure 221**

Whenever a vehicle is jump started, precautions must be followed in order to prevent the possibility of personal injury. Remember that batteries contain a small amount of explosive hydrogen gas which is a by-product of battery charging. Sparks should always be avoided when working around batteries, especially when attaching jumper cables. To minimize the possibility of accidental sparks, follow the procedure carefully.

❊❊ CAUTION

NEVER hook the batteries up in a series circuit or the entire electrical system will go up in smoke, including the starter!

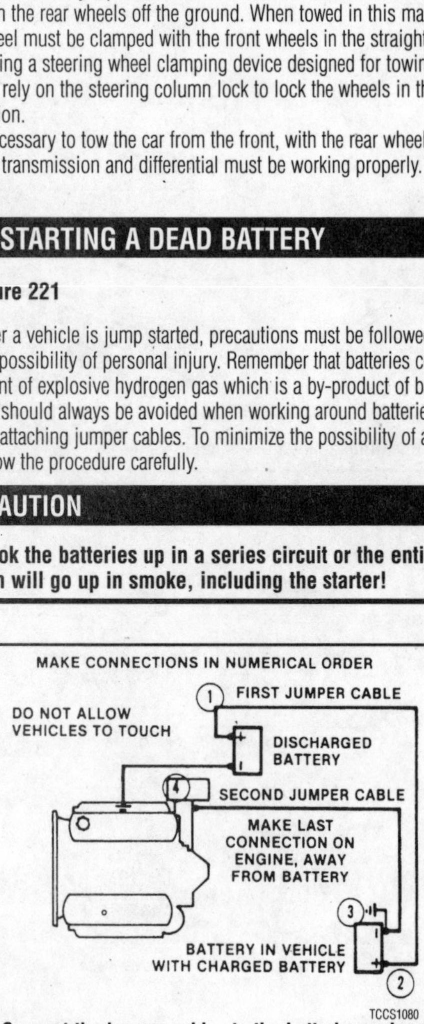

MAKE CONNECTIONS IN NUMERICAL ORDER

DO NOT ALLOW VEHICLES TO TOUCH

① FIRST JUMPER CABLE

DISCHARGED BATTERY

SECOND JUMPER CABLE

MAKE LAST CONNECTION ON ENGINE, AWAY FROM BATTERY

BATTERY IN VEHICLE WITH CHARGED BATTERY

TCCS1080

Fig. 221 Connect the jumper cables to the batteries and engine in the order shown

Vehicles equipped with a diesel engine may utilize two 12 volt batteries. If so, the batteries are connected in a parallel circuit (positive terminal to positive terminal, negative terminal to negative terminal). Hooking the batteries up in parallel circuit increases battery cranking power without increasing total battery voltage output. Output remains at 12 volts. On the other hand, hooking two 12 volt batteries up in a series circuit (positive terminal to negative terminal, positive terminal to negative terminal) increases total battery output to 24 volts (12 volts plus 12 volts).

Jump Starting Precautions

• Be sure that both batteries are of the same voltage. Vehicles covered by this manual and most vehicles on the road today utilize a 12 volt charging system.

• Be sure that both batteries are of the same polarity (have the same terminal, in most cases NEGATIVE grounded).

• Be sure that the vehicles are not touching or a short could occur.

• On serviceable batteries, be sure the vent cap holes are not obstructed.

• Do not smoke or allow sparks anywhere near the batteries.

• In cold weather, make sure the battery electrolyte is not frozen. This can occur more readily in a battery that has been in a state of discharge.

• Do not allow electrolyte to contact your skin or clothing.

Jump Starting Procedure

1. Make sure that the voltages of the 2 batteries are the same. Most batteries and charging systems are of the 12 volt variety.

2. Pull the jumping vehicle (with the good battery) into a position so the jumper cables can reach the dead battery and that vehicle's engine. Make sure that the vehicles do NOT touch.

3. Place the transmissions of both vehicles in **Neutral** (MT) or **P** (AT), as applicable, then firmly set their parking brakes.

➡️**If necessary for safety reasons, the hazard lights on both vehicles may be operated throughout the entire procedure without significantly increasing the difficulty of jumping the dead battery.**

4. Turn all lights and accessories OFF on both vehicles. Make sure the ignition switches on both vehicles are turned to the **OFF** position.

5. Cover the battery cell caps with a rag, but do not cover the terminals.

6. Make sure the terminals on both batteries are clean and free of corrosion or proper electrical connection will be impeded. If necessary, clean the battery terminals before proceeding.

7. Identify the positive (+) and negative (-) terminals on both batteries.

8. Connect the first jumper cable to the positive (+) terminal of the dead battery, then connect the other end of that cable to the positive (+) terminal of the booster (good) battery.

9. Connect one end of the other jumper cable to the negative (-) terminal on the booster battery and the final cable clamp to an engine bolt head, alternator bracket or other solid, metallic point on the engine with the dead battery. Try to pick a ground on the engine that is positioned away from the battery in order to minimize the possibility of the 2 clamps touching should one loosen during the procedure. DO NOT connect this clamp to the negative (-) terminal of the bad battery.

✳️ CAUTION

Be very careful to keep the jumper cables away from moving parts (cooling fan, belts, etc.) on both engines.

10. Check to make sure that the cables are routed away from any moving parts, then start the donor vehicle's engine. Run the engine at moderate speed for several minutes to allow the dead battery a chance to receive some initial charge.

11. With the donor vehicle's engine still running slightly above idle, try to start the vehicle with the dead battery. Crank the engine for no more than 10 seconds at a time and let the starter cool for at least 20 seconds between tries. If the vehicle does not start in 3 tries, it is likely that something else is also wrong or that the battery needs additional time to charge.

12. Once the vehicle is started, allow it to run at idle for a few seconds to make sure that it is operating properly.

13. Turn ON the headlights, heater blower and, if equipped, the rear defroster of both vehicles in order to reduce the severity of voltage spikes and subsequent risk of damage to the vehicles' electrical systems when the cables are disconnected. This step is especially important to any vehicle equipped with computer control modules.

14. Carefully disconnect the cables in the reverse order of connection. Start with the negative cable that is attached to the engine ground, then the negative cable on the donor battery. Disconnect the positive cable from the donor battery and finally, disconnect the positive cable from the formerly dead battery. Be careful when disconnecting the cables from the positive terminals not to allow the alligator clips to touch any metal on either vehicle or a short and sparks will occur.

JACKING

▶ **See Figures 222, 223, 224, 225 and 226**

Your vehicle was supplied with a jack for emergency road repairs. This jack is fine for changing a flat tire or other short term procedures not requiring you to go beneath the vehicle. If it is used in an emergency situation, carefully follow the instructions provided either with the jack or in your owner's manual. Do not attempt to use the jack on any portions of the vehicle other than specified by the vehicle manufacturer. Always block the diagonally opposite wheel when using a jack.

A more convenient way of jacking is the use of a garage or floor jack. You may use the floor jack on either side of the front of the vehicle by positioning the jack on the frame. However, it is usually easier to raise the front of the vehicle at the front crossmember.

Fig. 222 Place a suitable jack under the frame behind the front wheel(s) to raise the front of the vehicle

Fig. 223 Locate the jackstands under the frame as shown to support the front of the vehicle

Fig. 224 Place a suitable jack under the rear differential to raise the rear of the vehicle

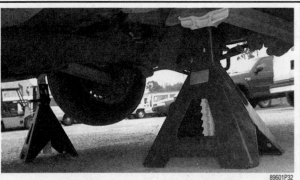

Fig. 225 Locate the jackstands under the frame as shown to support the rear of the vehicle

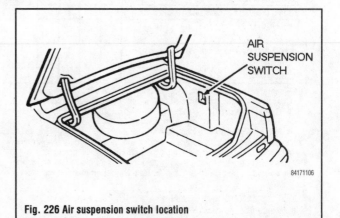

Fig. 226 Air suspension switch location

At the rear of the vehicle, the jack can be positioned under the rear axle housing tubes, between the suspension arm brackets and the differential housing. Do not raise the rear of the vehicle using the differential housing as a lift point.

❊❊ WARNING

If your vehicle is equipped with air suspension, the air suspension must be turned OFF. this is accomplished by flipping the switch located in the trunk to OFF.

Never place the jack under the radiator, engine or transmission components. Severe and expensive damage will result when the jack is raised. Additionally, never jack under the floorpan or bodywork; the metal will deform.

Whenever you plan to work under the vehicle, you must support it on jackstands or ramps. Never use cinder blocks or stacks of wood to support the vehicle, even if you're only going to be under it for a few minutes. Never crawl under the vehicle when it is supported only by the tire-changing jack or other floor jack.

➡**Always position a block of wood or small rubber pad on top of the jack or jackstand to protect the lifting point's finish when lifting or supporting the vehicle.**

Small hydraulic, screw, or scissors jacks are satisfactory for raising the vehicle. Drive-on trestles or ramps are also a handy and safe way to both raise and support the vehicle. Be careful though, some ramps may be too steep to drive your vehicle onto without scraping the front bottom panels. Never support the vehicle on any suspension member (unless specifically instructed to do so by a repair manual) or by an underbody panel.

Jacking Precautions

The following safety points cannot be overemphasized:
- Always block the opposite wheel or wheels to keep the vehicle from rolling off the jack.
- When raising the front of the vehicle, firmly apply the parking brake.
- When the drive wheels are to remain on the ground, leave the vehicle in gear to help prevent it from rolling.
- Always use jackstands to support the vehicle when you are working underneath. Place the stands beneath the vehicle's jacking brackets. Before climbing underneath, rock the vehicle a bit to make sure it is firmly supported.

Follow this Schedule if your driving habits MAINLY include one or more of the following conditions:

- Short trips of less than 16 km (10 miles) when outside temperatures remain below freezing.
- Operating during HOT WEATHER
  — Driving in stop-and-go "rush hour" traffic.
- Towing a trailer, using a car-top carrier.
- Operating in severe dust conditions.
- Extensive idling, such as police, taxi or door-to-door delivery service.

SERVICE INTERVAL Perform at the months or distances shown, whichever comes first. Miles × 1000	3	6	9	12	15	18	21	24	27	30	33	36	39	42	45	48	51	54	57	60
Kilometers × 1000	4.8	9.6	14.4	19.2	24	28.8	33.6	38.4	43.2	48	52.8	57.6	62.4	67.2	72	76.8	81.6	86.4	91.2	96
EMISSION CONTROL SERVICE																				
Replace Engine Oil and Oil Filter Every 3 Months OR	X	X	X	X	X	X	X	X	X	X	X	X	X	X	X	X	X	X	X	X
Replace Spark Plugs										X										X
Inspect Accessory Drive Belt(s)										X										X
Replace PCV Valve and Crankcase Emission Filter (5.0L Engine)					(X)					(X)					(X)					X
Replace Air Cleaner Filter①										X										X
Replace Crankcase Emission Filter① (5.8L Engine)										X										X
Check/Clean Choke Linkage (5.8L Engine)										X										X
Replace Engine Coolant, EVERY 36 Months OR										X										X
Check Engine Coolant Protection, Hoses and Clamps									ANNUALLY											
GENERAL MAINTENANCE																				
Inspect Exhaust Heat Shields										X										X
Change Automatic Transmission Fluid②										X										X
Lubricate Suspension										X										X
Lubricate Steering Linkage					X					X					X					X
Inspect Disc Brake Pads and Rotors③										X										X
Inspect Brake Linings and Drums (Rear)③										X										X
Inspect and Repack Front Wheel Bearings										X										X
Rotate Tires		X					X					X				X				

① If operating in severe dust, more frequent intervals may be required.
② Change automatic transmission fluid if your driving habits frequently include one or more of the following conditions:
  - Operation during hot weather (above 32°C (90°F)) carrying heavy loads and in hilly terrain.
  - Towing a trailer or using a car top carrrier.
  - Police, taxi or door to door delivery service.
③ If your driving includes continuous stop-and-go driving or driving in mountainous areas, more frequent intervals may be required.
X All items designated by an X must be performed in all states.
(X) This item not required to be performed, however, Ford recommends that you also perform maintenance on items designated by an (X) in order to achieve best vehicle operation. Failure to perform this recommended maintenance will not invalidate the vehicle emissions warranty or manufacturer recall liability.

84171117

Maintenance interval chart—1989–91 models

Follow Maintenance Schedule B if, generally, you drive your vehicle on a daily basis for more than 16 km (10 miles) and NONE OF THE UNIQUE DRIVING CONDITIONS SHOWN IN SCHEDULE A APPLY TO YOUR DRIVING HABITS.

SERVICE INTERVALS **Perform at the months or distances shown, whichever comes first.**	Miles x 1000	7.5	15	22.5	30	37.5	45	52.5	60
	Kilometers x 1000	12	24	36	48	60	72	84	96
EMISSIONS CONTROL SERVICE									
Replace Engine Oil and Filter (Every 6 Months) OR 7,500 Miles Whichever Occurs First		X	X	X	X	X	X	X	X
Replace Spark Plugs					X				X
Replace Crankcase Emission Filter①					X				X
Inspect Accessory Drive Belt(s)					X				X
Replace Air Cleaner Filter①					X				X
Replace PCV Valve and Crankcase Emission Filter — 5.0L Engine			(X)		(X)		(X)		X
Check/Clean Choke Linkage (5.8L only)					X				X
Change Engine Coolant Every 36 Months OR					X				X
Check Engine Coolant Protection, Hoses and Clamps		ANNUALLY							
GENERAL MAINTENANCE									
Check Exhaust Heat Shields					X				X
Lube Suspension			X		X		X		X
Lubricate Steering Linkage			X		X		X		X
Inspect Disc Brake Pads and Rotors (Front)②					X				X
Inspect Brake Linings and Drums (Rear)②					X				X
Inspect and Repack Front Wheel Bearings					X				X
Rotate Tires		X		X		X		X	

① If operating in severe dust, more frequent intervals may be required.
② If your driving includes continuous stop-and-go driving or driving in mountainous areas, more frequent intervals may be required.

X All items designated by an X must be performed in all states.
(X) This item not required to be performed, however, Ford recommends that you also perform maintenance on items designated by an (X) in order to achieve best vehicle operation. Failure to perform this recommended maintenance will not invalidate the vehicle emissions warranty or manufacturer recall liability.

84171118

Maintenance interval chart—1989–91 models

MANUFACTURER RECOMMENDED NORMAL MAINTENANCE INTERVALS

VEHICLE MAINTENANCE INTERVAL

Component	Type of Service	5 / 8	10 / 16	15 / 24	20 / 32	25 / 40	30 / 48	35 / 56	40 / 64	45 / 72	50 / 80	55 / 88	60 / 96	65 / 104	70 / 112	75 / 121	80 / 128
Miles (x1000) / km (x1000)		5 / 8	10 / 16	15 / 24	20 / 32	25 / 40	30 / 48	35 / 56	40 / 64	45 / 72	50 / 80	55 / 88	60 / 96	65 / 104	70 / 112	75 / 121	80 / 128
Engine oil and filter	Replace	✓	✓	✓	✓	✓	✓	✓	✓	✓	✓	✓	✓	✓	✓	✓	✓
Tires	Rotate	✓		✓		✓		✓		✓		✓		✓		✓	
Air cleaner	Replace						✓						✓				
Spark plugs ①	Replace																
Drive belt	Inspect												✓				
Cooling system	Inspect			✓			✓			✓			✓			✓	
Coolant	Replace										✓						✓
PCV valve	Replace												✓				
Automatic transmission fluid and filter	Replace						✓						✓				
Exhaust heat shields	Inspect						✓						✓				
Brake linings and drums	Inspect		✓		✓		✓		✓		✓		✓		✓		✓
Brake pads and rotors	Inspect		✓		✓		✓		✓		✓		✓		✓		✓
Fuel filter (NGV Crown Victoria) ②	Replace					✓					✓					✓	
Lubricate suspension	Inspect		✓		✓		✓		✓		✓		✓		✓		✓
Brake line hoses and connections	Inspect						✓						✓				
Front suspension	Inspect						✓						✓				
Bolts and nuts on chassis body	Inspect						✓						✓				
Steering linkage operation	Inspect						✓						✓				

Perform maintenance at the same intervals for mileage beyond that on this chart

Follow the normal service interval schedule if the vehicle is driven in the following conditions:

The vehicle is driven more than 10 miles on a daily basis

The vehicle is not used in the following conditions:

    towing a trailer or using a car-top carrier

    operating in severe dust conditions

    extensive idling such as a police car, taxi, or delivery service

    short trips of less than 10 miles when outside temperatures remain below 0°F (-18°C)

① Replace every 100,000 miles.

② Also drain coalescer

89601C05

Maintenance interval chart—1992–98 models

MANUFACTURER RECOMMENDED SEVERE MAINTENANCE INTERVALS
VEHICLE MAINTENANCE INTERVAL

Component	Type of Service	Miles (x1000) 3 / km 5	6 / 10	9 / 15	12 / 20	15 / 25	18 / 30	21 / 35	24 / 40	27 / 45	30 / 50	33 / 55	36 / 60	39 / 65	42 / 70	45 / 75	48 / 80	51 / 85	54 / 90	57 / 95	60 / 100
Engine oil and filter	Replace	✓	✓	✓	✓	✓	✓	✓	✓	✓	✓	✓	✓	✓	✓	✓	✓	✓	✓	✓	✓
Tires	Rotate		✓		✓		✓		✓		✓		✓		✓		✓		✓		✓
Air cleaner	Replace										✓										✓
Spark plugs ①	Replace																				
Drive belt	Inspect																				✓
Cooling system	Inspect				✓						✓					✓					✓
Coolant	Replace															✓					
PCV valve	Replace																				✓
Automatic transmission fluid & filter	Replace							✓							✓						
Exhaust heat shields	Inspect										✓										✓
Brake linings and drums	Inspect			✓			✓			✓			✓			✓			✓		
Brake pads and rotors	Inspect			✓			✓			✓			✓			✓			✓		
Fuel filter (NGV Crown Victoria) ②	Replace								✓								✓				
Lubricate suspension	Inspect				✓						✓					✓					✓
Brake line hoses and connections	Inspect				✓						✓					✓					✓
Front suspension	Inspect				✓						✓					✓					✓
Bolts and nuts on chassis body	Inspect				✓						✓					✓					✓
Steering linkage operation	Inspect				✓						✓					✓					✓

Perform maintenance at the same intervals for mileage beyond that on this chart

Follow the severe service interval schedule if the vehicle is driven in the following conditions:

    towing a trailer or using a car-top carrier

    operating in severe dust conditions

    extensive idling such as a police car, taxi, or delivery service

    short trips of less than 10 miles when outside temperatures remain below 0°F (-18°C)

① Replace every 100,000 miles.

② Also drain coalescer

89601C06

Maintenance interval chart—1992–98 models

CAPACITIES

Year	Model	Engine Displacement Liters (cc)	Engine ID/VIN	Engine Oil with Filter (qts.)	Automatic Transmission (pts.) ①	Rear Drive Axle (pts.)	Fuel Tank (gal.)	Cooling System (qts.)
1989	Crown Victoria	5.0 (4993)	F	5.0	24.6	4.0	18.0	14.1
	Crown Victoria	5.8 (5767)	G	5.0	24.6	4.0	20.0	14.1
	Grand Marquis	5.0 (4993)	F	5.0	24.6	4.0	18.0	14.1
	Grand Marquis	5.8 (5767)	G	5.0	24.6	4.0	20.0	14.1
1990	Crown Victoria	5.0 (4993)	F	5.0	24.6	4.0	18.0	14.1
	Crown Victoria	5.8 (5767)	G	5.0	24.6	4.0	20.0	14.1
	Grand Marquis	5.0 (4993)	F	5.0	24.6	4.0	18.0	14.1
	Grand Marquis	5.8 (5767)	G	5.0	24.6	4.0	20.0	14.1
1991	Crown Victoria	5.0 (4993)	F	5.0	24.6	4.0	18.0	14.1
	Crown Victoria	5.8 (5767)	G	5.0	24.6	4.0	20.0	14.1
	Grand Marquis	5.0 (4993)	F	5.0	24.6	4.0	18.0	14.1
	Grand Marquis	5.8 (5767)	G	5.0	24.6	4.0	20.0	14.1
1992	Crown Victoria	4.6 (4593)	W	5.0	27.2	②	20.0	14.1
	Grand Marquis	4.6 (4593)	W	5.0	28.2	②	20.0	15.1
1993	Crown Victoria	4.6 (4593)	W	5.0	27.2	②	20.0	14.1
	Grand Marquis	4.6 (4593)	W	5.0	28.2	②	20.0	15.1
1994	Crown Victoria	4.6 (4593)	W	5.0	27.2	②	20.0	14.1
	Grand Marquis	4.6 (4593)	W	5.0	28.2	②	20.0	15.1
1995	Crown Victoria	4.6 (4593)	W	5.0	27.2	②	20.0	14.1
	Grand Marquis	4.6 (4593)	W	5.0	28.2	②	20.0	15.1
1996	Crown Victoria	4.6 (4593)	W	5.0	27.2	②	20.0	14.1
	Grand Marquis	4.6 (4593)	W	5.0	28.2	②	20.0	15.1
1997	Crown Victoria	4.6 (4593)	W/9	5.0	27.2	②	20.0	14.1
	Grand Marquis	4.6 (4593)	W/9	5.0	28.2	②	20.0	15.1
1998	Crown Victoria	4.6 (4593)	W/9	5.0	27.2	②	20.0	14.1
	Grand Marquis	4.6 (4593)	W/9	5.0	28.2	②	20.0	15.1

NOTE: All capacities are approximate. Add fluid gradually and ensure a proper fluid level is obtained.

① Includes torque converter

② 7.50" axle: 3.0 pts.
   8.80" axle: 3.25 pts.

89601C04

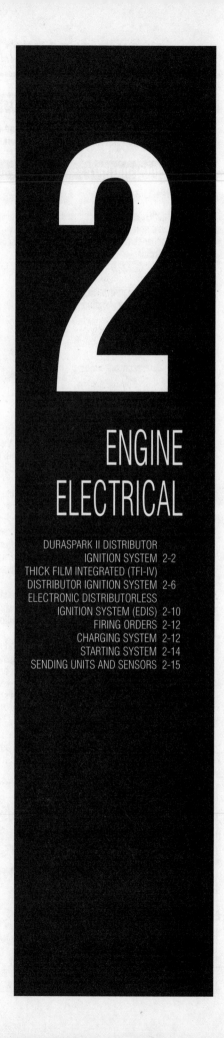

2

ENGINE
ELECTRICAL

DURASPARK II DISTRIBUTOR IGNITION SYSTEM

➡️**For information on understanding electricity and troubleshooting electrical circuits, please refer to Section 6 of this manual.**

General Information

♦ **See Figures 1, 2 and 3**

The Duraspark II ignition system consists of the typical electronic primary and conventional secondary circuits, designed to carry higher voltages. The primary and secondary circuits consists of the following components:

Primary Circuit
- Battery
- Ignition switch
- Ballast resistor start bypass (wires)
- Ignition coil primary winding
- Ignition module
- Distributor stator assembly

Secondary Circuit
- Battery
- Ignition coil secondary winding
- Distributor rotor
- Distributor cap
- Ignition wires
- Spark plugs

With the ignition switch in the **RUN** position, the primary circuit current is directed from the battery, through the ignition switch, the ballast resistor, the ignition coil (in the positive side, out the negative side), the ignition module and back to the battery through the ignition system ground in the distributor. This current flow causes a magnetic field to be built up in the ignition coil. When the poles on the armature and the stator assembly align, the ignition module turns the primary current flow off, collapsing the magnetic field in the ignition coil. The collapsing field induces a high voltage in the ignition coil secondary windings. The ignition coil wire then conducts the high voltage to the distributor where the cap and rotor distributes it to the appropriate spark plug.

A timing device in the ignition module turns the primary current back on after a very short period of time. High voltage is produced each time the magnetic field is built up and collapsed.

The red ignition module wire provides operating voltage for the ignition module electronic components in the run mode. The white ignition module wire and start bypass provide increased voltage for the ignition module and ignition coil, respectively, during start mode.

The distributor provides a signal to the ignition module, which controls the timing of the spark at the spark plugs. This signal is generated as the armature, attached to the distributor shaft, rotates past the stator assembly. The rotating armature causes fluctuations in a magnetic field produced by the stator assembly magnet. These fluctuations induce a voltage in the stator assembly pick-up coil. The signal is connected to the ignition module by the vehicle wiring harness.

The occurrence of the signal to the ignition module, in relation to the initial spark timing, is controlled by centrifugal and vacuum advance mechanisms. The centrifugal advance mechanism controls spark timing in response to engine

rpm. The vacuum advance mechanism controls spark timing in response to engine load.

The centrifugal advance mechanism varies the relationship of the armature to the stator assembly. The sleeve and plate assembly, on which the armature is mounted, rotates in relation to the distributor shaft. This rotation is caused by centrifugal weights moving in response to the engine rpm. The movement of the centrifugal weights change the initial relationship of the armature to the stator assembly by rotating the sleeve and plate assembly ahead of its static position on the distributor shaft. This results in spark advance. The rate of movement of the centrifugal weights is controlled by calibrated springs.

The vacuum spark control mechanism can provide spark advance if a single diaphragm assembly is used or spark advance and retard if a dual diaphragm assembly is used. The diaphragm assembly used depends on the engine calibration.

The single vacuum diaphragm assembly also varies the armature to stator assembly relationship. In this case the stator assembly position is changed by means of vacuum applied to the diaphragm assembly. The diaphragm assembly is attached to the stator assembly by the diaphragm rod. The stator assembly is mounted on the upper plate assembly. The vacuum applied to the diaphragm assembly causes the diaphragm and attached diaphragm rod to move, com-

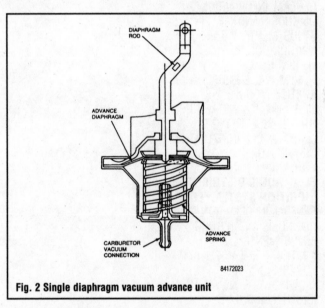

Fig. 2 Single diaphragm vacuum advance unit

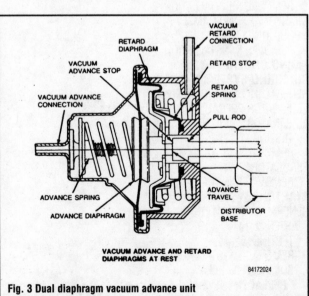

Fig. 3 Dual diaphragm vacuum advance unit

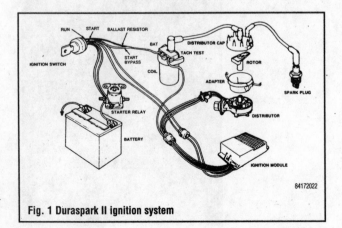

Fig. 1 Duraspark II ignition system

pressing the advance spring, which controls the rate of spark advance. The rate of spark advance is controlled by a calibrated spring.

Spark advance is obtained with a dual diaphragm assembly in the same manner as with a single diaphragm assembly. In this case, vacuum applied to the vacuum advance port cause the advance diaphragm rod to move, otherwise the action is the same. Spark retard is obtained by applying vacuum to the vacuum retard port. This causes the retard diaphragm to move, compressing the retard spring, which controls the rate of spark retard. Compressing the retard spring allows the diaphragm rod stop to move due to force applied by an advance spring pushing against it by means of a diaphragm rod. The result is the diaphragm rod moves, causing the attached stator assembly to change position with respect to the armature. In this instance, the direction of the stator assembly movement is opposite that occurring during vacuum advance, resulting in spark retard. It should be noted that vacuum applied to the advance port overrides any spark retard caused by vacuum applied to the retard port.

Diagnosis and Testing

SECONDARY SPARK TEST

▶ See Figures 4, 5, 6 and 7

The best way to perform this procedure is to use a spark tester (available at most automotive parts stores). Three types of spark testers are commonly available. The Neon Bulb type is connected to the spark plug wire and flashes with each ignition pulse. The Air Gap type must be adjusted to the individual spark plug gap specified for the engine. The last type of spark plug tester looks like a spark plug with a grounding clip on the side, but there is no side electrode for the spark to jump to. The last two types of testers allows the user to not only detect the presence of spark, but also the intensity (orange/yellow is weak, blue is strong).

1. Disconnect a spark plug wire at the spark plug end.
2. Connect the plug wire to the spark tester and ground the tester to an appropriate location on the engine.

3. Crank the engine and check for spark at the tester.
4. If spark exists at the tester, the ignition system is functioning properly.
5. If spark does not exist at the spark plug wire, perform diagnosis of the ignition system using individual component diagnosis procedures.

CYLINDER DROP TEST

▶ See Figures 8, 9 and 10

The cylinder drop test is performed when an engine misfire is evident. This test helps determine which cylinder is not contributing the proper power. The easiest way to perform this test is to remove the plug wires one at a time from the cylinders with the engine running.

1. Place the transmission in **P**, engage the emergency brake, and start the engine and let it idle.
2. Using a spark plug wire removing tool, preferably, the plier type, carefully remove the boot from one of the cylinders.

✳✳ CAUTION

Make sure your body is free from touching any part of the car which is metal. The secondary voltage in the ignition system is high and although it cannot kill you, it will shock you and it does hurt.

3. The engine will sputter, run worse, and possibly nearly stall. If this happens reinstall the plug wire and move to the next cylinder. If the engine runs no differently, or the difference is minimal, shut the engine off and inspect the spark plug wire, spark plug, and if necessary, perform component diagnostics as covered in this section. Perform the test on all cylinders to verify which cylinders are suspect.

Adjustments

The only adjustment available on the Duraspark II ignition system is the timing. Refer to Section 1 for timing inspection and adjustment.

Fig. 4 This spark tester looks just like a spark plug, attach the clip to ground and crank the engine to check for spark

Fig. 5 This spark tester has an adjustable air-gap for measuring spark strength and testing different voltage ignition systems

Fig. 6 Attach the clip to ground and crank the engine to check for spark

Fig. 7 This spark tester is the easiest to use just place it on a plug wire and the spark voltage is detected and the bulb on the top will flash with each pulse

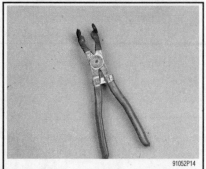

Fig. 8 These pliers are insulated and help protect the user from shock as well as the plug wires from being damaged

Fig. 9 To perform the cylinder drop test, remove one wire at a time and . . .

Fig. 10 . . . note the idle speed and idle characteristics of the engine. The cylinder(s) with the least drop is the non-contributing cylinder(s)

Ignition Coil

TESTING

▶ **See Figures 11 and 12**

1. To locate the coil, follow the coil wire from the center terminal on the distributor cap to the end at the ignition coil. Make sure that the transmission is in Park (AT) or Neutral (MT) and that the ignition is turned **OFF**.

2. Separate the wiring harness connector from the ignition module at the distributor. Inspect for dirt, corrosion and/or damage. Reconnect the harness if no problems are found.

3. Attach a 12 volt DC test light between the coil TACH terminal and an engine ground, then crank the engine. If the light flashes or is continuous:

    a. Turn the ignition switch **OFF**.

    b. Detach the ignition coil connector on top of the coil and inspect for dirt, corrosion and/or damage.

    c. Using an ohmmeter, measure the ignition coil primary resistance from the BATT to the TACH terminals.

    d. The ohmmeter reading should be 0.8–1.6 ohms. If the reading is less than 0.8 ohms or greater than 1.6 ohms, the ignition coil should be replaced.

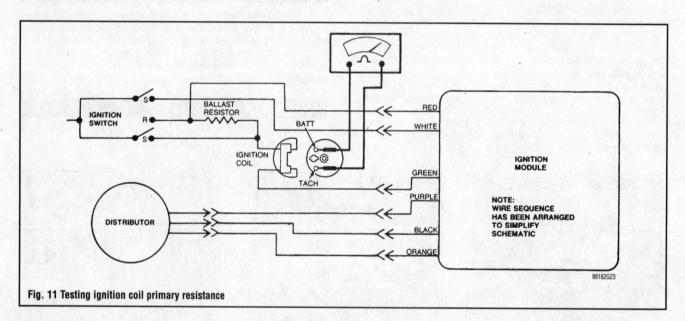

Fig. 11 Testing ignition coil primary resistance

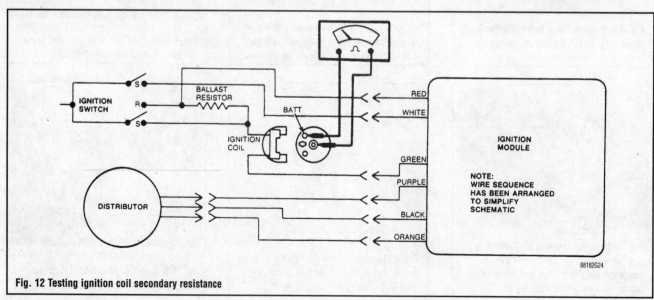

Fig. 12 Testing ignition coil secondary resistance

e. Using an ohmmeter, measure the ignition coil secondary resistance from the BATT terminal to the high voltage terminal.

f. The resistance should be 7,700–10,500 ohms. If the resistance is less that 7,700 ohms or greater than 10,500 ohms, replace the ignition coil.

REMOVAL & INSTALLATION

1. Disconnect the negative battery cable.
2. Detach the coil electrical connector(s).
3. Unfasten the retainers, then remove the ignition coil from the vehicle.
4. Installation is the reverse of the removal procedure.

Ignition Module

REMOVAL & INSTALLATION

1. Disconnect the negative battery cable.
2. Detach the electrical connectors for the ignition module.
3. Remove the ignition module retaining screws and remove the module.
4. The installation is the reverse of the removal.

Stator Assembly

REMOVAL & INSTALLATION

♦ See Figure 13

1. Disconnect the negative battery cable.
2. Remove the distributor cap, rotor and adapter.
3. Separate the distributor connector from the wiring harness.
4. Using a small gear puller or 2 small prybars, remove the armature from the sleeve and plate assembly. Use caution to avoid losing the roll pin.
5. Remove the C-clip securing the diaphragm rod to the stator assembly. Lift the diaphragm rod off the stator assembly pin.
6. Remove the screw retaining the ground strap at the stator assembly grommet. Remove the wire retaining clip from the lower plate assembly.
7. Remove the ground from the distributor base and lift the stator assembly off the lower plate assembly.

To install:

8. Place the stator assembly on the lower plate assembly bushing and install the wire retaining clip.
9. Place the diaphragm rod over the pin on the stator assembly and install the C-clip.
10. Insert the stator assembly grommet in the distributor base slot. Install and tighten the ground strap retaining screw to 15 inch lbs. (1.7 Nm).

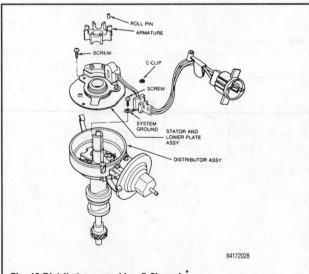

ROLL PIN
ARMATURE
SCREW
C-CLIP
SCREW
SYSTEM GROUND
STATOR AND LOWER PLATE ASSY
DISTRIBUTOR ASSY

84172028

Fig. 13 Distributor assembly—5.8L engine

11. Note there are 2 locating notches in the armature and install it on the sleeve and plate assembly with the unused notch and new roll pin.
12. Connect the distributor wiring harness. Install the distributor adapter, rotor and cap. Install the ignition wires. Verify that the spark plug wires are securely connected to the distributor cap and spark plugs.
13. Connect the negative battery cable and check the ignition timing.

Distributor

REMOVAL & INSTALLATION

Removal

1. Disconnect the negative battery cable.
2. Mark the position of the No. 1 cylinder wire tower on the distributor base.

➡**This reference is necessary in case the engine is disturbed while the distributor is removed.**

3. Remove the distributor cap and position the cap and ignition wires to the side. Detach the wiring harness plug from the distributor connector. Disconnect and plug the vacuum hoses from the vacuum diaphragm assembly, if equipped.
4. Scribe a mark on the distributor body to indicate the position of the rotor tip. Scribe a mark on the distributor housing and engine block to indicate the position of the distributor in the engine.
5. Remove the hold-down bolt and clamp located at the base of the distributor. Remove the distributor from the engine. Note the direction the rotor tip points if it moves from the No. 1 position when the drive gear disengages. For reinstallation purposes, the rotor should be at this point to insure proper gear mesh and timing.
6. Cover the distributor opening in the engine to prevent the entry of dirt or foreign material.
7. Avoid turning the engine, if possible, while the distributor is removed. If the engine is disturbed, the No. 1 cylinder piston will have to be brought to Top Dead Center (TDC) on the compression stroke before the distributor is installed.

Installation

➡**Before installing, visually inspect the distributor. The drive gear should be free of nicks, cracks and excessive wear. The distributor drive shaft should move freely, without binding. If equipped with an O-ring, it should fit tightly and be free of cuts.**

TIMING NOT DISTURBED

1. Position the distributor in the engine, aligning the rotor and distributor housing with the marks that were made during removal. If the distributor does not fully seat in the engine block or timing cover, it may be because the distributor is not engaging properly with the oil pump intermediate shaft. Remove the distributor and, using a screwdriver or similar tool, turn the intermediate shaft until the distributor will seat properly.
2. Install the hold-down clamp and bolt. Snug the mounting bolt so the distributor can be turned for ignition timing purposes.
3. Install the distributor cap and connect the distributor to the wiring harness.
4. Connect the negative battery cable. Check and, if necessary, set the ignition timing. Tighten the distributor hold-down clamp bolt to 17–25 ft. lbs. (23–34 Nm). Recheck the ignition timing after tightening the bolt.
5. If equipped, connect the vacuum diaphragm hoses.

TIMING DISTURBED

1. Disconnect the No. 1 cylinder spark plug wire and remove the No. 1 cylinder spark plug.

✳✳ CAUTION

Use care when performing the next step. Ensure that all body parts are clear of any moving components such as fans, belts, etc. Also ensure that any loose fitting or hanging clothing, jewelry and long hair is clear of the components.

2. Place a finger over the spark plug hole and have an assistant crank the engine slowly until compression is felt.

3. Align the TDC mark on the crankshaft pulley with the pointer on the timing cover. This places the piston in No. 1 cylinder at TDC on the compression stroke.

4. Turn the distributor shaft until the rotor points to the distributor cap No. 1 spark plug tower.

5. Install the distributor in the engine, aligning the rotor and distributor housing with the marks that were made during removal. If the distributor does not fully seat in the engine block or timing cover, it may be because the distributor is not engaging properly with the oil pump intermediate shaft. Remove the distributor and, using a screwdriver or similar tool, turn the intermediate shaft until the distributor will seat properly.

6. Install the hold-down clamp and bolt. Snug the mounting bolt so the distributor can be turned for ignition timing purposes.

7. Install the No. 1 cylinder spark plug and connect the spark plug wire. Install the distributor cap and connect the distributor to the wiring harness.

8. Connect the negative battery cable and set the ignition timing.

9. After the timing has been set, tighten the distributor hold-down clamp bolt to 17–25 ft. lbs. (23–34 Nm). Recheck the ignition timing after tightening the bolt.

10. If equipped, connect the vacuum diaphragm hoses.

THICK FILM INTEGRATED (TFI-IV) DISTRIBUTOR IGNITION SYSTEM

General Information

♦ **See Figures 14, 15, 16 and 17**

The Thick Film Integrated (TFI-IV) ignition system uses a camshaft driven distributor with no centrifugal or vacuum advance. The distributor has a diecast base, incorporating a Hall effect stator assembly. The TFI-IV system module is mounted on the distributor base, it has 6 pins and uses an E-Core ignition coil, named after the shape of the laminations making up the core.

The TFI-IV module supplies voltage to the Profile Ignition Pick-up (PIP) sensor, which sends the crankshaft position information to the TFI-IV module. The TFI-IV module then sends this information to the EEC-IV module, which determines the spark timing and sends an electronic signal to the TFI-IV ignition module to turn off the coil and produce a spark to fire the spark plug.

The operation of the universal distributor is accomplished through the Hall effect stator assembly, causing the ignition coil to be switched off and on by the ECC-IV computer and TFI-IV modules. The vane switch is an encapsulated package consisting of a Hall sensor on one side and a permanent magnet on the other side.

A rotary vane cup, made of ferrous metal, is used to trigger the Hall effect switch. When the window of the vane cup is between the magnet and the Hall effect device, a magnetic flux field is completed from the magnet through the Hall effect device back to the magnet. As the vane passes through the opening, the flux lines are shunted through the vane and back to the magnet. A voltage is produced while the vane passes through the opening. When the vane clears the opening, the window causes the signal to go to 0 volts. The signal is then used by the EEC-IV system for crankshaft position sensing and the computation of the desired spark advance based on the engine demand and calibration. The voltage distribution is accomplished through a conventional rotor, cap and ignition wires.

Diagnosis and Testing

Refer to Diagnosis and Testing under Dura-Spark Distributor Ignition in this section.

Adjustments

The only adjustment available on the TFI-IV system is the timing. Refer to Section 1 for Timing inspection and adjustment.

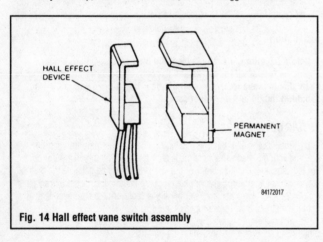

84172017

Fig. 14 Hall effect vane switch assembly

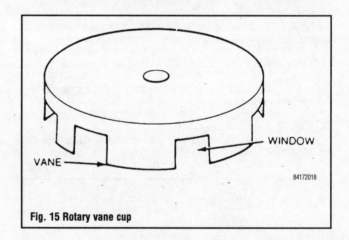

84172018

Fig. 15 Rotary vane cup

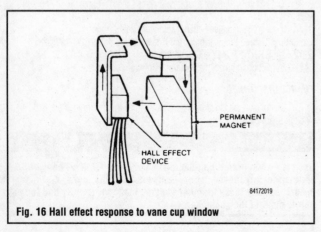

84172019

Fig. 16 Hall effect response to vane cup window

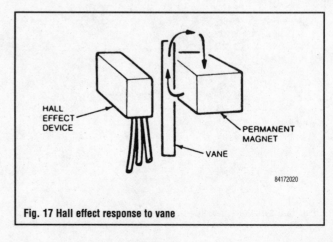

84172020

Fig. 17 Hall effect response to vane

Ignition Coil

TESTING

Primary Coil

▶ See Figures 18, 19 and 20

The first check of the primary ignition coil is to verify that there is battery voltage at the **BATT** terminal on the coil. A DVOM is recommended to test for voltage. Turn the ignition switch to the **RUN** position and connect the negative lead of the DVOM to a ground or the negative post/cable clamp on the battery. Connect the other lead of the DVOM to the **BATT** terminal on the coil. The voltage measured should be within 1 volt of the battery voltage as measure across the posts of the battery.

After verifying there is battery voltage present, the next check is to verify the operation of the coil primary ground which is received at the coil from the ICM (Ignition Control Module). This check is accomplished using a test lamp and connecting the lead of the test lamp to the ground or the battery negative post/cable clamp. Connect the test lamp to the ground side of the coil (the connection opposite the **BATT** terminal on the coil on the other side of the coil tower) and crank the engine. The light should blink on and off repeatedly as long as the engine cranks or runs. If the light does not blink the problem is either in the ICM or the **PIP** signal generated by the sensor inside the distributor.

The final check of the primary coil is to check the resistance of the coil. This is accomplished by using a DVOM and probing the **BATT** terminal and the coil ground terminal. Measure the resistance between the two terminals. If

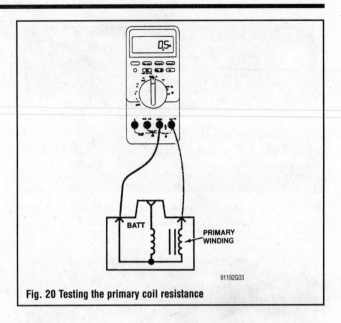
Fig. 20 Testing the primary coil resistance

the resistance is between 0.3 and 1.0 ohm, the primary ignition coil is within specifications. If the reading differs from this specification, replace the coil and retest.

Secondary Windings

▶ See Figure 21

The coil secondary resistance is the final check of the ignition coil. Use a DVOM to measure the resistance between the **BATT** terminal to the high voltage terminal of the ignition coil. If the reading is between 6,500–11,500 ohms, the ignition coil is OK. If the reading is less than 6,500 or more than 11,500 ohms, replace the ignition coil. If the secondary windings are within specifications and the primary circuit also tests within specifications, inspect and test the spark plug wires and the spark plugs, refer to Section 1.

REMOVAL & INSTALLATION

▶ See Figures 22, 23, 24 and 25

1. Pulling on the connector boot, detach the high tension lead at the coil.
2. Disconnect the wiring at the ignition coil.
3. Remove the ignition coil-to-bracket attaching screws, then remove the coil.

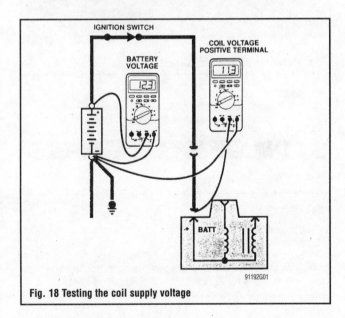
Fig. 18 Testing the coil supply voltage

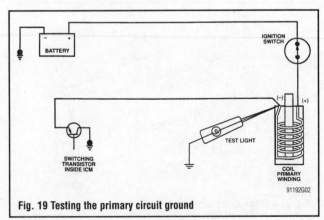
Fig. 19 Testing the primary circuit ground

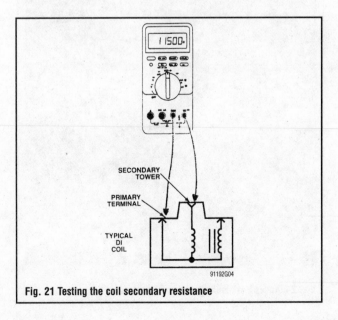
Fig. 21 Testing the coil secondary resistance

Fig. 22 Disengage the high tension wire by pulling on the connector boot

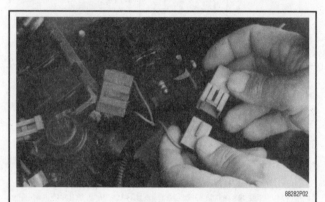

Fig. 23 Separate the wiring harness connection at the coil

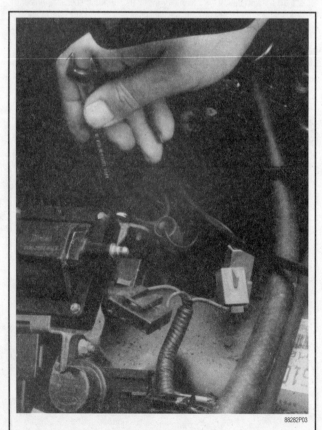

Fig. 24 Unscrew the coil from its bracket mount

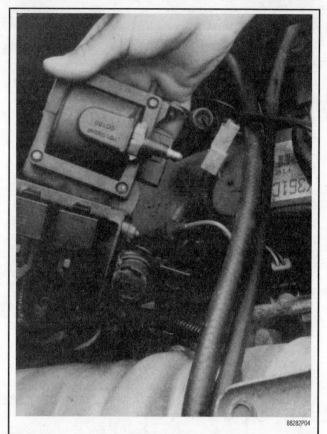

Fig. 25 Remove the coil from the engine

To install:

4. Install the coil, tightening the screws to 25–35 inch lbs. (3–4 Nm).
5. Connect the ignition coil wiring harness and the high tension lead.

Ignition Module

REMOVAL & INSTALLATION

▶ **See Figure 26**

1. Disconnect the negative battery cable.
2. Detach the ignition module connector.
3. Remove the module retaining screws. Pull the right side of the module down the distributor mounting flange and back up to disengage the module terminals from the connector in the distributor base. The module may be pulled toward the flange and away from the distributor.

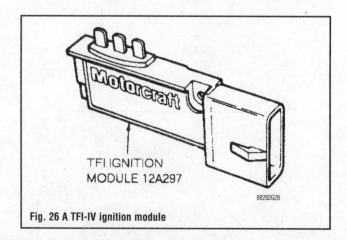

Fig. 26 A TFI-IV ignition module

➡Do not attempt to lift the module from the mounting surface except as explained in Step 3, as the pins will break at the distributor module connector.

To install:

4. Coat the base plate of the TFI-IV ignition module uniformly with a 1/32 (0.79mm) thick film of silicone dielectric compound.

5. Position the module on the distributor base mounting flange. Carefully position the module toward the distributor bowl and engage the 3 connector pins securely.

6. Install the retaining screws. Tighten to 15–35 inch lbs. (1.7–4.0 Nm), starting with the upper right screw.

7. Attach the module harness connector.

8. Connect the negative battery cable.

Stator Assembly

REMOVAL & INSTALLATION

▶ **See Figures 27 and 28**

1. Remove the distributor assembly from the engine; refer to the procedure in this section.

2. Remove the ignition rotor from the distributor shaft.

3. Remove the 2 TFI-IV module retaining screws and remove the module. Wipe the grease from the distributor and module, keeping the surfaces free of dirt.

4. Mark the armature and distributor drive gear with a felt tip pen or equivalent, to note their orientation. While holding the distributor gear, loosen the 2 armature retaining screws and remove the armature.

➡**Do not hold the armature to loosen the screws.**

5. Use a suitable punch to remove the roll pin from the distributor drive gear; discard the roll pin.

6. Position the distributor upside down in a suitable press. Using a press plate and suitable driver, press off the distributor drive gear.

7. Use a file and/or emery paper to remove any burrs or deposits from the distributor shaft, that would keep the shaft from sliding freely from the distributor housing. Remove the shaft assembly.

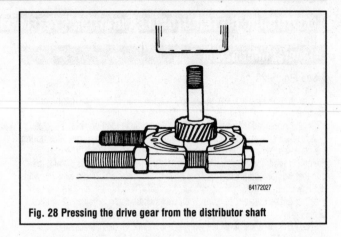

Fig. 28 Pressing the drive gear from the distributor shaft

8. Remove the 2 stator assembly retaining screws and remove the stator assembly.

9. Inspect the base bushing for wear or signs of excess heat concentration. If damage is evident, the entire distributor assembly must be replaced.

10. Inspect the base O-ring for cuts or damage and replace, as necessary.

11. Inspect the base for cracks and wear. Replace the entire distributor assembly if the base is damaged.

To install:

12. Position the stator assembly over the bushing and press down to seat.

13. Position the stator connector. The tab should fit in the notch on the base and the fastening eyelets should be aligned with the screw holes. Be sure the wires are positioned out of the way of moving parts.

14. Install the 2 stator retaining screws and tighten to 15–35 inch lbs. (1.7–4.0 Nm).

15. Apply a thin coat of clean engine oil to the distributor shaft below the armature. Insert the shaft into the distributor base.

16. Place a 1/2 in. deep well socket over the distributor shaft, invert the assembly and place on the press plate.

17. Position the distributor drive gear on the end of the distributor shaft, aligning the marks on the armature and gear. Make sure the holes in the shaft and drive gear are aligned, so the roll pin can be installed.

18. Place a 5/8 in. deep well socket over the shaft and gear and press the gear until the holes are aligned.

➡**If the shaft and gear holes do not align, the gear must be removed and repressed. Do not attempt to use a drift punch to align the holes.**

19. Drive a new roll pin through the gear and shaft.

20. Install the armature and tighten the screws to 25–35 inch lbs. (2.8–4.0 Nm).

21. Check that the distributor shaft moves freely over full rotation. If the armature contacts the stator, the entire distributor must be replaced.

22. Make sure the back of the TFI-IV module and the distributor mounting face are clean. Apply silicone dielectric compound to the back of the module, spreading thinly and evenly.

23. Turn the distributor base upside down, so the stator connector is in full view. Install the module, watching to make sure the 3 module pins are fully inserted into the stator connector. Fully seat the module into the connector and against the base.

24. Install the 2 module retaining screws and tighten to 15–35 inch lbs. (1.7–4.0 Nm).

25. Install the ignition rotor onto the distributor shaft. Install the distributor, as described in this Section.

Distributor

REMOVAL & INSTALLATION

Refer to The distributor removal and installation procedure in Dura-Spark Distributor Ignition in this section.

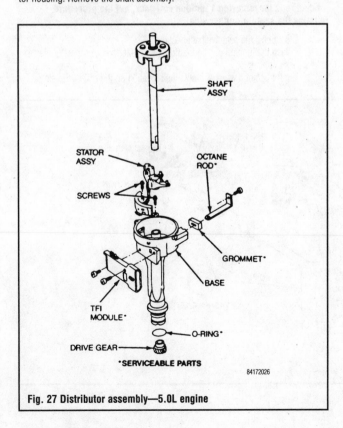

Fig. 27 Distributor assembly—5.0L engine

ELECTRONIC DISTRIBUTORLESS IGNITION SYSTEM (EDIS)

General Information

▶ See Figure 29

The ignition system used on the 4.6L engine is an Electronic Distributorless Ignition System (EDIS) known as the high data rate ignition system. The EDIS eliminates the need for a distributor by using multiple ignition coils. Each coil fires 2 spark plugs at the same time. The plugs are paired so as one fires during the compression cycle, the other fires during the exhaust stroke. The next time the coil is fired, the plug that was on exhaust will be on compression and the one that was on compression will be on exhaust. The spark in the exhaust cylinder is wasted but little of the coil energy is lost. The ignition coils are mounted together in coil packs. There are 2 coil packs used, each containing 2 ignition coils.

The EDIS consists of the following components: crankshaft sensor, ignition module, ignition coil pack, the spark angle portion of the Powertrain Control Module (PCM) and the related wiring. On 1996 and later models, the engines utilize what is known as an integrated ignition system in which the Powertrain Control Module (PCM) performs all the control functions and the Ignition control Module (ICM) is eliminated.

The system operates as follows: The CKP sensor produces a signal generated from the induced voltage created as the trigger wheel on the crankshaft or flywheel passes the sensor. The CKP signal provides engine position and rpm information. This signal is received at the ICM or PCM as a Profile Ignition Pickup (PIP) signal. The ICM or PCM processes the PIP signal along with signals received from other sensors on engine speed, engine temperature, and engine load, and determines the correct ignition timing and grounds the proper ignition coils in the coil pack or the individual coils. When the ignition coil is grounded, an Ignition Diagnostic Monitor (IDM) signal is sent to the ICM or PCM. This signal provides the ICM or PCM with diagnostic information and confirms that the coil fired and is also used to operate the vehicle's tachometer (if equipped).

Diagnosis and Testing

Refer to Diagnosis and Testing under Dura-Spark Distributor Ignition in this section.

Adjustments

All adjustments in the ignition system are controlled by the Powertrain Control Module (PCM) for optimum performance. No adjustments are possible.

Ignition Coil Pack

TESTING

Primary Winding Resistance

▶ See Figure 30

1. Turn the ignition **OFF**.
2. Disconnect the negative battery cable.
3. Disconnect the wiring harness from the ignition coil.
4. Check for dirt, corrosion or damage on the terminals and repair as necessary.
5. Measure coil primary resistance between ignition coil pin 2 (B+) and pins 1 (coil 2), 2 (coil 3) and 3 (coil 1).
6. Resistance should be 0.3–1.0 ohms. If resistance is out of specifications, replace the coil pack. If resistance is within specifications, proceed to secondary windings testing.

Secondary Winding Resistance

▶ See Figure 31

1. Measure coil secondary resistance between the corresponding spark plug wire towers on the coil.
   - Coil 1—cylinders 1 and 6
   - Coil 2—cylinders 3 and 5
   - Coil 3—cylinders 4 and 7
   - Coil 4—cylinders 2 and 8
2. Resistance should be 12.8–13.1 kilohms. If secondary resistance is not within specification, replace the coil pack.

REMOVAL & INSTALLATION

▶ See Figures 32, 33, 34 and 35

➡ Two ignition coil packs are used, one for each bank of cylinders. This procedure is for removing 1 ignition coil pack, but the procedure remains the same for either side.

1. Disconnect the negative battery cable.
2. Detach the ignition coil and radio ignition interference capacitor electrical harness connectors.
3. Tag the ignition wires and note their location on the coil pack before

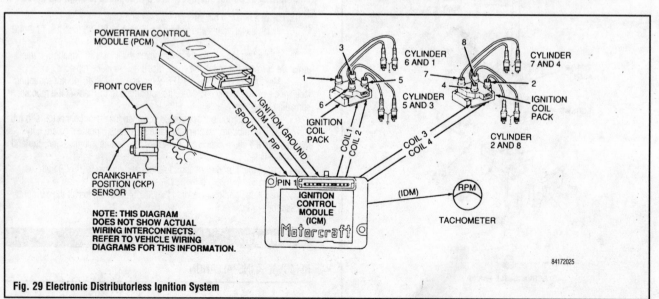

Fig. 29 Electronic Distributorless Ignition System

Fig. 30 Testing the primary ignition coil resistance—4.6L engine

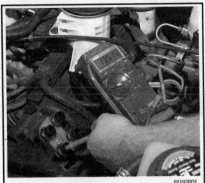

Fig. 31 Testing the secondary ignition coil resistance—4.6L engine

Fig. 32 Remove the ignition wires from the coil pack by squeezing the retaining tabs and carefully lifting up

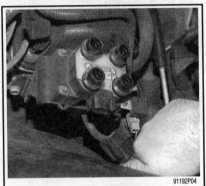

Fig. 33 Detach the connector for the coil pack

Fig. 34 Remove the four coil pack retaining screws and . . .

Fig. 35 . . . remove the coil pack from the bracket

removing. Remove the ignition wires by squeezing the locking tabs to release the coil boot retainers and twisting while pulling upward.

4. Remove 4 ignition coil retaining screws and remove the ignition coil and radio capacitor.

5. If replacing the ignition coil, save the radio capacitor for installation on the new ignition coil.

To install:

6. Place the ignition coil and radio capacitor on the mounting bracket.

7. Install 4 retaining screws and tighten to 40–61 inch lbs. (5–7 Nm).

8. Install the ignition wires to their proper terminals on the ignition coil. Apply silicone dielectric compound to the ignition wire boots prior to installation.

9. Connect the electrical harness connectors to the ignition coil and the radio ignition interference capacitor.

10. Connect the negative battery cable.

11. Road test the vehicle and check for proper engine operation.

Ignition Module

REMOVAL & INSTALLATION

◆ See Figures 36, 37 and 38

➡This procedure applies to 1992–95 models only.

1. Disconnect the negative battery cable.

2. Remove the module retaining screws and remove the module from the fender.

3. Detach the electrical connector at the module by pushing in on the connector finger ends while grasping the connector body and pulling away from the module.

To install:

4. Attach the electrical connector to the module by pushing until the connector fingers are locked over the locking wedge feature on the module.

Fig. 36 Remove the module retaining screws and . . .

Fig. 37 . . . remove the module from the fender

Fig. 38 Detach the electrical connectors at the module by pushing in on the connector finger ends while grasping the connector body and pulling away from the module

5. Install the module and the retaining screws. Tighten the screws to 24–35 inch lbs. (3–4 Nm).

➟Locking the connector is important to ensure sealing of the connector/module interface.

6. Connect the negative battery cable.

FIRING ORDERS

◆ See Figures 39, 40 and 41

➟To avoid confusion, remove and tag the spark plug wires one at a time, for replacement.

If a distributor is not keyed for installation with only one orientation, it could have been removed previously and rewired. The resultant wiring would hold the correct firing order, but could change the relative placement of the plug towers in relation to the engine. For this reason it is imperative that you label all wires before disconnecting any of them. Also, before removal, compare the current wiring with the accompanying illustrations. If the current wiring does not match, make notes in your book to reflect how your engine is wired.

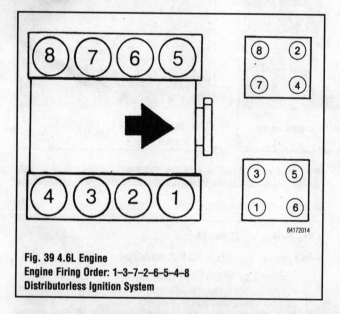

Fig. 39 4.6L Engine
Engine Firing Order: 1–3–7–2–6–5–4–8
Distributorless Ignition System

Crankshaft and Camshaft Position Sensors

For procedures on the position sensors, please refer to Section 4 in this manual.

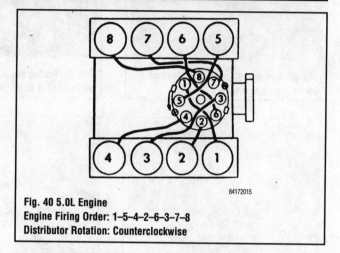

Fig. 40 5.0L Engine
Engine Firing Order: 1–5–4–2–6–3–7–8
Distributor Rotation: Counterclockwise

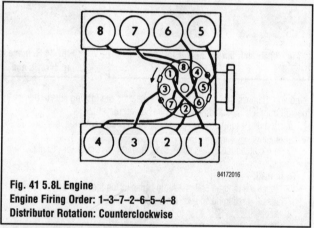

Fig. 41 5.8L Engine
Engine Firing Order: 1–3–7–2–6–5–4–8
Distributor Rotation: Counterclockwise

CHARGING SYSTEM

General Information

The automobile charging system provides electrical power for operation of the vehicle's ignition and starting systems and all the electrical accessories. The battery serves as an electrical surge or storage tank, storing (in chemical form) the energy originally produced by the engine driven alternator. The system also provides a means of regulating generator output to protect the battery from being overcharged and to avoid excessive voltage to the accessories.

The storage battery is a chemical device incorporating parallel lead plates in a tank containing a sulfuric acid/water solution. Adjacent plates are slightly dissimilar, and the chemical reaction of the 2 dissimilar plates produces electrical energy when the battery is connected to a load such as the starter motor. The chemical reaction is reversible, so that when the generator is producing a voltage (electrical pressure) greater than that produced by the battery, electricity is forced into the battery, and the battery is returned to its fully charged state.

The vehicle's alternator is driven mechanically, by a belt(s) that is driven by the engine crankshaft. In an alternator, the field rotates while all the current produced passes only through the stator winding. The brushes bear against continuous slip rings rather than a commutator. This causes the current produced to periodically reverse the direction of its flow creating alternating current (A/C).

Diodes (electrical one-way switches) block the flow of current from traveling in the wrong direction. A series of diodes is wired together to permit the alternating flow of the stator to be converted to a pulsating, but unidirectional flow at the alternator output. The alternator's field is wired in series with the voltage regulator.

The regulator consists of several circuits. Each circuit has a core, or magnetic coil of wire, which operates a switch. Each switch is connected to ground through one or more resistors. The coil of wire responds directly to system voltage. When the voltage reaches the required level, the magnetic field created by the winding of wire closes the switch and inserts a resistance into the generator field circuit, thus reducing the output. The contacts of the switch cycle open and close many times each second to precisely control voltage.

Alternator Precautions

Several precautions must be observed when performing work on alternator equipment.

• If the battery is removed for any reason, make sure that it is reconnected with the correct polarity. Reversing the battery connections may result in damage to the one-way rectifiers.

• Never operate the alternator with the main circuit broken. Make sure that the battery, alternator, and regulator leads are not disconnected while the engine is running.

• Never attempt to polarize an alternator.

• When charging a battery that is installed in the vehicle, disconnect the negative battery cable.

• When utilizing a booster battery as a starting aid, always connect it in parallel; negative to negative, and positive to positive.

• When arc (electric) welding is to be performed on any part of the vehicle, disconnect the negative battery cable and alternator leads.

• Never unplug the PCM while the engine is running or with the ignition in the **ON** position. Severe and expensive damage may result within the solid state equipment.

Alternator

TESTING

Voltage Test

1. Make sure the engine is **OFF**, and turn the headlights on for 15–20 seconds to remove any surface charge from the battery.
2. Using a DVOM set to volts DC, probe across the battery terminals.
3. Measure the battery voltage.
4. Write down the voltage reading and proceed to the next test.

No-Load Test

1. Connect a tachometer to the engine.

✳✳ CAUTION

Ensure that the transmission is in PARK and the emergency brake is set. Blocking a wheel is optional and an added safety measure.

2. Turn off all electrical loads (radio, blower motor, wipers, etc.)
3. Start the engine and increase engine speed to approximately 1500 rpm.
4. Measure the voltage reading at the battery with the engine holding a steady 1500 rpm. Voltage should have raised at least 0.5 volts, but no more than 2.5 volts.
5. If the voltage does not go up more than 0.5 volts, the alternator is not charging. If the voltage goes up more than 2.5 volts, the alternator is overcharging.

➡**Usually under and overcharging is caused by a defective alternator, or its related parts (regulator), and replacement will fix the problem; however, faulty wiring and other problems can cause the charging system to malfunction. Further testing, which is not covered by this book, will reveal the exact component failure. Many automotive parts stores have alternator bench testers available for use by customers. An alternator bench test is the most definitive way to determine the condition of your alternator.**

6. If the voltage is within specifications, proceed to the next test.

Load Test

1. With the engine running, turn on the blower motor and the high beams (or other electrical accessories to place a load on the charging system).
2. Increase and hold engine speed to 2000 rpm.
3. Measure the voltage reading at the battery.
4. The voltage should increase at least 0.5 volts from the voltage test. If the voltage does not meet specifications, the charging system is malfunctioning.

➡**Usually under and overcharging is caused by a defective alternator, or its related parts (regulator), and replacement will fix the problem; however, faulty wiring and other problems can cause the charging system to malfunction. Further testing, which is not covered by this book, will reveal the exact component failure. Many automotive parts stores have alternator bench testers available for use by customers. An alternator bench test is the most definitive way to determine the condition of your alternator.**

REMOVAL & INSTALLATION

5.0L and 5.8L Engines

1. Disconnect the negative battery cable.
2. Tag and detach the wiring connectors from the rear of the alternator. To detach push-on type terminals, depress the lock tab and pull straight off.
3. Loosen the alternator pivot bolt and remove the adjusting bolt. Disengage the drive belt from the alternator pulley.
4. Remove the alternator pivot bolt and the alternator.
   To install:
5. Position the alternator and install the retaining bolts.
6. Install the drive belt.
7. Tighten the retaining and pivot bolts to 15–21 ft. lbs. (21–29 Nm). Ensure that the drive belt is properly tensioned, refer to Section1 for more information.
8. Attach the alternator connectors.
9. Connect the battery ground cable.

4.6L Engine

▶ **See Figures 42 thru 49**

1. Disconnect the negative battery cable.
2. Rotate the drive belt tensioner away from the drive belt and remove the drive belt from the alternator pulley.
3. Detach the electrical harness connectors at the alternator assembly.
4. Disconnect the positive battery cable and remove the nut and washer.
5. Remove 2 front alternator bolts.
6. Remove the rear alternator support bracket retaining bolts and the support bracket.
7. Remove the alternator from the vehicle.
   To install:
8. Place the alternator in position and loosely install 2 front alternator retaining bolts.

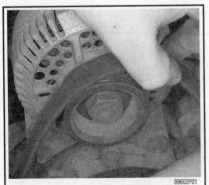

Fig. 42 Rotate the tensioner and remove the belt from around the alternator pulley

Fig. 43 Detach the 2 connectors from the alternator

Fig. 44 Slide the boot up to access the battery cable on the rear of the alternator

Fig. 45 Remove the nut retaining the battery cable and . . .

Fig. 46 . . . remove the battery cable from the post on the rear of the alternator

Fig. 47 Remove the three alternator rear mounting bolts

Fig. 48 Remove the two front alternator mounting bolts

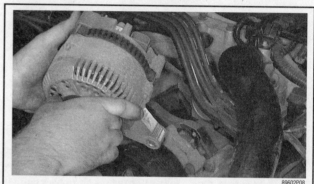

Fig. 49 Remove the alternator from the engine by carefully lifting it up and out of the engine compartment

9. Install the alternator bracket and 3 alternator bracket bolts. Tighten to 84 inch lbs. (10 Nm).
10. Tighten 2 front alternator retaining bolts to 19 ft. lbs. (26 Nm).
11. Connect 2 electrical harness connectors to the alternator assembly.
12. Connect the positive battery cable and install the nut and washer. Tighten the nut to 72 inch lbs. (8 Nm).
13. Rotate the drive belt tensioner away from the drive belt and install the drive belt on the alternator pulley.
14. Connect the negative battery cable.
15. Start the engine and check for proper charging system operation.

Regulator

REMOVAL & INSTALLATION

➡️**This procedure is for models with an external regulator only.**

1. Disconnect the negative battery cable.
2. Disconnect the regulator from the wiring harness.
3. Remove the regulator retaining screws and the regulator.
4. Installation is the reverse of the removal procedure.

STARTING SYSTEM

General Information

The starting system includes the battery, starter motor, solenoid, ignition switch, circuit protection and wiring connecting the components. An inhibitor switch located in the Transmission Range (TR) sensor is included in the starting system to prevent the vehicle from being started with the vehicle in gear.

When the ignition key is turned to the **START** position, current flows and energizes the starter's solenoid coil. The solenoid plunger and clutch shift lever are activated and the clutch pinion engages the ring gear on the flywheel. The switch contacts close and the starter cranks the engine until it starts.

To prevent damage caused by excessive starter armature rotation when the engine starts, the starter incorporates an over-running clutch in the pinion gear.

Starter

TESTING

Voltage Drop Test

➡️**The battery must be in good condition and fully charged prior to performing this test.**

1. Disable the ignition system by unplugging the coil pack. Verify that the vehicle will not start.
2. Connect a voltmeter between the positive terminal of the battery and the starter **B+** circuit.
3. Turn the ignition key to the **START** position and note the voltage on the meter.

4. If voltage reads 0.5 volts or more, there is high resistance in the starter cables or the cable ground, repair as necessary. If the voltage reading is ok proceed to the next step.

5. Connect a voltmeter between the positive terminal of the battery and the starter **M** circuit.

6. Turn the ignition key to the **START** position and note the voltage on the meter.

7. If voltage reads 0.5 volts or more, there is high resistance in the starter. Repair or replace the starter as necessary.

➡ **Many automotive parts stores have starter bench testers available for use by customers. A starter bench test is the most definitive way to determine the condition of your starter.**

REMOVAL & INSTALLATION

♦ **See Figures 50, 51, 52 and 53**

1. Disconnect the negative battery cable.
2. Raise the vehicle and support it safely.

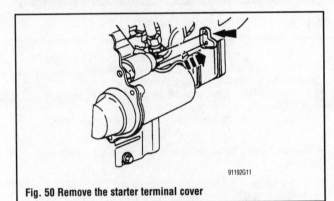

Fig. 50 Remove the starter terminal cover

3. Label and disconnect the starter cables from the starter. If equipped with starter mounted solenoid, detach the push-on connector from the solenoid.

➡ **To detach the hard-shell connector from the solenoid S terminal, grasp the plastic shell and pull off; do not pull on the wire. Pull straight off to prevent damage to the connector and S terminal.**

4. Remove the starter bolts and the starter.
To install:
5. Position the starter to the engine and tighten the mounting bolts to 15–20 ft. lbs. (20–27 Nm).
6. Reconnect the electrical leads.
7. Lower the vehicle.
8. Connect the negative battery cable.

SOLENOID OR RELAY REPLACEMENT

Starter Mounted Solenoid

1. Disconnect the negative battery cable.
2. Remove the starter.
3. Remove the positive brush connector from the solenoid M terminal.
4. Remove the solenoid retaining screws and remove the solenoid.
To install:
5. Attach the solenoid plunger rod to the slot in the lever and tighten the solenoid retaining screws to 45–54 inch lbs. (5.1–6.1 Nm).
6. Attach the positive brush connector to the solenoid M terminal and tighten the retaining nut to 80–120 inch lbs. (9.0–13.5 Nm).
7. Install the starter and connect the negative battery terminal.

Relay

1. Disconnect the negative battery cable.
2. Label and disconnect the wires from the relay.
3. Remove the relay retaining bolts and remove the relay.
4. Installation is the reverse of the removal procedure.

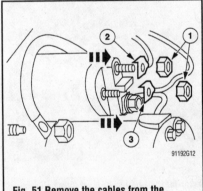

Fig. 51 Remove the cables from the starter terminals

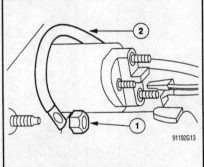

Fig. 52 If equipped, remove the ground cable retaining nut from the stud and remove the ground cable

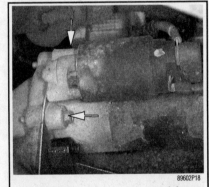

Fig. 53 Remove the two starter retaining bolts—4.6L engine

SENDING UNITS AND SENSORS

➡ **This section describes the operating principles of sending units, warning lights and gauges. Sensors which provide information to the Powertrain Control Module (PCM) are covered in Section 4 of this manual.**

Instrument panels contain a number of indicating devices (gauges and warning lights). These devices are composed of two separate components. One is the sending unit, mounted on the engine or other remote part of the vehicle, and the other is the actual gauge or light in the instrument panel.

Several types of sending units exist, however most can be characterized as being either a pressure type or a resistance type. Pressure type sending units convert liquid pressure into an electrical signal which is sent to the gauge. Resistance type sending units are most often used to measure temperature and use variable resistance to control the current flow back to the indicating device.

Both types of sending units are connected in series by a wire to the battery (through the ignition switch). When the ignition is turned **ON**, current flows from the battery through the indicating device and on to the sending unit.

Coolant Temperature Sender

TESTING

♦ **See Figure 54**

The sending unit is located in the front section of the intake manifold in the vicinity of the thermostat.

✳✳ CAUTION

Never open, service or drain the radiator or cooling system when hot; serious burns can occur from the steam and hot coolant. Also, when draining engine coolant, keep in mind that cats and dogs are attracted to ethylene glycol antifreeze and could drink any that is left in an uncovered container or in puddles on the ground. This will prove fatal in sufficient quantities. Always drain coolant into a sealable container. Coolant can be reused unless it is contaminated or is several years old.

1. Check the appropriate fuse before attempting any other diagnostics.
2. Disconnect the sending unit electrical harness.
3. Remove the radiator cap and place a mechanic's thermometer in the coolant.
4. Using an ohmmeter, check the resistance between the sending unit terminals.
5. Resistance should be high (74 ohms) with engine coolant cold and low (9.7 ohms) with engine coolant hot.

➥It is best to check resistance with the engine cool, then start the engine and watch the resistance change as the engine warms.

6. If resistance does not drop as engine temperature rises, the sending unit is faulty.

REMOVAL & INSTALLATION

▶ **See Figures 55, 56, 57 and 58**

1. Disconnect the negative battery cable.
2. Drain the cooling system into a suitable container.

Fig. 54 The temperature gauge sending unit is located in the front section of the intake manifold, just to the right of the alternator—4.6L engine

✳✳ CAUTION

When draining the coolant, keep in mind that cats and dogs are attracted by the ethylene glycol antifreeze, and are quite likely to drink any that is left in an uncovered container or in puddles on the ground. This will prove fatal in sufficient quantity. Always drain the coolant into a sealable container. Coolant should be reused unless it is contaminated or several years old.

3. Detach the electrical connector at the temperature sender/switch.
4. Remove the temperature sender/switch.
To install:
5. Apply pipe sealant or Teflon® tape to the threads of the new sender/switch.
6. Install the temperature sender/switch and connect the electrical connector.
7. Connect the negative battery cable. Fill the cooling system.
8. Run the engine and check for leaks.

Oil Pressure Sender/Switch

TESTING

1. Test and verify the engine oil pressure. See Section 3 for more information. If no or insufficient pressure exists, oil pressure problem exists and gauge and sensor are operational, repair oil pressure problem.
2. Check the appropriate fuse before attempting any other diagnostics.
3. Unplug the sensor electrical harness.
4. Using an ohmmeter, check continuity between the sensor terminals.
5. With the engine stopped, continuity should not exist.

➥The switch inside the oil pressure sensor opens at 6 psi or less of pressure.

6. With the engine running, continuity should exist.
7. If continuity does not exist as stated, the sensor is faulty.

Fig. 55 Detach the connector for the temperature sending unit

Fig. 56 Using a suitable size socket and drive tool, loosen the sending unit

Fig. 57 Remove the sending unit from the intake manifold by carefully unthreading it

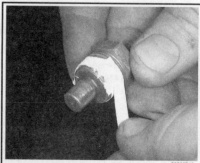
Fig. 58 Install some Teflon® tape on the threads of the new sending unit to help prevent a leak

REMOVAL & INSTALLATION

♦ See Figures 59 thru 64

※※ WARNING

The pressure switch used with the oil pressure warning light is not interchangeable with the sending unit used with the oil pressure gauge. If the incorrect part is installed the oil pressure indicating system will be inoperative and the sending unit or gauge will be damaged.

1. Disconnect the negative battery cable.
2. Detach the electrical connector and remove the oil pressure sender/switch.

To install:

3. Apply pipe sealant to the threads of the new sender/switch.
4. Install the oil pressure sender/switch and tighten to 9–11 ft. lbs. (12–16 Nm).
5. Connect the electrical connector to the sender/switch and connect the negative battery cable.
6. Run the engine and check for leaks and proper operation.

Low Oil Level Sensor

TESTING

1. Test and verify proper oil level and the engine oil pressure. See Sections 1 and 3 for more information. If no or insufficient pressure exists, oil pressure problem exists and gauge and sensor are operational, repair oil pressure problem.
2. Start the engine and observe the oil pressure warning lamp.
3. If the lamp stays on continuously, turn the engine off, then turn the ignition key to the run position.

4. Unplug the sensor electrical harness and observe the oil pressure warning lamp. If the lamp does not illuminate, the sensor is defective and should be replaced.

REMOVAL & INSTALLATION

♦ See Figure 65

➡This procedure requires draining some of the engine oil. However, it is recommended to drain all of the oil and perform a complete oil change procedure. Refer to

1. Disconnect the negative battery cable.
2. Raise and safely support the vehicle.
3. Drain at least 2 quarts of oil from the engine into a suitable container.
4. Detach the electrical connector from the sensor.
5. Remove the sensor using a 1 in. socket or wrench.

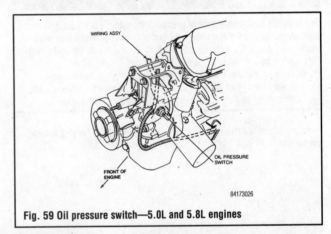

Fig. 59 Oil pressure switch—5.0L and 5.8L engines

Fig. 60 Oil pressure sender/switch—4.6L engine

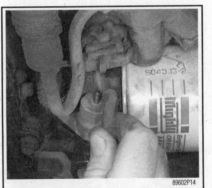

Fig. 61 Remove the wire connector from the sender/switch

Fig. 62 A special socket is available to remove the sender/switch

Fig. 63 Loosen the sender/switch using the socket and an appropriate drive tool and . . .

Fig. 64 . . . and remove the sender/switch from the engine. Be sure to place a drain pan under the area as oil typically will drip out

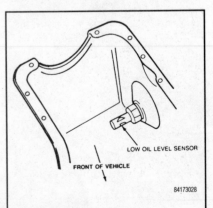

Fig. 65 Low oil level sensor

To install:

6. Install the sensor and tighten to 15–25 ft. lbs. (20–34 Nm).
7. Connect the electrical connector.
8. Tighten the oil pan drain plug to 8–12 ft. lbs. (11–16 Nm) on 4.6L engines or 15–25 ft. lbs. (20–34 Nm) on 5.0L and 5.8L engines.
9. Lower the vehicle.
10. Add oil to the proper level.
11. Connect the negative battery cable, start the engine and check for leaks.

Fuel Level Sending Unit

The fuel level sending unit is located on the fuel pump inside the fuel tank.

TESTING

✳✳ CAUTION

Observe all applicable safety precautions when working around fuel. Whenever servicing the fuel system, always work in a well ventilated area. Do not allow fuel spray or vapors to come in contact with a spark or open flame. Keep a dry chemical fire extinguisher near the work area. Always keep fuel in a container specifically designed for fuel storage; also, always properly seal fuel containers to avoid the possibility of fire or explosion.

➡**An assistant is recommended and extremely helpful for this testing procedure.**

1. Check the appropriate fuse before attempting any other diagnostics.
2. Raise and support the vehicle.
3. Unplug the fuel level sending unit connector from the top of the fuel tank.
4. Insert the leads of the Rotunda gauge tester number 021-00055 or equivalent into the fuel level sender connector and set the scale to 145 ohms.

➡**Although a gauge tester is recommended for the testing of the fuel level sending unit, you can purchase resistors of the equivalent value at any electrical store and form your own tool.**

5. Turn the ignition to the **ON** position and verify that the fuel gauge reads **EMPTY**. If the gauge reads **EMPTY**, proceed to the next step, if it does not, repair gauge and/or wiring as necessary.

➡**It may take as long as 60 seconds for the gauge to move.**

6. Slowly turn the resistance level on the gauge tester to 22 ohms and verify that the gauge reading moves to **FULL**. If the gauges moves to **FULL**, the gauge and wiring are operating as designed, most likely the sending unit is faulty, repair as necessary. If the gauge does not read **FULL**, repair gauge and/or wiring as necessary.

An alternative method requiring no special testers is to remove the fuel pump from the tank. Connect the wiring to the pump and sending unit and manually operate the sending unit arm while an assistant observes the gauge.

REMOVAL & INSTALLATION

The fuel level sending unit is attached to the fuel pump. Refer to Section 5 and the fuel pump removal and installation procedure.

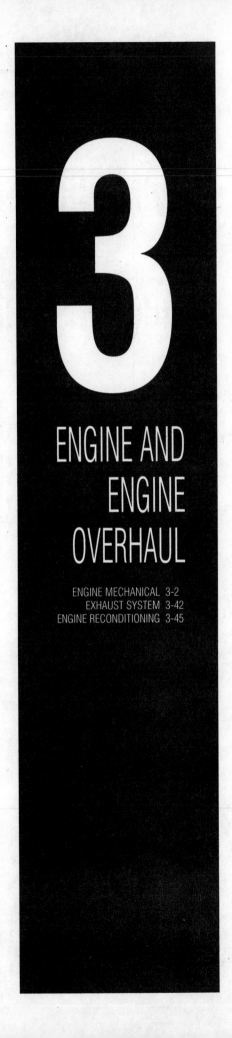

3

ENGINE AND ENGINE OVERHAUL

ENGINE MECHANICAL

4.6L ENGINE MECHANICAL SPECIFICATIONS

Description	English Specifications	Metric Specifications
General Information		
Type	Liquid Cooled, Overhead Camshaft	4.6L
Displacement	280 cid	
Number of cylinders	8	
Bore	3.55 in.	90.2mm
Stroke	3.54 in.	90.0mm
Compression ratio	9.0:1	
Firing order	1-3-7-2-6-5-4-8	
Oil Pressure	20-45 psi @ 1500 RPM (engine hot)	
Cylinder Head and Valve Train		
Valve guide bore diameter	0.3443-0.3433 in.	8.745-8.720
Valve seat width		
Intake	0.074-0.083 in.	1.9-2.1mm
Exhaust	0.074-0.083 in.	1.9-2.1mm
Valve seat angle	45 degrees	
Valve seat run-out	0.00094 in.	0.025mm
Valve stem-to-guide clearance		
Intake	0.00078-0.00272 in.	0.020-0.069mm
Exhaust	0.018-0.0037 in.	0.046-0.095mm
Valve guide inner diameter	0.2773-0.2762 in.	7.044-7.015mm
Valve head diameter		
Intake	1.75 in.	44.5mm
Exhaust	1.34 in.	34.0mm
Valve face run-out limit	0.001 in.	0.05mm
Valve face angle	45.5 degrees	
Valve stem diameter		
Intake	0.275-0.2746 in.	6.995-6.975mm
Exhaust	0.274-0.2736 in.	6.970-6.949mm
Free length		
Intake	1.976 in.	50.2mm
Exhaust	1.976 in.	50.2mm
Valve spring assembled length	1.566-1.637 in.	39.8-41.6mm
Rocker arm ratio	1.75:1	
Valve tappet diameter	0.63-0.629 in.	16.0-15.98mm
Valve tappet-to-bore clearance	0.00071-0.00272 in.	0.018-0.069mm
Valve tappet service limit	0.00063 in.	0.016mm
Valve tappet leakdown rate	5-25 seconds	
Valve tappet collapsed tappet gap (desired)	0.0335-0.0177 in.	0.85-0.45mm
Camshaft		
Lobe lift		
Intake	0.2594 in.	6.59mm
Exhaust	0.2594 in.	6.59mm
Lobe wear limit (all)	0.005 in.	0.127mm
Theoretical valve lift @ zero lash (all)	0.472 in.	12.0mm
End-play	0.00098-0.0065 in.	0.025-0.165mm
End-play wear limit	0.0075 in.	0.190mm
Bearing-to-journal clearance	0.00098-0.003 in.	0.025-0.076mm
Bearing-to-journal clearance service limit	0.0048 in.	0.121mm
Journal diameter	1.061-1.060 in.	26.962-26.936mm
Bearing journal inside diameter	1.063-1.0625 in.	27.012-26.987mm
Run-out	0.002 in.	0.05mm

89603C01

4.6L ENGINE MECHANICAL SPECIFICATIONS

Description	English Specifications	Metric Specifications
Cylinder Block		
Cylinder bore diameter		
Out-of-round	0.0006 in.	0.015mm
Out-of-round (service limit)	0.00079 in.	-0.020mm
Taper limit	0.00023 in.	0.006mm
Main bearing bore	2.85-2.851 in.	72.402-72.422mm
Crankshaft		
Main bearing journal diameter	2.65-2.657 in.	67.483-67.503mm
Main bearing journal taper	0.0007 in.	0.02mm
Main bearing journal run-out	0.002 in.	0.05mm
Main bearing-to-crankshaft clearance	0.0011-0.0026 in.	0.027-0.065mm
Bearing wall thickness	0.075-0.079 in.	1.920-1.928mm
Connecting rod bearing journal diameter	2.087-2.867 in.	52.988-53.003mm
Crankshaft free end-play	0.130-0.301 in.	0.0051-0.012mm
Crankshaft runout-to-rear face of the block	0.002 in.	0.05mm
Connecting Rod		
Connecting rod bearing-to-crankshaft clearance	0.001-0.0027 in.	0.027-0.069mm
Connecting rod bearing wall thickness	0.096-0.0965 in.	2.444-2.452mm
Connecting rod main bearing bore diameter	2.234-2.24 in.	56.756-56.876mm
Connecting rod length (center-to-center)	5.93 in.	150.7mm
Connecting rod-to-crank side clearance (standard)	0.0006-0.0177 in.	0.015-0.45mm
Connecting rod-to-crank side clearance (maximum)	0.02 in.	0.5mm
Connecting rod main bearing journal taper	0.0005 in.	0.015 mm
Pistons		
Piston diameter		
Coded red	3.550-3.551 in.	90.177-90.197mm
Coded blue	3.5507-3.5515 in.	90.190-90.210mm
Coded yellow	3.5513-3.5521 in.	90.203-90.223mm
Piston-to-bore clearance	0.0005-0.001 in.	0.012-0.026mm
Piston pin bore diameter	0.864-0.865 in.	21.959-21.979mm
Piston pin bore length	2.44-2.443 in.	61.93-62.05mm
Piston pin-to-rod clearance	0.0006-0.00157 in.	0.015-0.040mm
Piston pin-to-piston clearance	0.0002-0.0004 in.	0.005-0.010mm
Piston ring side clearance		
Upper compression ring	0.0016-0.0035 in.	0.040-0.090mm
Lower compression ring	0.0012-0.0031 in.	0.030-0.080mm
Oil control ring	0.05 in.	1.25mm
Piston ring groove width		
Upper compression ring	0.060-0.0610 in.	1.530-1.550mm
Lower compression ring	0.060-0.0602 in.	1.520-1.530mm
Oil control ring	0.2750-0.2844 in.	6.996-7.224mm
Piston ring gap		
Upper compression ring	0.01-0.02 in.	0.23-0.49mm
Lower compression ring	0.01-0.02 in.	0.23-0.49mm
Oil control ring	0.006-0.026 in.	0.15-0.66mm
Oil Pump		
Oil pump gear radial clearance (idler and drive)	0.0055-0.002 in.	0.125-0.050mm
Oil pump gear end height (extends below the housing)	0.0033-0.0004 in.	0.085-0.010mm

89603C02

5.0L ENGINE MECHANICAL SPECIFICATIONS

Description	English Specifications	Metric Specifications
General Information		
Type	90° V8 Overhead Valve Engine	5.0L (4949cc)
Displacement	302 cu. in.	
Number of Cylinders	8	
Bore	4.00 in.	101.6mm
Stroke	3.00 in.	76.2mm
Compression ratio	8.9:1	
Firing order	1-5-4-2-6-3-7-8	
Oil Pressure	40-60 psi @ 2000 RPM (engine hot)	
Cylinder head		
Cylinder head-to-engine block surface warpage	0.003 in. (0.0762mm) in a 6.0 in. (152.4mm) span	
Valve seat width		
Intake valves	0.060-0.080 in.	1.524-2.032mm
Exhaust valve	0.060-0.080 in.	1.524-2.032mm
Valve seat angle—Intake and exhaust valves	45°	
Valve guide bore diameter—Intake and exhaust valves	0.3433-0.3443	8.720-8.745mm
Valves, valve springs and camshaft		
Camshaft journal diameter		
No. 1	2.0815 in.	52.8701mm
No. 2	2.0665 in.	52.4891mm
No. 3	2.0515 in.	52.1081mm
No. 4	2.0365 in.	51.7271mm
No. 5	2.0215 in.	51.3461mm
Camshaft-to-bearing clearance	0.001-0.003 in.	0.0254-0.0762mm
Camshaft thrust clearance	0.007 in. max	0.1778mm max
Camshaft lobe lift		
Intake valve	0.2637 in.	6.69798mm
Exhaust valve	0.2801 in.	7.11454mm
Camshaft runout	0.005 in. max	0.127mm
Valve stem diameter		
Intake valves	0.3415-0.3423 in.	8.6741-8.6944mm
Exhaust valves	0.3410-0.3418 in.	8.6614-8.6817mm
Valve guide-to-valve stem clearance		
Intake valves	0.0010-0.0027 in.	0.0254-0.0686mm
Exhaust valves	0.0015-0.0032 in.	0.0381-0.08128mm
Valve face angle limit	44°	
Valve head diameter		
Intake valve	1.837-1.847 in.	46.660-46.914mm
Exhaust valve	1.536-1.546 in.	39.01-39.27mm
Valve head radial runout	0.002 in.	0.0508mm
Valve spring free length (approximate)	1.84 in.	46.7mm
Intake valve spring	2.06 in.	52.324mm
Exhaust valve spring	1.88 in.	47.752mm
Valve spring preload		
Intake valve spring	74-82 lbs. @ 1.78 in.	33.6-37.2kg @ 45.21mm
Exhaust valve spring	76-84 lbs. @ 1.60 in.	34.5-38.1kg @ 40.64mm
Valve spring installed height		
Intake valve spring	1.75-1.81 in.	44.45-45.974mm
Exhaust valve spring	1.58-1.64 in.	40.132-41.656mm
Valve spring out-of-square	0.078 in.	1.9812mm
Rocker arm ratio	1.62:1	

89603C03

5.0L ENGINE MECHANICAL SPECIFICATIONS

Description	English Specifications	Metric Specifications
Engine block		
Engine block-to-cylinder head surface warpage	0.003 in. (0.0762mm) in a 6.0 in. (152.4mm) span	
Standard cylinder bore	4.0000-4.0012 in.	101.6-101.6305mm
Cylinder bore out-of-round and taper	0.0015/0.010 in.	0.0381/0.254mm
Cylinder bore-to-piston clearance	0.0012-0.0020 in.	0.0305-0.0508mm
Pistons		
Standard piston diameter	3.9987-3.9993 in.	101.567-101.5822mm
Piston ring groove width		
Top compression ring	0.0602-0.0612 in.	1.530-1.555mm
Second compression ring	0.0602-0.0612 in.	1.530-1.555mm
Oil control ring	0.1587-0.1596 in.	4.030-4.055mm
Piston pin diameter	0.9121-0.9122 in.	23.1673-23.1699mm
Piston rings		
Thickness		
Top compression ring	0.0575-0.0587 in.	1.460-1.490mm
Second compression ring	0.0575-0.0587 in.	1.460-1.490mm
Oil Control ring	Side seal -Snug fit	
Side clearance		
Top compression ring	0.0013-0.0033 in.	0.0330-0.0838mm
Second compression ring	0.0013-0.0033 in.	0.0330-0.0838mm
End-gap		
Top compression ring	0.010-0.020 in.	0.25-0.50mm
Second compression ring	0.018-0.028 in.	0.4572-0.7112mm
Oil ring	0.010-0.040 in.	0.25-1.016mm
Crankshaft and connecting rods		
Crankshaft main journal diameter	2.2482-2.2490 in.	57.1043-57.1246mm
Main bearing-to-journal clearance (oil clearance)	0.0008-0.0026 in.	0.0203-0.0660mm
Crankshaft journal out-of-round and taper	0.0006 in.	0.01524mm
Crankshaft thrust play	0.004-0.008 in.	0.1016-0.2032mm
Crankshaft runout	0.002 in.	0.050mm
Connecting rod journal diameter	2.1228-2.1236 in.	53.9191-53.9191mm
Connecting rod journal out-of-round and taper	0.0006 in.	0.01524mm
Connecting rod journal-to-connecting rod clearance	0.0007-0.0024 in.	0.01778-0.06096mm
Connecting rod small and bore inside diameter	0.9097-0.9112 in.	23.1064-23.1445mm
Connecting rod big end side clearance	0.010-0.020 in.	0.254-0.508mm
Connecting rod twist	0.015 in.	0.381mm
Connecting rod bend	0.012 in.	0.3048mm

5.8L ENGINE MECHANICAL SPECIFICATIONS

Description	English Specifications	Metric Specifications
General Information		
Type	90° V8 Overhead Valve Engine	
Displacement	351 cu. in.	5.8L (5767cc)
Number of Cylinders	8	
Bore	4.00 in.	101.6mm
Stroke	3.50 in.	88.9mm
Compression ratio	8.3:1	
Firing order	1-3-7-2-6-5-4-8	
Oil Pressure	40-60 psi @ 2000 RPM (engine hot)	

89603C04

5.8L ENGINE MECHANICAL SPECIFICATIONS

Description	English Specifications	Metric Specifications
Cylinder Block		
Cylinder bore		
Standard size:	4.0000-4.0048	101.600-101.722
Maximum out-of-round:	0.0015	0.0381
Maximum taper:	0.0100	0.2540
Main bearing		
Bore diameter:	3.1922-3.1930	81.08-81.10
Crankshaft to rear face of block runout (TIR max.):	0.0050	0.1270
Distributor shaft bearing bore diameter:	.5155-.5170	13.09-13.13
Head gasket surface flatness:		
Overall:	0.0060	0.1524
In any 6 in. (152.4mm):	0.0030	0.0080
Head gasket Surface finish (RMS):	60-150	
Tappet bore diameter:	0.8752-0.8767	22.23-22.69
Cylinder Head		
Combustion chamber volume	3.70-3.88 cid	60.6-63.6 cc
Valve guide bore diameter		
Intake:	0.3433-0.3443	8.719-8.745
Exhaust:	0.3433-0.3443	8.719-8.745
Valve seat		
Maximum runout:	0.0020	0.0051
Gasket surface flatness		
Overall:	0.0060	0.1524
In any 6 in. (152.4mm):	0.0030	0.0762
Valve Rocker Arm Shaft, Pushrods and Tappets		
Rocker arm lift ration to 1: 1.59		
Pushrod runout TIR maximum:	0.0150	0.3810
Valve tappet or lifter		
Standard diameter:	0.8740-0.8745	22.199-22.212
Clearance to bore:	0.0007-0.0027	0.0178-0.0068
Hydraulic lifter leakdown rate:	10 to 50 seconds for 1/16 travel	
Collapsed tappet gap		
Allowable:	0.092-0.192	2.337-4.876
Desired:	0.112-0.172	2.845-4.369
Valves		
Valve stem to guide clearance		
Intake:	0.0010-0.0027	0.00254-0.0686
Exhaust:	0.0015-0.0032	0.0381-0.0813
Valve head diameter		
Intake:	1.770-1.794	44.958-45.567
Exhaust:	1.453-1.468	36.906-37.287
Maximum valve face runout:	0.0020	0.0508
Valve springs		
Valve spring compression pressure @ specified height		
Intake:	74-82 lbs. @ 1.78 in.	33.57-37.19 kg @ 45.21mm
	190-210 lbs. @ 1.20 in.	86.18-95.25 kg @ 30.48mm
Exhaust:	76-84 lbs. @ 1.6 in.	34.47-38.10 kg @ 40.64mm
	190-210 lbs. @ 1.20 in.	86.18-95.25 kg @ 30.48mm
Free length (approx.):		
Intake:	2.0600	52.3200
Exhaust:	1.8800	47.7500

89603C05

5.8L ENGINE MECHANICAL SPECIFICATIONS

Description	English Specifications	Metric Specifications
Valve springs (cont'd)		
Valve spring assembled height		
Intake:	1.75-1.81	44.45-45.97
Exhaust:	1.58-1.64	40.13-41.66
Valve spring out of square:	5/64 (0.078)	1.9800
Valve Stem Diameter		
Standard		
Intake:	0.3415-0.3423	8.67-8.69
Exhaust:	0.3410-0.3418	8.66-8.68
0.015 Oversize		
Intake:	0.3565-0.3573	9.06-9.08
Exhaust:	0.3561-0.3568	9.04-9.06
0.030 Oversize		
Intake:	0.3715-0.3723	9.44-9.46
Exhaust:	0.3711-0.3718	9.43-9.44
Crankshaft and Flywheel		
Main bearing journals		
Diameter:	2.9994-3.0002	76.185-76.205
TIR Maximum runout:	0.0020	0.0508
Maximum out of round:	0.0006	0.0152
Thrust face runout TIR maximum:	0.0010	0.0254
Maximum taper per inch/mm:	0.0005	0.0127
Thrust bearing journal length:	1.137-1.139	28.88-28.93
Main and rod bearing journal		
Finish RMS maximum: 12		
Main bearing thrust face		
Finish RMS maximum: 25 front/20 rear		
Connecting rod journal		
Diameter:	2.3103-2.3111	58.6816-58.7019
Taper per inch/om maximum:	0.0006	0.0152
Crankshaft free end-play:	0.004-0.008	0.102-0.203
Flywheel clutch face run-out:	0.0100	0.2540
Crankshaft Bearings		
Connecting rod bearing to crankshaft clearance selective fit		
Desired:	0.0008-0.0015	0.020-0.038
Allowable:	0.0008-0.0025	0.0203-0.0635
Bearing wall thickness		
Standard:	0.572-0.577	14.53-14.66
0.002 undersize:	0.573-0.578	14.55-14.68
Main bearing to crankshaft selective fit		
Desired:		
No. 1 bearing:	0.0008-0.0015	0.0200-0.0381
All other bearings:	0.0001-0.0015	0.00254-0.0381
Allowable:		
No. 1 bearing:	0.0005-0.0015	1.0127-1.0381
All other bearings:	1.0008-1.0026	1.020-1.066
Bearing wall thickness		
No. 1 bearing:	1.0001-1.0020	1.00254-1.0508
All other bearings:	1.0005-1.0024	1.0127-1.0609
No. 1 upper bearing:	0.0957-0.0960	2.430-2.438
All other bearings:	0.0961-0.0966	2.441-2.454
	0.0957-0.0962	2.431-2.443

89603C06

5.8L ENGINE MECHANICAL SPECIFICATIONS

Description	English Specifications	Metric Specifications
Crankshaft Bearings (cont'd)		
0.002 undersize		
No. 1 bearing:	0.0958-0.0962	2.433-2.443
All other bearings:	0.0958-0.0963	2.433-2.446
Connecting rods		
Piston pin bore or bushing I.D.:	0.9097-0.9112	23.106-23.144
Rod bearing bore I.D.:	2.4265-2.4273	61.633-61.653
Connecting rod bore max. out of round:	0.0004	0.0102
Rod length center to center:	5.9545-5.9575	151.244-151.321
Connecting rod alignment maximum total difference		
Twist:	0.0240	3.1500
Service limit:	0.0230	0.5840
Bend:	0.0120	0.3048
Rod to crankshaft assembled side clearance:	0.010-0.020	0.254-0.508
Service limit:	0.0230	0.5840
Pistons		
Diameter		
Coded red:	3.9978-3.9984	101.544-101.560
Coded blue:	3.9990-3.9996	101.575-101.590
.003 oversize:	4.0002-4.0008	101.605-101.620
Piston to bore clearance selective fit		
Standard engine:	0.0018-0.0026	0.0457-0.0660
Lightning engine:	0.0015-0.0023	0.0381-0.0584
Piston pin bore diameter:	0.9123-0.9126	23.172-23.180
Ring groove width compression		
Top:	0.080-0.081	2.032-2.057
Bottom:	0.080-0.081	2.032-2.057
Oil:	0.188-0.189	4.775-4.801
Piston pins		
Length:	3.010-3.040	76.45-77.21
Diameter		
Standard:	0.9119-0.9124	23.162-23.174
.001 oversize:	0.9130-0.9133	23.190-23.197
.002 oversize:	0.9140-0.9143	23.215-23.223
To piston pin bore clearance (selective fit):	0.0003-0.0005	0.0076-0.0127
To connecting rod bushing clearance: Interference fit		
Piston rings		
Ring width		
Top Compression:	0.077-0.087	1.9558-2.2098
Bottom compression:	0.077-0.087	1.9558-2.2098
Side clearance		
Top compression:	0.002-0.004	0.051-0.102
Bottom compression:	0.002-0.004	0.051-0.102
Oil: snug		
Ring gap		
Top compression:	0.010-0.020	0.254-0.508
Bottom compression:	0.010-0.020	0.254-0.508
Oil (steel rail):	0.015-0.040	0.381-1.016

89603C07

5.8L ENGINE MECHANICAL SPECIFICATIONS

Description	English Specifications	Metric Specifications
Camshaft		
Lobe lift		
Intake:	0.2780	7.0610
Exhaust:	0.2830	7.1880
End-play		
Standard:	0.001-0.007	0.0254-0.178
Maximum:	0.0090	0.2280
Camshaft journal to bearing clearance:	0.001-0.003	0.0254-0.076
Camshaft drive		
Journal diameter (standard)		
No. 1:	2.0815	52.8700
No. 2:	2.0655	52.4600
No. 3:	2.0515	51.1810
No. 4:	2.0365	51.7270
No. 5:	2.0215	51.3460
Bearing inside diameter		
No. 1:	2.0835	52.9210
No. 2:	2.0685	52.5400
No. 3:	2.0535	52.1590
No. 4:	2.0385	51.7780
No. 5:	2.0235	51.3970
Camshaft front bearing location	0.005-0.020	0.127-0.508
Oil pump and oil capacity		
Relief valve spring pressure @ specified length:	18.2-20.2 lbs. @ 2.49 in.	8.26-9.16 kg @ 63.25mm
Driveshaft to housing clearance:	0.0015-0.003	0.0381-0.076
Relief valve to housing clearance:	0.0015-0.003	0.0381-0.076
Rotor assembly end clearance:	0.004 maximum	0.100 maximum
Outer race to housing clearance:	0.001-0.003	0.0254-0.0762
Engine oil capacity		
U.S. quarts: 5		
Imperial quarts: 4.2		
Litres: 4.7		

89603C08

Engine

REMOVAL & INSTALLATION

In the process of removing the engine, you will come across a number of steps which call for the removal of a separate component or system, such as "disconnect the exhaust system" or "remove the radiator." In most instances, a detailed removal procedure can be found elsewhere in this manual.

It is virtually impossible to list each individual wire and hose which must be disconnected, simply because so many different model and engine combinations have been manufactured. Careful observation and common sense are the best possible approaches to any repair procedure.

Removal and installation of the engine can be made easier if you follow these basic points:

- If you have to drain any of the fluids, use a suitable container.
- Always tag any wires or hoses and, if possible, the components they came from before disconnecting them.
- Because there are so many bolts and fasteners involved, store and label the retainers from components separately in muffin pans, jars or coffee cans. This will prevent confusion during installation.
- After unbolting the transmission or transaxle, always make sure it is properly supported.
- If it is necessary to disconnect the air conditioning system, have this service performed by a qualified technician using a recovery/recycling station. If the system does not have to be disconnected, unbolt the compressor and set it aside.
- When unbolting the engine mounts, always make sure the engine is properly supported. When removing the engine, make sure that any lifting devices are properly attached to the engine. It is recommended that if your engine is supplied with lifting hooks, your lifting apparatus be attached to them.
- Lift the engine from its compartment slowly, checking that no hoses, wires or other components are still connected.
- After the engine is clear of the compartment, place it on an engine stand or workbench.
- After the engine has been removed, you can perform a partial or full teardown of the engine using the procedures outlined in this manual.

4.6L Engine

▶ See Figures 1, 2, 3 and 4

➡If your vehicle is equipped with air conditioning, refer to Section 1 for information regarding the implications of servicing your A/C system yourself. Only a MVAC-trained, EPA-certified, automotive technician should service the A/C system or its components.

1. Have the A/C system recovered by a MVAC-trained, EPA-certified, automotive technician.

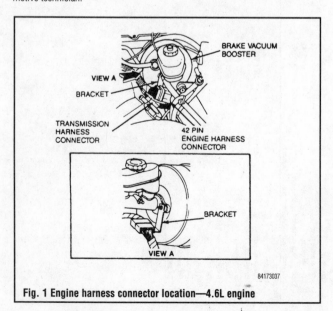

Fig. 1 Engine harness connector location—4.6L engine

2. Disconnect the negative, then the positive battery cable.
3. Drain the engine oil and the cooling system into suitable containers.

4. Relieve the fuel system pressure and disconnect the fuel lines; refer to Section 5.
5. Remove the hood. Refer to Section 10.
6. Remove the air inlet tube.
7. Remove the cooling fan, shroud and radiator. Refer to the procedure later in this section.
8. Remove the wiper module and support bracket. Refer to Section 6.
9. Remove the connector from the retaining bracket on the brake vacuum booster. Detach the connector and transmission harness connector and position aside.
10. Disconnect the accelerator and cruise control cables. Disconnect the throttle valve cable.
11. Detach the electrical connector and vacuum hose from the evaporative emissions valve.
12. Disconnect the power supply from the power distribution box and starter relay.
13. Disconnect the vacuum supply hose from the throttle body adapter vacuum port.
14. Disconnect the heater hoses.
15. Disconnect the alternator harness from the fender apron and junction block.
16. Disconnect the air conditioning hoses from the compressor.
17. Detach the power steering control valve connector from the power steering pump and disconnect the body ground strap from the dash panel.
18. Raise and safely support the vehicle.
19. Disconnect the exhaust system from the exhaust manifolds and support with wire hung from the crossmember.
20. Remove the retaining nut from the transmission line bracket and remove the 3 bolts and stud retaining the engine to the transmission knee braces.
21. Remove the starter.
22. Remove the 4 bolts retaining the power steering pump to the engine block and position aside.
23. Remove the plug from the engine block to access the torque converter retaining nuts. Rotate the crankshaft until each of the 4 nuts is accessible and remove the nuts.
24. Remove the 6 transmission-to-engine retaining bolts.
25. Remove the engine mount through bolts, 2 on the left mount and 1 on the right mount.
26. Lower the vehicle.
27. Support the transmission with a floor jack and remove the bolt retaining the right engine mount to the lower engine bracket.
28. Install an engine lifting bracket to the left cylinder head on the front and the right cylinder head on the rear.
29. Connect suitable engine lifting equipment to the lifting brackets.
30. Raise the engine slightly and carefully separate the engine from the transmission.
31. Carefully lift the engine out of the engine compartment and position on a workstand.
32. Remove the engine lifting equipment.
To install:
33. Install the engine lifting brackets to the engine.
34. Connect the engine lifting equipment to the brackets and remove the engine from the workstand.
35. Carefully lower the engine into the engine compartment.
36. Start the converter pilot into the flexplate and align the paint marks on the flexplate and torque converter. Make sure the studs on the torque converter align with the holes in the flexplate.
37. Fully engage the engine to the transmission and lower onto the mounts. Remove the engine lifting equipment and brackets. Install the bolt retaining the right engine mount to the frame.

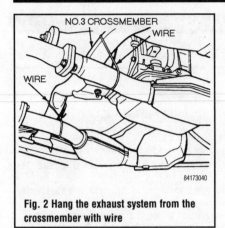

Fig. 2 Hang the exhaust system from the crossmember with wire

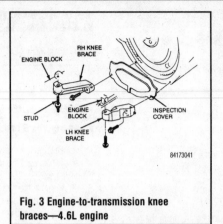

Fig. 3 Engine-to-transmission knee braces—4.6L engine

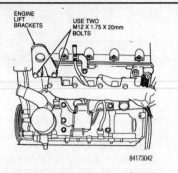

Fig. 4 Install an engine lifting bracket at the front of the left cylinder head—4.6L engine

38. Raise and safely support the vehicle.

39. Install the 6 engine-to-transmission bolts and tighten to 30–44 ft. lbs. (40–60 Nm).

40. Install the engine mount through bolts and tighten to 15–22 ft. lbs. (20–30 Nm).

41. Install the 4 torque converter retaining nuts and tighten to 22–25 ft. lbs. (20–30 Nm). Install the plug into the access hole in the engine block.

42. Position the power steering pump on the engine block and install the 4 retaining nuts. Tighten to 15–22 ft. lbs. (20–30 Nm).

43. Install the starter.

44. Position the engine to transmission braces and install the 3 bolts and 1 stud. Tighten the bolts and stud to 18–31 ft. lbs. (25–43 Nm).

45. Position the transmission line bracket to the knee brace stud and install the retaining nut. Tighten to 15–22 ft. lbs. (20–30 Nm).

46. Cut the wire and position the exhaust system to the manifolds. Install the 4 nuts and tighten to 20–30 ft. lbs. (27–41 Nm).

➡**Make sure the exhaust system clears the No. 3 crossmember. Adjust as necessary.**

47. Lower the vehicle and connect the power steering control valve.

48. Connect the air conditioner lines to the compressor.

49. Attach the alternator harness to the fender apron and junction block.

50. Connect the heater hoses and connect the vacuum supply hose to the throttle body adapter vacuum port.

51. Connect the power supply to the power distribution box and starter relay.

52. Attach the electrical connector and vacuum hose to the purge solenoid.

53. Connect and if necessary, adjust the throttle valve cable; refer to Section 7.

54. Connect the accelerator and cruise control cables.

55. Attach the engine harness connector and transmission harness connector. Install the connector to the retaining bracket on the brake vacuum booster.

56. Install the wiper module and support bracket.

57. Connect the fuel lines.

58. Install the radiator, cooling fan and shroud. Install the air inlet tube.

59. Fill the crankcase with the proper type and quantity of engine oil. Refer to Section 1.

60. Fill the cooling system. Refer to Section 1.

61. Install the hood, as outlined in Section 10.

62. Connect the battery cables.

63. Start the engine and bring to operating temperature.

64. Check for leaks. Check all fluid levels.

65. Have a MVAC-trained, EPA-certified, automotive technician evacuate and recharge the air conditioning system.

66. Road test the vehicle.

5.0L and 5.8L Engines

➡**If your vehicle is equipped with air conditioning, refer to Section 1 for information regarding the implications of servicing your A/C system yourself. Only a MVAC-trained, EPA-certified, automotive technician should service the A/C system or its components.**

1. Have the A/C system recovered by a MVAC-trained, EPA-certified, automotive technician.

2. Disconnect the negative, then the positive battery cable.

3. Drain the engine oil and the cooling system into suitable containers.

✳✳ CAUTION

When draining the coolant, keep in mind that cats and dogs are attracted by the ethylene glycol antifreeze, and are quite likely to drink any that is left in an uncovered container or in puddles on the ground. This will prove fatal in sufficient quantity. Always drain the coolant into a sealable container. Coolant should be reused unless it is contaminated or several years old.

4. Relieve the fuel system pressure; refer to Section 5.

5. Remove the hood. Refer to Section 10.

6. Disconnect the battery ground cables from the cylinder block.

7. Remove the air intake duct and the air cleaner, if engine mounted.

8. Disconnect the upper radiator hose from the thermostat housing and the lower hose from the water pump.

9. Disconnect the oil cooler lines from the radiator.

10. Remove the bolts attaching the radiator fan shroud to the radiator. Remove the radiator. Remove the fan, belt pulley and shroud. Refer to the procedure later in this section.

11. Remove the alternator bolts and position the alternator aside.

12. Disconnect the oil pressure sending unit wire from the sending unit. Disconnect the fuel lines; refer to Section 5.

13. Disconnect the accelerator cable from the carburetor or throttle body. Disconnect the throttle valve rod and disconnect the cruise control cable, if equipped.

14. Disconnect the throttle valve vacuum line from the intake manifold, if equipped.

15. Disconnect the transmission filler tube bracket from the cylinder block.

16. Detach the air conditioning lines and electrical connectors at the compressor and remove the compressor. Plug the lines and the compressor fittings to prevent the entrance of dirt and moisture.

17. Disconnect the power steering pump bracket from the cylinder head.

18. Remove the drive belt.

19. Position the power steering pump aside in a position that will prevent the fluid from leaking.

20. Disconnect the power brake vacuum line from the intake manifold.

21. On 5.0L engines, disconnect the heater hoses from the heater tubes.

22. On 5.8L engines, disconnect the heater hoses from the water pump and intake manifold.

23. Detach the electrical connector from the coolant temperature sending unit.

24. Remove the transmission-to-engine upper bolts.

25. On 5.8L engines, detach the primary wiring connector from the ignition coil.

26. Detach the wiring to the solenoid on the left rocker cover.

27. Remove the wire harness from the left rocker arm cover and position the wires aside. Disconnect the ground strap from the block.

28. On 5.0L engines, disconnect the wiring harness at the two 10-pin connectors.

29. Raise and safely support the vehicle.

30. Disconnect the starter cable from the starter and remove the starter.

31. Disconnect the muffler inlet pipes from the exhaust manifolds.
32. Disconnect the engine mounts from the chassis.
33. Disconnect the downstream thermactor tubing and check valve from the right exhaust manifold stud, if equipped.
34. Disconnect the transmission cooler lines from the retainer and remove the transmission inspection cover.
35. Disconnect the flywheel from the converter and secure the converter assembly in the transmission.
36. Remove the remaining transmission-to-engine bolts.
37. Lower the vehicle and then support the transmission.
38. Attach suitable engine lifting equipment and hoist the engine.
39. Raise the engine slightly and carefully pull it from the transmission.
40. Carefully lift the engine out of the engine compartment. Avoid bending or damaging the rear cover plate or other components.
41. Install the engine on a workstand.

To install:

42. Attach the engine lifting equipment and remove the engine from the workstand.
43. Lower the engine carefully into the engine compartment. Make sure the exhaust manifolds are properly aligned with the muffler inlet pipes.
44. Start the converter pilot into the crankshaft. Align the paint mark on the flywheel to the paint mark on the torque converter.
45. Install the transmission upper bolts, making sure the dowels in the cylinder block engage the transmission.
46. Install the engine mount-to-chassis attaching fasteners and remove the engine lifting equipment.
47. Raise and safely support the vehicle.
48. Connect both muffler inlet pipes to the exhaust manifolds.
49. Install the starter and connect the starter cable.
50. Remove the retainer holding the torque converter in the transmission. Attach the converter to the flywheel.
51. Install the converter housing inspection cover and install the remaining transmission attaching bolts.
52. Remove the support from the transmission and lower the vehicle.
53. On 5.8L engines, connect the wiring harness to the left rocker arm cover and attach the coil wiring connector.
54. On 5.0L engines, attach the wiring harness at the two 10-pin connectors.
55. Connect the coolant temperature sending unit wire and connect the heater hoses.
56. Attach the wiring to the metal heater tubes and the engine coolant temperature, air charge temperature and oxygen sensors.
57. Connect the transmission filler tube bracket.
58. Attach the manual shift rod and the retracting spring.
59. Connect the throttle valve vacuum line, if equipped.
60. Attach the accelerator cable and throttle valve cable. Connect the cruise control cable, if equipped.
61. Connect the fuel lines and the oil pressure sending unit wire.
62. Install the pulley, water pump belt and fan/clutch assembly.
63. Position the alternator bracket and install the alternator bolts.
64. Connect the alternator and ground cables.
65. Adjust the drive belt tension.
66. Install the air conditioning compressor.
67. Unplug and connect the refrigerant lines and connect the electrical connector to the compressor.
68. Install the power steering drive belt and power steering pump bracket. Connect the power brake vacuum line.
69. Place the shroud over the fan and install the radiator.
70. Connect the radiator hoses and the transmission oil cooler lines.
71. Position the fan shroud and install the bolts.
72. Connect the heater hoses to the heater tubes.
73. Fill the cooling system. Refer to Section 1.
74. Fill the crankcase with the proper type and quantity of engine oil.
75. Adjust the transmission throttle linkage; refer to Section 7.
76. Connect the negative battery cable.
77. Start the engine and bring to normal operating temperature.
78. Check for leaks. Check all fluid levels.
79. Install the air intake duct assembly.
80. Install the hood, Refer to Section 10.
81. Have a MVAC-trained, EPA-certified, automotive technician evacuate and recharge the air conditioning system.
82. Road test the vehicle.

Rocker Arm (Valve) Cover

REMOVAL & INSTALLATION

4.6L Engine

PASSENGER SIDE

▶ See Figures 5 and 6

1. Disconnect the negative battery cable.
2. Disconnect the positive battery cable at the battery and at the power distribution box.
3. Remove the retaining bolt from the positive battery cable bracket located on the side of the right cylinder head.
4. Detach the crankshaft position sensor, air conditioning compressor clutch and canister purge solenoid connectors. Position the harness out of the way.
5. Disconnect the vent hose from the purge solenoid and position the positive battery cable out of the way.
6. Disconnect the spark plug wires from the spark plugs. Remove the spark plug wire brackets from the camshaft cover studs and position the wires out of the way.

91193P34

Fig. 5 Loosen the valve cover retaining studs and remove the valve cover from the engine

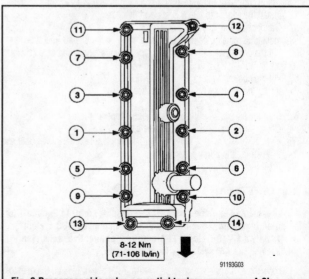

8-12 Nm
(71-106 lb/in)

91193G03

Fig. 6 Passenger side valve cover tightening sequence—4.6L

7. Remove the PCV valve from the valve cover grommet and position out of the way.

8. Remove the bolts and stud bolts (note their positions for reassembly) and remove the valve cover.

To install:

9. Clean the sealing surfaces of the valve covers and cylinder heads. Apply silicone sealer to the places where the front engine cover meets the cylinder head.

10. Attach new gaskets to the valve covers, using suitable sealant.

11. Install the covers with the bolts and stud bolts and tighten to 6–9 ft. lbs. (8–12 Nm).

12. Install the PCV into the valve cover grommet.

13. Install the spark plug wire brackets on the studs and connect the wires to the spark plugs.

14. Position the harness and connect the canister purge solenoid, air conditioning compressor clutch and crankshaft position sensor.

15. Position the positive battery cable harness on the right cylinder head.

16. Install the bolt retaining the cable bracket to the cylinder head.

17. Connect the positive battery cable at the power distribution box and the battery.

DRIVER'S SIDE

▶ **See Figure 7**

1. Disconnect the negative battery cable.

2. Remove the air inlet tube.

3. Relieve the fuel system pressure and disconnect the fuel lines; refer to Section 5.

4. Raise and safely support the vehicle.

5. If equipped, disconnect the power steering control valve and oil pressure sending unit and position the harness out of the way.

6. Lower the vehicle.

7. Remove the engine harness connector from the retaining bracket on the brake vacuum booster. Detach and position out of the way.

8. Remove the windshield wiper module. Refer to Section 6.

9. Tag and disconnect the spark plug wires from the spark plugs. Remove the spark plug wire brackets from the studs and position the wires out of the way.

10. Remove the bolts and stud bolts (noting their position for reassembly) and remove the valve cover.

To install:

11. Clean the sealing surfaces of the valve covers and cylinder heads. Apply silicone sealer to the places where the front engine cover meets the cylinder head.

12. Attach new gaskets to the valve covers, using suitable sealant.

13. Install the covers with the bolts and stud bolts and tighten to 6–9 ft. lbs. (8–12 Nm).

14. Install the spark plug wire brackets on the studs and connect the wires to the spark plugs.

15. Install the windshield wiper module. Refer to Section 6.

16. Connect the connector and transmission harness connector. Install the connector on the retaining bracket.

17. Raise and safely support the vehicle. Position and connect the power steering control valve and oil pressure sending unit harness.

18. Lower the vehicle.

19. Connect the fuel lines.

20. Connect the negative battery cable.

21. Start the engine and check for leaks.

5.0L Engine

▶ **See Figure 8**

1. Disconnect the negative battery cable.

2. If removing the right rocker arm cover, disconnect the PCV closure tube from the oil fill stand pipe at the rocker cover.

3. Remove the thermactor bypass valve and air supply hoses as necessary to provide clearance.

4. Tag and disconnect the spark plug wires from the spark plugs. Remove the wires and bracket assembly from the rocker arm cover attaching stud and position the wires out of the way.

5. Remove the upper intake manifold as described later in this section.

6. Remove the attaching bolts and remove the rocker arm covers.

To install:

7. Clean all gasket mating surfaces of the rocker arm covers and cylinder heads.

8. Attach new rocker arm cover gaskets to the rocker arm covers, using suitable sealant.

9. Install the rocker arm covers and tighten the bolts to 10–13 ft. lbs. (14–18 Nm), wait 2 minutes and tighten again to the same specification.

10. Install the crankcase ventilation tube in the right cover.

11. Install the upper intake manifold as described later in this section. Use a new gasket and tighten the retaining bolts to 12–18 ft. lbs. (16–24 Nm).

12. Install the spark plug wires and bracket assembly on the rocker cover attaching stud. Connect the spark plug wires.

13. Install the air cleaner and intake duct assembly.

14. Install the thermactor bypass valve and air supply hoses, if required.

15. Connect the negative battery cable.

16. Start the engine and check for leaks.

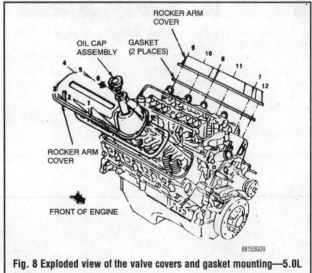

Fig. 8 Exploded view of the valve covers and gasket mounting—5.0L engine

5.8L Engine

1. Disconnect the negative battery cable.

2. If removing the right rocker arm cover, remove the air cleaner assembly.

3. Disconnect the automatic choke heat chamber air inlet hose from the inlet tube near the right rocker arm cover, if equipped.

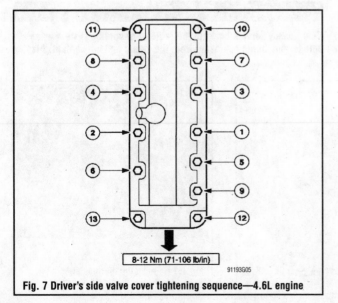

Fig. 7 Driver's side valve cover tightening sequence—4.6L engine

4. Remove the crankcase ventilation fresh air tube from the rocker arm cover.

5. Remove the thermactor bypass valve and air supply hoses as necessary to provide clearance.

6. Tag and disconnect the spark plug wires from the spark plugs. Remove the wires and bracket assembly from the rocker arm cover attaching stud and position the wires out of the way.

7. On the driver's side rocker arm cover, remove the wire harness from the retaining clips.

8. Disconnect the wires at the solenoid mounted on the left rocker cover.

9. Remove the rocker arm cover attaching bolts and remove the rocker arm cover.

To install:

10. Clean all gasket mating surfaces of the rocker arm covers and cylinder heads.

11. Attach new rocker arm cover gaskets to the rocker arm covers, using suitable sealant.

12. Install the rocker arm covers and tighten the bolts to 3–5 ft. lbs. (4–7 Nm) on 1989–90 vehicles or 10–13 ft. lbs. (14–18 Nm) on 1991 vehicles. Wait 2 minutes and tighten again to the same specification.

13. Install the crankcase ventilation hoses on the rocker arm covers.

14. Install the spark plug wires and bracket assembly on the rocker arm cover attaching stud. Connect the spark plug wires.

15. Install the thermactor bypass valve and air supply hoses.

16. Install the air cleaner assembly.

17. Connect the negative battery cable.

18. Start the engine and check for leaks.

Rocker Arms/Roller Followers

REMOVAL & INSTALLATION

4.6L Engine

♦ See Figure 9

1. Disconnect the negative battery cable.

2. Remove the valve cover(s) as described earlier in this section.

3. Position the piston of the cylinder being serviced at the bottom of its stroke and position the camshaft lobe on the base circle.

4. Install a suitable valve spring spacer tool, between the spring coils to prevent valve seal damage.

❊❊ WARNING

If the valve spring spacer tool is not used, the retainer will hit the valve stem seal and damage the seal.

5. Install a suitable valve spring compressor tool, under the camshaft and on top of the valve spring retainer.

6. Compress the valve spring and remove the roller follower. Remove the valve spring compressor and spacer.

7. Repeat Steps 3–;6 for each roller follower to be removed. Inspect the roller follower(s) for wear and/or damage and replace, as necessary.

To install:

8. Apply engine oil or assembly lubricant to the valve stem tip and roller follower contact surfaces.

9. Install a suitable valve spring spacer tool, between the spring coils. Compress the valve spring using a suitable valve spring compressor tool, and install the roller follower.

➡**The piston must be at the bottom of its stroke and the camshaft at the base circle.**

10. Remove the valve spring compressor and spacer.

11. Repeat Steps 8–10 for each roller follower to be installed.

12. Install the valve cover(s).

13. Connect the negative battery cable.

5.0L and 5.8L Engines

♦ See Figure 10

1. Disconnect the negative battery cable.

2. Remove the rocker arm cover(s).

3. Remove the rocker arm fulcrum bolt, fulcrum seat and rocker arm. Keep all rocker arm assemblies together. Identify each assembly so it may be reinstalled in its original position.

4. Inspect the rocker arm and fulcrum seat contact surfaces for wear and/or damage. Also check the rocker arm for wear on the valve stem tip contact surface and the pushrod socket. Replace complete rocker arm assemblies, as necessary.

5. Inspect the pushrod end and the valve stem tip. Replace pushrods, as necessary. If the valve stem tip is worn, the cylinder head must be removed to replace or machine the valve.

To install:

6. Apply engine oil or assembly lubricant to the valve stem tip and pushrod end. Also apply lubricant to the rocker arm and fulcrum seat contact surfaces.

7. Rotate the crankshaft until the lifter is on the camshaft base circle (all the way down) and install the rocker, fulcrum seat and fulcrum bolt. Tighten the bolts to 18–25 ft. lbs. (24–34 Nm).

8. Install the rocker arm cover(s).

9. Connect the negative battery cable.

Thermostat

REMOVAL & INSTALLATION

4.6L Engine

♦ See Figures 11 thru 16

1. Drain the cooling system to a level below the thermostat.

❊❊ CAUTION

Never open, service or drain the radiator or cooling system when hot; serious burns can occur from the steam and hot coolant. Also,

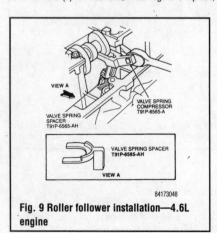

Fig. 9 Roller follower installation—4.6L engine

84173048

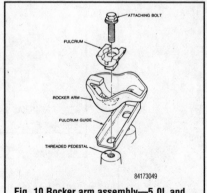
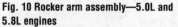

Fig. 10 Rocker arm assembly—5.0L and 5.8L engines

84173049

Fig. 11 Remove the thermostat housing bolts and . . .

89603P21

Fig. 12 . . . remove the housing from the intake manifold

Fig. 13 . . . remove the thermostat from the intake manifold

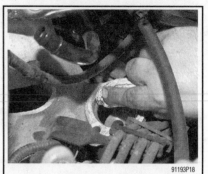

Fig. 14 Thoroughly clean the thermostat mounting surface before installing a new thermostat

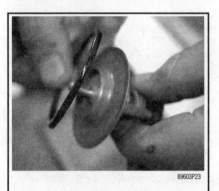

Fig. 15 Always replace the thermostat O-ring with a new one

Fig. 16 Make sure that the air valve is positioned in the 3 O'clock position after the thermostat is installed

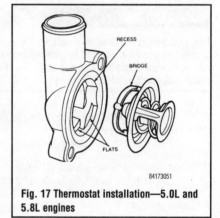

Fig. 17 Thermostat installation—5.0L and 5.8L engines

when draining engine coolant, keep in mind that cats and dogs are attracted to ethylene glycol antifreeze and could drink any that is left in an uncovered container or in puddles on the ground. This will prove fatal in sufficient quantities. Always drain coolant into a sealable container. Coolant should be reused unless it is contaminated or is several years old.

2. Disconnect the upper radiator hose from the thermostat housing.

3. Remove the 2 thermostat housing retaining bolts and remove the thermostat housing.

4. Remove the thermostat and O-ring seal. Inspect the O-ring for damage and replace, as necessary.

To install:

5. Make sure all mating surfaces are clean.

6. Install the thermostat, O-ring and thermostat housing. Make sure the thermostat is positioned in the 3 o'clock position.

7. Install and alternately tighten the thermostat housing retaining bolts to 15–22 ft. lbs. (20–30 Nm). Connect the upper radiator hose.

8. Fill the cooling system as described in Section 1. Check for leaks.

5.0L and 5.8L Engines

▶ See Figures 17 and 18

1. Drain the cooling system to a level below the thermostat.

✳✳ CAUTION

Never open, service or drain the radiator or cooling system when hot; serious burns can occur from the steam and hot coolant. Also, when draining engine coolant, keep in mind that cats and dogs are attracted to ethylene glycol antifreeze and could drink any that is left in an uncovered container or in puddles on the ground. This will prove fatal in sufficient quantities. Always drain coolant into a sealable container. Coolant should be reused unless it is contaminated or is several years old.

2. Disconnect the upper radiator hose and the bypass hose from the thermostat housing.

3. To gain access to the thermostat housing, either mark the location of the distributor, loosen the hold-down clamp and rotate the distributor, or remove the distributor cap and rotor.

4. Remove the thermostat housing retaining bolts and the housing and gasket.

5. Remove the thermostat from the housing.

To install:

6. Clean the gasket mating surfaces.

7. Position a new gasket on the intake manifold.

8. Install the thermostat in the housing, rotating slightly to lock the thermostat in place on the flats cast into the housing. Install the housing on the manifold and tighten the bolts to 12–18 ft. lbs. (16–24 Nm).

➡️If the thermostat has a bleeder valve, the thermostat should be positioned with the bleeder valve at the 12 o'clock position as viewed from the front of the engine.

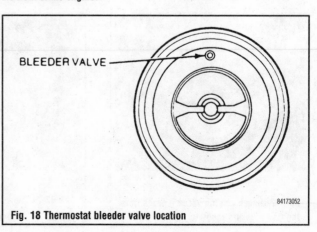

Fig. 18 Thermostat bleeder valve location

9. Install the distributor cap and rotor, or reposition the distributor for correct ignition timing, as necessary. Tighten the hold-down bolt to 18–26 ft. lbs. (24–35 Nm).

10. Connect the bypass hose and the upper radiator hose to the thermostat housing.

11. Fill the cooling system as described in Section 1.

12. Check for leaks.

Intake Manifold

REMOVAL & INSTALLATION

4.6L Engine

1992–95 MODELS

▶ See Figures 19 thru 28

❄❄ CAUTION

Fuel injection systems remain under pressure, even after the engine has been turned OFF. The fuel system pressure must be relieved before disconnecting any fuel lines. Failure to do so may result in fire and/or personal injury.

1. If equipped with air suspension, the air suspension switch, located on the right-hand side of the luggage compartment, must be turned to the OFF position before raising the vehicle.

2. Disconnect the negative battery cable.

3. Drain the engine cooling system.

4. Relieve the fuel system pressure as follows:

   a. Remove the fuel tank fill cap to relieve the pressure in the fuel tank.

   b. Remove the cap from the Schrader valve located on the fuel injection supply manifold.

   c. Attach Fuel Pressure Gauge T80L-9974-B or equivalent, to the Schrader valve and drain the fuel through the drain tube into a suitable container.

   d. After the fuel system pressure is relieved, remove the fuel pressure gauge and install the cap on the Schrader valve. Secure the fuel tank fill cap.

5. Disconnect the fuel supply and return lines.

6. Remove the windshield wiper governor (module).

7. Remove the engine air cleaner outlet tube.

8. Release the drive belt tensioner and remove the accessory drive belt.

9. Disconnect the alternator wiring harness from the junction block at the fender apron and alternator. Remove the bolts retaining the alternator brace to the intake manifold and the alternator to the cylinder block and remove the alternator.

10. Raise and safely support the vehicle.

11. Disconnect the oil pressure sensor and power steering control valve actuator wiring and position the wiring harness out of the way.

12. Disconnect the EGR valve to exhaust manifold tube from the right-hand exhaust manifold.

13. Lower the vehicle.

14. Remove and detach the engine/transmission harness connector from the retaining bracket on the power brake booster.

15. Detach the A/C compressor clutch, Crankshaft Position (CKP) sensor and the canister purge solenoid wiring connectors.

16. Remove the PCV valve from the cylinder head cover and disconnect the canister purge vent hose from the PCV valve.

17. Remove the heater hoses from the intake manifold.

18. Disconnect the accelerator and cruise control cables from the throttle body. Remove the accelerator cable bracket from the intake manifold and position out of the way.

19. Disconnect the vacuum hoses from the throttle body adapter port and the fuel pressure regulator.

20. Disconnect both Heated Oxygen Sensors (HO2S) and the heater water hose.

21. Remove 2 bolts retaining the thermostat housing to the intake manifold and position the upper hose and thermostat housing out of the way.

Fig. 19 Remove the fuel line connection safety clips and . . .

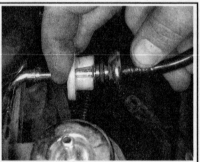

Fig. 20 . . . disconnect the fuel supply and return lines

Fig. 21 Remove the heater hoses from the intake manifold

Fig. 22 Disconnect the vacuum hoses from the fuel pressure regulator and . . .

Fig. 23 . . . the throttle body adapter port

Fig. 24 Disconnect the accelerator and cruise control cables from the throttle body

Fig. 25 Remove the accelerator cable bracket from the intake manifold and position out of the way

Fig. 26 Remove the three retaining bolts for the engine wiring harness and position the harness out of the way

Fig. 27 Carefully lift the intake manifold from the engine

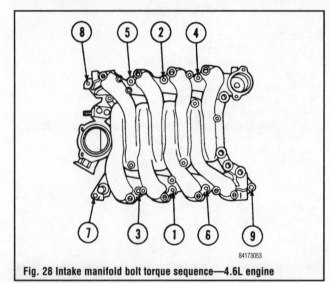

Fig. 28 Intake manifold bolt torque sequence—4.6L engine

➡ **The 2 thermostat housing bolts are also used to retain the intake manifold.**

22. Remove 9 bolts retaining the intake manifold to the cylinder heads and remove the intake manifold. Remove and discard the gaskets.

23. If replacing the intake manifold, swap over the necessary parts.

To install:

24. Clean all gasket mating surfaces.

25. Position new intake manifold gaskets on the cylinder heads. Make sure the alignment tabs on the gaskets are aligned with the holes in the cylinder heads.

26. Install the intake manifold and 9 retaining bolts. Hand tighten the right-rear bolt (viewed from the front of the engine) before final tightening, then torque the bolts, in sequence, to 15–22 ft. lbs. (20–30 Nm).

27. Inspect and if necessary, replace the O-ring seal on the thermostat housing. Position the housing and upper hose and install 2 retaining bolts. Torque to 15–22 ft. lbs. (20–30 Nm).

28. Reconnect the heater water hose.

29. Reconnect both HO2S wiring connectors.

30. Reconnect the vacuum hose to the throttle body adapter vacuum port and the fuel pressure regulator.

31. Install the accelerator cable bracket on the intake manifold and connect the accelerator and cruise control cables to the throttle body.

32. Install the PCV valve in the cylinder head cover and connect the canister purge solenoid vent hose. Reconnect the A/C compressor clutch, CKP sensor and canister purge solenoid wiring connectors.

33. Reconnect the engine/transmission harness connector. Install the connector on the retaining bracket on the power brake booster.

34. Raise and safely support the vehicle.

35. Reconnect the EGR valve to exhaust manifold tube to the right-hand exhaust manifold. Torque the tube nut to 26–33 ft. lbs. (35–45 Nm).

36. Reconnect the power steering control valve actuator and the oil pressure sensor wiring connectors.

37. Lower the vehicle.

38. Position the alternator and install 2 retaining bolts. Torque to 15–22 ft. lbs. (20–30 Nm). Install 2 bolts retaining the alternator brace to the intake manifold and torque to 71–106 inch lbs. (8–12 Nm).

39. Reconnect the alternator wiring harness to the alternator, right-hand fender apron and junction block.

40. Install the accessory drive belt.

41. Install the engine air cleaner outlet tube.

42. Install the windshield wiper governor.

43. Reconnect the fuel supply and return lines.

44. Fill and bleed the engine cooling system.

45. Reconnect the negative battery cable.

46. If equipped with air suspension, turn the air suspension switch to the ON position.

47. Start the engine and check for leaks.

48. Road test the vehicle and check for proper operation.

1996–98 MODELS

▸ See Figure 29

✳✳ CAUTION

Fuel injection systems remain under pressure, even after the engine has been turned OFF. The fuel system pressure must be relieved before disconnecting any fuel lines. Failure to do so may result in fire and/or personal injury.

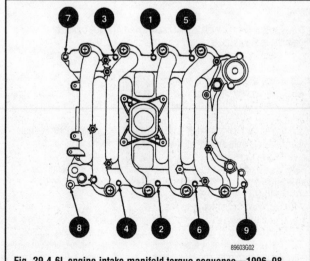

Fig. 29 4.6L engine intake manifold torque sequence—1996–98 Models

1. If equipped with air suspension, the air suspension switch, located on the right-hand side of the luggage compartment, must be turned to the OFF position before raising the vehicle.
2. Disconnect the negative battery cable.
3. Drain the engine cooling system.
4. Relieve the fuel system pressure as follows:
    a. Remove the fuel tank fill cap to relieve the pressure in the fuel tank.
    b. Remove the cap from the Schrader valve located on the fuel injection supply manifold.
    c. Attach Fuel Pressure Gauge T80L-9974-B or equivalent, to the Schrader valve and drain the fuel through the drain tube into a suitable container.
    d. After the fuel system pressure is relieved, remove the fuel pressure gauge and install the cap on the Schrader valve. Secure the fuel tank fill cap.
5. Disconnect the fuel supply and return lines.
6. Remove the windshield wiper governor (module).
7. Remove the engine air cleaner outlet tube.
8. Release the drive belt tensioner and remove the accessory drive belt.
9. Tag and disconnect the ignition wires from the spark plugs. Disconnect the ignition wire brackets from the cylinder head cover studs.
10. Disconnect the wiring from both ignition coils and the Camshaft Position (CMP) sensor. Tag and disconnect all ignition wires from both ignition coils. Remove 2 bolts retaining the ignition wire bracket to the ignition coil brackets and remove the ignition wire assembly.
11. Disconnect the alternator wiring harness from the junction block at the fender apron and alternator. Remove the bolts retaining the alternator brace to the intake manifold and the alternator to the cylinder block and remove the alternator.
12. Raise and safely support the vehicle.
13. Disconnect the oil pressure sensor and power steering control valve actuator wiring and position the wiring harness out of the way.
14. Disconnect the EGR valve to exhaust manifold tube from the right-hand exhaust manifold.
15. Lower the vehicle.
16. Remove and detach the engine/transmission harness connector from the retaining bracket on the power brake booster.
17. Detach the A/C compressor clutch, Crankshaft Position (CKP) sensor and the canister purge solenoid wiring connectors.
18. Remove the PCV valve from the cylinder head cover and disconnect the canister purge vent hose from the PCV valve.
19. Disconnect the accelerator and cruise control cables from the throttle body. Remove the accelerator cable bracket from the intake manifold and position out of the way.
20. Disconnect the vacuum hose from the throttle body adapter port.
21. Disconnect both Heated Oxygen Sensors (HO2S) and the heater water hose.
22. Remove 2 bolts retaining the thermostat housing to the intake manifold and position the upper hose and thermostat housing out of the way.

➡The 2 thermostat housing bolts are also used to retain the intake manifold.

23. Remove 9 bolts retaining the intake manifold to the cylinder heads and remove the intake manifold. Remove and discard the gaskets.
24. If replacing the intake manifold, swap over the necessary parts.
To install:
25. Clean all gasket mating surfaces.
26. Position new intake manifold gaskets on the cylinder heads. Make sure the alignment tabs on the gaskets are aligned with the holes in the cylinder heads.
27. Install the intake manifold and 9 retaining bolts. Hand tighten the right-rear bolt (viewed from the front of the engine) before final tightening, then torque the bolts, in sequence, to 15–22 ft. lbs. (20–30 Nm).
28. Inspect and if necessary, replace the O-ring seal on the thermostat housing. Position the housing and upper hose and install 2 retaining bolts. Torque to 15–22 ft. lbs. (20–30 Nm).
29. Reconnect the heater water hose.
30. Reconnect both HO2S wiring connectors.
31. Reconnect the vacuum hose to the throttle body adapter vacuum port.
32. Install the accelerator cable bracket on the intake manifold and connect the accelerator and cruise control cables to the throttle body.
33. Install the PCV valve in the cylinder head cover and connect the canister purge solenoid vent hose. Reconnect the A/C compressor clutch, CKP sensor

and canister purge solenoid wiring connectors.
34. Reconnect the engine/transmission harness connector. Install the connector on the retaining bracket on the power brake booster.
35. Raise and safely support the vehicle.
36. Reconnect the EGR valve to exhaust manifold tube to the right-hand exhaust manifold. Torque the tube nut to 26–33 ft. lbs. (35–45 Nm).
37. Reconnect the power steering control valve actuator and the oil pressure sensor wiring connectors.
38. Lower the vehicle.
39. Position the alternator and install 2 retaining bolts. Torque to 15–22 ft. lbs. (20–30 Nm). Install 2 bolts retaining the alternator brace to the intake manifold and torque to 71–106 inch lbs. (8–12 Nm).
40. Reconnect the alternator wiring harness to the alternator, right-hand fender apron and junction block.
41. Position the ignition wire assembly on the engine and install 2 bolts retaining the ignition wire bracket to the ignition coil brackets. Torque the bolts to 71–106 inch lbs. (8–12 Nm).
42. Reconnect the ignition wires to the ignition coils in their proper positions. Reconnect the ignition wires to the spark plugs.
43. Reconnect the ignition wire brackets on the cylinder head cover studs. Reconnect the wiring connectors to both ignition coils and the CMP sensor.
44. Install the accessory drive belt.
45. Install the engine air cleaner outlet tube.
46. Install the windshield wiper governor.
47. Reconnect the fuel supply and return lines.
48. Fill and bleed the engine cooling system.
49. Reconnect the negative battery cable.
50. If equipped with air suspension, turn the air suspension switch to the ON position.
51. Start the engine and check for leaks.
52. Road test the vehicle and check for proper operation.

5.0L Engine

▶ See Figures 30, 31, 32 and 33

1. Disconnect the negative battery cable.
2. Drain the cooling system. Relieve the fuel system pressure; refer to Section 5.

⁂⁂ CAUTION

When draining the coolant, keep in mind that cats and dogs are attracted by the ethylene glycol antifreeze, and are quite likely to drink any that is left in an uncovered container or in puddles on the ground. This will prove fatal in sufficient quantity. Always drain the coolant into a sealable container. Coolant should be reused unless it is contaminated or several years old.

3. Disconnect the accelerator cable and cruise control linkage, if equipped, from the throttle body. Disconnect the throttle valve cable, if equipped. Label and disconnect the vacuum lines at the intake manifold fitting.
4. Label and disconnect the spark plug wires from the spark plugs. Remove the wires and bracket assembly from the rocker arm cover attaching stud. Remove the distributor cap and wires assembly.
5. Detach the fuel lines (see Section 5) and the distributor wiring connector. Mark the position of the rotor on the distributor housing and the position of the distributor housing in the block. Remove the hold-down bolt and remove the distributor.
6. Disconnect the upper radiator hose from the thermostat housing and the water temperature sending unit wire from the sending unit. Disconnect the heater hose from the intake manifold and disconnect the 2 throttle body cooler hoses.
7. Disconnect the water pump bypass hose from the thermostat housing. Label and detach the connectors from the engine coolant temperature, air charge temperature, throttle position and EGR sensors and the idle speed control solenoid. Detach the injector wire connections and the fuel charging assembly wiring.
8. Remove the PCV valve from the grommet at the rear of the lower intake manifold. Detach the fuel evaporative purge hose from the plastic connector at the front of the upper intake manifold.
9. Remove the upper intake manifold cover plate and upper intake bolts. Remove the upper intake manifold.
10. Remove the heater tube assembly from the lower intake manifold studs.

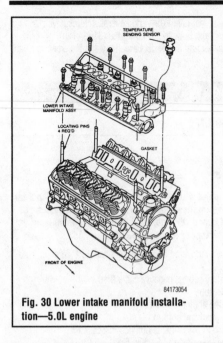

Fig. 30 Lower intake manifold installation—5.0L engine

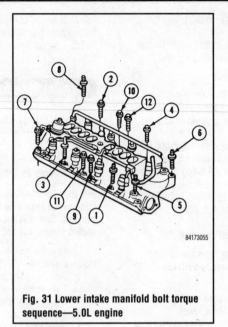

Fig. 31 Lower intake manifold bolt torque sequence—5.0L engine

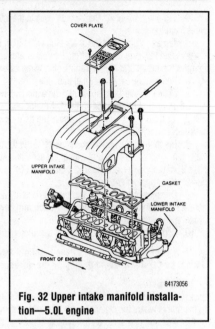

Fig. 32 Upper intake manifold installation—5.0L engine

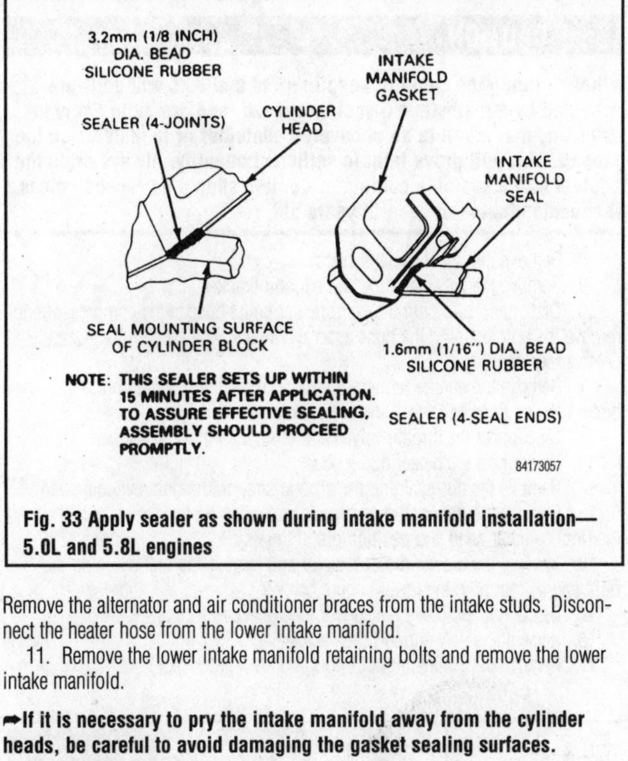

Fig. 33 Apply sealer as shown during intake manifold installation—5.0L and 5.8L engines

Remove the alternator and air conditioner braces from the intake studs. Disconnect the heater hose from the lower intake manifold.

11. Remove the lower intake manifold retaining bolts and remove the lower intake manifold.

➡️If it is necessary to pry the intake manifold away from the cylinder heads, be careful to avoid damaging the gasket sealing surfaces.

To install:

12. Clean all gasket mating surfaces. Apply a 1/8 in. (3mm) bead of silicone sealer to the points where the cylinder block rails meet the cylinder heads.

13. Position new seals on the cylinder block and new gaskets on the cylinder heads with the gaskets interlocked with the seal tabs. Make sure the holes in the gaskets are aligned with the holes in the cylinder heads.

14. Apply a 3/16 in. (5mm) bead of sealer to the outer end of each intake manifold seal for the full width of the seal.

15. Using guide pins to ease installation, carefully lower the intake manifold into position on the cylinder block and cylinder heads.

➡️After the intake manifold is in place, run a finger around the seal area to make sure the seals are in place. If the seals are not in place, remove the intake manifold and position the seals.

16. Make sure the holes in the manifold gaskets and the manifold are in alignment. Remove the guide pins. Install the intake manifold attaching bolts and tighten, in sequence, to 23–25 ft. lbs. (31–34 Nm).

17. If required, install the heater tube assembly to the lower intake manifold studs.

18. Install the water pump bypass hose and upper radiator hose on the thermostat housing. Install the hoses to the heater tubes and intake manifold. Connect the fuel lines.

19. Install the distributor, aligning the housing and rotor with the marks that were made during removal. Install the distributor cap. Position the spark plug wires in the harness brackets on the rocker arm cover attaching stud and connect the wires to the spark plugs.

20. Install a new gasket and the upper intake manifold. Tighten the bolts to 12–18 ft. lbs. (16–24 Nm). Install the cover plate and connect the crankcase vent tube.

21. Connect the accelerator, throttle valve cable and cruise control cable, if equipped, to the throttle body. Connect the electrical connectors and vacuum lines to their proper locations.

22. Attach the coolant hoses to the EGR spacer. Fill the cooling system.

23. Connect the negative battery cable, start the engine and check for leaks. Check the ignition timing.

24. Operate the engine at fast idle. When engine temperatures have stabilized, tighten the intake manifold bolts to 23–25 ft. lbs. (31–34 Nm).

25. Connect the air intake duct and the crankcase vent hose.

5.8L Engine

▶ See Figures 33, 34 and 35

1. Disconnect the negative battery cable and drain the cooling system.

☀️ CAUTION

When draining the coolant, keep in mind that cats and dogs are attracted by the ethylene glycol antifreeze, and are quite likely to drink any that is left in an uncovered container or in puddles on the ground. This will prove fatal in sufficient quantity. Always drain the coolant into a sealable container. Coolant should be reused unless it is contaminated or several years old.

2. Remove the air cleaner, crankcase ventilation hose and intake duct assembly. If equipped, disconnect the automatic choke heat tube.

3. Disconnect the accelerator cable and cruise control linkage, if equipped, from the carburetor. Disconnect the throttle valve rod, if equipped, and remove the accelerator cable bracket.

4. Tag and disconnect the vacuum lines at the intake manifold and the wires from the coil.

5. Tag and disconnect the spark plug wires from the spark plugs. Remove the wires and bracket assembly from the rocker arm cover attaching stud. Remove the distributor cap and spark plug wires assembly.

6. Remove the carburetor fuel inlet line.

7. Detach the vacuum hoses and the wiring connector from the distributor. Mark the position of the rotor on the distributor housing and the position of the distributor housing in the block. Remove the hold-down bolt and remove the distributor.

8. Disconnect the upper radiator hose at the thermostat housing and the water temperature sending unit wire at the sending unit. Disconnect the heater hose from the intake manifold. Disconnect the EGR cooler T-fitting from the heater return hose, if equipped.

9. Disconnect the water pump bypass hose at the thermostat housing. Disconnect the crankcase vent hose at the rocker arm cover. Disconnect the fuel evaporative purge tube, if equipped.

10. Remove the intake manifold and carburetor as an assembly.

➡ If it is necessary to pry the intake manifold away from the cylinder heads, be careful to avoid damaging the gasket sealing surfaces.

To install:

11. Clean all gasket mating surfaces. Apply a ⅛ in. bead of silicone sealer to the points where the cylinder block rails meet the cylinder heads.

12. Position new seals on the cylinder block and new gaskets on the cylinder heads with the gaskets interlocked with the seal tabs. Make sure the holes in the gaskets are aligned with the holes in the cylinder heads.

13. Apply a ³⁄₁₆ in. bead of sealer to the outer end of each intake manifold seal for the full width of the seal.

14. Using guide pins to ease installation, carefully lower the intake manifold into position on the cylinder block and cylinder heads.

➡ After the intake manifold is in place, run a finger around the seal area to make sure the seals are in place. If the seals are not in place, remove the intake manifold and position the seals.

15. Make sure the holes in the manifold gaskets and the manifold are in alignment. Remove the guide pins. Install the intake manifold attaching bolts and tighten, in sequence, to 23–25 ft. lbs. (31–34 Nm).

16. Install the water pump bypass hose on the thermostat housing. Connect the upper radiator hose and the heater hose. Install the carburetor fuel line.

17. Install the distributor, aligning the distributor housing and rotor with the marks that were made during removal. Install the distributor cap. Position the spark plug wires in the harness brackets on the rocker arm cover attaching stud and connect the wires to the spark plugs.

18. Connect the crankcase vent tube. Connect the coil wire and primary wiring connector.

19. Connect the accelerator cable and cable bracket. Connect the throttle valve rod and the cruise control linkage, if equipped.

20. Attach all electrical connections and vacuum lines detached during removal. Fill the cooling system.

21. Connect the negative battery cable, start the engine and check for leaks. Adjust the ignition timing and connect the vacuum hoses to the distributor.

22. Operate the engine at fast idle. When engine temperatures have stabilized, tighten the intake manifold bolts to 23–25 ft. lbs. (31–34 Nm).

23. Connect the air cleaner and intake duct assembly and the crankcase vent hose.

Exhaust Manifold

REMOVAL & INSTALLATION

4.6L Engine

▶ See Figures 36 thru 43

➡ If your vehicle is equipped with air conditioning, refer to Section 1 for information regarding the implications of servicing your A/C system yourself. Only a MVAC-trained, EPA-certified, automotive technician should service the A/C system or its components.

1. Have the A/C system recovered by a MVAC-trained, EPA-certified, automotive technician.

2. Disconnect the battery cables, negative cable first.

3. Remove the air inlet tube.

4. Drain and recycle the engine coolant.

5. Remove the cooling fan and shroud.

6. Relieve the fuel system pressure, as outlined in Section 5.

7. Disconnect the fuel lines; refer to Section 5.

✷✷ CAUTION

When draining the coolant, keep in mind that cats and dogs are attracted by the ethylene glycol antifreeze, and are quite likely to drink any that is left in an uncovered container or in puddles on the ground. This will prove fatal in sufficient quantity. Always drain the coolant into a sealable container. Coolant should be reused unless it is contaminated or several years old.

8. Remove the upper radiator hose.

9. Remove the wiper module and support bracket.

10. Disconnect and plug the compressor outlet hose at the compressor and remove the bolt retaining the hose assembly to the right coil bracket. Cap the compressor opening.

11. Remove the engine harness connector from the retaining bracket on the brake vacuum booster. Detach the connector.

12. Disconnect the throttle valve cable from the throttle body.

13. Disconnect the heater outlet hose.

14. Remove the nut retaining the ground strap to the right cylinder head.

15. Remove the upper stud and lower bolt retaining the heater outlet hose to the right cylinder head and position out of the way.

16. Remove the blower motor resistor and remove the bolt retaining the right engine mount to the lower engine bracket.

17. Disconnect both oxygen sensor electrical connectors.

18. Raise and safely support the vehicle.

19. Remove the engine mount through bolts.

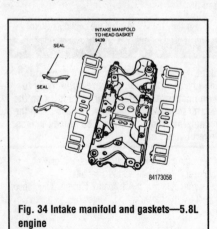

Fig. 34 Intake manifold and gaskets—5.8L engine

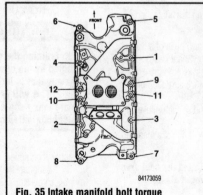

Fig. 35 Intake manifold bolt torque sequence—5.8L engine

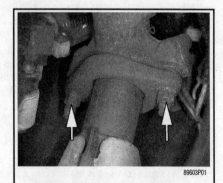

Fig. 36 Remove the catalytic converter-to-exhaust manifold flange bolts

Fig. 37 Remove the oil dipstick tube from the engine

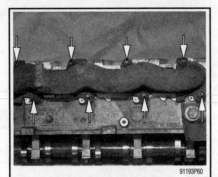

Fig. 38 Remove the exhaust manifold-to-cylinder head retaining nuts/studs and . . .

Fig. 39 . . . remove the manifold from the cylinder head

Fig. 40 Remove the exhaust manifold gaskets and . . .

Fig. 41 . . . thoroughly clean the cylinder head and exhaust manifold gasket mating surfaces

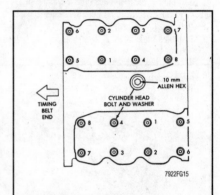

Fig. 42 Exhaust manifold torque sequence—1992–96

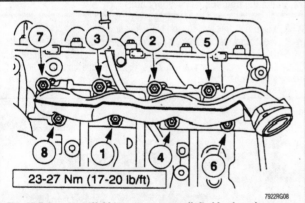

Fig. 43 Exhaust manifold torque sequence (left side shown)—1997–98

20. Remove the EGR tube line nut from the right exhaust manifold.
21. Disconnect the exhaust pipes from the manifolds.
22. Lower the exhaust system and hang it from the crossmember with wire.
23. To remove the left exhaust manifold, remove the engine mount from the engine block and remove the 8 bolts retaining the exhaust manifold.
24. Position a jack and a block of wood under the oil pan, rearward of the oil drain hole. Raise the engine approximately 4 in. (100mm).
25. Remove the 8 bolts retaining the right exhaust manifold and remove the manifold.

To install:

26. If the exhaust manifolds are being replaced, transfer the oxygen sensors and tighten to 27–33 ft. lbs. (37–45 Nm). On the right manifold, transfer the EGR tube connector and tighten to 33–48 ft. lbs. (45–65 Nm).

27. Clean the mating surfaces of the exhaust manifolds and cylinder heads.
28. Position the exhaust manifolds to the cylinder heads and install the retaining bolts. Tighten, in the sequence shown, to 15–22 ft. lbs. (20–30 Nm).
29. Position and connect the EGR valve and tube assembly to the exhaust manifold. Tighten the line nut to 26–33 ft. lbs. (35–45 Nm).
30. Install the left engine mount and tighten the bolts to 15–22 ft. lbs. (20–30 Nm). Lower the engine onto the mounts and remove the jack. Install the engine mount through bolts and tighten to 15–22 ft. lbs. (20–30 Nm).
31. Cut the wire and position the exhaust system. Tighten the nuts to 20–30 ft. lbs. (27–41 Nm).

➡Make sure the exhaust system clears the No. 3 crossmember. Adjust as necessary.

32. Lower the vehicle. Connect both oxygen sensors and install the bolt retaining the right engine mount to the frame. Tighten to 15–22 ft. lbs. (20–30 Nm).
33. Install the blower motor resistor. Position the heater outlet hoses. Install the upper stud and lower bolt and tighten to 15–22 ft. lbs. (20–30 Nm). Install the ground strap onto the stud and tighten the nut to 15–22 ft. lbs. (20–30 Nm).
34. Connect the heater outlet hose. Connect and if necessary, adjust the throttle valve cable.
35. Attach the engine connector and transmission harness connector. Install the connector to the retaining bracket on the brake vacuum booster.
36. Connect the air conditioning compressor outlet hose to the compressor and install the bolt retaining the hose assembly to the right coil bracket.
37. Install the upper radiator hose and connect the fuel lines. Install the wiper module and retaining bracket.
38. Install the cooling fan and shroud. Fill the cooling system.
39. Install the air inlet tube. Connect the battery cables, start the engine and check for leaks.
40. Have a MVAC-trained, EPA-certified, automotive technician evacuate and recharge the air conditioning system.

5.0L and 5.8L Engines

▶ **See Figures 44 and 45**

1. Disconnect the negative battery cable.
2. Remove the thermactor hardware from the right exhaust manifold. Remove the air cleaner and inlet duct, if necessary.
3. Tag and disconnect the spark plug wires. Remove the spark plugs.
4. Disconnect the engine oil dipstick tube from the exhaust manifold stud.
5. Raise and safely support the vehicle. Disconnect the exhaust pipes from the exhaust manifolds.
6. Remove the engine oil dipstick tube by carefully tapping upward on the tube. Detach the oxygen sensor connector.
7. Lower the vehicle.
8. Remove the attaching bolts and washers and remove the exhaust manifolds.

To install:

9. Clean the manifold, cylinder head and exhaust pipe mating surfaces.
10. Position the manifolds on the cylinder heads and install the mounting bolts and washers. Working from the center to the ends, tighten the bolts to 18–24 ft. lbs. (24–32 Nm).
11. Install the engine oil dipstick tube. Attach the oxygen sensor connector.

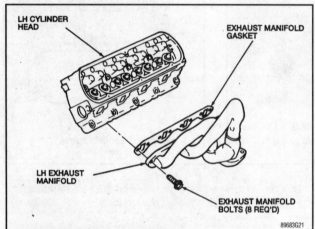

Fig. 44 Example of the 5.0L engine exhaust manifold. Left-hand manifold shown, right-hand manifold is similar

12. Install the spark plugs and connect the spark plug wires.
13. Install the thermactor hardware to the right exhaust manifold. Install the air cleaner and inlet duct, if removed.
14. Raise and safely support the vehicle. Position the exhaust pipes to the manifolds. Alternately tighten the exhaust pipe flange nuts to 20–30 ft. lbs. (27–41 Nm).
15. Lower the vehicle, start the engine and check for exhaust leaks.

Radiator

REMOVAL & INSTALLATION

▶ **See Figures 46 thru 60**

> ※※ **CAUTION**
>
> Never remove the radiator cap while the engine is running or personal injury from scalding hot coolant or steam may result. If possible, wait until the engine has cooled to remove the radiator cap. If this is not possible, wrap a thick cloth around the radiator cap and turn it slowly to the first stop. Step back while the pressure is released from the cooling system. When it is certain all the pressure has been released, press down on the cap, still with the cloth, and turn and remove it.

1. Disconnect the negative battery cable.
2. Remove the radiator cap. Place a drain pan under the radiator, open the draincock and drain the coolant.

> ※※ **CAUTION**
>
> When draining the coolant, keep in mind that cats and dogs are attracted by the ethylene glycol antifreeze, and are quite likely to drink any that is left in an uncovered container or in puddles on the ground. This will prove fatal in sufficient quantity. Always drain the coolant into a sealable container. Coolant should be reused unless it is contaminated or several years old.

3. Remove the radiator support brace trim cover.
4. Disconnect the upper, lower and coolant reservoir hoses at the radiator.
5. Disconnect the fluid cooler lines at the radiator. On 1989–90 vehicles, tool T82L–9500–AH or equivalent, is required to disconnect the fluid cooler lines.

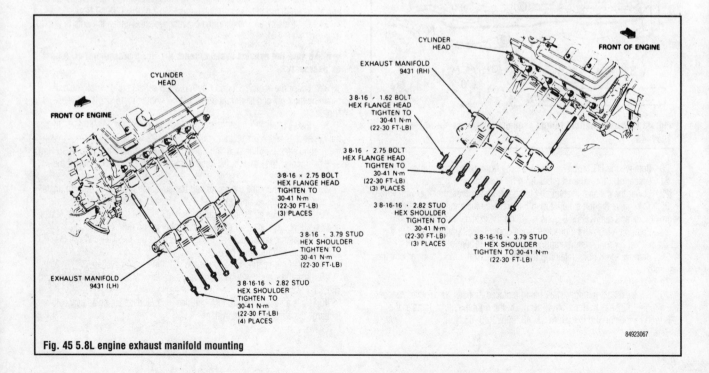

Fig. 45 5.8L engine exhaust manifold mounting

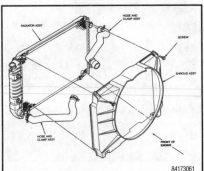

Fig. 46 Radiator and related components—1990–91 vehicles (except California)

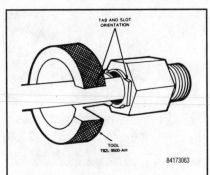

Fig. 47 Transmission fluid cooler line quick connect/disconnect tool, for 1989–90 vehicles

Fig. 48 Remove the retaining clips for the radiator support brace trim cover and . . .

Fig. 49 . . . remove the trim panel from the vehicle

Fig. 50 Remove the fan shroud-to-radiator retaining bolts

Fig. 51 Use a suitable pair of pliers to slide the hose clamps back and . . .

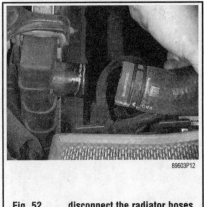

Fig. 52 . . . disconnect the radiator hoses

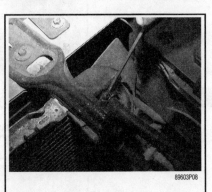

Fig. 53 Loosen the hose clamp retaining screw . . .

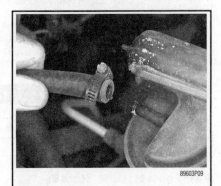

Fig. 54 . . . then remove the recovery tank hose from the radiator

Fig. 55 Using a back-up wrench to support the radiator fitting, loosen the transmission cooler lines from the radiator and . .

Fig. 56 . . . remove the lines from the radiator

Fig. 57 The radiator is retained by two upper support mounts

Fig. 58 Remove the radiator upper support mount bolts and . . .

Fig. 59 . . . remove the support mount brackets from the radiator

Fig. 60 Remove the radiator by carefully lifting it straight out of the engine compartment

6. On 1991–98 vehicles, use a backup wrench to hold the radiator fitting while loosening the fluid cooler lines.

7. Remove the 2 upper fan shroud retaining bolts at the radiator support, lift the fan shroud sufficiently to disengage the lower retaining clips and lay the shroud back over the fan.

8. Remove the radiator upper support retaining bolts and remove the supports.

9. Lift the radiator from the vehicle.

To install:

10. If a new radiator is to be installed, transfer the petcock from the old radiator to the new one. Remove the fluid cooler line fittings from the old radiator and install them on the new one, using an oil resistant sealer.

11. Position the radiator assembly into the vehicle. Install the upper supports and the retaining bolts. Connect the fluid cooler lines.

12. Place the fan shroud into the clips on the lower radiator support and install the 2 upper shroud retaining bolts. Position the shroud to maintain approximately 1 in. (25mm) clearance between the fan blades and the shroud.

13. Connect the radiator hoses.

14. Install the radiator support brace trim cover.

15. Close the radiator petcock.

16. Fill the cooling system as explained in Section 1.

17. Start the engine and bring to operating temperature.

18. Check for coolant and transmission fluid leaks. Check the coolant and transmission fluid levels.

Engine Fan

REMOVAL & INSTALLATION

1992–94 Models

▶ See Figures 61, 62, 63, 64 and 65

1. Disconnect the negative battery cable.

2. Loosen the fan clutch mounting shaft from the water pump hub.

3. Loosen the fan shroud from its radiator mounting and remove the lower hose from the shroud.

4. Lift the fan and clutch assembly and the fan shroud from the vehicle.

5. If necessary, remove the fan-to-fan clutch retaining bolts and separate the fan from the fan clutch.

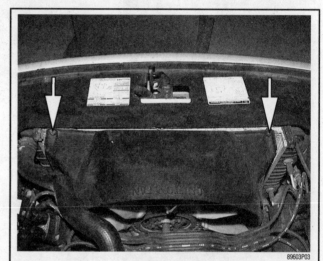

Fig. 62 Remove the fan shroud-to-radiator retaining bolts

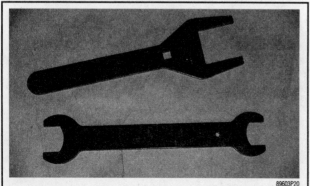

Fig. 61 Special wrenches to remove the fan clutch assembly like these are available from manufacturers such as Lisle®

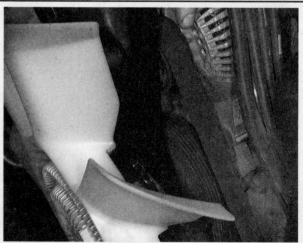

Fig. 63 Place the special fan removal tools over the water pump pulley bolts and onto the fan clutch hub and loosen the fan clutch assembly

Fig. 64 Remove the fan clutch from the water pump and . . .

Fig. 65 . . . remove the fan clutch and the shroud assembly from the vehicle

---

⁂ CAUTION

Closely examine the fan for cracks or separation, to avoid the possibility of personal injury or vehicle damage.

To install:
6. Assemble the fan and fan clutch. Tighten the retaining bolts to 15–20 ft. lbs. (20–27 Nm).
7. Install the fan and clutch assembly and the fan shroud. Mount the fan clutch shaft to the water pump hub and tighten to 37–46 ft. lbs. (50–62 Nm).
8. Slip the shroud into the lower mounting clips and install the shroud retaining screws.
9. Connect the negative battery cable.

1995–98 Models

⁂ CAUTION

Closely examine the fan for cracks or separation and replace as necessary. A damaged fan can cause serious personal injury or vehicle damage.

BELT DRIVEN COOLING FAN

▶ See Figure 66

1. Disconnect the negative battery cable.
2. Unplug the electric cooling fan wiring connector.
3. Separate the upper and lower fan shrouds.
4. Loosen the fan shroud from its radiator mounting and remove the lower radiator hose from the fan shroud.
5. Lift the fan shroud out of the vehicle.
6. Loosen the fan clutch mounting shaft by placing a suitable wrench on the flats of the shaft and remove from the water pump hub. Lift the fan and clutch assembly from the vehicle.
7. If necessary, remove 4 fan-to-fan clutch retaining bolts and separate the fan from the fan clutch.

To install:
8. Assemble the fan and fan clutch. Torque the 4 retaining bolts to 15–20 ft. lbs. (20–27 Nm).
9. Install the fan and clutch assembly. Mount the fan clutch shaft to the water pump hub and torque to 37–46 ft. lbs. (50–62 Nm).
10. Slip the shroud into the lower mounting clips and install the shroud retaining screws. Reconnect the lower radiator hose.
11. Plug in the electric cooling fan wire connector.
12. Reconnect the lower shroud to the upper shroud.
13. Reconnect the negative battery cable.
14. Start the engine and check for proper operation.

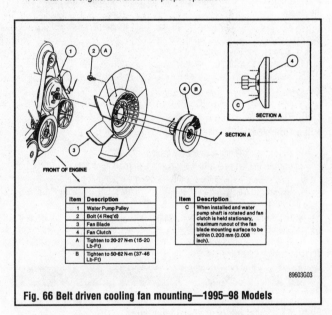

Fig. 66 Belt driven cooling fan mounting—1995–98 Models

ELECTRIC COOLING FAN

▶ See Figure 67

1. Disconnect the negative battery cable.
2. Unplug the electric cooling fan wiring connector from the side of the fan shroud.
3. Turn the lower fan shroud in the upper fan shroud to allow clearance for shroud removal.
4. Remove the radiator upper sight shield.
5. Loosen the fan shroud from its radiator mounting and remove the lower radiator hose from the supports on the fan shroud.
6. Lift the fan shroud from the vehicle.
7. Remove the retaining screws, then remove the fan blade and motor assembly.

To install:
8. Mount the fan blade and motor assembly. Torque the retaining screws to 27–53 inch lbs. (3–6 Nm).
9. Install the shroud and torque the retaining screws to 36 inch lbs. (5 Nm).

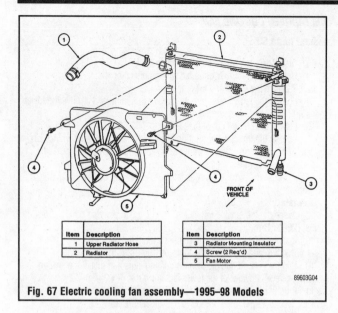

Fig. 67 Electric cooling fan assembly—1995–98 Models

Item	Description
1	Upper Radiator Hose
2	Radiator

Item	Description
3	Radiator Mounting Insulator
4	Screw (2 Req'd)
5	Fan Motor

89603G04

10. Install the lower radiator hose to the supports on the fan shroud.

11. Plug in the electric cooling fan wiring connector and secure the wire to the shroud.

12. Turn the lower fan shroud in the upper fan shroud to the closed position.

13. Install the radiator upper sight shield.

14. Reconnect the negative battery cable.

15. Start the engine and operate the A/C system to check cooling fan operation.

1989–91 Models

▶ **See Figure 68**

1. Disconnect the negative battery cable.

2. Loosen the fan clutch-to-water pump hub retaining bolts.

3. If necessary, remove the drive belt from the water pump pulley.

4. Remove the fan shroud upper retaining screws. Lift the shroud to disengage it from the lower retaining clips.

5. Remove the fan clutch-to-water pump hub bolts and remove the fan and clutch assembly and the fan shroud.

6. If necessary, remove the fan-to-fan clutch retaining bolts and separate the fan from the fan clutch.

⁂ CAUTION

Closely examine the fan for cracks or separation, to avoid the possibility of personal injury or vehicle damage.

To install:

7. Assemble the fan and fan clutch. Tighten the retaining bolts evenly and alternately to 12–18 ft. lbs. (16–24 Nm).

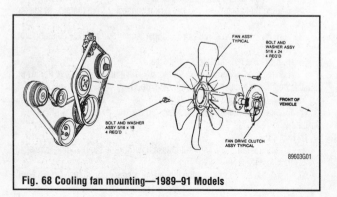

Fig. 68 Cooling fan mounting—1989–91 Models

89603G01

8. Install the fan and clutch assembly and the fan shroud.

9. Install the fan clutch-to-water pump hub bolts.

10. Slip the shroud into the lower mounting clips and install the shroud retaining screws.

11. If removed, install the water pump drive pulley and adjust the belt tension; refer to Section 1.

12. Tighten the fan clutch-to-water pump hub bolts evenly and alternately to 15–22 ft. lbs. (20–27 Nm). Recheck the belt tension.

13. Connect the negative battery cable.

Water Pump

REMOVAL & INSTALLATION

4.6L Engine

▶ **See Figures 61, 65 and 69 thru 72**

1. Disconnect the negative battery cable.

2. Drain the cooling system, remove the cooling fan and the shroud.

⁂ CAUTION

When draining the coolant, keep in mind that cats and dogs are attracted by the ethylene glycol antifreeze, and are quite likely to drink any that is left in an uncovered container or in puddles on the ground. This will prove fatal in sufficient quantity. Always drain the coolant into a sealable container. Coolant should be reused unless it is contaminated or several years old.

3. Release the belt tensioner and remove the accessory drive belt.

4. Remove the 4 bolts retaining the water pump pulley to the water pump and remove the pulley.

5. Remove the 4 bolts retaining the water pump to the engine assembly and remove the water pump.

To install:

6. Clean the sealing surfaces of the water pump and engine block.

7. Lubricate a new O-ring seal with clean antifreeze and install on the water pump.

8. Install the water pump and tighten the retaining bolts to 15–22 ft. lbs. (20–30 Nm).

9. Install the water pump pulley and tighten the retaining bolts to 15–22 ft. lbs. (20–30 Nm).

10. Install the accessory drive belt; refer to Section 1.

11. Install the cooling fan and shroud. Connect the negative battery cable and fill the cooling system as explained in Section 1.

12. Run the engine and check for leaks.

Fig. 69 Remove the four water pump retaining bolts and . . .

91193P75

Fig. 70 . . . remove the water pump from the engine

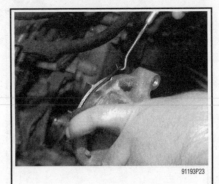

Fig. 71 Remove the water pump O-ring using a pick or other suitable tool

Fig. 72 Always replace the water pump O-ring with a quality replacement such as a Fel-Pro®

5.0L and 5.8L Engines

▶ See Figure 73

1. Disconnect the negative battery cable.
2. Drain the cooling system. Remove the air inlet tube.

❊❊ CAUTION

When draining the coolant, keep in mind that cats and dogs are attracted by the ethylene glycol antifreeze, and are quite likely to drink any that is left in an uncovered container or in puddles on the ground. This will prove fatal in sufficient quantity. Always drain the coolant into a sealable container. Coolant should be reused unless it is contaminated or several years old.

3. Remove the fan shroud attaching bolts and position the shroud over the fan. Remove the fan and clutch assembly from the water pump shaft and remove the shroud.
4. Remove the air conditioner drive belt and idler pulley bracket. Remove the alternator and power steering drive belts. Remove the power steering pump and position aside, leaving the hoses attached. Remove all accessory brackets that attach to the water pump.
5. Remove the water pump pulley. Disconnect the lower radiator hose, heater hose and water pump bypass hose at the water pump.
6. Remove the water pump attaching bolts and remove the water pump. Discard the gasket.

To install:

7. Clean all old gasket material from the timing cover and water pump.
8. Apply a suitable waterproof sealing compound to both sides of a new gasket and install the gasket on the timing cover.
9. Install the water pump and tighten the mounting bolts to 12–18 ft. lbs. (16–24 Nm).
10. Connect the hoses and accessory brackets to the water pump. Install the pulley on the water pump shaft.

11. Install the power steering pump and air conditioner idler pulley bracket. Install the accessory drive belts.
12. Install the fan and fan clutch assembly and the fan shroud.
13. Adjust the accessory drive belt tension; refer to Section 1.
14. Connect the negative battery cable and fill the cooling system, as explained in Section 1.
15. Run the engine and check for leaks.

Cylinder Head

REMOVAL & INSTALLATION

4.6L Engine

1992–95 MODELS

▶ See Figures 74 thru 81

❊❊ CAUTION

Fuel injection systems remain under pressure, even after the engine has been turned OFF. The fuel system pressure must be relieved before disconnecting any fuel lines. Failure to do so may result in fire and/or personal injury.

➡The cylinder head bolts are a torque-to-yield design and cannot be reused. Before beginning this procedure, make sure new cylinder head bolts are available.

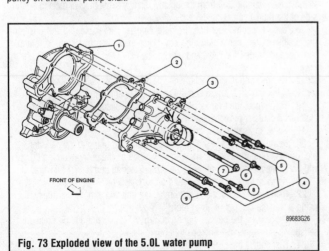

Fig. 73 Exploded view of the 5.0L water pump

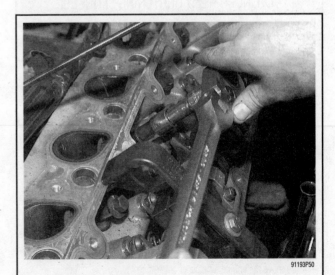

Fig. 74 Remove the cylinder head bolts and . . .

Fig. 75 . . . carefully lift the cylinder head off of the engine block and place it in a safe location

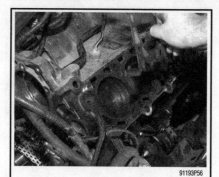

Fig. 76 Remove the head gasket from the engine block

Fig. 77 Thoroughly clean the cylinder head and . . .

Fig. 78 . . . engine block of any gasket material left

Fig. 79 After the gasket material has been removed, wipe the head and . . .

Fig. 80 . . . engine block clean using a suitable solvent

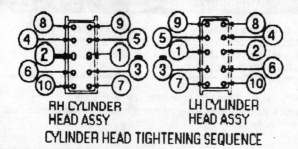

CYLINDER HEAD TIGHTENING SEQUENCE

Fig. 81 Tighten the cylinder head bolts in the proper sequence to prevent damage to the head and possible leaks

1. If equipped with air suspension, the air suspension switch, located on the right-hand side of the luggage compartment, must be turned to the OFF position before raising the vehicle.

2. Disconnect the negative battery cable.

3. Drain the engine cooling system.

4. Remove the cooling fan and shroud assembly.

5. Relieve the fuel system pressure as follows:

   a. Remove the fuel tank fill cap to relieve the pressure in the fuel tank.

   b. Remove the cap from the Schrader valve located on the fuel injection supply manifold.

   c. Attach Fuel Pressure Gauge T80L-9974-B or equivalent, to the Schrader valve and drain the fuel through the drain tube into a suitable container.

   d. After the fuel system pressure is relieved, remove the fuel pressure gauge and install the cap on the Schrader valve. Secure the fuel tank fill cap.

6. Remove the engine air cleaner outlet tube.

7. Remove the windshield wiper governor (module).

8. Release the drive belt tensioner and remove the accessory drive belt.

9. Tag and disconnect the ignition wires from the spark plugs. Disconnect the ignition wire brackets from the cylinder head cover studs and remove 2 bolts retaining the ignition wire tray to the ignition coil brackets.

10. Remove the bolt retaining the A/C pressure line to the right-hand ignition coil bracket.

11. Disconnect the wiring to both ignition coils and the Camshaft Position (CMP) sensor.

12. Remove the nuts retaining the ignition coil brackets to the engine front cover. Slide the ignition coil brackets and ignition wire assemblies off the mounting studs and remove from the vehicle.

13. Remove the water pump pulley.

14. Disconnect the alternator wiring harness from the junction block, fender apron and alternator. Disconnect the bolts retaining the alternator to the intake manifold and cylinder block and remove the alternator.

15. Disconnect the positive battery cable at the power distribution box. Remove the retaining bolt from the positive battery cable bracket located on the side of the right-hand cylinder head.

16. Disconnect the vent hose from the canister purge solenoid and position the positive battery cable out of the way. Disconnect the canister purge solenoid vent hose from the PCV valve and remove the PCV valve from the cylinder head cover.

17. Remove and disconnect the engine and transmission harness connectors from the retaining bracket on the power brake booster.

18. Disconnect the Crankshaft Position (CKP) sensor, A/C compressor clutch and canister purge solenoid electrical connectors.

19. Raise and safely support the vehicle.

20. Remove the bolts retaining the power steering pump to the cylinder block and engine front cover. The front lower bolt on the power steering pump will not come all the way out. Wire the power steering pump out of the way.

21. Remove the engine oil pan and oil pan gasket.

22. Remove the crankshaft pulley retaining bolt and remove the pulley, using a suitable damper remover tool.

23. Disconnect the power steering control valve actuator and oil pressure sensor wiring connectors and position out of the way.

24. Disconnect the EGR tube from the right-hand exhaust manifold.

25. Disconnect the exhaust pipes from the exhaust manifolds. Lower the exhaust pipes and hang with wire from the crossmember.

26. Remove the bolt retaining the starter wiring harness to the rear of the right-hand cylinder head.

27. Lower the vehicle.

28. Remove the bolts and stud bolts retaining the cylinder head covers to the cylinder heads and remove the covers.

29. Disconnect the accelerator and cruise control cables. Remove the accelerator cable bracket from the intake manifold and position out of the way.

30. Disconnect the vacuum hose from the throttle body elbow vacuum port, both Heated Oxygen Sensors (HO2S) and the heater water hose.

31. Remove 2 bolts retaining the thermostat housing to the intake manifold and position the upper hose and thermostat housing out of the way.

➡ **The 2 thermostat housing bolts also retain the intake manifold.**

32. Remove 9 bolts retaining the intake manifold to the cylinder heads and remove the intake manifold and gaskets.

33. Remove 7 stud bolts and 4 bolts retaining the engine front cover to the engine and remove the front cover.

34. Remove both timing chains.

✳ WARNING

This is not a freewheeling engine. A suitable cam positioning tool, must be installed on the camshafts to prevent the camshafts from rotating. Do not rotate the camshafts or crankshaft with the timing chains removed or the valves will contact the pistons.

35. Remove 10 bolts retaining the left-hand cylinder head to the cylinder block and remove the head. The lower rear cylinder head bolt must stay in the cylinder head until the cylinder head is removed due to lack of clearance for removal in the vehicle. Use a rubber band to secure the cylinder head bolt in the cylinder head during removal and installation of the cylinder head and to prevent the bolt from damaging the cylinder block or head gasket.

➡ **The lower rear cylinder head bolt cannot be removed due to interference with the power brake booster. Use a rubber band to hold the bolt away from the cylinder block.**

36. Remove the ground strap, 1 stud and 1 bolt retaining the heater return line to the right-hand cylinder head.

37. Remove 10 bolts retaining the right-hand cylinder head to the cylinder block and remove the head. The lower rear cylinder head bolt must stay in the cylinder head until the cylinder head is removed due to lack of clearance for removal in the vehicle. Use a rubber band to secure the cylinder head bolt in the cylinder head during removal and installation of the cylinder head and to prevent the bolt from damaging the cylinder block or head gasket.

➡ **The lower rear cylinder head bolt cannot be removed due to interference with the evaporator housing. Use a rubber band to hold the bolt away from the cylinder block.**

38. Clean all gasket mating surfaces. Check the cylinder heads and cylinder block for flatness. Check the cylinder heads for scratches near the coolant passages and combustion chambers that could provide leak paths.

To install:

39. Rotate the crankshaft counterclockwise 45 degrees. The crankshaft keyway should be at the 9 o'clock position viewed from the front of the engine. This ensures that all pistons are below the top of the engine block deck face.

40. Rotate the camshaft to a stable position where the valves do not extend below the head face.

41. Position new head gaskets on the cylinder block. Install new bolts in the lower rear bolt holes on both cylinder heads and retain with rubber bands as explained during the removal procedure.

➡ **New cylinder head bolts must be used whenever the cylinder head is removed and reinstalled. The cylinder head bolts used on these engines are a torque-to-yield design and cannot be reused.**

42. Position the cylinder heads on the cylinder block dowels, being careful not to score the surface of the head face. Apply clean oil to the new cylinder head bolts, remove the rubber bands from the lower rear bolts and install all bolts hand-tight.

43. Tighten the new cylinder head bolts as follows:

a. Torque the bolts in sequence, to 22–30 ft. lbs. (30–40 Nm).

b. Rotate each bolt in sequence 85–95 degrees.

c. Rotate each bolt in sequence an additional 85–95 degrees.

44. Position the heater return hose and install 2 retaining bolts.

45. Rotate the camshafts using the flats matched at the center of the camshaft until both are in time. Install suitable cam positioning tools, on the flats of the camshafts to keep them from rotating.

46. Rotate the crankshaft clockwise 45 degrees to position the crankshaft at TDC for No. 1 cylinder.

➡ **The crankshaft must only be rotated in the clockwise direction and only as far as TDC.**

47. Install both timing chains.

48. Install a new engine front cover seal and gasket. Apply silicone sealer to the lower corners of the cover where it meets the junction of the engine oil pan and cylinder block and to the points where the cover contacts the junction of the cylinder block and the cylinder heads.

49. Install the engine front cover and the stud bolts and bolts. Torque to 15–22 ft. lbs. (20–30 Nm).

50. Position new intake manifold gaskets on the cylinder heads. Make sure the alignment tabs on the gaskets are aligned with the holes in the cylinder heads.

➡ **Before installing the intake manifold, inspect it for nicks and cuts that could provide leak paths.**

51. Position the intake manifold on the cylinder heads and install the retaining bolts. Torque the bolts in sequence, to 15–22 ft. lbs. (20–30 Nm).

52. Install the thermostat and O-ring, then position the thermostat housing and upper hose and install 2 retaining bolts. Torque to 15–22 ft. lbs. (20–30 Nm).

53. Reconnect the heater water hose and both HO2S sensors.

54. Reconnect the vacuum hose to the throttle body adapter vacuum port.

55. Install the accelerator cable bracket on the intake manifold and connect the accelerator and cruise control cables to the throttle body.

56. Apply silicone sealer to both places where the engine front cover meets the cylinder heads. Install new gaskets on the cylinder head covers.

57. Install the cylinder head covers on the cylinder heads. Install the bolts and stud bolts and tighten to 71–106 inch lbs. (8–12 Nm).

58. Raise and safely support the vehicle.

59. Place the starter motor wiring harness to the right-hand cylinder head and install the retaining bolt.

60. Fit the exhaust pipes to the exhaust manifolds. Install and torque 4 nuts to 20–30 ft. lbs. (27–41 Nm).

➡ **Make sure the exhaust system clears the No. 3 crossmember. Adjust as necessary.**

61. Reconnect the EGR tube to the right-hand exhaust manifold and torque the line nut to 26–33 ft. lbs. (35–45 Nm).

62. Reconnect the power steering control valve actuator and oil pressure sensor electrical connectors.

63. Apply a small amount of silicone sealer in the rear of the keyway on the crankshaft pulley. Position the pulley on the crankshaft, making sure the crankshaft key and keyway are aligned.

64. Using a suitable damper installation tool, install the crankshaft pulley. Install the pulley bolt and washer and torque to 114–121 ft. lbs. (155–165 Nm).

65. Install the engine oil pan and a new gasket.

66. Place the power steering pump in position on the cylinder block and install 4 retaining bolts. Torque the bolts to 15–22 ft. lbs. (20–30 Nm).

67. Lower the vehicle.

68. Reconnect the A/C compressor, CKP sensor and canister purge solenoid electrical connectors.

69. Attach the engine and transmission harness connectors and install on the retaining bracket on the power brake booster.

70. Install the PCV valve in the right-hand cylinder head cover and connect the canister purge solenoid vent hose.

71. Position the positive battery cable harness on the right-hand cylinder head and install the bolt retaining the cable bracket to the cylinder head. Reconnect the positive battery cable at the power distribution box and battery.

72. Position the alternator and install 2 retaining bolts. Torque the bolts to 15–22 ft. lbs. (20–30 Nm). Install 2 bolts retaining the alternator brace to the intake manifold and torque to 6–8 ft. lbs. (8–12 Nm).

73. Install the water pump pulley and torque the bolts to 15–22 ft. lbs. (20–30 Nm).

74. Position the ignition coil brackets and ignition wire assemblies onto the mounting studs. Install 7 nuts retaining the ignition coil brackets to the engine front cover and torque to 15–22 ft. lbs. (20–30 Nm).

75. Install 2 bolts retaining the ignition wire tray to the ignition coil bracket and torque to 71–106 inch lbs. (8–12 Nm). Reconnect both ignition coil and CMP sensor harness connectors.

76. Place the A/C pressure line on the right-hand ignition coil bracket and install the retaining bolt. Reconnect the ignition wires to the spark plugs and install the bracket onto the cylinder head cover studs.

77. Install the accessory drive belt and the windshield wiper governor.

78. Reconnect the fuel supply and return lines.

79. Install the cooling fan and shroud.

80. Fill the engine cooling system.

81. Install the engine air cleaner outlet tube.

82. Reconnect the negative battery cable.

83. If equipped with air suspension, turn the air suspension switch to the ON position.

84. Check all fluid levels.

85. Replace the engine oil and filter if the oil is contaminated.

86. Start the engine and bring to normal operating temperature while checking for leaks.

87. Road test the vehicle and check for proper engine operation.

1996–98 MODELS

▶ See Figure 81

✳✳ CAUTION

Fuel injection systems remain under pressure, even after the engine has been turned OFF. The fuel system pressure must be relieved before disconnecting any fuel lines. Failure to do so may result in fire and/or personal injury.

➥The cylinder head bolts are a torque-to-yield design and cannot be reused. Before beginning this procedure, make sure new cylinder head bolts are available.

1. If equipped with air suspension, the air suspension switch, located on the right-hand side of the luggage compartment, must be turned to the OFF position before raising the vehicle.

2. Disconnect the negative battery cable.

3. Drain the engine cooling system.

4. Remove the cooling fan and shroud assembly.

5. Relieve the fuel system pressure as follows:

   a. Remove the fuel tank fill cap to relieve the pressure in the fuel tank.

   b. Remove the cap from the Schrader valve located on the fuel injection supply manifold.

   c. Attach a suitable fuel pressure gauge, to the Schrader valve and drain the fuel through the drain tube into a suitable container.

   d. After the fuel system pressure is relieved, remove the fuel pressure gauge and install the cap on the Schrader valve. Secure the fuel tank fill cap.

6. Remove the engine air cleaner outlet tube.

7. Remove the windshield wiper governor (module).

8. Release the drive belt tensioner and remove the accessory drive belt.

9. Tag and disconnect the ignition wires from the spark plugs. Disconnect the ignition wire brackets from the cylinder head cover studs and remove 2 bolts retaining the ignition wire tray to the ignition coil brackets.

10. Remove the bolt retaining the A/C pressure line to the right-hand ignition coil bracket.

11. Disconnect the wiring to both ignition coils and the Camshaft Position (CMP) sensor.

12. Remove the nuts retaining the ignition coil brackets to the engine front cover. Slide the ignition coil brackets and ignition wire assemblies off the mounting studs and remove from the vehicle.

13. Remove the water pump pulley.

14. Disconnect the alternator wiring harness from the junction block, fender apron and alternator. Disconnect the bolts retaining the alternator to the intake manifold and cylinder block and remove the alternator.

15. Disconnect the positive battery cable at the power distribution box.

Remove the retaining bolt from the positive battery cable bracket located on the side of the right-hand cylinder head.

16. Disconnect the vent hose from the canister purge solenoid and position the positive battery cable out of the way. Disconnect the canister purge solenoid vent hose from the PCV valve and remove the PCV valve from the cylinder head cover.

17. Remove and disconnect the engine/transmission harness connector from the retaining bracket on the power brake booster.

18. Disconnect the Crankshaft Position (CKP) sensor, A/C compressor clutch and canister purge solenoid electrical connectors.

19. Raise and safely support the vehicle.

20. Remove the bolts retaining the power steering pump to the cylinder block and engine front cover. The front lower bolt on the power steering pump will not come all the way out. Wire the power steering pump out of the way.

21. Remove the engine oil pan and oil pan gasket.

22. Remove the crankshaft pulley retaining bolt and remove the pulley, using a suitable damper removal tool.

23. Disconnect the power steering control valve actuator and oil pressure sensor wiring connectors and position out of the way.

24. Disconnect the EGR tube from the right-hand exhaust manifold.

25. Disconnect the exhaust pipes from the exhaust manifolds. Lower the exhaust pipes and hang with wire from the crossmember.

26. Remove the bolt retaining the starter wiring harness to the rear of the right-hand cylinder head.

27. Lower the vehicle.

28. Remove the bolts and stud bolts retaining the cylinder head covers to the cylinder heads and remove the covers.

29. Disconnect the accelerator and cruise control cables. Remove the accelerator cable bracket from the intake manifold and position out of the way.

30. Disconnect the vacuum hose from the throttle body elbow vacuum port, both Heated Oxygen Sensors (HO2S) and the heater water hose.

31. Remove 2 bolts retaining the thermostat housing to the intake manifold and position the upper hose and thermostat housing out of the way.

➥The 2 thermostat housing bolts also retain the intake manifold.

32. Remove 9 bolts retaining the intake manifold to the cylinder heads and remove the intake manifold and gaskets.

33. Remove 7 stud bolts and 4 bolts retaining the engine front cover to the engine and remove the front cover.

34. Remove both timing chains.

✳✳ WARNING

This is not a freewheeling engine. Suitable cam positioning tools must be installed on the camshafts to prevent the camshafts from rotating. Do not rotate the camshafts or crankshaft with the timing chains removed or the valves will contact the pistons.

35. Remove 10 bolts retaining the left-hand cylinder head to the cylinder block and remove the head. The lower rear cylinder head bolt must stay in the cylinder head until the cylinder head is removed due to lack of clearance for removal in the vehicle. Use a rubber band to secure the cylinder head bolt in the cylinder head during removal and installation of the cylinder head and to prevent the bolt from damaging the cylinder block or head gasket.

➥The lower rear cylinder head bolt cannot be removed due to interference with the power brake booster. Use a rubber band to hold the bolt away from the cylinder block.

36. Remove the ground strap, 1 stud and 1 bolt retaining the heater return line to the right-hand cylinder head.

37. Remove 10 bolts retaining the right-hand cylinder head to the cylinder block and remove the head. The lower rear cylinder head bolt must stay in the cylinder head until the cylinder head is removed due to lack of clearance for removal in the vehicle. Use a rubber band to secure the cylinder head bolt in the cylinder head during removal and installation of the cylinder head and to prevent the bolt from damaging the cylinder block or head gasket.

➥The lower rear cylinder head bolt cannot be removed due to interference with the evaporator housing. Use a rubber band to hold the bolt away from the cylinder block.

38. Clean all gasket mating surfaces. Check the cylinder heads and cylinder block for flatness. Check the cylinder heads for scratches near the coolant passages and combustion chambers that could provide leak paths.

To install:

39. Rotate the crankshaft counterclockwise 45 degrees. The crankshaft keyway should be at the 9 o'clock position viewed from the front of the engine. This ensures that all pistons are below the top of the engine block deck face.

40. Rotate the camshaft to a stable position where the valves do not extend below the head face.

41. Position new head gaskets on the cylinder block. Install new bolts in the lower rear bolt holes on both cylinder heads and retain with rubber bands as explained during the removal procedure.

➡**New cylinder head bolts must be used whenever the cylinder head is removed and reinstalled. The cylinder head bolts are a torque-to-yield design and cannot be reused.**

42. Position the cylinder heads on the cylinder block dowels, being careful not to score the surface of the head face. Apply clean oil to the new cylinder head bolts, remove the rubber bands from the lower rear bolts and install all bolts hand-tight.

43. Tighten the new cylinder head bolts as follows:
   a. Torque the bolts in sequence, to 28–31 ft. lbs. (37–43 Nm).
   b. Rotate each bolt in sequence 85–95 degrees.
   c. Loosen all bolts at least 1 full turn.
   d. Torque the bolts in sequence, to 28–31 ft. lbs. (37–43 Nm).
   e. Rotate each bolt in sequence 85–95 degrees.
   f. Rotate each bolt in sequence an additional 85–95 degrees.

44. Position the heater return hose and install 2 retaining bolts.

45. Rotate the camshafts using the flats matched at the center of the camshaft until both are in time. Install suitable cam positioning tools, on the flats of the camshafts to keep them from rotating.

46. Rotate the crankshaft clockwise 45 degrees to position the crankshaft at TDC for No. 1 cylinder.

➡**The crankshaft must only be rotated in the clockwise direction and only as far as TDC.**

47. Install both timing chains.

48. Install a new engine front cover seal and gasket. Apply silicone sealer to the lower corners of the cover where it meets the junction of the engine oil pan and cylinder block and to the points where the cover contacts the junction of the cylinder block and the cylinder heads.

49. Install the engine front cover and the stud bolts and bolts. Tighten to 15–22 ft. lbs. (20–30 Nm).

50. Position new intake manifold gaskets on the cylinder heads. Make sure the alignment tabs on the gaskets are aligned with the holes in the cylinder heads.

➡**Before installing the intake manifold, inspect it for nicks and cuts that could provide leak paths.**

51. Position the intake manifold on the cylinder heads and install the retaining bolts. Torque the bolts in sequence, to 15–22 ft. lbs. (20–30 Nm).

52. Install the thermostat and O-ring, then position the thermostat housing and upper hose and install 2 retaining bolts. Torque to 15–22 ft. lbs. (20–30 Nm).

53. Reconnect the heater water hose and both HO2S sensors.

54. Reconnect the vacuum hose to the throttle body adapter vacuum port.

55. Install the accelerator cable bracket on the intake manifold and connect the accelerator and cruise control cables to the throttle body.

56. Apply silicone sealer to both places where the engine front cover meets the cylinder heads. Install new gaskets on the cylinder head covers.

57. Install the cylinder head covers on the cylinder heads. Install the bolts and stud bolts and torque to 71–106 inch lbs. (8–12 Nm).

58. Raise and safely support the vehicle.

59. Place the starter motor wiring harness to the right-hand cylinder head and install the retaining bolt.

60. Fit the exhaust pipes to the exhaust manifolds. Install and torque the 4 nuts to 20–30 ft. lbs. (27–41 Nm).

➡**Make sure the exhaust system clears the No. 3 crossmember. Adjust as necessary.**

61. Reconnect the EGR tube to the right-hand exhaust manifold and torque the line nut to 26–33 ft. lbs. (35–45 Nm).

62. Reconnect the power steering control valve actuator and oil pressure sensor electrical connectors.

63. Apply a small amount of silicone sealer in the rear of the keyway on the

crankshaft pulley. Position the pulley on the crankshaft, making sure the crankshaft key and keyway are aligned.

64. Using Damper Installer T74P-6316-B or equivalent, install the crankshaft pulley. Install the pulley bolt and washer and torque to 114–121 ft. lbs. (155–165 Nm).

65. Install the engine oil pan and a new gasket.

66. Place the power steering pump in position on the cylinder block and install 4 retaining bolts. Torque the bolts to 15–22 ft. lbs. (20–30 Nm).

67. Lower the vehicle.

68. Reconnect the A/C compressor, CKP sensor and canister purge solenoid electrical connectors.

69. Reconnect the engine/transmission harness connector and install on the retaining bracket on the power brake booster.

70. Install the PCV valve in the right-hand cylinder head cover and connect the canister purge solenoid vent hose.

71. Position the positive battery cable harness on the right-hand cylinder head and install the bolt retaining the cable bracket to the cylinder head. Reconnect the positive battery cable at the power distribution box and battery.

72. Position the alternator and install 2 retaining bolts. Torque the bolts to 15–22 ft. lbs. (20–30 Nm). Install 2 bolts retaining the alternator brace to the intake manifold and torque to 6–8 ft. lbs. (8–12 Nm).

73. Install the water pump pulley and torque the bolts to 15–22 ft. lbs. (20–30 Nm).

74. Position the ignition coil brackets and ignition wire assemblies onto the mounting studs. Install 7 nuts retaining the ignition coil brackets to the engine front cover and torque to 15–22 ft. lbs. (20–30 Nm).

75. Install 2 bolts retaining the ignition wire tray to the ignition coil bracket and torque to 71–106 inch lbs. (8–12 Nm). Reconnect both ignition coil and CMP sensor harness connectors.

76. Place the A/C pressure line on the right-hand ignition coil bracket and install the retaining bolt. Reconnect the ignition wires to the spark plugs and install the bracket onto the cylinder head cover studs.

77. Install the accessory drive belt and the windshield wiper governor.

78. Reconnect the fuel supply and return lines.

79. Install the cooling fan and shroud.

80. Fill the engine cooling system.

81. Install the engine air cleaner outlet tube.

82. Reconnect the negative battery cable.

83. If equipped with air suspension, turn the air suspension switch to the **ON** position.

84. Check all fluid levels.

85. Replace the engine oil and filter if the oil is contaminated.

86. Start the engine and bring to normal operating temperature while checking for leaks.

87. Road test the vehicle and check for proper engine operation.

5.0L and 5.8L Engines

▶ **See Figures 82 and 83**

➡**If your vehicle is equipped with air conditioning, refer to Section 1 for information regarding the implications of servicing your A/C system yourself. Only a MVAC-trained, EPA-certified, automotive technician should service the A/C system or its components.**

1. Have the A/C system recovered by a MVAC-trained, EPA-certified, automotive technician.

2. Disconnect the negative battery cable.

3. Relieve the fuel system pressure; refer to Section 5. Drain the cooling system.

✳ CAUTION

When draining the coolant, keep in mind that cats and dogs are attracted by the ethylene glycol antifreeze, and are quite likely to drink any that is left in an uncovered container or in puddles on the ground. This will prove fatal in sufficient quantity. Always drain the coolant into a sealable container. Coolant should be reused unless it is contaminated or several years old.

---

4. On 5.0L engine, remove the upper and lower intake manifold and throttle body assembly. On 5.8L engine, remove the intake manifold and carburetor assembly.

Fig. 82 Keep the pushrods in order so they can be reinstalled in their original locations

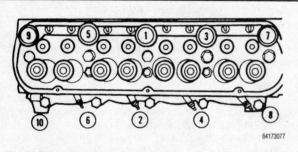

Fig. 83 Cylinder head bolt torque sequence—5.0L and 5.8L engines

5. If the air conditioning compressor is in the way of a cylinder head that is to be removed, proceed as follows:

a. Disconnect and plug the refrigerant lines at the compressor. Cap the openings on the compressor.

b. Detach the electrical connector from the compressor.

c. Remove the compressor and the necessary mounting brackets.

6. If the left cylinder head is to be removed, disconnect the power steering pump bracket from the cylinder head and remove the drive belt from the pump pulley. Position the pump out of the way in a position that will prevent the oil from draining out.

7. Disconnect the oil level dipstick tube bracket from the exhaust manifold stud, if necessary.

8. If the right cylinder head is to be removed, on some vehicles it is necessary to disconnect the alternator mounting bracket from the cylinder head.

9. Remove the thermactor crossover tube from the rear of the cylinder heads. If equipped, remove the fuel line from the clip at the front of the right cylinder head.

10. Raise and safely support the vehicle. Disconnect the exhaust manifolds from the muffler inlet pipes. Lower the vehicle.

11. Loosen the rocker arm fulcrum bolts so the rocker arms can be rotated to the side. Remove the pushrods in sequence so they may be installed in their original positions.

12. Remove the cylinder head attaching bolts and the cylinder heads. If necessary, remove the exhaust manifolds to gain access to the lower bolts. Remove and discard the head gaskets.

13. Clean all gasket mating surfaces. Check the flatness of the cylinder head using a straightedge and a feeler gauge. The cylinder head must not be warped any more than 0.003 in. in any 6.0 in. span; 0.006 in. overall. Machine as necessary.

To install:

14. Position the new cylinder head gasket over the dowels on the block. Position the cylinder heads on the block and install the attaching bolts.

15. On 5.0L engine, tighten the bolts, in sequence, in 2 steps, first to 55–65 ft. lbs. (75–88 Nm), then to 65–72 ft. lbs. (88–97 Nm).

16. On 5.8L engine, tighten the bolts, in sequence, in 3 steps, first to 85 ft. lbs. (116 Nm), then to 95 ft. lbs. (129 Nm), and finally to 105–112 ft. lbs. (142–152 Nm).

➥When the cylinder head bolts have been tightened following this procedure, it is not necessary to retighten the bolts after extended operation.

17. If removed, install the exhaust manifolds. Tighten the retaining bolts to 18–24 ft. lbs. (24–32 Nm).

18. Clean the pushrods, making sure the oil passages are clean. Check the ends of the pushrods for wear. Visually check the pushrods for straightness or check for run-out using a dial indicator. Replace pushrods, as necessary.

19. Apply a suitable grease to the ends of the pushrods and install them in their original positions. Position the rocker arms over the pushrods and the valves.

20. Before tightening each fulcrum bolt, bring the lifter for the fulcrum bolt to be tightened onto the base circle of the camshaft by rotating the engine. When the lifter is on the base circle of the camshaft, tighten the fulcrum bolt to 18–25 ft. lbs. (24–34 Nm).

➥If all the original valve train parts are reinstalled, a valve clearance check is not necessary. If any valve train components are replaced, a valve clearance check must be performed.

21. Install new rocker arm cover gaskets on the rocker arm covers and install the covers on the cylinder heads.

22. Raise and safely support the vehicle. Connect the exhaust manifolds to the muffler inlet pipes. Lower the vehicle.

23. If necessary, install the air conditioning compressor and brackets. Connect the refrigerant lines and electrical connector to the compressor.

24. If necessary, install the alternator bracket.

25. If the left cylinder head was removed, install the power steering pump.

26. Install the drive belts. Install the thermactor tube at the rear of the cylinder heads.

27. Install the intake manifold. Fill and bleed the cooling system.

28. Connect the negative battery cable, start the engine and bring to normal operating temperature. Check for leaks. Check all fluid levels.

29. Have a MVAC-trained, EPA-certified, automotive technician evacuate and recharge the air conditioning system.

CLEANING & INSPECTION

▶ See Figure 84

➥On the 4.6L engine, the roller followers, hydraulic lash adjusters and camshaft should be removed before proceeding further; refer to the procedures in this section.

✳✳ WARNING

Be careful when scraping and cleaning the 4.6L engine cylinder heads, as aluminum is easily damaged.

1. With the valves installed to protect the valve seats, remove deposits from the combustion chambers and valve heads with a scraper and drill-mounted wire brush. Be careful not to damage the cylinder head gasket surface. If the head is to be disassembled, proceed to Step 3. If the head is not to be disassembled, proceed to Step 2.

2. Remove all dirt, oil and old gasket material from the cylinder head with solvent. Clean the bolt holes and the oil passage. Be careful not to get solvent on the valve seals as the solvent may damage them. Dry the cylinder head with compressed air, if available. Check the head for cracks or other damage, and check the gasket surface for burrs, nicks and flatness. If you are in doubt about the head's serviceability, consult a reputable automotive machine shop.

3. Remove the valves, springs and retainers. If the valve seats are to be refaced, clean the carbon from the valve seat areas using a drill-mounted wire brush. Clean the valve guide bores with a valve guide cleaning tool. Remove all dirt, oil and old gasket material from the cylinder head with solvent. Clean the bolt holes and the oil passages.

4. Remove all deposits from the valves with a wire brush or buffing wheel.

5. Check the head for cracks in the valve seat area and ports, and check the gasket surface for burrs, nicks and flatness.

6. Refer to the valve, valve spring, valve seat and valve guide servicing procedures in this section. If you are in doubt about the head's serviceability, consult a reputable automotive machine shop.

➥If the cylinder head was removed due to an overheating condition and a crack is suspected, do not assume that the head is not cracked because a crack is not visually found. A crack can be so small that it cannot be seen by eye, but can pass coolant when the engine is at oper-

Fig. 84 Cleaning the combustion chamber with drill-mounted wire brush—5.0L engine shown

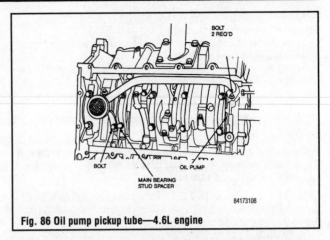

Fig. 86 Oil pump pickup tube—4.6L engine

ating temperature. Consult an automotive machine shop that has pressure testing equipment to make sure the head is not cracked.

Oil Pan

REMOVAL & INSTALLATION

4.6L Engine

▶ See Figures 85, 86 and 87

➡ If your vehicle is equipped with air conditioning, refer to Section 1 for information regarding the implications of servicing your A/C system yourself. Only a MVAC-trained, EPA-certified, automotive technician should service the A/C system or its components.

1. Have the A/C system recovered by a MVAC-trained, EPA-certified, automotive technician.
2. Disconnect the battery cables, negative cable first, and remove the air inlet tube.
3. Relieve the fuel system pressure and disconnect the fuel lines; refer to Section 5. Drain the cooling system and remove the cooling fan and shroud.

✳ CAUTION

When draining the coolant, keep in mind that cats and dogs are attracted by the ethylene glycol antifreeze, and are quite likely to drink any that is left in an uncovered container or in puddles on the

ground. This will prove fatal in sufficient quantity. Always drain the coolant into a sealable container. Coolant should be reused unless it is contaminated or several years old.

4. Remove the upper radiator hose. Remove the wiper module and support bracket.
5. Disconnect and plug the compressor outlet hose at the compressor and remove the bolt retaining the hose assembly to the right coil bracket. Cap the compressor outlet.
6. Remove the engine harness connector from the retaining bracket on the brake vacuum booster and detach the connector and transmission harness connector.
7. Disconnect the throttle valve cable from the throttle body and disconnect the heater outlet hose.
8. Remove the nut retaining the ground strap to the right cylinder head. Remove the upper stud and loosen the lower bolt retaining the heater outlet hose to the right cylinder head and position out of the way.
9. Remove the blower motor resistor. Remove the bolt retaining the right engine mount to the lower engine bracket.
10. Disconnect the vacuum hoses from the EGR valve and tube. Remove the 2 bolts retaining the EGR valve to the intake manifold.
11. Raise and safely support the vehicle. Drain the crankcase and remove the engine mount through bolts.

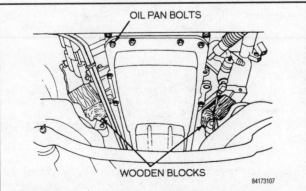

Fig. 85 Position of wood blocks under the engine mounts—4.6L engine

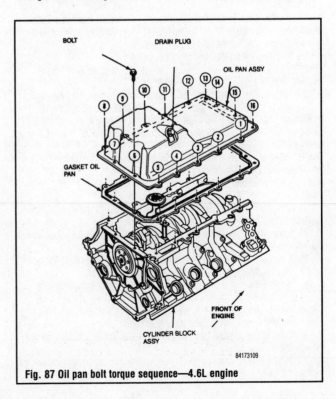

Fig. 87 Oil pan bolt torque sequence—4.6L engine

12. Remove the EGR tube line nut from the right exhaust manifold and remove the EGR valve and tube assembly.

13. Disconnect the exhaust from the exhaust manifolds. Lower the exhaust system and support it with wire from the crossmember.

14. Position a jack and a block of wood under the oil pan, rearward of the oil drain hole. Raise the engine approximately 4 in. and insert 2 wood blocks approximately 2½ in. thick under each engine mount. Lower the engine onto the wood blocks and remove the jack.

15. Remove the 16 bolts retaining the oil pan to the engine block and remove the oil pan.

➡**It may be necessary to loosen, but not remove, the 2 nuts on the rear transmission mount and with a jack, raise the transmission extension housing slightly to remove the pan.**

16. If necessary, remove the 2 bolts retaining the oil pickup tube to the oil pump and remove the bolt retaining the pickup tube to the main bearing stud spacer. Remove the pickup tube.

To install:

17. Clean the oil pan and inspect for damage. Clean the sealing surfaces of the front cover and engine block. Clean and inspect the oil pickup tube and replace the O-ring.

18. If removed, position the oil pickup tube on the oil pump and hand start the 2 bolts. Install the bolt retaining the pickup tube to the main bearing stud spacer hand tight.

19. Tighten the pickup tube-to-oil pump bolts to 6–9 ft. lbs. (8–12 Nm), then tighten the pickup tube-to-main bearing stud spacer bolt to 15–22 ft. lbs. (20–30 Nm).

20. Position a new gasket on the oil pan. Apply silicone sealer to where the front cover meets the cylinder block and rear seal retainer meets the cylinder block. Position the oil pan on the engine and install the bolts. Tighten the bolts, in sequence, to 15–22 ft. lbs. (20–30 Nm).

21. Position the jack and wood block under the oil pan, rearward of the oil drain hole, and raise the engine enough to remove the wood blocks. Lower the engine and remove the jack.

22. Install the engine mount through bolts and tighten to 15–22 ft. lbs. (20–30 Nm).

23. Position the EGR valve and tube assembly in the vehicle and connect to the exhaust manifold. Tighten the line nut to 26–33 ft. lbs. (35–45 Nm).

➡**Loosen the line nut at the EGR valve prior to installing the assembly into the vehicle. This will allow enough movement to align the EGR valve retaining bolts.**

24. Cut the wire and position the exhaust system to the manifolds. Install the 4 nuts and tighten to 20–30 ft. lbs. (27–41 Nm). Make sure the exhaust system clears the crossmember. Adjust as necessary.

25. Install a new oil filter and lower the vehicle.

26. Install the bolt retaining the right engine mount to the lower engine bracket. Tighten to 15–22 ft. lbs. (20–30 Nm).

27. Install a new gasket on the EGR valve and position on the intake manifold. Install the 2 bolts retaining the EGR valve to the intake manifold and tighten to 15–22 ft. lbs. (20–30 Nm). Tighten the EGR tube line nut at the EGR valve to 26–33 ft. lbs. (35–45 Nm). Connect the vacuum hoses to the EGR valve and tube.

28. Install the blower motor resistor. Position the heater outlet hose, install the upper stud and tighten the upper and lower bolts to 15–22 ft. lbs. (20–30 Nm). Install the ground strap on the stud and tighten to 15–22 ft. lbs. (20–30 Nm).

29. Connect the heater outlet hose and the throttle valve cable. If necessary, adjust the throttle valve cable.

30. Attach the engine connector and transmission harness connector. Install the harness connector on the brake vacuum booster.

31. Connect the air conditioning compressor outlet hose to the compressor and install the bolt retaining the hose to the right coil bracket.

32. Install the upper radiator hose and connect the fuel lines. Install the wiper module and retaining bracket.

33. Install the cooling fan and shroud and fill the cooling system. Fill the crankcase with the proper type and quantity of engine oil.

34. Connect the negative battery cable and install the air inlet tube. Start the engine and check for leaks.

35. Have a MVAC-trained, EPA-certified, automotive technician evacuate and recharge the air conditioning system.

5.0L and 5.8L Engines

▶ **See Figure 88**

1. Disconnect the negative battery cable. Relieve the fuel system pressure; refer to Section 5.

2. On 5.8L engine, remove the air cleaner assembly and air ducts.

3. Disconnect the accelerator and throttle valve cables at the throttle body or carburetor. On 5.8L engine, remove the accelerator mounting bracket retaining bolts and remove the bracket.

4. Remove the fan shroud attaching bolts, positioning the fan shroud back over the fan. Remove the dipstick and tube assembly.

5. Detach the wiper motor electrical connector and remove the wiper motor. Disconnect the windshield washer hose and remove the wiper motor mounting cover.

6. Remove the thermactor air dump tube retaining clamp on 5.0L engine. Remove the thermactor crossover tube at the rear of the vehicle.

7. Raise and safely support the vehicle. Drain the crankcase into a suitable container. Remove the filler tube from the oil pan and drain the transmission.

8. Disconnect the starter cable and remove the starter. Disconnect the fuel line.

9. Disconnect the exhaust system from the manifolds. Remove the oxygen sensors from the exhaust manifolds.

10. Remove the thermactor secondary air tube to torque converter housing clamps. Remove the converter inspection cover.

11. Disconnect the exhaust pipes to the catalytic converter outlet. Remove the catalytic converter secondary air tube and the inlet pipes to the exhaust manifold.

12. Loosen the rear engine mount attaching nuts and remove the engine mount through bolts. Remove the shift crossover bolts at the transmission.

13. Remove the brake line retainer from the front crossmember and disconnect the transmission kickdown rod.

14. Position a jack and wood block under the engine and raise the engine as high as it will go. Place wood blocks between the engine mounts and the chassis brackets, lower the engine and remove the jack.

15. Remove the oil pan retaining bolts and lower the oil pan. Remove the 2 bolts retaining the oil pump pickup tube and screen to the oil pump and the nut from the main bearing cap stud. Allow the pickup tube to drop into the oil pan.

16. Rotate the crankshaft, as required, for clearance and remove the oil pan from the vehicle.

To install:

17. Clean the oil pan and the gasket mating surfaces. Clean the oil pump pickup tube and screen assembly.

18. Install a new oil filter. Position a new oil pan gasket on the cylinder block. Place the oil pickup tube and screen in the oil pan and position the oil pan on the crossmember.

19. Install the pickup tube and screen with a new gasket. Install the bolts

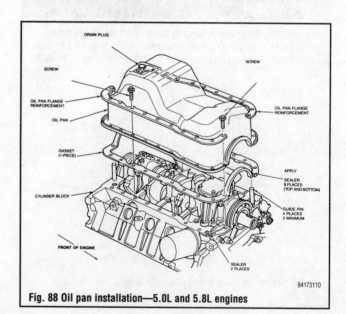

Fig. 88 Oil pan installation—5.0L and 5.8L engines

84173110

and tighten to 12–18 ft. lbs. (16–24 Nm). Position the oil pan and install the retaining bolts. Tighten to 7–10 ft. lbs. (9–14 Nm).

20. Position the jack and wood block under the engine and raise the engine enough to remove the wood blocks. Lower the engine and remove the jack. Install the engine mount through bolts and tighten to 33–46 ft. lbs. (45–62 Nm).

21. Connect the fuel lines. Install the converter inspection cover. Tighten the rear mount attaching nuts to 35–50 ft. lbs. (48–68 Nm).

22. Install the shift crossover. Position the catalytic converters, secondary air tube and inlet pipes to the exhaust manifold and install the retaining nuts.

23. Install the catalytic converter outlet attaching bolts and install the secondary air tube on the converter housing. Install the starter and connect the starter cable.

24. Install the oxygen sensors and lower the vehicle. Install the dipstick and tube. Install the thermactor air dump valve to exhaust manifold clamp.

25. Connect the windshield wiper hose and install the wiper motor mounting plate. Install the wiper motor.

26. Install the accelerator cable mounting bracket with the attaching screws on 5.8L engine. Connect the accelerator and throttle valve cables to the throttle body or carburetor.

27. Position the shroud and install the retaining bolts. Install the thermactor tube to the rear of the engine. Install the air cleaner assembly and air ducts.

28. Fill the crankcase with the proper type and quantity of engine oil. Fill the transmission with the proper type and quantity of transmission fluid.

29. Connect the negative battery cable. Start the engine and check for leaks.

Oil Pump

REMOVAL

4.6L Engine

1. Disconnect the negative battery cable.
2. Remove the valve covers, timing chain cover, and oil pan. Refer to the procedures in this section.
3. Remove the timing chains according to the procedure in this section.
4. Remove the 4 bolts retaining the oil pump to the cylinder block and remove the pump.
5. Remove the 2 bolts retaining the oil pickup tube to the oil pump and remove the bolt retaining the oil pickup tube to the main bearing stud spacer. Remove the pickup tube.

5.0L and 5.8L Engines

1. Disconnect the negative battery cable. Remove the oil pan; see the procedure in this section.
2. Remove the oil pump inlet tube and screen assembly.
3. Remove the oil pump attaching bolts and gasket. Remove the oil pump intermediate shaft.

INSPECTION & OVERHAUL

4.6L Engine

Internal components of the oil pump on the 4.6L engine are not serviceable. If the oil pump is suspect, the entire unit must be replaced.

5.0L and 5.8L Engines

▶ See Figures 89 and 90

1. Disassemble the pump and wash all parts in solvent. Use a brush to clean the inside of the pump housing and the pressure relief valve chamber. Make sure all dirt and metal particles are removed. After washing, dry the parts with compressed air, if available.

2. Check the inside of the pump housing and the inner and outer gears for damage or excessive wear.

3. Check the mating surface of the pump cover for wear. Minor scuff marks are normal, but if the cover, gears or housing surfaces are excessively worn, scored or grooved, replace the pump. Inspect the rotor for nicks, burrs or score marks. Remove minor imperfections with an oil stone.

4. Measure the inner to outer rotor tip clearance. With the rotor assembly

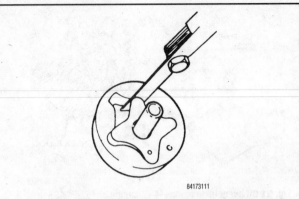

Fig. 89 Measuring inner-to-outer rotor tip clearance—5.0L and 5.8L engines

Fig. 90 Measuring oil pump rotor end-play—5.0L and 5.8L engines

removed from the pump and resting on a flat surface, the inner and outer rotor tip clearance must not exceed 0.012 in. (0.30mm) with the feeler gauge inserted 0.5 in. (13mm) minimum.

5. With the rotor assembly installed in the housing, place a straightedge over the rotor assembly and the housing. Measure the rotor end-play between the straightedge and both the inner and outer race. The maximum clearance must not exceed 0.005 in. (0.13mm).

6. Inspect the relief valve spring to see if it is collapsed or worn. Check the relief valve spring tension. Specifications are as follows:
  - 5.0L engine—10.6–12.2 lbs. @ 1.704 in.
  - 5.8L engine—18.2–20.2 lbs. @ 2.49 in.

7. If the spring tension is not within specification and/or the spring is worn or damaged, replace the pump. Check the relief valve piston for free operation in the bore.

8. If inspection proves the oil pump serviceable, lubricate the rotor assembly and pump housing with clean engine oil and reassemble the pump.

INSTALLATION

4.6L Engine

▶ See Figure 91

1. Clean the oil pickup tube and replace the O-ring.
2. Position the tube on the oil pump and hand-start the 2 bolts. Install the bolt retaining the pickup tube to the main bearing stud spacer hand tight.
3. Tighten the pickup tube-to-oil pump bolts to 6–9 ft. lbs. (8–12 Nm). Tighten the pickup tube to main bearing stud spacer bolt to 15–22 ft. lbs. (20–30 Nm).
4. Rotate the inner rotor of the oil pump to align with the flats on the crankshaft and install the oil pump flush with the cylinder block. Install the 4 retain-

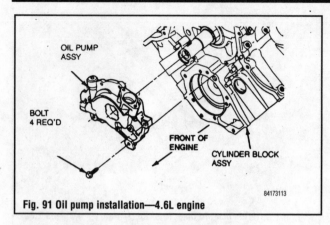

Fig. 91 Oil pump installation—4.6L engine

ing bolts and tighten to 6–9 ft. lbs. (8–12 Nm).

5. Install a new oil filter. Install the timing chains.
6. Install the oil pan, front cover and camshaft covers.
7. Fill the crankcase with the proper type and quantity of engine oil. Connect the negative battery cable, start the engine and check for leaks.

5.0L and 5.8L Engines

♦ See Figure 92

1. Prime the oil pump by filling either the inlet or outlet ports with engine oil and rotating the pump shaft to distribute the oil within the pump body.
2. Position the intermediate driveshaft into the distributor socket. With the shaft firmly seated in the distributor socket, the stop on the shaft should touch the roof of the crankcase. Remove the shaft and position the stop, as necessary.
3. Position a new gasket on the pump body, insert the intermediate shaft into the oil pump and install the pump and shaft as an assembly.

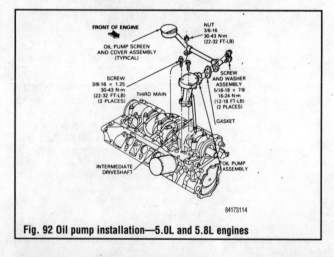

Fig. 92 Oil pump installation—5.0L and 5.8L engines

→Do not attempt to force the pump into position if it will not seat readily. The driveshaft hex may be misaligned with the distributor shaft. To align, rotate the intermediate shaft into a new position.

4. Tighten the oil pump attaching bolts to 22–32 ft. lbs. (30–43 Nm).
5. Clean and install the oil pump inlet tube and screen assembly.
6. Install the oil pan and the remaining components in the reverse order of removal. Start the engine and check for leaks.

Crankshaft Damper

REMOVAL & INSTALLATION

4.6L Engine

♦ See Figures 93, 94 and 95

1. Disconnect the negative battery cable.
2. Release the belt tensioner and remove the accessory drive belt.
3. Raise and safely support the vehicle.
4. Remove the crankshaft damper retaining bolt and washer. Remove the damper using a suitable puller.

To install:

5. Apply clean engine oil to the sealing surface of the damper. Apply a small amount of silicone sealer to the rear of the damper keyway. Using a damper installer, install the crankshaft damper. Be sure the key on the crankshaft aligns with the keyway in the damper.

✷✷ WARNING

Do not drive the damper onto the crankshaft with a hammer; damage to the crankshaft and/or thrust bearings may result. Always use a crankshaft damper installation tool.

6. Install the crankshaft damper retaining bolt and washer and tighten to 114–121 ft. lbs. (155–165 Nm).
7. Lower the vehicle and install the accessory drive belt.
8. Connect the negative battery cable, start the engine and check for leaks.

5.0L and 5.8L Engines

♦ See Figures 96 and 97

1. Disconnect the negative battery cable.
2. Remove the fan shroud and position it back over the fan. Remove the fan/clutch assembly and shroud.
3. Remove the accessory drive belts.
4. Remove the crankshaft pulley from the damper and remove the damper retaining bolt. Remove the damper using a suitable puller.

To install:

5. Apply clean engine oil to the sealing surface of the damper. Apply a small amount of silicone sealer to the damper keyway. Line up the crankshaft damper keyway with the crankshaft key and install the damper using a damper installation tool.

Fig. 93 Remove the crankshaft damper retaining bolt and . . .

Fig. 94 . . . install a suitable puller onto the damper assembly

Fig. 95 Tighten the puller forcing screw until the damper assembly releases from the crankshaft

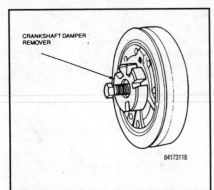

Fig. 96 Crankshaft damper puller installed on 5.0L/5.8L engine crankshaft damper

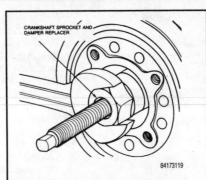

Fig. 97 Installing the crankshaft damper with the proper installation tool—5.0L and 5.8L engines

Fig. 98 The front crankshaft seal is located in the cover—4.6L engines

Fig. 99 Remove the seal from the cover using a suitable seal puller by carefully prying on the seal to . . .

Fig. 100 . . . remove the seal from the cover

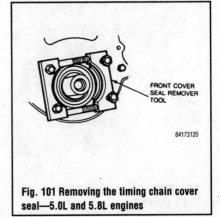

Fig. 101 Removing the timing chain cover seal—5.0L and 5.8L engines

✳ WARNING

Do not drive the damper onto the crankshaft with a hammer; damage to the crankshaft and/or thrust bearings may result. Always use a crankshaft damper installation tool.

6. Install the damper retaining bolt and tighten to 70–90 ft. lbs. (95–122 Nm).
7. Install the remaining components in the reverse order of their removal.

Timing Chain Cover Seal

REMOVAL & INSTALLATION

4.6L Engine

▶ See Figures 98, 99 and 100

1. Disconnect the negative battery cable.
2. Remove the engine cooling fan and fan shroud.
3. Release the drive belt tensioner and remove the accessory drive belt.
4. Remove the crankshaft pulley retaining bolt.
5. Remove the crankshaft pulley using a suitable crankshaft damper removal tool.
6. Remove the front cover oil seal using a suitable seal remover.

To install:

7. Clean the engine front cover seal bore, then lubricate the seal bore and the seal lip with clean engine oil.
8. Install the new front cover oil seal using a suitable seal installation tool. Make sure the seal is installed evenly and straight.
9. Use a suitable crankshaft damper replacement tool to install the crankshaft pulley.
10. Apply a suitable silicone sealer to the outer end of the crankshaft damper keyway.

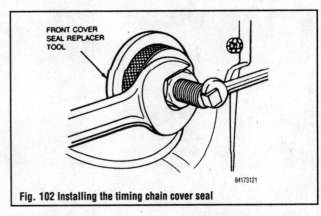

Fig. 102 Installing the timing chain cover seal

11. Using a suitable damper installation tool, install the crankshaft pulley. Install the pulley bolt and washer and torque to 114–121 ft. lbs. (155–165 Nm).
12. Release the drive belt tensioner and install the accessory drive belt.
13. Install the engine cooling fan and shroud assembly.
14. Check the engine oil level.
15. Connect the negative battery cable.
16. Start the engine and check for leaks.
17. Road test the vehicle and check for proper engine operation.

5.0 and 5.8L Engines

▶ See Figures 101 and 102

1. Remove the crankshaft damper as described in this section.
2. Use a suitable seal removal tool to remove the seal from the cover. Be careful not to damage the crankshaft or the seal bore in the timing chain cover.

To install:

3. Lubricate the seal bore in the front cover and the seal lip with clean engine oil.

4. Install the new seal using a suitable seal installation tool. Make sure the seal is installed evenly and straight.

5. Install the crankshaft damper. Be sure to lubricate the sealing surface of the damper with clean engine oil prior to installation.

6. Start the engine and check for leaks.

Timing Chain, Sprockets and Front Cover

REMOVAL & INSTALLATION

4.6L Engine

▶ See Figures 103 thru 125

1. Disconnect the negative battery cable.
2. Remove the radiator, fan blade and fan shroud assembly.

3. Remove the accessory drive belt.
4. Remove the water pump pulley.
5. Detach the electrical harness connectors from both ignition coils.
6. Remove both ignition coils with their brackets attached.
7. Remove the left-hand and right-hand cylinder head covers.
8. Raise and safely support the vehicle.
9. Remove the two upper power steering pump retaining bolts.
10. Remove the two lower power steering pump retaining bolts and move the pump aside.
11. Detach the Crankshaft Position (CKP) sensor electrical harness connector. Remove the retaining bolt and remove the CKP sensor.
12. Drain the engine oil into a suitable container.
13. Remove the four oil pan-to-engine front cover retaining bolts.
14. Lower the vehicle.
15. Remove the crankshaft damper retaining bolt and washer from the crankshaft.

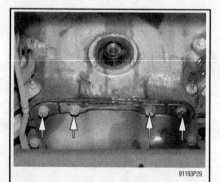
Fig. 103 Remove the driver's side ignition coil bracket bolts

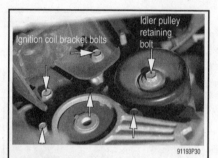
Fig. 104 Remove the passenger side ignition coil bracket bolts along with the belt tensioner retaining bolts and the idler pulley retaining bolt

Fig. 105 Remove the power steering pump mounting bolts and position the pump to the side

Fig. 106 Remove the four front oil pan-to-timing cover retaining bolts

Fig. 107 Once the necessary components are removed, the timing cover bolts are accessible, remove the bolts and . . .

Fig. 108 . . . remove the cover from the engine

Fig. 109 Install the camshaft holding tool

Fig. 110 Remove the crankshaft position sensor trigger wheel from the crankshaft

Fig. 111 Remove the timing chain tensioner retaining bolts and . . .

Fig. 112 . . . remove the tensioner from the engine

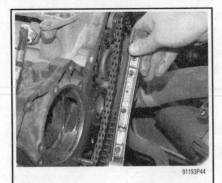

Fig. 113 Remove the tensioner arm from the engine

Fig. 114 Remove the timing chain from around the camshaft pulley

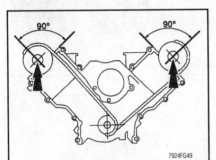

Fig. 115 When removing the timing chains, rotate the crankshaft so that the camshaft keyways are positioned as shown—4.6L engines

Fig. 116 Remove the timing chain guide retaining bolts and remove the guides from the engine

Fig. 117 Place the tensioner into a bench vise or other suitable device and retract the plunger

Fig. 118 Using a small screwdriver or other suitable tool, push back and hold the ratchet mechanism

Fig. 119 While holding the ratchet mechanism, push the ratchet arm back into the tensioner assembly

Fig. 120 After the ratchet mechanism is retracted, place a paper clip or other suitable tool into the hole in the tensioner body to hold the ratchet arm and plunger during installation

16. Install a suitable crankshaft damper removal tool and pull the damper from the crankshaft.

17. Remove the Camshaft Position (CMP) sensor retaining bolt and remove the CMP sensor.

18. Remove the idler pulley bolt and remove the pulley.

19. Remove the three belt tensioner retaining bolts and remove the tensioner.

20. Remove the eight engine front cover retaining bolts and the seven nuts. Swing the top of the cover out off the dowel pins and remove the cover.

21. Remove the sensor ring from the crankshaft.

22. Use a suitable camshaft positioning tool and camshaft positioning adapters, to position the camshaft.

23. Rotate the crankshaft until both camshaft keyways are 90 degrees from the cam cover surface. Be sure the copper links line up with the dots on the camshaft sprockets.

✳✳ WARNING

At no time, when the timing chains are removed and the cylinder heads are installed may the crankshaft or the camshaft be rotated. Severe piston and valve damage will occur.

24. Remove the two left-hand and right-hand tensioner bolts and remove the timing chain tensioners.

25. Slide the left-hand and right-hand tensioner guides off the dowel pins.

26. Remove the right-hand timing chain from the camshaft sprocket.

27. Remove the left-hand timing chain from the camshaft sprocket.

28. Remove the left-hand and right-hand timing chain guide bolts and remove the timing chain guides.

29. If necessary, remove the camshaft gear bolt and remove the camshaft gear.

Fig. 121 Place the tensioner assembly onto the engine and tighten the retaining bolts

Fig. 122 Remove the paper clip from the tensioner assembly

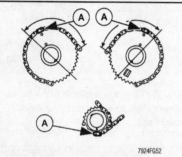

Fig. 123 When installing the timing chains, make certain that the copper colored links (A) are aligned with the timing marks—4.6L engine

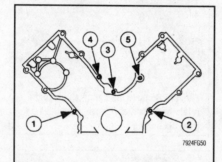

Fig. 124 Tighten the first five front cover fasteners in the sequence shown—4.6L engine

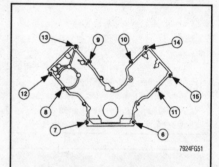

Fig. 125 Continue tightening the remaining fasteners in the sequence shown here—4.6L engine

To install:

30. Examine the timing chains, looking for the copper links. If the copper links are not visible, lay the chain on a flat surface and pull the chain taught until the opposite sides of the chain contact one another. Mark the links at each end of the chain and use these marks in place of the copper links.

➡ If the engine jumped time, damage has been done to valves and possibly pistons and/or connecting rods. Any damage must be corrected before installing the timing chains.

31. If removed, install the camshaft gears and tighten the retaining bolt to 81–95 ft. lbs. (110–130 Nm).

32. Install the left-hand and right-hand timing chain guides and retaining bolts. Tighten the retaining bolts to 71–106 inch lbs. (8–12 Nm).

33. If removed, install the left-hand crankshaft sprocket with the tapered part of the sprocket facing away from the engine block.

➡ The crankshaft sprockets are identical. They may only be installed one way, with the tapered part of the sprockets facing each other. Ensure that the keyway and timing marks on the crankshaft sprockets are aligned.

34. Install the left-hand timing chain on the camshaft and crankshaft sprockets. Be sure the copper links of the timing chain line up with the timing marks on both sprockets.

35. If removed, install the right-hand crankshaft sprocket with the tapered part of the sprocket facing the left-hand crankshaft sprocket.

36. Install the right-hand timing chain on the camshaft and crankshaft sprockets. Be sure the copper links of the timing chain line up with the timing marks on both sprockets.

37. It is necessary to bleed the timing chain tensioners before installation. Proceed as follows:

   a. Place the timing chain tensioner in a soft-jawed vise.

   b. Using a small pick or similar tool, hold the ratchet lock mechanism away from the ratchet stem and slowly compress the tensioner plunger by rotating the vise handle.

✳✳ WARNING

The tensioner must be compressed slowly or damage to the internal seals will result.

   c. Once the tensioner plunger bottoms in the tensioner bore, continue to hold the ratchet lock mechanism and push down on the ratchet stem until flush with the tensioner face.

   d. While holding the ratchet stem flush to the tensioner face, release the ratchet lock mechanism and install a paper clip or similar tool in the tensioner body to lock the tensioner in the collapsed position.

   e. The paper clip must not be removed until the timing chain, tensioner, tensioner arm and timing chain guide are completely installed on the engine.

38. Install the left-hand and right-hand timing chain tensioner guides on the dowel pins.

39. Place the left-hand and right-hand timing chain tensioners in position and install the retaining bolts. Tighten the bolts to 15–22 ft. lbs. (20–30 Nm).

40. Remove the retaining pins from the timing chain tensioners.

41. Remove the cam positioning tool and the positioning adapters from the camshaft.

42. Install the crankshaft sensor ring on the crankshaft.

43. Apply a bead of silicone sealer along the cylinder head-to-cylinder block and the oil pan-to-cylinder block sealing surfaces.

44. Install the engine front cover carefully onto the dowel pins.

45. Tighten the engine front cover bolts, in sequence, to 15–22 ft. lbs. (20–30 Nm).

46. Place the idler pulley in position and install the retaining bolt. Tighten the bolt to 15–22 ft. lbs. (20–30 Nm).

47. Install the drive belt tensioner and the three retaining bolts. Tighten the bolts to 15–22 ft. lbs. (20–30 Nm).

48. Install the CMP sensor and the retaining bolt. Tighten the bolt to 106 inch lbs. (12 Nm).

49. Place the damper on the crankshaft. Ensure the crankshaft key and keyway are aligned.

50. Using a suitable crankshaft damper replacement tool, install the crankshaft damper.

51. Raise and safely support the vehicle.

52. Install the four oil pan-to-engine front cover bolts and tighten, in sequence, in 2 steps:

   a. Tighten the bolts to 15 ft. lbs. (20 Nm).

   b. Rotate the bolts an additional 60 degrees.

53. Install the CKP sensor and the retaining bolt. Tighten the bolt to 106 inch lbs. (12 Nm). Connect the CKP sensor electrical harness connector.

54. Install the power steering pump and the two upper and two lower retaining bolts. Tighten the bolts to 15–20 ft. lbs. (20–30 Nm).

55. Lower the vehicle.

56. Place the ignition coil and brackets on the engine front cover and install the bracket bolts. Tighten the bolts to 15–22 ft. lbs. (20–30 Nm).

57. Connect the ignition coil and capacitor electrical harness connectors.

58. Connect the CMP electrical harness connector.

59. Install the water pump pulley and tighten the bolts to 15–22 ft. lbs. (20–30 Nm).

60. Install the radiator, fan blade and fan shroud assembly.

61. Install the accessory drive belt.

62. Connect the negative battery cable.

63. Start the engine and check for leaks.

64. Road test the vehicle and check for proper engine operation.

5.0L and 5.8L Engines

♦ See Figures 126 and 127

1. Disconnect the negative battery cable.
2. Drain the cooling system. Remove the air inlet tube.

※※ CAUTION

When draining the coolant, keep in mind that cats and dogs are attracted by the ethylene glycol antifreeze, and are quite likely to drink any that is left in an uncovered container or in puddles on the ground. This will prove fatal in sufficient quantity. Always drain the coolant into a sealable container. Coolant should be reused unless it is contaminated or several years old.

3. Remove the fan shroud attaching bolts and position the shroud over the fan. Remove the fan and clutch assembly from the water pump shaft and remove the shroud.

4. Remove the air conditioner drive belt and idler pulley bracket. Remove the alternator and power steering drive belts. Remove the power steering pump and position aside, leaving the hoses attached. Remove all accessory brackets that attach to the water pump.

5. Remove the water pump pulley. Disconnect the lower radiator hose, heater hose and water pump bypass hose from the water pump.

6. Remove the crankshaft pulley from the crankshaft vibration damper. Remove the damper attaching bolt and washer and remove the damper using a puller.

7. On 5.8L engines, disconnect the fuel pump outlet line from the fuel pump. Remove the fuel pump attaching bolts and lay the pump to 1 side with the flexible fuel line still attached.

8. Remove the fuel line from the clip on the front cover, if equipped.

9. Remove the oil pan-to-front cover attaching bolts. Use a thin blade knife to cut the oil pan gasket flush with the cylinder block face prior to separating the cover from the cylinder block.

10. Remove the cylinder front cover and water pump as an assembly.

11. Rotate the crankshaft until the timing marks on the sprockets are aligned.

12. Remove the camshaft retaining bolt, washer and eccentric. Slide both sprockets and the timing chain forward and remove them as an assembly.

To install:

13. Position the sprockets and timing chain on the camshaft and crankshaft simultaneously. Make sure the timing marks on the sprockets are aligned.

14. Install the washer, eccentric and camshaft sprocket retaining bolt. Tighten the bolt to 40–45 ft. lbs. (54–61 Nm).

15. If a new front cover is to be installed, remove the water pump from the old front cover and install it on the new front cover.

16. Clean all gasket mating surfaces. Pry the old oil seal from the front cover and install a new one, using a seal installer.

17. Coat the gasket surface of the oil pan with sealer, cut and position the required sections of a new gasket on the oil pan and apply silicone sealer at the corners. Apply sealer to a new front cover gasket and install on the block.

18. Position the front cover on the cylinder block. Use care to avoid seal damage or gasket mislocation. It may be necessary to force the cover downward to slightly compress the pan gasket. Use a suitable front cover aligner tool to assist the operation.

19. Coat the threads of the front cover attaching screws with pipe sealant and install. While pushing in on the alignment tool, tighten the oil pan to cover attaching screws to 9–11 ft. lbs. (12–15 Nm).

20. Tighten the front cover to cylinder block attaching bolts to 15–18 ft. lbs. (20–24 Nm). Remove the alignment tool.

21. Apply multi-purpose grease to the sealing surface of the vibration damper. Apply silicone sealer to the keyway of the vibration damper.

22. Line up the vibration damper keyway with the crankshaft key and install the damper using a suitable installation tool. Tighten the retaining bolt to 70–90 ft. lbs. (95–122 Nm). Install the crankshaft pulley.

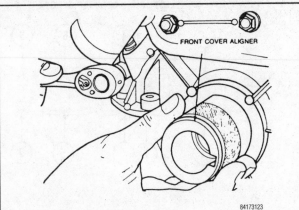

FRONT COVER ALIGNER

84173123

Fig. 126 Positioning the front cover aligner tool—5.0L and 5.8L engines

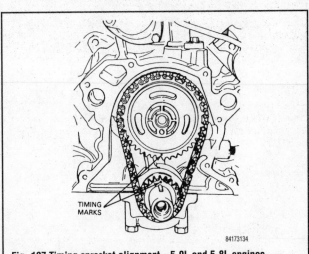

TIMING MARKS

84173134

Fig. 127 Timing sprocket alignment—5.0L and 5.8L engines

23. On 5.8L engines, install the fuel pump with a new gasket. Connect the fuel pump outlet line.

24. Install the remaining components in the reverse order of their removal.

25. Fill the crankcase with the proper type and quantity of engine oil. Fill the cooling system.

26. Connect the negative battery cable, start the engine and check for leaks.

Camshaft

REMOVAL & INSTALLATION

4.6L Engine

▶ **See Figures 128 thru 133**

1. Disconnect the negative battery cable and drain the cooling system. Relieve the fuel system pressure as described in Section 5.

❋❋ CAUTION

When draining the coolant, keep in mind that cats and dogs are attracted by the ethylene glycol antifreeze, and are quite likely to drink any that is left in an uncovered container or in puddles on the ground. This will prove fatal in sufficient quantity. Always drain the coolant into a sealable container. Coolant should be reused unless it is contaminated or several years old.

2. Remove the right and left valve covers.
3. Remove the timing chain front cover. Remove the timing chains.

4. Rotate the crankshaft counterclockwise 45 degrees from TDC to make sure all pistons are below the top of the engine block deck face.

❋❋ WARNING

The crankshaft must be in this position prior to rotating the camshafts or damage to the pistons and/or valve train will result.

5. Install a suitable valve spring compressor tool, under the camshaft and on top of the valve spring retainer.

➡ **The valve spring spacer tool must be installed between the spring coils and the camshaft must be at the base circle before compressing the valve spring.**

6. Compress the valve spring far enough to remove the roller follower. Repeat Steps 5 and 6 until all roller followers are removed.

7. Remove the bolts retaining the camshaft cap cluster assemblies to the cylinder heads. Tap upward on the camshaft caps at points near the upper bearing halves and gradually lift the camshaft clusters from the cylinder heads.

8. Remove the camshafts straight upward to avoid bearing damage.
   To install:

9. Apply heavy engine oil to the camshaft journals and lobes. Position the camshafts on the cylinder heads.

10. Install and seat the camshaft cap cluster assemblies. Hand start the bolts.

11. Tighten the camshaft cluster retaining bolts in sequence to 6–9 ft. lbs. (8–12 Nm).

➡ **Each camshaft cap cluster assembly is tightened individually.**

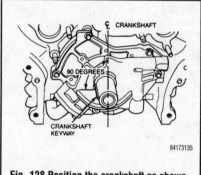

Fig. 128 Position the crankshaft as shown before rotating the camshafts—4.6L engine

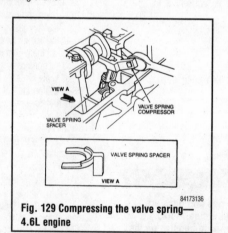

Fig. 129 Compressing the valve spring— 4.6L engine

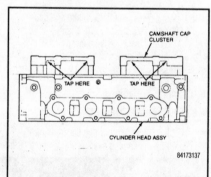

Fig. 130 Tap upward on the camshaft cap cluster assemblies at the points shown— 4.6L engine

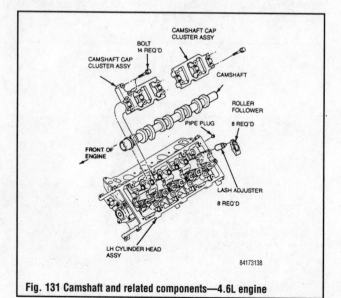

Fig. 131 Camshaft and related components—4.6L engine

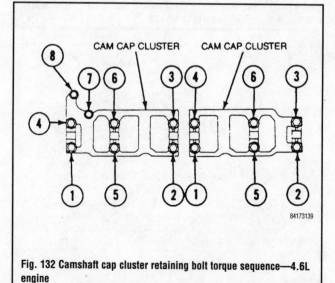

Fig. 132 Camshaft cap cluster retaining bolt torque sequence—4.6L engine

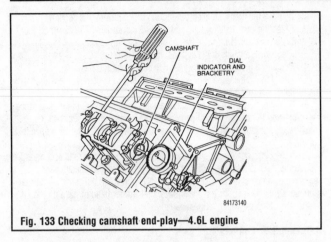

Fig. 133 Checking camshaft end-play—4.6L engine

12. Loosen the camshaft cap cluster retaining bolts approximately 2 turns or until the heads of the bolts are free. Retighten all bolts, in sequence, to 6–9 ft. lbs. (8–12 Nm).

➡ **The camshafts should turn freely with a slight drag.**

13. Check camshaft end-play as follows:
a. Install a suitable dial indicator on the front of the engine. Position it so the indicator foot is resting on the camshaft sprocket bolt or the front of the camshaft.
b. Push the camshaft toward the rear of the engine and zero the dial indicator.
c. Pull the camshaft forward and release it. Compare the dial indicator reading with specification.
d. If end-play is too tight, check for binding or foreign material in the camshaft thrust bearing. If end-play is excessive, check for worn camshaft thrust plate and replace the cylinder head, as required.
e. Remove the dial indicator.
14. If necessary, install cam positioning tools T92P–6256–A or equivalent, on the flats of the camshafts and install the spacers and camshaft sprockets. Install the bolts and washers and tighten to 81–95 ft. lbs. (110–130 Nm).
15. Install a suitable valve spring compressor tool, under the camshaft and on top of the valve spring retainer.

➡ **The valve spring spacer tool, must be installed between the spring coils and the camshaft must be at the base circle before compressing the valve spring.**

16. Compress the valve spring far enough to install the roller followers.
17. Repeat Steps 15 and 16 until all roller followers are installed.
18. Rotate the crankshaft clockwise 45 degrees to position the crankshaft at TDC.

➡ **The crankshaft must only be rotated in the clockwise direction and only as far as TDC.**

19. Install the timing chains and install the timing chain front cover. Install the valve covers.
20. Install the remaining components in the reverse order of removal.
21. Connect the negative battery cable. Start the engine and check for leaks.

5.0L and 5.8L Engines

▶ **See Figures 134 and 135**

1. Disconnect the negative battery cable and drain the cooling system.

❉❉ CAUTION

When draining the coolant, keep in mind that cats and dogs are attracted by the ethylene glycol antifreeze, and are quite likely to drink any that is left in an uncovered container or in puddles on the ground. This will prove fatal in sufficient quantity. Always drain the coolant into a sealable container. Coolant should be reused unless it is contaminated or several years old.

2. Relieve the fuel system pressure as described in Section 5. Discharge the air conditioning system.

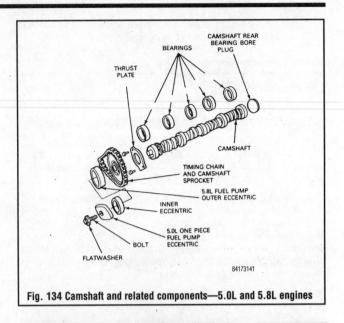

Fig. 134 Camshaft and related components—5.0L and 5.8L engines

Fig. 135 Checking camshaft end-play—5.0L and 5.8L engines

3. Remove the radiator and air conditioner condenser.
4. Remove the grille.
5. Remove the intake manifold and the lifters.
6. Remove the timing chain front cover, the timing chain and camshaft sprocket.
7. Check the camshaft end-play as follows:
a. Position a dial indicator on the front of the engine, with the indicator foot resting on the end of the camshaft.
b. Push the camshaft toward the rear of the engine and set the indicator pointer to 0.
c. Pull the camshaft forward and release it. Check the dial indicator reading.
d. If end-play exceeds specification, replace the thrust plate.
e. Recheck the end-play with the new thrust plate installed. If end-play is still excessive, check the camshaft and rear camshaft bore plug.
8. Remove the thrust plate. Remove the camshaft, being careful not to damage the bearing surfaces.
To install:
9. Lubricate the cam lobes and journals with heavy engine oil. Install the camshaft, being careful not to damage the bearing surfaces while sliding into position.
10. Install the thrust plate. Tighten the bolts to 9–12 ft. lbs. (12–16 Nm).
11. Install the timing chain and sprockets. Install the engine front cover.
12. Install the lifters and the intake manifolds.
13. Install the grille and the air conditioner condenser.
14. Install the radiator. Fill the cooling system.

15. Connect the negative battery cable. Start the engine and check for leaks.
16. Evacuate and recharge the air conditioning system.

INSPECTION

♦ **See Figure 136**

1. Clean the camshaft in solvent and allow to dry.
2. Inspect the camshaft for obvious signs of wear: scores, nicks or pits on the journals or lobes. Light scuffs or nicks can be removed with an oil stone.

➡**Lobe pitting except in the area shown in the figure will not hurt the operation of the camshaft; do not replace the camshaft because of pitting unless the pitting has occurred in the lobe lift area.**

3. Using a micrometer, measure the diameter of the journals and compare to specifications. Replace the camshaft if any journals are not within specification.
4. Measure the camshaft lobes at the major (A–A) and minor (B–B) diameters, using a micrometer. The difference in readings is the lobe height. Compare your measurements with the lobe height specifications. Replace the camshaft if any lobe heights are not within specification.

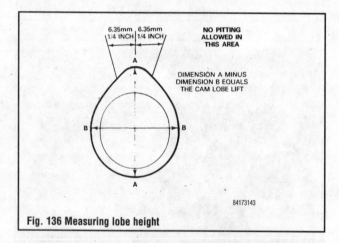

Fig. 136 Measuring lobe height

Camshaft Bearings

REMOVAL & INSTALLATION

4.6L Engine

The camshaft bearings are an integral part of the cylinder head on the 4.6L engine. If the camshaft bearing surfaces are damaged, or the oil clearance is excessive and the camshaft journals are within specification, the cylinder head must be replaced or rebored to accept a camshaft with oversize journals. Check the camshaft oil clearance as follows:

1. Remove the camshaft according to the procedure in this section.
2. Clean the camshaft journals and the bearing surface. The camshaft journal and bearing surface must be free of oil when using Plastigage®.
3. Place the camshaft in the cylinder head.
4. Position a piece of Plastigage® on the camshaft journal.
5. Install the camshaft cap cluster assemblies and tighten, as described in the installation procedure in this section.
6. Remove the camshaft cap cluster assemblies. Measure the oil clearance by comparing the piece of Plastigage® with the measurement scale on the Plastigage® packaging. Compare the measurement with the clearance specification.
7. If the clearance exceeds the maximum, remove the camshaft and measure the journal diameters. If the journal diameters are not within specification, replace the camshaft and repeat the oil clearance check. If the camshaft journal diameters are within specification, replace the cylinder head or have it rebored to accept a camshaft with oversize journals.

5.0L and 5.8L Engines

♦ **See Figures 137 and 138**

➡**The following procedure requires the use of camshaft bearing set tool T65L–6250–A or equivalent.**

1. Remove the engine assembly and mount it on a workstand.
2. Remove the camshaft, flywheel and crankshaft. Push the pistons to the top of the cylinders.
3. Using a sharp chisel or punch and hammer, cut a hole in the center of the rear bearing bore plug. Pry the plug from the bore using a prybar. Be careful not to damage the bore.
4. Select the proper size expanding collet and backup nut and assemble them on the expanding mandrel. With the expanding collet collapsed, install the collet assembly in the camshaft bearing, and tighten the backup nut on the expanding mandrel until the collet fits the camshaft bearing.
5. Assemble the puller screw and extension, if necessary, and install them on the expanding mandrel. Wrap a cloth around the threads of the puller screw to protect the bearing or journal. Tighten the puller nut against the thrust bearing and puller plate to remove the camshaft bearing. Hold the end of the puller screw to prevent it from turning.
6. Repeat Step 5 for each bearing. To remove the front bearing, install the puller from the rear of the block.

To install:

7. Position the new bearings at the bearing bores and install them with the camshaft bearing tool. Center the pulling plate and puller screw to avoid damage to the bearing. Failure to use the correct size collet can cause severe bearing damage. Align the holes in the bearings with the oil holes in the cylinder block before pressing the bearings into place.

➡**Make sure the front bearing is installed 0.005–0.020 in. below the front face of the cylinder block.**

8. Test fit the camshaft to make sure it turns easily in the bearings. If the camshaft does not turn easily, check if it is bent. If the camshaft is okay, it is possible that one or more of the bearings is cocked or installed incorrectly. If the bearings are okay, check the bearing bore alignment using a straightedge

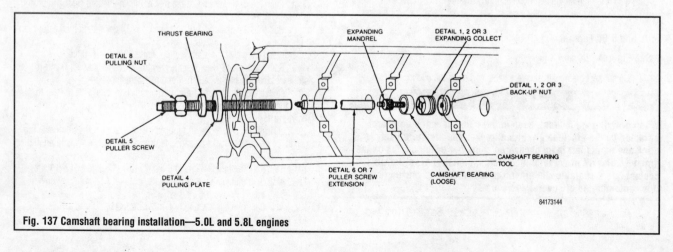

Fig. 137 Camshaft bearing installation—5.0L and 5.8L engines

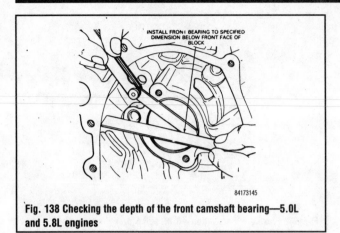

Fig. 138 Checking the depth of the front camshaft bearing—5.0L and 5.8L engines

and feeler gauge. If the bores are misaligned, consult an automotive machine shop for possible machining alternatives.

9. Apply a light coating of anaerobic sealer to the sealing edge of a new rear bearing bore plug. Install the plug using a suitable driver.

10. Install the camshaft, crankshaft and flywheel.

11. Install the engine assembly in the vehicle.

Rear Main Seal

REMOVAL & INSTALLATION

4.6L Engine

▶ See Figures 139 and 140

1. Disconnect the negative battery cable.
2. Remove the transmission; refer to Section 7.
3. Remove the flexplate from the crankshaft.
4. Remove the rear main seal retainer from the cylinder block.
5. Securely support the seal retainer and remove the seal, using a sharp pick.

To install:

6. Clean and inspect the retainer and retainer-to-cylinder block mating surfaces.

7. Apply a 0.060 in. (1.5mm) continuous bead of a suitable gasket maker to the cylinder block.

8. Install the seal retainer and tighten the bolts, in sequence, to 6–9 ft. lbs. (8–12 Nm).

9. Install the new rear main seal using a suitable rear main seal installation tool.

10. Install the flexplate and tighten the bolts, in a crisscross pattern, to 54–64 ft. lbs. (73–87 Nm).

11. Install the transmission and lower the vehicle.

12. Connect the negative battery cable, start the engine and check for leaks.

5.0L and 5.8L Engines

▶ See Figure 141

1. Disconnect the negative battery cable.
2. Remove the transmission; refer to Section 7.
3. Remove the flexplate from the crankshaft.
4. Punch 2 holes in the crankshaft rear oil seal on opposite sides of the crankshaft, just above the bearing cap to cylinder block split line. Install a sheet metal screw in each of the holes or use a small slide hammer and pry the crankshaft rear main oil seal from the block.

➡ **Use extreme caution not to scratch the crankshaft oil seal surface.**

To install:

5. Clean the oil seal recess in the cylinder block and main bearing cap.

6. Coat the seal and all of the seal mounting surfaces with oil. Position the seal on a suitable rear main seal installation tool, then position the tool and seal to the rear of the engine.

7. Alternate bolt tightening to seat the seal properly. The rear face of the seal must be within 0.005 in. (0.127mm) of the rear face of the block.

8. Install the flexplate. Apply pipe sealant to the flexplate bolt threads, then tighten them, in a crisscross pattern, to 75–85 ft. lbs. (102–115 Nm).

9. Install the transmission and lower the vehicle.

10. Connect the negative battery cable, start the engine and check for leaks.

Flexplate

REMOVAL & INSTALLATION

▶ See Figures 142 and 143

1. Disconnect the negative battery cable.
2. Remove the transmission; refer to Section 7.
3. Remove the retaining bolts and remove the flexplate from the crankshaft.
4. Inspect the flexplate for cracks or other damage. Check the ring gear for worn, chipped or cracked teeth. If the teeth are damaged, the entire flexplate must be replaced.

To install:

5. Make sure the crankshaft flange and flexplate mating surfaces are clean.

6. Position the flexplate on the crankshaft and install the retaining bolts.

➡ **On 5.0L and 5.8L engines, apply suitable pipe sealant to the flexplate bolt threads prior to installation.**

7. On 4.6L engine, tighten the flexplate retaining bolts, in a crisscross pattern, to 54–64 ft. lbs. (73–87 Nm).

8. On 5.0L and 5.8L engines, tighten the flexplate retaining bolts, in a crisscross pattern, to 75–85 ft. lbs. (102–115 Nm).

9. Install the transmission and lower the vehicle. Connect the negative battery cable.

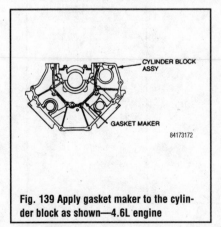

Fig. 139 Apply gasket maker to the cylinder block as shown—4.6L engine

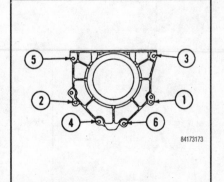

Fig. 140 Rear main seal retainer bolt torque sequence—4.6L engine

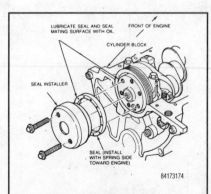

Fig. 141 Rear main seal installation—5.0L and 5.8L engines shown

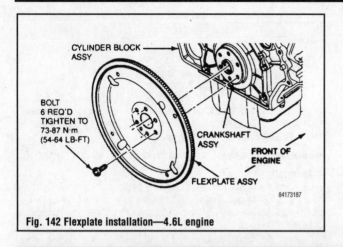

Fig. 142 Flexplate installation—4.6L engine

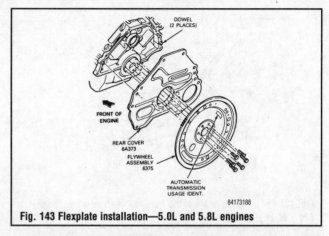

Fig. 143 Flexplate installation—5.0L and 5.8L engines

EXHAUST SYSTEM

Inspection

◆ See Figures 144 thru 152

➡Safety glasses should be worn at all times when working on or near the exhaust system. Older exhaust systems will almost always be covered with loose rust particles which will shower you when disturbed. These particles are more than a nuisance and could injure your eye.

✺✺ CAUTION

DO NOT perform exhaust repairs or inspection with the engine or exhaust hot. Allow the system to cool completely before attempting any work. Exhaust systems are noted for sharp edges, flaking metal and rusted bolts. Gloves and eye protection are required. A healthy supply of penetrating oil and rags is highly recommended.

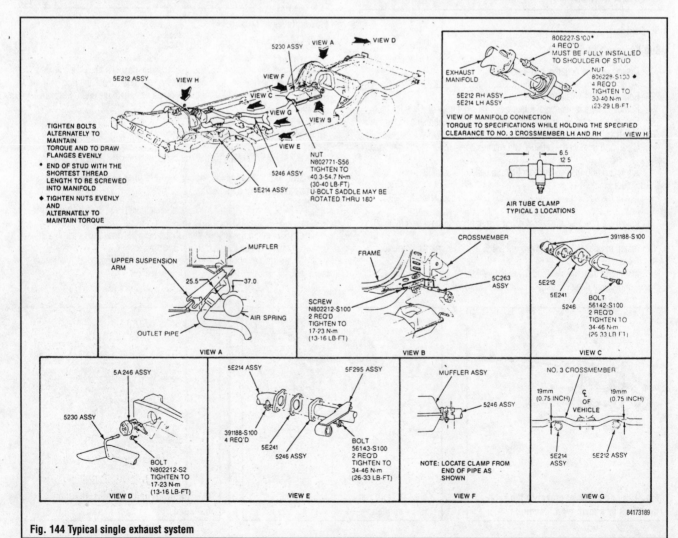

Fig. 144 Typical single exhaust system

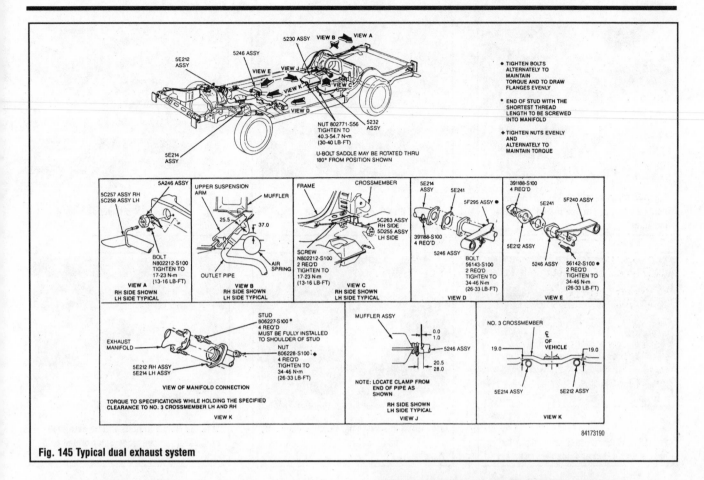

Fig. 145 Typical dual exhaust system

Your vehicle must be raised and supported safely to inspect the exhaust system properly. By placing 4 safety stands under the vehicle for support should provide enough room for you to slide under the vehicle and inspect the system completely. Start the inspection at the exhaust manifold or turbocharger pipe where the header pipe is attached and work your way to the back of the vehicle. On dual exhaust systems, remember to inspect both sides of the vehicle. Check the complete exhaust system for open seams, holes loose connections, or other deterioration which could permit exhaust fumes to seep into the passenger compartment. Inspect all mounting brackets and hangers for deterioration, some models may have rubber O-rings that can be overstretched and non-supportive. These components will need to be replaced if found. It has always been a prac-

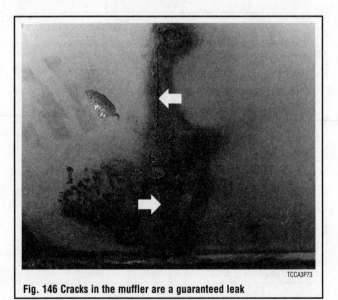

Fig. 146 Cracks in the muffler are a guaranteed leak

Fig. 147 Check the muffler for rotted spot welds and seams

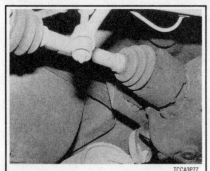

Fig. 148 Make sure the exhaust components are not contacting the body or suspension

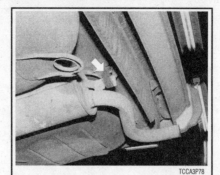

Fig. 149 Check for overstretched or torn exhaust hangers

Fig. 150 Example of a badly deteriorated exhaust pipe

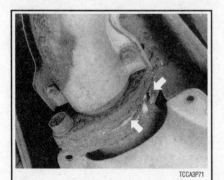

Fig. 151 Inspect flanges for gaskets that have deteriorated and need replacement

Fig. 152 Some systems, like this one, use large O-rings (doughnuts) in between the flanges

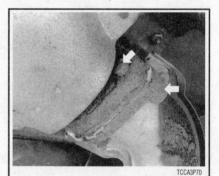

Fig. 153 Nuts and bolts will be extremely difficult to remove when deteriorated with rust

tice to use a pointed tool to poke up into the exhaust system where the deterioration spots are to see whether or not they crumble. Some models may have heat shield covering certain parts of the exhaust system , it will be necessary to remove these shields to have the exhaust visible for inspection also.

REPLACEMENT

▶ **See Figure 153**

There are basically two types of exhaust systems. One is the flange type where the component ends are attached with bolts and a gasket in-between. The other exhaust system is the slip joint type. These components slip into one another using clamps to retain them together.

> ⚹⚹ **CAUTION**
>
> **Allow the exhaust system to cool sufficiently before spraying a solvent exhaust fasteners. Some solvents are highly flammable and could ignite when sprayed on hot exhaust components.**

Before removing any component of the exhaust system, ALWAYS squirt a liquid rust dissolving agent onto the fasteners for ease of removal. A lot of knuckle skin will be saved by following this rule. It may even be wise to spray the fasteners and allow them to sit overnight.

Flange Type

▶ **See Figure 154**

> ⚹⚹ **CAUTION**
>
> **Do NOT perform exhaust repairs or inspection with the engine or exhaust hot. Allow the system to cool completely before attempting any work. Exhaust systems are noted for sharp edges, flaking metal and rusted bolts. Gloves and eye protection are required. A**

healthy supply of penetrating oil and rags is highly recommended. Never spray liquid rust dissolving agent onto a hot exhaust component.

Before removing any component on a flange type system, ALWAYS squirt a liquid rust dissolving agent onto the fasteners for ease of removal. Start by unbolting the exhaust piece at both ends (if required). When unbolting the headpipe from the manifold, make sure that the bolts are free before trying to remove them. if you snap a stud in the exhaust manifold, the stud will have to be removed with a bolt extractor, which often means removal of the manifold itself. Next, disconnect the component from the mounting; slight twisting and turning

Fig. 154 Example of a flange type exhaust system joint

may be required to remove the component completely from the vehicle. You may need to tap on the component with a rubber mallet to loosen the component. If all else fails, use a hacksaw to separate the parts. An oxy-acetylene cutting torch may be faster but the sparks are DANGEROUS near the fuel tank, and at the very least, accidents could happen, resulting in damage to the under-car parts, not to mention yourself.

Slip Joint Type

▶ **See Figure 155**

Before removing any component on the slip joint type exhaust system, ALWAYS squirt a liquid rust dissolving agent onto the fasteners for ease of removal. Start by unbolting the exhaust piece at both ends (if required). When unbolting the headpipe from the manifold, make sure that the bolts are free before trying to remove them. if you snap a stud in the exhaust manifold, the stud will have to be removed with a bolt extractor, which often means removal of the manifold itself. Next, remove the mounting U-bolts from around the exhaust pipe you are extracting from the vehicle. Don't be surprised if the U-bolts break while removing the nuts. Loosen the exhaust pipe from any mounting brackets retaining it to the floor pan and separate the components.

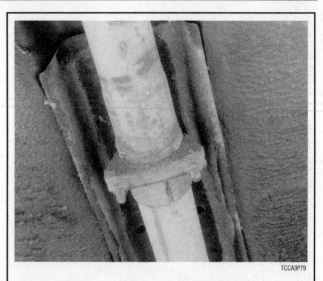

TCCA3P79

Fig. 155 Example of a common slip joint type system

ENGINE RECONDITIONING

Determining Engine Condition

Anything that generates heat and/or friction will eventually burn or wear out (for example, a light bulb generates heat, therefore its life span is limited). With this in mind, a running engine generates tremendous amounts of both; friction is encountered by the moving and rotating parts inside the engine and heat is created by friction and combustion of the fuel. However, the engine has systems designed to help reduce the effects of heat and friction and provide added longevity. The oiling system reduces the amount of friction encountered by the moving parts inside the engine, while the cooling system reduces heat created by friction and combustion. If either system is not maintained, a break-down will be inevitable. Therefore, you can see how regular maintenance can affect the service life of your vehicle. If you do not drain, flush and refill your cooling system at the proper intervals, deposits will begin to accumulate in the radiator, thereby reducing the amount of heat it can extract from the coolant. The same applies to your oil and filter; if it is not changed often enough it becomes laden with contaminates and is unable to properly lubricate the engine. This increases friction and wear.

There are a number of methods for evaluating the condition of your engine. A compression test can reveal the condition of your pistons, piston rings, cylinder bores, head gasket(s), valves and valve seats. An oil pressure test can warn you of possible engine bearing, or oil pump failures. Excessive oil consumption, evidence of oil in the engine air intake area and/or bluish smoke from the tailpipe may indicate worn piston rings, worn valve guides and/or valve seals. As a general rule, an engine that uses no more than one quart of oil every 1000 miles is in good condition. Engines that use one quart of oil or more in less than 1000 miles should first be checked for oil leaks. If any oil leaks are present, have them fixed before determining how much oil is consumed by the engine, especially if blue smoke is not visible at the tailpipe.

COMPRESSION TEST

▶ **See Figure 156**

A noticeable lack of engine power, excessive oil consumption and/or poor fuel mileage measured over an extended period are all indicators of internal engine wear. Worn piston rings, scored or worn cylinder bores, blown head gaskets, sticking or burnt valves, and worn valve seats are all possible culprits. A check of each cylinder's compression will help locate the problem.

➡**A screw-in type compression gauge is more accurate than the type you simply hold against the spark plug hole. Although it takes slightly longer to use, it's worth the effort to obtain a more accurate reading.**

1. Make sure that the proper amount and viscosity of engine oil is in the crankcase, then ensure the battery is fully charged.

2. Warm-up the engine to normal operating temperature, then shut the engine **OFF**.
3. Disable the ignition system.
4. Label and disconnect all of the spark plug wires from the plugs.
5. Thoroughly clean the cylinder head area around the spark plug ports, then remove the spark plugs.
6. Set the throttle plate to the fully open (wide-open throttle) position. You can block the accelerator linkage open for this, or you can have an assistant fully depress the accelerator pedal.
7. Install a screw-in type compression gauge into the No. 1 spark plug hole until the fitting is snug.

✻✻ WARNING

Be careful not to crossthread the spark plug hole.

8. According to the tool manufacturer's instructions, connect a remote starting switch to the starting circuit.
9. With the ignition switch in the **OFF** position, use the remote starting switch to crank the engine through at least five compression strokes (approximately 5 seconds of cranking) and record the highest reading on the gauge.

TCCS3801

Fig. 156 A screw-in type compression gauge is more accurate and easier to use without an assistant

10. Repeat the test on each cylinder, cranking the engine approximately the same number of compression strokes and/or time as the first.

11. Compare the highest readings from each cylinder to that of the others. The indicated compression pressures are considered within specifications if the lowest reading cylinder is within 75 percent of the pressure recorded for the highest reading cylinder. For example, if your highest reading cylinder pressure was 150 psi (1034 kPa), then 75 percent of that would be 113 psi (779 kPa). So the lowest reading cylinder should be no less than 113 psi (779 kPa).

12. If a cylinder exhibits an unusually low compression reading, pour a tablespoon of clean engine oil into the cylinder through the spark plug hole and repeat the compression test. If the compression rises after adding oil, it means that the cylinder's piston rings and/or cylinder bore are damaged or worn. If the pressure remains low, the valves may not be seating properly (a valve job is needed), or the head gasket may be blown near that cylinder. If compression in any two adjacent cylinders is low, and if the addition of oil doesn't help raise compression, there is leakage past the head gasket. Oil and coolant in the combustion chamber, combined with blue or constant white smoke from the tailpipe, are symptoms of this problem. However, don't be alarmed by the normal white smoke emitted from the tailpipe during engine warm-up or from cold weather driving. There may be evidence of water droplets on the engine dipstick and/or oil droplets in the cooling system if a head gasket is blown.

OIL PRESSURE TEST

Check for proper oil pressure at the sending unit passage with an externally mounted mechanical oil pressure gauge (as opposed to relying on a factory installed dash-mounted gauge). A tachometer may also be needed, as some specifications may require running the engine at a specific rpm.

1. With the engine cold, locate and remove the oil pressure sending unit.

2. Following the manufacturer's instructions, connect a mechanical oil pressure gauge and, if necessary, a tachometer to the engine.

3. Start the engine and allow it to idle.

4. Check the oil pressure reading when cold and record the number. You may need to run the engine at a specified rpm, so check the specifications.

5. Run the engine until normal operating temperature is reached (upper radiator hose will feel warm).

6. Check the oil pressure reading again with the engine hot and record the number. Turn the engine **OFF**.

7. Compare your hot oil pressure reading to that given in the chart. If the reading is low, check the cold pressure reading against the chart. If the cold pressure is well above the specification, and the hot reading was lower than the specification, you may have the wrong viscosity oil in the engine. Change the oil, making sure to use the proper grade and quantity, then repeat the test.

Low oil pressure readings could be attributed to internal component wear, pump related problems, a low oil level, or oil viscosity that is too low. High oil pressure readings could be caused by an overfilled crankcase, too high of an oil viscosity or a faulty pressure relief valve.

Buy or Rebuild?

Now that you have determined that your engine is worn out, you must make some decisions. The question of whether or not an engine is worth rebuilding is largely a subjective matter and one of personal worth. Is the engine a popular one, or is it an obsolete model? Are parts available? Will it get acceptable gas mileage once it is rebuilt? Is the car it's being put into worth keeping? Would it be less expensive to buy a new engine, have your engine rebuilt by a pro, rebuild it yourself or buy a used engine from a salvage yard? Or would it be simpler and less expensive to buy another car? If you have considered all these matters and more, and have still decided to rebuild the engine, then it is time to decide how you will rebuild it.

➡The editors at Chilton feel that most engine machining should be performed by a professional machine shop. Don't think of it as wasting money, rather, as an assurance that the job has been done right the first time. There are many expensive and specialized tools required to perform such tasks as boring and honing an engine block or having a valve job done on a cylinder head. Even inspecting the parts requires expensive micrometers and gauges to properly measure wear and clearances. Also, a machine shop can deliver to you clean, and ready to assemble parts, saving you time and aggravation. Your maximum savings will come from performing the removal, disassembly, assembly and instal-

lation of the engine and purchasing or renting only the tools required to perform the above tasks. Depending on the particular circumstances, you may save 40 to 60 percent of the cost doing these yourself.

A complete rebuild or overhaul of an engine involves replacing all of the moving parts (pistons, rods, crankshaft, camshaft, etc.) with new ones and machining the non-moving wearing surfaces of the block and heads. Unfortunately, this may not be cost effective. For instance, your crankshaft may have been damaged or worn, but it can be machined undersize for a minimal fee.

So, as you can see, you can replace everything inside the engine, but, it is wiser to replace only those parts which are really needed, and, if possible, repair the more expensive ones. Later in this section, we will break the engine down into its two main components: the cylinder head and the engine block. We will discuss each component, and the recommended parts to replace during a rebuild on each.

Engine Overhaul Tips

Most engine overhaul procedures are fairly standard. In addition to specific parts replacement procedures and specifications for your individual engine, this section is also a guide to acceptable rebuilding procedures. Examples of standard rebuilding practice are given and should be used along with specific details concerning your particular engine.

Competent and accurate machine shop services will ensure maximum performance, reliability and engine life. In most instances it is more profitable for the do-it-yourself mechanic to remove, clean and inspect the component, buy the necessary parts and deliver these to a shop for actual machine work.

Much of the assembly work (crankshaft, bearings, piston rods, and other components) is well within the scope of the do-it-yourself mechanic's tools and abilities. You will have to decide for yourself the depth of involvement you desire in an engine repair or rebuild.

TOOLS

The tools required for an engine overhaul or parts replacement will depend on the depth of your involvement. With a few exceptions, they will be the tools found in a mechanic's tool kit (see Section 1 of this manual). More in-depth work will require some or all of the following:

• A dial indicator (reading in thousandths) mounted on a universal base
• Micrometers and telescope gauges
• Jaw and screw-type pullers
• Scraper
• Valve spring compressor
• Ring groove cleaner
• Piston ring expander and compressor
• Ridge reamer
• Cylinder hone or glaze breaker
• Plastigage®
• Engine stand

The use of most of these tools is illustrated in this section. Many can be rented for a one-time use from a local parts jobber or tool supply house specializing in automotive work.

Occasionally, the use of special tools is called for. See the information on Special Tools and the Safety Notice in the front of this book before substituting another tool.

OVERHAUL TIPS

Aluminum has become extremely popular for use in engines, due to its low weight. Observe the following precautions when handling aluminum parts:

• Never hot tank aluminum parts (the caustic hot tank solution will eat the aluminum.
• Remove all aluminum parts (identification tag, etc.) from engine parts prior to the tanking.
• Always coat threads lightly with engine oil or anti-seize compounds before installation, to prevent seizure.
• Never overtighten bolts or spark plugs especially in aluminum threads.

When assembling the engine, any parts that will be exposed to frictional contact must be prelubed to provide lubrication at initial start-up. Any product specifically formulated for this purpose can be used, but engine oil is not recommended as a prelube in most cases.

When semi-permanent (locked, but removable) installation of bolts or nuts is desired, threads should be cleaned and coated with Loctite• or another similar, commercial non-hardening sealant.

CLEANING

♦ See Figures 157, 158, 159 and 160

Before the engine and its components are inspected, they must be thoroughly cleaned. You will need to remove any engine varnish, oil sludge and/or carbon deposits from all of the components to insure an accurate inspection. A crack in the engine block or cylinder head can easily become overlooked if hidden by a layer of sludge or carbon.

Most of the cleaning process can be carried out with common hand tools and readily available solvents or solutions. Carbon deposits can be chipped away using a hammer and a hard wooden chisel. Old gasket material and varnish or sludge can usually be removed using a scraper and/or cleaning solvent. Extremely stubborn deposits may require the use of a power drill with a wire brush. If using a wire brush, use extreme care around any critical machined surfaces (such as the gasket surfaces, bearing saddles, cylinder bores, etc.). USE OF A WIRE BRUSH IS NOT RECOMMENDED ON ANY ALUMINUM COMPONENTS. Always follow any safety recommendations given by the manufacturer of the tool and/or solvent. You should always wear eye protection during any cleaning process involving scraping, chipping or spraying of solvents.

An alternative to the mess and hassle of cleaning the parts yourself is to drop them off at a local garage or machine shop. They will, more than likely, have the necessary equipment to properly clean all of the parts for a nominal fee.

✳✳ CAUTION

Always wear eye protection during any cleaning process involving scraping, chipping or spraying of solvents.

Remove any oil galley plugs, freeze plugs and/or pressed-in bearings and carefully wash and degrease all of the engine components including the fasteners and bolts. Small parts such as the valves, springs, etc., should be placed in a metal basket and allowed to soak. Use pipe cleaner type brushes, and clean all passageways in the components. Use a ring expander and remove the rings from the pistons. Clean the piston ring grooves with a special tool or a piece of broken ring. Scrape the carbon off of the top of the piston. You should never use a wire brush on the pistons. After preparing all of the piston assemblies in this manner, wash and degrease them again.

✳✳ WARNING

Use extreme care when cleaning around the cylinder head valve seats. A mistake or slip may cost you a new seat.

When cleaning the cylinder head, remove carbon from the combustion chamber with the valves installed. This will avoid damaging the valve seats.

REPAIRING DAMAGED THREADS

♦ See Figures 161, 162, 163, 164 and 165

Several methods of repairing damaged threads are available. Heli-Coil• (shown here), Keenserts• and Microdot• are among the most widely used. All involve basically the same principle—drilling out stripped threads, tapping the hole and installing a prewound insert—making welding, plugging and oversize fasteners unnecessary.

Two types of thread repair inserts are usually supplied: a standard type for most inch coarse, inch fine, metric course and metric fine thread sizes and a spark lug type to fit most spark plug port sizes. Consult the individual tool manufacturer's catalog to determine exact applications. Typical thread repair kits will contain a selection of prewound threaded inserts, a tap (corresponding to the outside diameter threads of the insert) and an installation tool. Spark plug inserts usually differ because they require a tap equipped with pilot threads and a combined reamer/tap section. Most manufacturers also supply blister-packed thread repair inserts separately in addition to a master kit containing a variety of taps and inserts plus installation tools.

Fig. 157 Thoroughly clean all gasket mating surfaces

Fig. 158 Use a ring expander tool to remove the piston rings

Fig. 159 Clean the piston ring grooves using a ring groove cleaner tool, or . . .

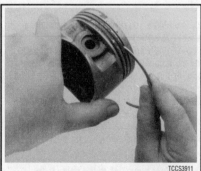
Fig. 160 . . . use a piece of an old ring to clean the grooves. Be careful, the ring can be quite sharp

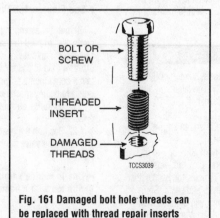
Fig. 161 Damaged bolt hole threads can be replaced with thread repair inserts

Fig. 162 Standard thread repair insert (left), and spark plug thread insert

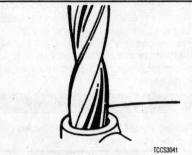

Fig. 163 Drill out the damaged threads with the specified size bit. Be sure to drill completely through the hole or to the bottom of a blind hole

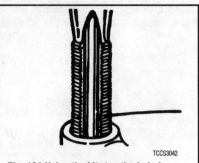

Fig. 164 Using the kit, tap the hole in order to receive the thread insert. Keep the tap well oiled and back it out frequently to avoid clogging the threads

Fig. 165 Screw the insert onto the installer tool until the tang engages the slot. Thread the insert into the hole until it is ¼–½ turn below the top surface, then remove the tool and break off the tang using a punch

Before attempting to repair a threaded hole, remove any snapped, broken or damaged bolts or studs. Penetrating oil can be used to free frozen threads. The offending item can usually be removed with locking pliers or using a screw/stud extractor. After the hole is clear, the thread can be repaired, as shown in the series of accompanying illustrations and in the kit manufacturer's instructions.

Engine Preparation

To properly rebuild an engine, you must first remove it from the vehicle, then disassemble and diagnose it. Ideally you should place your engine on an engine stand. This affords you the best access to the engine components. Follow the manufacturer's directions for using the stand with your particular engine. Remove the flywheel or flexplate before installing the engine to the stand.

Now that you have the engine on a stand, and assuming that you have drained the oil and coolant from the engine, it's time to strip it of all but the necessary components. Before you start disassembling the engine, you may want to take a moment to draw some pictures, or fabricate some labels or containers to mark the locations of various components and the bolts and/or studs which fasten them. Modern day engines use a lot of little brackets and clips which hold wiring harnesses and such, and these holders are often mounted on studs and/or bolts that can be easily mixed up. The manufacturer spent a lot of time and money designing your vehicle, and they wouldn't have wasted any of it by haphazardly placing brackets, clips or fasteners on the vehicle. If it's present when you disassemble it, put it back when you assemble, you will regret not remembering that little bracket which holds a wire harness out of the path of a rotating part.

You should begin by unbolting any accessories still attached to the engine, such as the water pump, power steering pump, alternator, etc. Then, unfasten any manifolds (intake or exhaust) which were not removed during the engine removal procedure. Finally, remove any covers remaining on the engine such as the rocker arm, front or timing cover and oil pan. Some front covers may require the vibration damper and/or crank pulley to be removed beforehand. The idea is to reduce the engine to the bare necessities (cylinder head(s), valve train, engine block, crankshaft, pistons and connecting rods), plus any other `in block' components such as oil pumps, balance shafts and auxiliary shafts.

Finally, remove the cylinder head(s) from the engine block and carefully place on a bench. Disassembly instructions for each component follow later in this section.

Cylinder Head

There are two basic types of cylinder heads used on today's automobiles: the Overhead Valve (OHV) and the Overhead Camshaft (OHC). The latter can also be broken down into two subgroups: the Single Overhead Camshaft (SOHC) and the Dual Overhead Camshaft (DOHC). Generally, if there is only a single camshaft on a head, it is just referred to as an OHC head. Also, an engine with an OHV cylinder head is also known as a pushrod engine.

Most cylinder heads these days are made of an aluminum alloy due to its light weight, durability and heat transfer qualities. However, cast iron was the material of choice in the past, and is still used on many vehicles today. Whether made from aluminum or iron, all cylinder heads have valves and seats. Some use two valves per cylinder, while the more hi-tech engines will utilize a multi-valve configuration using 3, 4 and even 5 valves per cylinder. When the valve

contacts the seat, it does so on precision machined surfaces, which seals the combustion chamber. All cylinder heads have a valve guide for each valve. The guide centers the valve to the seat and allows it to move up and down within it. The clearance between the valve and guide can be critical. Too much clearance and the engine may consume oil, lose vacuum and/or damage the seat. Too little, and the valve can stick in the guide causing the engine to run poorly if at all, and possibly causing severe damage. The last component all cylinder heads have are valve springs. The spring holds the valve against its seat. It also returns the valve to this position when the valve has been opened by the valve train or camshaft. The spring is fastened to the valve by a retainer and valve locks (sometimes called keepers). Aluminum heads will also have a valve spring shim to keep the spring from wearing away the aluminum.

An ideal method of rebuilding the cylinder head would involve replacing all of the valves, guides, seats, springs, etc. with new ones. However, depending on how the engine was maintained, often this is not necessary. A major cause of valve, guide and seat wear is an improperly tuned engine. An engine that is running too rich, will often wash the lubricating oil out of the guide with gasoline, causing it to wear rapidly. Conversely, an engine which is running too lean will place higher combustion temperatures on the valves and seats allowing them to wear or even burn. Springs fall victim to the driving habits of the individual. A driver who often runs the engine rpm to the redline will wear out or break the springs faster then one that stays well below it. Unfortunately, mileage takes it toll on all of the parts. Generally, the valves, guides, springs and seats in a cylinder head can be machined and re-used, saving you money. However, if a valve is burnt, it may be wise to replace all of the valves, since they were all operating in the same environment. The same goes for any other component on the cylinder head. Think of it as an insurance policy against future problems related to that component.

Unfortunately, the only way to find out which components need replacing, is to disassemble and carefully check each piece. After the cylinder head(s) are disassembled, thoroughly clean all of the components.

DISASSEMBLY

5.0/5.8L Engines

♦ See Figures 166 thru 171

Before disassembling the cylinder head, you may want to fabricate some containers to hold the various parts, as some of them can be quite small (such as keepers) and easily lost. Also keeping yourself and the components organized will aid in assembly and reduce confusion. Where possible, try to maintain a components original location; this is especially important if there is not going to be any machine work performed on the components.

1. If you haven't already removed the rocker arms and/or shafts, do so now.

2. Position the head so that the springs are easily accessed.

3. Use a valve spring compressor tool, and relieve spring tension from the retainer.

➡**Due to engine varnish, the retainer may stick to the valve locks. A gentle tap with a hammer may help to break it loose.**

4. Remove the valve locks from the valve tip and/or retainer. A small magnet may help in removing the locks.

Fig. 166 When removing an OHV valve spring, use a compressor tool to relieve the tension from the retainer

Fig. 167 A small magnet will help in removal of the valve locks (keepers)

Fig. 168 Be careful not to lose the small valve locks (keepers)

Fig. 169 Remove the valve seal from the valve stem—O-ring type seal shown

Fig. 170 Removing an umbrella/positive type seal

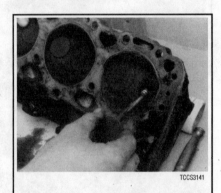

Fig. 171 Invert the cylinder head and withdraw the valve from the valve guide bore

5. Lift the valve spring, tool and all, off of the valve stem.

6. If equipped, remove the valve seal. If the seal is difficult to remove with the valve in place, try removing the valve first, then the seal. Follow the steps below for valve removal.

7. Position the head to allow access for withdrawing the valve.

➡**Cylinder heads that have seen a lot of miles and/or abuse may have mushroomed the valve lock grove and/or tip, causing difficulty in removal of the valve. If this has happened, use a metal file to carefully remove the high spots around the lock grooves and/or tip. Only file it enough to allow removal.**

8. Remove the valve from the cylinder head.

9. If equipped, remove the valve spring shim. A small magnetic tool or screwdriver will aid in removal.

10. Repeat Steps 3 though 9 until all of the valves have been removed.

4.6L Engine

▶ **See Figures 172 thru 176**

Whether it is a single or dual overhead camshaft cylinder head, the disassembly procedure is relatively unchanged. One aspect to pay attention to is careful labeling of the parts on the dual camshaft cylinder head. There will be an intake camshaft and followers as well as an exhaust camshaft and followers and they must be labeled as such. In some cases, the components are identical and could easily be installed incorrectly. DO NOT MIX THEM UP! Determining which is which is very simple; the intake camshaft and components are on the same side of the head as was the intake manifold. Conversely, the exhaust camshaft and components are on the same side of the head as was the exhaust manifold.

Most cylinder heads with cup type camshaft followers will have the valve spring, retainer and locks recessed within the follower's bore. You will need a C-clamp style valve spring compressor tool, an OHC spring removal tool (or equivalent) and a small magnet to disassemble the head.

1. If not already removed, remove the camshaft(s) and/or followers. Mark their positions for assembly.

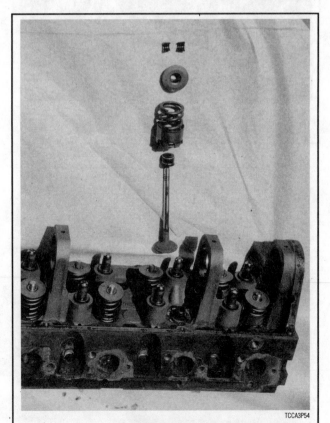

Fig. 172 Exploded view of a valve, seal, spring, retainer and locks from an OHC cylinder head

2. Position the cylinder head to allow use of a C-clamp style valve spring compressor tool.

➡️**It is preferred to position the cylinder head gasket surface facing you with the valve springs facing the opposite direction and the head laying horizontal.**

3. With the OHC spring removal adapter tool positioned inside of the follower bore, compress the valve spring using the C-clamp style valve spring compressor.

4. Remove the valve locks. A small magnetic tool or screwdriver will aid in removal.

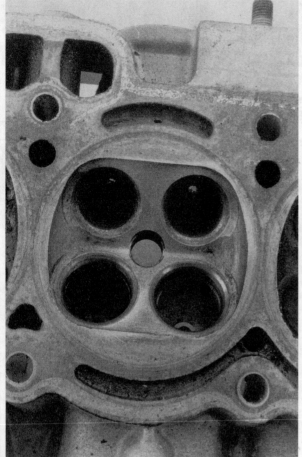

Fig. 173 Example of a multi-valve cylinder head. Note how it has 2 intake and 2 exhaust valve ports

Fig. 174 C-clamp type spring compressor and an OHC spring removal tool (center) for cup type followers

Fig. 175 Most cup type follower cylinder heads retain the camshaft using bolt-on bearing caps

Fig. 176 Position the OHC spring tool in the follower bore, then compress the spring with a C-clamp type tool

5. Release the compressor tool and remove the spring assembly.
6. Withdraw the valve from the cylinder head.
7. If equipped, remove the valve seal.

➡**Special valve seal removal tools are available. Regular or needlenose type pliers, if used with care, will work just as well. If using ordinary pliers, be sure not to damage the follower bore. The follower and its bore are machined to close tolerances and any damage to the bore will effect this relationship.**

8. If equipped, remove the valve spring shim. A small magnetic tool or screwdriver will aid in removal.
9. Repeat Steps 3 through 8 until all of the valves have been removed.

INSPECTION

Now that all of the cylinder head components are clean, it's time to inspect them for wear and/or damage. To accurately inspect them, you will need some specialized tools:
- A 0–1 in. micrometer for the valves
- A dial indicator or inside diameter gauge for the valve guides
- A spring pressure test gauge

If you do not have access to the proper tools, you may want to bring the components to a shop that does.

Valves

▶ **See Figures 177 and 178**

The first thing to inspect are the valve heads. Look closely at the head, margin and face for any cracks, excessive wear or burning. The margin is the best

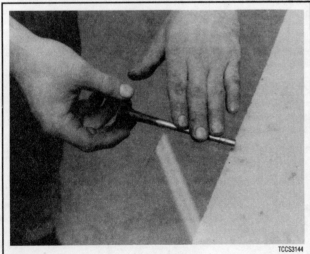

TCCS3144

Fig. 177 Valve stems may be rolled on a flat surface to check for bends

place to look for burning. It should have a squared edge with an even width all around the diameter. When a valve burns, the margin will look melted and the edges rounded. Also inspect the valve head for any signs of tulipping. This will show as a lifting of the edges or dishing in the center of the head and will usually not occur to all of the valves. All of the heads should look the same, any that seem dished more than others are probably bad. Next, inspect the valve lock grooves and valve tips. Check for any burrs around the lock grooves, especially if you had to file them to remove the valve. Valve tips should appear flat, although slight rounding with high mileage engines is normal. Slightly worn valve tips will need to be machined flat. Last, measure the valve stem diameter with the micrometer. Measure the area that rides within the guide, especially towards the tip where most of the wear occurs. Take several measurements along its length and compare them to each other. Wear should be even along the length with little to no taper. If no minimum diameter is given in the specifications, then the stem should not read more than 0.001 in. (0.025mm) below the unworn area of the valve stem. Any valves that fail these inspections should be replaced.

Springs, Retainers and Valve Locks

▶ **See Figures 179 and 180**

The first thing to check is the most obvious, broken springs. Next check the free length and squareness of each spring. If applicable, insure to distinguish between intake and exhaust springs. Use a ruler and/or carpenter's square to measure the length. A carpenter's square should be used to check the springs for squareness. If a spring pressure test gauge is available, check each springs rating and compare to the specifications chart. Check the readings against the specifications given. Any springs that fail these inspections should be replaced.

The spring retainers rarely need replacing, however they should still be checked as a precaution. Inspect the spring mating surface and the valve lock retention area for any signs of excessive wear. Also check for any signs of cracking. Replace any retainers that are questionable.

Valve locks should be inspected for excessive wear on the outside contact area as well as on the inner notched surface. Any locks which appear worn or broken and its respective valve should be replaced.

Cylinder Head

There are several things to check on the cylinder head: valve guides, seats, cylinder head surface flatness, cracks and physical damage.

VALVE GUIDES

▶ **See Figure 181**

Now that you know the valves are good, you can use them to check the guides, although a new valve, if available, is preferred. Before you measure anything, look at the guides carefully and inspect them for any cracks, chips or breakage. Also if the guide is a removable style (as in most aluminum heads), check them for any looseness or evidence of movement. All of the guides should appear to be at the same height from the spring seat. If any seem lower (or higher) from another, the guide has moved. Mount a dial indicator onto the spring side of the cylinder head. Lightly oil the valve stem and insert it into the cylinder head. Position the dial indicator against the valve stem near the tip and

TCCS3910

Fig. 178 Use a micrometer to check the valve stem diameter

TCCS3907

Fig. 179 Use a caliper to check the valve spring free-length

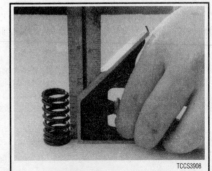

TCCS3908

Fig. 180 Check the valve spring for squareness on a flat surface; a carpenter's square can be used

Fig. 181 A dial gauge may be used to check valve stem-to-guide clearance; read the gauge while moving the valve stem

TCCS3142

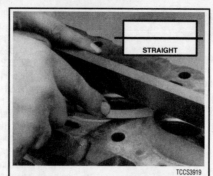

Fig. 182 Check the head for flatness across the center of the head surface using a straightedge and feeler gauge

TCCS3919

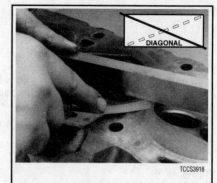

Fig. 183 Checks should also be made along both diagonals of the head surface

TCCS3918

zero the gauge. Grasp the valve stem and wiggle towards and away from the dial indicator and observe the readings. Mount the dial indicator 90 degrees from the initial point and zero the gauge and again take a reading. Compare the two readings for a out of round condition. Check the readings against the specifications given. An Inside Diameter (I.D.) gauge designed for valve guides will give you an accurate valve guide bore measurement. If the I.D. gauge is used, compare the readings with the specifications given. Any guides that fail these inspections should be replaced or machined.

VALVE SEATS

A visual inspection of the valve seats should show a slightly worn and pitted surface where the valve face contacts the seat. Inspect the seat carefully for severe pitting or cracks. Also, a seat that is badly worn will be recessed into the cylinder head. A severely worn or recessed seat may need to be replaced. All cracked seats must be replaced. A seat concentricity gauge, if available, should be used to check the seat run-out. If run-out exceeds specifications the seat must be machined (if no specification is given use 0.002 in. or 0.051mm).

CYLINDER HEAD SURFACE FLATNESS

♦ See Figures 182 and 183

After you have cleaned the gasket surface of the cylinder head of any old gasket material, check the head for flatness.

Place a straightedge across the gasket surface. Using feeler gauges, determine the clearance at the center of the straightedge and across the cylinder head at several points. Check along the centerline and diagonally on the head surface. If the warpage exceeds 0.003 in. (0.076mm) within a 6.0 in. (15.2cm) span, or 0.006 in. (0.152mm) over the total length of the head, the cylinder head must be resurfaced. After resurfacing the heads of a V-type engine, the intake manifold flange surface should be checked, and if necessary, milled proportionally to allow for the change in its mounting position.

CRACKS AND PHYSICAL DAMAGE

Generally, cracks are limited to the combustion chamber, however, it is not uncommon for the head to crack in a spark plug hole, port, outside of the head or in the valve spring/rocker arm area. The first area to inspect is always the hottest: the exhaust seat/port area.

A visual inspection should be performed, but just because you don't see a crack does not mean it is not there. Some more reliable methods for inspecting for cracks include Magnaflux®, a magnetic process or Zyglo®, a dye penetrant. Magnaflux® is used only on ferrous metal (cast iron) heads. Zyglo® uses a spray on fluorescent mixture along with a black light to reveal the cracks. It is strongly recommended to have your cylinder head checked professionally for cracks, especially if the engine was known to have overheated and/or leaked or consumed coolant. Contact a local shop for availability and pricing of these services.

Physical damage is usually very evident. For example, a broken mounting ear from dropping the head or a bent or broken stud and/or bolt. All of these defects should be fixed or, if unrepairable, the head should be replaced.

Camshaft and Followers

Inspect the camshaft(s) and followers as described earlier in this section.

REFINISHING & REPAIRING

Many of the procedures given for refinishing and repairing the cylinder head components must be performed by a machine shop. Certain steps, if the inspected part is not worn, can be performed yourself inexpensively. However, you spent a lot of time and effort so far, why risk trying to save a couple bucks if you might have to do it all over again?

Valves

Any valves that were not replaced should be refaced and the tips ground flat. Unless you have access to a valve grinding machine, this should be done by a machine shop. If the valves are in extremely good condition, as well as the valve seats and guides, they may be lapped in without performing machine work.

It is a recommended practice to lap the valves even after machine work has been performed and/or new valves have been purchased. This insures a positive seal between the valve and seat.

LAPPING THE VALVES

➡**Before lapping the valves to the seats, read the rest of the cylinder head section to insure that any related parts are in acceptable enough condition to continue.**

➡**Before any valve seat machining and/or lapping can be performed, the guides must be within factory recommended specifications.**

1. Invert the cylinder head.
2. Lightly lubricate the valve stems and insert them into the cylinder head in their numbered order.
3. Raise the valve from the seat and apply a small amount of fine lapping compound to the seat.
4. Moisten the suction head of a hand-lapping tool and attach it to the head of the valve.
5. Rotate the tool between the palms of both hands, changing the position of the valve on the valve seat and lifting the tool often to prevent grooving.
6. Lap the valve until a smooth, polished circle is evident on the valve and seat.
7. Remove the tool and the valve. Wipe away all traces of the grinding compound and store the valve to maintain its lapped location.

❋❋ WARNING

Do not get the valves out of order after they have been lapped. They must be put back with the same valve seat with which they were lapped.

Springs, Retainers and Valve Locks

There is no repair or refinishing possible with the springs, retainers and valve locks. If they are found to be worn or defective, they must be replaced with new (or known good) parts.

Cylinder Head

Most refinishing procedures dealing with the cylinder head must be performed by a machine shop. Read the sections below and review your inspection data to determine whether or not machining is necessary.

VALVE GUIDE

➡**If any machining or replacements are made to the valve guides, the seats must be machined.**

Unless the valve guides need machining or replacing, the only service to perform is to thoroughly clean them of any dirt or oil residue.

There are only two types of valve guides used on automobile engines: the replaceable-type (all aluminum heads) and the cast-in integral-type (most cast iron heads). There are four recommended methods for repairing worn guides.

- Knurling
- Inserts
- Reaming oversize
- Replacing

Knurling is a process in which metal is displaced and raised, thereby reducing clearance, giving a true center, and providing oil control. It is the least expensive way of repairing the valve guides. However, it is not necessarily the best, and in some cases, a knurled valve guide will not stand up for more than a short time. It requires a special knurlizer and precision reaming tools to obtain proper clearances. It would not be cost effective to purchase these tools, unless you plan on rebuilding several of the same cylinder head.

Installing a guide insert involves machining the guide to accept a bronze insert. One style is the coil-type which is installed into a threaded guide. Another is the thin-walled insert where the guide is reamed oversize to accept a split-sleeve insert. After the insert is installed, a special tool is then run through the guide to expand the insert, locking it to the guide. The insert is then reamed to the standard size for proper valve clearance.

Reaming for oversize valves restores normal clearances and provides a true valve seat. Most cast-in type guides can be reamed to accept an valve with an oversize stem. The cost factor for this can become quite high as you will need to purchase the reamer and new, oversize stem valves for all guides which were reamed. Oversizes are generally 0.003 to 0.030 in. (0.076 to 0.762mm), with 0.015 in. (0.381mm) being the most common.

To replace cast-in type valve guides, they must be drilled out, then reamed to accept replacement guides. This must be done on a fixture which will allow centering and leveling off of the original valve seat or guide, otherwise a serious guide-to-seat misalignment may occur making it impossible to properly machine the seat.

Replaceable-type guides are pressed into the cylinder head. A hammer and a stepped drift or punch may be used to install and remove the guides. Before removing the guides, measure the protrusion on the spring side of the head and record it for installation. Use the stepped drift to hammer out the old guide from the combustion chamber side of the head. When installing, determine whether or not the guide also seals a water jacket in the head, and if it does, use the recommended sealing agent. If there is no water jacket, grease the valve guide and its bore. Use the stepped drift, and hammer the new guide into the cylinder head from the spring side of the cylinder head. A stack of washers the same thickness as the measured protrusion may help the installation process.

VALVE SEATS

➡**Before any valve seat machining can be performed, the guides must be within factory recommended specifications.**

➡**If any machining or replacements were made to the valve guides, the seats must be machined.**

If the seats are in good condition, the valves can be lapped to the seats, and the cylinder head assembled. See the valves section for instructions on lapping.

If the valve seats are worn, cracked or damaged, they must be serviced by a machine shop. The valve seat must be perfectly centered to the valve guide, which requires very accurate machining.

CYLINDER HEAD SURFACE

If the cylinder head is warped, it must be machined flat. If the warpage is extremely severe, the head may need to be replaced. In some instances, it may be possible to straighten a warped head enough to allow machining. In either case, contact a professional machine shop for service.

➡**Any OHC cylinder head that shows excessive warpage should have the camshaft bearing journals align bored after the cylinder head has been resurfaced.**

✳✳ WARNING

Failure to align bore the camshaft bearing journals could result in severe engine damage including but not limited to: valve and piston damage, connecting rod damage, camshaft and/or crankshaft breakage.

CRACKS AND PHYSICAL DAMAGE

Certain cracks can be repaired in both cast iron and aluminum heads. For cast iron, a tapered threaded insert is installed along the length of the crack. Aluminum can also use the tapered inserts, however welding is the preferred method. Some physical damage can be repaired through brazing or welding. Contact a machine shop to get expert advice for your particular dilemma.

ASSEMBLY

The first step for any assembly job is to have a clean area in which to work. Next, thoroughly clean all of the parts and components that are to be assembled. Finally, place all of the components onto a suitable work space and, if necessary, arrange the parts to their respective positions.

5.0/5.8L Engines

1. Lightly lubricate the valve stems and insert all of the valves into the cylinder head. If possible, maintain their original locations.
2. If equipped, install any valve spring shims which were removed.
3. If equipped, install the new valve seals, keeping the following in mind:
   - If the valve seal presses over the guide, lightly lubricate the outer guide surfaces.
   - If the seal is an O-ring type, it is installed just after compressing the spring but before the valve locks.
4. Place the valve spring and retainer over the stem.
5. Position the spring compressor tool and compress the spring.
6. Assemble the valve locks to the stem.
7. Relieve the spring pressure slowly and insure that neither valve lock becomes dislodged by the retainer.
8. Remove the spring compressor tool.
9. Repeat Steps 2 through 8 until all of the springs have been installed.

4.6L Engine

♦ **See Figure 184**

To install the springs, retainers and valve locks on heads which have these components recessed into the camshaft follower's bore, you will need a small screwdriver-type tool, some clean white grease and a lot of patience. You will also need the C-clamp style spring compressor and the OHC tool used to disassemble the head.

1. Lightly lubricate the valve stems and insert all of the valves into the cylinder head. If possible, maintain their original locations.
2. If equipped, install any valve spring shims which were removed.
3. If equipped, install the new valve seals, keeping the following in mind:
   - If the valve seal presses over the guide, lightly lubricate the outer guide surfaces.
   - If the seal is an O-ring type, it is installed just after compressing the spring but before the valve locks.
4. Place the valve spring and retainer over the stem.
5. Position the spring compressor and the OHC tool, then compress the spring.
6. Using a small screwdriver as a spatula, fill the valve stem side of the lock with white grease. Use the excess grease on the screwdriver to fasten the lock to the driver.
7. Carefully install the valve lock, which is stuck to the end of the screwdriver, to the valve stem then press on it with the screwdriver until the grease squeezes out. The valve lock should now be stuck to the stem.
8. Repeat Steps 6 and 7 for the remaining valve lock.

Fig. 184 Once assembled, check the valve clearance and correct as needed

9. Relieve the spring pressure slowly and insure that neither valve lock becomes dislodged by the retainer.

10. Remove the spring compressor tool.

11. Repeat Steps 2 through 10 until all of the springs have been installed.

12. Install the followers, camshaft(s) and any other components that were removed for disassembly.

Engine Block

GENERAL INFORMATION

A thorough overhaul or rebuild of an engine block would include replacing the pistons, rings, bearings, timing belt/chain assembly and oil pump. For OHV engines also include a new camshaft and lifters. The block would then have the cylinders bored and honed oversize (or if using removable cylinder sleeves, new sleeves installed) and the crankshaft would be cut undersize to provide new wearing surfaces and perfect clearances. However, your particular engine may not have everything worn out. What if only the piston rings have worn out and the clearances on everything else are still within factory specifications? Well, you could just replace the rings and put it back together, but this would be a very rare example. Chances are, if one component in your engine is worn, other components are sure to follow, and soon. At the very least, you should always replace the rings, bearings and oil pump. This is what is commonly called a "freshen up".

Cylinder Ridge Removal

Because the top piston ring does not travel to the very top of the cylinder, a ridge is built up between the end of the travel and the top of the cylinder bore.

Pushing the piston and connecting rod assembly past the ridge can be difficult, and damage to the piston ring lands could occur. If the ridge is not removed before installing a new piston or not removed at all, piston ring breakage and piston damage may occur.

➡ It is always recommended that you remove any cylinder ridges before removing the piston and connecting rod assemblies. If you know that new pistons are going to be installed and the engine block will be bored oversize, you may be able to forego this step. However, some ridges may actually prevent the assemblies from being removed, necessitating its removal.

There are several different types of ridge reamers on the market, none of which are inexpensive. Unless a great deal of engine rebuilding is anticipated, borrow or rent a reamer.

1. Turn the crankshaft until the piston is at the bottom of its travel.
2. Cover the head of the piston with a rag.
3. Follow the tool manufacturers instructions and cut away the ridge, exercising extreme care to avoid cutting too deeply.

4. Remove the ridge reamer, the rag and as many of the cuttings as possible. Continue until all of the cylinder ridges have been removed.

DISASSEMBLY

◆ See Figures 185 and 186

The engine disassembly instructions following assume that you have the engine mounted on an engine stand. If not, it is easiest to disassemble the engine on a bench or the floor with it resting on the bell housing or transmission mounting surface. You must be able to access the connecting rod fasteners and turn the crankshaft during disassembly. Also, all engine covers (timing, front, side, oil pan, whatever) should have already been removed. Engines which are seized or locked up may not be able to be completely disassembled, and a core (salvage yard) engine should be purchased.

5.0/5.8L Engines

If not done during the cylinder head removal, remove the pushrods and lifters, keeping them in order for assembly. Remove the timing gears and/or timing chain assembly, then remove the oil pump drive assembly and withdraw the camshaft from the engine block. Remove the oil pick-up and pump assembly. If equipped, remove any balance or auxiliary shafts. If necessary, remove the cylinder ridge from the top of the bore. See the cylinder ridge removal procedure earlier in this section.

4.6L Engine

If not done during the cylinder head removal, remove the timing chain/belt and/or gear/sprocket assembly. Remove the oil pick-up and pump assembly and, if necessary, the pump drive. If equipped, remove any balance or auxiliary shafts. If necessary, remove the cylinder ridge from the top of the bore. See the cylinder ridge removal procedure earlier in this section.

All Engines

Rotate the engine over so that the crankshaft is exposed. Use a number punch or scribe and mark each connecting rod with its respective cylinder number. The cylinder closest to the front of the engine is always number 1. However, depending on the engine placement, the front of the engine could either be the flywheel or damper/pulley end. Generally the front of the engine faces the front of the vehicle. Use a number punch or scribe and also mark the main bearing caps from front to rear with the front most cap being number 1 (if there are five caps, mark them 1 through 5, front to rear).

✳✳ WARNING

Take special care when pushing the connecting rod up from the crankshaft because the sharp threads of the rod bolts/studs will

Fig. 185 Place rubber hose over the connecting rod studs to protect the crankshaft and cylinder bores from damage

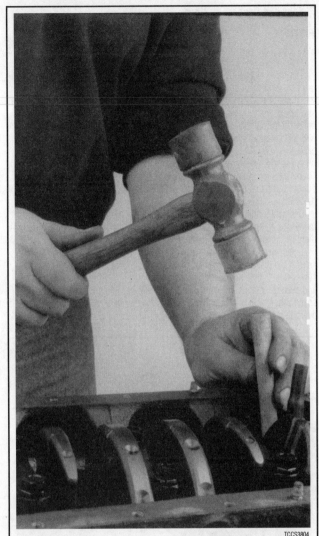

Fig. 186 Carefully tap the piston out of the bore using a wooden dowel

score the crankshaft journal. Insure that special plastic caps are installed over them, or cut two pieces of rubber hose to do the same.

Again, rotate the engine, this time to position the number one cylinder bore (head surface) up. Turn the crankshaft until the number one piston is at the bottom of its travel, this should allow the maximum access to its connecting rod. Remove the number one connecting rods fasteners and cap and place two lengths of rubber hose over the rod bolts/studs to protect the crankshaft from damage. Using a sturdy wooden dowel and a hammer, push the connecting rod up about 1 in. (25mm) from the crankshaft and remove the upper bearing insert. Continue pushing or tapping the connecting rod up until the piston rings are out of the cylinder bore. Remove the piston and rod by hand, put the upper half of the bearing insert back into the rod, install the cap with its bearing insert installed, and hand-tighten the cap fasteners. If the parts are kept in order in this manner, they will not get lost and you will be able to tell which bearings came form what cylinder if any problems are discovered and diagnosis is necessary. Remove all the other piston assemblies in the same manner. On V-style engines, remove all of the pistons from one bank, then reposition the engine with the other cylinder bank head surface up, and remove that banks piston assemblies.

The only remaining component in the engine block should now be the crankshaft. Loosen the main bearing caps evenly until the fasteners can be turned by hand, then remove them and the caps. Remove the crankshaft from the engine block. Thoroughly clean all of the components.

INSPECTION

Now that the engine block and all of its components are clean, it's time to inspect them for wear and/or damage. To accurately inspect them, you will need some specialized tools:
- Two or three separate micrometers to measure the pistons and crankshaft journals
- A dial indicator
- Telescoping gauges for the cylinder bores
- A rod alignment fixture to check for bent connecting rods

If you do not have access to the proper tools, you may want to bring the components to a shop that does.

Generally, you shouldn't expect cracks in the engine block or its components unless it was known to leak, consume or mix engine fluids, it was severely overheated, or there was evidence of bad bearings and/or crankshaft damage. A visual inspection should be performed on all of the components, but just because you don't see a crack does not mean it is not there. Some more reliable methods for inspecting for cracks include Magnaflux®, a magnetic process or Zyglo®, a dye penetrant. Magnaflux® is used only on ferrous metal (cast iron). Zyglo® uses a spray on fluorescent mixture along with a black light to reveal the cracks. It is strongly recommended to have your engine block checked professionally for cracks, especially if the engine was known to have overheated and/or leaked or consumed coolant. Contact a local shop for availability and pricing of these services.

Engine Block

ENGINE BLOCK BEARING ALIGNMENT

Remove the main bearing caps and, if still installed, the main bearing inserts. Inspect all of the main bearing saddles and caps for damage, burrs or high spots. If damage is found, and it is caused from a spun main bearing, the block will need to be align-bored or, if severe enough, replacement. Any burrs or high spots should be carefully removed with a metal file.

Place a straightedge on the bearing saddles, in the engine block, along the centerline of the crankshaft. If any clearance exists between the straightedge and the saddles, the block must be align-bored.

Align-boring consists of machining the main bearing saddles and caps by means of a flycutter that runs through the bearing saddles.

DECK FLATNESS

The top of the engine block where the cylinder head mounts is called the deck. Insure that the deck surface is clean of dirt, carbon deposits and old gasket material. Place a straightedge across the surface of the deck along its centerline and, using feeler gauges, check the clearance along several points. Repeat the checking procedure with the straightedge placed along both diagonals of the deck surface. If the reading exceeds 0.003 in. (0.076mm) within a 6.0 in. (15.2cm) span, or 0.006 in. (0.152mm) over the total length of the deck, it must be machined.

CYLINDER BORES

▶ See Figure 187

The cylinder bores house the pistons and are slightly larger than the pistons themselves. A common piston-to-bore clearance is 0.0015–0.0025 in. (0.0381mm–0.0635mm). Inspect and measure the cylinder bores. The bore should be checked for out-of-roundness, taper and size. The results of this inspection will determine whether the cylinder can be used in its existing size and condition, or a rebore to the next oversize is required (or in the case of removable sleeves, have replacements installed).

The amount of cylinder wall wear is always greater at the top of the cylinder than at the bottom. This wear is known as taper. Any cylinder that has a taper of 0.0012 in. (0.305mm) or more, must be rebored. Measurements are taken at a number of positions in each cylinder: at the top, middle and bottom and at two points at each position; that is, at a point 90 degrees from the crankshaft centerline, as well as a point parallel to the crankshaft centerline. The measurements are made with either a special dial indicator or a telescopic gauge and micrometer. If the necessary precision tools to check the bore are not available, take the block to a machine shop and have them mike it. Also if you don't have the tools to check the cylinder bores, chances are you will not have the necessary devices

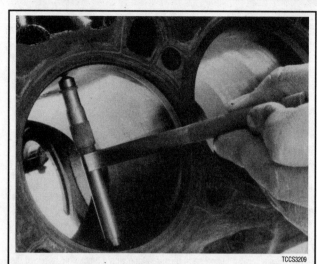

Fig. 187 Use a telescoping gauge to measure the cylinder bore diameter—take several readings within the same bore

to check the pistons, connecting rods and crankshaft. Take these components with you and save yourself an extra trip.

For our procedures, we will use a telescopic gauge and a micrometer. You will need one of each, with a measuring range which covers your cylinder bore size.

1. Position the telescopic gauge in the cylinder bore, loosen the gauges lock and allow it to expand.

➡**Your first two readings will be at the top of the cylinder bore, then proceed to the middle and finally the bottom, making a total of six measurements.**

2. Hold the gauge square in the bore, 90 degrees from the crankshaft centerline, and gently tighten the lock. Tilt the gauge back to remove it from the bore.

3. Measure the gauge with the micrometer and record the reading.

4. Again, hold the gauge square in the bore, this time parallel to the crankshaft centerline, and gently tighten the lock. Again, you will tilt the gauge back to remove it from the bore.

5. Measure the gauge with the micrometer and record this reading. The difference between these two readings is the out-of-round measurement of the cylinder.

6. Repeat steps 1 through 5, each time going to the next lower position, until you reach the bottom of the cylinder. Then go to the next cylinder, and continue until all of the cylinders have been measured.

The difference between these measurements will tell you all about the wear in your cylinders. The measurements which were taken 90 degrees from the crankshaft centerline will always reflect the most wear. That is because at this position is where the engine power presses the piston against the cylinder bore the hardest. This is known as thrust wear. Take your top, 90 degree measurement and compare it to your bottom, 90 degree measurement. The difference between them is the taper. When you measure your pistons, you will compare these readings to your piston sizes and determine piston-to-wall clearance.

Crankshaft

Inspect the crankshaft for visible signs of wear or damage. All of the journals should be perfectly round and smooth. Slight scores are normal for a used crankshaft, but you should hardly feel them with your fingernail. When measuring the crankshaft with a micrometer, you will take readings at the front and rear of each journal, then turn the micrometer 90 degrees and take two more readings, front and rear. The difference between the front-to-rear readings is the journal taper and the first-to-90 degree reading is the out-of-round measurement. Generally, there should be no taper or out-of-roundness found, however, up to 0.0005 in. (0.0127mm) for either can be overlooked. Also, the readings should fall within the factory specifications for journal diameters.

If the crankshaft journals fall within specifications, it is recommended that it be polished before being returned to service. Polishing the crankshaft insures that any minor burrs or high spots are smoothed, thereby reducing the chance of scoring the new bearings.

Pistons and Connecting Rods

PISTONS

◆ See Figure 188

The piston should be visually inspected for any signs of cracking or burning (caused by hot spots or detonation), and scuffing or excessive wear on the skirts. The wrist pin attaches the piston to the connecting rod. The piston should move freely on the wrist pin, both sliding and pivoting. Grasp the connecting rod securely, or mount it in a vise, and try to rock the piston back and forth along the centerline of the wrist pin. There should not be any excessive play evident between the piston and the pin. If there are C-clips retaining the pin in the piston then you have wrist pin bushings in the rods. There should not be any excessive play between the wrist pin and the rod bushing. Normal clearance for the wrist pin is approx. 0.001–0.002 in. (0.025mm–0.051mm).

Use a micrometer and measure the diameter of the piston, perpendicular to the wrist pin, on the skirt. Compare the reading to its original cylinder measurement obtained earlier. The difference between the two readings is the piston-to-wall clearance. If the clearance is within specifications, the piston may be used as is. If the piston is out of specification, but the bore is not, you will need a new piston. If both are out of specification, you will need the cylinder rebored and oversize pistons installed. Generally if two or more pistons/bores are out of specification, it is best to rebore the entire block and purchase a complete set of oversize pistons.

Fig. 188 Measure the piston's outer diameter, perpendicular to the wrist pin, with a micrometer

CONNECTING ROD

You should have the connecting rod checked for straightness at a machine shop. If the connecting rod is bent, it will unevenly wear the bearing and piston, as well as place greater stress on these components. Any bent or twisted connecting rods must be replaced. If the rods are straight and the wrist pin clearance is within specifications, then only the bearing end of the rod need be checked. Place the connecting rod into a vice, with the bearing inserts in place, install the cap to the rod and torque the fasteners to specifications. Use a telescoping gauge and carefully measure the inside diameter of the bearings. Compare this reading to the rods original crankshaft journal diameter measurement. The difference is the oil clearance. If the oil clearance is not within specifications, install new bearings in the rod and take another measurement. If the clearance is still out of specifications, and the crankshaft is not, the rod will need to be reconditioned by a machine shop.

➡**You can also use Plastigage® to check the bearing clearances. The assembling section has complete instructions on its use.**

Camshaft

Inspect the camshaft and lifters/followers as described earlier in this section.

Bearings

All of the engine bearings should be visually inspected for wear and/or damage. The bearing should look evenly worn all around with no deep scores or pits. If the bearing is severely worn, scored, pitted or heat blued, then the bearing, and the components that use it, should be brought to a machine shop for inspection. Full-circle bearings (used on most camshafts, auxiliary shafts, balance shafts, etc.) require specialized tools for removal and installation, and should be brought to a machine shop for service.

Oil Pump

➡**The oil pump is responsible for providing constant lubrication to the whole engine and so it is recommended that a new oil pump be installed when rebuilding the engine.**

Completely disassemble the oil pump and thoroughly clean all of the components. Inspect the oil pump gears and housing for wear and/or damage. Insure that the pressure relief valve operates properly and there is no binding or sticking due to varnish or debris. If all of the parts are in proper working condition, lubricate the gears and relief valve, and assemble the pump.

REFINISHING

◆ **See Figure 189**

Almost all engine block refinishing must be performed by a machine shop. If the cylinders are not to be rebored, then the cylinder glaze can be removed with a ball hone. When removing cylinder glaze with a ball hone, use a light or penetrating type oil to lubricate the hone. Do not allow the hone to run dry as this may cause excessive scoring of the cylinder bores and wear on the hone. If new pistons are required, they will need to be installed to the connecting rods. This should be performed by a machine shop as the pistons must be installed in the correct relationship to the rod or engine damage can occur.

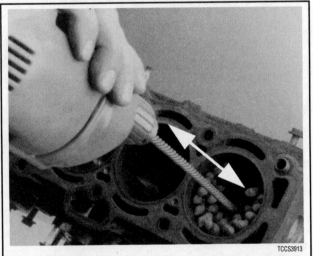

Fig. 189 Use a ball type cylinder hone to remove any glaze and provide a new surface for seating the piston rings

Pistons and Connecting Rods

◆ **See Figure 190**

Only pistons with the wrist pin retained by C-clips are serviceable by the home-mechanic. Press fit pistons require special presses and/or heaters to remove/install the connecting rod and should only be performed by a machine shop.

All pistons will have a mark indicating the direction to the front of the engine and the must be installed into the engine in that manner. Usually it is a notch or arrow on the top of the piston, or it may be the letter F cast or stamped into the piston.

Fig. 190 Most pistons are marked to indicate positioning in the engine (usually a mark means the side facing the front)

C-CLIP TYPE PISTONS

1. Note the location of the forward mark on the piston and mark the connecting rod in relation.
2. Remove the C-clips from the piston and withdraw the wrist pin.

➡**Varnish build-up or C-clip groove burrs may increase the difficulty of removing the wrist pin. If necessary, use a punch or drift to carefully tap the wrist pin out.**

3. Insure that the wrist pin bushing in the connecting rod is usable, and lubricate it with assembly lube.
4. Remove the wrist pin from the new piston and lubricate the pin bores on the piston.
5. Align the forward marks on the piston and the connecting rod and install the wrist pin.
6. The new C-clips will have a flat and a rounded side to them. Install both C-clips with the flat side facing out.
7. Repeat all of the steps for each piston being replaced.

ASSEMBLY

Before you begin assembling the engine, first give yourself a clean, dirt free work area. Next, clean every engine component again. The key to a good assembly is cleanliness.

Mount the engine block into the engine stand and wash it one last time using water and detergent (dishwashing detergent works well). While washing it, scrub the cylinder bores with a soft bristle brush and thoroughly clean all of the oil passages. Completely dry the engine and spray the entire assembly down with an anti-rust solution such as WD-40® or similar product. Take a clean lint-free rag and wipe up any excess anti-rust solution from the bores, bearing saddles, etc. Repeat the final cleaning process on the crankshaft. Replace any freeze or oil galley plugs which were removed during disassembly.

Crankshaft

◆ **See Figures 191, 192, 193 and 194**

1. Remove the main bearing inserts from the block and bearing caps.
2. If the crankshaft main bearing journals have been refinished to a definite undersize, install the correct undersize bearing. Be sure that the bearing inserts and bearing bores are clean. Foreign material under inserts will distort bearing and cause failure.
3. Place the upper main bearing inserts in bores with tang in slot.

➡**The oil holes in the bearing inserts must be aligned with the oil holes in the cylinder block.**

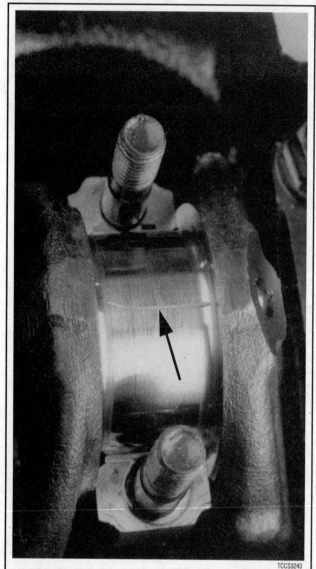

Fig. 191 Apply a strip of gauging material to the bearing journal, then install and torque the cap

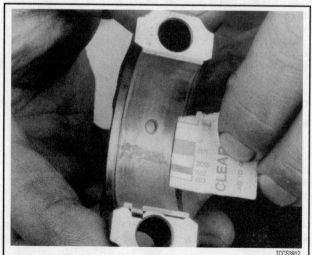

Fig. 192 After the cap is removed again, use the scale supplied with the gauging material to check the clearance

Fig. 193 A dial gauge may be used to check crankshaft end-play

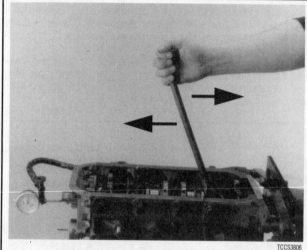

Fig. 194 Carefully pry the crankshaft back and forth while reading the dial gauge for end-play

4. Install the lower main bearing inserts in bearing caps.

5. Clean the mating surfaces of block and rear main bearing cap.

6. Carefully lower the crankshaft into place. Be careful not to damage bearing surfaces.

7. Check the clearance of each main bearing by using the following procedure:

   a. Place a piece of Plastigage® or its equivalent, on bearing surface across full width of bearing cap and about ¼ in. off center.

   b. Install cap and tighten bolts to specifications. Do not turn crankshaft while Plastigage® is in place.

   c. Remove the cap. Using the supplied Plastigage® scale, check width of Plastigage® at widest point to get maximum clearance. Difference between readings is taper of journal.

   d. If clearance exceeds specified limits, try a 0.001 in. or 0.002 in. undersize bearing in combination with the standard bearing. Bearing clearance must be within specified limits. If standard and 0.002 in. undersize bearing does not bring clearance within desired limits, refinish crankshaft journal, then install undersize bearings.

8. Install the rear main seal.

9. After the bearings have been fitted, apply a light coat of engine oil to the journals and bearings. Install the rear main bearing cap. Install all bearing caps except the thrust bearing cap. Be sure that main bearing caps are installed in original locations. Tighten the bearing cap bolts to specifications.

10. Install the thrust bearing cap with bolts finger-tight.

11. Pry the crankshaft forward against the thrust surface of upper half of bearing.

12. Hold the crankshaft forward and pry the thrust bearing cap to the rear. This aligns the thrust surfaces of both halves of the bearing.

13. Retain the forward pressure on the crankshaft. Tighten the cap bolts to specifications.

14. Measure the crankshaft end-play as follows:

    a. Mount a dial gauge to the engine block and position the tip of the gauge to read from the crankshaft end.

    b. Carefully pry the crankshaft toward the rear of the engine and hold it there while you zero the gauge.

    c. Carefully pry the crankshaft toward the front of the engine and read the gauge.

    d. Confirm that the reading is within specifications. If not, install a new thrust bearing and repeat the procedure. If the reading is still out of specifications with a new bearing, have a machine shop inspect the thrust surfaces of the crankshaft, and if possible, repair it.

15. Rotate the crankshaft so as to position the first rod journal to the bottom of its stroke.

Pistons and Connecting Rods

▶ **See Figures 195, 196, 197 and 198**

1. Before installing the piston/connecting rod assembly, oil the pistons, piston rings and the cylinder walls with light engine oil. Install connecting rod bolt protectors or rubber hose onto the connecting rod bolts/studs. Also perform the following:

    a. Select the proper ring set for the size cylinder bore.

    b. Position the ring in the bore in which it is going to be used.

Fig. 195 Checking the piston ring-to-ring groove side clearance using the ring and a feeler gauge

    c. Push the ring down into the bore area where normal ring wear is not encountered.

    d. Use the head of the piston to position the ring in the bore so that the ring is square with the cylinder wall. Use caution to avoid damage to the ring or cylinder bore.

    e. Measure the gap between the ends of the ring with a feeler gauge. Ring gap in a worn cylinder is normally greater than specification. If the ring gap is greater than the specified limits, try an oversize ring set.

    f. Check the ring side clearance of the compression rings with a feeler gauge inserted between the ring and its lower land according to specification. The gauge should slide freely around the entire ring circumference without binding. Any wear that occurs will form a step at the inner portion of the lower land. If the lower lands have high steps, the piston should be replaced.

2. Unless new pistons are installed, be sure to install the pistons in the cylinders from which they were removed. The numbers on the connecting rod and bearing cap must be on the same side when installed in the cylinder bore. If a connecting rod is ever transposed from one engine or cylinder to another, new bearings should be fitted and the connecting rod should be numbered to correspond with the new cylinder number. The notch on the piston head goes toward the front of the engine.

3. Install all of the rod bearing inserts into the rods and caps.

4. Install the rings to the pistons. Install the oil control ring first, then the second compression ring and finally the top compression ring. Use a piston ring expander tool to aid in installation and to help reduce the chance of breakage.

5. Make sure the ring gaps are properly spaced around the circumference of the piston. Fit a piston ring compressor around the piston and slide the piston and connecting rod assembly down into the cylinder bore, pushing it in with the wooden hammer handle. Push the piston down until it is only slightly below the top of the cylinder bore. Guide the connecting rod onto the crankshaft bearing journal carefully, to avoid damaging the crankshaft.

6. Check the bearing clearance of all the rod bearings, fitting them to the crankshaft bearing journals. Follow the procedure in the crankshaft installation above.

7. After the bearings have been fitted, apply a light coating of assembly oil to the journals and bearings.

8. Turn the crankshaft until the appropriate bearing journal is at the bottom of its stroke, then push the piston assembly all the way down until the connecting rod bearing seats on the crankshaft journal. Be careful not to allow the bearing cap screws to strike the crankshaft bearing journals and damage them.

9. After the piston and connecting rod assemblies have been installed, check the connecting rod side clearance on each crankshaft journal.

10. Prime and install the oil pump and the oil pump intake tube.

5.0/5.8L Engines

CAMSHAFT, LIFTERS AND TIMING ASSEMBLY

1. Install the camshaft.
2. Install the lifters/followers into their bores.
3. Install the timing gears/chain assembly.

CYLINDER HEAD(S)

1. Install the cylinder head(s) using new gaskets.
2. Assemble the rest of the valve train (pushrods and rocker arms and/or shafts).

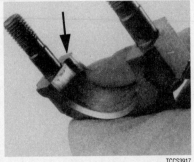

Fig. 196 The notch on the side of the bearing cap matches the tang on the bearing insert

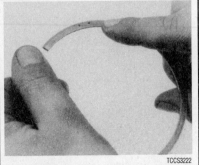

Fig. 197 Most rings are marked to show which side of the ring should face up when installed to the piston

Fig. 198 Install the piston and rod assembly into the block using a ring compressor and the handle of a hammer

4.6L Engine

CYLINDER HEAD(S)

1. Install the cylinder head(s) using new gaskets.
2. Install the timing sprockets/gears and the belt/chain assemblies.

Engine Covers and Components

Install the timing cover(s) and oil pan. Refer to your notes and drawings made prior to disassembly and install all of the components that were removed. Install the engine into the vehicle.

Engine Start-up and Break-in

STARTING THE ENGINE

Now that the engine is installed and every wire and hose is properly connected, go back and double check that all coolant and vacuum hoses are connected. Check that your oil drain plug is installed and properly tightened. If not already done, install a new oil filter onto the engine. Fill the crankcase with the proper amount and grade of engine oil. Fill the cooling system with a 50/50 mixture of coolant/water.

1. Connect the vehicle battery.
2. Start the engine. Keep your eye on your oil pressure indicator; if it does not indicate oil pressure within 10 seconds of starting, turn the vehicle off.

✳✳ WARNING

Damage to the engine can result if it is allowed to run with no oil pressure. Check the engine oil level to make sure that it is full.

Check for any leaks and if found, repair the leaks before continuing. If there is still no indication of oil pressure, you may need to prime the system.

3. Confirm that there are no fluid leaks (oil or other).
4. Allow the engine to reach normal operating temperature (the upper radiator hose will be hot to the touch).
5. At this point you can perform any necessary checks or adjustments, such as checking the ignition timing.
6. Install any remaining components or body panels which were removed.

BREAKING IT IN

Make the first miles on the new engine, easy ones. Vary the speed but do not accelerate hard. Most importantly, do not lug the engine, and avoid sustained high speeds until at least 100 miles. Check the engine oil and coolant levels frequently. Expect the engine to use a little oil until the rings seat. Change the oil and filter at 500 miles, 1500 miles, then every 3000 miles past that.

KEEP IT MAINTAINED

Now that you have just gone through all of that hard work, keep yourself from doing it all over again by thoroughly maintaining it. Not that you may not have maintained it before, heck you could have had one to two hundred thousand miles on it before doing this. However, you may have bought the vehicle used, and the previous owner did not keep up on maintenance. Which is why you just went through all of that hard work. See?

TORQUE SPECIFICATIONS

Components	English	Metric
Belt driven engine fan		
4.6L engine		
Fan-to-fan clutch bolts	15-20 ft. lbs.	20-27 Nm
Fan clutch shaft-to-water pump	37-46 ft. lbs.	50-62 Nm
5.0/5.8L engines		
Fan-to-fan clutch bolts	12-18 ft. lbs.	16-25 Nm
Fan clutch shaft-to-water pump	15-22 ft. lbs.	20-30 Nm
Camshaft		
4.6L engine		
Timing gear retaining bolt	81-95 ft. lbs.	110-130 Nm
Bearing caps	①	①
5.0/5.8L engines		
Thrust plate bolts	9-12 ft. lbs.	12-16 Nm
Crankshaft damper retaining bolt		
4.6L engine	114-121 ft. lbs.	155-165 Nm
5.0/5.8L engines	70-90 ft. lbs.	95-122 Nm
Cylinder head bolts		
All engines	①	①
EGR tube-to-valve/manifold nut	26-33 ft. lbs.	35-45 Nm
EGR valve-to-manifold bolts	15-22 ft. lbs.	20-30 Nm
Electric cooling fan retaining screws	27-53 inch lbs.	3-6 Nm
Engine mounts		
4.6L engine	15-22 ft. lbs.	20-30 Nm
5.0/5.8L engines		
Through-bolts	80 ft. lbs.	108 Nm
Nuts	70 ft. lbs.	95 Nm
Engine-to-transmission retaining bolts		
4.6L engine	30-44 ft. lbs.	40-60 Nm
5.0/5.8L engines	50 ft. lbs.	68 Nm
Exhaust manifold retaining bolts		
4.6L engine	18-24 ft. lbs.	24-32 Nm
Exhaust manifold-to-exhaust pipe/catalytic converter bolts		
All engines	20-30 ft. lbs.	27-41 Nm
Flywheel/flexplate retaining bolts		
4.6L engine	54-64 ft. lbs.	73-87 Nm
5.0/5.8L engines	75-85 ft. lbs.	103-115 Nm
Intake manifold retaining bolts		
4.6L engine		
Lower intake-to-upper intake	①	①
Upper intake-to-engine	①	①
5.0L engine		
Lower intake	23-25 ft. lbs.	31-34 Nm
Upper intake	12-18 ft. lbs.	16-25 Nm
5.8L engine	23-25 ft. lbs.	31-34 Nm
Oil pan retaining bolts		
4.6L engine	①	①
5.0/5.8L engines	7-10 ft. lbs.	9-14 Nm
Oil pump pickup tube and screen retaining bolts		
4.6L engine	6-9 ft. lbs.	8-12 Nm
5.0/5.8L engines	12-18 ft. lbs.	16-25 Nm

89603C09

TORQUE SPECIFICATIONS

Components	English	Metric
Oil pump retaining bolts		
4.6L engine	6-9 ft. lbs.	8-12 Nm
Oil pump screen and cover spacer bolts	15-22 ft. lbs.	20-30 Nm
5.0/5.8L engines	22-32 ft. lbs.	30-43 Nm
Rocker arm retaining bolts		
5.0/5.8L engines	18-25 ft. lbs.	25-34 Nm
Thermostat housing retaining bolts		
4.6L engine	15-22 ft. lbs.	20-30 Nm
5.0/5.8L engines	12-18 ft. lbs.	16-24 Nm
Timing chain guide retaining bolts		
4.6L engine	71-106 inch lbs.	8-12 Nm
Timing chain tensioner retaining bolts		
4.6L engine	15-22 ft. lbs.	20-30 Nm
Timing cover retaining bolts		
4.6L engine	①	①
5.0/5.8L engines	9-11 ft. lbs.	12-15 Nm
Oil pan-to-timing cover retaining bolts	15-18 ft. lbs.	20-24 Nm
Timing cover-to-engine block retaining bolts		
Torque converter retaining nuts		
4.6L engine	22-25 ft. lbs.	20-30 Nm
5.0/5.8L engines	30 ft. lbs.	41 Nm
Valve cover retaining bolts		
4.6L engine	6-9 ft. lbs.	8-12 Nm
5.0L engine	10-13 ft. lbs.	14-18 Nm
5.8L engine		
1989-90 Models	3-5 ft. lbs.	4-7 Nm
1991 Models	10-13 ft. lbs.	14-18 Nm
Water pump bolts		
4.6L engine	15-22 ft. lbs.	20-30 Nm
5.0/5.8L engines	18 ft. lbs.	25 Nm
Water pump pulley-to-water pump bolts		
4.6L engine	15-22 ft. lbs.	20-30 Nm
5.0/5.8L engines	12-18 ft. lbs.	16-25 Nm

① Refer to procedure for specific directions on tightening torque/sequence

89603C10

USING A VACUUM GAUGE

White needle = steady needle   *Dark needle = drifting needle*

The vacuum gauge is one of the most useful and easy-to-use diagnostic tools. It is inexpensive, easy to hook up, and provides valuable information about the condition of your engine.

Indication: Normal engine in good condition

Gauge reading: Steady, from 17–22 in./Hg.

Indication: Sticking valve or ignition miss

Gauge reading: Needle fluctuates from 15–20 in./Hg. at idle

Indication: Late ignition or valve timing, low compression, stuck throttle valve, leaking carburetor or manifold gasket.

Gauge reading: Low (15–20 in./Hg.) but steady

Indication: Improper carburetor adjustment, or minor intake leak at carburetor or manifold

NOTE: Bad fuel injector O-rings may also cause this reading.

Gauge reading: Drifting needle

Indication: Weak valve springs, worn valve stem guides, or leaky cylinder head gasket (vibrating excessively at all speeds).

NOTE: A plugged catalytic converter may also cause this reading.

Gauge reading: Needle fluctuates as engine speed increases

Indication: Burnt valve or improper valve clearance. The needle will drop when the defective valve operates.

Gauge reading: Steady needle, but drops regularly

Indication: Choked muffler or obstruction in system. Speed up the engine. Choked muffler will exhibit a slow drop of vacuum to zero.

Gauge reading: Gradual drop in reading at idle

Indication: Worn valve guides

Gauge reading: Needle vibrates excessively at idle, but steadies as engine speed increases

TCCS3C01

4

DRIVEABILITY AND EMISSION CONTROLS

AIR POLLUTION

The earth's atmosphere, at or near sea level, consists approximately of 78 percent nitrogen, 21 percent oxygen and 1 percent other gases. If it were possible to remain in this state, 100 percent clean air would result. However, many varied sources allow other gases and particulates to mix with the clean air, causing our atmosphere to become unclean or polluted.

Some of these pollutants are visible while others are invisible, with each having the capability of causing distress to the eyes, ears, throat, skin and respiratory system. Should these pollutants become concentrated in a specific area and under certain conditions, death could result due to the displacement or chemical change of the oxygen content in the air. These pollutants can also cause great damage to the environment and to the many man made objects that are exposed to the elements.

To better understand the causes of air pollution, the pollutants can be categorized into 3 separate types, natural, industrial and automotive.

Natural Pollutants

Natural pollution has been present on earth since before man appeared and continues to be a factor when discussing air pollution, although it causes only a small percentage of the overall pollution problem. It is the direct result of decaying organic matter, wind born smoke and particulates from such natural events as plain and forest fires (ignited by heat or lightning), volcanic ash, sand and dust which can spread over a large area of the countryside.

Such a phenomenon of natural pollution has been seen in the form of volcanic eruptions, with the resulting plume of smoke, steam and volcanic ash blotting out the sun's rays as it spreads and rises higher into the atmosphere. As it travels into the atmosphere the upper air currents catch and carry the smoke and ash, while condensing the steam back into water vapor. As the water vapor, smoke and ash travel on their journey, the smoke dissipates into the atmosphere while the ash and moisture settle back to earth in a trail hundreds of miles long. In some cases, lives are lost and millions of dollars of property damage result.

Industrial Pollutants

Industrial pollution is caused primarily by industrial processes, the burning of coal, oil and natural gas, which in turn produce smoke and fumes. Because the burning fuels contain large amounts of sulfur, the principal ingredients of smoke and fumes are sulfur dioxide and particulate matter. This type of pollutant occurs most severely during still, damp and cool weather, such as at night. Even in its less severe form, this pollutant is not confined to just cities. Because of air movements, the pollutants move for miles over the surrounding countryside, leaving in its path a barren and unhealthy environment for all living things.

Working with Federal, State and Local mandated regulations and by carefully monitoring emissions, big business has greatly reduced the amount of pollutant introduced from its industrial sources, striving to obtain an acceptable level. Because of the mandated industrial emission clean up, many land areas and streams in and around the cities that were formerly barren of vegetation and life, have now begun to move back in the direction of nature's intended balance.

Automotive Pollutants

The third major source of air pollution is automotive emissions. The emissions from the internal combustion engines were not an appreciable problem years ago because of the small number of registered vehicles and the nation's small highway system. However, during the early 1950's, the trend of the American people was to move from the cities to the surrounding suburbs. This caused an immediate problem in transportation because the majority of suburbs were not afforded mass transit conveniences. This lack of transportation created an attractive market for the automobile manufacturers, which resulted in a dramatic increase in the number of vehicles produced and sold, along with a marked increase in highway construction between cities and the suburbs. Multi-vehicle families emerged with a growing emphasis placed on an individual vehicle per family member. As the increase in vehicle ownership and usage occurred, so did pollutant levels in and around the cities, as suburbanites drove daily to their businesses and employment, returning at the end of the day to their homes in the suburbs.

It was noted that a smoke and fog type haze was being formed and at times, remained in suspension over the cities, taking time to dissipate. At first this "smog," derived from the words "smoke" and "fog," was thought to result from industrial pollution but it was determined that automobile emissions shared the

blame. It was discovered that when normal automobile emissions were exposed to sunlight for a period of time, complex chemical reactions would take place.

It is now known that smog is a photochemical layer which develops when certain oxides of nitrogen (NOx) and unburned hydrocarbons (HC) from automobile emissions are exposed to sunlight. Pollution was more severe when smog would become stagnant over an area in which a warm layer of air settled over the top of the cooler air mass, trapping and holding the cooler mass at ground level. The trapped cooler air would keep the emissions from being dispersed and diluted through normal air flows. This type of air stagnation was given the name "Temperature Inversion."

TEMPERATURE INVERSION

In normal weather situations, surface air is warmed by heat radiating from the earth's surface and the sun's rays. This causes it to rise upward, into the atmosphere. Upon rising it will cool through a convection type heat exchange with the cooler upper air. As warm air rises, the surface pollutants are carried upward and dissipated into the atmosphere.

When a temperature inversion occurs, we find the higher air is no longer cooler, but is warmer than the surface air, causing the cooler surface air to become trapped. This warm air blanket can extend from above ground level to a few hundred or even a few thousand feet into the air. As the surface air is trapped, so are the pollutants, causing a severe smog condition. Should this stagnant air mass extend to a few thousand feet high, enough air movement with the inversion takes place to allow the smog layer to rise above ground level but the pollutants still cannot dissipate.

This inversion can remain for days over an area, with the smog level only rising or lowering from ground level to a few hundred feet high. Meanwhile, the pollutant levels increase, causing eye irritation, respiratory problems, reduced visibility, plant damage and in some cases, even disease. This inversion phenomenon was first noted in the Los Angeles, California area. The city lies in terrain resembling a basin and with certain weather conditions, a cold air mass is held in the basin while a warmer air mass covers it like a lid.

Because this type of condition was first documented as prevalent in the Los Angeles area, this type of trapped pollution was named Los Angeles Smog, although it occurs in other areas where a large concentration of automobiles are used and the air remains stagnant for any length of time.

HEAT TRANSFER

Consider the internal combustion engine as a machine in which raw materials must be placed so a finished product comes out. As in any machine operation, a certain amount of wasted material is formed. When we relate this to the internal combustion engine, we find that through the input of air and fuel, we obtain power during the combustion process to drive the vehicle. The by-product or waste of this power is, in part, heat and exhaust gases with which we must dispose.

The heat from the combustion process can rise to over 4000°F (2204°C). The dissipation of this heat is controlled by a ram air effect, the use of cooling fans to cause air flow and a liquid coolant solution surrounding the combustion area to transfer the heat of combustion through the cylinder walls and into the coolant. The coolant is then directed to a thin-finned, multi-tubed radiator, from which the excess heat is transferred to the atmosphere by 1 of the 3 heat transfer methods, conduction, convection or radiation.

The cooling of the combustion area is an important part in the control of exhaust emissions. To understand the behavior of the combustion and transfer of its heat, consider the air/fuel charge. It is ignited and the flame front burns progressively across the combustion chamber until the burning charge reaches the cylinder walls. Some of the fuel in contact with the walls is not hot enough to burn, thereby snuffing out or quenching the combustion process. This leaves unburned fuel in the combustion chamber. This unburned fuel is then forced out of the cylinder and into the exhaust system, along with the exhaust gases.

Many attempts have been made to minimize the amount of unburned fuel in the combustion chambers due to quenching, by increasing the coolant temperature and lessening the contact area of the coolant around the combustion area. However, design limitations within the combustion chambers prevent the complete burning of the air/fuel charge, so a certain amount of the unburned fuel is still expelled into the exhaust system, regardless of modifications to the engine.

AUTOMOTIVE EMISSIONS

Before emission controls were mandated on internal combustion engines, other sources of engine pollutants were discovered along with the exhaust emissions. It was determined that engine combustion exhaust produced approximately 60 percent of the total emission pollutants, fuel evaporation from the fuel tank and carburetor vents produced 20 percent, with the final 20 percent being produced through the crankcase as a by-product of the combustion process.

Exhaust Gases

The exhaust gases emitted into the atmosphere are a combination of burned and unburned fuel. To understand the exhaust emission and its composition, we must review some basic chemistry.

When the air/fuel mixture is introduced into the engine, we are mixing air, composed of nitrogen (78 percent), oxygen (21 percent) and other gases (1 percent) with the fuel, which is 100 percent hydrocarbons (HC), in a semi-controlled ratio. As the combustion process is accomplished, power is produced to move the vehicle while the heat of combustion is transferred to the cooling system. The exhaust gases are then composed of nitrogen, a diatomic gas (N_2), the same as was introduced in the engine, carbon dioxide (CO_2), the same gas that is used in beverage carbonation, and water vapor (H_2O). The nitrogen (N_2), for the most part, passes through the engine unchanged, while the oxygen (O_2) reacts (burns) with the hydrocarbons (HC) and produces the carbon dioxide (CO_2) and the water vapors (H_2O). If this chemical process would be the only process to take place, the exhaust emissions would be harmless. However, during the combustion process, other compounds are formed which are considered dangerous. These pollutants are hydrocarbons (HC), carbon monoxide (CO), oxides of nitrogen (NOx) oxides of sulfur (SOx) and engine particulates.

HYDROCARBONS

Hydrocarbons (HC) are essentially fuel which was not burned during the combustion process or which has escaped into the atmosphere through fuel evaporation. The main sources of incomplete combustion are rich air/fuel mixtures, low engine temperatures and improper spark timing. The main sources of hydrocarbon emission through fuel evaporation on most vehicles used to be the vehicle's fuel tank and carburetor float bowl.

To reduce combustion hydrocarbon emission, engine modifications were made to minimize dead space and surface area in the combustion chamber. In addition, the air/fuel mixture was made more lean through the improved control which feedback carburetion and fuel injection offers and by the addition of external controls to aid in further combustion of the hydrocarbons outside the engine. Two such methods were the addition of air injection systems, to inject fresh air into the exhaust manifolds and the installation of catalytic converters, units that are able to burn traces of hydrocarbons without affecting the internal combustion process or fuel economy.

To control hydrocarbon emissions through fuel evaporation, modifications were made to the fuel tank to allow storage of the fuel vapors during periods of engine shut-down. Modifications were also made to the air intake system so that at specific times during engine operation, these vapors may be purged and burned by blending them with the air/fuel mixture.

CARBON MONOXIDE

Carbon monoxide is formed when not enough oxygen is present during the combustion process to convert carbon (C) to carbon dioxide (CO_2). An increase in the carbon monoxide (CO) emission is normally accompanied by an increase in the hydrocarbon (HC) emission because of the lack of oxygen to completely burn all of the fuel mixture.

Carbon monoxide (CO) also increases the rate at which the photo chemical smog is formed by speeding up the conversion of nitric oxide (NO) to nitrogen dioxide (NO_2). To accomplish this, carbon monoxide (CO) combines with oxygen (O_2) and nitric oxide (NO) to produce carbon dioxide (CO_2) and nitrogen dioxide (NO_2). ($CO + O_2 + NO = CO_2 + NO_2$).

The dangers of carbon monoxide, which is an odorless and colorless toxic gas are many. When carbon monoxide is inhaled into the lungs and passed into the blood stream, oxygen is replaced by the carbon monoxide in the red blood cells, causing a reduction in the amount of oxygen supplied to the many parts of the body. This lack of oxygen causes headaches, lack of coordination, reduced mental alertness and, should the carbon monoxide concentration be high enough, death could result.

NITROGEN

Normally, nitrogen is an inert gas. When heated to approximately 2500°F (1371°C) through the combustion process, this gas becomes active and causes an increase in the nitric oxide (NO) emission.

Oxides of nitrogen (NOx) are composed of approximately 97–98 percent nitric oxide (NO). Nitric oxide is a colorless gas but when it is passed into the atmosphere, it combines with oxygen and forms nitrogen dioxide (NO_2). The nitrogen dioxide then combines with chemically active hydrocarbons (HC) and when in the presence of sunlight, causes the formation of photo-chemical smog.

Ozone

To further complicate matters, some of the nitrogen dioxide (NO_2) is broken apart by the sunlight to form nitric oxide and oxygen. (NO_2 + sunlight = NO + O). This single atom of oxygen then combines with diatomic (meaning 2 atoms) oxygen (O_2) to form ozone (O_3). Ozone is one of the smells associated with smog. It has a pungent and offensive odor, irritates the eyes and lung tissues, affects the growth of plant life and causes rapid deterioration of rubber products. Ozone can be formed by sunlight as well as electrical discharge into the air.

The most common discharge area on the automobile engine is the secondary ignition electrical system, especially when inferior quality spark plug cables are used. As the surge of high voltage is routed through the secondary cable, the circuit builds up an electrical field around the wire, which acts upon the oxygen in the surrounding air to form the ozone. The faint glow along the cable with the engine running that may be visible on a dark night, is called the "corona discharge." It is the result of the electrical field passing from a high along the cable, to a low in the surrounding air, which forms the ozone gas. The combination of corona and ozone has been a major cause of cable deterioration. Recently, different and better quality insulating materials have lengthened the life of the electrical cables.

Although ozone at ground level can be harmful, ozone is beneficial to the earth's inhabitants. By having a concentrated ozone layer called the "ozonosphere," between 10 and 20 miles (16–32 km) up in the atmosphere, much of the ultra violet radiation from the sun's rays are absorbed and screened. If this ozone layer were not present, much of the earth's surface would be burned, dried and unfit for human life.

OXIDES OF SULFUR

Oxides of sulfur (SOx) were initially ignored in the exhaust system emissions, since the sulfur content of gasoline as a fuel is less than $\frac{1}{10}$ of 1 percent. Because of this small amount, it was felt that it contributed very little to the overall pollution problem. However, because of the difficulty in solving the sulfur emissions in industrial pollution and the introduction of catalytic converters to automobile exhaust systems, a change was mandated. The automobile exhaust system, when equipped with a catalytic converter, changes the sulfur dioxide (SO_2) into sulfur trioxide (SO_3).

When this combines with water vapors (H_2O), a sulfuric acid mist (H_2SO_4) is formed and is a very difficult pollutant to handle since it is extremely corrosive. This sulfuric acid mist that is formed, is the same mist that rises from the vents of an automobile battery when an active chemical reaction takes place within the battery cells.

When a large concentration of vehicles equipped with catalytic converters are operating in an area, this acid mist may rise and be distributed over a large ground area causing land, plant, crop, paint and building damage.

PARTICULATE MATTER

A certain amount of particulate matter is present in the burning of any fuel, with carbon constituting the largest percentage of the particulates. In gasoline, the remaining particulates are the burned remains of the various other compounds used in its manufacture. When a gasoline engine is in good internal condition, the particulate emissions are low but as the engine wears internally, the particulate emissions increase. By visually inspecting the tail pipe emissions, a determination can be made as to where an engine defect may exist. An engine with light gray or blue smoke emitting from the tail pipe normally indicates an increase in the oil consumption through burning due to internal engine wear. Black smoke would indicate a defective fuel delivery system, causing the engine to operate in a rich mode. Regardless of the color of the smoke, the internal part of the engine or the fuel delivery system should be repaired to prevent excess particulate emissions.

Diesel and turbine engines emit a darkened plume of smoke from the exhaust system because of the type of fuel used. Emission control regulations are mandated for this type of emission and more stringent measures are being used to prevent excess emission of the particulate matter. Electronic components are being introduced to control the injection of the fuel at precisely the proper time of piston travel, to achieve the optimum in fuel ignition and fuel usage. Other particulate after-burning components are being tested to achieve a cleaner emission.

Good grades of engine lubricating oils should be used, which meet the manufacturer's specification. Cut-rate oils can contribute to the particulate emission problem because of their low flash or ignition temperature point. Such oils burn prematurely during the combustion process causing emission of particulate matter.

The cooling system is an important factor in the reduction of particulate matter. The optimum combustion will occur, with the cooling system operating at a temperature specified by the manufacturer. The cooling system must be maintained in the same manner as the engine oiling system, as each system is required to perform properly in order for the engine to operate efficiently for a long time.

Crankcase Emissions

Crankcase emissions are made up of water, acids, unburned fuel, oil fumes and particulates. These emissions are classified as hydrocarbons (HC) and are formed by the small amount of unburned, compressed air/fuel mixture entering the crankcase from the combustion area (between the cylinder walls and piston rings) during the compression and power strokes. The head of the compression and combustion help to form the remaining crankcase emissions.

Since the first engines, crankcase emissions were allowed into the atmosphere through a road draft tube, mounted on the lower side of the engine block. Fresh air came in through an open oil filler cap or breather. The air passed through the crankcase mixing with blow-by gases. The motion of the vehicle and the air blowing past the open end of the road draft tube caused a low pressure area (vacuum) at the end of the tube. Crankcase emissions were simply drawn out of the road draft tube into the air.

To control the crankcase emission, the road draft tube was deleted. A hose and/or tubing was routed from the crankcase to the intake manifold so the blow-by emission could be burned with the air/fuel mixture. However, it was found that intake manifold vacuum, used to draw the crankcase emissions into the manifold, would vary in strength at the wrong time and not allow the proper emission flow. A regulating valve was needed to control the flow of air through the crankcase.

Testing, showed the removal of the blow-by gases from the crankcase as quickly as possible, was most important to the longevity of the engine. Should large accumulations of blow-by gases remain and condense, dilution of the engine oil would occur to form water, soot, resins, acids and lead salts, resulting in the formation of sludge and varnishes. This condensation of the blow-by gases occurs more frequently on vehicles used in numerous starting and stopping conditions, excessive idling and when the engine is not allowed to attain normal operating temperature through short runs.

Evaporative Emissions

Gasoline fuel is a major source of pollution, before and after it is burned in the automobile engine. From the time the fuel is refined, stored, pumped and transported, again stored until it is pumped into the fuel tank of the vehicle, the gasoline gives off unburned hydrocarbons (HC) into the atmosphere. Through the redesign of storage areas and venting systems, the pollution factor was diminished, but not eliminated, from the refinery standpoint. However, the automobile still remained the primary source of vaporized, unburned hydrocarbon (HC) emissions.

Fuel pumped from an underground storage tank is cool but when exposed to a warmer ambient temperature, will expand. Before controls were mandated, an owner might fill the fuel tank with fuel from an underground storage tank and park the vehicle for some time in warm area, such as a parking lot. As the fuel would warm, it would expand and should no provisions or area be provided for the expansion, the fuel would spill out of the filler neck and onto the ground, causing hydrocarbon (HC) pollution and creating a severe fire hazard. To correct this condition, the vehicle manufacturers added overflow plumbing and/or gasoline tanks with built in expansion areas or domes.

However, this did not control the fuel vapor emission from the fuel tank. It was determined that most of the fuel evaporation occurred when the vehicle was stationary and the engine not operating. Most vehicles carry 5–25 gallons (19–95 liters) of gasoline. Should a large concentration of vehicles be parked in one area, such as a large parking lot, excessive fuel vapor emissions would take place, increasing as the temperature increases.

To prevent the vapor emission from escaping into the atmosphere, the fuel systems were designed to trap the vapors while the vehicle is stationary, by sealing the system from the atmosphere. A storage system is used to collect and hold the fuel vapors from the carburetor (if equipped) and the fuel tank when the engine is not operating. When the engine is started, the storage system is then purged of the fuel vapors, which are drawn into the engine and burned with the air/fuel mixture.

EMISSION CONTROLS

Crankcase Ventilation System

OPERATION

▶ See Figures 1 and 2

When the engine is running, a small portion of the gases which are formed in the combustion chamber leak by the piston rings and enter the crankcase. Since these gases are under pressure they tend to escape from the crankcase and enter into the atmosphere. If these gases are allowed to remain in the crankcase for any length of time, they would contaminate the engine oil and cause sludge to build up. If the gases are allowed to escape into the atmosphere, they would pollute the air, as they contain unburned hydrocarbons. The crankcase ventilation system recycles these gases back into the engine combustion chamber, where they are burned.

Crankcase gases are recycled in the following manner. While the engine is running, clean filtered air is drawn into the crankcase through the intake air filter and then through a hose leading to the oil filler cap or the valve cover . As the air passes through the crankcase it picks up the combustion gases and carries them out of the crankcase, up through the PCV valve, and into the intake manifold. After they enter the intake manifold they are drawn into the combustion chamber and are burned.

The most critical component of the system is the PCV valve. This vacuum-controlled valve regulates the amount of gases that are recycled into the combustion chamber. At low engine speeds the valve is partially closed, limiting the

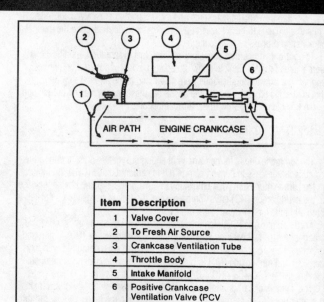

AIR PATH   ENGINE CRANKCASE

Item	Description
1	Valve Cover
2	To Fresh Air Source
3	Crankcase Ventilation Tube
4	Throttle Body
5	Intake Manifold
6	Positive Crankcase Ventilation Valve (PCV Valve)

91054G01

Fig. 1 Typical PCV air flow diagram

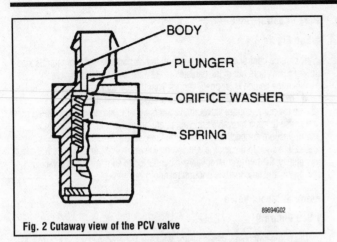

Fig. 2 Cutaway view of the PCV valve

flow of gases into the intake manifold. As engine speed increases, the valve opens to admit greater quantities of the gases into the intake manifold. If the valve should become blocked or plugged, the gases will be prevented from escaping the crankcase by the normal route. Since these gases are under pressure, they will find their own way out of the crankcase. This alternate route is usually a weak oil seal or gasket in the engine. As the gas escapes by the gasket, it also creates an oil leak. Besides causing oil leaks, a clogged PCV valve also allows these gases to remain in the crankcase for an extended period of time, promoting the formation of sludge in the engine.

COMPONENT TESTING

♦ See Figure 3

1. Remove the PCV valve from the valve cover grommet.
2. Shake the PCV valve.
   a. If the valve rattles when shaken, reinstall it and proceed to Step 3.
   b. If the valve does not rattle, it is sticking and must be replaced.
3. Start the engine and allow it to reach normal operating temperature.
4. Check the PCV valve for vacuum by placing your finger over the end of the valve.
   a. If vacuum exists, proceed to Step 5.
   b. If vacuum does not exist, check for loose hose connections, vacuum leaks or blockage. Correct as necessary.
5. Disconnect the fresh air intake hose from the air inlet tube (connects the air cleaner housing to the throttle body).
6. Place a stiff piece of paper over the hose end and wait 1 minute.
   a. If vacuum holds the paper in place, the system is OK; reconnect the hose.
   b. If the paper is not held in place, check for loose hose connections, vacuum leaks or blockage. Correct as necessary.

REMOVAL & INSTALLATION

Refer to Section 1 for removal and installation of the PCV valve.

OPERATION

♦ See Figures 4 and 5

Changes in atmospheric temperature cause fuel tanks to breathe, that is, the air within the tank expands and contracts with outside temperature changes. If an unsealed system was used, when the temperature rises, air would escape through the tank vent tube or the vent in the tank cap. The air that escapes contains gasoline vapors.

The Evaporative Emission Control System provides a sealed fuel system with the capability to store and condense fuel vapors. When the fuel evaporates expand in the fuel tank, the vapor passes through the EVAP emission valve, through vent hoses or tubes to a carbon filled evaporative canister. When the engine is operating the vapors are drawn into the intake manifold and burned during combustion..

A sealed, maintenance free evaporative canister is used. The canister is filled with granules of an activated carbon mixture. Fuel vapors entering the canister are absorbed by the charcoal granules. A vent cap is located on the top of the canister to provide fresh air to the canister when it is being purged. The vent cap opens to provide fresh air into the canister, which circulates through the charcoal, releasing trapped vapors and carrying them to the engine to be burned.

Fuel tank pressure vents fuel vapors into the canister. They are held in the canister until they can be drawn into the intake manifold. The canister purge valve allows the canister to be purged at a pre-determined time and engine operating conditions.

Vacuum to the canister is controlled by the canister purge valve. The valve is operated by the PCM. The PCM regulates the valve by switching the ground circuit on and off based on engine operating conditions. When energized, the valve prevents vacuum from reaching the canister. When not energized the valve allows vacuum to purge the vapors from the canister.

During warm up and for a specified time after hot starts, the PCM energizes (grounds) the valve preventing vacuum from reaching the canister. When the engine temperature reaches the operating level of about 120°F (49°C), the PCM removes the ground from the valve allowing vacuum to flow through the canister and purges vapors through the throttle body. During certain idle conditions, the purge valve may be grounded to control fuel mixture calibrations.

The fuel tank is sealed with a pressure-vacuum relief filler cap. The relief valve in the cap is a safety feature, preventing excessive pressure or vacuum in the fuel tank. If the cap is malfunctioning, and needs to be replaced, ensure that the replacement is the identical cap to ensure correct system operation.

On vehicles with 5.8L engine, fuel vapors from the carburetor fuel bowl are vented to the carbon canister for storage. The flow of vapors is controlled by the fuel bowl solenoid vent valve and/or fuel bowl thermal vent valve.

Purging the carbon canister removes the fuel vapor stored in the carbon canister. The fuel vapor flow from the canister to the engine is controlled by a purge solenoid or vacuum controlled purge valve. Purging occurs

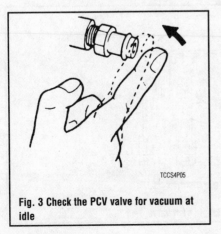

Fig. 3 Check the PCV valve for vacuum at idle

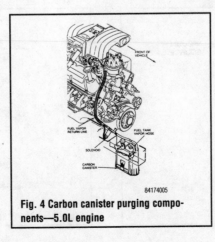

Fig. 4 Carbon canister purging components—5.0L engine

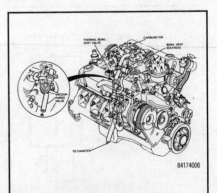

Fig. 5 Carbon canister purging components—5.8L engine

when the engine is at operating temperature and, in most systems, off idle.

OBD-II EVAP System Monitor

Some of the models covered in this manual have added system components due to the EVAP system monitor incorporated in the OBD-II engine control system. A pressure sensor is mounted on the fuel tank which measures pressure inside the tank, and a purge flow sensor measures the flow of the gases from the canister into the engine. The purge valve is now called the Vapor Management Valve (VMV). It performs the same functions as the purge valve, however it looks slightly different. A canister vent solenoid is mounted on the canister, taking the place of the vent cap, providing a source of fresh air to the canister.

The PCM can store trouble codes for EVAP system performance, a list of the codes is provided later in this section. Normal testing procedure can be used, see EVAP System Component Testing in this Section.

Carbon Canister

▶ See Figure 6

The fuel vapors from the fuel tank (and carburetor, if equipped) are stored in the carbon canister until the vehicle is operated, at which time, the vapors will purge from the canister into the engine for consumption. The carbon canister contains activated carbon, which absorbs the fuel vapor. The canister is located in the engine compartment or along the frame rail.

Fuel Tank Vapor Orifice and Roll over Valve Assembly

▶ See Figure 7

Fuel vapor in the fuel tank is vented to the carbon canister through the vapor valve assembly. The valve is mounted in a rubber grommet at a central location in the upper surface of the fuel tank. A vapor space between the fuel level and the tank upper surface is combined with a small orifice and float shut-off valve in the vapor valve assembly to prevent liquid fuel from passing to the carbon canister. The vapor space also allows for thermal expansion of the fuel.

Purge Control Valve

▶ See Figure 8

The purge control valve is in-line with the carbon canister and controls the flow of fuel vapors out of the canister.

When the engine is stopped, vapors from the fuel tank and carburetor fuel bowl flow into the canister. On systems using spark port or EGR port vacuum to actuate the purge control valve, the vacuum signal is strong enough during normal cruise to open the valve and vapors are drawn from the canister to the engine vacuum connection. At the same time, vapors from the fuel tank are routed directly into the engine. On some systems where purging does not affect idle quality, the purge control valve is connected to engine manifold vacuum and opens any time there is enough manifold vacuum.

Purge Solenoid Valve

▶ See Figure 9

The purge solenoid valve is in-line with the carbon canister and controls the flow of fuel vapors out of the canister. It is normally closed. When the engine is shut off, the vapors from the fuel tank flow into the canister. After the engine is started, the solenoid is engaged and opens, purging the vapors into the engine. With the valve open, vapors from the fuel tank are routed directly into the engine.

Fuel Bowl Solenoid Vent Valve

▶ See Figure 10

The fuel bowl solenoid vent valve is located in the fuel bowl vent line on carbureted engines. The valve is open when the ignition switch is in the **OFF** position and closes when the engine is running.

➡ **If lean fuel mixture is suspected as the cause of improper engine operation, check either the solenoid vent valve or the carburetor's built-in fuel bowl vent valve to make sure they are closed when the engine is running. If the valve is open, purge vacuum will affect the fuel bowl bal-**

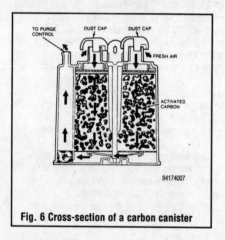

Fig. 6 Cross-section of a carbon canister

Fig. 7 Fuel tank vapor orifice and roll over valve assembly

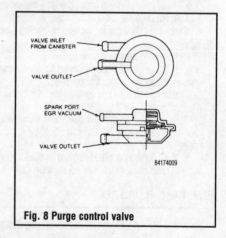

Fig. 8 Purge control valve

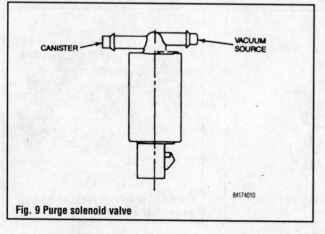

Fig. 9 Purge solenoid valve

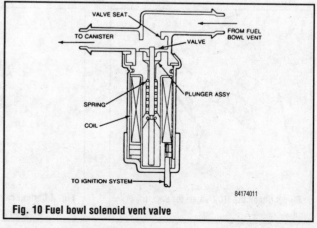

Fig. 10 Fuel bowl solenoid vent valve

anced air pressure, and the carburetor will have a leaner air/fuel mixture.

Fuel Bowl Thermal Vent Valve

▶ See Figure 11

The thermal vent valve is located in the carburetor-to-carbon canister vent line. The valve's function is to prevent fuel tank vapors from being vented through the carburetor fuel bowl when the engine is cold.

The valve is closed when the engine compartment is cold, blocking fuel vapors from entering the now-open carburetor fuel bowl vent, and instead routing them to the carbon canister. When the engine runs and the engine compartment warms up, the thermal vent valve opens. When the engine is turned off, the fuel bowl (or solenoid) vent valve opens, allowing fuel vapor to flow through the open thermal vent valve and into the carbon canister. The thermal vent valve closes as it cools, and the cycle repeats.

Auxiliary Fuel Bowl Vent Tube

On some carbureted vehicles, an auxiliary fuel bowl vent tube is connected to the fuel bowl vent tube to vent the fuel bowl when the internal fuel bowl vent or the solenoid vent valve is closed and the thermal vent valve is also closed. An air filter is installed on the air cleaner end of the tube to prevent the entrance of contaminants into the carburetor fuel bowl.

Pressure/Vacuum Relief Fuel Cap

The fuel cap contains an integral pressure and vacuum relief valve. The vacuum valve acts to allow air into the fuel tank to replace the fuel as it is used, while preventing vapors from escaping the tank through the atmosphere. The vacuum relief valve opens after a vacuum of 0.5hg. The pressure valve acts as a backup pressure relief valve in the event the normal venting system is overcome by excessive generation of internal pressure or restriction of the normal venting system. The pressure relief range is 1.6–2.1 psi. Fill cap damage or contamination that stops the pressure vacuum valve from working may result in deformation of the fuel tank.

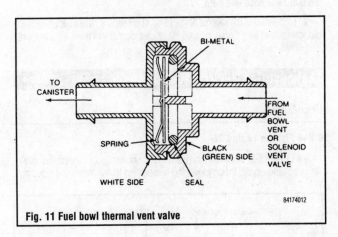

Fig. 11 Fuel bowl thermal vent valve

TESTING

Evaporative Emissions Canister

▶ See Figure 12

Generally, the only testing done to the canister is a visual inspection. Look the canister over and replace it with a new one if there is any evidence of cracks or other damage.

Evaporative Hoses and Tubes

Inspect all system hoses and tubes for signs of damage, cracks or blockage. Any damage or leakage must be repaired. Inspect for blockages by disconnecting both ends of the hose or tube and blowing through it. Replace any hoses or tubes that are blocked.

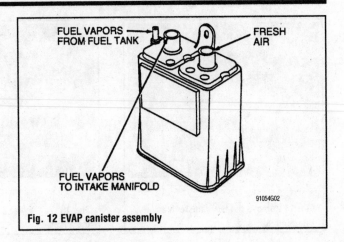

Fig. 12 EVAP canister assembly

Evaporative Emissions Valve

Inspect the valve for open air passage through the orifice. The valve is molded directly to the fuel tank and is not serviceable separately. If the orifice is blocked, replace the fuel tank.

Canister Purge Valve/Vapor Management Valve

▶ See Figure 13

1. Remove the canister purge valve.
2. Measure the resistance between the two valve terminals.
   a. If the resistance is between 30–36 ohms, proceed to the Step 3.
   b. If the resistance is not between 30–36 ohms, replace the valve.
3. Attach a hand-held vacuum pump to the intake manifold vacuum side of the valve, then apply 16 in. Hg (53 kPa) of vacuum to the valve.
   a. If the valve will not hold vacuum for at least 20 seconds replace it with a new one.
   b. If the valve holds vacuum, proceed to Step 4. Keep the vacuum applied to the valve.
4. Using an external voltage source, apply 9–14 DC volts to the valve electrical terminals.
   a. If the valve opens and the vacuum drops, the valve is working properly. Check power and ground circuits.
   b. If the valve does not open and the vacuum remains, replace the valve is faulty.

REMOVAL & INSTALLATION

Carbon Canister

▶ See Figures 14, 15, 16 and 17

1. Disconnect the negative battery cable.
2. Remove the canister bracket retaining nuts and lower the canister.

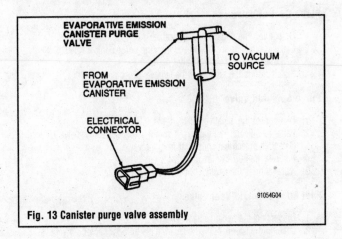

Fig. 13 Canister purge valve assembly

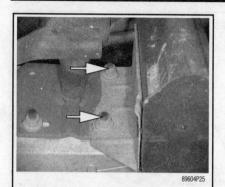

Fig. 14 Remove the two canister bracket retaining nuts and . . .

Fig. 15 . . . lower the canister to access the hoses

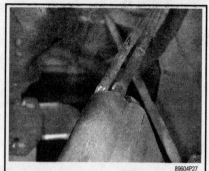

Fig. 16 Label the hoses for the canister before removing them to aid in the installation

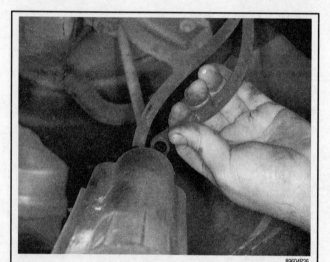

Fig. 17 Disconnect the canister hoses and remove the canister from the vehicle

3. Label and disconnect the vapor hoses from the carbon canister and remove the canister from the vehicle.
4. Installation is the reverse of the removal procedure.

Fuel Tank Vapor Orifice and Roll over Valve Assembly

1. Disconnect the negative battery cable.
2. Remove the fuel tank as described in Section 5.
3. Remove the vapor orifice and roll over valve assembly from the fuel tank.
4. Installation is the reverse of the removal procedure.

Purge Control Valve

1. Disconnect the negative battery cable.
2. Label and disconnect the hoses from the purge control valve.
3. Remove the purge control valve.
4. Installation is the reverse of the removal procedure.

Purge Solenoid Valve

1. Disconnect the negative battery cable.
2. Label and disconnect the hoses from the purge solenoid valve.
3. Detach the electrical connector from the valve.
4. Remove the purge solenoid valve.
5. Installation is the reverse of the removal procedure.

Fuel Bowl Solenoid Vent Valve

1. Disconnect the negative battery cable.
2. Label and disconnect the hoses from the fuel bowl solenoid vent valve.
3. Detach the electrical connector from the valve.

4. Remove the fuel bowl solenoid vent valve.
5. Installation is the reverse of the removal procedure.

Fuel Bowl Thermal Vent Valve

1. Disconnect the negative battery cable.
2. Label and disconnect the hoses from the fuel bowl thermal vent valve.
3. Remove the fuel bowl thermal vent valve.
4. Installation is the reverse of the removal procedure.

Pressure/Vacuum Relief Fuel Cap

1. Unscrew the fuel filler cap. The cap has a pre-vent feature that allows the tank to vent for the first ¾ turn before unthreading.
2. Remove the screw retaining the fuel cap tether and remove the fuel cap.

➡Use care when removing the screw to not drop it down into the fuel filler neck. Use of a magnetic screwdriver or placing a clean rag over the fuel filler neck will help.

3. Installation is the reverse of the removal procedure. When installing the cap, continue to turn clockwise until the ratchet mechanism gives off 3 or more loud clicks.

Exhaust Gas Recirculation System

OPERATION

◆ See Figures 18 thru 25

The Exhaust Gas Recirculation (EGR) system reintroduces exhaust gas into the combustion cycle, thereby lowering combustion temperatures and reducing

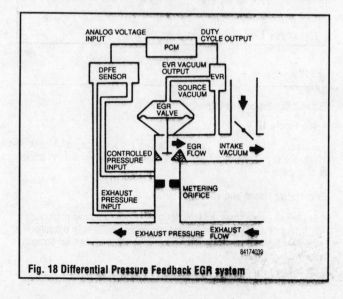

Fig. 18 Differential Pressure Feedback EGR system

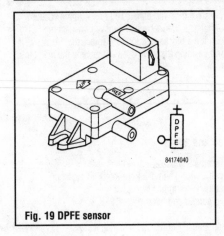

Fig. 19 DPFE sensor

84174040

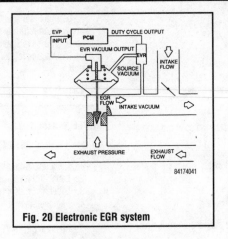

Fig. 20 Electronic EGR system

84174041

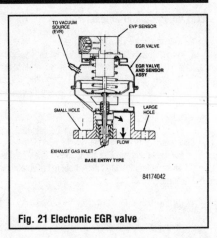

Fig. 21 Electronic EGR valve

84174042

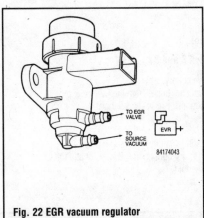

Fig. 22 EGR vacuum regulator

84174043

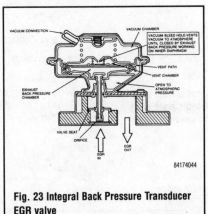

Fig. 23 Integral Back Pressure Transducer EGR valve

84174044

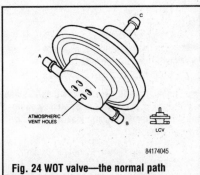

Fig. 24 WOT valve—the normal path between ports A and B is vented to atmosphere when sufficient vacuum is applied to port C

84174045

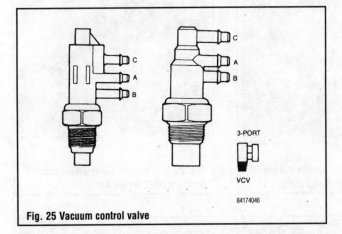

Fig. 25 Vacuum control valve

84174046

the formation of Nitrous Oxide. The amount of exhaust gas reintroduced and the timing of the cycle varies by calibration and is controlled by factors such as engine speed, engine vacuum, exhaust system back pressure, coolant temperature and throttle angle. All EGR valves are vacuum actuated.

There are 3 systems used: The 4.6L engine is equipped with the Differential Pressure Feedback EGR (DPFE) system, the 5.0L engine uses the Electronic EGR (EEGR) system and the 5.8L engine is equipped with the Integral Back Pressure Transducer EGR system.

The DPFE is a subsonic closed loop EGR system that controls EGR flow rate by directly monitoring the pressure drop across a remotely located sharp-edged orifice. The DPFE sensor then converts the pressure signal into a proportional analog voltage which is sent to the Powertrain Control Module (PCM). The PCM digitizes the signal and computes the optimum EGR flow. The output signal from the PCM is varied by valve modulation using vacuum output of the EGR Vacuum Regulator (EVR). In the DPFE system, the EGR valve serves as a pressure regulator rather than a flow metering device.

In the EEGR system, EGR flow is controlled according to computer demands by means of an EGR Valve Position (EVP) sensor attached to the valve. The valve is operated by a vacuum signal from the electronic vacuum regulator which actuates the valve diaphragm. As supply vacuum overcomes the spring load, the diaphragm is actuated. This lifts the pintle off its seat allowing exhaust gas to recirculate. The amount of flow is proportional to the pintle position. The EVP sensor mounted on the valve sends an electrical signal of its position to the PCM.

The Integral Back Pressure Transducer EGR valve combines inputs of back pressure and EGR port vacuum into one unit. Both inputs are required for the valve to operate, it will not operate on vacuum alone. The Integral Back Pressure Transducer EGR system also includes the EGR Load Control (WOT) valve and the Vacuum Control Valve (VCV). The WOT valve dumps EGR vacuum at or near wide open throttle and the VCV controls vacuum to the EGR valve during engine warm-up.

COMPONENT TESTING

DPFE Sensor

1. Disconnect the pressure hoses at the DPFE sensor.
2. Connect a hand vacuum pump to the downstream pickup marked **REF** on the sensor.
3. Using a multimeter, backprobe the SIG RTN circuit at the DPFE connector.
4. With the ignition **ON**, signal voltage should be 0.20–0.70 volts.
5. Apply 8–9 in. Hg of vacuum to the sensor. Voltage should be greater than 4 volts.
6. Quickly release the vacuum from the sensor. Voltage should drop to less than 1 volt in 3 seconds.
7. If the sensor does not respond as specified, check the power and ground circuits.
8. If power and ground circuits are functional, the sensor is faulty.

EGR Valve Control Solenoid

1. Remove the EVR solenoid.
2. Attempt to lightly blow air into the EVR solenoid.
   a. If air blows through the solenoid, replace the solenoid with a new one.
   b. If air does not pass freely through the solenoid, continue with the test.
3. Apply battery voltage (approximately 12 volts) and a ground to the EVR solenoid electrical terminals. Attempt to lightly blow air, once again, through the solenoid.
   a. If air does not pass through the solenoid, replace the solenoid with a new one.
   b. If air does not flow through the solenoid, the solenoid is OK.
4. If the solenoid is functional but the problem still exists, check the power and ground circuits.

EGR Valve

1. Install a tachometer on the engine, following the manufacturer's instructions.
2. Detach the engine wiring harness connector from the Idle Air Control (IAC) solenoid.
3. Disconnect and plug the vacuum supply hose from the EGR valve.
4. Start the engine, then apply the parking brake, block the rear wheels and position the transmission in Neutral.
5. Observe and note the idle speed.

➡If the engine will not idle with the IAC solenoid disconnected, provide an air bypass to the engine by slightly opening the throttle plate or by creating an intake vacuum leak. Do not allow the idle speed to exceed typical idle rpm.

6. Using a hand-held vacuum pump, slowly apply 5–10 in. Hg (17–34 kPa) of vacuum to the EGR valve nipple.
   a. If the idle speed drops more than 100 rpm with the vacuum applied and returns to normal after the vacuum is removed, the EGR valve is OK.

b. If the idle speed does not drop more than 100 rpm with the vacuum applied and return to normal after the vacuum is removed, inspect the EGR valve for a blockage; clean it if a blockage is found. Replace the EGR valve if no blockage is found, or if cleaning the valve does not remedy the malfunction.

REMOVAL & INSTALLATION

DPFE Sensor

▶ See Figures 26, 27, 28 and 29

1. Disconnect the negative battery cable.
2. Label and disconnect the wiring harness from the DPFE sensor.
3. Label and disconnect the vacuum hoses.
4. Remove the mounting screws and remove the DPFE sensor.

To install:

5. Position the DPFE sensor and tighten the mounting screws.
6. Attach all necessary hoses and wiring to the sensor.
7. Connect the negative battery cable.

EGR Valve Control Solenoid

▶ See Figures 30, 31, 32, 33 and 34

1. Disconnect the negative battery cable.
2. Label and detach the vacuum hoses from the EVR solenoid.
3. Detach the electrical connector from the solenoid.
4. Remove the retaining hardware, and remove the solenoid.

To install:

5. Position the solenoid and install the retaining hardware.
6. Attach the main emission vacuum control connector and the wiring harness connector to the EVR solenoid.
7. Connect the negative battery cable.

Fig. 26 Detach the connector for the DPFE sensor

Fig. 27 Matchmark and remove the vacuum hoses for the DPFE sensor and . . .

Fig. 28 . . . remove the retaining nuts from the DPFE sensor and . . .

Fig. 29 . . . remove the DPFE sensor from the intake manifold

Fig. 30 Detach the connector for the EVR solenoid

Fig. 31 Match mark the vacuum hoses for the EVR solenoid and . . .

Fig. 32 . . . remove the vacuum hoses from the EVR solenoid

Fig. 33 Remove the retaining nut for the solenoid and . . .

Fig. 34 . . . remove the solenoid from the intake manifold

EGR Valve

4.6L ENGINE

▶ See Figures 35 thru 42

1. Disconnect the negative battery cable.
2. Remove the vacuum hose from the EGR valve.
3. On the 4.6L engine, remove the nut and the brake booster bracket.
4. Disconnect the EGR valve-to-exhaust manifold tube from the EGR valve.
5. Remove the EGR valve mounting bolts, then separate the valve from the intake manifold.
6. Remove and discard the old EGR valve gasket, and clean the gasket mating surfaces on the valve and the intake manifold.

To install:

7. Install the EGR valve, along with a new gasket, on the intake manifold, then install and tighten the mounting bolts.

8. Connect the EGR valve-to-exhaust manifold tube to the valve, then tighten the tube nut to 25–35 ft. lbs. (34–47 Nm).
9. Connect the vacuum hose to the EGR valve.
10. On the 4.6L engine install the brake booster bracket and the retaining nut.
11. Connect the negative battery cable.

5.0L ENGINE

1. Disconnect the negative battery cable.
2. Remove the air cleaner outlet tube.
3. Detach the EVP sensor connector.
4. Disconnect the EGR valve-to-exhaust manifold tube from the EGR valve.
5. Remove the vacuum hose from the EGR valve.
6. Remove the EGR valve mounting bolts, then separate the valve from the intake manifold.

Fig. 35 Remove the vacuum hose from the EGR valve

Fig. 36 On the 4.6L engine, remove the nut and the brake booster bracket from the EGR mounting stud

Fig. 37 Using a suitable size wrench, loosen the EGR valve-to-exhaust manifold tube and . . .

Fig. 38 . . . remove the tub from the EGR valve

Fig. 39 Remove the EGR valve mounting bolts and . . .

Fig. 40 . . . remove the EGR valve from the intake manifold

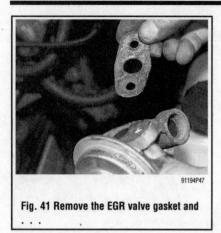

Fig. 41 Remove the EGR valve gasket and . . .

Fig. 42 . . . thoroughly clean the EGR valve mounting surface

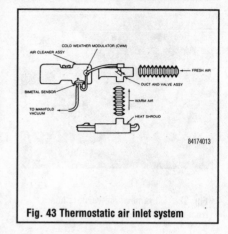

Fig. 43 Thermostatic air inlet system

7. Remove and discard the old EGR valve gasket, and clean the gasket mating surfaces on the valve and the intake manifold.

To install:

➡️**If replacing the EGR valve, transfer the EVP sensor onto the new valve.**

8. Install the EGR valve, along with a new gasket, on the upper intake manifold, then install and tighten the mounting bolts.
9. Connect the EGR valve-to-exhaust manifold tube to the valve, then tighten the tube nut to 25–35 ft. lbs. (34–47 Nm).
10. Connect the vacuum hose to the EGR valve.
11. Attach the EVP sensor connector.
12. Install the air cleaner outlet tube.
13. Connect the negative battery cable.

Thermostatic Air Inlet System

OPERATION

▶ **See Figure 43**

The thermostatic air inlet system is used on the 5.8L engine. The thermostatic air inlet system regulates the air inlet temperature by drawing air in from a cool air source as well as heated air from a heat shroud which is mounted on the exhaust manifold. The system consists of the following components: duct and valve assembly, heat shroud, bimetal sensor, cold weather modulator and the necessary vacuum lines and air ducts.

Duct and Valve Assembly

The duct and valve assembly which regulates the air flow from the cool and heated air sources is attached to the air cleaner. The flow is regulated by means of a door that is operated by a vacuum motor. The operation of the motor is controlled by the bimetal sensor and cold weather modulator.

Bimetal Sensor

The core of the bimetal sensor is made of 2 different types of metals bonded together, each having different temperature expansion rates. At a given increase in temperature, the shape of the sensor core changes, bleeding off vacuum available at the vacuum motor. This permits the vacuum motor to open the duct door to allow fresh air in while shutting off full heat. The bimetal sensor is calibrated according to the needs of each particular application.

Cold Weather Modulator

The cold weather modulator modifies the vacuum signal to the duct and valve assembly vacuum motor, based on temperature calibration.

TESTING

Duct and Valve Assembly

▶ **See Figure 44**

1. If the duct door is in the closed to fresh air position, remove the hose from the air cleaner vacuum motor.
2. The door should go to the open to fresh air position. If it sticks or binds, service or replace, as required.
3. If the door is in the open to fresh air position, check the door by applying 8 in. Hg or greater of vacuum to the vacuum motor.
4. The door should move freely to the closed to fresh air position. If it binds or sticks, service or replace, as required.

➡️**Make sure the vacuum motor is functional before changing the duct and valve assembly.**

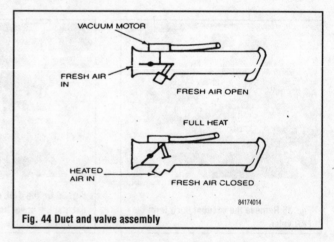

Fig. 44 Duct and valve assembly

Bimetal Sensor

▶ **See Figure 45**

1. Bring the temperature of the bimetal sensor below 75°F (24°C) and apply 16 in. Hg of vacuum with a vacuum pump at the vacuum source port of the sensor.
2. The duct door should stay closed. If not, replace the bimetal sensor.
3. The sensor will bleed off vacuum to allow the duct door to open and let in fresh air at or above the following temperatures:
   a. Brown—75°F (24°C)
   b. Pink, black or red—90°F (32.2°C)
   c. Blue, yellow or green—105°F (40.6°C)

➡️**Do not cool the bimetal sensor while the engine is running.**

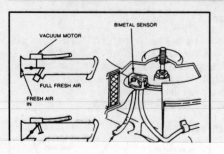

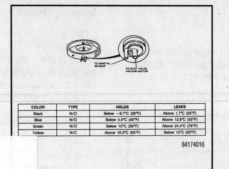

COLOR	TYPE	HOLDS	LEAKS
Black	N/O	Below − 6.7°C (20°F)	Above 1.7°C (35°F)
Blue	N/O	Below 4.4°C (40°F)	Above 12.8°C (55°F)
Green	N/O	Below 10°C (50°F)	Above 24.4°C (76°F)
Yellow	N/C	Above 18.3°C (65°F)	Below 10°C (50°F)

84174016

46 Cold weather modulator

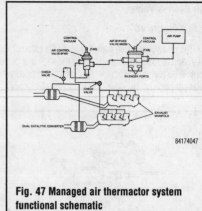

84174047

Fig. 47 Managed air thermactor system functional schematic

84174049

Fig. 49 Thermactor air supply pump

Thermactor Air Injection System

OPERATION

▶ See Figures 47 and 48

The thermactor air injection system reduces the hydrocarbon and carbon monoxide content of the exhaust gases by continuing the combustion of unburned gases after they leave the combustion chamber. This is done by injecting fresh air into the hot exhaust stream leaving the exhaust ports or into the catalyst. At this point, the fresh air mixes with hot exhaust gases to promote further oxidation of both the hydrocarbons and carbon monoxide, thereby reducing their concentration and converting some of them into harmless carbon dioxide and water.

All vehicles with 5.0L and 5.8L engines are equipped with a managed air thermactor system. This system is utilized in electronic control systems to divert thermactor air either upstream to the exhaust manifold check valve or downstream to the rear section check valve and dual bed catalyst. The system will also dump thermactor air to atmosphere during some operating modes.

The thermactor air injection system consists of the air supply pump, air bypass valve, check valves, air supply control valve, combination air bypass/air control valve, solenoid vacuum valve, thermactor idle vacuum valve and vacuum control valve. Components will vary according to year and application.

Air Supply Pump

▶ See Figure 49

The air supply pump is a belt-driven, positive displacement, vane-type pump that provides air for the thermactor system. It is available in 19 and 22 cu. in. sizes, either of which may be driven with different pulley ratios for different applications. The pump receives air from a remote silencer filter on the rear side of the engine air cleaner attached to the pump's air inlet nipple or through an impeller-type centrifugal filter fan.

3. Installation is the reverse of the removal procedure.

Bimetal Sensor

1. Remove the air cleaner housing lid to gain access to the sensor.
2. Label and disconnect the vacuum hoses from the sensor. It may be necessary to move the air cleaner housing to accomplish this.
3. Remove the sensor from the air cleaner housing.
4. Installation is the reverse of the removal procedure.

Cold Weather Modulator

1. Remove the air cleaner housing lid to gain access to the modulator.
2. Label and disconnect the vacuum hoses from the modulator.
3. Remove the modulator from the air cleaner housing.
4. Installation is the reverse of the removal procedure.

Air Bypass Valve

▶ **See Figure 50**

The air bypass valve supplies air to the exhaust system with medium and high applied vacuum signals when the engine is at normal operating temperature. With low or no vacuum applied, the pumped air is dumped through the silencer ports of the valve or through the dump port.

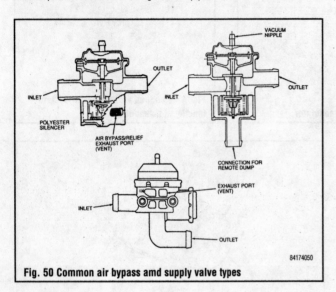

Fig. 50 Common air bypass amd supply valve types

Air Check Valve

▶ **See Figure 51**

The air check valve is a 1-way valve that allows thermactor air to pass into the exhaust system while preventing exhaust gases from passing in the opposite direction.

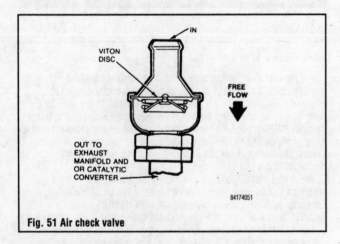

Fig. 51 Air check valve

Air Supply Control Valve

The air supply control valve directs air pump output to the exhaust manifold or downstream to the catalyst system depending upon the engine control strategy. It may also be used to dump air to the air cleaner or dump silencer.

Combination Air Bypass/Air Control Valve

The combination air control/bypass valve combines the secondary air bypass and air control functions. The valve is located in the air supply line between the air pump and the upstream/downstream air supply check valves.

The air bypass portion controls the flow of thermactor air to the exhaust system or allows thermactor air to be bypassed to atmosphere. When air is not being bypassed, the air control portion of the valve switches the air injection point to either an upstream or downstream location.

Solenoid Vacuum Valve

The normally closed solenoid valve assembly consists of 2 vacuum ports with an atmospheric vent. The valve assembly can be with or without control bleed. The outlet port of the valve is opened to atmospheric vent and closed to the inlet port when de-energized. When energized, the outlet port is opened to the inlet port and closed to atmospheric vent. The control bleed is provided to prevent contamination entering the solenoid valve assembly from the intake manifold.

Thermactor Idle Vacuum Valve

The Thermactor Idle Vacuum (TIV) valve vents the vacuum signal to atmosphere when the preset manifold vacuum or pressure is exceeded. It is used to divert thermactor airflow during cold starts to control exhaust backfire.

Vacuum Control Valve

The Vacuum Control Valve (VCV) controls vacuum to other emission devices during engine warm-up. The 2-port VCV opens when engine coolant reaches a pre-determined calibration temperature. The 4-port VCV functions in the same manner, as it is nothing more than two 2-port VCVs in one housing. The 3-port VCV switches the vacuum source to the center port from the top or bottom ports. Electrical switches can be either open or closed until the VCV is fully cycled. The VCV responds to a sensing bulb immersed in engine coolant by utilizing a wax pellet principle.

Vacuum Check Valve

The vacuum check valve blocks airflow in one direction, allowing free airflow in the other direction. The check valve side of the valve will hold the highest vacuum seen on the vacuum side.

TESTING

Air Supply Pump

1. Check belt tension and adjust if needed.

> ❊❊❊ **WARNING**

Do not pry on the pump to adjust the belt. The aluminum housing is likely to collapse.

2. Disconnect the air supply hose from the bypass control valve.
3. The pump is operating properly if airflow is felt at the pump outlet and the flow increases as engine speed increases.
4. If the pump is not operating as described in Step 3 and the system is equipped with a silencer/filter, check the silencer/filter for possible obstruction before replacing the pump.

Air Bypass Valve

1. Turn the ignition key **OFF**.
2. Remove the control vacuum line from the bypass valve.
3. Start the engine and bring to normal operating temperature.
4. Check for vacuum at the vacuum line. If there is no vacuum, check the solenoid vacuum valve assembly. If vacuum is present, inspect the air bypass valve.
5. Turn the engine **OFF** and disconnect the air hose at the bypass valve outlet.
6. Inspect the outlet for damage from the hot exhaust gas.
7. If the valve is damaged, replace it. If the valve is not damaged, check the bypass valve diaphragm.
8. Connect a vacuum pump to the bypass valve and apply 10 in. Hg of vacuum.
9. If the valve holds vacuum, leave the vacuum applied and go to Step 10. If the valve does not hold vacuum, it must be replaced.
10. Start the engine and increase the engine speed to 1500 rpm.
11. Check for air flow at the valve outlet, either audibly or by feel. If there is air flow, go to Step 12. If there is no air flow, replace the air bypass valve.
12. Release the vacuum applied by the vacuum pump and check that the air flow switches from the valve outlet to the dump port or silencer ports, either audibly or by feel.

13. If the air flow does not switch, replace the air bypass valve. If the air flow switches, the air bypass valve is okay, check the air supply control valve, or check the air check valve.

Air Check Valve

1. Turn the ignition **OFF**.
2. Visually inspect the thermactor system hoses, tubes, control valve(s) and check valve(s) for leaks or external signs of damage, from the back flow of hot exhaust gases.
3. If the hoses and valves are okay, go to Step 4. If they are not, service or replace the damaged parts, including the check valve.
4. Remove the hose from the check valve inlet and visually check the inside of the hose for damage from hot exhaust gas.
5. If the hose is clean and undamaged, go to Step 6. If not, replace the hose and check valve.
6. Start the engine and listen for escaping exhaust gas from the check valve. Feel for the gas only if the engine temperature is at an acceptable level.
7. If any exhaust gas is escaping, replace the check valve.

Air Supply Control Valve

▶ See Figure 50

1. Turn the ignition **OFF**.
2. Remove the hoses from the air control valve outlets and inspect the outlets for damage from hot exhaust gases.
3. If the air supply control valve is damaged, it must be replaced, then check the air check valve. If the air supply control valve is not damaged, go to Step 4.
4. Remove the vacuum line from the air supply control valve. Start the engine and bring to normal operating temperature, then shut the engine **OFF**.
5. Restart the engine and immediately check for vacuum at the hose. If vacuum was present at the start, go to Step 6. If vacuum was not present at the start, check the solenoid vacuum valve.
6. Start the engine and let it run. Check for the vacuum to change from high to low.
7. If the vacuum dropped to 0 within a few minutes after the engine started, go to Step 8. If not, check the solenoid vacuum valve.
8. Connect a vacuum pump to the air supply control valve and apply 10 in. Hg of vacuum.
9. If the valve holds vacuum, go to Step 10. If it does not hold vacuum, replace the air supply control valve.
10. Start the engine and bring to normal operating temperature. Make sure air is being supplied to the air supply control valve.
11. If air is present, go to Step 12. If air is not present, check air pump operation.
12. Leave the engine running and apply 10 in. Hg of vacuum to the air supply control valve. Increase engine speed to 1500 rpm.
13. If air flow comes out of outlet A, go to Step 14. If not, replace the air supply control valve.
14. Leave the engine running. Vent the vacuum pump until there is 0 vacuum.
15. If the air flow switches from outlet A to outlet B, the air supply control valve is okay. If the air flow does not switch, replace the air supply control valve.

Combination Air Bypass/Air Control Valve

▶ See Figure 52

1. Turn the ignition **OFF**.
2. Remove the hoses from the combination air control valve outlets A and B and inspect the outlets for damage from hot exhaust gases.
3. If the valve appears damaged, replace it, then check the air check valve. If the valve is not damaged, go to Step 4.
4. Leave the hoses disconnected from the valve. Disconnect and plug the vacuum line to port D.
5. Start the engine and run at 1500 rpm. If air flow is present at the valve, go to Step 6. If it is not, check the air pump. If the air pump is okay, replace the combination air control valve.
6. Leave the engine running. Disconnect both vacuum lines from ports D and S.
7. Measure the manifold vacuum at both ports. If the proper vacuum is present, go to Step 8. If not, check the solenoid vacuum valve.
8. Turn the ignition **OFF**. Reconnect the vacuum line to port D but leave the vacuum line to port S disconnected and plugged.

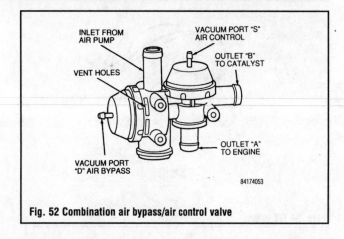

Fig. 52 Combination air bypass/air control valve

9. Start the engine and run it at 1500 rpm. If air flow is present at outlet B but not at outlet A, go to Step 10. If not, replace the combination air control valve and reconnect all hoses.
10. Turn the ignition **OFF** and leave the vacuum line to port S disconnected and unplugged.
11. Apply 8–10 in. Hg of vacuum to port S on the combination valve. Start the engine and run at 1500 rpm. If air flow is present at outlet A, the combination valve is okay. If not, replace the combination air control valve.

➡If the combination valve is a bleed type, this will affect the amount of air flow.

Solenoid Vacuum Valve

▶ See Figure 53

1. The ports should flow air when the solenoid is energized.
2. Check the resistance at the solenoid terminals with an ohmmeter. The resistance should be 51–108 ohms.
3. If the resistance is not as specified, replace the solenoid.

➡The valve can be expected to have a very small leakage rate when energized or de-energized. This leakage is not measurable in the field and is not detrimental to valve function.

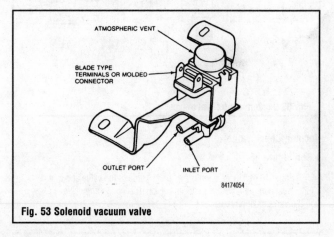

Fig. 53 Solenoid vacuum valve

TIV Valve

▶ See Figure 54

➡The following tests apply to valves with the words ASH or RED on the decal.

1. Start the engine and let it idle. Apply the parking brake, block the drive wheels and place the transmission in **N**.
2. Apply vacuum to the small nipple and place your fingers over the TIV valve atmospheric vent holes. If no vacuum is sensed, the TIV valve is damaged and must be replaced.

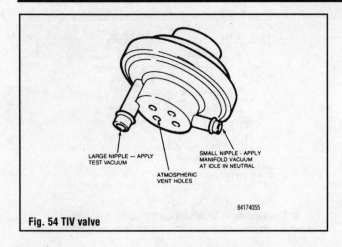

LARGE NIPPLE — APPLY TEST VACUUM

ATMOSPHERIC VENT HOLES

SMALL NIPPLE - APPLY MANIFOLD VACUUM AT IDLE IN NEUTRAL

84174055

Fig. 54 TIV valve

3. With the engine still idling in **N**, use a suitable vacuum source to apply 1.5–3.0 in. Hg vacuum to the ASH TIV valve large nipple, or 3.5–4.5 in. Hg vacuum to the RED TIV valve large nipple. If vacuum is still sensed when placing your fingers over the vent holes, the TIV valve is damaged and must be replaced.

Vacuum Control Valve

♦ See Figure 55

1. When the engine is cold, passage A to B should be closed and passage A to C should be open.

2. When the engine is at normal operating temperature, the valve should be open between A and B and closed between A and C.

➡ **On 4-port valves, check A₁ to B₁ and A₂ to B₂ separately.**

On 4-port valves, check A_1 to B_1 and A_2 to B_2 separately.

3. If the valve does not operate as specified in Steps 2 and 3, it must be replaced.

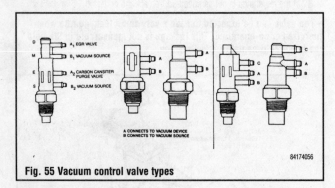

D A₁ EGR VALVE
M B₁ VACUUM SOURCE
E A₂ CARBON CANISTER PURGE VALVE
S B₂ VACUUM SOURCE

A CONNECTS TO VACUUM DEVICE
B CONNECTS TO VACUUM SOURCE

84174056

Fig. 55 Vacuum control valve types

Vacuum Check Valve

♦ See Figure 56

1. Apply 16 in. Hg vacuum to the "check" side of the valve and trap.

2. If vacuum remains above 15 in. Hg for 10 seconds, the valve is okay. If not, the valve must be replaced.

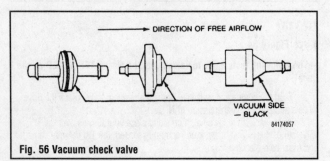

DIRECTION OF FREE AIRFLOW

VACUUM SIDE — BLACK

84174057

Fig. 56 Vacuum check valve

REMOVAL & INSTALLATION

Air Supply Pump

1. Disconnect the negative battery cable.
2. Remove the drive belt from the air pump pulley.
3. Label and disconnect the air hose(s) from the air pump.
4. Remove the mounting bolts and, if necessary, the mounting brackets.
5. Remove the air pump from the vehicle.
6. Installation is the reverse of the removal procedure. Adjust the drive belt tension as explained in Section 1.

Air Bypass Valve

1. Disconnect the negative battery cable.
2. Label and disconnect the air inlet and outlet hoses and the vacuum hose from the bypass valve.
3. Remove the bypass valve from the vehicle.
4. Installation is the reverse of the removal procedure.

Air Check Valve

1. Disconnect the negative battery cable.
2. Disconnect the input hose from the check valve.
3. Remove the check valve from the connecting tube.
4. Installation is the reverse of the removal procedure.

Air Supply Control Valve

1. Disconnect the negative battery cable.
2. Label and disconnect the air hoses and the vacuum line from the air control valve.
3. Remove the air control valve from the vehicle.
4. Installation is the reverse of the removal procedure.

Combination Air Bypass/Air Control Valve

1. Disconnect the negative battery cable.
2. Label and disconnect the air hoses and vacuum lines from the valve.
3. Remove the valve from the vehicle.
4. Installation is the reverse of the removal procedure.

Solenoid Vacuum Valve

1. Disconnect the negative battery cable.
2. Detach the electrical connector from the solenoid valve. Label and disconnect the vacuum lines.
3. Remove the mounting bolts and remove the solenoid valve.
4. Installation is the reverse of the removal procedure.

TIV Valve

1. Disconnect the negative battery cable.
2. Label and disconnect the vacuum lines from the valve.
3. Remove the valve from the vehicle.
4. Installation is the reverse of the removal procedure.

Vacuum Control Valve

1. Disconnect the negative battery cable.
2. Drain the cooling system, as necessary.

❄❄ CAUTION

When draining the coolant, keep in mind that cats and dogs are attracted by the ethylene glycol antifreeze, and are quite likely to drink any that is left in an uncovered container or in puddles on the ground. This will prove fatal in sufficient quantity. Always drain the coolant into a sealable container. Coolant should be reused unless it is contaminated or several years old.

3. Label and disconnect the vacuum lines from the valve.
4. Remove the valve.
5. Installation is the reverse of the removal procedure. Fill the cooling system as explained in Section 1.

ELECTRONIC ENGINE CONTROLS

Powertrain Control Module (PCM)

OPERATION

▶ **See Figure 57**

The Powertrain Control Module (PCM) performs many functions on your vehicle. The module accepts information from various engine sensors and computes the required fuel flow rate necessary to maintain the correct amount of air/fuel ratio throughout the entire engine operational range.

Based on the information that is received and programmed into the PCM's memory, the PCM generates output signals to control relays, actuators and solenoids. The PCM also sends out a command to the fuel injectors that meters the appropriate quantity of fuel. The module automatically senses and compensates for any changes in altitude when driving your vehicle.

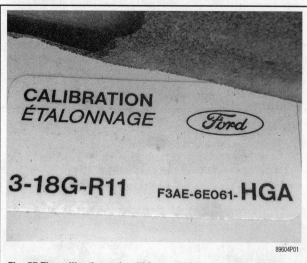

89604P01

Fig. 57 The calibration code will be needed to replace the PCM or any electrical engine control sensors. The calibration code can typically be found on a label affixed on the driver's door or the door jam

REMOVAL & INSTALLATION

It is located in the engine compartment, attached to the firewall on the driver's side, near the master cylinder.

✳✳ WARNING

Never detach the Powertrain Control Module (PCM) with the battery connected. Be sure to wear a grounding device when removing or installing a PCM to prevent damage to the unit due to static electricity.

1. Disconnect the negative battery cable.
2. Wearing a grounding device, loosen the engine control sensor wiring harness connector retaining bolt and carefully detach the harness connector from the PCM.
3. Remove the PCM bracket clip from the module bracket and remove the PCM.

To install:

4. Wearing a grounding device, install the PCM to the mounting bracket and secure the bracket clip.
5. Carefully fit the engine control sensor wiring harness connector to the PCM and secure with the retaining bolt. Torque the retaining bolt to 32 inch lbs. (3.7 Nm).
6. Reconnect the negative battery cable.
7. Check for proper operation.

Oxygen Sensor

OPERATION

The oxygen (O_2) sensor is a device which produces an electrical voltage when exposed to the oxygen present in the exhaust gases. The sensor is mounted in the exhaust system, usually in the manifold or a boss located on the down pipe before the catalyst.. Some of the oxygen sensors used on the Ford Crown Victoria/Mercury Grand Marquis are electrically heated internally for faster switching when the engine is started cold. The oxygen sensor produces a voltage within 0 and 1 volt. When there is a large amount of oxygen present (lean mixture), the sensor produces a low voltage (less than 0.4v). When there is a lesser amount present (rich mixture) it produces a higher voltage (0.6–1.0v).The stoichiometric or correct fuel to air ratio will read between 0.4 and 0.6v. By monitoring the oxygen content and converting it to electrical voltage, the sensor acts as a rich-lean switch. The voltage is transmitted to the PCM.

Some models have two or more sensors, before the catalyst and after. This is done for a catalyst efficiency monitor that is a part of the OBD-II engine controls that are on all models from the 1995 model year on. The sensor before the catalyst measures the exhaust emissions right out of the engine, and sends the signal to the PCM about the state of the mixture as previously talked about. The second sensor reports the difference in the emissions after the exhaust gases have gone through the catalyst. This sensor reports to the PCM the amount of emissions reduction the catalyst is performing.

The oxygen sensor will not work until a predetermined temperature is reached, until this time the PCM is running in what as known as OPEN LOOP operation. OPEN LOOP means that the PCM has not yet begun to correct the air-to-fuel ratio by reading the oxygen sensor. After the engine comes to operating temperature, the PCM will monitor the oxygen sensor and correct the air/fuel ratio from the sensor's readings. This is what is known as CLOSED LOOP operation.

A heated oxygen sensor (HO2S) has a heating element that keeps the sensor at proper operating temperature during all operating modes. Maintaining correct sensor temperature at all times allows the system to enter into CLOSED LOOP operation sooner.

In CLOSED LOOP operation the PCM monitors the sensor input (along with other inputs) and adjusts the injector pulse width accordingly. During OPEN LOOP operation the PCM ignores the sensor input and adjusts the injector pulse to a preprogrammed value based on other inputs.

TESTING

▶ **See Figure 58**

✳✳ WARNING

Do not pierce the wires when testing this sensor; this can lead to wiring harness damage. Backprobe the connector to properly read the voltage of the HO2S.

91054P13

Fig. 58 The HO2S can be monitored with an appropriate and Data-stream capable scan tool

1. Disconnect the HO2S.
2. Measure the resistance between PWR and GND terminals of the sensor. Resistance should be approximately 6 ohms at 68°F (20°C). If resistance is not within specification, the sensor's heater element is faulty.
3. With the HO2S connected and engine running, measure the voltage with a Digital Volt-Ohmmeter (DVOM) between terminals **HO2S** and **SIG RTN** (GND) of the oxygen sensor connector. Voltage should fluctuate between 0.01–1.0 volts. If voltage fluctuation is slow or voltage is not within specification, the sensor may be faulty.

REMOVAL & INSTALLATION

▶ **See Figures 59 thru 64**

➡An oxygen sensor socket/wrench is available from Ford or aftermarket manufacturers to ease the removal and installation of the oxygen sensor(s). If one is not available, an open end wrench can be used.

※ WARNING

The sensor uses a permanently attached pigtail and connector. This pigtail should not be removed from the sensor. Damage or removal of the pigtail or connector will affect the proper operation of the sensor. Keep the electrical connector and louvered end of the sensor clean and free of grease. NEVER use cleaning solvents of any type on the sensor! The oxygen sensor may be difficult to remove when the temperature of the engine is below 120°F (49°C). Excessive force may damage the threads in the exhaust manifold or exhaust pipe.

1. Disconnect the negative battery cable.
2. Raise and support the vehicle.
3. Unplug the electrical connector and any attaching hardware.

➡Lubricate the sensor with penetrating oil prior to removal.

4. Remove the sensor using an appropriate tool. Special oxygen sensor sockets are available to remove the sensor and can be purchased at many parts stores or where automotive tools are sold. The proper size wrench can be used, most sensors are ⅞ inch or 22 mm sizes.
To install:
5. Coat the threads of the sensor with a suitable anti-seize compound before installation. New sensors are precoated with this compound.
6. Install the sensor and tighten it. Use care in making sure the silicone boot is in the correct position to avoid melting it during operation.
7. Attach the electrical connector.
8. Lower the vehicle.
9. Connect the negative battery cable.

Idle Air Control Valve

OPERATION

The Idle Air Control (IAC) valve adjusts the engine idle speed. The valve is located on the side of the throttle body. The valve is controlled by a duty cycle signal from the PCM and allows air to bypass the throttle plate in order to maintain the proper idle speed.

➡Do not attempt to clean the IAC valve. Carburetor tune-up cleaners or any type of solvent cleaners will damage the internal components of the valve.

TESTING

▶ **See Figure 65**

1. Turn the ignition switch to the **OFF** position.
2. Disconnect the wiring harness from the IAC valve.
3. Measure the resistance between the terminals of the valve.

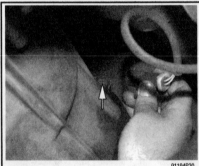

Fig. 59 Detach the connector for the H_2O sensor

Fig. 60 A special socket is available to remove the H2O sensor that contains a slot for the wire harness to slide out of

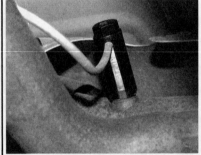

Fig. 61 Place the socket onto the sensor and . . .

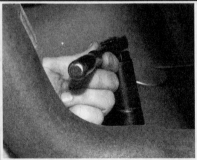

Fig. 62 loosen the sensor using a suitable drive tool

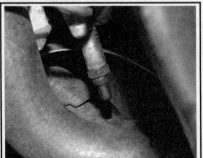

Fig. 63 After the sensor is sufficiently loose using the drive tool, remove the sensor from the exhaust pipe by hand

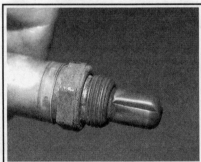

Fig. 64 Inspect the sensor tip for any signs of build-up or damage

➡**Due to the diode in the solenoid, place the ohmmeter positive lead on the VPWR terminal and the negative lead on the ISC terminal.**

4. Resistance should be 6–13 ohms.
5. If resistance is not within specification, the valve may be faulty.

REMOVAL & INSTALLATION

▶ **See Figure 66**

1. Disconnect the negative battery cable.
2. Detach the IAC solenoid connector.
3. Remove the 2 retaining bolts and remove the IAC solenoid and gasket from the throttle body.
4. Installation is the reverse of the removal procedure. Use a new gasket and tighten the retaining bolts to 71–97 inch lbs. (8–11 Nm).

➡**If scraping is necessary to remove old gasket material, be careful not to damage the IAC solenoid or the throttle body gasket surfaces or drop material into the throttle body.**

Engine Coolant Temperature (ECT) Sensor

OPERATION

The Engine Coolant Temperature (ECT) sensor resistance changes in response to engine coolant temperature. The sensor resistance decreases as the coolant temperature increases, and increases as the coolant temperature decreases. This provides a reference signal to the PCM, which indicates engine coolant temperature. The signal sent to the PCM by the ECT sensor helps the PCM to determine spark advance, EGR flow rate, air/fuel ratio, and engine temperature. The ECT is a two wire sensor, a 5-volt reference signal is sent to the sensor and the signal return is based upon the change in the measured resistance due to temperature.

TESTING

▶ **See Figures 67, 68 and 69**

1. Disconnect the engine wiring harness from the ECT sensor.
2. Connect an ohmmeter between the ECT sensor terminals.
3. With the engine cold and the ignition switch in the **OFF** position, measure and note the ECT sensor resistance.
4. Connect the engine wiring harness to the sensor.
5. Start the engine and allow the engine to reach normal operating temperature.
6. Once the engine has reached normal operating temperature, turn the engine **OFF**.
7. Once again, disconnect the engine wiring harness from the ECT sensor.
8. Measure and note the ECT sensor resistance with the engine hot.
9. Compare the cold and hot ECT sensor resistance measurements with the accompanying chart.
10. If readings do not approximate those in the chart, the sensor may be faulty.

REMOVAL & INSTALLATION

▶ **See Figures 70 thru 75**

1. Disconnect the negative battery cable.
2. Drain and recycle the engine coolant.

❄❄❄ CAUTION

Never open, service or drain the radiator or cooling system when hot; serious burns can occur from the steam and hot coolant. Also, when draining engine coolant, keep in mind that cats and dogs are attracted to ethylene glycol antifreeze and could drink any that is left in an uncovered container or in puddles on the ground. This will prove fatal in sufficient quantities. Always drain coolant into a sealable container. Coolant should be reused unless it is contaminated or is several years old.

Fig. 65 The IAC can be monitored with an appropriate and Data-stream capable scan tool

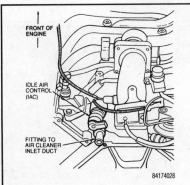

Fig. 66 IAC solenoid location—4.6L engine

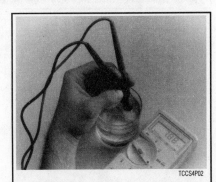

Fig. 67 Another method of testing the ECT is to submerge it in cold or hot water and check resistance

Temperature		Engine Coolant/Intake Air Temperature Sensor Values
		Resistance (K ohms)
°F	°C	
248	120	1.18
230	110	1.55
212	100	2.07
194	90	2.80
176	80	3.84
158	70	5.37
140	60	7.70
122	50	10.97
104	40	16.15
86	30	24.27
68	20	37.30
50	10	58.75

Fig. 68 ECT/IAT resistance-to-temperature specifications

3. Remove the air cleaner outlet tube.
4. Detach the ECT sensor connector.
5. Remove the ECT sensor from the intake manifold.

To install:

6. Coat the sensor threads with Teflon® sealant.
7. Thread the sensor into position and tighten to:
- 10–15 ft. lbs. (13–20 Nm) on the 5.0L engine
- 12–17 ft. lbs. (16–24 Nm) on the 4.6L engine
8. Attach the ECT sensor connector.
9. Install the air cleaner outlet tube.
10. Connect the negative battery cable.
11. Refill the engine cooling system.

12. Start the engine and check for coolant leaks.
13. Bleed the cooling system.

Intake Air Temperature Sensor

OPERATION

▶ **See Figure 76**

The Intake Air Temperature (IAT) sensor determines the air temperature inside the intake manifold. Resistance changes in response to the ambient air temperature. The sensor has a negative temperature coefficient. As the temperature of the sensor rises the resistance across the sensor decreases. This provides a signal to the PCM indicating the temperature of the incoming air

Fig. 69 Test the ECT resistance across the two sensor terminals

Fig. 70 Detach the connector for the ECT sensor and . . .

Fig. 71 . . . and loosen the sensor using a suitable socket or other drive tool

Fig. 72 Once the sensor is sufficiently loose, remove the sensor from the intake manifold by hand

Fig. 73 Use a quality thread sealant to . . .

Fig. 74 . . . coat the threads of the ECT sensor before installation

Fig. 75 The ECT sensor must be tightened with a torque wrench to specifications

Fig. 76 The tip of the IAT sensor has an exposed thermistor that changes the resistance of the sensor based upon the force of the air rushing past it

charge. This sensor helps the PCM to determine spark timing and air/fuel ratio. Information from this sensor is added to the pressure sensor information to calculate the air mass being sent to the cylinders. The IAT is a two wire sensor, a 5-volt reference signal is sent to the sensor and the signal return is based upon the change in the measured resistance due to temperature.

TESTING

▶ **See Figures 68, 77 and 78**

1. Turn the ignition switch **OFF**.
2. Disconnect the wiring harness from the IAT sensor.
3. Measure the resistance between the sensor terminals.
4. Compare the resistance reading with the accompanying chart.
5. If the resistance is not within specification, the IAT may be faulty.
6. Connect the wiring harness to the sensor.

Fig. 77 The IAT sensor can be monitored with an appropriate and Data-stream capable scan tool

REMOVAL & INSTALLATION

1992–95 Models

▶ **See Figures 79, 80, 81 and 82**

1. Disconnect the negative battery cable.
2. Detach the electrical connector from the IAT sensor.
3. Using a suitable socket and drive tool, remove the IAT sensor from the air cleaner lid.
   To install:
4. Coat the sensor threads with Teflon® sealant.
5. Thread the sensor into position and tighten it to 6–8 ft. lbs. (8–13 Nm)..
6. Attach the electrical connector to the IAT sensor.
7. Connect the negative battery cable.

1996–98 Models

1. Disconnect the negative battery cable.
2. Detach the electrical connector from the IAT sensor.
3. Turn the sensor 90° counterclockwise and remove the IAT sensor from the air cleaner lid.
4. Remove the sensor O-ring and inspect it. Replace as necessary.
   To install:
5. The installation is the reverse of the removal.

Mass Airflow Sensor

OPERATION

▶ **See Figure 83**

The Mass Air Flow (MAF) sensor directly measures the mass of air being drawn into the engine. The sensor output is used to calculate injec-

Fig. 78 Measure the resistance of the IAT sensor across the two sensor pins

Fig. 79 Using a suitable socket and drive tool, loosen the IAT sensor

Fig. 80 Remove the IAT sensor from the air cleaner assembly

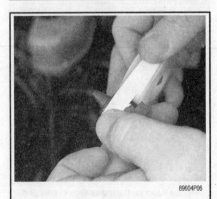

Fig. 81 It is advisable to use Teflon® to . . .

Fig. 82 . . . coat the threads of the sensor before installing it into the air cleaner assembly

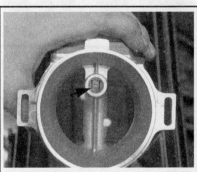

Fig. 83 The exposed "hot wire" of the MAF sensor

tor pulse width. The MAF sensor is what is referred to as a "hot-wire sensor". The sensor uses a thin platinum wire filament, wound on a ceramic bobbin and coated with glass, that is heated to 200°C (417°F) above the ambient air temperature and subjected to the intake airflow stream. A "cold-wire" is used inside the MAF sensor to determine the ambient air temperature.

Battery voltage from the EEC power relay, and a reference signal and a ground signal from the PCM are supplied to the MAF sensor. The sensor returns a signal proportionate to the current flow required to keep the "hot-wire" at the required temperature. The increased airflow across the "hot-wire" acts as a cooling fan, lowering the resistance and requiring more current to maintain the temperature of the wire. The increased current is measured by the voltage in the circuit, as current increases, voltage increases. As the airflow increases the signal return voltage of a normally operating MAF sensor will increase.

TESTING

▶ **See Figures 84 and 85**

1. Using a multimeter, check for voltage by backprobing the MAF sensor connector.
2. With the key **ON**, and the engine **OFF**, verify that there is at least 10.5 volts between the VPWR and GND terminals of the MAF sensor connector. If voltage is not within specification, check power and ground circuits and repair as necessary.
3. With the key **ON**, and the engine **ON**, verify that there is at least 4.5 volts between the SIG and GND terminals of the MAF sensor connector. If voltage is not within specification, check power and ground circuits and repair as necessary.
4. With the key **ON**, and the engine **ON**, check voltage between GND and SIG RTN terminals. Voltage should be approximately 0.34–1.96 volts. If voltage is not within specification, the sensor may be faulty.

REMOVAL & INSTALLATION

▶ **See Figures 86, 87, 88 and 89**

1. Disconnect the negative battery cable.
2. Remove the air intake tube from the MAF sensor and the throttle body.
3. Detach the connector from the MAF sensor.
4. Remove the four sensor retaining screws and remove the sensor.
5. Remove the sensor gasket.

To install:

6. Installation is the reverse of removal.

Manifold Air Pressure (MAP) Sensor

OPERATION

➡ **The Manifold Absolute Pressure (MAP) sensor is used on the 5.0L engine, except on 1990–91 sedans sold in California.**

The most important information for measuring engine fuel requirements comes from the pressure sensor. Using the pressure and temperature data, the PCM calculates the intake air mass. It is connected to the engine intake manifold through a hose and takes readings of the absolute pressure. A piezoelectric crystal changes a voltage input to a frequency output which reflects the pressure in the intake manifold.

Atmospheric pressure is measured both when the engine is started and when driving fully loaded, then the pressure sensor information is adjusted accordingly.

TESTING

▶ **See Figures 90, 91, 92 and 93**

1. Connect MAP/BARO tester to the sensor connector and sensor harness connector. With ignition **ON** and engine **OFF**, use DVOM to measure voltage

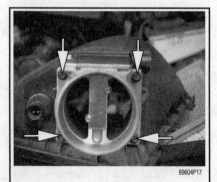

Fig. 84 Testing the SIG circuit of the MAF sensor

Fig. 85 Testing the VPWR circuit of the MAF sensor

Fig. 86 Remove the air intake tube from the MAF sensor

Fig. 87 Remove the four sensor retaining screws and . . .

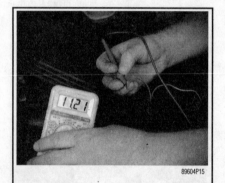

Fig. 88 . . . remove the sensor from the air cleaner assembly

Fig. 89 Remove the old sensor gasket and replace it

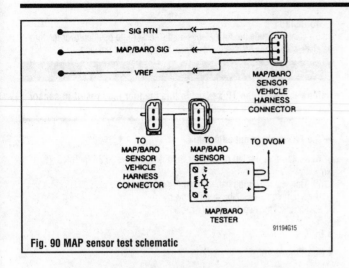

Fig. 90 MAP sensor test schematic

Approximate Altitude (Feet)	Signal Voltage (±0.04V)
0	1.59
1000	1.56
2000	1.53
3000	1.50
4000	1.47
5000	1.44
6000	1.41
7000	1.39

Fig. 91 MAP sensor altitude/voltage output relationship

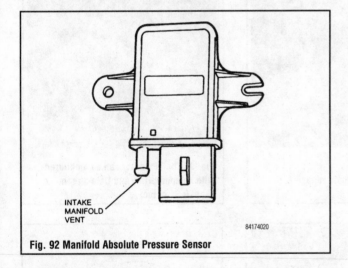

Fig. 92 Manifold Absolute Pressure Sensor

across tester terminals. If the tester's 4-6V indicator is ON, the reference voltage input to the sensor is okay.

2. Measure the reference signal of the MAP sensor. If the DVOM voltage reading is as indicated in the table, the sensor is okay.

REMOVAL & INSTALLATION

1. Disconnect the negative battery cable.
2. Detach the electrical connector and the vacuum line from the sensor.

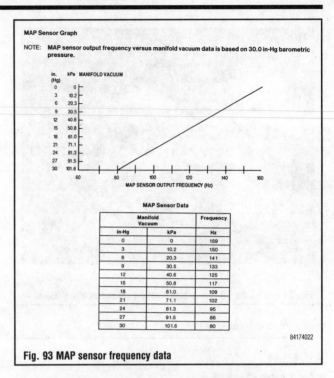

Fig. 93 MAP sensor frequency data

MAP Sensor Graph

NOTE: MAP sensor output frequency versus manifold vacuum data is based on 30.0 in-Hg barometric pressure.

MAP Sensor Data

Manifold Vacuum		Frequency
in-Hg	kPa	Hz
0	0	159
3	10.2	150
6	20.3	141
9	30.5	133
12	40.6	125
15	50.8	117
18	61.0	109
21	71.1	102
24	81.3	95
27	91.5	88
30	101.6	80

3. Remove the sensor mounting bolts and remove the sensor.
4. Installation is the reverse of the removal procedure.

Throttle Position Sensor

OPERATION

The Throttle Position (TP) sensor is a potentiometer that provides a signal to the PCM that is directly proportional to the throttle plate position. The TP sensor is mounted on the side of the throttle body and is connected to the throttle plate shaft. The TP sensor monitors throttle plate movement and position, and transmits an appropriate electrical signal to the PCM. These signals are used by the PCM to adjust the air/fuel mixture, spark timing and EGR operation according to engine load at idle, part throttle, or full throttle. The TP sensor is not adjustable.

The TP sensor receives a 5 volt reference signal and a ground circuit from the PCM. A return signal circuit is connected to a wiper that runs on a resistor internally on the sensor. The further the throttle is opened, the wiper moves along the resistor, at wide open throttle, the wiper essentially creates a loop between the reference signal and the signal return returning the full or nearly full 5 volt signal back to the PCM. At idle the signal return should be approximately 0.9 volts.

TESTING

▶ See Figures 94, 95, 96 and 97

1. With the engine **OFF** and the ignition **ON**, check the voltage at the signal return circuit of the TP sensor by carefully backprobing the connector using a DVOM.
2. Voltage should be between 0.2 and 1.4 volts at idle.
3. Slowly move the throttle pulley to the wide open throttle (WOT) position and watch the voltage on the DVOM. The voltage should slowly rise to slightly less than 4.8v at Wide Open Throttle (WOT).
4. If no voltage is present, check the wiring harness for supply voltage (5.0v) and ground (0.3v or less), by referring to your corresponding wiring guide. If supply voltage and ground are present, but no output voltage from TP, replace the TP sensor. If supply voltage and ground do not meet specifications, make necessary repairs to the harness or PCM.

Fig. 94 Testing the TP sensor signal return voltage at idle position

REMOVAL & INSTALLATION

4.6L Engine

▶ See Figures 98 and 99

1. Disconnect the negative battery cable.
2. If necessary, remove the throttle cover from the engine.
3. Disconnect the wiring harness from the TP sensor.
4. Remove the two sensor mounting screws, then pull the TP sensor off of the throttle shaft.

To install:
5. Carefully slide the rotary tangs on the sensor into position over the throttle shaft, then rotate the sensor clockwise to the installed position..

✸✸ CAUTION

Failure to install the TP sensor in this manner may result in sensor damage or high idle speeds.

➡ **The TP sensor is not adjustable.**

6. Install and tighten the sensor mounting screws to 27 inch lbs. (3 Nm).
7. Connect the wiring harness to the sensor.
8. If removed, install the throttle cover.
9. Connect the negative battery cable.

5.0L Engine

▶ See Figure 100

1. Disconnect the negative battery cable.
2. Detach the TP sensor connector.
3. Scribe a reference mark across the edge of the sensor and the throttle body so the sensor can be reinstalled in the same position.
4. Remove the TP sensor retaining screws and remove the sensor.

To install:
5. The TP sensor bushing, if present, must be reused. Install the bushing with the larger diameter facing outward.
6. Install the TP sensor on the throttle shaft and rotate the TP sensor 10–20 degrees counterclockwise to align the screw holes.
7. Install the 2 TP sensor retaining screws and tighten to 11–16 inch lbs. (1.2–1.8 Nm).
8. Cycle the throttle lever to WOT; it should return without interference.
9. Connect the TP sensor connector and connect the negative battery cable.

Fig. 95 Test the operation of the TP sensor by gently opening the throttle while observing the signal return voltage. The voltage should move smoothly according to the amount the throttle is opened

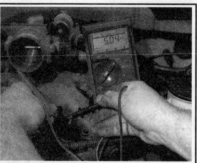

Fig. 96 Testing the supply voltage at the TP sensor connector

Fig. 97 The TP sensor can be monitored with an appropriate and Data-stream capable scan tool

Fig. 98 Disconnect the wiring harness from the TP sensor

Fig. 99 Remove the two retaining screws for the TP sensor and remove the sensor from the throttle body

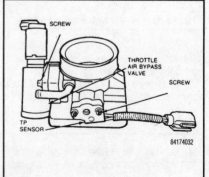

Fig. 100 Throttle position sensor location—5.0L engine

Knock Sensor

OPERATION

➡️ **The Knock Sensor (KS) is only outfitted on the 4.6L engine.**

The operation of the Knock Sensor (KS) is to monitor preignition or "engine knocks" and send the signal to the PCM. The PCM responds by adjusting ignition timing until the "knocks" stop. The sensor works by generating a signal produced by the frequency of the knock as recorded by the piezoelectric ceramic disc inside the KS. The disc absorbs the shock waves from the knocks and exerts a pressure on the metal diaphragm inside the KS. This compresses the crystals inside the disc and the disc generates a voltage signal proportional to the frequency of the knocks ranging from zero to 1 volt.

TESTING

There is no real test for this sensor, the sensor produces it's own signal based on information gathered while the engine is running. The sensors also are usually inaccessible without major component removal. The sensors can be monitored with an appropriate scan tool using a data display or other data stream information. Follow the instructions included with the scan tool for information on accessing the data. The only test available is to test the continuity of the harness from the PCM to the sensor.

REMOVAL & INSTALLATION

4.6L Engine

▶ **See Figure 101**

1. Disconnect the negative battery cable.
2. Remove the upper intake manifold. Refer to Section 3.
3. Detach the knock sensor connector.
4. Remove the knock sensor from the engine.
   To install:
5. The installation is the reverse of removal.

Camshaft Position Sensor

➡️ **The Camshaft Position Sensor (CMP) is only outfitted on the 4.6L engine.**

The camshaft position sensor (CMP) is a variable reluctance sensor that is triggered by a high point on the left-hand exhaust camshaft sprocket. The CMP sends a signal relating camshaft position back to the PCM which is used by the PCM to control engine timing.

TESTING

1. Check voltage between the camshaft position sensor terminals PWR GND and CID.
2. With engine running, voltage should be greater than 0.1 volt AC and vary with engine speed.

3. If voltage is not within specification, check for proper voltage at the VPWR terminal.
4. If VPWR voltage is greater than 10.5 volts, sensor may be faulty.

REMOVAL & INSTALLATION

4.6L Engine

▶ **See Figures 102, 103 and 104**

1. Disconnect the negative battery cable.
2. Detach the electrical connector for the CMP sensor.
3. Remove the CMP sensor retaining bolt(s) and remove the CMP sensor from the front cover.
   To install:
4. Installation is the reverse of removal.

Crankshaft Position Sensor

OPERATION

▶ **See Figure 105**

The Crankshaft Position (CKP) sensor is a variable reluctance sensor that uses a trigger wheel to induce voltage. The CKP sensor is a fixed magnetic sensor mounted to the engine block and monitors the trigger or "pulse" wheel which is attached to the crank pulley/damper. As the pulse wheel rotates by the CKP sensor, teeth on the pulse wheel induce voltage inside the sensor through magnetism. The pulse wheel has a missing tooth that changes the reading of the sensor. This is used for the Cylinder Identification (CID) function to properly monitor and adjust engine timing by locating the number 1 cylinder. The voltage created by the CKP sensor is alternating current (A/C). This voltage reading is sent to the PCM and is used to determine engine RPM, engine timing, and is used to fire the ignition coils.

TESTING

1. Measure the voltage between the sensor CKP sensor terminals by back-probing the sensor connector.

➡️ **If the connector cannot be backprobed, fabricate or purchase a test harness.**

2. Sensor voltage should be more than 0.1 volt AC with the engine running and should vary with engine RPM.
3. If voltage is not within specification, the sensor may be faulty.

REMOVAL & INSTALLATION

▶ **See Figure 106**

1. Disconnect the negative battery cable.
2. Remove the accessory drive belt from the engine.
3. Raise and safely support the vehicle.
4. Remove the A/C compressor mounting bolts, but do not disconnect the A/C lines. Remove and support the compressor out of the way.

Fig. 101 The knock sensor is located under the intake manifold—4.6L Engine

Fig. 102 Detach the connector for the CMP sensor and . . .

Fig. 103 . . . remove the bolt retaining the CMP sensor to the front cover and . . .

Fig. 104 . . . remove the sensor

Fig. 105 The CKP sensor trigger wheel rides on the front of the crankshaft. The missing tooth creates a fluctuation of voltage in the sensor

Fig. 106 Remove the retaining bolt for the CKP sensor and remove the sensor from the front cover

5. Detach the electrical connector for the CKP sensor.
6. Remove the CKP sensor retaining bolts and remove the CKP sensor.
To install:
7. Installation is the reverse of removal.

Vehicle Speed Sensor

OPERATION

The Vehicle Speed Sensor (VSS) is a magnetic pick-up sensor that sends a signal to the Powertrain Control Module (PCM) and the speedometer. The sensor measures the rotation of the transmission output shaft or the ring gear on the differential and sends an AC voltage signal to the PCM which determines the corresponding vehicle speed.

TESTING

1. Disconnect the negative battery cable.
2. Disengage the wiring harness connector from the VSS.

3. Using a Digital Volt-Ohmmeter (DVOM), measure the resistance (ohmmeter function) between the sensor terminals. If the resistance is 190–250 ohms, the sensor is okay.

REMOVAL & INSTALLATION

▶ See Figures 107, 108, 109, 110 and 111

1. Disconnect the negative battery cable.
2. Raise and safely support the vehicle securely on jackstands.
3. Detach the connector for the VSS.
4. Remove the VSS retaining bolt and remove the VSS from the transmission.
5. Remove the driven gear retainer and the drive gear.
To install:
6. Inspect the O-ring on the sensor and replace if necessary.
7. Install the driven gear and the retainer.
8. Place the VSS into the transmission.
9. Tighten the retaining bolt to 98–115 inch lbs. (11–13 Nm).
10. Attach the VSS electrical connector.
11. Lower the vehicle.
12. Connect the negative battery cable.

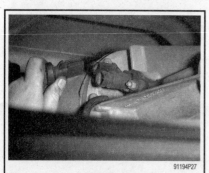

Fig. 107 Detach the connector for the VSS sensor

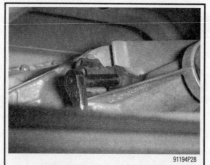

Fig. 108 Remove the retaining bolt for the VSS sensor and . . .

Fig. 109 . . . remove the VSS sensor from the transmission

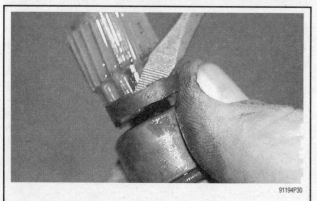

Fig. 110 Pry the retainer for the VSS gear off and . . .

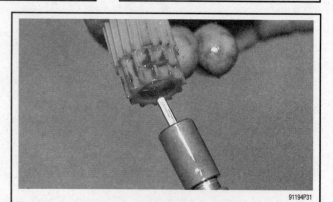

Fig. 111 . . . remove the gear from the VSS

COMPONENT LOCATIONS

COMMON EMISSIONS AND ELECTRONIC ENGINE CONTROL COMPONENT LOCATIONS—4.6L ENGINE

1. Positive Crankcase Ventilation (PCV) valve
2. Exhaust Gas Recirculation (EGR) valve
3. EGR vacuum control solenoid
4. Throttle Position (TP) sensor
5. Idle Air Control (IAC) valve—located on the backside of throttle body
6. Engine Coolant Temperature (ECT) sensor
7. Camshaft Position (CMP) sensor
8. Powertrain Control Module (PCM)
9. Mass Airflow (MAF) sensor
10. Intake Air Temperature (IAT) sensor
11. Electronic Engine Control self-test connector (EEC-IV only)

89604P30

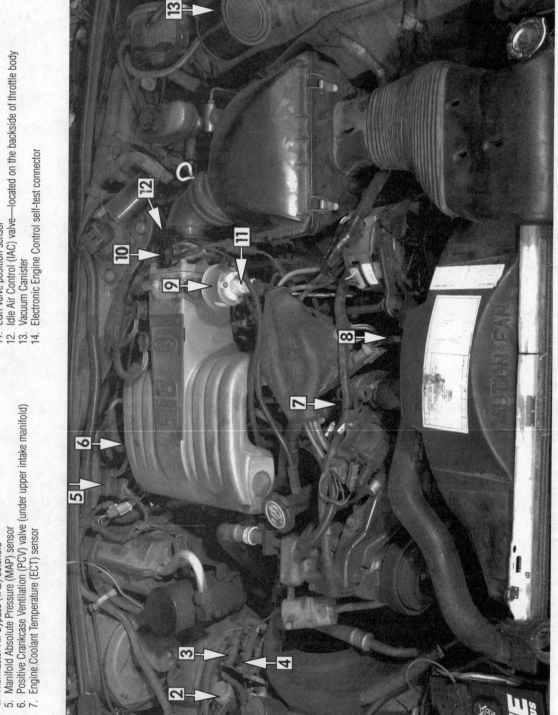

COMMON EMISSIONS AND ELECTRONIC ENGINE CONTROL COMPONENT LOCATIONS—5.0L ENGINE

1. Reserve vacuum reservoir
2. EGR vacuum control solenoid
3. Thermactor Air Diverter (TAD) solenoid
4. Thermactor Air Bypass (TAB) solenoid
5. Manifold Absolute Pressure (MAP) sensor
6. Positive Crankcase Ventilation (PCV) valve (under upper intake manifold)
7. Engine Coolant Temperature (ECT) sensor
8. Spark Output (SPOUT) connector
9. Exhaust Gas Recirculation (EGR) valve
10. Throttle Position (TP) sensor
11. EGR valve position sensor
12. Idle Air Control (IAC) valve—located on the backside of throttle body
13. Vacuum Canister
14. Electronic Engine Control self-test connector

TROUBLE CODES—EEC-IV SYSTEM

General Information

The EEC-IV system is outfitted on the 1989–94 Crown Victoria and Mercury Grand Marquis models equipped with the 5.0L and 4.6L engines only.

One part of the Powertrain Control Module (PCM) is devoted to monitoring both input and output functions within the system. This ability forms the core of the self-diagnostic system. If a problem is detected within a circuit, the controller will recognize the fault, assign it an identification code, and store the code in a memory section. Depending on the year and model, the fault code(s) may be represented by two or three-digit numbers. The stored code(s) may be retrieved during diagnosis.

While the EEC-IV system is capable of recognizing many internal faults, certain faults will not be recognized. Because the computer system sees only electrical signals, it cannot sense or react to mechanical or vacuum faults affecting engine operation. Some of these faults may affect another component which will set a code. For example, the PCM monitors the output signal to the fuel injectors, but cannot detect a partially clogged injector. As long as the output driver responds correctly, the computer will read the system as functioning correctly. However, the improper flow of fuel may result in a lean mixture. This would, in turn, be detected by the oxygen sensor and noticed as a constantly lean signal by the PCM. Once the signal falls outside the pre-programmed limits, the engine control assembly would notice the fault and set an identification code.

FAILURE MODE EFFECTS MANAGEMENT (FMEM)

The PCM contains back-up programs which allow the engine to operate if a sensor signal is lost. If a sensor input is seen to be out of range—either high or low—the FMEM program is used. The processor substitutes a fixed value for the missing sensor signal. The engine will continue to operate, although performance and driveability may be noticeably reduced. This function of the controller is sometimes referred to as the limp-in or fail-safe mode. If the missing sensor signal is restored, the FMEM system immediately returns the system to normal operation. The dashboard warning lamp will be lit when FMEM is in effect.

HARDWARE LIMITED OPERATION STRATEGY (HLOS)

This mode is only used if the fault is too extreme for the FMEM circuit to handle. In this mode, the processor has ceased all computation and control; the entire system is run on fixed values. The vehicle may be operated but performance and driveability will be greatly reduced. The fixed or default settings provide minimal calibration, allowing the vehicle to be carefully driven in for service. The dashboard warning lamp will be lit when HLOS is engaged. Codes cannot be read while the system is operating in this mode.

Diagnostic Link Connector

➡**Some of the vehicles covered by this manual utilize two Diagnostic Link Connectors (DLCs), both of which are in the same vicinity.**

The Diagnostic Link Connector(s) (DLC) may be found in the following location:
- Under the hood near the firewall behind the driver's side strut tower.

The DLC is rectangular in design and capable of allowing access to 16 terminals. The connector has keying features that allow easy connection. The test equipment and the DLC have a latching feature to ensure a good mated connection.

HAND-HELD SCAN TOOLS

▶ **See Figures 112, 113, 114 and 115**

Although stored codes may be read through the flashing of the CHECK ENGINE or SERVICE ENGINE SOON lamp, the use of hand-held scan tools such as Ford's Self-Test Automatic Readout (STAR) tester or the second generation SUPER STAR II tester or their equivalent is highly recommended. There are many manufacturers of these tools; the purchaser must be certain that the tool is proper for the intended use.

The scan tool allows any stored faults to be read from the engine controller memory. Use of the scan tool provides additional data during troubleshooting, but does not eliminate the use of the charts. The scan tool makes collecting information easier, but the data must be correctly interpreted by an operator familiar with the system.

ELECTRICAL TOOLS

The most commonly required electrical diagnostic tool is the digital multimeter, also known as a Digital Volt Ohmmeter (DVOM), which permits voltage, resistance (ohms) and amperage to be read by one instrument.

The multimeter must be a high impedance unit, with 10 megaohms of impedance in the voltmeter. This type of meter will not place an additional load on the circuit it is testing; this is extremely important in low voltage circuits. The multimeter must be of high quality in all respects. It should be handled carefully and protected from impact or damage. Replace the batteries frequently in the unit.

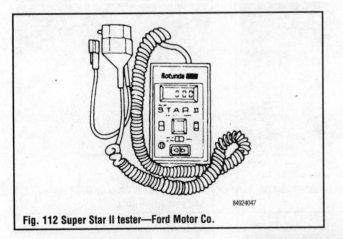

Fig. 112 Super Star II tester—Ford Motor Co.

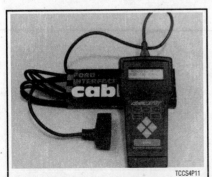

Fig. 113 Inexpensive scan tools, such as this Auto Xray ®, are available to interface with your Ford vehicle

Fig. 114 An economically friendly alternative is this Code Scanner ® from SunPro. They are purchased according to manufacturer and are available at many parts stores

Fig. 115 The Code Scanner ® from SunPro has no LCD display, just a LED that will flash out the codes and an audible buzzer to alert that the test is in progress

Additionally, an analog (needle type) voltmeter may be used to read stored fault codes if the STAR tester is not available. The codes are transmitted as visible needle sweeps on the face of the instrument.

Almost all diagnostic procedures will require the use of a Breakout Box, a device which connects into the EEC-IV harness and provides testing ports for the 60 wires in the harness. Direct testing of the harness connectors at the terminals or by backprobing is not recommended; damage to the wiring and terminals is almost certain to occur.

Other necessary tools include a quality tachometer with inductive (clip-on) pickup, a fuel pressure gauge with system adapters and a vacuum gauge with an auxiliary source of vacuum.

Reading Codes

Diagnosis of a driveability problem requires attention to detail and following the diagnostic procedures in the correct order. Resist the temptation to begin extensive testing before completing the preliminary diagnostic steps. The preliminary or visual inspection must be completed in detail before diagnosis begins. In many cases this will shorten diagnostic time and often cure the problem without electronic testing.

VISUAL INSPECTION

This is possibly the most critical step of diagnosis. A detailed examination of all connectors, wiring and vacuum hoses can often lead to a repair without further diagnosis. Performance of this step relies on the skill of the technician performing it; a careful inspector will check the undersides of hoses as well as the integrity of hard-to-reach hoses blocked by the air cleaner or other components. Wiring should be checked carefully for any sign of strain, burning, crimping or terminal pull-out from a connector.

Checking connectors at components or in harnesses is required; usually, pushing them together will reveal a loose fit. Pay particular attention to ground circuits, making sure they are not loose or corroded. Remember to inspect connectors and hose fittings at components not mounted on the engine, such as the evaporative canister or relays mounted on the fender aprons. Any component or wiring in the vicinity of a fluid leak or spillage should be given extra attention during inspection.

Additionally, inspect maintenance items such as belt condition and tension, battery charge and condition and the radiator cap carefully. Any of these very simple items may affect the system enough to set a fault.

ELECTRONIC TESTING

If a code was set before a problem self-corrected (such as a momentarily loose connector), the code will be erased if the problem does not reoccur within 80 warm-up cycles. Codes will be output and displayed as numbers on the hand-held scan tool, such as 23. If the codes are being read on an analog voltmeter, the needle sweeps indicate the code digits. code 23 will appear as two needle pulses (sweeps) then, after a 1.6 second pause, the needle will pulse (sweep) three times.

Key On Engine Off (KOEO) Test

♦ See Figures 116 thru 122

1. Connect the scan tool to the self-test connectors. Make certain the test button is unlatched or up.
2. Start the engine and run it until normal operating temperature is reached.
3. Turn the engine **OFF** for 10 seconds.
4. Activate the test button on the STAR tester.
5. Turn the ignition switch **ON** but do not start the engine.
6. The KOEO codes will be transmitted. Six to nine seconds after the last KOEO code, a single separator pulse will be transmitted. Six to nine seconds after this pulse, the codes from the Continuous Memory will be transmitted.
7. Record all service codes displayed. Do not depress the throttle on gasoline engines during the test.

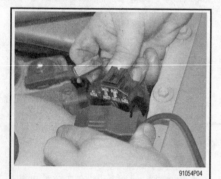

Fig. 116 Connect the scan tool to the DLC connector

Fig. 117 The scan tool menu will be displayed, follow the instructions included with the scan tool

Fig. 118 This PCM had no DTC's stored and passed the KOEO

Fig. 119 This PCM had a DTC 113 stored. Most scan tools will give a code definition on-screen as the Auto X-ray shown here informs what code 113 is for the IAT sensor

Fig. 120 If the A/C or Blower motor is left on, a code 539 will be tripped. Turn the A/C or blower motor off and retest

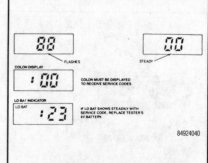

Fig. 121 STAR tester displays; note that the colon must be present before codes can be received

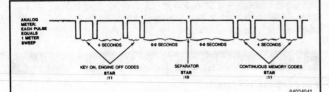

Fig. 122 Code transmission during KOEO test. Note that the continuous memory codes are transmitted after a pause and a separator pulse

Key On Engine Running (KOER) Test

▶ **See Figures 112, 121 thru 123**

1. Make certain the self-test button is released or de-activated on the STAR tester.

2. Start the engine and run it at 2000 rpm for two minutes. This action warms up the oxygen sensor.

3. Turn the ignition switch **OFF** for 10 seconds.

4. Activate or latch the self-test button on the scan tool.

5. Start the engine. The engine identification code will be transmitted. This is a single digit number representing ½ the number of cylinders in a gasoline engine. On the STAR tester, this number may appear with a zero, such as 20 = 2. The code is used to confirm that the correct processor is installed and that the self-test has begun.

6. If the vehicle is equipped with a Brake On/Off (BOO) switch, the brake pedal must be depressed and released after the ID code is transmitted.

7. If the vehicle is equipped with a Power Steering Pressure Switch (PSPS), the steering wheel must be turned at least ½ turn and released within 2 seconds after the engine ID code is transmitted.

8. Certain Ford vehicles will display a Dynamic Response code 6–20 seconds after the engine ID code. This will appear as one pulse on a meter or as a 10 on the STAR tester. When this code appears, briefly take the engine to wide open throttle. This allows the system to test the throttle position, MAF and MAP sensors.

9. All relevant codes will be displayed and should be recorded. Remember that the codes refer only to faults present during this test cycle. Codes stored in Continuous Memory are not displayed in this test mode.

10. Do not depress the throttle during testing unless a dynamic response code is displayed.

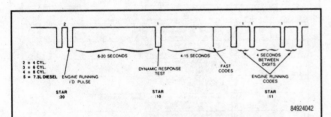

Fig. 123 Code transmission during KOER testing begins with the engine identification pulse and may include a dynamic response prompt

Reading Codes With Analog Voltmeter

▶ **See Figures 124**

In the absence of a scan tool, an analog voltmeter may be used to retrieve stored fault codes. Set the meter range to read DC 0–15 volts. Connect the + lead of the meter to the battery positive terminal and connect the −; lead of the meter to the self-test output pin of the diagnostic connector.

Follow the directions given previously for performing the KOEO and KOER tests. To activate the tests, use a jumper wire to connect the signal return pin on the diagnostic connector to the self-test input connector. The self-test input line is the separate wire and connector with or near the diagnostic connector.

The codes will be transmitted as groups of needle sweeps. This method may be used to read either 2 or 3-digit codes. The Continuous Memory codes are separated from the KOEO codes by 6 seconds, a single sweep and another 6 second delay.

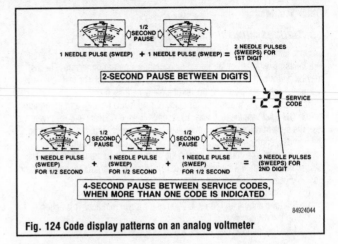

Fig. 124 Code display patterns on an analog voltmeter

Malfunction Indicator Lamp Method

▶ **See Figures 125 and 126**

The Malfunction Indicator Lamp (MIL) on the dashboard may also be used to retrieve the stored codes. This method displays only the stored codes and does not allow any system investigation. It should only be used in field conditions where a quick check of stored codes is needed.

Follow the directions given previously for performing the scan tool procedure. To activate the tests, use a jumper wire to connect the signal return pin on the diagnostic connector to the Self-Test Input (STI) connector. The self-test input line is the separate wire and connector with or near the diagnostic connector.

Codes are transmitted by place value with a pause between the digits; for example, code 32 would be sent as 3 flashes, a pause and 2 flashes. A slightly longer pause divides codes from each other. Be ready to count and record codes; the only way to repeat a code is to recycle the system. This method may be used to read either 2 or 3-digit codes. The Continuous Memory codes are separated from the other codes by 6 seconds, a single flash and another 6 second delay.

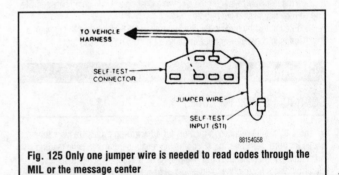

Fig. 125 Only one jumper wire is needed to read codes through the MIL or the message center

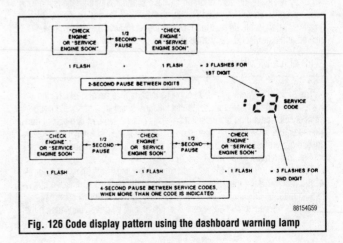

Fig. 126 Code display pattern using the dashboard warning lamp

Other Test Modes

CONTINUOUS MONITOR OR WIGGLE TEST

Once entered, this mode allows the operator to attempt to recreate intermittent faults by wiggling or tapping components, wiring or connectors. The test may be performed during either KOEO or KOER procedures. The test requires the use of either an analog voltmeter or a hand-held scan tool.

To enter the continuous monitor mode during KOEO testing, turn the ignition switch **ON** . Activate the test, wait 10 seconds, then deactivate and reactivate the test; the system will enter the continuous monitor mode. Tap, move or wiggle the harness, component or connector suspected of causing the problem; if a fault is detected, the code will store in the memory. When the fault occurs, the dash warning lamp will illuminate, the STAR tester will light a red indicator (and possibly beep) and the analog meter needle will sweep once.

To enter this mode in the KOER test:

1. Start the engine and run it at 2000 rpm for two minutes. This action warms up the oxygen sensor.

2. Turn the ignition switch **OFF** for 10 seconds.

3. Start the engine.

4. Activate the test, wait 10 seconds, then deactivate and reactivate the test; the system will enter the continuous monitor mode.

5. Tap, move or wiggle the harness, component or connector suspected of causing the problem; if a fault is detected, the code will store in the memory.

6. When the fault occurs, the dash warning lamp will illuminate, the STAR tester will light a red indicator (and possibly beep) and the analog meter needle will sweep once.

OUTPUT STATE CHECK

This testing mode allows the operator to energize and de-energize most of the outputs controlled by the EEC-IV system. Many of the outputs may be checked at the component by listening for a click or feeling the item move or engage by a hand placed on the case. To enter this check:

1. Enter the KOEO test mode.

2. When all codes have been transmitted, depress the accelerator all the way to the floor and release it.

3. The output actuators are now all ON. Depressing the throttle pedal to the floor again switches the all the actuator outputs OFF.

4. This test may be performed as often as necessary, switching between ON and OFF by depressing the throttle.

5. Exit the test by turning the ignition switch **OFF**, detaching the jumper at the diagnostic connector or releasing the test button on the scan tool.

Clearing Codes

CONTINUOUS MEMORY CODES

These codes are retained in memory for 40 warm-up cycles. To clear the codes for purposes of testing or confirming repair, perform the code reading procedure. When the fault codes begin to be displayed, de-activate the test either by disconnecting the jumper wire (if using a meter, MIL or message center) or by releasing the test button on the hand scanner. Stopping the test during code transmission will erase the Continuous Memory. Do not disconnect the negative battery cable to clear these codes; the Keep Alive memory will be cleared and a new code, 19, will be stored for loss of PCM power.

KEEP ALIVE MEMORY

The Keep Alive Memory (KAM) contains the adaptive factors used by the processor to compensate for component tolerances and wear. It should not be routinely cleared during diagnosis. If an emissions related part is replaced during repair, the KAM must be cleared. Failure to clear the KAM may cause severe driveability problems since the correction factor for the old component will be applied to the new component.

To clear the Keep Alive Memory, disconnect the negative battery cable for at least 5 minutes. After the memory is cleared and the battery reconnected, the vehicle must be driven at least 10 miles (16 km) so that the processor may relearn the needed correction factors. The distance to be driven depends on the engine and vehicle, but all drives should include steady-throttle cruise on open roads. Certain driveability problems may be noted during the drive because the adaptive factors are not yet functioning.

EEC-IV Diagnostic Trouble Codes

♦ **See Figures 127 thru 135**

SERVICE CODE		SERVICE CODE DEFINITION
11	orc	System PASS
12	r	Unable to control rpm to Self-Test upper limit band
13	r	Unable to control rpm to Self-Test lower limit band
14	c	PIP circuit failure
15	o	ROM test failure
15	c	Power interruption to Keep Alive Memory (KAM)
16	r	RPM too low to perform fuel test
18	r	SPOUT circuit open
18	c	Loss of tach input to Processor/SPOUT circuit grounded
19	o	Failure of EEC power supply
21	or	ECT sensor input is out of Self-Test range
22	orc	MAP sensor input is out of Self-Test range
23	or	TP sensor input is out of Self-Test range
24	or	ACT sensor input is out of Self-Test range
29	c	Insufficient input from the Vehicle Speed Sensor (VSS)
31	orc	EVP circuit is below minimum voltage
32	orc	EVP voltage is below closed limit (SONIC)
33	rc	EGR valve is not opening (SONIC)
34	orc	EVP voltage is above closed limit (SONIC)
35	orc	EVP circuit is above maximum voltage
41	r	HEGO sensor circuit indicates system lean (right HEGO)
41	c	No HEGO switching detected (right HEGO)
42	r	HEGO sensor circuit indicates system rich (right HEGO)
44	r	Thermactor air system inoperative (cyl. 1-4)
45	r	Thermactor air upstream during Self-Test
46	r	Thermactor air not bypassed during Self-Test
51	oc	ECT sensor input is greater than Self-Test maximum
53	oc	TP sensor input is greater than Self-Test maximum
54	oc	ACT sensor input is greater than Self-Test maximum
61	oc	ECT sensor input is less than Self-Test minimum
63	oc	TP sensor input is less than Self-Test minimum
64	oc	ACT sensor input is less than Self-Test minimum
67	o	Neutral Drive Switch (NDS) circuit open
74	r	Brake On/Off (BOO) circuit open — not actuated during test
75	r	Brake On/Off (BOO) circuit closed - always high
79	o	A/C on during Self-Test
81	o	Air Management 2 (AM2) circuit failure
82	o	Air Management 1 (AM1) circuit failure
84	o	EGR Vacuum Regulator (EVR) circuit failure
85	o	Canister Purge (CANP) circuit failure
87	oc	Fuel pump primary circuit failure
91	r	HEGO sensor circuit indicates system lean (left HEGO)
91	c	No HEGO switching detected (left HEGO)
92	r	HEGO sensor circuit indicates system rich (left HEGO)
94	r	Thermactor air system inoperative (cyl. 5-8)
98	r	Hard fault is present
NO CODES		Unable to initiate Self-Test or unable to output Self-Test codes
CODES NOT LISTED	►	Service codes displayed are not applicable to the vehicle being tested

KEY: o = Key On Engine Off (KOEO) r = Engine Running (ER) c = Continuous Memory

84174208

Fig. 127 Diagnostic service codes; 1989 5.0L engine only

SERVICE CODE		SERVICE CODE DEFINITION
11	orc	System PASS
12	r	Cannot control rpm during Self-Test high rpm check
13	r	Cannot control rpm during Self-Test low rpm check
14	c	PIP circuit failure
15	o	ECA Read Only Memory (ROM) test failed
15	c	ECA Keep Alive Memory (KAM) test failed
16	r	Rpm too low to perform EGO test
18	r	SPOUT circuit open
18	c	IDM circuit failure/SPOUT circuit grounded
19	o	Failure in ECA internal voltage
21	or	ECT out of Self-Test range
22	oc	MAP/BP out of Self-Test range
23	or	TP out of Self-Test range
24	or	ACT out of Self-Test range
26	or	MAF out of Self-Test range (MA only)
29	c	Insufficient input from the Vehicle Speed Sensor (VSS)
31	orc	EVP circuit below minimum voltage
32	orc	EVP voltage below closed limit (SONIC)
33	rc	EGR valve opening not detected (SONIC)
34	orc	EVP voltage above closed limit (SONIC)
35	orc	EVP circuit above maximum voltage
41	r	HEGO sensor circuit indicates system lean (right HEGO)
41	c	No HEGO switch detected (right HEGO)
42	r	HEGO sensor circuit indicates system rich (right HEGO)
44	r	Thermactor air system inoperative (right side)
45	r	Thermactor air upstream during Self-Test
46	r	Thermactor air not bypassed during Self-Test
51	oc	ECT indicated −40°F/circuit open
53	oc	TP above maximum voltage
54	oc	ACT indicated −40°F/circuit open
56	oc	MAF circuit above maximum voltage (MA only)
61	oc	ECT indicated 254°F/circuit grounded
63	oc	TP circuit below minimum voltage
64	oc	ACT indicated 254°F/circuit grounded
66	oc	MAF circuit below minimum voltage (MA only)
67	o	Neutral Drive Switch (NDS) circuit open
74	r	Brake ON/OFF (BOO) circuit open/not actuated during Self-Test
75	r	Brake ON/OFF (BOO) circuit closed/ECA input open
77	r	Brief WOT not sensed during Self-Test/Operator error
79	o	A/C on/Defrost on during Self-Test
81	o	Air Management 2 (AM2) circuit failure
82	o	Air Management 1 (AM1) circuit failure
84	o	EGR Vacuum Regulator (EVR) circuit failure
85	o	Canister Purge (CANP) circuit failure
87	oc	Fuel pump primary circuit failure
91	r	HEGO sensor circuit indicates system lean (left HEGO)
91	c	No HEGO switching detected (left HEGO)
92	r	HEGO sensor circuit indicates system rich (left HEGO)
94	r	Thermactor air system inoperative (left side)
95	oc	Fuel pump secondary circuit failure
96	oc	Fuel pump secondary circuit failure
98	r	Hard fault is present - FMEM mode
NO CODES		Unable to initiate Self-Test or unable to output Self-Test codes
CODES NOT LISTED	►	Service codes displayed are not applicable to the vehicle being tested

KEY: o = Key On Engine Off (KOEO) r = Engine Running (ER) c = Continuous Memory

84174209

Fig. 128 Diagnostic service codes; 1990 5.0L engine only

SERVICE CODE		SERVICE CODE DEFINITION
11	orc	System PASS
12	r	Cannot control rpm during Self-Test high rpm check
13	r	Cannot control rpm during Self-Test low rpm check
14	c	PIP circuit failure
15	o	EEC processor Read Only Memory (ROM) test failed
15	o	EEC processor Keep Alive Memory (KAM) test failed
16	r	Rpm too low to perform EGO test
18	r	SPOUT circuit open
18	c	IDM circuit failure/SPOUT circuit grounded
19	o	Failure in EEC processor internal voltage
21	or	ECT out of Self-Test range
22	orc	MAP/BP out of Self-Test range
23	or	TP out of Self-Test range
24	or	ACT out of Self-Test range
26	or	MAF out of Self-Test range
29	c	Insufficient input from the Vehicle Speed Sensor (VSS)
31	orc	EVP circuit below minimum voltage
32	orc	EVP voltage above closed limit (SONIC)
33	rc	EGR valve opening not detected (SONIC)
34	orc	EVP voltage above closed limit (SONIC)
35	orc	EVP circuit above maximum voltage
41	r	HEGO sensor circuit indicates system lean (right HEGO)
41	c	No HEGO switch detected (right HEGO)
42	r	HEGO sensor circuit indicates system rich (right HEGO)
44	r	Thermactor air system inoperative (right side)
45	r	Thermactor air upstream during Self-Test
46	r	Thermactor air not bypassed during Self-Test
51	oc	ECT indicated −40°F/circuit open
53	oc	TP circuit above maximum voltage
54	oc	ACT indicated −40°F/circuit open
56	oc	MAF circuit above maximum voltage (MA only)
61	oc	ECT indicated 254°F/circuit grounded
63	oc	TP circuit below minimum voltage
64	oc	ACT indicated 254°F/circuit grounded
66	c	MAF circuit below minimum voltage (MA only)
67	o	Neutral Drive Switch (NDS) circuit open
74	r	Brake On/Off (BOO) circuit open/not actuated during Self-Test
75	r	Brake On/Off (BOO) circuit closed/ECA input open
77	r	Brief WOT not sensed during Self-Test/Operator error
79	o	A/C on/Defrost on during Self-Test
81	o	Air Management 2 (AM2) circuit failure
82	o	Air Management 1 (AM1) circuit failure
84	o	EGR Vacuum Regulator (EVR) circuit failure
85	o	Canister Purge (CANP) circuit failure
87	oc	Fuel pump primary circuit failure
91	r	HEGO sensor circuit indicates system lean (left HEGO)
91	c	No HEGO switching detected (left HEGO)
92	r	HEGO sensor circuit indicates system rich (left HEGO)
94	r	Thermactor air system inoperative (left side)
95	oc	Fuel pump secondary circuit failure
96	oc	Fuel pump secondary circuit failure
98	r	Hard fault is present - FMEM mode
NO CODES		Unable to initiate Self-Test or unable to output Self-Test codes
CODES NOT LISTED		Service codes displayed are not applicable to the vehicle being tested

KEY: o = Key On Engine Off (KOEO) r = Engine Running (ER) c = Continuous Memory

84174210

Fig. 129 Diagnostic service codes; 1991 5.0L engine only

SERVICE CODE		SERVICE CODE DEFINITION
111	orc	System PASS
112	or	ACT indicated 123°C (254°F)/circuit grounded
113	or	ACT indicated -40°C (-40°F)/circuit grounded
114	or	ACT out of Self-Test range
116	or	ECT out of Self-Test range
117	oc	ECT indicated 123°C (254°F)/circuit grounded
118	oc	ECT indicated -40°C (-40°F)/circuit open
121	orc	TP out of Self-Test range
122	oc	TP circuit below minimum voltage
123	oc	TP circuit above maximum voltage
124	c	TP circuit output higher than expected
125	c	TP circuit output lower than expected
129	r	Insufficient MAF change during Dynamic Response Test
136	r	HEGO sensor indicates system lean (left side)
137	r	HEGO sensor indicates system rich (left side)
139	c	No HEGO switching detected (left side)
144	c	No HEGO switching detected (right side)
157	rc	MAF circuit below minimum voltage
158	orc	MAF circuit above maximum voltage
159	or	MAF out of Self-Test range
167	r	Insufficient TP change during Dynamic Response Test
171	c	No HEGO switching detected/adaptive fuel at limit (right side)
172	rc	HEGO sensor indicates system lean (right side)
173	rc	HEGO sensor indicates system rich (right side)
174	c	HEGO switching time is slow (right side)
175	c	No HEGO switching detected/adaptive fuel at limit (left side)
176	c	HEGO sensor indicates system lean (left side)
177	c	HEGO sensor indicates system rich (left side)
178	c	HEGO switching time is slow (left side)
179	c	Adaptive fuel lean limit is reached (right side)
181	c	Adaptive fuel lean limit is reached (right side)
182	c	Adaptive fuel lean limit is reached at idle (right side)
183	c	Adaptive fuel rich limit is reached at idle (right side)
184	c	MAF circuit output higher than expected
185	c	MAF circuit output lower than expected
186	c	Injector pulsewidth higher than expected
187	c	Injector pulsewidth lower than expected
188	c	Adaptive fuel lean limit is reached (left side)
189	c	Adaptive fuel rich limit is reached (left side)
191	c	Adaptive fuel lean limit is reached at idle (left side)
192	c	Adaptive fuel rich limit is reached at idle (left side)
211	c	PIP circuit failure
212	c	IDM circuit failure/SPOUT circuit grounded
213	r	SPOUT circuit open
327	orc	DPFE circuit output below minimum voltage
326	rc	DPFE circuit voltage lower than expected
332	rc	EGR valve opening not detected
335	o	DPFE sensor voltage higher or lower than expected

84174211

Fig. 130 Diagnostic service codes: 1992 models only

SERVICE CODE		SERVICE CODE DEFINITION
337	orc	DPFE circuit above maximum voltage
341	o	Octane Adjust circuit open
519	o	Power Steering Pressure Switch (PSPS) circuit open
521	r	Power Steering Pressure Switch (PSPS) circuit did not change states
536	rc	Brake On/Off (BOO) circuit failure
411	r	Cannot control rpm during Self-Test low rpm check
412	r	Cannot control rpm during Self-Test high rpm check
452	c	Insufficient input from the Vehicle Speed Sensor (VSS)
511	o	EEC processor Read Only Memory (ROM) test failed
512	c	EEC processor Keep Alive Memory (KAM) test failed
513	o	Failure in EEC processor internal voltage
522	o	Indicates vehicle in gear
538	r	Operator error (Dynamic response/Cylinder Balance Test)
539	o	A/C on/Defrost on during Self-Test
542	oc	Fuel pump secondary circuit failure
543	oc	Fuel pump secondary circuit failure
556	oc	Fuel pump primary circuit failure
558	o	EGR Vacuum Regulator (EVR) circuit failure
565	o	Canister Purge Solenoid (CANP) circuit failure
617	c	1-2 Shift error
618	c	2-3 Shift error
619	c	3-4 Shift error
621	oc	Shift Solenoid 1 (SS1) circuit failure
622	oc	Shift Solenoid 2 (SS2) circuit failure
624	c	Electronic Pressure Control (EPC) circuit failure
625	o	Electronic Pressure Control (EPC) driver open in ECA
628	c	Excessive Converter Clutch slippage
634	oc	Manual Lever Position (MLP) sensor out of range
636	or	Transmission Oil Temperature (TOT) out of Self-Test range
637	oc	TOT indicated -40°C (140°F)/circuit open
638	oc	TOT indicated 143°C (290°F)/circuit grounded
639	rc	Ouput Shaft Speed Sneosr (OSS) circuit failure
652	c	Modulated/Converter Clutch Control (M/CCC) circuit failure
998	r	Hard fault is present - FMEM mode
NO CODES		Unable to initiate Self-Test or unable to output Self-Test codes
CODES NOT LISTED		Service codes displayed are not applicable to the vehicle being tested

KEY: o = Key On Engine Off (KOEO), r = Engine Running (ER), c = Continuous Memory

84174212

Fig. 131 Diagnostic service codes; 1992 models only, continued

DIAGNOSTIC TROUBLE CODES	DEFINITIONS
111	System Pass
112	Intake Air Temp (IAT) sensor circuit below minimum voltage/254°F indicated
113	Intake Air Temp (IAT) sensor circuit above maximum voltage/-40°F indicated
114	Intake Air Temp (IAT) higher or lower than expected
116	Engine Coolant Temp (ECT) higher or lower than expected
117	Engine Coolant Temp (ECT) sensor circuit below minimum voltage/254°F indicated
118	Engine Coolant Temp (ECT) sensor circuit above maximum voltage/-40°F indicated
121	Closed throttle voltage higher or lower than expected
121	Indicates throttle position voltage inconsistent with the MAF sensor
122	Throttle Position (TP) sensor circuit below minimum voltage
123	Throttle Position (TP) sensor circuit above maximum voltage
124	Throttle Position (TP) sensor voltage higher than expected
125	Throttle Position (TP) sensor voltage lower than expected
126	MAP/BARO sensor higher or lower than expected
128	MAP sensor vacuum hose damaged/disconnected
129	Insufficient MAP/Mass Air Flow (MAF) change during dynamic response test KOER
136	Lack of Heated Oxygen Sensor (HO2S-2) switch during KOER, indicates lean (Bank #2)
137	Lack of Heated Oxygen Sensor (HO2S-2) switch during KOER, indicates rich (Bank #2)
138	Cold Start Injector (CSI) flow insufficient KOER
139	No Heated Oxygen Sensor (HO2S-2) switches detected (Bank #2)
144	No Heated Oxygen Sensor (HO2S-1) switches detected (Bank #1)
157	Mass Air Flow (MAF) sensor circuit below minimum voltage
158	Mass Air Flow (MAF) sensor circuit above maximum voltage
159	Mass Air Flow (MAF) higher or lower than expected
167	Insufficient throttle position change during dynamic response test KOER
171	Fuel system at adaptive limits, Heated Oxygen Sensor (HO2S-1) unable to switch (Bank #1)
172	Lack of Heated Oxygen Sensor (HO2S-1) switches, indicates lean (Bank #1)
173	Lack of Heated Oxygen Sensor (HO2S-1) switches, indicates rich (Bank #1)
175	Fuel system at adaptive limits, Heated Oxygen Sensor (HO2S-2) unable to switch (Bank #2)
176	Lack of Heated Oxygen Sensor (HO2S-2) switches, indicates lean (Bank #2)
177	Lack of Heated Oxygen Sensor (HO2S-2) switches, indicates rich (Bank #2)
179	Fuel system at lean adaptive limit at part throttle, system rich (Bank #1)
181	Fuel system at rich adaptive limit at part throttle, system lean (Bank #1)
184	Mass Air Flow (MAF) higher than expected
185	Mass Air Flow (MAF) lower than expected
186	Injector pulsewidth higher than expected (with BARO sensor)
186	Injector pulsewidth higher or MAF lower than expected (without BARO sensor)
187	Injector pulsewidth lower than expected (with BARO sensor)
187	Injector pulsewidth lower or MAF higher than expected (without BARO sensor)
188	Fuel system at lean adaptive limit at part throttle, system rich (Bank #2)
189	Fuel system at rich adaptive limit at part throttle, system lean (Bank #2)
193	Flexible Fuel (FF) sensor circuit failure

84174213

Fig. 132 Diagnostic service codes; 1993–94 models only

DIAGNOSTIC TROUBLE CODES	DEFINITIONS
211	Profile Ignition Pickup (PIP) circuit failure
212	Loss of Ignition Diagnostic Monitor (IDM) input to PCM/SPOUT circuit grounded
213	SPOUT circuit open
214	Cylinder Identification (CID) circuit failure
215	PCM detected coil 1 primary circuit failure (EI)
216	PCM detected coil 2 primary circuit failure (EI)
217	PCM detected coil 3 primary circuit failure (EI)
218	Loss of Ignition Diagnostic Monitor (IDM) signal-left side (dual plug EI)
219	Spark timing defaulted to 10 degrees-SPOUT circuit open (EI)
221	Spark timing error (EI)
222	Loss of Ignition Diagnostic Monitor (IDM) signal-right side (dual plug EI)
223	Loss of Dual Plug Inhibit (DPI) control (dual plug EI)
224	PCM detected coil 1, 2, 3 or 4 primary circuit failure (dual plug EI)
225	Knock not sensed during dynamic response test KOER
226	Ignition Diagnostic Module (IDM) signal not received (EI)
232	PCM detected coil 1, 2, 3 or 4 primary circuit failure (EI)
238	PCM detected coil 4 primary circuit failure (EI)
241	ICM to PCM IDM pulsewidth transmission error (EI)
244	CID circuit fault present when cylinder balance test requested
311	AIR system inoperative during KOER (Bank #1 w/dual HO2S)
312	AIR misdirected during KOER
313	AIR not bypassed during KOER
314	AIR system inoperative during KOER (Bank #2 w/dual HO2S)
326	EGR (PFE/DPFE) circuit voltage lower than expected
327	EGR (EVP/PFE/DPFE) circuit below minimum voltage
328	EGR (EVP) closed valve voltage lower than expected
332	Insufficient EGR flow detected (EVP/PFE/DPFE)
334	EGR (EVP) closed valve voltage higher than expected
335	EGR (PFE/DPFE) sensor voltage higher or lower than expected during KOEO
336	Exhaust pressure high/EGR (PFE/DPFE) circuit voltage higher than expected
337	EGR (EVP/PFE/DPFE) circuit above maximum voltage
338	Engine Coolant Temperature (ECT) lower than expected (thermostat test)
339	Engine Coolant Temperature (ECT) higher than expected (thermostat test)
341	Octane adjust service pin open
411	Cannot control RPM during KOER low RPM check
412	Cannot control RPM during KOER high RPM check
415	Idle Air Control (IAC) system at maximum adaptive lower limit
416	Idle Air Control (IAC) system at upper adaptive learning limit
452	Insufficient input from Vehicle Speed Sensor (VSS) to PCM
453	Servo leaking down (KOER IVSC test)
454	Servo leaking up (KOER IVSC test)
455	Insufficient RPM increase (KOER IVSC test)
456	Insufficient RPM decrease (KOER IVSC test)
457	Speed control command switch(s) circuit not functioning (KOEO IVSC test)

84174214

Fig. 133 Diagnostic service codes; 1993–94 models only, continued

DIAGNOSTIC TROUBLE CODES	DEFINITIONS
458	Speed control command switch(s) stuck/circuit grounded (KOEO IVSC test)
459	Speed control ground circuit open (KOEO IVSC test)
511	PCM Read Only Memory (ROM) test failure KOEO
512	PCM Keep Alive Memory (KAM) test failure
513	PCM internal voltage failure (KOEO)
519	Power Steering Pressure (PSP) switch circuit open KOEO
521	Power Steering Pressure (PSP) switch circuit did not change states KOER
522	Vehicle not in PARK or NEUTRAL during KOEO/PNP switch circuit open
524	Low speed fuel pump circuit open—battery to PCM
525	Indicates vehicle in gear/A/C on
527	Park/Neutral Position (PNP) switch circuit open—A/C on KOEO
528	Clutch Pedal Position (CPP) switch circuit failure
529	Data Communication Link (DCL) or PCM circuit failure
532	Cluster Control Assembly (CCA) circuit failure
533	Data Communication Link (DCL) or Electronic Instrument Cluster (EIC) circuit failure
536	Brake On/Off (BOO) circuit failure/not actuated during KOER
538	Insufficient RPM change during KOER dynamic response test
538	Invalid cylinder balance test due to throttle movement during test (SFI only)
538	Invalid cylinder balance test due to CID circuit failure
539	A/C on/Defrost on during Self-Test
542	Fuel pump secondary circuit failure
543	Fuel pump secondary circuit failure
551	Idle Air Control (IAC) circuit failure KOEO
552	Secondary Air Injection Bypass (AIRB) circuit failure KOEO
553	Secondary Air Injection Diverter (AIRD) circuit failure KOEO
554	Fuel Pressure Regulator Control (FPRC) circuit failure
556	Fuel pump relay primary circuit failure
557	Low speed fuel pump primary circuit failure
558	EGR Vacuum Regulator (EVR) circuit failure KOEO
559	Air Conditioning On (ACON) relay circuit failure KOEO
563	High Fan Control (HFC) circuit failure KOEO
564	Fan Control (FC) circuit failure KOEO
565	Canister Purge (CANP) circuit failure KOEO
566	3-4 shift solenoid circuit failure KOEO (A4LD)
567	Speed Control Vent (SCVNT) circuit failure (KOEO IVSC test)
568	Speed Control Vacuum (SCVAC) circuit failure (KOEO IVSC test)
569	Auxiliary Canister Purge (CANP2) circuit failure KOEO
578	A/C pressure sensor circuit shorted (VCRM module)
579	Insufficient A/C pressure change (VCRM module)
581	Power to Fan circuit over current (VCRM module)
582	Fan circuit open (VCRM module)
583	Power to Fuel pump over current (VCRM module)
584	Power ground circuit open (Pin 1) (VCRM module)

84174215

Fig. 134 Diagnostic service codes; 1993–94 models only, continued

DIAGNOSTIC TROUBLE CODES	DEFINITIONS
585	Power to A/C clutch over current (VCRM module)
586	A/C clutch circuit open (VCRM module)
587	Variable Control Relay Module (VCRM) communication failure
617	1-2 shift error
618	2-3 shift error
619	3-4 shift error
621	Shift Solenoid 1 (SS1) circuit failure KOEO
622	Shift Solenoid 2 (SS2) circuit failure KOEO
624	Electronic Pressure Control (EPC) circuit failure
625	Electronic Pressure Control (EPC) driver open in PCM
626	Coast Clutch Solenoid (CCS) circuit failure KOEO
627	Torque Converter Clutch (TCC) solenoid circuit failure
628	Excessive converter clutch slippage
629	Torque Converter Clutch (TCC) solenoid circuit failure
631	Transmission Control Indicator Lamp (TCIL) circuit failure KOEO
632	Transmission Control Switch (TCS) circuit did not change states during KOER
633	4x4L switch closed during KOEO
634	Manual Lever Position (MLP) voltage higher or lower than expected
636	Transmission Oil Temp (TOT) higher or lower than expected
637	Transmission Oil Temp (TOT) sensor circuit above maximum voltage/ -40°F (-40°C) indicated/circuit open
638	Transmission Oil Temp (TOT) sensor circuit below minimum voltage/ 290°F (143°C) indicated/circuit shorted
639	Insufficient input from Transmission Speed Sensor (TSS)
641	Shift Solenoid 3 (SS3) circuit failure
643	Torque Converter Clutch (TCC) circuit failure
645	Incorrect gear ratio obtained for first gear
646	Incorrect gear ratio obtained for second gear
647	Incorrect gear ratio obtained for third gear
648	Incorrect gear ratio obtained for fourth gear
649	Electronic Pressure Control (EPC) higher or lower than expected
651	Electronic Pressure Control (EPC) circuit failure
652	Torque Converter Clutch (TCC) solenoid circuit failure
654	Manual Lever Position (MLP) sensor not indicating PARK during KOEO
656	Torque Converter Clutch continuous slip error
657	Transmission over temperature condition occurred
998	Hard fault present ****FMEM MODE****

84174216

Fig. 135 Diagnostic service codes; 1993–94 models only, continued

TROUBLE CODES—EEC-V SYSTEM (OBD-II)

General Information

The Powertrain Control Module (PCM) is given responsibility for the operation of the emission control devices, cooling fans, ignition and advance and in some cases, automatic transmission functions. Because the EEC-V oversees both the ignition timing and the fuel injection operation, a precise air/fuel ratio will be maintained under all operating conditions. The PCM is a microprocessor or small computer which receives electrical inputs from several sensors, switches and relays on and around the engine.

Based on combinations of these inputs, the PCM controls various output devices concerned with engine operation and emissions. The control module relies on the signals to form a correct picture of current vehicle operation. If any of the input signals is incorrect, the PCM reacts to whatever picture is painted for it. For example, if the coolant temperature sensor is inaccurate and reads too low, the PCM may see a picture of the engine never warming up. Consequently, the engine settings will be maintained as if the engine were cold. Because so many inputs can affect one output, correct diagnostic procedures are essential on these systems.

One part of the PCM is devoted to monitoring both input and output functions within the system. This ability forms the core of the self-diagnostic system. If a problem is detected within a circuit, the control module will recognize the fault, assign it an Diagnostic Trouble Code (DTC), and store the code in memory. The stored code(s) may be retrieved during diagnosis.

While the EEC-V system is capable of recognizing many internal faults, certain faults will not be recognized. Because the control module sees only electrical signals, it cannot sense or react to mechanical or vacuum faults affecting engine operation. Some of these faults may affect another component which will set a code. For example, the PCM monitors the output signal to the fuel injectors, but cannot detect a partially clogged injector. As long as the output driver responds correctly, the computer will read the system as functioning correctly. However, the improper flow of fuel may result in a lean mixture. This would, in turn, be detected by the oxygen sensor and noticed as a constantly lean signal by the PCM. Once the signal falls outside the pre-programmed limits, the control module would notice the fault and set an trouble code.

Additionally, the EEC-V system employs adaptive fuel logic. This process is used to compensate for normal wear and variability within the fuel system. Once the engine enters steady-state operation, the control module watches the oxygen sensor signal for a bias or tendency to run slightly rich or lean. If such a bias is detected, the adaptive logic corrects the fuel delivery to bring the air/fuel mixture towards a centered or 14.7:1 ratio. This compensating shift is stored in a non-volatile memory which is retained by battery power even with the ignition switched **OFF**. The correction factor is then available the next time the vehicle is operated.

Malfunction Indicator Lamp

The Malfunction Indicator Lamp (MIL) is located on the instrument panel. The lamp is connected to the PCM and will alert the driver to certain malfunctions within the EEC-V system. When the lamp is illuminated, the PCM has detected a fault and stored an DTC in memory.

The light will stay illuminated as long as the fault is present. Should the fault self-correct, the MIL will extinguish but the stored code will remain in memory.

Under normal operating conditions, the MIL should illuminate briefly when the ignition key is turned **ON** . This is commonly known as a prove-out. As soon as the PCM receives a signal that the engine is cranking, the lamp should extinguish. The lamp should remain extinguished during the normal operating cycle.

Data Link Connector

The Data Link Connector (DLC) may be found in the following location:
- Under the driver's side dash , near the steering column.

The DLC is rectangular in design and capable of allowing access to 16 terminals. The connector has keying features that allow easy connection. The test equipment and the DLC have a latching feature to ensure a good mated connection.

ELECTRICAL TOOLS

The most commonly required electrical diagnostic tool is the Digital Multimeter, allowing voltage, resistance, and amperage to be read by one instrument.

The multimeter must be a high impedance unit, with 10 megaohms of impedance in the voltmeter. This type of meter will not place an additional load on the circuit it is testing; this is extremely important in low voltage circuits. The multimeter must be of high quality in all respects. It should be handled carefully and protected from impact or damage. Replace the batteries frequently in the unit.

Reading Codes

♦ See Figure 136

The EEC-V equipped engines utilize On Board Diagnostic II (OBD-II) DTC's, which are alpha-numeric (they use letters and numbers). The letters in the OBD-II DTC's make it highly difficult to convey the codes through the use of anything but a scan tool. Therefore, to read the codes on these vehicles it is necessary to utilize an OBD-II compatible scan tool.

Since each manufacturers scan tool is different, please follow the manufacturer's instructions for connecting the tool and obtaining code information.

Fig. 136 When using a scan tool, make sure to follow all of the manufacturer's instructions carefully to ensure proper diagnosis

Clearing Codes

CONTINUOUS MEMORY CODES

These codes are retained in memory for 40 warm-up cycles. To clear the codes for the purposes of testing or confirming repair, perform the code reading procedure. When the fault codes begin to be displayed, de-activate the test by either disconnecting the jumper wire (meter, MIL or message center) or releasing the test button on the hand scanner. Stopping the test during code transmission will erase the Continuous Memory. Do not disconnect the negative battery cable to clear these codes; the Keep Alive memory will be cleared and a new code, 19, will be stored for loss of PCM power.

KEEP ALIVE MEMORY

The Keep Alive Memory (KAM) contains the adaptive factors used by the processor to compensate for component tolerances and wear. It should not be routinely cleared during diagnosis. If an emissions related part is replaced during repair, the KAM must be cleared. Failure to clear the KAM may cause severe driveability problems since the correction factor for the old component will be applied to the new component.

To clear the Keep Alive Memory, disconnect the negative battery cable for at least 5 minutes. After the memory is cleared and the battery reconnected, the vehicle must be driven at least 10 miles so that the processor may relearn the needed correction factors. The distance to be driven depends on the engine and vehicle, but all drives should include steady-throttle cruise on open roads. Certain driveability problems may be noted during the drive because the adaptive factors are not yet functioning.

EEC-V Diagnostic Trouble Codes (DTC's)

P0000 No Failures
P0100 Mass or Volume Air Flow Circuit Malfunction
P0101 Mass or Volume Air Flow Circuit Range/Performance Problem
P0102 Mass or Volume Air Flow Circuit Low Input
P0103 Mass or Volume Air Flow Circuit High Input
P0104 Mass or Volume Air Flow Circuit Intermittent
P0105 Manifold Absolute Pressure/Barometric Pressure Circuit Malfunction
P0106 Manifold Absolute Pressure/Barometric Pressure Circuit Range/Performance Problem
P0107 Manifold Absolute Pressure/Barometric Pressure Circuit Low Input
P0108 Manifold Absolute Pressure/Barometric Pressure Circuit High Input
P0109 Manifold Absolute Pressure/Barometric Pressure Circuit Intermittent
P0110 Intake Air Temperature Circuit Malfunction
P0111 Intake Air Temperature Circuit Range/Performance Problem
P0112 Intake Air Temperature Circuit Low Input
P0113 Intake Air Temperature Circuit High Input
P0114 Intake Air Temperature Circuit Intermittent
P0115 Engine Coolant Temperature Circuit Malfunction
P0116 Engine Coolant Temperature Circuit Range/Performance Problem
P0117 Engine Coolant Temperature Circuit Low Input
P0118 Engine Coolant Temperature Circuit High Input
P0119 Engine Coolant Temperature Circuit Intermittent
P0120 Throttle/Pedal Position Sensor/Switch "A" Circuit Malfunction
P0121 Throttle/Pedal Position Sensor/Switch "A" Circuit Range/Performance Problem
P0122 Throttle/Pedal Position Sensor/Switch "A" Circuit Low Input
P0123 Throttle/Pedal Position Sensor/Switch "A" Circuit High Input
P0124 Throttle/Pedal Position Sensor/Switch "A" Circuit Intermittent
P0125 Insufficient Coolant Temperature For Closed Loop Fuel Control
P0126 Insufficient Coolant Temperature For Stable Operation
P0130 O2 Circuit Malfunction (Bank no. 1 Sensor no. 1)
P0131 O2 Sensor Circuit Low Voltage (Bank no. 1 Sensor no. 1)
P0132 O2 Sensor Circuit High Voltage (Bank no. 1 Sensor no. 1)
P0133 O2 Sensor Circuit Slow Response (Bank no. 1 Sensor no. 1)
P0134 O2 Sensor Circuit No Activity Detected (Bank no. 1 Sensor no. 1)
P0135 O2 Sensor Heater Circuit Malfunction (Bank no. 1 Sensor no. 1)
P0136 O2 Sensor Circuit Malfunction (Bank no. 1 Sensor no. 2)
P0137 O2 Sensor Circuit Low Voltage (Bank no. 1 Sensor no. 2)
P0138 O2 Sensor Circuit High Voltage (Bank no. 1 Sensor no. 2)
P0139 O2 Sensor Circuit Slow Response (Bank no. 1 Sensor no. 2)
P0140 O2 Sensor Circuit No Activity Detected (Bank no. 1 Sensor no. 2)
P0141 O2 Sensor Heater Circuit Malfunction (Bank no. 1 Sensor no. 2)
P0142 O2 Sensor Circuit Malfunction (Bank no. 1 Sensor no. 3)
P0143 O2 Sensor Circuit Low Voltage (Bank no. 1 Sensor no. 3)
P0144 O2 Sensor Circuit High Voltage (Bank no. 1 Sensor no. 3)
P0145 O2 Sensor Circuit Slow Response (Bank no. 1 Sensor no. 3)
P0146 O2 Sensor Circuit No Activity Detected (Bank no. 1 Sensor no. 3)
P0147 O2 Sensor Heater Circuit Malfunction (Bank no. 1 Sensor no. 3)
P0150 O2 Sensor Circuit Malfunction (Bank no. 2 Sensor no. 1)
P0151 O2 Sensor Circuit Low Voltage (Bank no. 2 Sensor no. 1)
P0152 O2 Sensor Circuit High Voltage (Bank no. 2 Sensor no. 1)
P0153 O2 Sensor Circuit Slow Response (Bank no. 2 Sensor no. 1)
P0154 O2 Sensor Circuit No Activity Detected (Bank no. 2 Sensor no. 1)
P0155 O2 Sensor Heater Circuit Malfunction (Bank no. 2 Sensor no. 1)
P0156 O2 Sensor Circuit Malfunction (Bank no. 2 Sensor no. 2)
P0157 O2 Sensor Circuit Low Voltage (Bank no. 2 Sensor no. 2)
P0158 O2 Sensor Circuit High Voltage (Bank no. 2 Sensor no. 2)
P0159 O2 Sensor Circuit Slow Response (Bank no. 2 Sensor no. 2)
P0160 O2 Sensor Circuit No Activity Detected (Bank no. 2 Sensor no. 2)
P0161 O2 Sensor Heater Circuit Malfunction (Bank no. 2 Sensor no. 2)

P0162 O2 Sensor Circuit Malfunction (Bank no. 2 Sensor no. 3)
P0163 O2 Sensor Circuit Low Voltage (Bank no. 2 Sensor no. 3)
P0164 O2 Sensor Circuit High Voltage (Bank no. 2 Sensor no. 3)
P0165 O2 Sensor Circuit Slow Response (Bank no. 2 Sensor no. 3)
P0166 O2 Sensor Circuit No Activity Detected (Bank no. 2 Sensor no. 3)
P0167 O2 Sensor Heater Circuit Malfunction (Bank no. 2 Sensor no. 3)
P0170 Fuel Trim Malfunction (Bank no. 1)
P0171 System Too Lean (Bank no. 1)
P0172 System Too Rich (Bank no. 1)
P0173 Fuel Trim Malfunction (Bank no. 2)
P0174 System Too Lean (Bank no. 2)
P0175 System Too Rich (Bank no. 2)
P0176 Fuel Composition Sensor Circuit Malfunction
P0177 Fuel Composition Sensor Circuit Range/Performance
P0178 Fuel Composition Sensor Circuit Low Input
P0179 Fuel Composition Sensor Circuit High Input
P0180 Fuel Temperature Sensor "A" Circuit Malfunction
P0181 Fuel Temperature Sensor "A" Circuit Range/Performance
P0182 Fuel Temperature Sensor "A" Circuit Low Input
P0183 Fuel Temperature Sensor "A" Circuit High Input
P0184 Fuel Temperature Sensor "A" Circuit Intermittent
P0185 Fuel Temperature Sensor "B" Circuit Malfunction
P0186 Fuel Temperature Sensor "B" Circuit Range/Performance
P0187 Fuel Temperature Sensor "B" Circuit Low Input
P0188 Fuel Temperature Sensor "B" Circuit High Input
P0189 Fuel Temperature Sensor "B" Circuit Intermittent
P0190 Fuel Rail Pressure Sensor Circuit Malfunction
P0191 Fuel Rail Pressure Sensor Circuit Range/Performance
P0192 Fuel Rail Pressure Sensor Circuit Low Input
P0193 Fuel Rail Pressure Sensor Circuit High Input
P0194 Fuel Rail Pressure Sensor Circuit Intermittent
P0195 Engine Oil Temperature Sensor Malfunction
P0196 Engine Oil Temperature Sensor Range/Performance
P0197 Engine Oil Temperature Sensor Low
P0198 Engine Oil Temperature Sensor High
P0199 Engine Oil Temperature Sensor Intermittent
P0200 Injector Circuit Malfunction
P0201 Injector Circuit Malfunction—Cylinder no. 1
P0202 Injector Circuit Malfunction—Cylinder no. 2
P0203 Injector Circuit Malfunction—Cylinder no. 3
P0204 Injector Circuit Malfunction—Cylinder no. 4
P0205 Injector Circuit Malfunction—Cylinder no. 5
P0206 Injector Circuit Malfunction—Cylinder no. 6
P0207 Injector Circuit Malfunction—Cylinder no. 7
P0208 Injector Circuit Malfunction—Cylinder no. 8
P0215 Engine Shutoff Solenoid Malfunction
P0216 Injection Timing Control Circuit Malfunction
P0217 Engine Over Temperature Condition
P0218 Transmission Over Temperature Condition
P0219 Engine Over Speed Condition
P0220 Throttle/Pedal Position Sensor/Switch "B" Circuit Malfunction
P0221 Throttle/Pedal Position Sensor/Switch "B" Circuit Range/Performance Problem
P0222 Throttle/Pedal Position Sensor/Switch "B" Circuit Low Input
P0223 Throttle/Pedal Position Sensor/Switch "B" Circuit High Input
P0224 Throttle/Pedal Position Sensor/Switch "B" Circuit Intermittent
P0225 Throttle/Pedal Position Sensor/Switch "C" Circuit Malfunction
P0226 Throttle/Pedal Position Sensor/Switch "C" Circuit Range/Performance Problem
P0227 Throttle/Pedal Position Sensor/Switch "C" Circuit Low Input
P0228 Throttle/Pedal Position Sensor/Switch "C" Circuit High Input
P0229 Throttle/Pedal Position Sensor/Switch "C" Circuit Intermittent
P0230 Fuel Pump Primary Circuit Malfunction
P0231 Fuel Pump Secondary Circuit Low
P0232 Fuel Pump Secondary Circuit High
P0233 Fuel Pump Secondary Circuit Intermittent
P0261 Cylinder no. 1 Injector Circuit Low
P0262 Cylinder no. 1 Injector Circuit High
P0263 Cylinder no. 1 Contribution/Balance Fault
P0264 Cylinder no. 2 Injector Circuit Low
P0265 Cylinder no. 2 Injector Circuit High

P0266 Cylinder no. 2 Contribution/Balance Fault
P0267 Cylinder no. 3 Injector Circuit Low
P0268 Cylinder no. 3 Injector Circuit High
P0269 Cylinder no. 3 Contribution/Balance Fault
P0270 Cylinder no. 4 Injector Circuit Low
P0271 Cylinder no. 4 Injector Circuit High
P0272 Cylinder no. 4 Contribution/Balance Fault
P0273 Cylinder no. 5 Injector Circuit Low
P0274 Cylinder no. 5 Injector Circuit High
P0275 Cylinder no. 5 Contribution/Balance Fault
P0276 Cylinder no. 6 Injector Circuit Low
P0277 Cylinder no. 6 Injector Circuit High
P0278 Cylinder no. 6 Contribution/Balance Fault
P0279 Cylinder no. 7 Injector Circuit Low
P0280 Cylinder no. 7 Injector Circuit High
P0281 Cylinder no. 7 Contribution/Balance Fault
P0282 Cylinder no. 8 Injector Circuit Low
P0283 Cylinder no. 8 Injector Circuit High
P0284 Cylinder no. 8 Contribution/Balance Fault
P0300 Random/Multiple Cylinder Misfire Detected
P0301 Cylinder no. 1—Misfire Detected
P0302 Cylinder no. 2—Misfire Detected
P0303 Cylinder no. 3—Misfire Detected
P0304 Cylinder no. 4—Misfire Detected
P0305 Cylinder no. 5—Misfire Detected
P0306 Cylinder no. 6—Misfire Detected
P0307 Cylinder no. 7—Misfire Detected
P0308 Cylinder no. 8—Misfire Detected
P0320 Ignition/Distributor Engine Speed Input Circuit Malfunction
P0321 Ignition/Distributor Engine Speed Input Circuit Range/Performance
P0322 Ignition/Distributor Engine Speed Input Circuit No Signal
P0323 Ignition/Distributor Engine Speed Input Circuit Intermittent
P0325 Knock Sensor no. 1—Circuit Malfunction (Bank no. 1 or Single Sensor)
P0326 Knock Sensor no. 1—Circuit Range/Performance (Bank no. 1 or Single Sensor)
P0327 Knock Sensor no. 1—Circuit Low Input (Bank no. 1 or Single Sensor)
P0328 Knock Sensor no. 1—Circuit High Input (Bank no. 1 or Single Sensor)
P0329 Knock Sensor no. 1—Circuit Input Intermittent (Bank no. 1 or Single Sensor)
P0330 Knock Sensor no. 2—Circuit Malfunction (Bank no. 2)
P0331 Knock Sensor no. 2—Circuit Range/Performance (Bank no. 2)
P0332 Knock Sensor no. 2—Circuit Low Input (Bank no. 2)
P0333 Knock Sensor no. 2—Circuit High Input (Bank no. 2)
P0334 Knock Sensor no. 2—Circuit Input Intermittent (Bank no. 2)
P0335 Crankshaft Position Sensor "A" Circuit Malfunction
P0336 Crankshaft Position Sensor "A" Circuit Range/Performance
P0337 Crankshaft Position Sensor "A" Circuit Low Input
P0338 Crankshaft Position Sensor "A" Circuit High Input
P0339 Crankshaft Position Sensor "A" Circuit Intermittent
P0340 Camshaft Position Sensor Circuit Malfunction
P0341 Camshaft Position Sensor Circuit Range/Performance
P0342 Camshaft Position Sensor Circuit Low Input
P0343 Camshaft Position Sensor Circuit High Input
P0344 Camshaft Position Sensor Circuit Intermittent
P0350 Ignition Coil Primary/Secondary Circuit Malfunction
P0351 Ignition Coil "A" Primary/Secondary Circuit Malfunction
P0352 Ignition Coil "B" Primary/Secondary Circuit Malfunction
P0353 Ignition Coil "C" Primary/Secondary Circuit Malfunction
P0354 Ignition Coil "D" Primary/Secondary Circuit Malfunction
P0355 Ignition Coil "E" Primary/Secondary Circuit Malfunction
P0356 Ignition Coil "F" Primary/Secondary Circuit Malfunction
P0357 Ignition Coil "G" Primary/Secondary Circuit Malfunction
P0358 Ignition Coil "H" Primary/Secondary Circuit Malfunction
P0359 Ignition Coil "I" Primary/Secondary Circuit Malfunction
P0360 Ignition Coil "J" Primary/Secondary Circuit Malfunction
P0361 Ignition Coil "K" Primary/Secondary Circuit Malfunction
P0362 Ignition Coil "L" Primary/Secondary Circuit Malfunction
P0370 Timing Reference High Resolution Signal "A" Malfunction

P0371 Timing Reference High Resolution Signal "A" Too Many Pulses
P0372 Timing Reference High Resolution Signal "A" Too Few Pulses
P0373 Timing Reference High Resolution Signal "A" Intermittent/Erratic Pulses
P0374 Timing Reference High Resolution Signal "A" No Pulses
P0375 Timing Reference High Resolution Signal "B" Malfunction
P0376 Timing Reference High Resolution Signal "B" Too Many Pulses
P0377 Timing Reference High Resolution Signal "B" Too Few Pulses
P0378 Timing Reference High Resolution Signal "B" Intermittent/Erratic Pulses
P0379 Timing Reference High Resolution Signal "B" No Pulses
P0385 Crankshaft Position Sensor "B" Circuit Malfunction
P0386 Crankshaft Position Sensor "B" Circuit Range/Performance
P0387 Crankshaft Position Sensor "B" Circuit Low Input
P0388 Crankshaft Position Sensor "B" Circuit High Input
P0389 Crankshaft Position Sensor "B" Circuit Intermittent
P0400 Exhaust Gas Recirculation Flow Malfunction
P0401 Exhaust Gas Recirculation Flow Insufficient Detected
P0402 Exhaust Gas Recirculation Flow Excessive Detected
P0403 Exhaust Gas Recirculation Circuit Malfunction
P0404 Exhaust Gas Recirculation Circuit Range/Performance
P0405 Exhaust Gas Recirculation Sensor "A" Circuit Low
P0406 Exhaust Gas Recirculation Sensor "A" Circuit High
P0407 Exhaust Gas Recirculation Sensor "B" Circuit Low
P0408 Exhaust Gas Recirculation Sensor "B" Circuit High
P0410 Secondary Air Injection System Malfunction
P0411 Secondary Air Injection System Incorrect Flow Detected
P0412 Secondary Air Injection System Switching Valve "A" Circuit Malfunction
P0413 Secondary Air Injection System Switching Valve "A" Circuit Open
P0414 Secondary Air Injection System Switching Valve "A" Circuit Shorted
P0415 Secondary Air Injection System Switching Valve "B" Circuit Malfunction
P0416 Secondary Air Injection System Switching Valve "B" Circuit Open
P0417 Secondary Air Injection System Switching Valve "B" Circuit Shorted
P0418 Secondary Air Injection System Relay "A" Circuit Malfunction
P0419 Secondary Air Injection System Relay "B" Circuit Malfunction
P0420 Catalyst System Efficiency Below Threshold (Bank no. 1)
P0421 Warm Up Catalyst Efficiency Below Threshold (Bank no. 1)
P0422 Main Catalyst Efficiency Below Threshold (Bank no. 1)
P0423 Heated Catalyst Efficiency Below Threshold (Bank no. 1)
P0424 Heated Catalyst Temperature Below Threshold (Bank no. 1)
P0430 Catalyst System Efficiency Below Threshold (Bank no. 2)
P0431 Warm Up Catalyst Efficiency Below Threshold (Bank no. 2)
P0432 Main Catalyst Efficiency Below Threshold (Bank no. 2)
P0433 Heated Catalyst Efficiency Below Threshold (Bank no. 2)
P0434 Heated Catalyst Temperature Below Threshold (Bank no. 2)
P0440 Evaporative Emission Control System Malfunction
P0441 Evaporative Emission Control System Incorrect Purge Flow
P0442 Evaporative Emission Control System Leak Detected (Small Leak)
P0443 Evaporative Emission Control System Purge Control Valve Circuit Malfunction
P0444 Evaporative Emission Control System Purge Control Valve Circuit Open
P0445 Evaporative Emission Control System Purge Control Valve Circuit Shorted
P0446 Evaporative Emission Control System Vent Control Circuit Malfunction
P0447 Evaporative Emission Control System Vent Control Circuit Open
P0448 Evaporative Emission Control System Vent Control Circuit Shorted
P0449 Evaporative Emission Control System Vent Valve/Solenoid Circuit Malfunction
P0450 Evaporative Emission Control System Pressure Sensor Malfunction
P0451 Evaporative Emission Control System Pressure Sensor Range/Performance
P0452 Evaporative Emission Control System Pressure Sensor Low Input
P0453 Evaporative Emission Control System Pressure Sensor High Input
P0454 Evaporative Emission Control System Pressure Sensor Intermittent
P0455 Evaporative Emission Control System Leak Detected (Gross Leak)
P0460 Fuel Level Sensor Circuit Malfunction
P0461 Fuel Level Sensor Circuit Range/Performance

P0462 Fuel Level Sensor Circuit Low Input
P0463 Fuel Level Sensor Circuit High Input
P0464 Fuel Level Sensor Circuit Intermittent
P0465 Purge Flow Sensor Circuit Malfunction
P0466 Purge Flow Sensor Circuit Range/Performance
P0467 Purge Flow Sensor Circuit Low Input
P0468 Purge Flow Sensor Circuit High Input
P0469 Purge Flow Sensor Circuit Intermittent
P0470 Exhaust Pressure Sensor Malfunction
P0471 Exhaust Pressure Sensor Range/Performance
P0472 Exhaust Pressure Sensor Low
P0473 Exhaust Pressure Sensor High
P0474 Exhaust Pressure Sensor Intermittent
P0475 Exhaust Pressure Control Valve Malfunction
P0476 Exhaust Pressure Control Valve Range/Performance
P0477 Exhaust Pressure Control Valve Low
P0478 Exhaust Pressure Control Valve High
P0479 Exhaust Pressure Control Valve Intermittent
P0480 Cooling Fan no. 1 Control Circuit Malfunction
P0481 Cooling Fan no. 2 Control Circuit Malfunction
P0482 Cooling Fan no. 3 Control Circuit Malfunction
P0483 Cooling Fan Rationality Check Malfunction
P0484 Cooling Fan Circuit Over Current
P0485 Cooling Fan Power/Ground Circuit Malfunction
P0500 Vehicle Speed Sensor Malfunction
P0501 Vehicle Speed Sensor Range/Performance
P0502 Vehicle Speed Sensor Circuit Low Input
P0503 Vehicle Speed Sensor Intermittent/Erratic/High
P0505 Idle Control System Malfunction
P0506 Idle Control System RPM Lower Than Expected
P0507 Idle Control System RPM Higher Than Expected
P0510 Closed Throttle Position Switch Malfunction
P0520 Engine Oil Pressure Sensor/Switch Circuit Malfunction
P0521 Engine Oil Pressure Sensor/Switch Range/Performance
P0522 Engine Oil Pressure Sensor/Switch Low Voltage
P0523 Engine Oil Pressure Sensor/Switch High Voltage
P0530 A/C Refrigerant Pressure Sensor Circuit Malfunction
P0531 A/C Refrigerant Pressure Sensor Circuit Range/Performance
P0532 A/C Refrigerant Pressure Sensor Circuit Low Input
P0533 A/C Refrigerant Pressure Sensor Circuit High Input
P0534 A/C Refrigerant Charge Loss
P0550 Power Steering Pressure Sensor Circuit Malfunction
P0551 Power Steering Pressure Sensor Circuit Range/Performance
P0552 Power Steering Pressure Sensor Circuit Low Input
P0553 Power Steering Pressure Sensor Circuit High Input
P0554 Power Steering Pressure Sensor Circuit Intermittent
P0560 System Voltage Malfunction
P0561 System Voltage Unstable
P0562 System Voltage Low
P0563 System Voltage High
P0565 Cruise Control On Signal Malfunction
P0566 Cruise Control Off Signal Malfunction
P0567 Cruise Control Resume Signal Malfunction
P0568 Cruise Control Set Signal Malfunction
P0569 Cruise Control Coast Signal Malfunction
P0570 Cruise Control Accel Signal Malfunction
P0571 Cruise Control/Brake Switch "A" Circuit Malfunction
P0572 Cruise Control/Brake Switch "A" Circuit Low
P0573 Cruise Control/Brake Switch "A" Circuit High
P0574 **Through P0580** Reserved for Cruise Codes
P0600 Serial Communication Link Malfunction
P0601 Internal Control Module Memory Check Sum Error
P0602 Control Module Programming Error
P0603 Internal Control Module Keep Alive Memory (KAM) Error
P0604 Internal Control Module Random Access Memory (RAM) Error
P0605 Internal Control Module Read Only Memory (ROM) Error
P0606 PCM Processor Fault
P0608 Control Module VSS Output "A" Malfunction
P0609 Control Module VSS Output "B" Malfunction
P0620 Generator Control Circuit Malfunction
P0621 Generator Lamp "L" Control Circuit Malfunction

P0622 Generator Field "F" Control Circuit Malfunction
P0650 Malfunction Indicator Lamp (MIL) Control Circuit Malfunction
P0654 Engine RPM Output Circuit Malfunction
P0655 Engine Hot Lamp Output Control Circuit Malfunction
P0656 Fuel Level Output Circuit Malfunction
P0700 Transmission Control System Malfunction
P0701 Transmission Control System Range/Performance
P0702 Transmission Control System Electrical
P0703 Torque Converter/Brake Switch "B" Circuit Malfunction
P0704 Clutch Switch Input Circuit Malfunction
P0705 Transmission Range Sensor Circuit Malfunction (PRNDL Input)
P0706 Transmission Range Sensor Circuit Range/Performance
P0707 Transmission Range Sensor Circuit Low Input
P0708 Transmission Range Sensor Circuit High Input
P0709 Transmission Range Sensor Circuit Intermittent
P0710 Transmission Fluid Temperature Sensor Circuit Malfunction
P0711 Transmission Fluid Temperature Sensor Circuit Range/Performance
P0712 Transmission Fluid Temperature Sensor Circuit Low Input
P0713 Transmission Fluid Temperature Sensor Circuit High Input
P0714 Transmission Fluid Temperature Sensor Circuit Intermittent
P0715 Input/Turbine Speed Sensor Circuit Malfunction
P0716 Input/Turbine Speed Sensor Circuit Range/Performance
P0717 Input/Turbine Speed Sensor Circuit No Signal
P0718 Input/Turbine Speed Sensor Circuit Intermittent
P0719 Torque Converter/Brake Switch "B" Circuit Low
P0720 Output Speed Sensor Circuit Malfunction
P0721 Output Speed Sensor Circuit Range/Performance
P0722 Output Speed Sensor Circuit No Signal
P0723 Output Speed Sensor Circuit Intermittent
P0724 Torque Converter/Brake Switch "B" Circuit High
P0725 Engine Speed Input Circuit Malfunction
P0726 Engine Speed Input Circuit Range/Performance
P0727 Engine Speed Input Circuit No Signal
P0728 Engine Speed Input Circuit Intermittent
P0730 Incorrect Gear Ratio
P0731 Gear no. 1 Incorrect Ratio
P0732 Gear no. 2 Incorrect Ratio
P0733 Gear no. 3 Incorrect Ratio
P0734 Gear no. 4 Incorrect Ratio
P0735 Gear no. 5 Incorrect Ratio
P0736 Reverse Incorrect Ratio
P0740 Torque Converter Clutch Circuit Malfunction
P0741 Torque Converter Clutch Circuit Performance or Stuck Off
P0742 Torque Converter Clutch Circuit Stuck On
P0743 Torque Converter Clutch Circuit Electrical
P0744 Torque Converter Clutch Circuit Intermittent
P0745 Pressure Control Solenoid Malfunction
P0746 Pressure Control Solenoid Performance or Stuck Off
P0747 Pressure Control Solenoid Stuck On
P0748 Pressure Control Solenoid Electrical
P0749 Pressure Control Solenoid Intermittent
P0750 Shift Solenoid "A" Malfunction
P0751 Shift Solenoid "A" Performance or Stuck Off
P0752 Shift Solenoid "A" Stuck On
P0753 Shift Solenoid "A" Electrical
P0754 Shift Solenoid "A" Intermittent
P0755 Shift Solenoid "B" Malfunction
P0756 Shift Solenoid "B" Performance or Stuck Oft
P0757 Shift Solenoid "B" Stuck On
P0758 Shift Solenoid "B" Electrical
P0759 Shift Solenoid "B" Intermittent
P0760 Shift Solenoid "C" Malfunction
P0761 Shift Solenoid "C" Performance Or Stuck Oft
P0762 Shift Solenoid "C" Stuck On
P0763 Shift Solenoid "C" Electrical
P0764 Shift Solenoid "C" Intermittent
P0765 Shift Solenoid "D" Malfunction
P0766 Shift Solenoid "D" Performance Or Stuck Oft
P0767 Shift Solenoid "D" Stuck On
P0768 Shift Solenoid "D" Electrical
P0769 Shift Solenoid "D" Intermittent

P0770 Shift Solenoid "E" Malfunction
P0771 Shift Solenoid "E" Performance Or Stuck Oft
P0772 Shift Solenoid "E" Stuck On
P0773 Shift Solenoid "E" Electrical
P0774 Shift Solenoid "E" Intermittent
P0780 Shift Malfunction
P0781 1–2 Shift Malfunction
P0782 2–3 Shift Malfunction
P0783 3–4 Shift Malfunction
P0784 4–5 Shift Malfunction
P0785 Shift/Timing Solenoid Malfunction
P0786 Shift/Timing Solenoid Range/Performance
P0787 Shift/Timing Solenoid Low
P0788 Shift/Timing Solenoid High
P0789 Shift/Timing Solenoid Intermittent
P0790 Normal/Performance Switch Circuit Malfunction
P0801 Reverse Inhibit Control Circuit Malfunction
P0803 1–4 Upshift (Skip Shift) Solenoid Control Circuit Malfunction
P0804 1–4 Upshift (Skip Shift) Lamp Control Circuit Malfunction
P1000 OBD II Monitor Testing Not Complete More Driving Required
P1001 Key On Engine Running (KOER) Self-Test Not Able To Complete, KOER Aborted
P1100 Mass Air Flow (MAF) Sensor Intermittent
P1101 Mass Air Flow (MAF) Sensor Out Of Self-Test Range
P1111 System Pass 49 State Except Econoline
P1112 Intake Air Temperature (IAT) Sensor Intermittent
P1116 Engine Coolant Temperature (ECT) Sensor Out Of Self-Test Range
P1117 Engine Coolant Temperature (ECT) Sensor Intermittent
P1120 Throttle Position (TP) Sensor Out Of Range (Low)
P1121 Throttle Position (TP) Sensor Inconsistent With MAF Sensor
P1124 Throttle Position (TP) Sensor Out Of Self-Test Range
P1125 Throttle Position (TP) Sensor Circuit Intermittent
P1127 Exhaust Not Warm Enough, Downstream Heated Oxygen Sensors (HO2S) Not Tested
P1128 Upstream Heated Oxygen Sensors (HO2 S) Swapped From Bank To Bank
P1129 Downstream Heated Oxygen Sensors (HO2 S) Swapped From Bank To Bank
P1130 Lack Of Upstream Heated Oxygen Sensor (HO2 S 11) Switch, Adaptive Fuel At Limit (Bank #1)
P1131 Lack Of Upstream Heated Oxygen Sensor (HO2 S 11) Switch, Sensor Indicates Lean (Bank #1)
P1132 Lack Of Upstream Heated Oxygen Sensor (HO2S 11) Switch, Sensor Indicates Rich (Bank#1)
P1137 Lack Of Downstream Heated Oxygen Sensor (HO2 S 12) Switch, Sensor Indicates Lean (Bank#1)
P1138 Lack Of Downstream Heated Oxygen Sensor (HO2 S 12) Switch, Sensor Indicates Rich (Bank#1)
P1150 Lack Of Upstream Heated Oxygen Sensor (HO2 S 21) Switch, Adaptive Fuel At Limit (Bank #2)
P1151 Lack Of Upstream Heated Oxygen Sensor (HO2 S 21) Switch, Sensor Indicates Lean (Bank#2)
P1152 Lack Of Upstream Heated Oxygen Sensor (HO2 S 21) Switch, Sensor Indicates Rich (Bank #2)
P1157 Lack Of Downstream Heated Oxygen Sensor (HO2 S 22) Switch, Sensor Indicates Lean (Bank #2)
P1158 Lack Of Downstream Heated Oxygen Sensor (HO2 S 22) Switch, Sensor Indicates Rich (Bank#2)
P1169 (HO2 S 12) Signal Remained Unchanged For More Than 20 Seconds After Closed Loop
P1170 (HO2 S 11) Signal Remained Unchanged For More Than 20 Seconds After Closed Loop
P1173 Feedback A/F Mixture Control (HO2S 21) Signal Remained Unchanged For More Than 20 Seconds After Closed Loop
P1184 Engine Oil Temp Sensor Circuit Performance
P1195 Barometric (BARO) Pressure Sensor Circuit Malfunction (Signal Is From EGR Boost Sensor)
P1196 Starter Switch Circuit Malfunction
P1218 Cylinder Identification (CID) Stuck High
P1219 Cylinder Identification (CID) Stuck Low
P1220 Series Throttle Control Malfunction (Traction Control System)

P1224 Throttle Position Sensor "B" (TP-B) Out Of Self-Test Range (Traction Control System)
P1230 Fuel Pump Low Speed Malfunction
P1231 Fuel Pump Secondary Circuit Low With High Speed Pump On
P1232 Low Speed Fuel Pump Primary Circuit Malfunction
P1233 Fuel Pump Driver Module Off-line (MIL DTC)
P1234 Fuel Pump Driver Module Disabled Or Off-line (No MIL)
P1235 Fuel Pump Control Out Of Range (MIL DTC)
P1236 Fuel Pump Control Out Of Range (No MIL)
P1237 Fuel Pump Secondary Circuit Malfunction (MIL DTC)
P1238 Fuel Pump Secondary Circuit Malfunction (No DMIL)
P1260 THEFT Detected—Engine Disabled
P1261 High To Low Side Short—Cylinder #1 (Indicates Low side Circuit Is Shorted To B+ Or To The High Side Between The IDM And The Injector)
P1262 High To Low Side Short—Cylinder #2 (Indicates Low side Circuit Is Shorted To B+ Or To The High Side Between The IDM And The Injector)
P1263 High To Low Side Short—Cylinder #3 (Indicates Low side Circuit Is Shorted To B+ Or To The High Side Between The IDM And The Injector)
P1264 High To Low Side Short—Cylinder #4 (Indicates Low side Circuit Is Shorted To B+ Or To The High Side Between The IDM And The Injector)
P1265 High To Low Side Short—Cylinder #5 (Indicates Low side Circuit Is Shorted To B+ Or To The High Side Between The IDM And The Injector)
P1266 High To Low Side Short—Cylinder #6 (Indicates Low side Circuit Is Shorted To B+ Or To The High Side Between The IDM And The Injector)
P1267 High To Low Side Short—Cylinder #7 (Indicates Low side Circuit Is Shorted To B+ Or To The High Side Between The IDM And The Injector)
P1268 High To Low Side Short—Cylinder #8 (Indicates Low side Circuit Is Shorted To B+ Or To The High Side Between The IDM And The Injector)
P1270 Engine RPM Or Vehicle Speed Limiter Reached
P1271 High To Low Side Open—Cylinder #1 (Indicates A High To Low Side Open Between The Injector And The IDM)
P1272 High To Low Side Open—Cylinder #2 (Indicates A High To Low Side Open Between The Injector And The IDM)
P1273 High To Low Side Open—Cylinder #3 (Indicates A High To Low Side Open Between The Injector And The IDM)
P1274 High To Low Side Open—Cylinder #4 (Indicates A High To Low Side Open Between The Injector And The IDM)
P1275 High To Low Side Open—Cylinder #5 (Indicates A High To Low Side Open Between The Injector And The IDM)
P1276 High To Low Side Open—Cylinder #6 (Indicates A High To Low Side Open Between The Injector And The IDM)
P1277 High To Low Side Open—Cylinder #7 (Indicates A High To Low Side Open Between The Injector And The IDM)
P1278 High To Low Side Open—Cylinder #8 (Indicates A High To Low Side Open Between The Injector And The IDM)
P1285 Cylinder Head Temperature (CHT) Over Temperature Sensed
P1288 Cylinder Head Temperature (CHT) Sensor Out Of Self-Test Range
P1289 Cylinder Head Temperature (CHT) Sensor Circuit Low Input
P1290 Cylinder Head Temperature (CHT) Sensor Circuit High Input
P1299 Engine Over Temperature Condition
P1309 Misfire Detection Monitor Is Not Enabled
P1320 Distributor Signal Interrupt
P1336 Crankshaft Position Sensor (Gear)
P1345 No Camshaft Position Sensor Signal
P1351 Ignition Diagnostic Monitor (IDM) Circuit Input Malfunction
P1351 Indicates Ignition System Malfunction
P1352 Indicates Ignition System Malfunction
P1353 Indicates Ignition System Malfunction
P1354 Indicates Ignition System Malfunction
P1355 Indicates Ignition System Malfunction
P1356 PIPs Occurred While IDM Pulse width Indicates Engine Not Turning
P1357 Ignition Diagnostic Monitor (IDM) Pulse width Not Defined
P1358 Ignition Diagnostic Monitor (IDM) Signal Out Of Self-Test Range
P1359 Spark Output Circuit Malfunction
P1364 Spark Output Circuit Malfunction
P1390 Octane Adjust (OCT ADJ) Out Of Self-Test Range
P1397 System Voltage Out Of Self Test Range
P1400 Differential Pressure Feedback EGR (DPFE) Sensor Circuit Low Voltage Detected
P1401 Differential Pressure Feedback EGR (DPFE) Sensor Circuit High Voltage Detected/EGR Temperature Sensor

P1402 EGR Valve Position Sensor Open Or Short
P1403 Differential Pressure Feedback EGR (DPFE) Sensor Hoses Reversed
P1405 Differential Pressure Feedback EGR (DPFE) Sensor Upstream Hose Off Or Plugged
P1406 Differential Pressure Feedback EGR (DPFE) Sensor Downstream Hose Off Or Plugged
P1407 Exhaust Gas Recirculation (EGR) No Flow Detected (Valve Stuck Closed Or Inoperative)
P1408 Exhaust Gas Recirculation (EGR) Flow Out Of Self-Test Range
P1409 Electronic Vacuum Regulator (EVR) Control Circuit Malfunction
P1410 Check That Fuel Pressure Regulator Control Solenoid And The EGR Check Solenoid Connectors Are Not Swapped
P1411 Secondary Air Injection System Incorrect Downstream Flow Detected
P1413 Secondary Air Injection System Monitor Circuit Low Voltage
P1414 Secondary Air Injection System Monitor Circuit High Voltage
P1442 Evaporative Emission Control System Small Leak Detected
P1443 Evaporative Emission Control System—Vacuum System, Purge Control Solenoid Or Purge Control Valve Malfunction
P1444 Purge Flow Sensor (PFS) Circuit Low Input
P1445 Purge Flow Sensor (PFS) Circuit High Input
P1449 Evaporative Emission Control System Unable To Hold Vacuum
P1450 Unable To Bleed Up Fuel Tank Vacuum
P1455 Evaporative Emission Control System Control Leak Detected (Gross Leak)
P1460 Wide Open Throttle Air Conditioning Cut-Off Circuit Malfunction
P1461 Air Conditioning Pressure (ACP) Sensor Circuit Low Input
P1462 Air Conditioning Pressure (ACP) Sensor Circuit High Input
P1463 Air Conditioning Pressure (ACP) Sensor Insufficient Pressure Change
P1464 Air Conditioning (A/C) Demand Out Of Self-Test Range/A/C On During KOER Or CCT Test
P1469 Low Air Conditioning Cycling Period
P1473 Fan Secondary High, With Fan(s) Off
P1474 Low Fan Control Primary Circuit Malfunction
P1479 High Fan Control Primary Circuit Malfunction
P1480 Fan Secondary Low, With Low Fan On
P1481 Fan Secondary Low, With High Fan On
P1483 Power To Fan Circuit Over current
P1484 Open Power/Ground To Variable Load Control Module (VLCM)
P1485 EGR Control Solenoid Open Or Short
P1486 EGR Vent Solenoid Open Or Short
P1487 EGR Boost Check Solenoid Open Or Short
P1500 Vehicle Speed Sensor (VSS) Circuit Intermittent
P1501 Vehicle Speed Sensor (VSS) Out Of Self-Test Range/Vehicle Moved During Test
P1502 Invalid Self Test—Auxiliary Powertrain Control Module (APCM) Functioning
P1504 Idle Air Control (IAC) Circuit Malfunction
P1505 Idle Air Control (IAC) System At Adaptive Clip
P1506 Idle Air Control (IAC) Overspeed Error
P1507 Idle Air Control (IAC) Underspeed Error
P1512 Intake Manifold Runner Control (IMRC) Malfunction (Bank#1 Stuck Closed)
P1513 Intake Manifold Runner Control (IMRC) Malfunction (Bank#2 Stuck Closed)
P1516 Intake Manifold Runner Control (IMRC) Input Error (Bank #1)
P1517 Intake Manifold Runner Control (IMRC) Input Error (Bank #2)
P1518 Intake Manifold Runner Control (IMRC) Malfunction (Stuck Open)
P1519 Intake Manifold Runner Control (IMRC) Malfunction (Stuck Closed)
P1520 Intake Manifold Runner Control (IMRC) Circuit Malfunction
P1521 Variable Resonance Induction System (VRIS) Solenoid #1 Open Or Short
P1522 Variable Resonance Induction System (VRIS) Solenoid#2 Open Or Short
P1523 High Speed Inlet Air (HSIA) Solenoid Open Or Short
P1530 Air Condition (A/C) Clutch Circuit Malfunction
P1531 Invalid Test—Accelerator Pedal Movement
P1536 Parking Brake Applied Failure
P1537 Intake Manifold Runner Control (IMRC) Malfunction (Bank#1 Stuck Open)

P1538 Intake Manifold Runner Control (IMRC) Malfunction (Bank#2 Stuck Open)
P1539 Power To Air Condition (A/C) Clutch Circuit Overcurrent
P1549 Problem In Intake Manifold Tuning (IMT) Valve System
P1550 Power Steering Pressure (PSP) Sensor Out Of Self-Test Range
P1601 Serial Communication Error
P1605 Powertrain Control Module (PCM)—Keep Alive Memory (KAM) Test Error
P1608 PCM Internal Circuit Malfunction
P1609 PCM Internal Circuit Malfunction (2.5L Only)
P1625 B+ Supply To Variable Load Control Module (VLCM) Fan Circuit Malfunction
P1626 B+ Supply To Variable Load Control Module (VLCM) Air Conditioning (A/C) Circuit
P1650 Power Steering Pressure (PSP) Switch Out Of Self-Test Range
P1651 Power Steering Pressure (PSP) Switch Input Malfunction
P1660 Output Circuit Check Signal High
P1661 Output Circuit Check Signal Low
P1662 Injection Driver Module Enable (IDM EN) Circuit Failure
P1663 Fuel Delivery Command Signal (FDCS) Circuit Failure
P1667 Cylinder Identification (CID) Circuit Failure
P1668 PCM—IDM Diagnostic Communication Error
P1670 EF Feedback Signal Not Detected
P1701 Reverse Engagement Error
P1701 Fuel Trim Malfunction (Villager)
P1703 Brake On/Off (BOO) Switch Out Of Self-Test Range
P1704 Digital Transmission Range (TR) Sensor Failed To Transition State
P1705 Transmission Range (TR) Sensor Out Of Self-Test Range
P1705 Clutch Pedal Position (CPP) Or Park Neutral Position (PNP) Problem
P1706 High Vehicle Speed In Park
P1709 Park Or Neutral Position (PNP) Or Clutch Pedal Position (CPP) Switch Out Of Self-Test Range
P1709 Throttle Position (TP) Sensor Malfunction (Aspire 1.3L, Escort/Tracer 1.8L, Probe 2.5L)
P1711 Transmission Fluid Temperature (TFT) Sensor Out Of Self-Test Range
P1714 Shift Solenoid "A" Inductive Signature Malfunction
P1715 Shift Solenoid "B" Inductive Signature Malfunction
P1716 Transmission Malfunction
P1717 Transmission Malfunction
P1719 Transmission Malfunction
P1720 Vehicle Speed Sensor (VSS) Circuit Malfunction
P1727 Coast Clutch Solenoid Inductive Signature Malfunction
P1728 Transmission Slip Error—Converter Clutch Failed
P1731 Improper 1–2 Shift
P1732 Improper 2–3 Shift
P1733 Improper 3–4 Shift
P1734 Improper 4–5 Shift
P1740 Torque Converter Clutch (TCC) Inductive Signature Malfunction
P1741 Torque Converter Clutch (TCC) Control Error
P1742 Torque Converter Clutch (TCC) Solenoid Failed On (Turns On MIL)
P1743 Torque Converter Clutch (TCC) Solenoid Failed On (Turns On TCIL)
P1744 Torque Converter Clutch (TCC) System Mechanically Stuck In Off Position
P1744 Torque Converter Clutch (TCC) Solenoid Malfunction (2.5L Only)
P1746 Electronic Pressure Control (EPC) Solenoid Open Circuit (Low Input)
P1747 Electronic Pressure Control (EPC) Solenoid Short Circuit (High Input)
P1748 Electronic Pressure Control (EPC) Malfunction
P1749 Electronic Pressure Control (EPC) Solenoid Failed Low
P1751 Shift Solenoid#1 (SS1) Performance
P1754 Coast Clutch Solenoid (CCS) Circuit Malfunction
P1756 Shift Solenoid#2 (SS2) Performance
P1760 Overrun Clutch SN
P1761 Shift Solenoid #(SS2) Performance
P1762 Transmission Malfunction
P1765 3–2 Timing Solenoid Malfunction (2.5L Only)
P1779 TCIL Circuit Malfunction
P1780 Transmission Control Switch (TCS) Circuit Out Of Self-Test Range

P1783 Transmission Over Temperature Condition
P1784 Transmission Malfunction
P1785 Transmission Malfunction
P1786 Transmission Malfunction
P1787 Transmission Malfunction
P1788 3–2 Timing/Coast Clutch Solenoid (3–2/CCS) Circuit Open
P1789 3–2 Timing/Coast Clutch Solenoid (3–2/CCS) Circuit Shorted
P1792 Idle (IDL) Switch (Closed Throttle Position Switch) Malfunction
P1794 Loss Of Battery Voltage Input
P1795 EGR Boost Sensor Malfunction
P1797 Clutch Pedal Position (CPP) Switch Or Neutral Switch Circuit Malfunction

P1900 Cooling Fan
U1021 SCP Indicating The Lack Of Air Conditioning (A/C) Clutch Status Response
U1039 Vehicle Speed Signal (VSS) Missing Or Incorrect
U1051 Brake Switch Signal Missing Or Incorrect
U1073 SCP Indicating The Lack Of Engine Coolant Fan Status Response
U1131 SCP Indicating The Lack Of Fuel Pump Status Response
U1135 SCP Indicating The Ignition Switch Signal Missing Or Incorrect
U1256 SCP Indicating A Communications Error
U1451 Lack Of Response From Passive Anti-Theft System (PATS) Module—Engine Disabled

VACUUM DIAGRAMS

▶ **See Figure 137**

Following are vacuum diagrams for most of the engine and emissions package combinations covered by this manual. Because vacuum circuits will vary based on various engine and vehicle options, always refer first to the vehicle emission control information label, if present. Should the label be missing, or should vehicle be equipped with a different engine from the vehicle's original equipment, refer to the diagrams below for the same or similar configuration.

If you wish to obtain a replacement emissions label, most manufacturers make the labels available for purchase. The labels can usually be ordered from a local dealer.

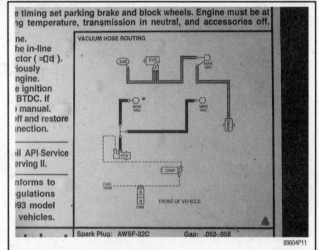

Fig. 137 A vacuum diagram is usually located on the underside of the hood on the emission control label

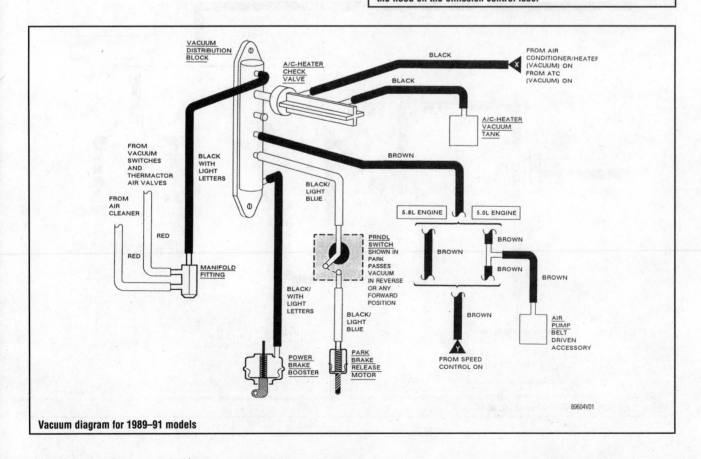

Vacuum diagram for 1989–91 models

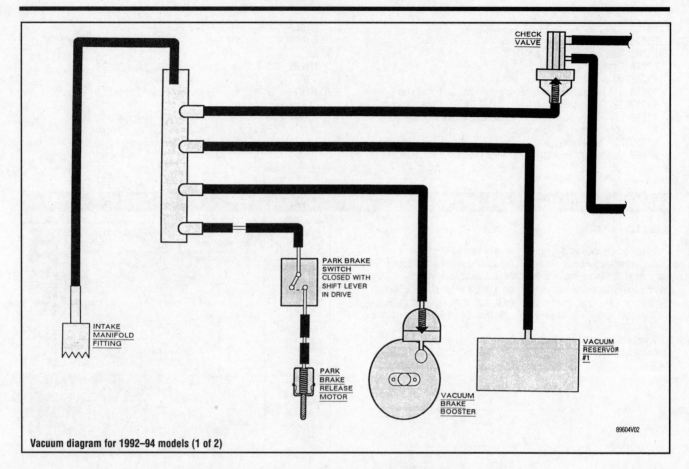

Vacuum diagram for 1992–94 models (1 of 2)

89604V02

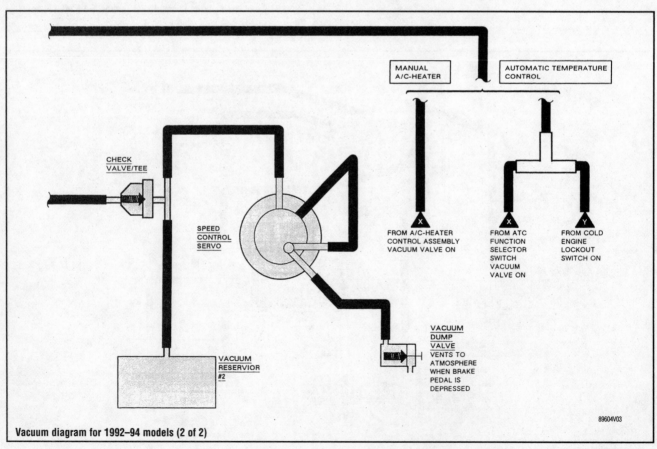

Vacuum diagram for 1992–94 models (2 of 2)

89604V03

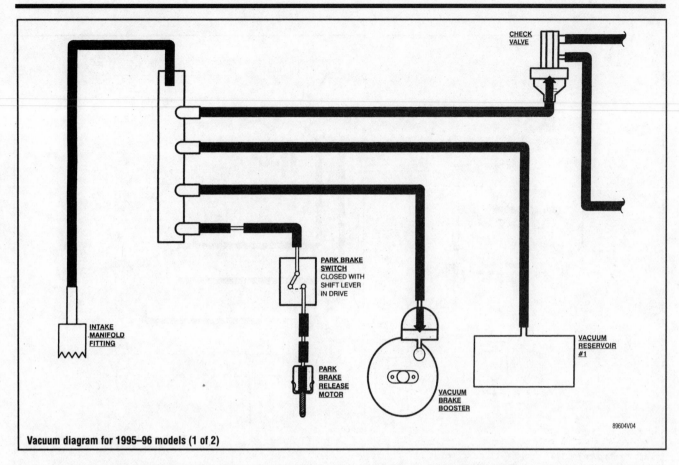

CHECK VALVE

PARK BRAKE SWITCH CLOSED WITH SHIFT LEVER IN DRIVE

INTAKE MANIFOLD FITTING

PARK BRAKE RELEASE MOTOR

VACUUM BRAKE BOOSTER

VACUUM RESERVOIR #1

89604V04

Vacuum diagram for 1995–96 models (1 of 2)

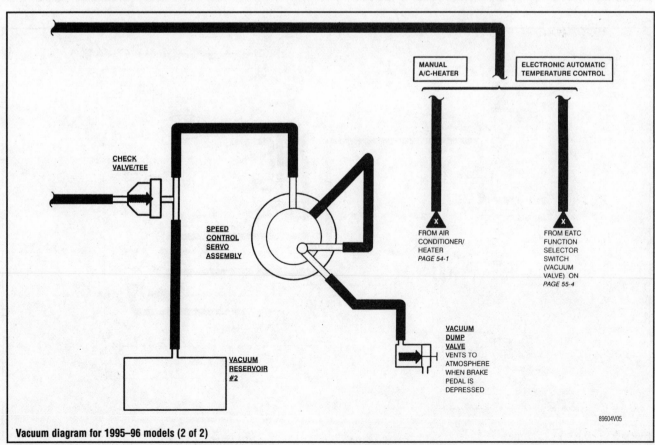

MANUAL A/C-HEATER

ELECTRONIC AUTOMATIC TEMPERATURE CONTROL

CHECK VALVE/TEE

SPEED CONTROL SERVO ASSEMBLY

X

FROM AIR CONDITIONER/ HEATER
PAGE 54-1

X

FROM EATC FUNCTION SELECTOR SWITCH (VACUUM VALVE) ON
PAGE 55-4

VACUUM DUMP VALVE VENTS TO ATMOSPHERE WHEN BRAKE PEDAL IS DEPRESSED

VACUUM RESERVOIR #2

89604V05

Vacuum diagram for 1995–96 models (2 of 2)

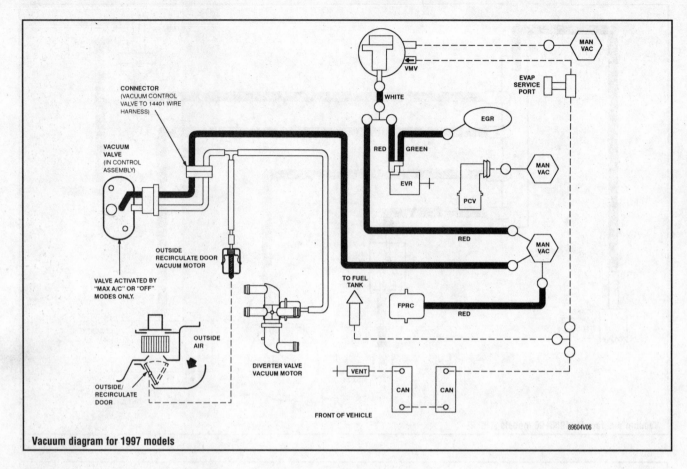

Vacuum diagram for 1997 models

89604V06

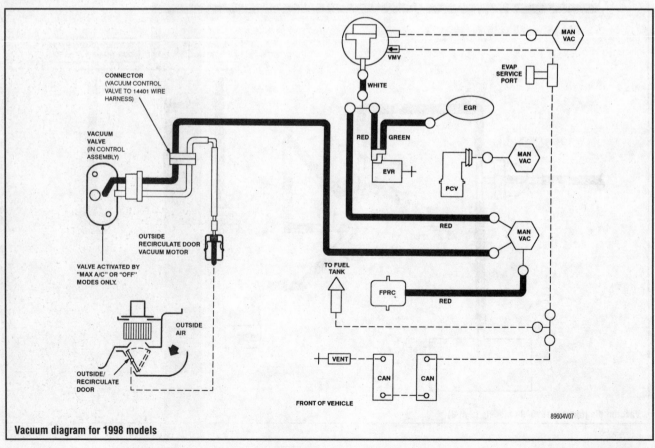

Vacuum diagram for 1998 models

89604V07

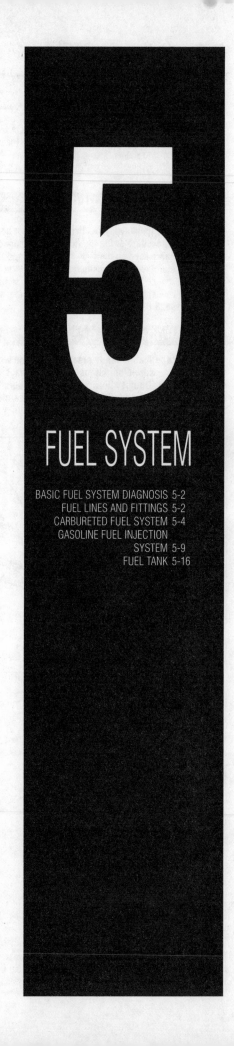

5

FUEL SYSTEM

BASIC FUEL SYSTEM DIAGNOSIS

When there is a problem starting or driving a vehicle, two of the most important checks involve the ignition and the fuel systems. The questions most mechanics attempt to answer first, "is there spark?" and "is there fuel?" will often lead to solving most basic problems. For ignition system diagnosis and testing, please refer to the information on engine electrical components and ignition systems found earlier in this manual. If the ignition system checks out (there is spark), then you must determine if the fuel system is operating properly (is there fuel?).

FUEL LINES AND FITTINGS

➡Quick-connect (push type) fuel line fittings must be disconnected using proper procedure or the fitting may be damaged. There are two types of retainers used on the push connect fittings. Line sizes of ⅜ and ⁵⁄₁₆ in. diameter use a hairpin clip retainer. The ¼ in. diameter line connectors use a duck-bill clip retainer. In addition, some engines use spring-lock connections, secured by a garter spring, which require Ford Tool T81P-19623-G (or equivalent) for removal.

✳✳ CAUTION

Observe all applicable safety precautions when working around fuel. Whenever servicing the fuel system, always work in a well ventilated area. Do not allow fuel spray or vapors to come in contact with a spark or open flame. Keep a dry chemical fire extinguisher near the work area. Always keep fuel in a container specifically designed for fuel storage; also, always properly seal fuel containers to avoid the possibility of fire or explosion.

Hairpin Clip Fitting

REMOVAL & INSTALLATION

▶ **See Figures 1 and 2**

1. Clean all dirt and grease from the fitting. Spread the two clip legs about ⅛ in. (3mm) each to disengage from the fitting and pull the clip outward from the fitting. Use finger pressure only; do not use any tools.
2. Grasp the fitting and hose assembly and pull away from the steel line. Twist the fitting and hose assembly slightly while pulling, if the assembly sticks.
3. Inspect the hairpin clip for damage, replacing the clip if necessary. Reinstall the clip in position on the fitting.
4. Inspect the fitting and inside of the connector to ensure freedom from dirt or obstruction. Install the fitting into the connector and push together. A click will be heard when the hairpin snaps into the proper connection. Pull on the line to insure full engagement.

Duckbill Clip Fitting

REMOVAL & INSTALLATION

▶ **See Figure 3**

1. A special tool is available from Ford and other manufacturers for removing the retaining clips. Use Ford Tool T90T-9550-B or C or equivalent. If the tool is not on hand, go onto step 2. Align the slot on the push connector disconnect tool with either tab on the retaining clip. Pull the line from the connector.
2. If the special clip tool is not available, use a pair of narrow 6-inch slip-jaw pliers with a jaw width of 0.2 in (5mm) or less. Align the jaws of the pliers with the openings of the fitting case and compress the part of the retaining clip that engages the case. Compressing the retaining clip will release the fitting,

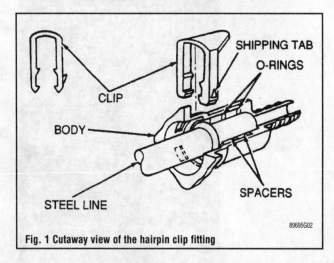

Fig. 1 Cutaway view of the hairpin clip fitting

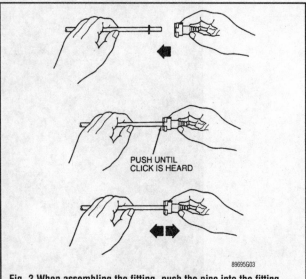

Fig. 2 When assembling the fitting, push the pipe into the fitting until a click is heard

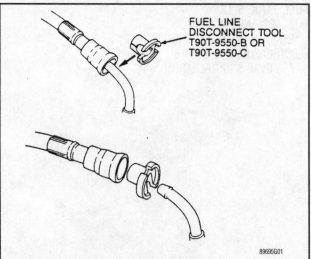

Fig. 3 A fuel line disconnect tool is required to properly separate a duckbill clip fitting

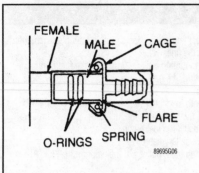

Fig. 4 Cutaway view of a spring lock coupling

Fig. 5 Remove the safety clip from the fuel lines, the clip is attached to a small wire that keeps it from getting lost

Fig. 6 This type of removal tool has a hinged center section that allows you to fit it around the fuel line

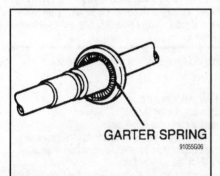

Fig. 7 The garter spring is located inside the fitting and holds the fitting together

Fig. 8 Slide the tool back to unseat the garter spring on the fitting, and pull back on the fuel line to separate them

Fig. 9 This type of removal tool snaps over the line

Fig. 10 Slide the tool back to unseat the garter spring on the fitting, and pull back on the fuel line to separate them

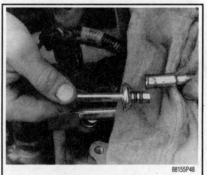

Fig. 11 Be sure to check the O-rings for damage; replace them if necessary

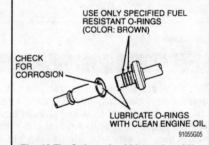

Fig. 12 The O-rings should be replaced if necessary with the specific ones used for the fuel system, a non-specific O-ring could leak

which may be pulled from the connector. Both sides of the clip must be compressed at the same time to disengage.

3. Inspect the retaining clip, fitting end and connector. Replace the clip if any damage is apparent.

4. Push the line into the steel connector until a click is heard, indicating the clip is in place. Pull on the line to check engagement.

Spring Lock Coupling

REMOVAL & INSTALLATION

♦ See Figures 4 thru 13

The spring lock coupling is held together by a garter spring inside a circular cage. When the coupling is connected together, the flared end of the female fitting slips behind the garter spring inside the cage of the male fitting. The garter spring and cage then prevent the flared end of the female fitting from pulling out of the cage. As an additional locking feature, most vehicles have a horseshoe-shaped retaining clip that improves the retaining reliability of the spring lock coupling.

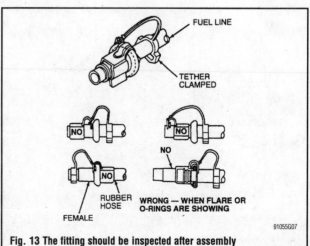

Fig. 13 The fitting should be inspected after assembly

CARBURETED FUEL SYSTEM

Description

All vehicles with the 5.8L engine are equipped with a Motorcraft 7200 Variable Venturi (VV) carburetor. Fuel is supplied to the carburetor by a mechanical fuel pump mounted on the engine. The fuel pump is driven by an eccentric attached to the front of the camshaft.

The 7200 VV carburetor is unique in that it is able to vary the venturi area according to engine speed and load, which is quite different from standard carburetors which have a fixed venturi area. The venturi area is varied by dual venturi valves that are controlled by engine vacuum and throttle position. The position of the venturi valves change, depending on engine demands, to determine the area for airflow to the two throats of the carburetor.

The venturi valves are connected to two tapered main metering rods that ride in the main metering jets. When the venturi valve position varies, the metering rods vary the fuel flow by changing the flow area of the main metering jets. During engine operation, air speed through the carburetor is fairly constant, causing more even air/fuel mixtures throughout the engine operating range.

In a traditional fixed venturi carburetor, airflow speed varies according to throttle opening and engine speed, making a supplementary idle system and power enrichment system necessary in order to work with the changing flow speed. In the variable venturi carburetor, these supplementary systems are not necessary.

The variable venturi carburetor varies the air/fuel ratio in response to signals from a control module. The air bleed feedback system used on the variable venturi carburetor uses a stepper motor, activated by a signal from the control module, to regulate bleed air admitted into the main fuel metering system. The stepper motor modulates the pintle movement in the metering orifice, varying the air bleed into the main system. The air/fuel mixture becomes leaner as the amount of air becomes greater.

Mechanical Fuel Pump

REMOVAL & INSTALLATION

▶ See Figure 14

✳ CAUTION

Observe all applicable safety precautions when working around fuel. Whenever servicing the fuel system, always work in a well ventilated area. Do not allow fuel spray or vapors to come in contact with a spark or open flame. Keep a dry chemical fire extinguisher near the work area. Always keep fuel in a container specifically designed for fuel storage; also, always properly seal fuel containers to avoid the possibility of fire or explosion.

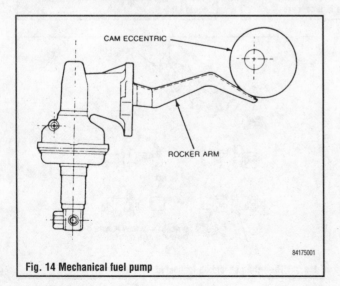

CAM ECCENTRIC

ROCKER ARM

84175001

Fig. 14 Mechanical fuel pump

1. Loosen the threaded fuel line connection(s) with a tubing wrench, then tighten snugly. Do not remove the lines yet.
2. Loosen the fuel pump mounting bolts 1–2 turns. If the fuel pump does not come loose from its mounting, the gasket is probably stuck; apply force with your hands to loosen the pump.
3. Rotate the crankshaft with the starter until the fuel pump eccentric is near its low position, reducing the tension on the fuel pump rocker arm. It will now be easier to remove and install the fuel pump.
4. Disconnect the negative battery cable.
5. Disconnect the fuel pump inlet, outlet and fuel vapor return line, if equipped.

✳ CAUTION

The outlet line is pressurized. Wrap a rag around the line, release pressure slowly and contain spillage. Observe no smoking/no open flame precautions. Have a class B-C (dry powder) fire extinguisher within arm's reach at all times.

6. Remove the fuel pump mounting bolts and remove the fuel pump. Discard the old gasket.
To install:
7. Clean all old gasket material from the pump mounting surface on the engine and from the fuel pump, if it is to be reused.
8. Apply a coat of oil resistant sealer to a new gasket.
9. Install the mounting bolts into the fuel pump and install the gasket on the bolts. Position the pump on the engine. Turn the mounting bolts alternately and evenly and tighten to 19–27 ft. lbs. (26–37 Nm).
10. Connect the fuel pump outlet line. If it is a threaded connection, start the fitting by hand to avoid cross-threading. Tighten the fitting to 15–18 ft. lbs. (20–24 Nm).
11. Connect the inlet line and fuel vapor return line, if equipped. Tighten the hose clamp(s).

➡**Prior to installation, check the rubber fuel lines and make sure they are not cracked, hardened or frayed. If replacement is necessary, use only rubber hose made for fuel line use.**

12. Connect the negative battery cable, start the engine and check for leaks.
13. Stop the engine and check all fuel line connections for leaks. Check the fuel pump mounting pad for oil leaks.

TESTING

Capacity Test

1. Remove the air cleaner assembly.
2. Using a backup wrench on the carburetor inlet nut, slowly disconnect the fuel line from the carburetor.

✳ CAUTION

The fuel line is pressurized. Wrap a rag around the line, release pressure slowly and contain spillage. Observe no smoking/no open flame precautions. Have a class B-C (dry powder) fire extinguisher within arm's reach at all times.

3. Attach a piece of rubber hose to the end of the fuel line and direct the other end of the hose into a suitable container.
4. Crank the engine 10 revolutions. If little or no fuel flows from the fuel line during the tenth revolution, check the following:
   a. Make sure there is fuel in the fuel tank and the fuel tank outlet is not plugged or restricted.
   b. If there is an in-line filter between the fuel pump and carburetor, make sure it is not plugged.
   c. Check all fuel lines for kinks, cracks and leaks.
   d. Check the fuel pump diaphragm crimp area and breather hole(s) for fuel or oil leaks.
5. If there is an adequate fuel supply and there are no restrictions or leaks, replace the fuel pump.
6. If the fuel flow is adequate, perform the pressure test.

Pressure Test

1. Connect a suitable pressure gauge to the carburetor end of the fuel line.
2. Start the engine and read the pressure after 10 seconds. The engine should be able to run for over 30 seconds on the fuel in the carburetor bowl.
3. The fuel pump pressure should be 6–8 psi. If pump pressure is too low or too high, install a new fuel pump.
4. Connect the fuel line to the carburetor, using a backup wrench on the carburetor inlet fitting.
5. Install the air cleaner assembly.

Carburetor

ADJUSTMENTS

Choke

COLD ENRICHMENT ROD (CER) ADJUSTMENT

♦ **See Figures 15 and 16**

➡ **The CER mechanism affects carburetor air/fuel mixtures throughout engine operation, cold and warm. Several adjustments are required. Although each adjustment affects a particular phase of operation, and a** maladjustment can lead to a particular performance symptom, the adjustment procedure must be performed completely and in the following sequence.

If adjustment cannot be accomplished due to epoxy in the adjustment nut, a new service assembly must be installed.

1. Remove the carburetor from the engine.
2. Install a suitable dial indicator on the carburetor, as shown in the Fig. 3.

➡ **The CER adjustment specifications are listed on a tag attached to the carburetor above the choke cap, as shown in figure given.**

3. Remove the choke diaphragm cover and spring.
4. Remove the choke cap.
5. Compress the idle speed positioner where applicable and insert a 5/16–1/2 in. spacer between the positioner stem and the throttle lever contact paddle. Retain in this position with a rubber band. This will locate the fast idle pick-up lever away from the cam and allow the cam to rotate freely.
6. Install Stator Cap T77L–9848–A or equivalent as a weight to rotate the bimetal lever counterclockwise and seat the CER.
7. Position the dial indicator with the tip centered on the top surface of the CER. Zero the dial indicator, then raise the weight slightly and release to check for accurate zero.

➡ **This adjustment will be the reference for other adjustments. Make sure the dial indicator reading is accurate.**

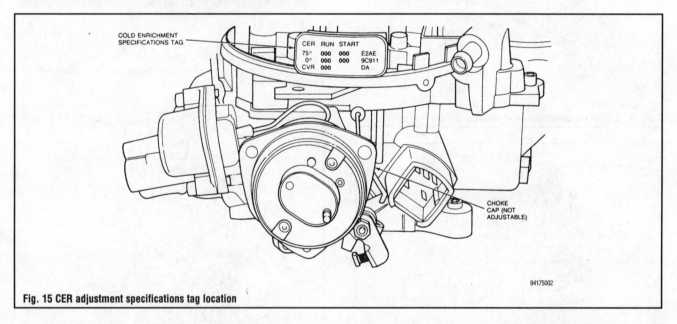

Fig. 15 CER adjustment specifications tag location

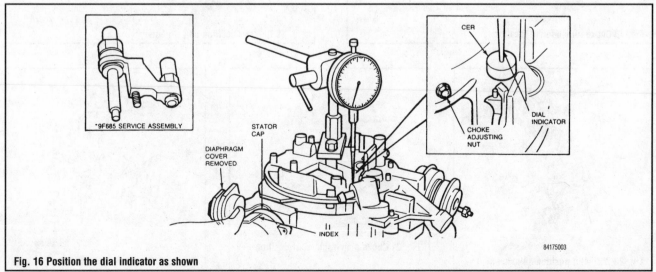

Fig. 16 Position the dial indicator as shown

CONTROL VACUUM REGULATOR (CVR) SWIVEL ASSEMBLY REPLACEMENT

▶ **See Figures 17 and 18**

The CVR/CER nuts have cylindrical projections above the threads which are filled with epoxy after final adjustment. To adjust, the existing parts must be removed and a new assembly installed.

1. Remove the E-clip and hinge pin.
2. Turn the CER adjusting nut counterclockwise until the nut disengages from the rod.
3. Remove the CVR and replace with a new assembly.
4. The unbroken rod must be in place first before further assembly. Install the assembly and tighten the CER adjusting nut to lower and locate into position. Connect the lever to the swivel.
5. Install the hinge pin and E-clip.

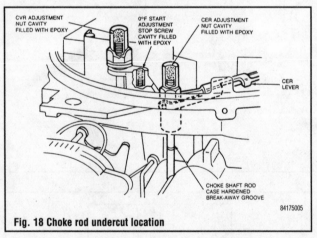

Fig. 17 CVR swivel assembly replacement

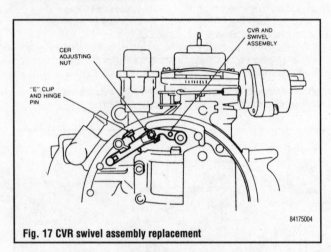

Fig. 18 Choke rod undercut location

➡The rod has an undercut designed to break. If breakage does occur, a new rod assembly must be installed. The upper body must be loosened to position the rod through the opening. Replace the upper body gasket as necessary.

CER RUN POSITION ADJUSTMENT

▶ **See Figure 19**

1. Install the stator cap and rotate clockwise to index. The dial should indicate the tag specification for Run at 75°F (24°C) plus or minus 0.010 in.
2. Adjust by turning the choke adjusting nut clockwise to increase or counterclockwise to decrease the height.

CER START (CRANK) POSITION ADJUSTMENT

▶ **See Figure 20**

1. Remove the stator cap.
2. Rotate the choke bimetal lever clockwise until the CER travel stop screw bottoms on the choke seal retainer (full travel). The dial should indicate the tag specification for Start at 0°F (18°C) plus or minus 0.005 in.
3. Adjust by turning the CER travel stop screw with a 5/64 in. hex wrench, clockwise to decrease or counterclockwise to increase height.

CHOKE DIAPHRAGM START (CRANK) POSITION FOR WARM ENGINE

▶ **See Figure 21**

1. Push in the diaphragm assembly. The dial should indicate the tag specification for Start at 75°F (24°C) plus or minus 0.020 in.
2. Adjust by rotating the diaphragm assembly clockwise to decrease or counterclockwise to increase height.

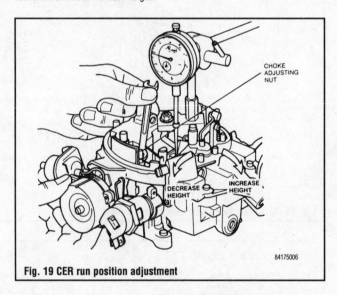

Fig. 19 CER run position adjustment

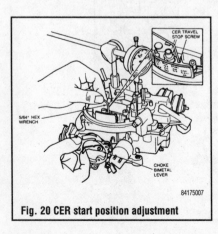

Fig. 20 CER start position adjustment

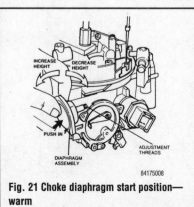

Fig. 21 Choke diaphragm start position— warm

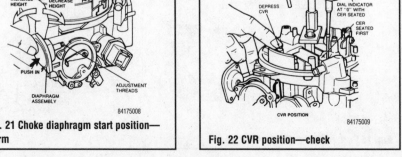

Fig. 22 CVR position—check

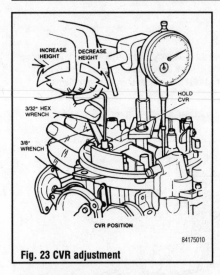

Fig. 23 CVR adjustment

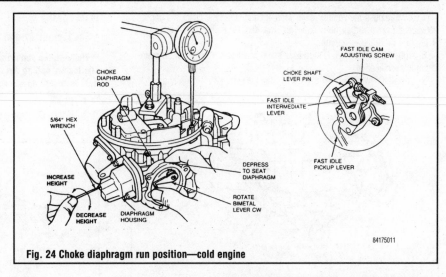

Fig. 24 Choke diaphragm run position—cold engine

CONTROL VACUUM ROD (CVR) POSITION

▶ **See Figures 22 and 23**

1. Seat the CER again using the stator cap weight and check for zero dial indicator reading. Reset the zero position of the indicator, if required. Remove the stator cap weight.

2. Depress the CVR until seated. The dial should indicate the tag specification for CVR plus or minus 0.10 in.

3. Adjust by holding the CVR with a ⅜ in. wrench and turning the adjustment with a 3⁄32 in. hex wrench, clockwise to decrease or counterclockwise to increase height.

4. Reinstall the original choke diaphragm cover with the original spring.

CHOKE DIAPHRAGM RUN POSITION FOR COLD ENGINE

▶ **See Figure 24**

1. Apply vacuum to the choke diaphragm cover, or depress the choke diaphragm rod to the seated position.

2. Rotate the choke bimetal lever clockwise until the choke shaft lever pin contacts the fast idle intermediate lever. The dial should indicate the tag specification for Run at 0°F plus or minus 0.005 in.

3. If an adjustment is required, remove the choke diaphragm cover and install a new cover with the original spring. This is necessary because of the tamper-resistant material on the adjustment screw.

4. Adjust by rotating the screw in the diaphragm housing with a 5⁄64 in. hex wrench, clockwise to increase or counterclockwise to decrease height.

5. Apply sealing liquid on the adjustment screw to secure the adjustment.

6. Install lead ball plug in the adjusting screw hole.

FAST IDLE CAM SETTING

▶ **See Figure 25**

1. Position the fast idle pick-up lever on the second step of the fast idle cam against the shoulder of the high step.

2. Install the stator cap and rotate clockwise until the fast idle pick-up lever contacts the fast idle cam adjusting screw. The dial should indicate specification 0.360 in. plus or minus 0.005 in.

3. Adjust by rotating the fast idle cam adjusting screw.

4. Remove the stator cap.

5. Assemble the choke cap, gasket and retainer with breakaway screws.

6. Remove the dial indicator and rubber band.

7. Install the carburetor and adjust the idle speeds.

Venturi Valve Wide Open Throttle(WOT) Opening

▶ **See Figures 26, 27, 28, 29 and 30**

1. Remove the carburetor from the engine.

2. Remove the expansion plug covering the venturi valve limiter adjustment screw (center punch until loose).

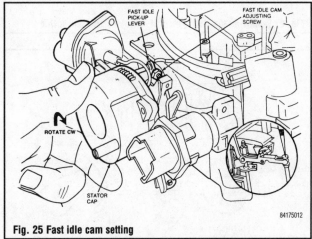

Fig. 25 Fast idle cam setting

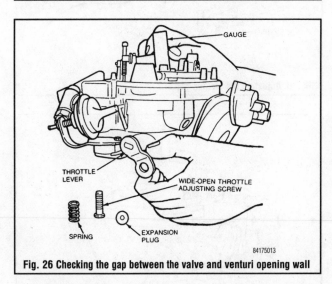

Fig. 26 Checking the gap between the valve and venturi opening wall

3. Remove the (WOT) stop adjustment screw and spring, using a 5⁄32 in. Allen wrench.

4. Hold the throttle plates wipe open, lightly push the venturi valve toward "close position" and check the gap between the valve and venturi opening wall. Set the closing gap specification at 0.39–0.41 in. (9.91–10.41mm).

5. Using a 5⁄64 in. Allen wrench, turn the venturi valve limiter adjustment screw (on the venturi valve arm) to set the closing gap to specification.

6. Install the throttle (WOT) stop adjustment screw and spring, using a 5⁄32 in. Allen wrench.

7. Lightly push the venturi valve "wide open to stop" and check the gap between the valve and air horn wall. This "maximum opening specification" is 0.99–1.01 in. (25.15–25.65mm).

8. Turn the throttle (WOT) stop adjustment screw until the maximum opening is to specification.

9. Install a new expansion plug and install the carburetor on the engine.

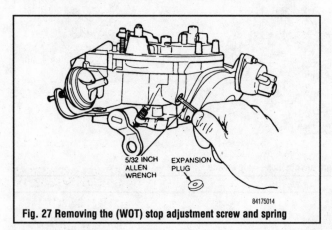

Fig. 27 Removing the (WOT) stop adjustment screw and spring

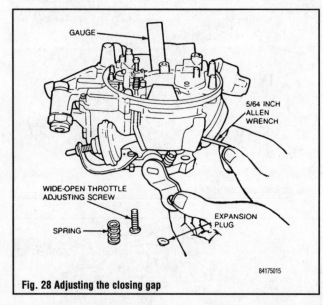

Fig. 28 Adjusting the closing gap

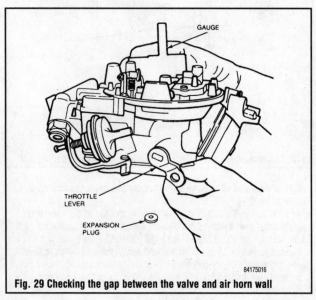

Fig. 29 Checking the gap between the valve and air horn wall

Float Level

◗ **See Figures 31 and 32**

➡ **The variable venturi carburetor is very insensitive to float level settings. The factory setting does not change with time and usage. Adjusting the float level setting will not correct any typical start/drive problems.**

1. Remove the carburetor.
2. Remove the upper body assembly and the upper body gasket.

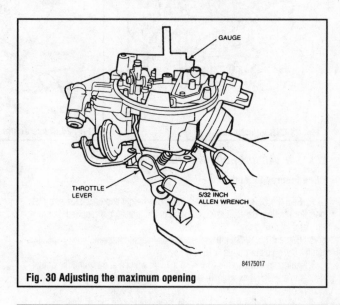

Fig. 30 Adjusting the maximum opening

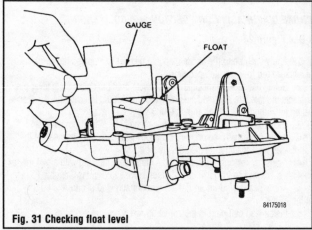

Fig. 31 Checking float level

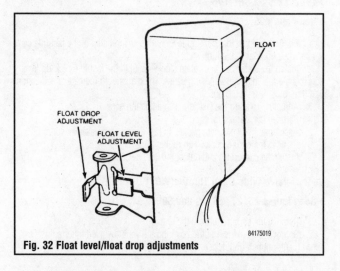

Fig. 32 Float level/float drop adjustments

3. If necessary, fabricate a gauge to the specified dimension.
4. With the upper body inverted, place the float level gauge on the cast surface of the upper body and measure the vertical distance from the cast surface of the upper body and the bottom of the float.
5. The float level specification is 1.010–1.070 in. (25.66–27.17mm).
6. To adjust, bend the float operating lever away from the fuel inlet needle to decrease the setting and toward the needle to increase the setting.
7. Check and/or adjust the float drop.

Float Drop

▶ See Figures 33

1. If necessary, fabricate a gauge to 1.430–1.490 in. (36.33–37.84mm).
2. With the carburetor upper body assembly held in an upright position, place the gauge against the cast surface of the upper body and measure the vertical distance between the cast surface of the upper body and the bottom of the float.
3. The float drop specification is 1.430–1.490 in. (36.33–37.84mm).

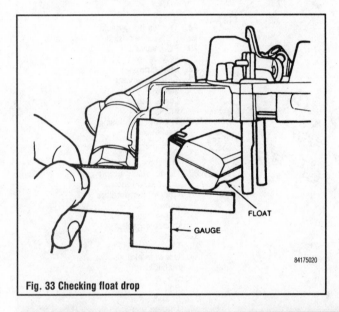

FLOAT

GAUGE

84175020

Fig. 33 Checking float drop

GASOLINE FUEL INJECTION SYSTEM

General Information

▶ See Figure 34

All vehicles with the 4.6L and 5.0L engines are equipped with a Sequential Electronic Fuel Injection (SEFI) system. In this system, fuel is metered into each intake port in sequence with the engine firing order, according to engine demand, through fuel injectors mounted on a tuned intake manifold.

The SEFI system consists of two subsystems, the fuel delivery system and the electronic control system. The fuel delivery system supplies fuel to the fuel injectors at a specified pressure. The electronic control system regulates the flow of fuel from the injectors into the engine.

The fuel delivery system consists of an electric fuel pump, fuel filters, fuel supply manifold (fuel rail), fuel pressure regulator and fuel injectors. The electric fuel pump, mounted in the fuel tank, draws fuel through a filter screen attached to the fuel pump/sending unit assembly. Fuel is pumped through a frame mounted fuel filter, to the engine compartment, and into the fuel supply manifold. The fuel supply manifold supplies fuel directly to the injectors. A constant fuel pressure to the injectors is maintained by the fuel pressure regulator. The fuel pressure regulator is mounted on the fuel supply manifold, downstream from the fuel injectors. The excess fuel supplied by the fuel pump but not required by the engine, passes through the regulator and returns to the fuel tank through the fuel return line. The fuel injectors spray a metered quantity of fuel into the intake air stream when they are energized. The quantity of fuel is determined by the electronic control system.

4. To adjust, bend the stop tab on the float lever away from the hinge pin to increase the setting and toward the hinge pin to decrease the setting.
5. Install a new upper body gasket and install the upper body assembly.

REMOVAL & INSTALLATION

➡**In many instances, flooding, stumble on acceleration, and other performance complaints are caused by the presence of dirt, water or other foreign material in the carburetor. To aid in complaint diagnosis, the carburetor should be carefully removed from the engine without removing the fuel from the bowl. The contents of the bowl can then be examined for contamination as the carburetor is disassembled.**

1. Disconnect the negative battery cable. Remove the air cleaner.
2. Remove the throttle cable and transmission kickdown levers from the throttle lever. Tag and detach all vacuum lines, emission hoses, and electrical connections.
3. Using a backup wrench on the carburetor inlet nut, slowly disconnect the fuel line from the carburetor.

❋❖❋ CAUTION

The fuel line is pressurized. Wrap a rag around the line, release pressure slowly and contain spillage. Observe no smoking/no open flame precautions. Have a class B-C (dry powder) fire extinguisher within arm's reach at all times.

4. Remove the carburetor mounting nuts; then remove the carburetor. Remove the carburetor mounting gasket spacer, if equipped, and lower gasket from the intake manifold.
To install:
5. Clean the gasket mounting surfaces of the spacer and carburetor. Place the spacer between 2 new gaskets and place the spacer and gaskets on the intake manifold. Position the carburetor on the spacer and gasket.
6. Install the spark and EGR vacuum lines and fuel fitting before bolting the carburetor in place. Install the carburetor mounting nuts and hand tighten them. Then, alternately tighten each nut in a crisscross pattern to 12–15 ft. lbs. (16–20 Nm).
7. Connect the throttle cable and all emission and vacuum lines. Observe the color coded vacuum line connections on the carburetor.
8. Run the engine and adjust the idle speeds. Check for fuel leaks. Adjust the throttle valve lever.

Air entering the engine is monitored by speed, pressure and temperature sensors. The outputs of these sensors are processed by the Powertrain Control Module (PCM). The PCM computes the required fuel flow rate and determines the needed injector pulse width (injector "on" time) and sends a signal to the injector to meter the exact quantity of fuel. Each fuel injector is energized once every other crankshaft revolution, in sequence with the ignition firing order.

➡**For description and testing of electronic control system components, see Section 4.**

FUEL SYSTEM SERVICE PRECAUTIONS

Safety is the most important factor when performing not only fuel system maintenance, but any type of maintenance. Failure to conduct maintenance and repairs in a safe manner may result in serious personal injury or death. Work on a vehicle's fuel system components can be accomplished safely and effectively by adhering to the following rules and guidelines.

• To avoid the possibility of fire and personal injury, always disconnect the negative battery cable unless the repair or test procedure requires that battery voltage by applied.

• Always relieve the fuel system pressure prior to detaching any fuel system component (injector, fuel rail, pressure regulator, etc.) fitting or fuel line connection. Exercise extreme caution whenever relieving fuel system pressure to avoid exposing skin, face and eyes to fuel spray. Please be advised that fuel under pressure may penetrate the skin or any part of the body that it contacts.

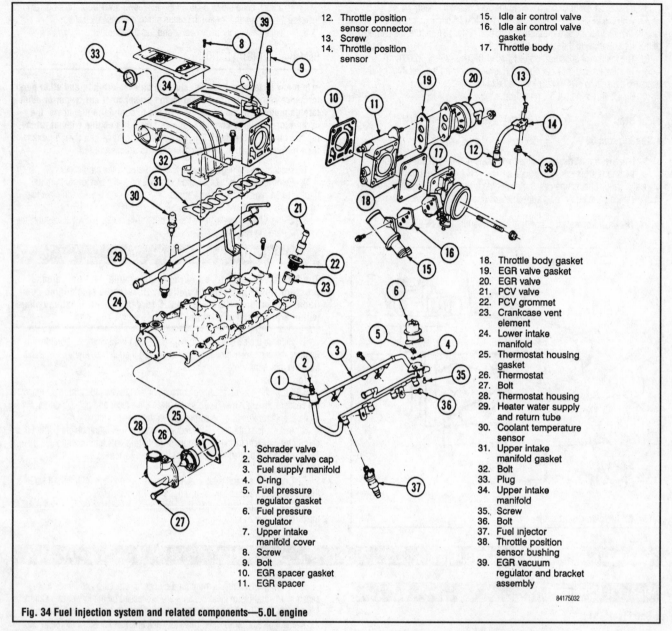

12. Throttle position
    sensor connector
13. Screw
14. Throttle position
    sensor
15. Idle air control valve
16. Idle air control valve
    gasket
17. Throttle body

1. Schrader valve
2. Schrader valve cap
3. Fuel supply manifold
4. O-ring
5. Fuel pressure
   regulator gasket
6. Fuel pressure
   regulator
7. Upper intake
   manifold cover
8. Screw
9. Bolt
10. EGR spacer gasket
11. EGR spacer

18. Throttle body gasket
19. EGR valve gasket
20. EGR valve
21. PCV valve
22. PCV grommet
23. Crankcase vent
    element
24. Lower intake
    manifold
25. Thermostat housing
    gasket
26. Thermostat
27. Bolt
28. Thermostat housing
29. Heater water supply
    and return tube
30. Coolant temperature
    sensor
31. Upper intake
    manifold gasket
32. Bolt
33. Plug
34. Upper intake
    manifold
35. Screw
36. Bolt
37. Fuel injector
38. Throttle position
    sensor bushing
39. EGR vacuum
    regulator and bracket
    assembly

84175032

Fig. 34 Fuel injection system and related components—5.0L engine

• Always place a shop towel or cloth around the fitting or connection prior to loosening to absorb any excess fuel due to spillage. Ensure that all fuel spillage is quickly remove from engine surfaces. Ensure that all fuel-soaked cloths or towels are deposited into a flame-proof waste container with a lid.

• Always keep a dry chemical (Class B) fire extinguisher near the work area.

• Do not allow fuel spray or fuel vapors to come into contact with a spark or open flame.

• Always use a second wrench when loosening or tightening fuel line connections fittings. This will prevent unnecessary stress and torsion to fuel piping. Always follow the proper torque specifications.

• Always replace worn fuel fitting O-rings with new ones. Do not substitute fuel hose where rigid pipe is installed.

Relieving Fuel System Pressure

✳✳ CAUTION

Fuel supply lines on fuel injected vehicles will remain pressurized for some time after the engine is shut off. Fuel pressure must be relieved before servicing the fuel system.

1. Disconnect the negative battery cable.
2. Remove the fuel tank cap to relieve the pressure in the fuel tank.
3. Remove the cap from the Schrader valve located on the fuel supply manifold.
4. Attach fuel pressure gauge T80L–9974–A or equivalent, to the Schrader valve and drain the fuel through the drain tube into a suitable container.
5. After the fuel system pressure is relieved, remove the fuel pressure gauge and install the cap on the Schrader valve.

Fuel Pump

TESTING

▶ See Figure 35

✳✳ CAUTION

Observe all applicable safety precautions when working around fuel. Whenever servicing the fuel system, always work in a well ventilated area. Do not allow fuel spray or vapors to come in contact with a spark or open flame. Keep a dry chemical fire extin-

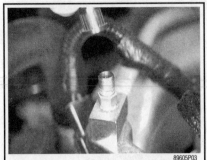

Fig. 35 The fuel pressure test port is located on the fuel rail, under a protective cap

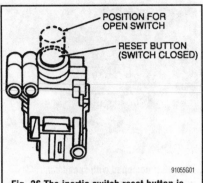

POSITION FOR OPEN SWITCH

RESET BUTTON (SWITCH CLOSED)

Fig. 36 The inertia switch reset button is located on the top of the switch

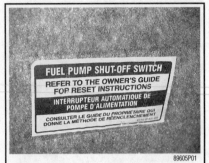

FUEL PUMP SHUT-OFF SWITCH
REFER TO THE OWNER'S GUIDE FOP RESET INSTRUCTIONS
INTERRUPTEUR AUTOMATIQUE DE POMPE D'ALIMENTATION
CONSULTER LE GUIDE DU PROPRIETAIRE QUI DONNE LA METHODE DE REENCLENCHEMENT

Fig. 37 The inertia switch location is typically identified by this label affixed in the trunk

guisher near the work area. Always keep fuel in a container specifically designed for fuel storage; also, always properly seal fuel containers to avoid the possibility of fire or explosion.

1. Check all hoses and lines for kinks and leaking. Repair as necessary.
2. Check all electrical connections for looseness and corrosion. Repair as necessary.
3. Turn the ignition key from the **OFF** position to the **RUN** position several times (do not start the engine) and verify that the pump runs briefly each time, (you will here a low humming sound from the fuel tank).

➡️**Check that the inertia switch is reset before diagnosing power supply problems to the fuel pump.**

The use of a scan tool is required to perform these tests.
4. Turn the ignition key **OFF**.
5. Connect a suitable fuel pressure gauge to the fuel test port (Schrader valve) on the fuel rail.
6. Connect the scan tool and turn the ignition key **ON** but do not start the engine.
7. Following the scan tool manufacturer's instructions, enter the output test mode and run the fuel pump to obtain the maximum fuel pressure.
8. The fuel pressure should be between 30–45 psi (210–310 kPa).
9. If the fuel pressure is within specification the pump is working properly. If not, continue with the test.
10. Check the pump ground connection and service as necessary.
11. Turn the ignition key **ON**.
12. Using the scan tool, enter output test mode and turn on the fuel pump circuit.
13. Using a Digital Volt Ohmmeter (DVOM), check for voltage (approximately 10.5 volts) at the fuel pump electrical connector.
14. If the pump is getting a good voltage supply, the ground connection is good and the fuel pressure is not within specification, then replace the pump.

REMOVAL & INSTALLATION

See fuel pump under fuel tank in this section.

Inertia Switch

GENERAL INFORMATION

This switch shuts off the fuel pump in the event of a collision. Once the switch has been tripped, it must be reset manually in order to start the engine.
The inertia switch is located in the trunk behind the side panel on all models covered by this manual.

RESETTING THE SWITCH

▶ **See Figures 36 and 37**

1. Turn the ignition switch **OFF**.
2. Ensure that there is no fuel leaking in the engine compartment, along any of the lines or at the tank. There should be no odor of fuel as well.

3. If no leakage and/or odor is apparent, reset the switch by pushing the reset button on top of the switch. The reset switch is usually accessible through an opening in the kick panel or by reaching over the top of the panel.
4. Cycle the ignition switch from the **ON** to **OFF** positions several times, allowing five seconds at each position, to build fuel pressure within the system.
5. Again, check the fuel system for leaks. There should be no odor of fuel as well.
6. If there is no leakage and/or odor of fuel, it is safe to operate the vehicle. However, it is recommended that the entire system be checked by a professional, especially if the vehicle was in an accident severe enough to trip the inertia switch.

REMOVAL & INSTALLATION

1. Disconnect the negative battery cable.
2. Remove the any necessary trim to access the switch.
3. Unplug the connector on the inertia switch.
4. Remove the retaining bolts and remove the switch.
To install:
5. Installation is the reverse of removal.

Throttle Body

REMOVAL & INSTALLATION

4.6L Engine

▶ **See Figures 38 thru 45**

1. Disconnect the negative battery cable.
2. Remove the air cleaner outlet tube from the throttle body.

Fig. 38 Detach the TP sensor connector

Fig. 39 Disconnect the accelerator cable from the throttle lever

Fig. 40 If equipped with speed control, disconnect the speed control actuator from the throttle lever

Fig. 41 Disconnect the accelerator return spring from the throttle body

Fig. 42 Remove the four retaining bolts and . . .

Fig. 43 . . . remove the throttle body from the intake manifold

Fig. 44 Remove and discard the gasket from the throttle body

Fig. 45 Thoroughly clean the throttle body mating surfaces

3. Disconnect the throttle position sensor and throttle linkage at the throttle lever.

4. Remove the 4 throttle body mounting bolts.

5. Carefully separate the throttle body from the intake manifold adapter.

6. Remove and discard the gasket between the throttle body adapter.

To install:

7. Clean all gasket mating surfaces, being careful not to damage them or allow material to drop into the manifold.

8. Install the throttle body, a new gasket and the 4 mounting bolts. Tighten the bolts to 6–8.5 ft. lbs. (8–11.5 Nm).

9. Connect the throttle position sensor and the throttle linkage.

10. Install the air cleaner outlet tube.

11. Connect the negative battery cable.

5.0L Engine

▶ **See Figure 46**

1. Disconnect the negative battery cable.

2. Remove the air cleaner outlet tube from the throttle body.

3. Detach the throttle position sensor and idle air control valve connectors.

4. Remove the PCV vent closure hose at the throttle body.

5. Remove the 4 throttle body mounting nuts.

6. Carefully separate the throttle body from the EGR spacer and intake manifold.

7. Remove and discard the gasket between the throttle body and EGR spacer.

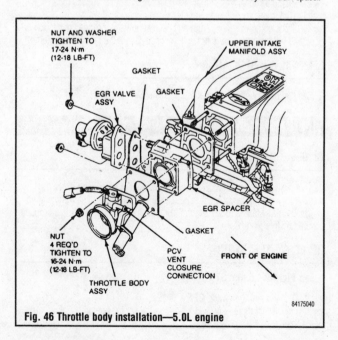

Fig. 46 Throttle body installation—5.0L engine

To install:

8. Clean all gasket mating surfaces, being careful not to damage them or allow material to drop into the manifold.

9. Install the throttle body with a new gasket on the 4 studs of the EGR spacer. Install the nuts and tighten to 12–18 ft. lbs. (16–24 Nm).

10. Connect the PCV vent closure hose.

11. Connect the throttle position sensor and idle air control valve connectors.

12. Install the air cleaner outlet tube.

13. Connect the negative battery cable.

Fuel Rail And Fuel Injector(s)

REMOVAL & INSTALLATION

4.6L Engine

▶ **See Figures 47 thru 52**

1. Disconnect the negative battery cable.

2. Remove the fuel tank cap and relieve the fuel system pressure, as explained in this Section.

3. Disconnect the vacuum line at the pressure regulator.

4. Disconnect the fuel lines from the fuel rail.

5. Detach the electrical connectors from the injectors.

6. Remove the fuel rail assembly retaining bolts.

7. Carefully disengage the fuel rail from the fuel injectors and remove the fuel rail.

➡ **It may be easier to remove the injectors with the fuel rail as an assembly.**

8. Grasping the injector body, pull while gently rocking the injector from side-to-side to remove the injector from the fuel rail or intake manifold.

9. Inspect the pintle protection cap and washer for signs of deterioration. Replace the complete injector, as required. If the cap is missing, look for it in the intake manifold.

➡ **The pintle protection cap is not available as a separate part.**

To install:

10. Lubricate new O-rings with light grade oil and install 2 on each injector.

➡ **Never use silicone grease as it will clog the injectors.**

11. Install the injectors using a light, twisting, pushing motion.

12. Install the fuel rail, pushing it down to ensure all injector O-rings are fully seated in the fuel rail cups and intake manifold.

13. Install the retaining bolts while holding the fuel rail down and tighten to 71–106 inch lbs. (8–12 Nm).

14. Connect the fuel lines to the fuel rail and the vacuum line to the pressure regulator.

15. With the injector wiring disconnected, connect the negative battery cable and turn the ignition switch to the **RUN** position to allow the fuel pump to pressurize the system.

16. Check for fuel leaks.

17. Disconnect the negative battery cable.

18. Connect the electrical connectors to the fuel injectors.

19. Connect the negative battery cable and start the engine. Let it idle for 2 minutes.

20. Turn the engine **OFF** and check for leaks.

5.0L Engine

▶ **See Figure 53**

1. Disconnect the negative battery cable.

2. Remove the fuel tank cap and relieve the fuel system pressure, as explained in this Section.

3. Partially drain the cooling system into a suitable container.

✳✳ CAUTION

When draining the coolant, keep in mind that cats and dogs are attracted by the ethylene glycol antifreeze, and are quite likely to drink any that is left in an uncovered container or in puddles on the ground. This will prove fatal in sufficient quantity. Always drain the coolant into a sealable container. Coolant should be reused unless it is contaminated or several years old.

Fig. 47 Detach the electrical connectors from the injectors

Fig. 48 Remove the fuel rail assembly retaining bolts. There are two on each side of the engine

Fig. 49 Lift the rail from the intake manifold and . . .

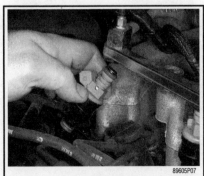

Fig. 50 . . . remove the injectors by gently pulling them out of the rail

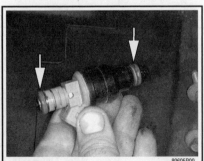

Fig. 51 Replace the injector O-rings before installing the injectors back into the engine

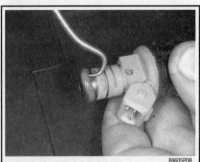

Fig. 52 Remove the O-rings from the injectors using a small pick or other suitable tool

4. Label and detach the electrical connectors at the idle air control valve, throttle position sensor and EGR sensor.

5. Disconnect the throttle linkage at the throttle ball and transmission linkage from the throttle body. Remove the 2 bolts securing the bracket to the intake manifold and position the bracket with the cables aside.

6. Label and disconnect the upper intake manifold vacuum fitting connections by disconnecting all vacuum lines to the vacuum tree, EGR valve, fuel pressure regulator and evaporative canister.

7. Disconnect the PCV hose from the fitting on the rear of the upper manifold and disconnect the PCV vent closure tube at the throttle body.

8. Remove the 2 EGR coolant lines from the fittings on the EGR spacer.

9. Remove the 6 upper intake manifold retaining bolts.

10. Remove the upper intake and throttle body as an assembly from the lower intake manifold.

11. Disconnect the fuel lines from the fuel rail.

12. Remove the 4 fuel rail assembly retaining bolts.

13. Detach the electrical connectors from the injectors.

14. Carefully disengage the fuel rail from the fuel injectors.

➡**It may be easier to remove the injectors with the fuel rail as an assembly.**

15. Grasping the injector body, pull up while gently rocking the injector from side-to-side to remove the injector from the fuel rail or intake manifold.

16. Inspect the pintle protection cap and washer for signs of deterioration. Replace the complete injector, as required. If the cap is missing, look for it in the intake manifold.

➡**The pintle protection cap is not available as a separate part.**

To install:
17. Lubricate new O-rings with light grade oil and install 2 on each injector.

➡**Never use silicone grease as it will clog the injectors.**

18. Install the injectors using a light, twisting, pushing motion.

19. Install the fuel rail, pushing it down to ensure all the injector O-rings are fully seated in the fuel rail cups and intake manifold.

20. Install the retaining bolts while holding the fuel rail down and tighten to 71–106 inch lbs. (8–12 Nm).

21. Connect the fuel lines to the fuel rail.

22. With the injector wiring disconnected, connect the negative battery cable and turn the ignition switch to the **RUN** position to allow the fuel pump to pressurize the system.

23. Check for fuel leaks.

24. Disconnect the negative battery cable.

25. Connect the electrical connectors to the injectors.

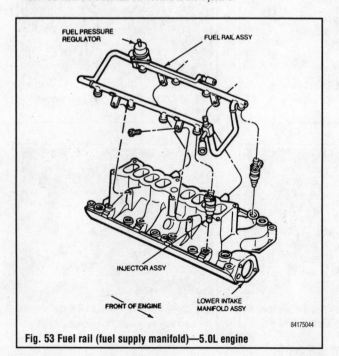

FUEL PRESSURE REGULATOR

FUEL RAIL ASSY

INJECTOR ASSY

FRONT OF ENGINE

LOWER INTAKE MANIFOLD ASSY

84175044

Fig. 53 Fuel rail (fuel supply manifold)—5.0L engine

26. Install the upper intake manifold and throttle body assembly by reversing the removal procedure. Use a new gasket and tighten the retaining bolts to 12–18 ft. lbs. (16–24 Nm).

27. Refill the cooling system and connect the negative battery cable.

28. Start the engine and let it idle for 2 minutes. Turn the engine **OFF** and check for leaks.

TESTING

The easiest way to test the operation of the fuel injectors is to listen for a clicking sound coming from the injectors while the engine is running. This is accomplished using a mechanic's stethoscope, or a long screwdriver. Place the end of the stethoscope or the screwdriver (tip end, not handle) onto the body of the injector. Place the ear pieces of the stethoscope in your ears, or if using a screwdriver, place your ear on top of the handle. An audible clicking noise should be heard; this is the solenoid operating. If the injector makes this noise, the injector driver circuit and computer are operating as designed. Continue testing all the injectors this way.

❊❊ CAUTION

Be extremely careful while working on an operating engine, make sure you have no dangling jewelry, extremely loose clothes, power tool cords or other items that might get caught in a moving part of the engine.

All Injectors Clicking

If all the injectors are clicking, but you have determined that the fuel system is the cause of your driveability problem, continue diagnostics. Make sure that you have checked fuel pump pressure as outlined earlier in this section. An easy way to determine a weak or unproductive cylinder is a cylinder drop test. This is accomplished by removing one spark plug wire at a time, and seeing which cylinder causes the least difference in the idle. The one that causes the least change is the weak cylinder.

If the injectors were all clicking and the ignition system is functioning properly, remove the injector of the suspect cylinder and bench test it. This is accomplished by checking for a spray pattern from the injector itself. Install a fuel supply line to the injector (or rail if the injector is left attached to the rail) and momentarily apply 12 volts DC and a ground to the injector itself; a visible fuel spray should appear. If no spray is achieved, replace the injector and check the running condition of the engine.

One or More Injectors Are Not Clicking

⬦ **See Figures 54, 55, 56 and 57**

If one or more injectors are found to be not operating, testing the injector driver circuit and computer can be accomplished using a "noid" light. First, with the engine not running and the ignition key in the **OFF** position, remove the connector from the injector you plan to test, then plug the "noid" light tool into the injector connector. Start the engine and the "noid" light should flash, signaling that the injector driver circuit is working. If the "noid" light flashes, but the injector does not click when plugged in, test the injector's resistance. resistance should be between 11–18 ohms.

If the "noid" light does not flash, the injector driver circuit is faulty. Disconnect the negative battery cable. Unplug the "noid" light from the injector connector and also unplug the PCM. Check the harness between the appropriate pins on the harness side of the PCM connector and the injector connector. Resistance should be less than 5.0 ohms; if not, repair the circuit. If resistance is within specifications, the injector driver inside the PCM is faulty and replacement of the PCM will be necessary.

Fuel Pressure Regulator

REMOVAL & INSTALLATION

⬦ **See Figures 58, 59, 60 and 61**

1. Disconnect the negative battery cable.

2. Remove the fuel tank cap and relieve the fuel system pressure, as explained in this section.

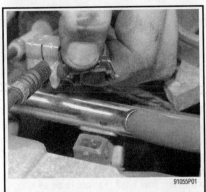

Fig. 54 Unplug the fuel injector connector

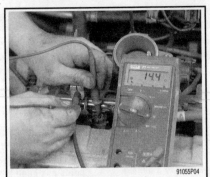

Fig. 55 Probe the two terminals of a fuel injector to check it's resistance

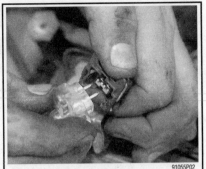

Fig. 56 Plug the correct "noid" light directly into the injector harness connector

Fig. 57 If the correct "noid" light flashes while the engine is running, the injector driver circuit inside the PCM is working

Fig. 58 Remove the vacuum hose from the pressure regulator

Fig. 59 Remove the pressure regulator retaining screws and . . .

Fig. 60 . . . lift the regulator off of the rail

Fig. 61 Replace the O-ring on the bottom of the fuel pressure regulator

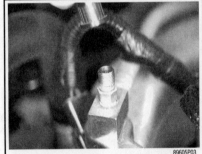

Fig. 62 The fuel pressure relief valve is located on the fuel rail, under the protective cap

3. Disconnect the vacuum line at the pressure regulator.

4. Remove and discard the 3 Allen head screws retaining the regulator housing.

5. Remove the pressure regulator, gasket and O-ring.

6. If scraping is necessary to remove old gasket material, be careful not to damage the pressure regulator or fuel supply manifold gasket surfaces.

To install:

7. Lubricate a new fuel pressure regulator O-ring with clean engine oil.

➡ **Never use silicone grease as it will clog the injectors.**

8. Make sure the pressure regulator and fuel supply manifold gasket mating surfaces are clean.

9. Install the new O-ring and new gasket on the pressure regulator.

10. Install the fuel pressure regulator on the fuel supply manifold. Install new Allen screws and tighten to 27–40 inch lbs. (3–4.5 Nm).

11. Connect the vacuum line to the pressure regulator.

12. Connect the negative battery cable and turn the ignition switch to the **RUN** position to allow the fuel pump to pressurize the system.

13. Check for fuel leaks.

14. Start the engine and let it idle for 2 minutes. Turn the engine **OFF** and check for leaks.

Pressure Relief Valve

REMOVAL & INSTALLATION

♦ See Figure 62

1. Disconnect the negative battery cable.

2. Properly relieve the fuel system pressure.

3. Remove the air cleaner outlet tube(s).

4. Remove any necessary components to access the pressure relief valve.

5. Remove the cap from the pressure relief valve.

6. Remove the pressure relief valve from the fuel rail using the proper size socket and drive tool.

To install:

7. The installation is the reverse of the removal.

FUEL TANK

Tank Assembly

REMOVAL & INSTALLATION

1. Disconnect the negative battery cable and relieve the fuel system pressure.
2. Siphon or pump as much fuel as possible out through the fuel filler pipe.

➡ Fuel injected vehicles have reservoirs inside the fuel tank to maintain fuel near the fuel pickup during cornering and under low fuel operating conditions. These reservoirs could block siphon tubes or hoses from reaching the bottom of the fuel tank. Repeated attempts using different hose orientations can overcome this obstacle.

3. Raise and safely support the vehicle.
4. If equipped with a metal retainer that fastens the filler pipe to the fuel tank, remove the screw attaching the retainer to the fuel tank flange.
5. Detach the fuel lines and the electrical connector to the fuel tank sending unit. On some vehicles, these are inaccessible on top of the tank. In these cases they must be disconnected with the tank partially removed.
6. Place a safety support under the fuel tank and remove the bolts or nuts from the fuel tank straps. Allow the straps to swing out of the way.
7. Partially remove the tank and detach the fuel lines and electrical connector from the sending unit, if not detached previously.
8. Remove the tank from the vehicle.

To install:

9. Raise the fuel tank into position in the vehicle. Connect the fuel lines and sending unit electrical connector if it is necessary to connect them before the tank is in the final installed position.
10. Lubricate the fuel filler pipe with water base tire mounting lubricant and install the tank onto the filler pipe, then bring the tank into final position. Be careful not to deform the tank.
11. Bring the fuel tank straps around the tank and start the retaining nut or bolt. Align the tank with the straps. If equipped, make sure the fuel tank shields are installed with the straps and are positioned correctly on the tank.
12. Check the hoses and wiring mounted on the tank top to make sure they are correctly routed and will not be pinched between the tank and body.
13. Tighten the fuel tank strap retaining nuts or bolts to 20-30 ft. lbs. (28-40 Nm).
14. If not already connected, connect the fuel hoses and lines which were detached. Make sure the fuel supply, fuel return, if present, and vapor vent connections are made correctly. If not already connected, connect the sending unit electrical connector.
15. Lower the vehicle.
16. Replace the fuel that was drained from the tank.
17. Check all connections for leaks.

Electric Fuel Pump

REMOVAL & INSTALLATION

▶ **See Figures 63, 64 and 65**

✳✳ CAUTION

Fuel injection systems remain under pressure, even after the engine has been turned OFF. The fuel system pressure must be relieved before disconnecting any fuel lines. Failure to do so may result in fire and/or personal injury.

1. If equipped with air suspension, the air suspension switch, located on the right-hand side of the luggage compartment, must be turned to the **OFF** position before raising the vehicle.
2. Disconnect the negative battery cable.
3. Relieve fuel system pressure using the recommended procedure.
4. Raise and safely support the vehicle.
5. Remove the fuel tank from the vehicle and place on a suitable work bench.
6. Remove any dirt that has accumulated around the fuel pump retaining flange so it will not enter the tank during pump removal and installation.
7. On 1989-94 models, turn the fuel pump locking ring counterclockwise and remove the locking ring.
8. On 1995-98 models, remove 6 retaining bolts around the perimeter of the fuel pump module.
9. Remove the fuel pump/sending unit assembly. Remove and discard the seal ring.

To install:

10. Clean the fuel pump mounting flange, fuel tank mounting surface and seal ring groove.
11. Apply a light coating of grease on a new seal ring to hold it in place during assembly and install in the seal ring groove.
12. Install the fuel pump/sending unit assembly carefully to ensure the filter is not damaged. Make sure the locating keys are in the keyways and the seal ring remains in the groove.
13. Hold the pump assembly in place and install the locking ring finger-tight. Make sure all the locking tabs are under the tank lock ring tabs.
14. Rotate the locking ring clockwise until the ring is against the stops.
15. Install the fuel tank into the vehicle.
16. Lower the vehicle.
17. If equipped with air suspension, turn the air suspension switch to the **ON** position.
18. Add a minimum of 10 gallons of fuel to the tank and check for leaks.
19. Reconnect the negative battery cable.
20. Turn the ignition switch to the **RUN** position several times to pressurize the fuel system. Check for fuel leaks and correct as necessary.
21. Start the engine and check for leaks.
22. Road test the vehicle and check for proper operation.

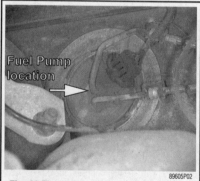

Fig. 63 The fuel pump is located in the fuel tank. On some models it can be viewed from the side as shown here

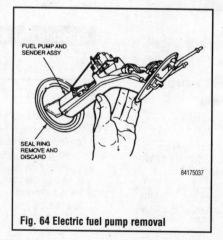

Fig. 64 Electric fuel pump removal

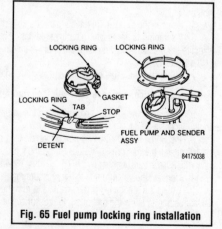

Fig. 65 Fuel pump locking ring installation

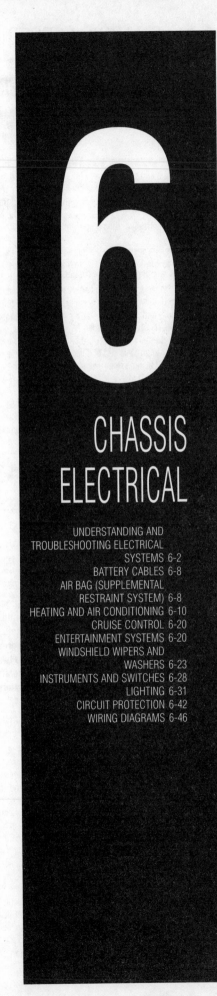

6

CHASSIS ELECTRICAL

UNDERSTANDING AND TROUBLESHOOTING ELECTRICAL SYSTEMS

Basic Electrical Theory

♦ **See Figure 1**

For any 12 volt, negative ground, electrical system to operate, the electricity must travel in a complete circuit. This simply means that current (power) from the positive (+) terminal of the battery must eventually return to the negative (-) terminal of the battery. Along the way, this current will travel through wires, fuses, switches and components. If, for any reason, the flow of current through the circuit is interrupted, the component fed by that circuit will cease to function properly.

Perhaps the easiest way to visualize a circuit is to think of connecting a light bulb (with two wires attached to it) to the battery—one wire attached to the negative (-) terminal of the battery and the other wire to the positive (+) terminal. With the two wires touching the battery terminals, the circuit would be complete and the light bulb would illuminate. Electricity would follow a path from the battery to the bulb and back to the battery. It's easy to see that with longer wires on our light bulb, it could be mounted anywhere. Further, one wire could be fitted with a switch so that the light could be turned on and off.

The normal automotive circuit differs from this simple example in two ways. First, instead of having a return wire from the bulb to the battery, the current travels through the frame of the vehicle. Since the negative (-) battery cable is attached to the frame (made of electrically conductive metal), the frame of the vehicle can serve as a ground wire to complete the circuit. Secondly, most automotive circuits contain multiple components which receive power from a single circuit. This lessens the amount of wire needed to power components on the vehicle.

Fig. 1 This example illustrates a simple circuit. When the switch is closed, power from the positive (+) battery terminal flows through the fuse and the switch, and then to the light bulb. The light illuminates and the circuit is completed through the ground wire back to the negative (-) battery terminal. In reality, the two ground points shown in the illustration are attached to the metal frame of the vehicle, which completes the circuit back to the battery

HOW DOES ELECTRICITY WORK: THE WATER ANALOGY

Electricity is the flow of electrons—the subatomic particles that constitute the outer shell of an atom. Electrons spin in an orbit around the center core of an atom. The center core is comprised of protons (positive charge) and neutrons (neutral charge). Electrons have a negative charge and balance out the positive charge of the protons. When an outside force causes the number of electrons to unbalance the charge of the protons, the electrons will split off the atom and look for another atom to balance out. If this imbalance is kept up, electrons will continue to move and an electrical flow will exist.

Many people have been taught electrical theory using an analogy with water. In a comparison with water flowing through a pipe, the electrons would be the water and the wire is the pipe.

The flow of electricity can be measured much like the flow of water through a pipe. The unit of measurement used is amperes, frequently abbreviated as amps (a). You can compare amperage to the volume of water flowing through a pipe. When connected to a circuit, an ammeter will measure the actual amount of current flowing through the circuit. When relatively few electrons flow through a circuit, the amperage is low. When many electrons flow, the amperage is high.

Water pressure is measured in units such as pounds per square inch (psi);

The electrical pressure is measured in units called volts (v). When a voltmeter is connected to a circuit, it is measuring the electrical pressure.

The actual flow of electricity depends not only on voltage and amperage, but also on the resistance of the circuit. The higher the resistance, the higher the force necessary to push the current through the circuit. The standard unit for measuring resistance is an ohm. Resistance in a circuit varies depending on the amount and type of components used in the circuit. The main factors which determine resistance are:

• Material—some materials have more resistance than others. Those with high resistance are said to be insulators. Rubber materials (or rubber-like plastics) are some of the most common insulators used in vehicles as they have a very high resistance to electricity. Very low resistance materials are said to be conductors. Copper wire is among the best conductors. Silver is actually a superior conductor to copper and is used in some relay contacts, but its high cost prohibits its use as common wiring. Most automotive wiring is made of copper.

• Size—the larger the wire size being used, the less resistance the wire will have. This is why components which use large amounts of electricity usually have large wires supplying current to them.

• Length—for a given thickness of wire, the longer the wire, the greater the resistance. The shorter the wire, the less the resistance. When determining the proper wire for a circuit, both size and length must be considered to design a circuit that can handle the current needs of the component.

• Temperature—with many materials, the higher the temperature, the greater the resistance (positive temperature coefficient). Some materials exhibit the opposite trait of lower resistance with higher temperatures (negative temperature coefficient). These principles are used in many of the sensors on the engine.

OHM'S LAW

There is a direct relationship between current, voltage and resistance. The relationship between current, voltage and resistance can be summed up by a statement known as Ohm's law.

Voltage (E) is equal to amperage (I) times resistance ®: $E = I \times R$

Other forms of the formula are $R = E/I$ and $I = E/R$

In each of these formulas, E is the voltage in volts, I is the current in amps and R is the resistance in ohms. The basic point to remember is that as the resistance of a circuit goes up, the amount of current that flows in the circuit will go down, if voltage remains the same.

The amount of work that the electricity can perform is expressed as power. The unit of power is the watt (w). The relationship between power, voltage and current is expressed as:

Power (w) is equal to amperage (I) times voltage (E): $W = I \times E$

This is only true for direct current (DC) circuits; The alternating current formula is a tad different, but since the electrical circuits in most vehicles are DC type, we need not get into AC circuit theory.

Electrical Components

POWER SOURCE

Power is supplied to the vehicle by two devices: The battery and the alternator. The battery supplies electrical power during starting or during periods when the current demand of the vehicle's electrical system exceeds the output capacity of the alternator. The alternator supplies electrical current when the engine is running. Just not does the alternator supply the current needs of the vehicle, but it recharges the battery.

The Battery

In most modern vehicles, the battery is a lead/acid electrochemical device consisting of six 2 volt subsections (cells) connected in series, so that the unit is capable of producing approximately 12 volts of electrical pressure. Each subsection consists of a series of positive and negative plates held a short distance apart in a solution of sulfuric acid and water.

The two types of plates are of dissimilar metals. This sets up a chemical reaction, and it is this reaction which produces current flow from the battery when its positive and negative terminals are connected to an electrical load. The power removed from the battery is replaced by the alternator, restoring the battery to its original chemical state.

The Alternator

On some vehicles there isn't an alternator, but a generator. The difference is that an alternator supplies alternating current which is then changed to direct current for use on the vehicle, while a generator produces direct current. Alternators tend to be more efficient and that is why they are used.

Alternators and generators are devices that consist of coils of wires wound together making big electromagnets. One group of coils spins within another set and the interaction of the magnetic fields causes a current to flow. This current is then drawn off the coils and fed into the vehicles electrical system.

GROUND

Two types of grounds are used in automotive electric circuits. Direct ground components are grounded to the frame through their mounting points. All other components use some sort of ground wire which is attached to the frame or chassis of the vehicle. The electrical current runs through the chassis of the vehicle and returns to the battery through the ground (-) cable; if you look, you'll see that the battery ground cable connects between the battery and the frame or chassis of the vehicle.

➡**It should be noted that a good percentage of electrical problems can be traced to bad grounds.**

PROTECTIVE DEVICES

◗ See Figure 2

It is possible for large surges of current to pass through the electrical system of your vehicle. If this surge of current were to reach the load in the circuit, the surge could burn it out or severely damage it. It can also overload the wiring, causing the harness to get hot and melt the insulation. To prevent this, fuses, circuit breakers and/or fusible links are connected into the supply wires of the electrical system. These items are nothing more than a built-in weak spot in the system. When an abnormal amount of current flows through the system, these protective devices work as follows to protect the circuit:

• Fuse—when an excessive electrical current passes through a fuse, the

fuse "blows" (the conductor melts) and opens the circuit, preventing the passage of current.

• Circuit Breaker—a circuit breaker is basically a self-repairing fuse. It will open the circuit in the same fashion as a fuse, but when the surge subsides, the circuit breaker can be reset and does not need replacement.

• Fusible Link—a fusible link (fuse link or main link) is a short length of special, high temperature insulated wire that acts as a fuse. When an excessive electrical current passes through a fusible link, the thin gauge wire inside the link melts, creating an intentional open to protect the circuit. To repair the circuit, the link must be replaced. Some newer type fusible links are housed in plug-in modules, which are simply replaced like a fuse, while older type fusible links must be cut and spliced if they melt. Since this link is very early in the electrical path, it's the first place to look if nothing on the vehicle works, yet the battery seems to be charged and is properly connected.

✳✳ CAUTION

Always replace fuses, circuit breakers and fusible links with identically rated components. Under no circumstances should a component of higher or lower amperage rating be substituted.

SWITCHES & RELAYS

◗ See Figures 3 and 4

Switches are used in electrical circuits to control the passage of current. The most common use is to open and close circuits between the battery and the various electric devices in the system. Switches are rated according to the amount of amperage they can handle. If a sufficient amperage rated switch is not used in a circuit, the switch could overload and cause damage.

Some electrical components which require a large amount of current to operate use a special switch called a relay. Since these circuits carry a large amount of current, the thickness of the wire in the circuit is also greater. If this large wire were connected from the load to the control switch, the switch would have to carry the high amperage load and the fairing or dash would be twice as large to accommodate the increased size of the wiring harness. To prevent these problems, a relay is used.

Relays are composed of a coil and a set of contacts. When the coil has a current passed though it, a magnetic field is formed and this field causes the contacts to move together, completing the circuit. Most relays are normally open, preventing current from passing through the circuit, but they can take any electrical form depending on the job they are intended to do. Relays can be considered "remote control switches." They allow a smaller current to operate devices that require higher amperages. When a small current operates the coil, a larger current is allowed to pass by the contacts. Some common circuits which may use relays are the horn, headlights, starter, electric fuel pump and other high draw circuits.

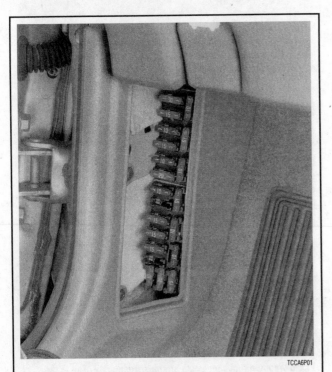

TCCA6P01

Fig. 2 Most vehicles use one or more fuse panels. This one is located on the driver's side kick panel

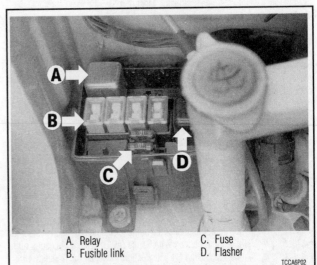

A. Relay   C. Fuse
B. Fusible link   D. Flasher

TCCA6P02

Fig. 3 The underhood fuse and relay panel usually contains fuses, relays, flashers and fusible links

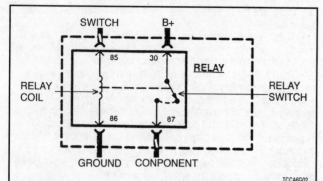

TCCA6G02

Fig. 4 Relays are composed of a coil and a switch. These two components are linked together so that when one operates, the other operates at the same time. The large wires in the circuit are connected from the battery to one side of the relay switch (B+) and from the opposite side of the relay switch to the load (component). Smaller wires are connected from the relay coil to the control switch for the circuit and from the opposite side of the relay coil to ground

LOAD

Every electrical circuit must include a "load" (something to use the electricity coming from the source). Without this load, the battery would attempt to deliver its entire power supply from one pole to another. This is called a "short circuit." All this electricity would take a short cut to ground and cause a great amount of damage to other components in the circuit by developing a tremendous amount of heat. This condition could develop sufficient heat to melt the insulation on all the surrounding wires and reduce a multiple wire cable to a lump of plastic and copper.

WIRING & HARNESSES

The average vehicle contains meters and meters of wiring, with hundreds of individual connections. To protect the many wires from damage and to keep them from becoming a confusing tangle, they are organized into bundles, enclosed in plastic or taped together and called wiring harnesses. Different harnesses serve different parts of the vehicle. Individual wires are color coded to help trace them through a harness where sections are hidden from view.

Automotive wiring or circuit conductors can be either single strand wire, multi-strand wire or printed circuitry. Single strand wire has a solid metal core and is usually used inside such components as alternators, motors, relays and other devices. Multi-strand wire has a core made of many small strands of wire twisted together into a single conductor. Most of the wiring in an automotive electrical system is made up of multi-strand wire, either as a single conductor or grouped together in a harness. All wiring is color coded on the insulator, either as a solid color or as a colored wire with an identification stripe. A printed circuit is a thin film of copper or other conductor that is printed on an insulator backing. Occasionally, a printed circuit is sandwiched between two sheets of plastic for more protection and flexibility. A complete printed circuit, consisting of conductors, insulating material and connectors for lamps or other components is called a printed circuit board. Printed circuitry is used in place of individual wires or harnesses in places where space is limited, such as behind instrument panels.

Since automotive electrical systems are very sensitive to changes in resistance, the selection of properly sized wires is critical when systems are repaired. A loose or corroded connection or a replacement wire that is too small for the circuit will add extra resistance and an additional voltage drop to the circuit.

The wire gauge number is an expression of the cross-section area of the conductor. Vehicles from countries that use the metric system will typically describe the wire size as its cross-sectional area in square millimeters. In this method, the larger the wire, the greater the number. Another common system for expressing wire size is the American Wire Gauge (AWG) system. As gauge number increases, area decreases and the wire becomes smaller. An 18 gauge wire is smaller than a 4 gauge wire. A wire with a higher gauge number will carry less current than a wire with a lower gauge number. Gauge wire size refers to the size of the strands of the conductor, not the size of the complete wire with

insulator. It is possible, therefore, to have two wires of the same gauge with different diameters because one may have thicker insulation than the other.

It is essential to understand how a circuit works before trying to figure out why it doesn't. An electrical schematic shows the electrical current paths when a circuit is operating properly. Schematics break the entire electrical system down into individual circuits. In a schematic, usually no attempt is made to represent wiring and components as they physically appear on the vehicle; switches and other components are shown as simply as possible. Face views of harness connectors show the cavity or terminal locations in all multi-pin connectors to help locate test points.

CONNECTORS

♦ See Figures 5 and 6

Three types of connectors are commonly used in automotive applications—weatherproof, molded and hard shell.

• Weatherproof—these connectors are most commonly used where the connector is exposed to the elements. Terminals are protected against moisture and dirt by sealing rings which provide a weathertight seal. All repairs require the use of a special terminal and the tool required to service it. Unlike standard blade type terminals, these weatherproof terminals cannot be straightened once they are bent. Make certain that the connectors are properly seated and all of the sealing rings are in place when connecting leads.

• Molded—these connectors require complete replacement of the connector if found to be defective. This means splicing a new connector assembly into

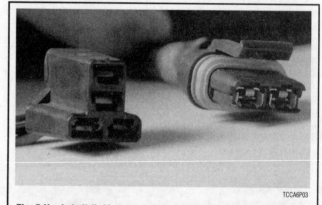

TCCA6P03

Fig. 5 Hard shell (left) and weatherproof (right) connectors have replaceable terminals

TCCA6P04

Fig. 6 Weatherproof connectors are most commonly used in the engine compartment, or where the connector is exposed to the elements

the harness. All splices should be soldered to insure proper contact. Use care when probing the connections or replacing terminals in them, as it is possible to create a short circuit between opposite terminals. If this happens to the wrong terminal pair, it is possible to damage certain components. Always use jumper wires between connectors for circuit checking and NEVER probe through weatherproof seals.

• Hard Shell—unlike molded connectors, the terminal contacts in hardshell connectors can be replaced. Replacement usually involves the use of a special terminal removal tool that depresses the locking tangs (barbs) on the connector terminal and allows the connector to be removed from the rear of the shell. The connector shell should be replaced if it shows any evidence of burning, melting, cracks, or breaks. Replace individual terminals that are burnt, corroded, distorted or loose.

Test Equipment

Pinpointing the exact cause of trouble in an electrical circuit is most times accomplished by the use of special test equipment. The following describes different types of commonly used test equipment and briefly explains how to use them in diagnosis. In addition to the information covered below, the tool manufacturer's instructions booklet (provided with the tester) should be read and clearly understood before attempting any test procedures.

JUMPER WIRES

✳✳ CAUTION

Never use jumper wires made from a thinner gauge wire than the circuit being tested. If the jumper wire is of too small a gauge, it may overheat and possibly melt. Never use jumpers to bypass high resistance loads in a circuit. Bypassing resistances, in effect, creates a short circuit. This may, in turn, cause damage and fire. Jumper wires should only be used to bypass lengths of wire or to simulate switches.

Jumper wires are simple, yet extremely valuable, pieces of test equipment. They are basically test wires which are used to bypass sections of a circuit. Although jumper wires can be purchased, they are usually fabricated from lengths of standard automotive wire and whatever type of connector (alligator clip, spade connector or pin connector) that is required for the particular application being tested. In cramped, hard-to-reach areas, it is advisable to have insulated boots over the jumper wire terminals in order to prevent accidental grounding. It is also advisable to include a standard automotive fuse in any jumper wire. This is commonly referred to as a "fused jumper". By inserting an in-line fuse holder between a set of test leads, a fused jumper wire can be used for bypassing open circuits. Use a 5 amp fuse to provide protection against voltage spikes.

Jumper wires are used primarily to locate open electrical circuits, on either the ground (-) side of the circuit or on the power (+) side. If an electrical component fails to operate, connect the jumper wire between the component and a good ground. If the component operates only with the jumper installed, the ground circuit is open. If the ground circuit is good, but the component does not operate, the circuit between the power feed and component may be open. By moving the jumper wire successively back from the component toward the power source, you can isolate the area of the circuit where the open is located. When the component stops functioning, or the power is cut off, the open is in the segment of wire between the jumper and the point previously tested.

You can sometimes connect the jumper wire directly from the battery to the "hot" terminal of the component, but first make sure the component uses 12 volts in operation. Some electrical components, such as fuel injectors or sensors, are designed to operate on about 4 to 5 volts, and running 12 volts directly to these components will cause damage.

TEST LIGHTS

♦ See Figure 7

The test light is used to check circuits and components while electrical current is flowing through them. It is used for voltage and ground tests. To use a 12 volt test light, connect the ground clip to a good ground and probe wherever necessary with the pick. The test light will illuminate when voltage is detected. This does not necessarily mean that 12 volts (or any particular amount of volt-

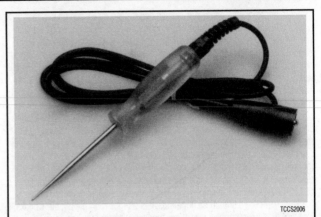

Fig. 7 A 12 volt test light is used to detect the presence of voltage in a circuit

age) is present; it only means that some voltage is present. It is advisable before using the test light to touch its ground clip and probe across the battery posts or terminals to make sure the light is operating properly.

✳✳ WARNING

Do not use a test light to probe electronic ignition, spark plug or coil wires. Never use a pick-type test light to probe wiring on computer controlled systems unless specifically instructed to do so. Any wire insulation that is pierced by the test light probe should be taped and sealed with silicone after testing.

Like the jumper wire, the 12 volt test light is used to isolate opens in circuits. But, whereas the jumper wire is used to bypass the open to operate the load, the 12 volt test light is used to locate the presence of voltage in a circuit. If the test light illuminates, there is power up to that point in the circuit; if the test light does not illuminate, there is an open circuit (no power). Move the test light in successive steps back toward the power source until the light in the handle illuminates. The open is between the probe and a point which was previously probed.

The self-powered test light is similar in design to the 12 volt test light, but contains a 1.5 volt penlight battery in the handle. It is most often used in place of a multimeter to check for open or short circuits when power is isolated from the circuit (continuity).

The battery in a self-powered test light does not provide much current. A weak battery may not provide enough power to illuminate the test light even when a complete circuit is made (especially if there is high resistance in the circuit). Always make sure that the test battery is strong. To check the battery, briefly touch the ground clip to the probe; if the light glows brightly, the battery is strong enough for testing.

➡**A self-powered test light should not be used on any computer controlled system or component. The small amount of electricity transmitted by the test light is enough to damage many electronic automotive components.**

MULTIMETERS

Multimeters are an extremely useful tool for troubleshooting electrical problems. They can be purchased in either analog or digital form and have a price range to suit any budget. A multimeter is a voltmeter, ammeter and ohmmeter (along with other features) combined into one instrument. It is often used when testing solid state circuits because of its high input impedance (usually 10 megaohms or more). A brief description of the multimeter main test functions follows:

• Voltmeter—the voltmeter is used to measure voltage at any point in a circuit, or to measure the voltage drop across any part of a circuit. Voltmeters usually have various scales and a selector switch to allow the reading of different voltage ranges. The voltmeter has a positive and a negative lead. To avoid damage to the meter, always connect the negative lead to the negative (-) side of the circuit (to ground or nearest the ground side of the circuit) and connect the positive lead to the positive (+) side of the circuit (to the power source or the nearest power source). Note that the negative voltmeter lead will always be black and that the positive voltmeter will always be some color other than black (usually red).

• Ohmmeter—the ohmmeter is designed to read resistance (measured in ohms) in a circuit or component. Most ohmmeters will have a selector switch which permits the measurement of different ranges of resistance (usually the selector switch allows the multiplication of the meter reading by 10, 100, 1,000 and 10,000). Some ohmmeters are "auto-ranging" which means the meter itself will determine which scale to use. Since the meters are powered by an internal battery, the ohmmeter can be used like a self-powered test light. When the ohmmeter is connected, current from the ohmmeter flows through the circuit or component being tested. Since the ohmmeter's internal resistance and voltage are known values, the amount of current flow through the meter depends on the resistance of the circuit or component being tested. The ohmmeter can also be used to perform a continuity test for suspected open circuits. In using the meter for making continuity checks, do not be concerned with the actual resistance readings. Zero resistance, or any ohm reading, indicates continuity in the circuit. Infinite resistance indicates an opening in the circuit. A high resistance reading where there should be none indicates a problem in the circuit. Checks for short circuits are made in the same manner as checks for open circuits, except that the circuit must be isolated from both power and normal ground. Infinite resistance indicates no continuity, while zero resistance indicates a dead short.

✷✷ WARNING

Never use an ohmmeter to check the resistance of a component or wire while there is voltage applied to the circuit.

• Ammeter—an ammeter measures the amount of current flowing through a circuit in units called amperes or amps. At normal operating voltage, most circuits have a characteristic amount of amperes, called "current draw" which can be measured using an ammeter. By referring to a specified current draw rating, then measuring the amperes and comparing the two values, one can determine what is happening within the circuit to aid in diagnosis. An open circuit, for example, will not allow any current to flow, so the ammeter reading will be zero. A damaged component or circuit will have an increased current draw, so the reading will be high. The ammeter is always connected in series with the circuit being tested. All of the current that normally flows through the circuit must also flow through the ammeter; if there is any other path for the current to follow, the ammeter reading will not be accurate. The ammeter itself has very little resistance to current flow and, therefore, will not affect the circuit, but it will measure current draw only when the circuit is closed and electricity is flowing. Excessive current draw can blow fuses and drain the battery, while a reduced current draw can cause motors to run slowly, lights to dim and other components to not operate properly.

Troubleshooting Electrical Systems

When diagnosing a specific problem, organized troubleshooting is a must. The complexity of a modern automotive vehicle demands that you approach any problem in a logical, organized manner. There are certain troubleshooting techniques, however, which are standard:

• Establish when the problem occurs. Does the problem appear only under certain conditions? Were there any noises, odors or other unusual symptoms? Isolate the problem area. To do this, make some simple tests and observations, then eliminate the systems that are working properly. Check for obvious problems, such as broken wires and loose or dirty connections. Always check the obvious before assuming something complicated is the cause.

• Test for problems systematically to determine the cause once the problem area is isolated. Are all the components functioning properly? Is there power going to electrical switches and motors. Performing careful, systematic checks will often turn up most causes on the first inspection, without wasting time checking components that have little or no relationship to the problem.

• Test all repairs after the work is done to make sure that the problem is fixed. Some causes can be traced to more than one component, so a careful verification of repair work is important in order to pick up additional malfunctions that may cause a problem to reappear or a different problem to arise. A blown fuse, for example, is a simple problem that may require more than another fuse to repair. If you don't look for a problem that caused a fuse to blow, a shorted wire (for example) may go undetected.

Experience has shown that most problems tend to be the result of a fairly simple and obvious cause, such as loose or corroded connectors, bad grounds or damaged wire insulation which causes a short. This makes careful visual inspection of components during testing essential to quick and accurate troubleshooting.

Testing

OPEN CIRCUITS

♦ See Figure 8

This test already assumes the existence of an open in the circuit and it is used to help locate the open portion.

1. Isolate the circuit from power and ground.
2. Connect the self-powered test light or ohmmeter ground clip to the ground side of the circuit and probe sections of the circuit sequentially.
3. If the light is out or there is infinite resistance, the open is between the probe and the circuit ground.
4. If the light is on or the meter shows continuity, the open is between the probe and the end of the circuit toward the power source.

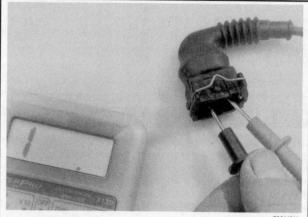

TCCA6P10

Fig. 8 The infinite reading on this multimeter indicates that the circuit is open

SHORT CIRCUITS

➥**Never use a self-powered test light to perform checks for opens or shorts when power is applied to the circuit under test. The test light can be damaged by outside power.**

1. Isolate the circuit from power and ground.
2. Connect the self-powered test light or ohmmeter ground clip to a good ground and probe any easy-to-reach point in the circuit.
3. If the light comes on or there is continuity, there is a short somewhere in the circuit.
4. To isolate the short, probe a test point at either end of the isolated circuit (the light should be on or the meter should indicate continuity).
5. Leave the test light probe engaged and sequentially open connectors or switches, remove parts, etc. until the light goes out or continuity is broken.
6. When the light goes out, the short is between the last two circuit components which were opened.

VOLTAGE

This test determines voltage available from the battery and should be the first step in any electrical troubleshooting procedure after visual inspection. Many electrical problems, especially on computer controlled systems, can be caused by a low state of charge in the battery. Excessive corrosion at the battery cable terminals can cause poor contact that will prevent proper charging and full battery current flow.

1. Set the voltmeter selector switch to the 20V position.
2. Connect the multimeter negative lead to the battery's negative (-) post or terminal and the positive lead to the battery's positive (+) post or terminal.
3. Turn the ignition switch **ON** to provide a load.
4. A well charged battery should register over 12 volts. If the meter reads below 11.5 volts, the battery power may be insufficient to operate the electrical system properly.

VOLTAGE DROP

▶ **See Figure 9**

When current flows through a load, the voltage beyond the load drops. This voltage drop is due to the resistance created by the load and also by small resistances created by corrosion at the connectors and damaged insulation on the wires. The maximum allowable voltage drop under load is critical, especially if there is more than one load in the circuit, since all voltage drops are cumulative.

1. Set the voltmeter selector switch to the 20 volt position.
2. Connect the multimeter negative lead to a good ground.
3. Operate the circuit and check the voltage prior to the first component (load).
4. There should be little or no voltage drop in the circuit prior to the first component. If a voltage drop exists, the wire or connectors in the circuit are suspect.
5. While operating the first component in the circuit, probe the ground side of the component with the positive meter lead and observe the voltage readings. A small voltage drop should be noticed. This voltage drop is caused by the resistance of the component.
6. Repeat the test for each component (load) down the circuit.
7. If a large voltage drop is noticed, the preceding component, wire or connector is suspect.

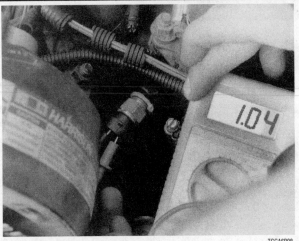

Fig. 10 Checking the resistance of a coolant temperature sensor with an ohmmeter. Reading is 1.04 kilohms

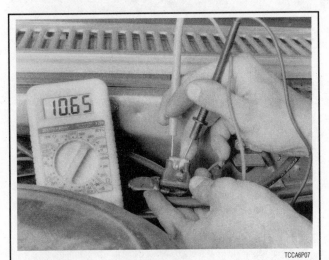

Fig. 9 This voltage drop test revealed high resistance (low voltage) in the circuit

RESISTANCE

▶ **See Figures 10 and 11**

❊❊ WARNING

Never use an ohmmeter with power applied to the circuit. The ohmmeter is designed to operate on its own power supply. The normal 12 volt electrical system voltage could damage the meter!

1. Isolate the circuit from the vehicle's power source.
2. Ensure that the ignition key is **OFF** when disconnecting any components or the battery.
3. Where necessary, also isolate at least one side of the circuit to be checked, in order to avoid reading parallel resistances. Parallel circuit resistances will always give a lower reading than the actual resistance of either of the branches.
4. Connect the meter leads to both sides of the circuit (wire or component) and read the actual measured ohms on the meter scale. Make sure the selector switch is set to the proper ohm scale for the circuit being tested, to avoid misreading the ohmmeter test value.

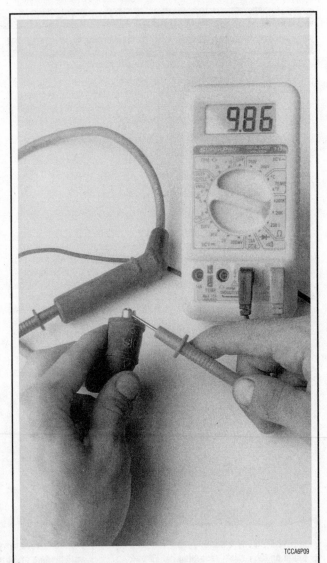

Fig. 11 Spark plug wires can be checked for excessive resistance using an ohmmeter

Wire and Connector Repair

Almost anyone can replace damaged wires, as long as the proper tools and parts are available. Wire and terminals are available to fit almost any need. Even the specialized weatherproof, molded and hard shell connectors are now available from aftermarket suppliers.

Be sure the ends of all the wires are fitted with the proper terminal hardware and connectors. Wrapping a wire around a stud is never a permanent solution and will only cause trouble later. Replace wires one at a time to avoid confusion. Always route wires exactly the same as the factory.

➡If connector repair is necessary, only attempt it if you have the proper tools. Weatherproof and hard shell connectors require special tools to release the pins inside the connector. Attempting to repair these connectors with conventional hand tools will damage them.

BATTERY CABLES

Disconnecting the Cables

When working on any electrical component on the vehicle, it is always a good idea to disconnect the negative (-) battery cable. This will prevent potential damage to many sensitive electrical components such as the Powertrain Control Module (PCM), radio, alternator, etc.

➡Any time you disengage the battery cables, it is recommended that you disconnect the negative (-) battery cable first. This will prevent your accidentally grounding the positive (+) terminal to the body of the vehicle when disconnecting it, thereby preventing damage to the above mentioned components.

Before you disconnect the cable(s), first turn the ignition to the OFF position. This will prevent a draw on the battery which could cause arcing (electricity trying to ground itself to the body of a vehicle, just like a spark plug jumping the gap) and, of course, damaging some components such as the alternator diodes.

When the battery cable(s) are reconnected (negative cable last), be sure to check that your lights, windshield wipers and other electrically operated safety components are all working correctly. If your vehicle contains an Electronically Tuned Radio (ETR), don't forget to also reset your radio stations. Ditto for the clock.

AIR BAG (SUPPLEMENTAL RESTRAINT SYSTEM)

General Information

The Air Bag system or Supplemental Restraint System (SRS) is designed to provide additional protection for front seat occupants when used in conjunction with a seat belt. The system is an electronically controlled, mechanically operated system. The system contains two basic subsytems: the air bag module(s) (the actual air bag(s) themselves), and the electrical system. The system consists of:

- The crash sensors
- The safing sensor
- The air bag module(s)
- The diagnostic monitor
- The back-up power supply (1990–91 models only)
- The instrument cluster indicator
- The sliding contacts (clock spring assembly)

The system is operates as follows: The system remains out of sight until activated in an accident that is determined to be the equivalent of hitting a parked car of the same size and weight at 28 mph (40 km/h) with the vehicle receiving severe front end damage. This determination is made by crash and safing sensors mounted on the vehicle which when an sufficient impact occurs, close their contacts completing the electrical circuit and inflating the air bags. When not activated the system is monitored by the air bag diagnostic monitor and system readiness is indicated by the lamp located on the instrument cluster. Any fault detected by the diagnostic monitor will illuminate the lamp and store a Diagnostic Trouble Code (DTC).

SERVICE PRECAUTIONS

▶ See Figures 12, 13 and 14

Whenever working around, or on, the air bag supplemental restraint system, ALWAYS adhere to the following warnings and cautions.

- Always wear safety glasses when servicing an air bag vehicle and when handling an air bag module.
- Carry a live air bag module with the bag and trim cover facing away from your body, so that an accidental deployment of the air bag will have a small chance of personal injury.
- Place an air bag module on a table or other flat surface with the bag and trim cover pointing up.
- Wear gloves, a dust mask and safety glasses whenever handling a deployed air bag module. The air bag surface may contain traces of sodium hydroxide, a by-product of the gas that inflates the air bag and which can cause skin irritation.
- Ensure to wash your hands with mild soap and water after handling a deployed air bag.
- All air bag modules with discolored or damaged cover trim must be replaced, not repainted.
- All component replacement and wiring service must be made with the negative and positive battery cables disconnected from the battery for a minimum of one minute prior to attempting service or replacement.
- NEVER probe the air bag electrical terminals. Doing so could result in air bag deployment, which can cause serious physical injury.

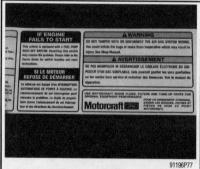

Fig. 12 Typically a warning label will be found on the vehicle regarding the air bag system

Fig. 13 Always carry a live air bag module with the bag and trim cover facing away from your body

Fig. 14 Always place an air bag module on a table or other flat surface with the bag and trim cover pointing up

• If the vehicle is involved in a fender-bender which results in a damaged front bumper or grille, have the air bag sensors inspected by a qualified automotive technician to ensure that they were not damaged.

• If at any time, the air bag light indicates that the computer has noted a problem, have your vehicle's SRS serviced immediately by a qualified automotive technician. A faulty SRS can cause severe physical injury or death.

DISARMING THE SYSTEM

1990–91 Vehicles

▶ See Figures 15 and 16

1. Disconnect the negative battery cable.
2. Detach the electrical connector from the backup power supply.

➡ **The backup power supply allows air bag deployment if the battery or battery cables are damaged in an accident before the crash sensors close. The power supply is a capacitor that will leak down in approximately 15 minutes after the battery is disconnected or in 1 minute if the battery positive cable is grounded. It is located in the instrument panel and is combined with the diagnostic monitor. The backup power supply must be disconnected before any air bag related service is performed.**

3. Remove the 4 nut and washer assemblies retaining the driver air bag module to the steering wheel.
4. Detach the driver air bag module connector and attach a jumper wire to the air bag terminals on the clockspring.
5. Connect the backup power supply and negative battery cable.

1992–98 Vehicles

> ☀ **CAUTION**
>
> **The air bag system must be disarmed before performing service around air bag components or wiring. Failure to do so may cause accidental deployment of the air bag, resulting in unnecessary repairs and/or personal injury.**

1. Position the vehicle with the front wheels in a straight ahead position.
2. Disconnect the negative battery cable.
3. Disconnect the positive battery cable.
4. Wait at least one minute for the air bag back-up power supply to drain before continuing.

   a. Remove the air bag module retaining bolts. Detach the electrical connector and remove the module.

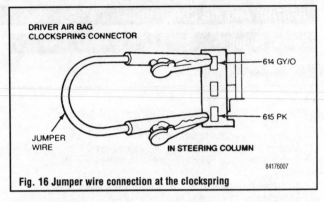

Fig. 16 Jumper wire connection at the clockspring

   b. Attach air bag simulator tool 105–00010 or equivalent, to the vehicle harness connector.
5. Connect the positive, then the negative battery cables.

ARMING THE SYSTEM

1990–91 Vehicles

1. Disconnect the negative battery cable and the backup power supply.
2. Remove the jumper wire from the air bag terminals on the clockspring assembly and reattach the air bag connector.
3. Position the driver air bag on the steering wheel with the 4 nut and washer assemblies. Tighten the nuts to 24–32 inch lbs. (2.7–3.7 Nm).
4. Connect the backup power supply and negative battery cable. Verify the air bag light.

1992–98 Vehicles

1. Connect the positive battery cable.
2. Connect the negative battery cable.
3. Stand outside the vehicle and carefully turn the ignition to the **RUN** position. Be sure that no part of your body is in front of the air bag module on the steering wheel, to prevent injury in case of an accidental air bag deployment.
4. Ensure the air bag indicator light turns off after approximately 6 seconds. If the light does not illuminate at all, does not turn off, or starts to flash, have the system tested by a qualified automotive technician. If the light does turn off after 6 seconds and does not flash, the SRS is working properly.

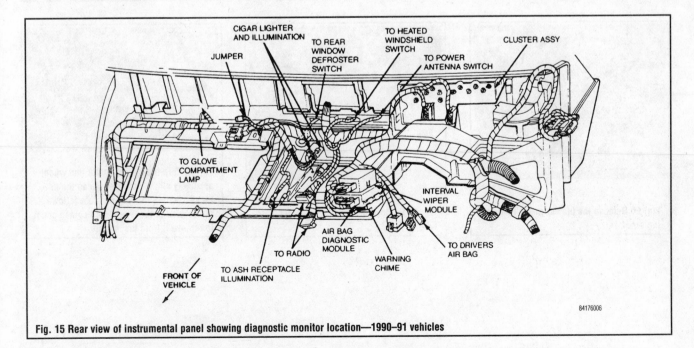

Fig. 15 Rear view of instrumental panel showing diagnostic monitor location—1990–91 vehicles

HEATING AND AIR CONDITIONING

Blower Motor

REMOVAL & INSTALLATION

▶ **See Figures 17 thru 22**

1. Disconnect the negative battery cable.
2. Remove the radiator coolant recovery tank.
3. Slide the connector from the top of the blower motor.
4. Detach the blower motor lead connector from the wiring harness connector.
5. Remove the blower motor cooling tube from the blower motor.
6. Remove the 4 retaining screws.
7. Turn the blower motor and wheel assembly slightly to the right so the bottom edge of the mounting plate follows the contour of the wheel well splash panel. While still in the blower housing, lift the motor and wheel assembly up and maneuver it out of the blower housing.
8. If necessary, remove the pushnut from the motor shaft and slide the wheel from the shaft.
9. Installation is the reverse of removal. If the wheel was removed from the motor shaft, make sure it is reinstalled so the outside of the wheel is 3.62–3.70 in. (92–94mm) from the blower motor mounting plate.
10. Connect the negative battery cable and check for proper blower motor operation.

Heater Core

REMOVAL & INSTALLATION

▶ **See Figures 23 thru 29**

1. Disconnect the negative battery cable.
2. Drain the cooling system and disconnect the heater hoses from the heater core tubes. Plug the hoses and the heater core tubes to prevent coolant leakage.

✳✳ CAUTION

Never open, service or drain the radiator or cooling system when hot; serious burns can occur from the steam and hot coolant. Also, when draining engine coolant, keep in mind that cats and dogs are attracted to ethylene glycol antifreeze and could drink any that is left in an uncovered container or in puddles on the ground. This will prove fatal in sufficient quantities. Always drain coolant into a sealable container. Coolant should be reused unless it is contaminated or is several years old.

3. Remove the 3 nuts located below the windshield wiper motor attaching the left end of the plenum to the dash panel. Remove the 1 nut retaining the upper left corner of the evaporator case to the dash panel.

89606P85

Fig. 17 Remove the radiator recovery tank assembly

89606P80

Fig. 18 Slide the connector from the top of the blower motor

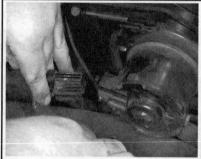
89606P81

Fig. 19 Detach the connector for the blower motor

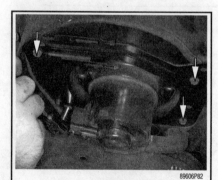
89606P82

Fig. 20 Remove the blower motor retaining screw

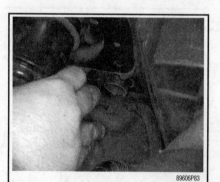
89606P83

Fig. 21 Remove the blower motor cooling tube

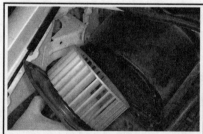
89606P84

Fig. 22 Turn the blower motor and wheel assembly slightly to the right so the bottom edge of the mounting plate follows the contour of the wheel well splash panel to remove it from the vehicle

4. Disconnect the vacuum supply hose(s) from the vacuum source. Push the grommet and vacuum supply hose(s) into the passenger compartment.

5. Remove the right and left lower instrument panel insulators.

6. On 1989 vehicles:

a. Remove the 3 glove compartment hinge screws, disconnect the check arms and remove the glove compartment.

b. Loosen the right door sill plate and remove the right side cowl trim panel.

c. Remove the bolt attaching the lower right end of the instrument panel to the side cowl.

d. Remove the instrument panel pad as follows:

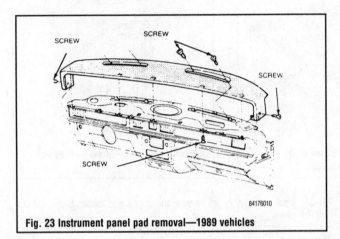

Fig. 23 Instrument panel pad removal—1989 vehicles

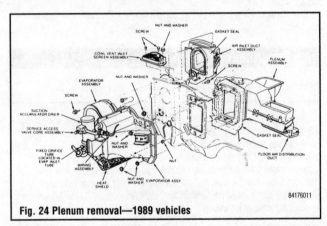

Fig. 24 Plenum removal—1989 vehicles

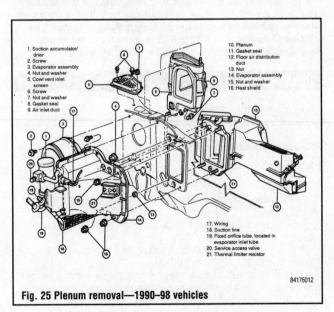

1. Suction accumulator/drier
2. Screw
3. Evaporator assembly
4. Nut and washer
5. Cowl vent inlet screen
6. Screw
7. Nut and washer
8. Gasket seal
9. Air inlet duct
10. Plenum
11. Gasket seal
12. Floor air distribution duct
13. Nut
14. Evaporator assembly
15. Nut and washer
16. Heat shield
17. Wiring
18. Suction line
19. Fixed orifice tube, located in evaporator inlet tube
20. Service access valve
21. Thermal limiter resistor

Fig. 25 Plenum removal—1990–98 vehicles

• Remove the 2 screws attaching the pad to the instrument panel at each defroster opening. Be careful not to drop the screws into the defroster openings.

• Remove the one screw attaching each outboard end of the pad to the instrument panel.

• On Crown Victoria, remove one pad attaching screw near the upper right corner of the glove compartment door.

• Remove the 5 screws attaching the lower edge of the pad to the instrument panel. Pull the instrument panel pad rearward and remove it from the vehicle.

7. On 1990–98 vehicles:

a. Remove all instrument panel mounting screws and pull the instrument panel back as far as it will go without disconnecting any wiring harnesses.

b. Make sure the nuts attaching the instrument panel braces to the dash panel are removed.

c. Loosen the right door sill plate and remove the right side cowl trim panel.

d. If equipped with manual air conditioning, disengage the temperature control cable housing from the bracket on top of the plenum. Disconnect the cable from the temperature blend door crank arm.

8. If equipped with Automatic Temperature Control (ATC), proceed as follows:

a. On 1989 vehicles, disconnect the temperature control cable from the ATC sensor.

b. Detach the vacuum harness line connector from the ATC sensor harness and detach the electrical connector from the ATC servo connector.

c. On 1990–98 vehicles, remove the cross body brace and disconnect the wiring harness from the temperature blend door actuator. Detach the ATC sensor tube from the evaporator case connector.

9. Detach the vacuum jumper harness at the multiple vacuum connector near the floor air distribution duct.

10. Disconnect the white vacuum hose from the outside-recirculating door vacuum motor.

11. Remove the 2 hush panels.

12. Remove 1 plastic push fastener retaining the floor air distribution duct to the left end of the plenum.

13. Remove the left screw and loosen the right screw on the rear face of the plenum and remove the floor air distribution duct.

14. Remove the 2 nuts from the 2 studs along the lower flange of the plenum.

15. Carefully move the plenum rearward to allow the heater core tubes and the stud at the top of the plenum to clear the holes in the dash panel. Remove the plenum from the vehicle by rotating the top of the plenum forward, down and out from under the instrument panel. Carefully pull the lower edge of the instrument panel rearward, as necessary, while rolling the plenum from behind the instrument panel.

16. On 1989 vehicles with ATC, remove the ATC servo from the plenum.

17. Remove the 4 retaining screws from the heater core cover and remove the cover from the plenum assembly.

18. Pull the heater core and seal assembly from the plenum assembly.

To install:

19. Carefully install the heater core and seal assembly into the plenum assembly. Visually check to ensure that the core seal is properly positioned. Position the heater core cover and install the 4 retaining screws.

20. On 1989 vehicles with ATC, install the ATC servo on the plenum.

21. Route the vacuum supply hose through the dash panel and seat the grommet in the opening.

22. Position the plenum under the instrument panel with the register duct opening up and the heater core tubes down. Rotate the plenum up behind the instrument panel and position the plenum to the dash panel. Insert the heater core tubes and mounting studs through their respective holes in the dash panel and the evaporator case.

23. Install the 3 nuts on the studs along the lower flange and one on the upper flange of the plenum. Install the 3 nuts below the windshield wiper motor to attach the left end of the plenum to the dash panel and the one nut to retain the upper left corner of the evaporator case to the dash panel.

24. Position the floor air distribution duct on the plenum. Install the 2 screws and plastic push fastener. If removed, position the panel door vacuum motor to the mounting bracket and install the 2 attaching screws.

25. Connect the white vacuum hose to the outside-recirculating door vacuum motor. Attach the vacuum jumper harness to the plenum harness at the multiple vacuum connector near the floor air distribution duct. Install the floor duct.

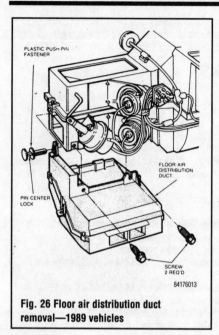

Fig. 26 Floor air distribution duct removal—1989 vehicles

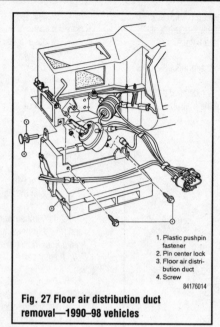

1. Plastic pushpin fastener
2. Pin center lock
3. Floor air distribution duct
4. Screw

84176014

Fig. 27 Floor air distribution duct removal—1990–98 vehicles

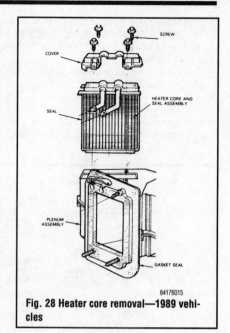

84176015

Fig. 28 Heater core removal—1989 vehicles

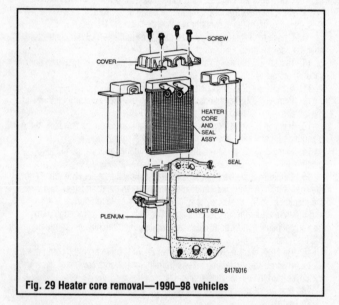

84176016

Fig. 29 Heater core removal—1990–98 vehicles

26. If equipped with manual air conditioning, connect the temperature control cable housing to the bracket on top of the plenum and connect the temperature control cable to the temperature blend door crank arm. Adjust the temperature cable.

27. If equipped with ATC, proceed as follows:

a. On 1989 vehicles, connect the temperature control cable to the ATC sensor and adjust the cable. Route and attach the vacuum harness connector to the ATC sensor and attach the electrical connector to the ATC servo connector. Do not block the sensor aspirator exhaust port with the excess vacuum harness. Install the ATC sensor tube between the sensor and the evaporator connector.

b. On 1990–98 vehicles, attach the ATC sensor tube to the evaporator case connector. Install the cross body brace and connect the wiring harness to the blend door actuator.

28. Install the bolt to attach the lower right end of the instrument panel to the side cowl. Install the right side cowl trim panel and tighten the right door sill plate attaching screws.

29. On 1989 vehicles, install the instrument panel pad and the glove compartment door. On 1990–98 vehicles, push the instrument panel back into position and install all instrument panel mounting screws. Install the right and left lower instrument panel insulators.

30. Connect the vacuum supply hose(s) to the vacuum source.

31. Install the right and left lower instrument panel insulators and install the 2 hush panels.

32. Unplug the heater core tubes and the heater hoses and connect the heater hoses to the heater core tubes. Fill the cooling system.

33. Connect the negative battery cable and check the system for proper operation.

Air Conditioning Components

REMOVAL & INSTALLATION

Repair or service of air conditioning components is not covered by this manual, because of the risk of personal injury or death, and because of the legal ramifications of servicing these components without the proper EPA certification and experience. Cost, personal injury or death, environmental damage, and legal considerations (such as the fact that it is a federal crime to vent refrigerant into the atmosphere), dictate that the A/C components on your vehicle should be serviced only by a Motor Vehicle Air Conditioning (MVAC) trained, and EPA certified automotive technician.

➡**If your vehicle's A/C system uses R-12 refrigerant and is in need of recharging, the A/C system can be converted over to R-134a refrigerant (less environmentally harmful and expensive). Refer to Section 1 for additional information on R-12 to R-134a conversions, and for additional considerations dealing with your vehicle's A/C system.**

Control Cables

REMOVAL & INSTALLATION

Vehicles with Manual Climate Control

▶ **See Figures 30 and 31**

1. Disconnect the negative battery cable.
2. Press the glove compartment door stops inward and allow the door to hang by the hinge.
3. Remove the control panel from the instrument panel, as explained in this Section.
4. Disconnect the cable housing from the control assembly and disengage the cable from the temperature control lever.
5. Working through the glove compartment opening, disconnect the cable from the plenum temperature blend door crank arm and cable mounting bracket.
6. Note the cable routing and remove the cable from the vehicle.

To install:

7. Make sure the self-adjusting clip is at least 1 in. (25.4mm) from the end loop of the control cable.

8. Route the cable behind the instrument panel and connect the control cable to the mounting bracket on the plenum.

9. Install the self-adjusting clip on the temperature blend door crank arm.

10. Connect the other end of the cable to the temperature lever arm on the control assembly. Snap the cable housing into place at the control assembly.

11. Install the control panel in the instrument panel.

12. Return the glove compartment door to the normal position and connect the negative battery cable.

13. Check the system for proper operation.

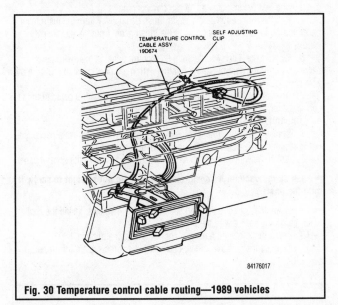

Fig. 30 Temperature control cable routing—1989 vehicles

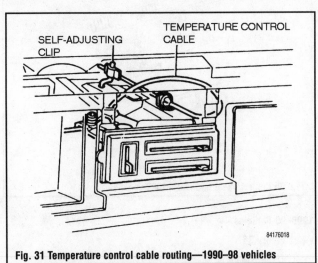

Fig. 31 Temperature control cable routing—1990–98 vehicles

1989 Vehicles with Automatic Temperature Control (ATC)

♦ **See Figure 32**

1. Disconnect the negative battery cable.

2. Remove the instrument panel pad as follows:

   a. Remove the 2 screws attaching the pad to the instrument panel at each defroster opening. Be careful not to drop the screws into the defroster openings.

   b. Remove the one screw attaching each outboard end of the pad to the instrument panel.

   c. On Crown Victoria, remove one pad attaching screw near the upper right corner of the glove compartment door.

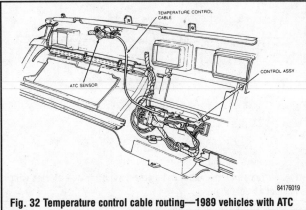

Fig. 32 Temperature control cable routing—1989 vehicles with ATC

   d. Remove the 5 screws attaching the lower edge of the pad to the instrument panel. Pull the instrument panel pad rearward and remove it from the vehicle.

3. Remove the one screw attaching the cable to the ATC sensor and remove the cable from the sensor.

4. If equipped with a mechanically controlled radio, pull the knobs from the radio control shafts.

5. Open the ash tray and remove the 2 screws attaching the center finish panel to the instrument panel at the ash tray opening.

6. Pull the lower edge of the center finish panel away from the instrument panel and disengage the upper tabs of the finish panel from the instrument panel.

7. Remove the 4 screws attaching the control panel to the instrument panel and pull the control out from the opening.

8. Remove the pushnut retaining the cable end loop on the temperature lever arm. Disconnect the cable housing from the control panel.

9. Note the cable routing and remove the cable from the vehicle.

To install:

10. Route the cable behind the instrument panel and connect the cable to the sensor. Loosely assemble; do not tighten the attaching screw at this time.

11. Connect the other end of the cable to the temperature lever arm of the control panel. Snap the cable housing into place at the control panel.

12. Install a new pushnut to retain the cable end loop on the temperature lever arm.

13. Install the control panel and secure with the 4 screws. Install the center finish panel and secure with the 2 screws.

14. Install the knobs on the radio control shafts, if equipped.

15. Adjust the cable according to the procedure in this Section.

16. Install the instrument panel pad in the reverse order of removal.

17. Connect the negative battery cable and check the system for proper operation.

ADJUSTMENT

Vehicles with Manual Climate Control

♦ **See Figure 33**

The temperature control cable is self-adjusting with a firm movement of the temperature control lever to the extreme right of the slot (WARM) in the face of the control panel. To prevent kinking of the control cable wire during cable installation, a preset adjustment should be made before attempting to perform the self-adjustment procedure. The preset adjustment can be performed either in the vehicle, with the cable installed or before installation.

1. Grip the self-adjusting clip and the cable with pliers and slide the clip down the control wire (away from the end) approximately 1 in. (25.4mm).

2. With the temperature selector lever in the maximum COOL position, snap the temperature cable housing into the mounting bracket. Attach the self-adjusting clip to the temperature door crank arm.

3. Firmly move the temperature selector lever to the extreme right of the slot (WARM) to position the self-adjusting clip.

4. Check for proper control operation.

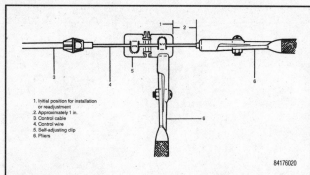

Fig. 33 Temperature control cable preset adjustment—vehicles with manual air conditioning

1989 Vehicles with Automatic Temperature Control (ATC)

◊ See Figure 34

1. Remove the instrument panel pad as follows:

a. Remove the 2 screws attaching the pad to the instrument panel at each defroster opening. Be careful not to drop the screws into the defroster openings.

b. Remove the one screw attaching each outboard end of the pad to the instrument panel.

c. On Crown Victoria, remove one pad attaching screw near the upper right corner of the glove compartment door.

d. Remove the 5 screws attaching the lower edge of the pad to the instrument panel. Pull the instrument panel pad rearward and remove it from the vehicle.

2. Move the temperature selector lever to the 75°F position.

3. The control arm of the ATC sensor should be aligned with the arrow on the sensor body.

4. If it is not, loosen the cable housing-to-sensor attaching screw and align the sensor control arm with the arrow while maintaining the 75°F position of the temperature selector control lever.

5. Tighten the cable housing-to-sensor attaching screw. Make sure the temperature control stays at 75°F and the sensor arm stays locked.

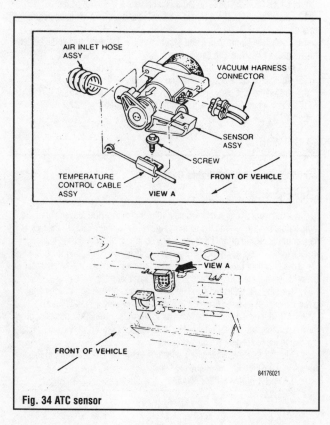

Fig. 34 ATC sensor

REMOVAL & INSTALLATION

1989 Vehicles

◊ See Figure 35

1. Disconnect the negative battery cable.

2. If equipped with a mechanically controlled radio, pull the knobs from the radio control shafts.

3. Open the ash tray and remove the 2 screws attaching the center finish panel to the instrument panel at the ash tray opening.

4. Pull the lower edge of the center finish panel away from the instrument panel and disengage the upper tabs of the finish panel from the instrument panel.

5. Remove the 4 screws attaching the control panel to the instrument panel, then pull the control panel from the instrument panel opening. Detach the wire connectors.

6. Disconnect the vacuum harness and temperature control cable from the control panel.

To install:

7. Connect the temperature cable to the control panel and use a new push-nut to retain the cable end loop to the control arm.

8. Attach the wire connectors and the vacuum harness to the control panel.

➡Push on the vacuum harness retaining nut. Do not attempt to screw it onto the post.

9. Install the control panel and secure with the 4 screws. Install the center finish panel and secure with the 2 screws.

10. Install the knobs on the radio control shafts, if equipped.

11. Connect the negative battery cable and check the system for proper operation.

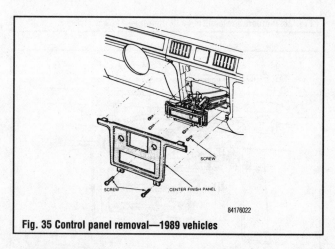

Fig. 35 Control panel removal—1989 vehicles

1990–98 Vehicles

◊ See Figure 36

1. Disconnect the negative battery cable.

2. Remove the left and right instrument panel mouldings.

3. Remove the cluster finish panel screws made visible in Step 2 as well as the 6 screws along the top surface of the cluster finish panel.

4. Pull off the knob from the headlight auto dim switch.

5. Remove the headlight switch shaft as follows:

a. Locate the headlight switch assembly body under the instrument panel.

b. Push the spring loaded shaft release button located on the side of the switch body and simultaneously pull out the headlight switch shaft.

6. Remove 2 screws on the left side, one screw on the right side and the 3 screws from the bottom and remove the steering column close out bolster panel.

7. Remove the 2 screws retaining the steering column close out bolster panel bracket and remove the bracket.

8. Lower the steering column as follows:

  a. Place the gearshift lever in **1**.

  b. Remove the transmission range indicator cable from the steering column arm and remove the bolt from the steering column transmission range indicator bracket. Remove the transmission range indicator cable assembly.

  c. Remove the 4 nuts retaining the steering column and let the steering column rest on the front seat.

9. Detach the electrical connectors from the accessory pushbutton switches and remove the cluster finish panel.

10. Remove the top 2 screws from the center finish panel. Gently rock the top of the center finish panel back while unsnapping the bottom tabs from the instrument panel. Detach the electrical connector from the clock and remove the center finish panel.

11. Remove the 4 retaining screws and pull the control panel out of the instrument panel.

12. Detach the electrical connectors, temperature control cable (manual air conditioning), and vacuum connector from the control panel.

To install:

13. Attach the temperature cable, if equipped, electrical connectors and vacuum connector to the control panel.

14. Install the control panel and secure with the 4 screws.

15. Attach the clock electrical connector. Snap in the bottom of the center finish panel and secure the top of the panel with the 2 screws.

16. Attach the electrical connectors and install the cluster finish panel.

17. Raise the steering column and install the 4 nuts to the steering column bracket. Tighten the nuts to 9–14 ft. lbs. (13–19 Nm).

18. Install the bolt to the steering column transmission range indicator bracket and connect the transmission range indicator cable to the steering column arm.

19. Install the steering column close out bolster panel bracket and secure with the 2 screws. Install the steering column close out bolster panel.

20. Install the cluster finish panel screws.

21. Install the headlight switch knob/shaft assembly, which is a snap lock fit. Install the headlight auto dim knob.

22. Snap the left and right instrument panel mouldings in place.

23. Connect the negative battery cable and check the system for proper operation.

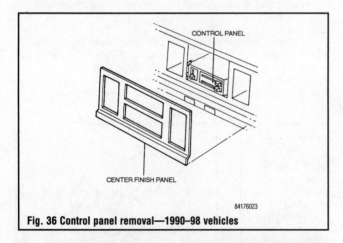

Fig. 36 Control panel removal—1990–98 vehicles

Vacuum Motors

REMOVAL & INSTALLATION

Panel Door Vacuum Motor

▶ **See Figures 37 and 38**

1. Disconnect the negative battery cable.

2. Drain the cooling system and disconnect the heater hoses from the heater core tubes. Plug the hoses and the heater core tubes to prevent coolant leakage.

3. Remove the 3 nuts located below the windshield wiper motor attaching the left end of the plenum to the dash panel. Remove the 1 nut retaining the upper left corner of the evaporator case to the dash panel.

4. Disconnect the vacuum supply hose(s) from the vacuum source. Push the grommet and vacuum supply hose(s) into the passenger compartment.

5. Remove the right and left lower instrument panel insulators.

6. On 1989 vehicles, remove the 3 glove compartment hinge screws, disconnect the check arms and remove the glove compartment. Loosen the right door sill plate and remove the right side cowl trim panel. Remove the bolt attaching the lower right end of the instrument panel to the side cowl. Remove the instrument panel pad as follows:

  a. Remove the 2 screws attaching the pad to the instrument panel at each defroster opening. Be careful not to drop the screws into the defroster openings.

  b. Remove the one screw attaching each outboard end of the pad to the instrument panel.

  c. On Crown Victoria, remove one pad attaching screw near the upper right corner of the glove compartment door.

  d. Remove the 5 screws attaching the lower edge of the pad to the instrument panel. Pull the instrument panel pad rearward and remove it from the vehicle.

7. On 1990–98 vehicles, remove all instrument panel mounting screws and pull the instrument panel back as far as it will go without disconnecting any wiring harnesses. Make sure the nuts attaching the instrument panel braces to the dash panel are removed. Loosen the right door sill plate and remove the right side cowl trim panel.

8. If equipped with manual air conditioning, disengage the temperature control cable housing from the bracket on top of the plenum. Disconnect the cable from the temperature blend door crank arm.

9. If equipped with Automatic Temperature Control (ATC), proceed as follows:

  a. On 1989 vehicles, disconnect the temperature control cable from the ATC sensor. Detach the vacuum harness line connector from the ATC sensor harness and detach the electrical connector from the ATC servo connector.

  b. On 1990–98 vehicles, remove the cross body brace and disconnect the wiring harness from the temperature blend door actuator. Detach the ATC sensor tube from the evaporator case connector.

10. Detach the vacuum jumper harness at the multiple vacuum connector near the floor air distribution duct. Disconnect the white vacuum hose from the outside-recirculating door vacuum motor.

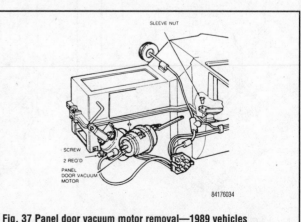

Fig. 37 Panel door vacuum motor removal—1989 vehicles

11. Remove the 2 hush panels.

12. Remove 1 plastic push fastener retaining the floor air distribution duct to the left end of the plenum. Remove the left screw and loosen the right screw on the rear face of the plenum and remove the floor air distribution duct.

13. Remove the 2 nuts from the 2 studs along the lower flange of the plenum.

14. Carefully move the plenum rearward to allow the heater core tubes and the stud at the top of the plenum to clear the holes in the dash panel. Remove the plenum from the vehicle by rotating the top of the plenum forward, down and out from under the instrument panel. Carefully pull the lower edge of the instrument panel rearward, as necessary, while rolling the plenum from behind the instrument panel.

15. Reach through the defroster nozzle opening and remove the sleeve nut attaching the vacuum motor arm to the door.

16. Remove the 2 screws attaching the vacuum motor to the mounting bracket. Disengage the vacuum motor from the plenum and disconnect the vacuum hose from the vacuum motor.

To install:

17. Position the vacuum motor to the mounting bracket and the door bracket. Install the 2 screws to attach the motor to the mounting bracket.

18. Connect the vacuum motor arm to the panel door with a new sleeve nut and connect the vacuum hose to the vacuum motor.

19. Route the vacuum supply hose through the dash panel and seat the grommet in the opening.

20. Position the plenum under the instrument panel with the register duct opening up and the heater core tubes down. Rotate the plenum up behind the instrument panel and position the plenum to the dash panel. Insert the heater core tubes and mounting studs through their respective holes in the dash panel and the evaporator case.

21. Install the 3 nuts on the studs along the lower flange and one on the upper flange of the plenum. Install the 3 nuts below the windshield wiper motor to attach the left end of the plenum to the dash panel and the one nut to retain the upper left corner of the evaporator case to the dash panel.

22. Position the floor air distribution duct on the plenum. Install the 2 screws and plastic push fastener. If removed, position the panel door vacuum motor to the mounting bracket and install the 2 attaching screws.

23. Connect the white vacuum hose to the outside-recirculating door vacuum motor. Attach the vacuum jumper harness to the plenum harness at the multiple vacuum connector near the floor air distribution duct. Install the floor duct.

24. If equipped with manual air conditioning, connect the temperature control cable housing to the bracket on top of the plenum and connect the temperature control cable to the temperature blend door crank arm. Adjust the temperature cable.

25. If equipped with ATC, proceed as follows:

   a. On 1989 vehicles, connect the temperature control cable to the ATC sensor and adjust the cable. Route and attach the vacuum harness connector to the ATC sensor and attach the electrical connector to the ATC servo connector. Do not block the sensor aspirator exhaust port with the excess vacuum harness. Install the ATC sensor tube between the sensor and the evaporator connector.

   b. On 1990–98 vehicles, attach the ATC sensor tube to the evaporator case connector. Install the cross body brace and connect the wiring harness to the blend door actuator.

26. Install the bolt to attach the lower right end of the instrument panel to the side cowl. Install the right side cowl trim panel and tighten the right door sill plate attaching screws.

27. On 1989 vehicles, install the instrument panel pad and the glove compartment door. On 1990–98 vehicles, push the instrument panel back into position and install all instrument panel mounting screws. Install the right and left lower instrument panel insulators.

28. Connect the vacuum supply hose(s) to the vacuum source.

29. Install the right and left lower instrument panel insulators and install the 2 hush panels.

30. Unplug the heater core tubes and the heater hoses and connect the heater hoses to the heater core tubes. Fill the cooling system.

31. Connect the negative battery cable and check the system for proper operation.

Floor-Defrost Door Vacuum Motor

▶ **See Figures 39 and 40**

1. Remove the 2 screws retaining the passenger (rear) side of the floor air distribution duct to the plenum. It may be necessary to remove the 2 nuts retaining the vacuum motor to the mounting bracket to gain access to the right duct screw.

2. Remove the one plastic push pin fastener retaining the floor air distribution duct to the left end of the plenum and remove the floor air distribution duct.

3. Remove the pushnut retaining the vacuum motor arm to the floor-defrost door crank arm.

4. If not previously removed, remove the 2 nuts retaining the vacuum motor to the motor bracket.

5. Disengage the motor from the mounting bracket and the motor arm from the door crank arm.

6. Disconnect the vacuum hoses from the motor and remove the motor from the plenum.

To install:

7. Connect the yellow vacuum hose to the vacuum motor end nipple and the red vacuum hose to the vacuum motor side nipple. Position the motor to the floor-defrost door crank arm and the motor mounting bracket.

8. Install the 2 nuts to retain the vacuum motor to the mounting bracket and install a new pushnut to retain the motor arm on the door crank arm.

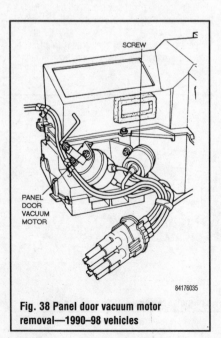

Fig. 38 Panel door vacuum motor removal—1990–98 vehicles

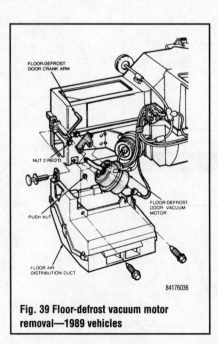

Fig. 39 Floor-defrost vacuum motor removal—1989 vehicles

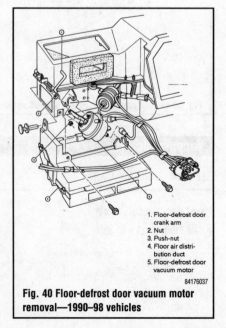

Fig. 40 Floor-defrost door vacuum motor removal—1990–98 vehicles

9. Position the floor air distribution duct to the plenum air duct opening. Install the plastic push pin fastener to the left end of the plenum and duct.

10. Install the 2 screws that attach the passenger (rear) side of the floor air distribution duct to the plenum.

11. If not previously installed, install the 2 nuts retaining the vacuum motor to the mounting bracket.

12. Check the system for proper operation.

Outside-Recirculating Door Vacuum Motor

▶ See Figures 41 and 42

1. Remove the spring nut retaining the outside-recirculating air door vacuum motor arm to the door crank arm.

2. Disengage the vacuum motor arm and washer from the crank arm.

3. Disengage the assist spring and the second washer from the crank arm.

4. Detach the white vacuum hose connector from the vacuum motor.

5. Remove the 2 nuts retaining the vacuum motor and the assist spring bracket to the air inlet duct mounting bracket. Remove the vacuum motor and the assist spring mounting bracket.

To install:

6. Install the vacuum motor and the assist spring bracket to the air inlet duct mounting bracket and secure with the retaining nuts.

7. Install one of the washers on the crank arm and install the loop end of the assist spring.

8. Install the second washer and the vacuum motor arm on the crank arm. Secure the 2 washers, the assist spring and the vacuum motor arm on the crank arm with a new spring nut.

9. Attach the white vacuum hose connector onto the vacuum motor.

10. Check the system for proper operation.

Thermal Blower Lock Out Switch

REMOVAL & INSTALLATION

Vehicles with Automatic Temperature Control

▶ See Figure 43

1. Disconnect the negative battery cable and drain the cooling system.

✖✖ CAUTION

Never open, service or drain the radiator or cooling system when hot; serious burns can occur from the steam and hot coolant. Also, when draining engine coolant, keep in mind that cats and dogs are attracted to ethylene glycol antifreeze and could drink any that is left in an uncovered container or in puddles on the ground. This will prove fatal in sufficient quantities. Always drain coolant into a sealable container. Coolant should be reused unless it is contaminated or is several years old.

2. Detach the electrical and vacuum connections at the switch.

3. Loosen the hose clamps at the switch remove the switch from the hose.

To install:

4. Slide new hose clamps over the ends of the hoses.

5. Apply soapy water to the ends of the hoses.

6. Insert the switch in the hose ends and tighten the clamps to 16–21 inch lbs. (1.8–2.5 Nm).

7. Attach the electrical and vacuum connectors to the switch.

8. Connect the negative battery cable and fill the cooling system.

9. Check the system for proper operation.

Servo Motor

REMOVAL & INSTALLATION

1989 Vehicles with Automatic Temperature Control

▶ See Figure 44

1. Disconnect the negative battery cable.

2. Disconnect the glove compartment door stop (one screw) and let the door hang by the hinges.

3. Detach the vacuum hose and electrical connector from the servo motor.

4. Remove the 2 screws from the servo motor mounting bracket and position the servo for access to the vacuum diverter valve.

5. Remove the retaining pushnut and vacuum connector clip, then unplug the multiple vacuum connector from the vacuum diverter valve.

6. Remove the pushnut that retains the servo motor overtravel spring and arm link to the blend door crank arm. Remove the servo assembly.

To install:

7. Connect the servo motor overtravel spring and arm link to the blend door crank arm. Install a new pushnut.

8. Attach the multiple vacuum connector to the vacuum diverter valve and secure it with a vacuum connector and a new retaining pushnut.

9. Position the servo motor and install the 2 mounting screws.

10. Connect the vacuum hose to the servo motor and attach the electrical connector to the harness.

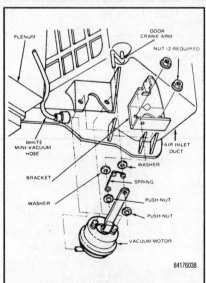

Fig. 41 Outside-recirculating air door vacuum motor removal—1989 vehicles

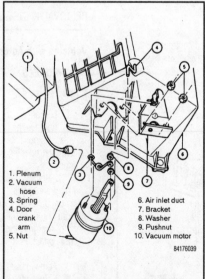

1. Plenum
2. Vacuum hose
3. Spring
4. Door crank arm
5. Nut
6. Air inlet duct
7. Bracket
8. Washer
9. Pushnut
10. Vacuum motor

Fig. 42 Outside-recirculating air door vacuum motor removal—1990–98 vehicles

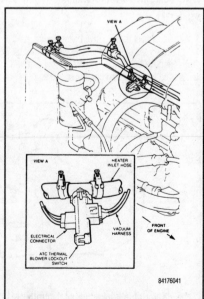

Fig. 43 Thermal blower lock out switch

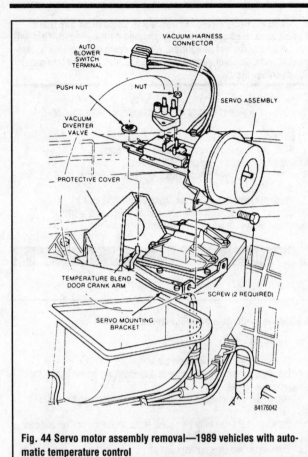

Fig. 44 Servo motor assembly removal—1989 vehicles with automatic temperature control

11. Replace the glove compartment door stop screw and connect the negative battery cable.

12. Check the system for proper operation.

Variable Blower Speed Controller

REMOVAL & INSTALLATION

1990–98 Vehicles with Automatic Temperature Control

▶ See Figure 45

1. Disconnect the negative battery cable.
2. Detach the electrical connector from the blower speed controller.
3. Remove the 2 screws attaching the controller to the evaporator case and remove the blower speed controller.

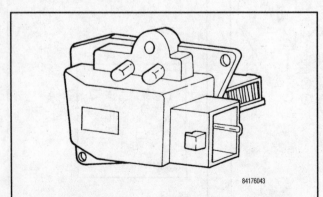

Fig. 45 Variable blower speed controller—1990–98 vehicles with automatic temperature control

4. Installation is the reverse of the removal procedure. Check the blower for proper operation.

Temperature Blend Door Actuator

REMOVAL & INSTALLATION

1990–98 Vehicles with Automatic Temperature Control

▶ See Figure 46

1. Disconnect the negative battery cable.
2. Remove the instrument panel; refer to Section 10.
3. Disconnect the electrical harness to the temperature controller on the control assembly, from the blend door actuator.
4. Remove the 4 screws and remove the blend door actuator from the plenum.

To install:

5. Position the blend door actuator on the plenum. Make sure the actuator cam is properly engaged with the temperature blend door crank arm.
6. Secure the blend door actuator to the plenum with the 4 screws.
7. Connect the temperature controller electrical harness to the blend door actuator.
8. Install the instrument panel and connect the negative battery cable.

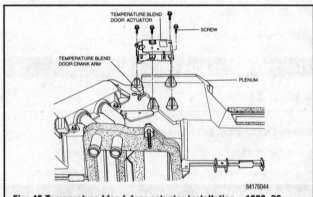

Fig. 46 Temperature blend door actuator installation—1990–98 vehicles with automatic temperature control

In-Vehicle Temperature Sensor

REMOVAL & INSTALLATION

Vehicles with Automatic Temperature Control

1989 MODELS

▶ See Figure 47

1. Disconnect the negative battery cable.
2. Remove the instrument panel pad as follows:

   a. Remove the 2 screws attaching the pad to the instrument panel at each defroster opening. Be careful not to drop the screws into the defroster openings.

   b. Remove the one screw attaching each outboard end of the pad to the instrument panel.

   c. On Crown Victoria, remove one pad attaching screw near the upper right corner of the glove compartment door.

   d. Remove the 5 screws attaching the lower edge of the pad to the instrument panel. Pull the instrument panel pad rearward and remove it from the vehicle.

3. Remove the 2 mounting screws from the sensor.
4. Remove the control cable housing-to-sensor attachment screw.
5. Disconnect the cable end loop from the lever arm and remove the cable from the sensor.

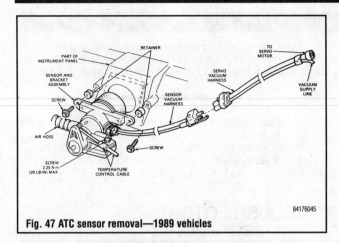

Fig. 47 ATC sensor removal—1989 vehicles

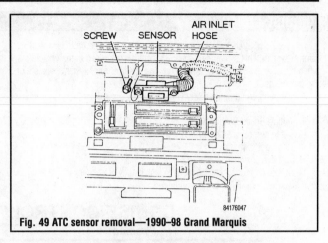

Fig. 49 ATC sensor removal—1990–98 Grand Marquis

➡Secure the control cable with tape or wire to prevent it from falling from sight behind the instrument panel.

6. Disconnect the sensor vacuum harness from the servo vacuum harness.

7. Remove the ambient air hose from the end of the sensor by rotating the sensor in a clockwise direction.

8. Remove the sensor from the vehicle.

To install:

9. Connect the ambient air hose to the sensor by turning it counterclockwise.

10. Route and attach the vacuum harness connector to the jumper line connector. Make sure the locking tab is snapped onto the jumper line connector.

11. Position the sensor to the screw mounting bosses and install the mounting screws.

➡Use a mirror to help align the sensor screw holes to the mounting bosses. If necessary, position a trouble light on the windshield for additional light. A small amount of body caulk in the end of the ratchet socket will help prevent the screws from falling from the socket.

12. Remove the tape or wire securing the cable and connect the control cable to the lever arm. Loosely install the attaching screw. Adjust the cable according to the procedure in this Section.

13. Do not block the sensor aspirator exhaust port with the excess vacuum harness.

14. Install the instrument panel pad and connect the negative battery cable. Check the system for proper operation.

1990–98 MODELS

▶ See Figures 48 and 49

1. Disconnect the negative battery cable.
2. Remove the left and right instrument panel mouldings.

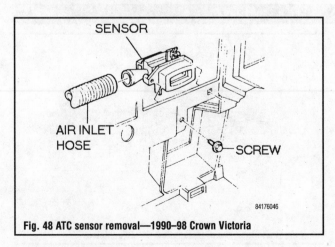

Fig. 48 ATC sensor removal—1990–98 Crown Victoria

3. Remove the cluster finish panel screws made visible in Step 2 as well as the 6 screws along the top surface of the cluster finish panel.

4. Pull off the knob from the headlight auto dim switch.

5. Remove the headlight switch shaft as follows:

a. Locate the headlight switch assembly body under the instrument panel.

b. Push the spring loaded shaft release button located on the side of the switch body and simultaneously pull out the headlight switch shaft.

6. Remove 2 screws on the left side, one screw on the right side and the 3 screws from the bottom and remove the steering column close out bolster panel.

7. Remove the 2 screws retaining the steering column close out bolster panel bracket and remove the bracket.

8. Lower the steering column as follows:

a. Place the gearshift lever in **1**.

b. Remove the transmission range indicator cable from the steering column arm and remove the bolt from the steering column transmission range indicator bracket. Remove the transmission range indicator cable assembly.

c. Remove the 4 nuts retaining the steering column and let the steering column rest on the front seat.

9. Detach the electrical connectors from the accessory pushbutton switches and remove the cluster finish panel.

10. Remove the top 2 screws from the center finish panel. Gently rock the top of the center finish panel back while unsnapping the bottom tabs from the instrument panel. Detach the electrical connector from the clock and remove the center finish panel.

11. Grasp the sensor, remove the 2 screws and rotate the sensor down and out of the instrument panel.

12. Detach the electrical connector and the air hose from the sensor.

To install:

13. Connect the electrical lead and the air hose to the sensor.

14. Position the sensor on the instrument panel and install the 2 retaining screws.

15. Attach the clock electrical connector. Snap in the bottom of the center finish panel and secure the top of the panel with the 2 screws.

16. Attach the electrical connectors and install the cluster finish panel.

17. Raise the steering column and install the 4 nuts to the steering column bracket. Tighten the nuts to 9–14 ft. lbs. (13–19 Nm).

18. Install the bolt to the steering column transmission range indicator bracket and connect the transmission range indicator cable to the steering column arm.

19. Install the steering column close out bolster panel bracket and secure with the 2 screws. Install the steering column close out bolster panel.

20. Install the cluster finish panel screws.

21. Install the headlight switch knob/shaft assembly, which is a snap lock fit. Install the headlight auto dim knob.

22. Snap the left and right instrument panel mouldings in place.

23. Connect the negative battery cable and check the system for proper operation.

CRUISE CONTROL

All models covered by this manual were available with an optional speed control system. This system automatically controls the speed of the vehicle when cruising at a stable highway speed. The speed control system consists of the following:

- Speed control amplifier/servo assembly
- Speed control cable
- Vehicle Speed Sensor (VSS)
- Speed control actuator switch
- Stop light switch
- Deactivator switch

The speed control system operates independently of engine vacuum and, therefore, does not utilize any vacuum lines.

The speed control amplifier integrates the system electronics, thereby eliminating any other electronic control modules in the vehicle. The amplifier controls the vehicle's speed via a cable attached to the throttle body lever.

The speed control actuator switch assembly is mounted on the steering wheel and allows the driver to control the system's operation. The switch assembly contains five control buttons for system functioning, namely: ON, OFF, RESUME, SET ACCEL, COAST.

The system will continue to control the vehicle's speed until the OFF button is used, or the brake pedal or clutch pedal (manual transmissions only) is depressed.

CRUISE CONTROL TROUBLESHOOTING

Problem	Possible Cause
Will not hold proper speed	Incorrect cable adjustment
	Binding throttle linkage
	Leaking vacuum servo diaphragm
	Leaking vacuum tank
	Faulty vacuum or vent valve
	Faulty stepper motor
	Faulty transducer
	Faulty speed sensor
	Faulty cruise control module
Cruise intermittently cuts out	Clutch or brake switch adjustment too tight
	Short or open in the cruise control circuit
	Faulty transducer
	Faulty cruise control module
Vehicle surges	Kinked speedometer cable or casing
	Binding throttle linkage
	Faulty speed sensor
	Faulty cruise control module
Cruise control inoperative	Blown fuse
	Short or open in the cruise control circuit
	Faulty brake or clutch switch
	Leaking vacuum circuit
	Faulty cruise control switch
	Faulty stepper motor
	Faulty transducer
	Faulty speed sensor
	Faulty cruise control module

Note: Use this chart as a guide. Not all systems will use the components listed.

TCCA6C01

ENTERTAINMENT SYSTEMS

Radio Receiver/Tape Player/CD Player (Except Changer)

REMOVAL & INSTALLATION

1989 Vehicles

▶ **See Figure 50**

1. Disconnect the negative battery cable.
2. Remove the screws attaching the bezel to the instrument panel. Remove the radio attaching screws.
3. Pull the radio to disengage it from the lower rear support bracket. Disconnect the power antenna and speaker leads and remove the radio.
4. Remove the lower rear support retaining nut and remove the support.
5. Installation is the reverse of the removal procedure.

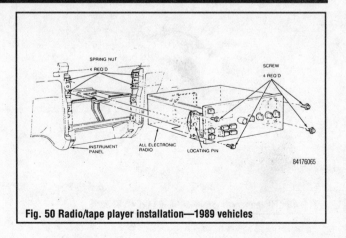

Fig. 50 Radio/tape player installation—1989 vehicles

Fig. 51 The radio is equipped with quick release retainers. There are two holes on either side of the radio chassis to insert a special tool to release the clips

Fig. 52 Install Radio Removal Tool (T87P-19061-A) or equivalent into the radio face place

Fig. 53 Apply a slight outward spreading force on both sides and . . .

Fig. 54 . . . pull the radio chassis out of the instrument panel

Fig. 55 Detach the antenna and the . . .

Fig. 56 . . . electrical connectors from the back of the radio and remove the radio

1990–98 Models

▶ See Figures 51 thru 56

1. Disconnect the negative battery cable.

➡Do not use excessive force when installing the radio removal tool. This will damage the retaining clips, making radio chassis removal difficult and may cause other internal damage.

2. Install Radio Removal Tool (T87P-19061-A) or equivalent into the radio face plate. Push the tool in approximately 1 in. (25mm) to release the retaining clips.
3. Apply a slight outward spreading force on both sides and pull the radio chassis out of the instrument panel.
4. Disconnect the radio wiring harness and antenna cable.
5. Remove the radio chassis.

To install:
6. Position the radio chassis in the vehicle.
7. Connect the radio wiring harness and antenna cable.
8. Push the radio chassis inward until the retaining clips are fully engaged.
9. Connect the negative battery cable.

Amplifier

REMOVAL & INSTALLATION

Sedan

▶ See Figure 57

1. Disconnect the negative battery cable.
2. Lift and remove the rear seat cushion.
3. Remove the 2 safety belt retaining bolts.

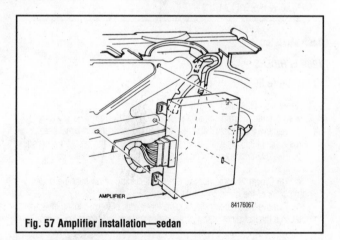

Fig. 57 Amplifier installation—sedan

4. Carefully remove the sound insulation material.
5. Remove the retaining screws.
6. Remove the spare tire.
7. Detach the hardshell connectors and remove the amplifier.
8. Installation is the reverse of the removal procedure.

Station Wagon

▶ See Figure 58

1. Disconnect the negative battery cable.
2. Remove the spare tire cover and the spare tire.
3. Remove the 4 amplifier retaining screws from the mounting bracket.
4. Remove the 2 amplifier retaining screws.
5. Detach the hardshell connectors and remove the amplifier.
6. Installation is the reverse of the removal procedure.

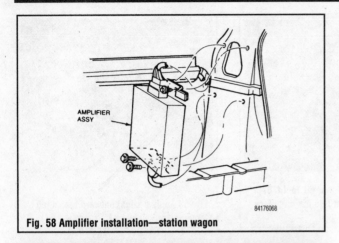

Fig. 58 Amplifier installation—station wagon

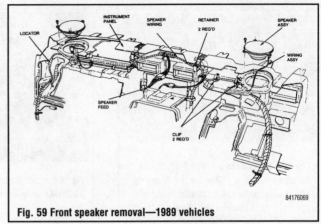

Fig. 59 Front speaker removal—1989 vehicles

Compact Disc Changer

REMOVAL & INSTALLATION

1. Disconnect the negative battery cable.
2. Remove the luggage compartment trim cover.
3. Remove the screws retaining the compact disc changer bracket to the body.
4. Detach the connectors and remove the compact disc changer and bracket assembly.
5. Remove the screws retaining the compact disc changer to the bracket.
6. Installation is the reverse of the removal procedure. Tighten the screws retaining the compact disc changer to the bracket to 24–32 inch lbs. (2.7–3.7 Nm).

Speakers

REMOVAL & INSTALLATION

Dash Mounted

1989 VEHICLES

▶ See Figure 59

1. Disconnect the negative battery cable.
2. Remove the instrument panel pad as follows:
   a. Remove the 2 screws attaching the pad to the instrument panel at each defroster opening. Be careful not to drop the screws into the defroster openings.
   b. Remove the one screw attaching each outboard end of the pad to the instrument panel.
   c. On Crown Victoria, remove one pad attaching screw near the upper right corner of the glove compartment door.
   d. Remove the 5 screws attaching the lower edge of the pad to the instrument panel. Pull the instrument panel pad rearward and remove it from the vehicle.

3. Remove the 3 retaining screws for each of the front speakers.
4. Raise the speakers and detach the leads at the connectors.
5. Installation is the reverse of the removal procedure.

Door Mounted

1989 AND 1992–98 VEHICLES

▶ See Figures 60, 61 and 62

1. Disconnect the negative battery cable.
2. Remove the door panel as explained in Section 10.
3. Remove the retaining screws and pull the speaker from the opening.
4. Detach the speaker lead at the connector and remove the speaker.
5. Installation is the reverse of the removal procedure.

1990–91 VEHICLES

▶ See Figure 63

1. Disconnect the negative battery cable.
2. Remove the door speaker grille.
3. Remove the 3 retaining screws for the door speakers.
4. Remove the speaker and disconnect the lead.

Rear

1989–91 SEDAN

▶ See Figure 64

1. Disconnect the negative battery cable.
2. Remove the spare tire and jack assembly from the luggage compartment, if necessary.
3. Working inside the luggage compartment, disconnect the speaker lead from the wire harness.
4. Disengage the strap from the retaining clips and remove the speaker.
5. Installation is the reverse of the removal procedure.

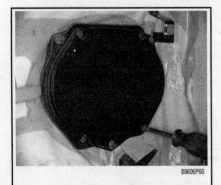

Fig. 60 Remove the speaker retaining screws

Fig. 61 Pull the speaker from the door to access the connector and . . .

Fig. 62 . . . detach the connector and remove the speaker

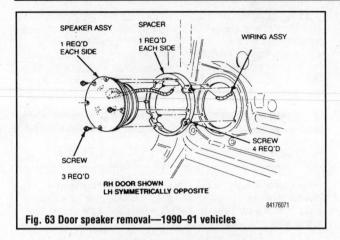

Fig. 63 Door speaker removal—1990–91 vehicles

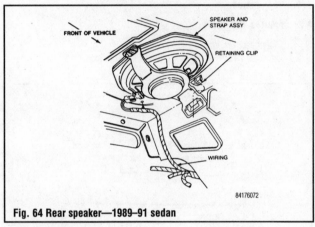

Fig. 64 Rear speaker—1989–91 sedan

1992–98 SEDAN

▶ **See Figure 65**

1. Disconnect the negative battery cable.
2. Remove the package tray trim.

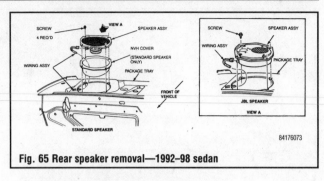

Fig. 65 Rear speaker removal—1992–98 sedan

3. Remove the 4 speaker retaining screws.
4. Detach the connector and lift out the speaker.
5. If equipped with standard speakers, remove the NVH cover if necessary.
6. Installation is the reverse of the removal procedure.

STATION WAGON

1. Disconnect the negative battery cable.
2. Remove the speaker and grille assembly retaining screws from the quarter trim panel.
3. Lift the speaker and grille assembly from the trim panel and detach the speaker connector lead.
4. Remove the retaining nuts and remove the speaker from the grille.
5. Installation is the reverse of the removal procedure.

Subwoofer

1. Disconnect the negative battery cable.
2. Remove the spare tire.
3. Remove the 4 nut and washer assemblies from the bottom of the subwoofer. Remove the subwoofer by lowering straight down.
4. Detach the power connector and amplifier input connector located on the forward face of the subwoofer enclosure.
5. The subwoofer and amplifier assembly is now free of the vehicle.
6. To remove the subwoofer amplifier from the enclosure, detach the power and input connectors.
7. Remove the 4 retaining screws from the amplifier and remove the amplifier from the subwoofer enclosure.
8. Installation is the reverse of the removal procedure.

WINDSHIELD WIPERS AND WASHERS

Windshield Wiper Blade and Arm

REMOVAL & INSTALLATION

1989–91 Vehicles

▶ **See Figures 66 and 67**

Raise the blade end of the arm off of the windshield and move the slide latch away from the pivot shaft. This will unlock the wiper arm from the pivot shaft and hold the blade end of the arm off of the glass at the same time. The wiper arm can now be pulled off of the pivot shaft without the aid of any tools.

➡**To prevent glass and/or paint damage, do not pry the arm from the pivot with metal or sharp tools.**

Turn on the wiper switch and allow the motor to move the pivot shafts 3–4 cycles, then turn off the wiper switch. This will place the pivot shafts in the PARK position. Make sure the switch is not rotated into the INTERVAL position, before installing the blade and arm assembly.

Position the auxiliary arm over the pivot pin, hold it down and push the main arm head over the pivot shaft. Install the blade and arm assemblies to dimension X, as shown in the figure. Dimension X is the distance between the centerline of the blade element and the arm stop. At the lower settings the arm will be beyond the stop. This is normal. In operation, the arms will assume slightly different positions.

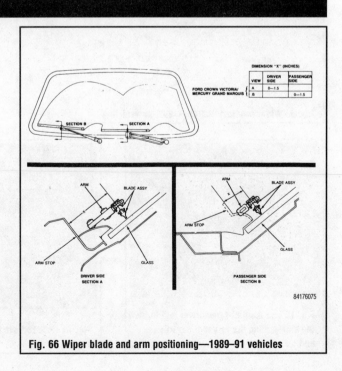

Fig. 66 Wiper blade and arm positioning—1989–91 vehicles

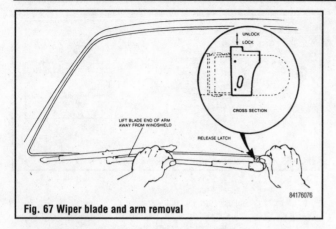

Fig. 67 Wiper blade and arm removal

1992–98 Vehicles

▶ **See Figures 67, 68, 69, 70 and 71**

Raise the blade end of the arm off of the windshield and move the slide latch away from the pivot shaft. This will unlock the wiper arm from the pivot shaft and hold the blade end of the arm off of the glass at the same time. The wiper arm can now be pulled off of the pivot shaft without the aid of any tools.

➡ **To prevent glass and/or paint damage, do not pry the arm from the pivot with metal or sharp tools.**

To install the blade and arm assembly, line up the key on the wiper arm with the keyway in the pivot shaft. Push the arm onto the pivot shaft.

Hold the main arm head onto the pivot shaft while raising the blade end of the wiper arm and push the slide latch into the lock under the pivot shaft. Then lower the blade to the windshield. If the blade does not touch the windshield, the slide latch is not completely in place.

After blade and arm installation, operate the wiper switch to cycle the linkage and bring the blade and arm back to the parked position. Check dimension X in the figure. Dimension X in Section A should be 0.2–1.3 in. and dimension X in Section B should be 0.08–1.02 in.

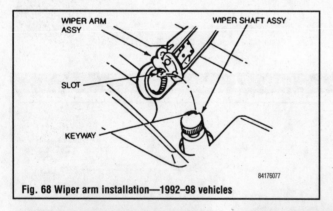

Fig. 68 Wiper arm installation—1992–98 vehicles

If adjustment is necessary, remove the blade and arm assemblies and use a small prybar to remove the plastic key from the arm. Turn on the wiper switch and allow the motor to move the pivot shafts 3–4 cycles, then turn off the wiper switch. Reinstall the blade and arm assemblies to dimension X. Install the arm on the pivot shaft, then apply downward pressure on the arm head. Allow the latch to slide under the pivot shaft and slide latch using finger pressure only.

Windshield Wiper Motor

REMOVAL & INSTALLATION

➡ **The internal permanent magnets used in the wiper motor are a ceramic (glass-like) material. Be careful when handling the motor to avoid damaging the magnets. The motor must not be struck or tapped with a hammer or other object.**

1989–91 Vehicles

▶ **See Figures 72 and 73**

1. Disconnect the negative battery cable.
2. Detach the 2 push-on wire connectors from the motor.

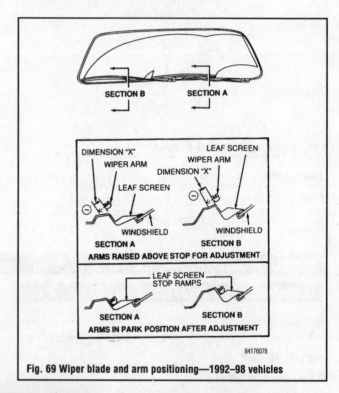

Fig. 69 Wiper blade and arm positioning—1992–98 vehicles

Fig. 70 Use a small screwdriver to release the clip holding the arm to the pivot and . . .

Fig. 71 . . . remove the arm from the pivot

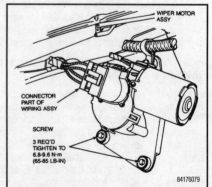

Fig. 72 Windshield wiper motor—1989–91 vehicles

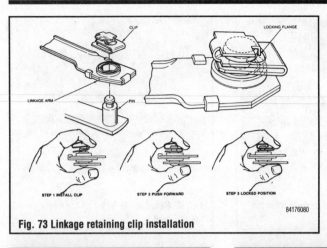

Fig. 73 Linkage retaining clip installation

3. Remove the hood seal. Remove the right wiper arm and blade assembly from the pivot shaft.

4. Remove the windshield wiper linkage cover by removing the 2 attaching screws and hose clip.

5. Remove the linkage retaining clip from the operating arm on the motor by lifting the locking tab up and pulling the clip away from the pin.

6. Remove the 3 bolts that retain the motor to the dash panel extension and remove the motor.

7. Installation is the reverse of the removal procedure.

1992–98 Vehicles

▶ See Figures 74 thru 88

1. Disconnect the negative battery cable.

2. Remove the rear hood seal. Remove the wiper arm assemblies by raising the wiper blade off the windshield. Move the slide latch away from the pivot shaft and slowly lower the arm onto the latch. This unlocks the arm from

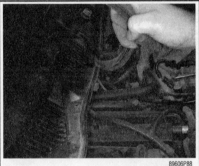

Fig. 74 Lift up to release the clips and remove the hood-to-cowl weather strip

Fig. 75 Remove the washer fluid hose from the nipple

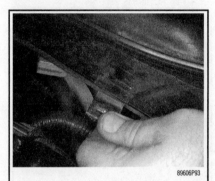

Fig. 76 Remove the cowl panel-to-firewall retaining clips

Fig. 77 Remove the driver's side then the . . .

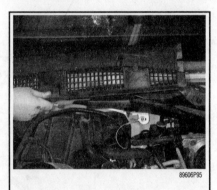

Fig. 78 . . . passenger side cowl panel from the vehicle

Fig. 79 Detach the electrical connector for the wiper motor

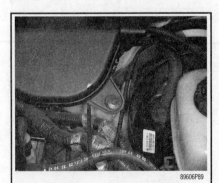

Fig. 80 Remove the wiper motor cover retaining bolt

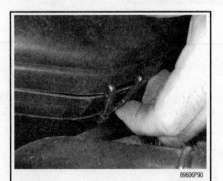

Fig. 81 Release the wiper motor retaining clips and . . .

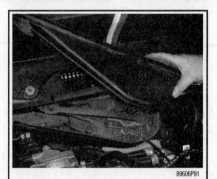

Fig. 82 . . . remove the cover from the vehicle

Fig. 83 Remove the wiper module assembly retaining bolts and . . .

Fig. 84 . . . remove the module from the vehicle

Fig. 85 Remove the wiper linkage retaining clip and . . .

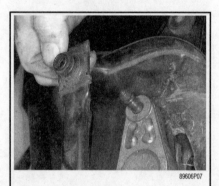

Fig. 86 . . . remove the linkage from the wiper motor

Fig. 87 Remove the wiper motor retaining bolts and . . .

Fig. 88 . . . remove the wiper motor from the vehicle

the pivot shaft and holds the blade off the glass. Pull the arm from the pivot shaft.

   3. Remove the cowl vent screws and disconnect the washer hoses from the washer jets.

   4. Detach the electrical connectors from the wiper motor.

   5. Remove the wiper assembly attaching screws, lift the assembly out and disconnect the washer hose.

   6. Unsnap and remove the linkage cover.

   7. Remove the wiper module assembly retaining bolts and remove the module from the vehicle.

   8. Remove the linkage retaining clip from the motor operating arm by lifting the locking tab and pulling the clip away from the pin.

   9. Remove the motor retaining screws and remove the motor from the vehicle.

   10. The installation is the reverse of the removal.

Windshield Washer Fluid Reservoir

REMOVAL & INSTALLATION

1989–91 Vehicles

▶ See Figures 89 and 90

➥1991 California vehicles with 5.0L engine are equipped with a reservoir similar to that installed in 1992–98 vehicles, therefore the procedure for 1992–98 vehicles should be followed.

   1. Disconnect the negative battery cable.

   2. Use a small prybar to unlock the lock-tab wire connectors.

   3. Remove the retaining screws and lift the reservoir from the left fender apron.

   4. Disconnect the hose and drain the reservoir into a container.

   5. Installation is the reverse of the removal procedure. Refill the reservoir after installation and check for leaks and proper operation.

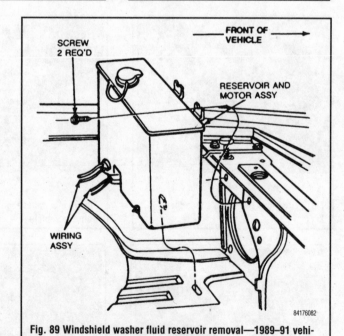

Fig. 89 Windshield washer fluid reservoir removal—1989–91 vehicles (except 1991 California 5.0L engine)

1992–98 Vehicles

▶ See Figure 91

   1. Disconnect the negative battery cable.

   2. Remove the wheel well apron.

➥Air cleaner removal may aid in reservoir removal and installation.

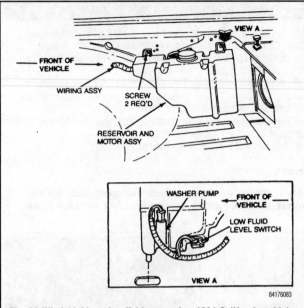

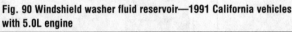

Fig. 90 Windshield washer fluid reservoir—1991 California vehicles with 5.0L engine

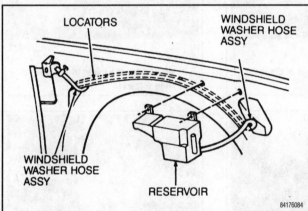

Fig. 91 Windshield washer fluid reservoir removal—1992–98 vehicles

3. Remove the reservoir retaining screws and lift the assembly from the apron.
4. Detach the electrical connector and washer hose. The reservoir will drain with the hose disconnected.
5. Installation is the reverse of the removal procedure. Refill the reservoir and check for leaks and proper operation.

Windshield Washer Motor

REMOVAL & INSTALLATION

1989–91 Vehicles

▶ **See Figures 92 and 93**

➡**1991 California vehicles with 5.0L engine are equipped with a motor similar to that installed in 1992–98 vehicles, therefore the procedure for 1992–98 vehicles should be followed.**

1. Disconnect the negative battery cable.
2. Remove the fluid reservoir from the vehicle and drain the fluid into a container.
3. Using a small prybar, pry out the retaining ring.

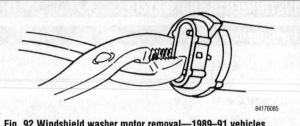

Fig. 92 Windshield washer motor removal—1989–91 vehicles (except 1991 California 5.0L engine)

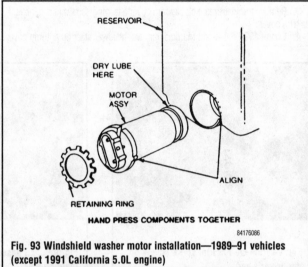

Fig. 93 Windshield washer motor installation—1989–91 vehicles (except 1991 California 5.0L engine)

4. Using pliers to grip one wall around the electrical terminals, pull out the motor, seal and impeller assembly.
To install:
5. Make sure the reservoir pump chamber is free of foreign material prior to installing the motor in the reservoir.
6. Lubricate the outside diameter of the seal with a dry lubricant such as powdered graphite. This will prevent the seal from sticking to the wall of the reservoir motor cavity and make assembly easier.
7. Align the small projection on the motor end cap with the slot in the reservoir and assemble so the seal seats against the bottom of the motor cavity.
8. Using a 1-inch 12-point socket, hand press the retaining ring securely against the motor end plate.
9. Attach the electrical connector and hose. Install the fluid reservoir in the vehicle.
10. Fill the reservoir and connect the negative battery cable. Operate the washer system and check for leaks and hose kinks.

➡**Do not operate the pump until fluid is added to the reservoir.**

1992–98 Vehicles

1. Disconnect the negative battery cable.
2. Remove the fluid reservoir.
3. Using a small prybar, pry out the pump, being careful not to damage the plastic housing.
4. Remove the one-piece seal/filter and inspect for damage or debris.
To install:
5. Insert the seal.
6. Lubricate the inside diameter of the seal with a soapy solution and insert the pump into the cavity until it is firmly seated in the seal.
7. Attach the electrical connectors and hoses and install the fluid reservoir.
8. Fill the reservoir slowly (otherwise air will be trapped in the reservoir causing it to overflow). Connect the negative battery cable.
9. Operate the washer system and check for leaks.

➡**Do not operate the pump until fluid is added to the reservoir.**

INSTRUMENTS AND SWITCHES

Instrument Cluster

REMOVAL & INSTALLATION

Conventional Cluster

▶ See Figures 94 thru 102

1. Disconnect the negative battery cable.
2. On 1989 vehicles, disconnect the speedometer cable. On 1989 Crown Victoria and Grand Marquis, remove the headlight switch knob and shaft assembly.
3. Remove the instrument cluster trim cover attaching screws and remove the trim cover.
4. Except 1992–98 Grand Marquis, remove the lower steering column cover retaining screws and remove the lower cover. On 1992–98 Grand Marquis, remove the knee bolster retaining screws and remove the knee bolster.
5. On all except 1992–98 Grand Marquis, remove the lower half of the steering column shroud.
6. Remove the screw holding the transmission range indicator column bracket to the steering column. Detach the cable loop from the pin and cane shift lever. Remove the column bracket from the column.
7. Remove the 4 cluster retaining screws. Disconnect the cluster feed plugs from the receptacle and remove the cluster assembly.
8. Installation is the reverse of the removal procedure.

Electronic Cluster

➡The electronics within the electronic instrument cluster are not serviceable. In the event of an electronic failure, the entire instru-

Fig. 94 Remove the trim screw covers on the driver's and . . .

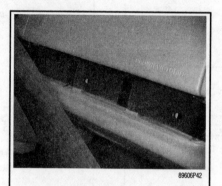

Fig. 95 . . . passenger side of the instrument cluster

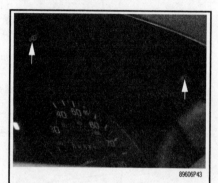

Fig. 96 Remove the upper trim panel retaining screws

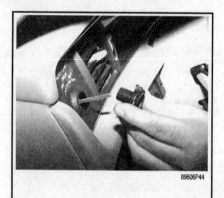

Fig. 97 Remove the headlight switch knob

Fig. 98 Detach the electrical connectors for the trim panel and remove it from the vehicle

Fig. 99 Remove the instrument cluster retaining screws from either side of the cluster

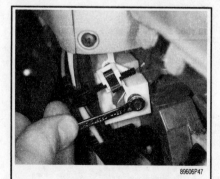

Fig. 100 Remove the transmission range indicator cable

Fig. 101 Slide the cluster out and detach the electrical connectors and . . .

Fig. 102 . . . . remove the instrument cluster from the vehicle

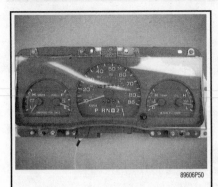

Fig. 103 The instrument cluster assembly as removed from the vehicle

Fig. 104 Remove the cluster lens and cover

Fig. 105 To remove a gauge, grasp the gauge and gently pull it straight out, such as for this temperature/oil gauge assembly

Fig. 106 The fuel/volt gauge is removed in the same manner as well as . . .

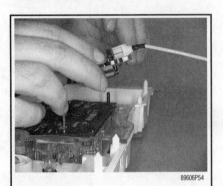

Fig. 107 . . . the transmission range indicator

Fig. 108 The speedometer/odometer assembly is also replaceable

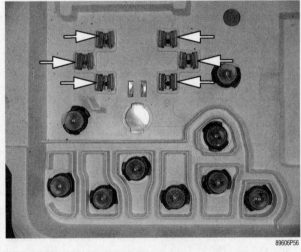

Fig. 109 When installing the gauges, make sure the prongs line up with the proper slots in the cluster assembly

ment cluster must be replaced or returned to the manufacturer for repair.

1. Disconnect the negative battery cable and set the parking brake.
2. Unsnap the center moulding on the left and right sides of the instrument panel. Remove the steering column cover and column shroud.
3. Remove the knobs from the auto dim and auto lamp switches, if equipped. Remove the 13 screws retaining the instrument panel and pull the panel out.

4. Move the shift lever to the **1** position, if required, for easier access.
5. Detach the electrical connectors from the warning lamp module, switch module and center panel switches, if equipped.
6. Remove the instrument cluster carefully so as not to scratch the cluster lens. Detach the electrical connector from the front of the cluster.
7. Disconnect the transmission range indicator assembly from the cluster by carefully bending the bottom tab down and pulling the indicator assembly forward.
8. Pull the cluster out and detach the electrical connectors on the rear of the cluster. Remove the instrument cluster.
9. Installation is the reverse of the removal procedure.

Gauges

REMOVAL & INSTALLATION

♦ **See Figures 103 thru 109**

1. Disconnect the negative battery cable.
2. Remove the instrument cluster.
3. Remove the retaining screws for the instrument cluster lens and cover assembly. Remove the cover and lens.
4. Remove the retaining screws for the gauge or warning lamp to be replaced and remove the gauge or warning lamp.
To install:
5. Place the gauge or warning lamp into place and tighten the retaining screws.
6. Install the instrument cluster lens and cover assembly.
7. Install the instrument cluster.
8. Connect the negative battery cable.

Back-up Light Switch

REMOVAL & INSTALLATION

1. Disconnect the negative battery cable.
2. Detach the back-up light switch wires at the plug connector.
3. If equipped, disconnect the 2 parking brake release vacuum hoses.
4. Remove the 2 screws retaining the back-up light switch to the steering column and lift the switch from the column.
5. Check the column to be sure the metal switch actuator is secured to the shift tube and that it is seated as far forward against the shift tube bearing as is possible. Check for a broken or damaged actuator.@INSTALL:To install:
6. Before installing a new switch to the column, make sure the drive position gauge is inserted in the drive pinning hole. If the pin is missing, align the 2 holes at the drive pinning hole on top of the switch and install a No. 43 drill bit or 0.092–0.093 in. gauge pin.
7. While holding the selector lever against the stop in the drive detent position, place the switch on the column and install the 2 retaining screws.
8. Remove the drill bit or gauge pin.
9. Attach the switch wires to the plug connector. If equipped, connect the 2 parking brake release vacuum hoses.
10. Connect the negative battery cable. Check the back-up lights for proper operation.

Headlight Switch

REMOVAL & INSTALLATION

1989 Vehicles

♦ **See Figure 110**

1. Disconnect the negative battery cable.
2. Pull the headlight switch shaft out to the headlight **ON** position.
3. From under the instrument panel, depress the headlight switch knob and shaft retainer button on the headlight switch. Hold the button in and pull the knob and shaft assembly straight out.
4. Remove the autolamp control bezel and remove the locknut.
5. From under the instrument panel, move the switch toward the front of the vehicle while tilting it downward.
6. Disconnect the wiring from the switch and remove the switch from the vehicle.
7. Installation is the reverse of removal.

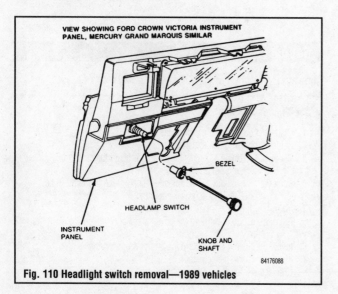

VIEW SHOWING FORD CROWN VICTORIA INSTRUMENT PANEL, MERCURY GRAND MARQUIS SIMILAR

BEZEL
HEADLAMP SWITCH
INSTRUMENT PANEL
KNOB AND SHAFT

84176088

Fig. 110 Headlight switch removal—1989 vehicles

1990–95 Vehicles

♦ **See Figure 111**

1. Disconnect the negative battery cable.
2. Remove the right and left mouldings from the instrument panel by pulling up and snapping out of the retainers.
3. Remove the screws retaining the finish panel to the instrument panel.
4. Remove the headlight switch knob from the shaft by depressing the spring, in the knob slot, with a hooked tool. Remove the finish panel.
5. Remove the 2 headlight bracket retaining screws and pull the bracket and switch from the instrument panel.
6. Remove the nut retaining the switch to the bracket.
7. Detach the electrical connector and remove the switch.
8. Installation is the reverse of removal.

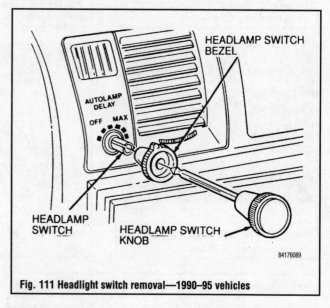

AUTOLAMP DELAY
OFF   MAX
HEADLAMP SWITCH BEZEL
HEADLAMP SWITCH
HEADLAMP SWITCH KNOB

84176089

Fig. 111 Headlight switch removal—1990–95 vehicles

1996–98 Models

1. Disconnect the negative battery cable.
2. Remove the headlight switch knob by grasping and pulling off.
3. Remove the left-hand and right-hand mouldings from the instrument panel by pulling away from the instrument panel and snapping out of the retainers.
4. Remove the radio and disconnect the clock and heated rear defrost switch.
5. Remove the screws retaining the finish panel to the instrument panel.
6. Pull the finish panel away from the instrument panel unsnapping the retainers and disconnecting wiring.
7. Detach the wiring connector, remove the retaining nut from the headlight switch bracket assembly and remove the headlight switch.
   To install:
8. Attach the wiring connector to the headlight switch, position the headlight switch into the bracket assembly and install the retaining nut. Torque the nut to 26 inch lbs. (3 Nm).
9. Reconnect the wiring to the finish panel and install the finish panel making sure all the snaps are in their proper holes.
10. Install the screws retaining the finish panel to the instrument panel and tighten securely.
11. Install the radio and connect the clock and heated rear defrost switch.
12. Install the left-hand and right-hand mouldings to the instrument panel by snapping them into their retainers.
13. Install the headlight switch knob.
14. Reconnect the negative battery cable.
15. Check for proper headlight switch operation.

LIGHTING

Headlights

REMOVAL & INSTALLATION

All 1989–91 vehicles are equipped with sealed-beam halogen headlights. All 1992–98 vehicles are equipped with aerodynamically styled headlight bodies using replaceable halogen bulbs.

❈❈ CAUTION

The halogen headlight bulb contains gas under pressure. The bulb may shatter if the glass envelope is scratched or the bulb is dropped. Handle the bulb carefully. Grasp the bulb only by its plastic base. Avoid touching the glass envelope. Keep the bulb out of the reach of children.

1989–91 VEHICLES

▶ See Figure 112

1. Remove the headlight door mounting screws and remove the headlight door.
2. Remove the 4 retainer ring screws and remove the retainer ring from the headlight.
3. Pull the headlight bulb forward and detach the wiring connector.

To install:

4. Attach the wiring connector to the headlight bulb and place the bulb in position, locating the bulb glass tabs in the positioning slots.

5. Attach the bulb retainer ring to the assembly with the retainer ring screws.
6. Install the headlight door and secure with the screws.
7. Check the headlight bulb aim and adjust as necessary.

1992–98 VEHICLES

▶ See Figures 113, 114, 115 and 116

1. Make sure the headlight switch is in the OFF position.
2. Lift the hood and remove the trim panel located above the headlight bulb.
3. Rotate the bulb counterclockwise (when viewed from the rear) about an ⅛–¼ turn.
4. Carefully remove the bulb from the socket in the reflector by gently pulling straight out of the socket. Do not rotate the bulb during removal.
5. Detach the electrical connector from the bulb.

To install:

6. Attach the electrical connector to the bulb.
7. Insert the glass envelope of the bulb into the socket while aligning the locking tabs.
8. Rotate the bulb ¼ turn.
9. Turn the headlights on and check for proper operation.

➡A properly aimed headlight normally does not need to be re-aimed after bulb installation. A burned out bulb should not be removed from the headlight reflector until just before a replacement bulb is to be installed. Removal of a bulb for an extended period of time may allow contaminants to enter the headlight body and affect the performance of the headlight. The headlight bulb should be energized only while it is contained within the headlight body.

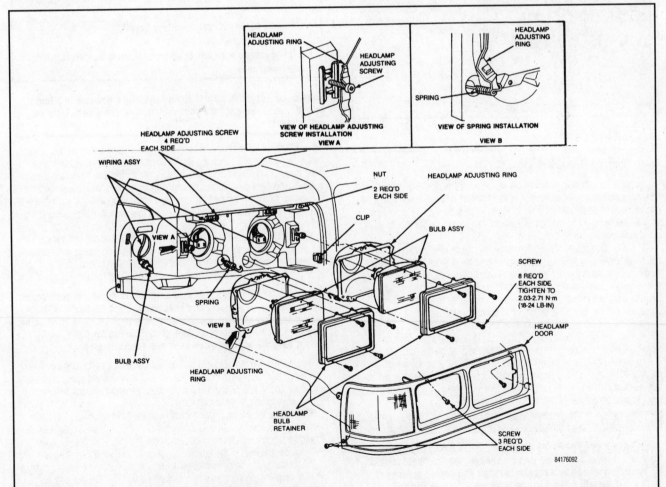

Fig. 112 Headlight and turn signal/parking light assembly—1989–91 Grand Marquis

84176092

Fig. 113 Headlight bulb in installed position

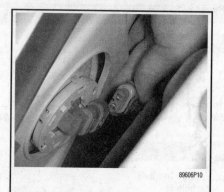

Fig. 114 Detach the electrical connector from the bulb

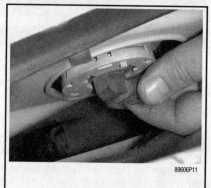

Fig. 115 Rotate the bulb ⅛–¼ turn counterclockwise to . . .

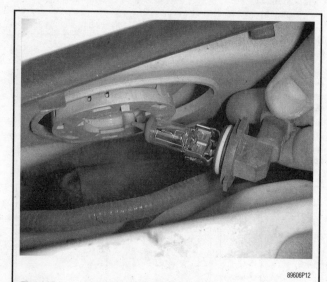

Fig. 116 . . . remove the bulb from the lens

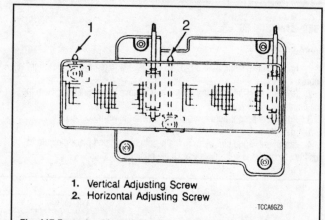

1. Vertical Adjusting Screw
2. Horizontal Adjusting Screw

Fig. 117 Example of headlight adjustment screw location for composite headlamps

AIMING THE HEADLIGHTS

▶ See Figures 117, 118 and 119

On 1989–91 vehicles, the headlights can be aimed using the adjusting screws located above and to the side of the headlight bulbs. A rough adjustment can be made while shining the headlights on a wall or on the rear of another vehicle, but headlight adjustment should really be made using proper headlight aiming equipment.

On 1992–98 vehicles, the aerodynamically styled headlights necessitate the use of headlight aiming kit 107–00003 or equivalent. The adjustable aimer adapters provided in the kit must be used to aim the headlights. Adjustment aimer adapter positions are moulded into the bottom edge of the headlight lens. Set and lock the adjustable adapters, attach each adapter to its mechanical aimer and aim the headlights according to the instructions in the kit.

Headlight aim adjustment should be made with the fuel tank approximately half full, the vehicle unloaded and the trunk empty, except for the spare tire and jacking equipment. Make sure all tires are inflated to the proper pressure.

The headlights must be properly aimed to provide the best, safest road illumination. The lights should be checked for proper aim and adjusted as necessary. Certain state and local authorities have requirements for headlight aiming; these should be checked before adjustment is made.

✳✳ CAUTION

About once a year, when the headlights are replaced or any time front end work is performed on your vehicle, the headlight should be accurately aimed by a reputable repair shop using the proper equipment. Headlights not properly aimed can make it virtually impossible to see and may blind other drivers on the road, possibly causing an accident. Note that the following procedure is a temporary fix, until you can take your vehicle to a repair shop for a proper adjustment.

Headlight adjustment may be temporarily made using a wall, as described below, or on the rear of another vehicle. When adjusted, the lights should not glare in oncoming car or truck windshields, nor should they illuminate the passenger compartment of vehicles driving in front of you. These adjustments are rough and should always be fine-tuned by a repair shop which is equipped with headlight aiming tools. Improper adjustments may be both dangerous and illegal.

For most of the vehicles covered by this manual, horizontal and vertical aiming of each sealed beam unit is provided by two adjusting screws which move the retaining ring and adjusting plate against the tension of a coil spring. There is no adjustment for focus; this is done during headlight manufacturing.

➡Because the composite headlight assembly is bolted into position, no adjustment should be necessary or possible. Some applications, however, may be bolted to an adjuster plate or may be retained by adjusting screws. If so, follow this procedure when adjusting the lights, BUT always have the adjustment checked by a reputable shop.

Before removing the headlight bulb or disturbing the headlamp in any way, note the current settings in order to ease headlight adjustment upon reassembly. If the high or low beam setting of the old lamp still works, this can be done using the wall of a garage or a building:

1. Park the vehicle on a level surface, with the fuel tank about ½ full and with the vehicle empty of all extra cargo (unless normally carried). The vehicle should be facing a wall which is no less than 6 feet (1.8m) high and 12 feet (3.7m) wide. The front of the vehicle should be about 25 feet from the wall.

2. If aiming is to be performed outdoors, it is advisable to wait until dusk in order to properly see the headlight beams on the wall. If done in a garage, darken the area around the wall as much as possible by closing shades or hanging cloth over the windows.

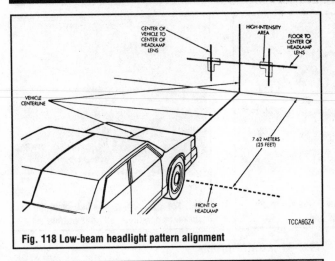

Fig. 118 Low-beam headlight pattern alignment

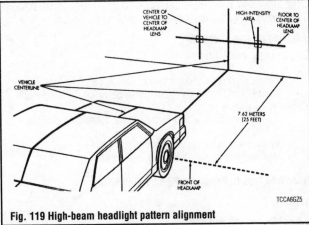

Fig. 119 High-beam headlight pattern alignment

3. Turn the headlights **ON** and mark the wall at the center of each light's low beam, then switch on the brights and mark the center of each light's high beam. A short length of masking tape which is visible from the front of the vehicle may be used. Although marking all four positions is advisable, marking one position from each light should be sufficient.

4. If neither beam on one side is working, and if another like-sized vehicle is available, park the second one in the exact spot where the vehicle was and mark the beams using the same-side light. Then switch the vehicles so the one to be aimed is back in the original spot. It must be parked no closer to or farther away from the wall than the second vehicle.

5. Perform any necessary repairs, but make sure the vehicle is not moved, or is returned to the exact spot from which the lights were marked. Turn the headlights **ON** and adjust the beams to match the marks on the wall.

6. Have the headlight adjustment checked as soon as possible by a reputable repair shop.

Signal and Marker Lights

REMOVAL & INSTALLATION

Front Turn Signal and Parking Lights

1989–91 VEHICLES

◆ See Figure 112

1. Remove the screws retaining the headlight door to the grille opening panel.

2. Pull the headlight door and turn signal/parking light assembly away from the grille opening panel.

3. Remove the turn signal/parking light bulb and socket assembly from the headlight door by rotating the socket ⅓ turn counterclockwise.

4. Remove the bulb from the socket.

5. Installation is the reverse of the removal procedure.

➡On Crown Victoria, if only bulb replacement is necessary, the bulb socket can be accessed by reaching up behind the bumper reinforcement and grille opening panel.

1992–98 CROWN VICTORIA

◆ See Figures 120, 121, 122, 123 and 124

1. Remove the headlight body as described in this Section.

2. Remove the nut and screw retaining the turn signal/parking light assembly to the fender.

3. Pull the light assembly away from the fender, rotate the socket and remove it from the light.

Fig. 120 The parking lamp assembly is retained by a Torx® headed screw

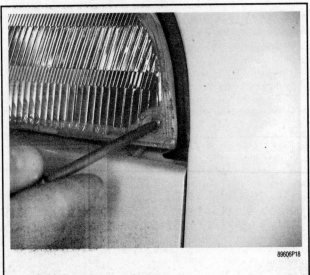

Fig. 121 Remove the retaining screw . . .

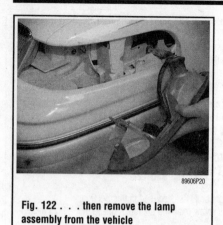

Fig. 122 . . . then remove the lamp assembly from the vehicle

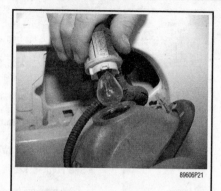

Fig. 123 Remove the bulb and connector from the lens assembly and . . .

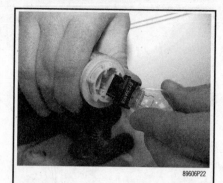

Fig. 124 . . . remove the bulb from the socket by carefully pulling it straight out

4. Remove the bulb from the socket.
5. Installation is the reverse of the removal procedure.

1992–98 GRAND MARQUIS

▶ See Figure 125

1. Remove the 2 screws retaining the turn signal/parking light assembly to the bumper cover.
2. Pull the light assembly away from the cover, rotate the socket and remove it from the light.
3. Remove the bulb from the socket.
4. Installation is the reverse of the removal procedure.

Side Marker/Cornering Lights

1989–91 VEHICLES—FRONT

▶ See Figure 126

1. If only bulb replacement is necessary, reach up behind the fender, rotate the bulb socket ⅓ turn and remove the bulb and socket assembly. Remove the bulb from the socket.
2. If the light body is to be removed, first remove the bezel retaining screws and the bezel.
3. Remove the exposed housing retaining screws and remove the housing from behind the fender. Disconnect the harness locator.
4. Installation is the reverse of the removal procedure.

1989–91 CROWN VICTORIA STATION WAGON/COUNTRY SQUIRE— REAR

1. Remove the 4 screws retaining the side marker light to the quarter panel.
2. Pull the light body away from the opening.
3. Remove the socket from the light body.
4. Remove the bulb from the socket.
5. Installation is the reverse of the removal procedure.

1992–98 CROWN VICTORIA

For side marker light removal and installation, refer to the turn signal/parking light removal and installation procedure in this Section.

1992–98 GRAND MARQUIS

▶ See Figure 127

1. Remove the headlight body as described in this Section.
2. Remove the nut and screw retaining the side marker/cornering light assembly to the fender.
3. Pull the light assembly away from the fender, rotate the socket and remove it from the light.
4. Remove the bulb from the socket.
5. Installation is the reverse of the removal procedure.

Rear Turn Signal, Brake and Parking Lights

1989–91 SEDAN

▶ See Figures 128 and 129

1. Remove the luggage compartment rear trim panel.
2. Turn the light sockets counterclockwise to the stop and remove the bulb and socket assemblies from the light assembly. Remove the bulb from the socket.
3. If the light assembly is to be removed, remove the nuts and remove the light assembly from the vehicle.
4. Installation is the reverse of the removal procedure.

1992–98 SEDAN

▶ See Figures 130 thru 138

1. Remove the screw(s) and wing nut retainers at the rear of the luggage compartment and push the trim away from the back of the light.
2. Remove the wing nuts retaining the light assembly to the vehicle and the retaining nut from either side of the luggage compartment and pull the light body assembly from the vehicle.

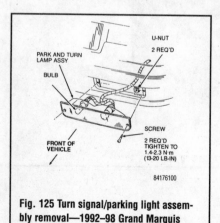

Fig. 125 Turn signal/parking light assembly removal—1992–98 Grand Marquis

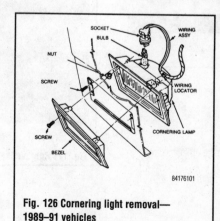

Fig. 126 Cornering light removal— 1989–91 vehicles

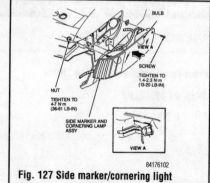

Fig. 127 Side marker/cornering light assembly removal—1992–98 Grand Marquis

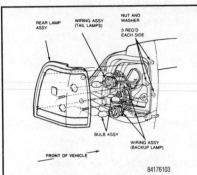

Fig. 128 Rear turn signal/brake/parking light assembly removal—1989–91 Crown Victoria sedan

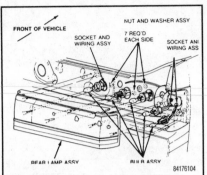

Fig. 129 Rear turn signal/brake/parking light assembly removal—1989–91 Grand Marquis sedan

Fig. 130 Push the trim away from the back of the light—1992–98 Crown Victoria

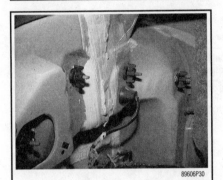

Fig. 131 The rear tailamp assembly is held by various fasteners

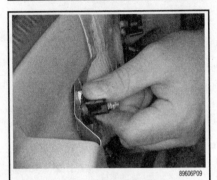

Fig. 132 Remove the wing nuts retaining the light assembly to the lower back panel—1992–98 Crown Victoria

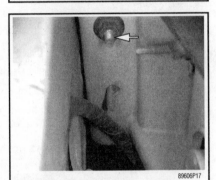

Fig. 133 Remove the nut retaining the light assembly from the side of the luggage compartment

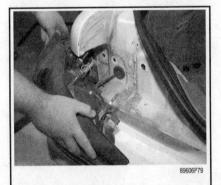

Fig. 134 Pull the light assembly away from the vehicle—1992–98 Crown Victoria

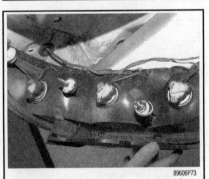

Fig. 135 The tailamp assembly contains bulbs for the brake, tailamp, and reverse lamps

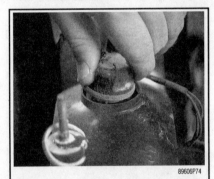

Fig. 136 Turn the bulb and socket assembly counterclockwise to remove it from the light assembly to . . .

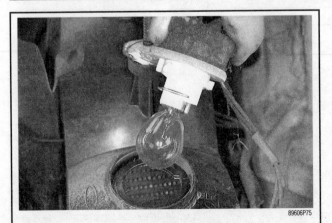

Fig. 137 . . . remove it from the lamp assembly

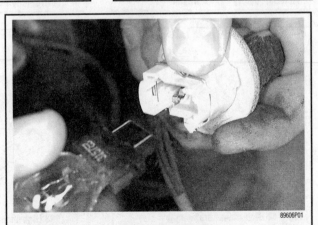

Fig. 138 Pull the bulb straight out of the socket

3. Turn the bulb socket(s) counterclockwise to the stop and remove the socket(s) from the light assembly. Remove the bulb(s) from the socket(s).

4. Installation is the reverse of the removal procedure.

STATION WAGON

♦ **See Figures 139 and 140**

1. On Crown Victoria/Country Squire, remove the screws retaining the light assembly to the quarter panel. Pull the light from the quarter panel opening, remove the light socket and remove the bulb from the socket.

2. On Grand Marquis/Colony Park, remove the quarter trim panel to gain access to the attaching nuts. Remove the nuts and the bulb sockets, then remove the light assembly from the quarter panel opening. Remove the bulb from the socket.

3. Installation is the reverse of the removal procedure.

High-Mount Brake Light

1989–92 SEDAN

♦ **See Figures 141 and 142**

1. If equipped, remove the retainer screw covers from each side of the light assembly. Remove the screws from the retainer.

2. Pull the light assembly up and forward to detach from the retainer brackets.

➡**Be careful not to move the plastic attachment brackets.**

3. On the bottom of the light body, pull the wire locator from the light body.

4. From the bottom of the light, remove the bulb and socket assembly by twisting counterclockwise.

5. Installation is the reverse of the removal procedure.

1993–98 VEHICLES

♦ **See Figures 143, 144, 145 and 146**

1. Remove the 2 screws retaining the light to the adjustable attaching brackets.

2. Lift up the light and detach the wiring connector.

3. Remove the 2 screws and adjustable attaching brackets from the replacement light. The brackets from the old light can be reused.

4. If the bulb needs to be replaced, pull the bulb out of the socket and install a new one.

5. Installation is the reverse of the removal procedure.

STATION WAGON

♦ **See Figure 147**

1. Remove the 2 screws from the light assembly.

2. Pull the light rearward and remove from the tailgate moulding.

3. Disengage the wiring harness strain relief clip by pulling straight out from the light assembly.

4. Remove the bulb and socket assembly by gently twisting and pulling straight out of the light assembly.

5. Installation is the reverse of the removal procedure.

Dome Light

♦ **See Figures 148 thru 155**

1. If equipped with standard dome light, remove the lens by squeezing it inward to release the locking tabs.

2. If equipped with combination dome/map light, remove the lens using a small thin-bladed prybar to release the locking tabs.

3. Pull the bulb from the socket.

4. Installation is the reverse of the removal procedure.

Cargo Light

STATION WAGON

♦ **See Figure 156**

1. Carefully pry the end of the lens that is furthest away from the switch down and away from the light housing.

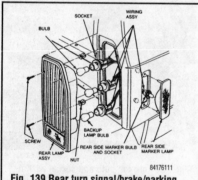

Fig. 139 Rear turn signal/brake/parking light assembly removal—Crown Victoria/Country Squire wagon

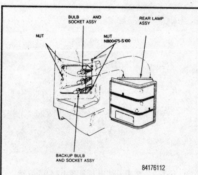

Fig. 140 Rear turn signal/brake/parking light assembly removal—Grand Marquis/Colony Park wagon

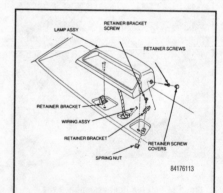

Fig. 141 High-mount brake light removal—1989–91 sedan

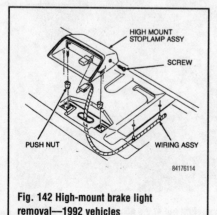

Fig. 142 High-mount brake light removal—1992 vehicles

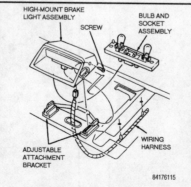

Fig. 143 High-mount brake light removal—1993–98 vehicles

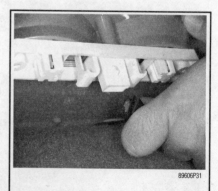

Fig. 144 Detach the connector for the high mount brake lamp

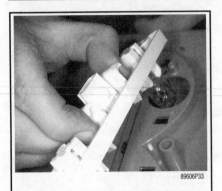

Fig. 145 Remove the lamp assembly from the lens

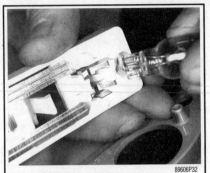

Fig. 146 Remove the bulb by gently pulling it straight out of the lamp assembly

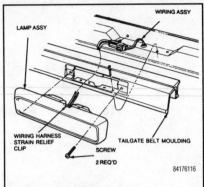

Fig. 147 High-mount brake light removal—station wagon

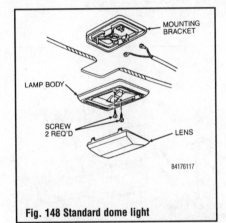

Fig. 148 Standard dome light

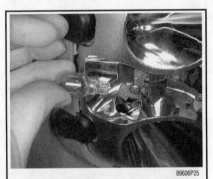

Fig. 149 Combination dome/map light—1992–98 vehicles

Fig. 150 Carefully pry the dome/map lamp lens and . . .

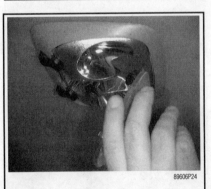

Fig. 151 . . . remove the lens from the lamp

Fig. 152 Grasp the dome light bulb and pull it straight out to remove it from the vehicle

Fig. 153 Remove the retaining screws to lower the lamp and access the map lamp bulbs

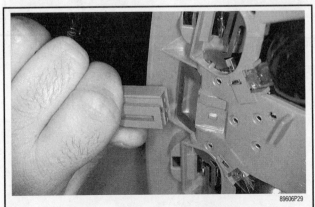

Fig. 154 Detach the connector for the lamp assembly

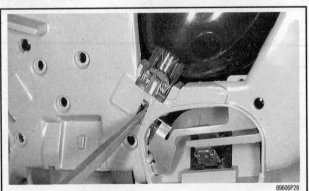

Fig. 155 A small screwdriver may be needed to remove the bulbs from the lamp assembly

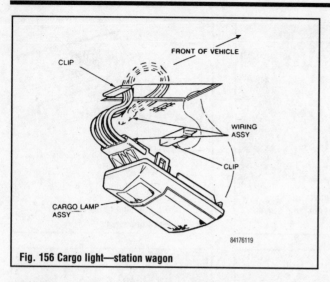

Fig. 156 Cargo light—station wagon

2. Pull the bulb from its socket.
3. Installation is the reverse of the removal procedure.

License Plate Lights

♦ See Figures 157, 158, 159, 160 and 161

1. On 1989–91 sedan, raise the trunk lid. With the trunk lid open, twist the light socket approximately ⅛ turn counterclockwise and pull the socket and bulb assembly from the light housing.

2. On 1989–91 station wagon, remove the 2 screws retaining the light assembly to the tailgate. Pull the light assembly from the tailgate, grasp and twist the light socket approximately ⅛ turn counterclockwise and pull the socket and bulb assembly from the light housing.

3. On 1992–98 vehicles, use a Phillips head screwdriver to remove the 2 plastic rivets retaining the light assembly to the rear bumper. With a small pry-bar, remove the rivet retainer and pull the light assembly from the bumper. Grasp and twist the light socket approximately ⅛ turn counterclockwise and pull the socket and bulb assembly from the light housing.

4. Installation is the reverse of the removal procedure.

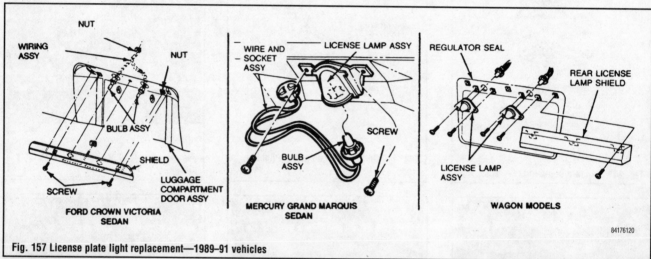

Fig. 157 License plate light replacement—1989–91 vehicles

Fig. 158 Use a Phillips head screwdriver to remove the 2 plastic rivets retaining the light assembly to the rear bumper

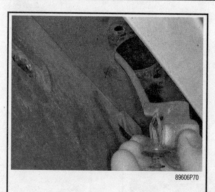

Fig. 159 Lower the lamp assembly and . . .

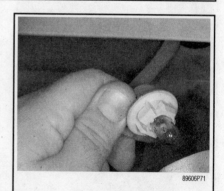

Fig. 160 . . . remove the connector and bulb

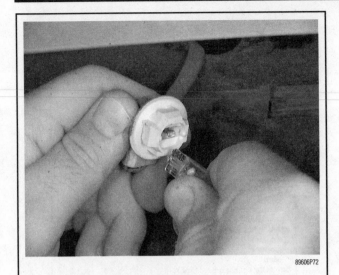

Fig. 161 Pull the bulb straight out to remove it from the socket

Function	Trade number
Exterior lights	
Rear	
Tail lamp, brakelamp, turn lamp (sedan)	3157
Tail lamp (sedan)	916
Side marker (sedan)	194
Front	
Parklamp, turnlamp, side marker	2357A
Backup lamp (sedan)	3156
Backup lamp (wagon)	1156
Cornering lamp	3156
License plate lamp	168
High-mounted brakelamp (sedan)	912
High-mounted brakelamp (wagon)	922
Headlamps (hi & lo)	H4656
Headlamps (high beam)	H4651
Interior lights	
Luggage compartment lamp	98
Cargo lamp (wagon)	906
Dome lamp	906
Dome/map lamp (opt.)	
Dome	561
Map	105
Courtesy lamp	89
Courtesy lamp (c-pillar)	105
Door courtesy lamp	906
Visor vanity lamp	194
Coach lamp (opt.)	161
Engine compartment lamp (opt.)	912
Instrument panel lights	
Glove box	194
High beam indicator	194
I/P ashtray lamp	161
Radio illumination	•
Turn signal indicator	194
Warning lights (all)	194
"PRN Ⓓ D1" bulb	194
Heater or heater — A/C	161
Gauge illumination lamps	194

• Refer bulb replacement to a Ford authorized radio service center.

89606G01

1989–90 Grand Marquis light bulb application chart

Function	Trade number
Exterior lights	
Rear	
Tail lamp, stoplamp, turn lamp (sedan)	3157
Tail lamp, stoplamp, turn lamp (wagon)	1157
Side marker	194
Front	
Parklamp, turn lamp	3157
Side marker	916
Parklamp only	916
Backup lamp (sedan)	3156
Backup lamp (wagon)	1156
Cornering lamp	3156
License plate lamp (sedan)	194
License plate lamp (wagon)	168
High-mounted brakelamp (opt.)	912
Headlamps (hi and lo)	H4656
Headlamps (high beam)	H4651
Interior lights	
Luggage compartment lamp	912
Cargo lamp (wagon)	906
Dome lamp	561
Dome/map lamp (opt.)	
Dome	561
Map	105
Visor vanity lamp (opt.)	168
Engine compartment lamp (opt.)	912
Instrument panel lights	
Glove box	194
High beam indicator	194
I/P ashtray lamp	161
Radio illumination	•
Turn signal indicator	194
Warning lights (all)	194
"PRN Ⓓ D1" bulb	194
Heater or heater — A/C	161
Parking brakelamp (opt.)	194
Rear window defroster lamp (opt.)	2162
Instrument illumination lamp	194

• Refer bulb replacement to a Ford authorized radio service center.

89606G07

1989–91 Crown Victoria light bulb application chart

Function	Trade number
Exterior lights	
Rear	
Tail lamp, brakelamp, turn lamp	3157
Tail lamp (sedan)	916
Side marker (sedan)	194
Front	
Parklamp, turnlamp, side marker	2357A
Backup lamp	3156
Cornering lamp	3156
License plate lamp	168
High-mounted brakelamp	912
Headlamps (hi & lo)	H4656
Headlamps (high beam)	H4651
Interior lights	
Luggage compartment lamp	98
Cargo lamp (wagon)	906
Dome lamp	906
Dome/map lamp (opt.)	
Dome	561
Map	105
Courtesy lamp	89
Courtesy lamp (c-pillar)	105
Door courtesy lamp	906
Visor vanity lamp	194
Coach lamp (opt.)	161
Engine compartment lamp (opt.)	912
Instrument panel lights	
Glove box	194
High beam indicator	194
I/P ashtray lamp	161
Radio illumination	•
Turn signal indicator	194
Warning lights (all)	194
"PRN Ⓓ D1" bulb	194
Heater or heater — A/C	161
Gauge illumination lamps	194

• Refer bulb replacement to a Ford authorized radio service center.

89606G02

1991 Grand Marquis light bulb application chart

Function	Trade number
Exterior lights front	
Headlamps lo beam	9006
Headlamps hi beam	9005
Parklamp, turnlamp and side marker	3157NA*
Cornering lamp (opt.)	3156
Exterior lights rear	
Tail, stop, turn and side marker	3157
Backup lamp	921
License plate lamp	194
High-mounted brakelamp	912
Interior lights	
Luggage compartment lamp	904
Engine compartment lamp	906
Dome lamp	906
Dome/map lamp (opt.)	
Dome	906
Map	168
Sun visor lighted mirror (opt.)	194
Front door courtesy lamp	904
Visor vanity lamp	168
Dual floorwell lamps	906
Instrument panel	
Glove compartment	194
Ashtray lamp	161
Radio illumination	**
Cluster — standard	
Warning lamps	194
Illumination	194
Cluster — electronic	***
PRN(D)D1	***

*NA means Natural Amber
** Refer bulb replacement to a Ford authorized radio service center.
*** Refer bulb replacement to a Ford or Lincoln-Mercury dealer.

89606G08

1992 Crown Victoria light bulb application chart

Function	Trade number
Exterior lights front	
Headlamps lo beam	9006
Headlamps hi beam	9005
Parklamp and turnlamp	3157NA*
Park	916NA*
Side marker	194NA*
Cornering lamp (opt.)	3156
Exterior lights rear	
Tail, stop and turn	3157
Side marker	194
Backup lamp	3156
License plate lamp	194
High-mounted brakelamp	912
Interior lights	
Luggage compartment lamp	906
Engine compartment lamp	906
Dome lamp	906
Reading lamp rear (opt.)	211-2
Dome/map lamp (opt.)	
Dome	906
Map	168
Sun visor lighted mirror (opt.)	194
Front door courtesy lamp	904
Visor vanity lamp	168
Dual floorwell lamps	906
Instrument panel	
Glove compartment	168
Radio illumination	**
Cluster — standard	
Warning lamps	194
Illumination	194
Cluster — electronic	***
PRN(D)D1	***

* NA means Natural Amber
** Refer bulb replacement to a Ford authorized radio service center.
*** Refer bulb replacement to a Ford or Lincoln-Mercury dealer.

89606G09

1993–95 Crown Victoria light bulb application chart

Function	Trade number
Exterior lights front	
Headlamps lo beam	9006
Headlamps hi beam	9005
Parklamp and turnlamp	3157NA*
Park	916NA*
Side marker	194NA*
Cornering lamp (opt.)	3156
Exterior lights rear	
Tail, stop and turn	3157
Side marker	194
Backup lamp	3156
License plate lamp	194
High-mounted brakelamp	912
Interior lights	
Luggage compartment lamp	906
Engine compartment lamp	906
Dome lamp	906
Reading lamp rear (opt.)	211-2
Dome/map lamp (opt.)	
Dome	906
Map	168
Sun visor lighted mirror (opt.)	194
Front door courtesy lamp	904
Visor vanity lamp	168
Dual floorwell lamps	906
Instrument panel	
Glove compartment	168
Radio illumination	**
Cluster — standard	
Warning lamps	194
Illumination	194
Cluster — electronic	***
PRN(D)D1	***

* NA means Natural Amber
** Refer bulb replacement to a Ford authorized radio service center.
*** Refer bulb replacement to a Ford or Lincoln-Mercury dealer.

89606G03

1992–95 Grand Marquis light bulb application chart

Function	Trade number
Exterior lights front	
Headlamps lo beam	9006
Headlamps hi beam	9005
Parklamp, turnlamp and side marker	3157NAK*
Cornering lamp (opt.)	3156K
Exterior lights rear	
Tail, stop, turn and side marker	3157K
Backup lamp	3156K
License plate lamp	168
High-mounted brakelamp	912
Interior lights	
Luggage compartment lamp	906
Dome lamp	906
Dome/map lamp (opt.)	
Dome	906
Map	168
Sun visor lighted mirror (opt.)	194
Front door courtesy lamp	904
Visor vanity lamp	168
Dual floorwell lamps	906
Instrument panel	
Glove compartment	194
Radio illumination	**
Cluster — standard	
Warning lamps	194
Illumination	194
Cluster — electronic	***
PRN(D)21	***

* NA means Natural Amber
** Refer bulb replacement to a Ford authorized radio service center.
*** Refer bulb replacement to a Ford or Lincoln-Mercury dealer.

89606G10

1996 Crown Victoria light bulb application chart

Function	Trade number
Exterior lights front	
Headlamps lo beam	9006
Headlamps hi beam	9005
Parklamp and turnlamp	3457NAK*
Side marker	194NA*
Cornering lamp (opt.)	3156K
Exterior lights rear	
Tail, stop and turn	3157K
Side marker	194
Backup lamp	3156
License plate lamp	168
High-mounted brakelamp	912
Interior lights	
Luggage compartment lamp	212-2
Dome lamp	906
Reading lamp rear (opt.)	211-2
Dome/map lamp (opt.)	
Dome	906
Map	168
Sun visor lighted mirror (opt.)	194
Front door courtesy lamp	194
Visor vanity lamp	168
Dual floorwell lamps	906
Instrument panel	
Glove compartment	168
Radio illumination	**
Cluster — standard	
Warning lamps	194
Illumination	194
Cluster — electronic	***
PRN(D)D1	***

* NA means Natural Amber
** Refer bulb replacement to a Ford authorized radio service center.
*** Refer bulb replacement to a Ford or Lincoln-Mercury dealer.

89606G04

1996 Grand Marquis light bulb application chart

Function	Trade number
Exterior lights front	
Headlamps lo beam	9006
Headlamps hi beam	9005
Parklamp, turnlamp and side marker	3157NAK*
Cornering lamp (opt.)	3156K
Exterior lights rear	
Tail, stop, turn and side marker	3157K
Backup lamp	3156K
License plate lamp	168
High-mounted brakelamp	912
Interior lights	
Luggage compartment lamp	906
Dome lamp	906
Dome/map lamp (opt.)	
Dome	906
Map	168
Sun visor lighted mirror (opt.)	194
Visor vanity lamp	168
Dual floorwell lamps	906
Instrument panel	
Glove compartment	194
Radio illumination	**
Cluster — standard	
Warning lamps	194
Illumination	194
Cluster — electronic	***
PRN(D)21	***

* NA means Natural Amber
**Refer bulb replacement to a Ford authorized radio service center.
***Refer bulb replacement to a Ford or Lincoln-Mercury dealer.

89606G05

1997 Grand Marquis light bulb application chart

Function	Trade number
Exterior lights front	
Headlamps lo beam	9006
Headlamps hi beam	9005
Parklamp and turnlamp	3457NAK*
Side marker	194NA*
Cornering lamp (opt.)	3156K
Exterior lights rear	
Tail, stop and turn	3157K
Side marker	194
Backup lamp	3156
License plate lamp	168
High-mounted brakelamp	912
Interior lights	
Luggage compartment lamp	212-2
Dome lamp	906
Reading lamp rear (opt.)	211-2
Dome/map lamp (opt.)	
Dome	906
Map	168
Sun visor lighted mirror (opt.)	194
Visor vanity lamp	168
Dual floorwell lamps	906
Instrument panel	
Glove compartment	168
Radio illumination	**
Cluster — standard	
Warning lamps	194
Illumination	194
Cluster — electronic	***
PRN(D)D1	***

* NA means Natural Amber
** Refer bulb replacement to a Ford authorized radio service center.
*** Refer bulb replacement to a Ford or Lincoln-Mercury dealer.

89606G11

1997 Crown Victoria light bulb application chart

Function	Trade Number
Headlamp (low beam)	9006
Headlamp (high beam)	9005
Park lamp and turn lamp (front)	3457 NAK
Side marker (front)	194 NA
Cornering lamp (front)	3156 K
Tail, stop, turn (rear)	3157 K
Side marker (rear)	194
Backup lamp	3156
License plate lamp	168
High-mount brakelamp	912
Luggage compartment lamp	212-2
Dome lamp	906
Rear reading lamp	211-2
Map lamp	168
Illuminated visor mirror	168
Dual floorwell lamp	906
Glove compartment	168
To replace all instrument panel lights - see your dealer.	

89606G06

1998 Grand Marquis/Crown Victoria light bulb application chart

CIRCUIT PROTECTION

Fuses

All vehicles are equipped with a fuse panel located on the left side of the lower instrument panel. In addition, 1992–98 vehicles are equipped with a combination fuse/relay panel called the "power distribution box" which is located in the right front of the engine compartment.

REPLACEMENT

▶ **See Figures 162 thru 168**

1. Locate the fuse panel and remove the cover, if necessary.
2. Look through the clear side of the fuse in question, to see if the metal wire inside is separated. If the wire is separated, the fuse is blown and must be replaced.

3. Remove the fuse by pulling it from its cavity; no special tools are required.
4. Replace the blown fuse only with one having the same amp rating for that particular circuit. Push the fuse straight in until the fuse seats fully in the cavity.

Fusible Links

▶ **See Figure 169**

Fuse links are used to protect the main wiring harness and selected branches from complete burn-out, should a short circuit or electrical overload occur. A fuse link is a short length of insulated wire, integral with the engine compartment wiring harness. It is several wire gauges smaller than the circuit it protects and generally located in-line directly from the positive terminal of the battery.

Fig. 162 The interior fuse box is located underneath the driver's side of the instrument panel

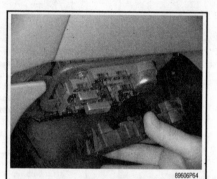

Fig. 163 Remove the fuse box cover by grasping it and gently pulling it straight out

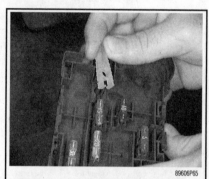

Fig. 164 Typically there is a fuse removal tool and spare fuses on the underside of the cover

Fig. 165 Use the removal tool to grasp the fuse and . . .

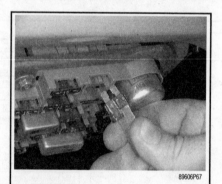

Fig. 166 . . . remove the fuse from the fusebox

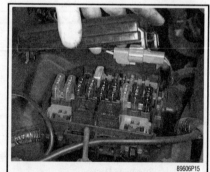

Fig. 167 The engine fuse box (power distribution box) is located in the engine compartment

Fig. 168 Grasp the fuse and pull it straight out to remove fuses from the engine fuse box

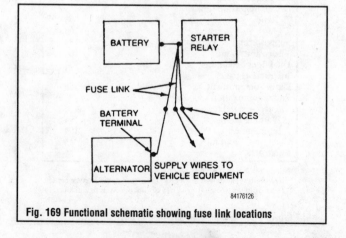

Fig. 169 Functional schematic showing fuse link locations

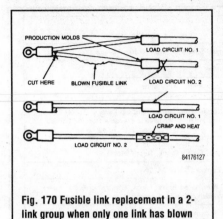

Fig. 170 Fusible link replacement in a 2-link group when only one link has blown

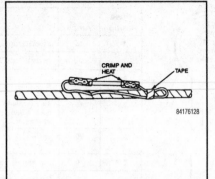

Fig. 171 Fusible link replacement in a single circuit

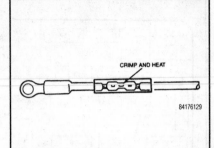

Fig. 172 Fusible link repair using the eyelet terminal fuse link of the specified gauge for attachment to a circuit wire end.

Production fuse links are color coded as follows:
- Gray: 12 gauge
- Dark Green: 14 gauge
- Black: 16 gauge
- Brown: 18 gauge
- Dark Blue: 20 gauge

When a heavy current flows, such as when a booster battery is connected incorrectly or when a short to ground occurs in the wiring harness, the fuse link burns out and protects the alternator or wiring.

A burned out fuse link may have bare wire ends protruding from the insulation, or it may have only expanded or bubbled insulation with illegible identification. When it is hard to determine if the fuse link is burned out, perform the continuity test:

1. Make sure the battery is okay, then turn on the headlights or an accessory. If the headlights or accessory do not work, the fuse link is probably burned out.

2. If equipped with more than one fuse link, use the same procedure as in Step 1 to test each link separately.

3. To test the fuse link that protects the alternator, make sure the battery is okay, then check with a voltmeter for voltage at the BAT terminal of the alternator. No voltage indicates that the fuse link is probably burned out.

REPLACEMENT

♦ See Figures 170, 171 and 172

When replacing a fuse link, always make sure the replacement fuse link is a duplicate of the one removed with respect to gauge, length and insulation. Original equipment and original equipment specification replacement fuse links have insulation that is flame proof. Do not fabricate a fuse link from ordinary wire because the insulation may not be flame proof.

If a circuit protected by a fuse link becomes inoperative, inspect for a blown fuse link. If the fuse link wire insulation is burned or opened, disconnect the feed as close as possible behind the splice in the harness. If the damaged fuse link is between 2 splices (weld points in the harness), cut out the damaged portion as close as possible to the weld points.

Replace the fuse link as follows:

1. To service a 2-link group when only one link has blown and the other link is not damaged, proceed as follows:

a. Disconnect the negative battery cable.

b. Cut out the blown fusible link (2 places).

c. Position the correct eyelet type service fusible link with the bare end to the correct size wire connector and crimp to the wire ends.

d. Heat the splice insulation until the tubing shrinks and adhesive flows from each end of the connector.

e. Connect the negative battery cable.

2. To service a fuse link in a multi-feed or single circuit, proceed as follows:

a. Disconnect the negative battery cable.

b. Determine which circuit is damaged, its location and the cause of the open fuse link. If the damaged fuse link is one of 3 fed by a common number 10 or 12 gauge feed wire, determine the specific affected circuit.

c. Cut the damaged fuse link from the wiring harness and discard. If the fuse link is one of 3 circuits fed by a single feed wire, cut it out of the harness at each splice end and discard.

d. Obtain the proper fuse link and butt connectors for attaching the fuse link to the harness.

e. Strip ⁵⁄₁₆in. (7.6mm) of insulation from the wire ends and insert into the proper size wire connector. Crimp and heat the splice insulation until the tubing shrinks and adhesive flows from each end of the connector.

f. To replace a fuse link on a single circuit in a harness, cut out the damaged portion. Strip approximately ½ in. (12.7mm) of insulation from the 2 wire ends and attach the correct size fuse link to each wire end with the proper gauge wire connectors. Crimp and heat the splice insulation until the tubing shrinks and adhesive flows from each end of the connector.

g. Connect the negative battery cable.

3. To service a fuse link with an eyelet terminal on one end, such as the charging circuit, proceed as follows:

a. Disconnect the negative battery cable.

b. Cut off the fuse link behind the weld, strip approximately ½ in. (12.7mm) of insulation from the cut end, and attach the appropriate new eyelet fuse link to the cut stripped wire with the proper size connector.

c. Crimp and heat the splice insulation until the tubing shrinks and adhesive flows from each end of the connector.

d. Connect the negative battery cable.

➡ **Do not mistake a resistor wire for a fuse link. The resistor wire is generally longer and has print stating "Resistor—do not cut or splice."When attaching a No. 16, 18 or 20 gauge fuse link to a heavy gauge wire, always double the stripped wire end of the fuse link before inserting and crimping it into the wire connector for positive wire retention.**

Circuit Breakers

Circuit breakers are located inside the fuse panel. They are automatically reset when the problem corrects itself, is repaired, or the circuit cools down to allow operation again.

Flashers

REPLACEMENT

The turn signal and emergency flashers are attached to the interior fuse panel. They are replaced in the same manner as the fuses and circuit breakers.

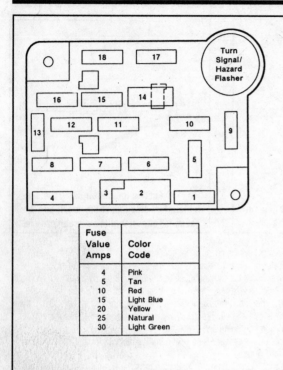

Fuse Position	Amps	Circuits Protected
1	15	Stop/Hazard Lamps, Speed Control, Trailer Towing
2	8.25 c.b.	Interval Wiper/Washer
4	15	Exterior Lamps, Instrument Illumination, Trailer Towing Relays, Automatic Headlamps (Autolamp)
5	15	Air Conditioning Clutch, Turn Lamps, Backup Lamps, Trailer Circuits, Load Leveling, Heated Windshield, Daytime Running Lamps, Air Bag Module
6	20	Speed Control, Trunk Lid Release, Police Circuits, Illuminated Entry, Power Window Relay, Digital Clock, Rear Defrost
7	10	Daytime Running Lamps (CANADA ONLY)
8	10	Courtesy Lamps, Illuminated Entry, Clock, Electronic Radio, Power Mirrors, Heated Windshield, ATC Control
9	30	A/C Blower, ATC Blower
10	20	Passing Beam, Daytime Running Lamps
11	15	Radio, Power Antenna, Premium Sound
12	30 c.b.	Rear Lighters, Tailgate Window Key Switch, Door Locks, Power Seats
13	5	Instrument Illumination
14	20 c.b.	Power Windows
15	—	Not Used
16	20	Cigar Lighter, Horn
17	15	Air Bag Restraint System
18	10	Warning Indicators, Seat Belt Warning, Automatic Headlamps/Delayed Exit (Autolamp), Carburetor Circuits, Dual Warning Buzzer, Thermactor Dump Timer and Relay

89606G12

1989–90 models fuse box locations

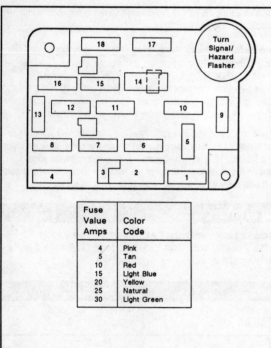

Fuse Position	Amps	Circuits Protected
1	15	Turn/Stop/Hazard Lamps, Speed Control
2	8.25 c.b.	Interval Wiper/Washer
3	—	Not Used
4	15	Exterior Lamps, Instrument Illumination, Trailer Towing Relays, Automatic Headlamps/Delayed Exit (Autolamp), Digital Clock
5	15	Air Conditioning Clutch, Turn Lamps, Backup Lamps, Trailer Circuits, Load Leveling, Heated Windshield, Daytime Running Lamps, Air Bag Module
6	20	Speed Control, Trunk Lid Release, Police Circuits, Illuminated Entry, Power Window Relay, Digital Clock, Rear Defrost
7	10	Daytime Running Lamps (CANADA ONLY)
8	10	Courtesy Lamps, Illuminated Entry, Clock, Electronic Radio, Power Mirrors, Heated Windshield, ATC Control
9	30	A/C Blower, ATC Blower
10	20	Passing Beam, Daytime Running Lamps
11	15	Radio, Power Antenna, Premium Sound
12	30 c.b.	Rear Lighters, Tailgate Window Key Switch, Door Locks, Power Seats
13	5	Instrument Illumination
14	20 c.b.	Power Windows
15	—	Not Used
16	20	Cigar Lighters, Horn
17	15	Air Bag Restraint System
18	10	Warning Indicators, Automatic Headlamps/Delayed Exit (Autolamp), Carburetor Circuits, Thermactor Dump Timer and Relay, Warning Chime

89606G13

1991 model fuse box locations

* WITH POLICE

ENGINE COMPARTMENT FUSE BOX

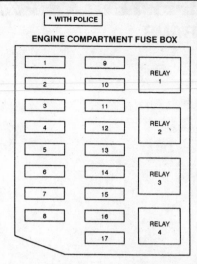

MAXI−FUSE	AMPS	CIRCUITS PROTECTED
8	30	Air Suspension System
9	50	See Fuses 5 and 9
10	50	See Fuses 1, 2, 6, 7, 10, 11 & 13 and Circuit Breaker 14
11	40	See Fuses 4, 8, 16 and Circuit Breaker 12
12	30	PCM Power Relay, PCM, Natural Gas Vehicle Module
13	50	High Speed Cooling Fan Relay
14	40	Rear Window Defrost Relay, Also see Fuse 17
15	50	Anti−Lock Brake Module
*16	50	Police Option Fuse Holder
FUSE	**AMPS**	**CIRCUITS PROTECTED**
1	20	Electric Fuel Pump Relay
2	30	Starter Relay, Generator, and Fuses 15 & 18
3	25	Radio, Subwoofer Amplifier, and CD Changer
*4	30	Police Power Relay
5	15	Horn Relay
6	20	DRL Module
CIRCUIT BREAKER	**AMPS**	**CIRCUITS PROTECTED**
7	20	Power Door Locks, Power Seats, and Trunk Lid Release
17	30	Low Speed Cooling Fan Relay

RELAY NUMBER	NAME
1	Rear Defrost Relay
2	Horn Relay
3	Cooling Fan Relay
4	Air Suspension Pump Relay
*4	Police Power Relay

89606G18

1998 model engine fuse box locations

INSTRUMENT PANEL FUSE PANEL

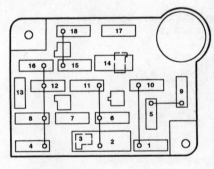

FUSE	AMPS	CIRCUITS PROTECTED
1	15	Multi−Function Switch, BPP Switch, Speed Control
2	30	Wiper Control Module, Windshield Wiper Motor
3	—	NOT USED
4	15	Lighting Control Module (LCM), Main Light Switch
5	15	Backup Lamps, Variable Assist Power Steering (VAPS), Turn Signals, Air Suspension, Daytime Running Lamps (DRL), Speed Chime Warning, Electronic Day/Night Mirror, Shift Lock, EATC
6	15	Speed Control, Main Light Switch, Lighting Control Module (LCM), Clock, Police Power Relay
7	25	Powertrain Control Module (PCM) Power Diode, Ignition Coils
8	15	Lighting Control Module (LCM), Power Mirrors, Keyless Entry, Clock Memory, PATS Module, EATC, Power Windows, Police Spot Lamps
9	30	Blower Motor, A/C−Heater Mode Switch
10	10	Air Bag Module
11	5	Radio
12	18 c.b.	Lighting Control Module (LCM), Flash−to−Pass, Main Light Switch
13	15	Warning Lamps, Analog Cluster Gauges and Indicators, EATC, Lighting Control Module (LCM)
14	20 c.b.	Window/Door Lock Control, Driver's Door Module, One Touch Down
15	10	ABS, Instrument Cluster, Transmission Control Switch
16	20	Cigar Lighter
17	10	Rear Defrost
18	10	Air Bag Module

89606G19

1998 model interior fuse box locations

WIRING DIAGRAMS

INDEX OF WIRING DIAGRAMS

89606W01

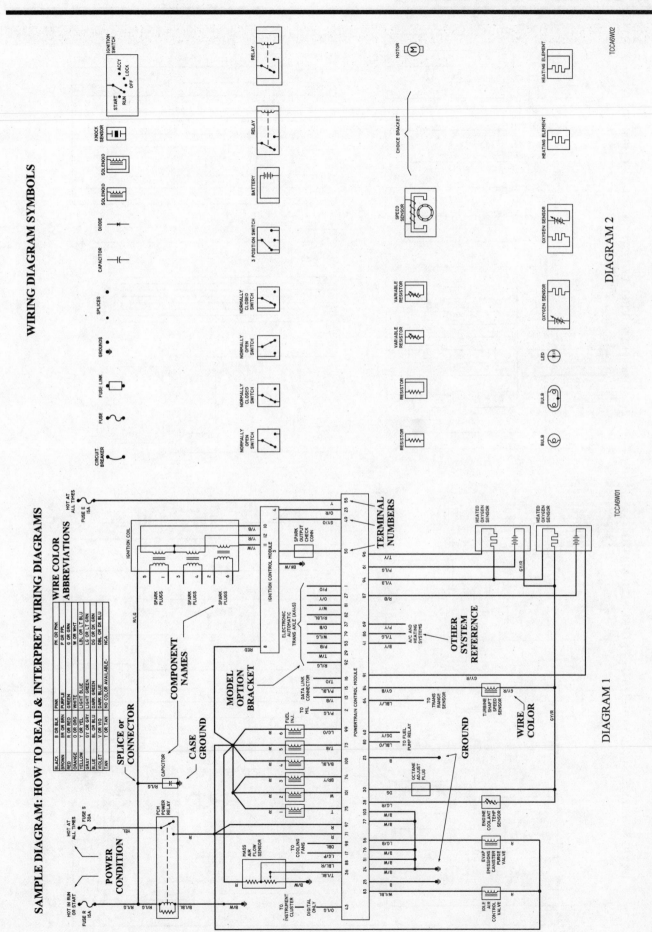

WIRING DIAGRAM SYMBOLS

DIAGRAM 2

SAMPLE DIAGRAM: HOW TO READ & INTERPRET WIRING DIAGRAMS

DIAGRAM 1

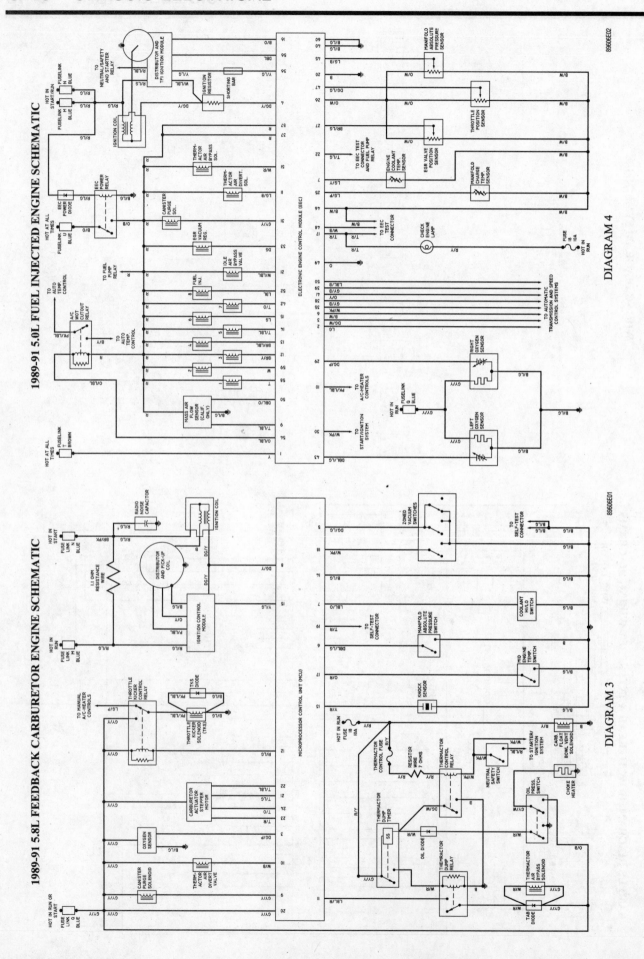

1989-91 5.0L FUEL INJECTED ENGINE SCHEMATIC

DIAGRAM 4

1989-91 5.8L FEEDBACK CARBURETOR ENGINE SCHEMATIC

DIAGRAM 3

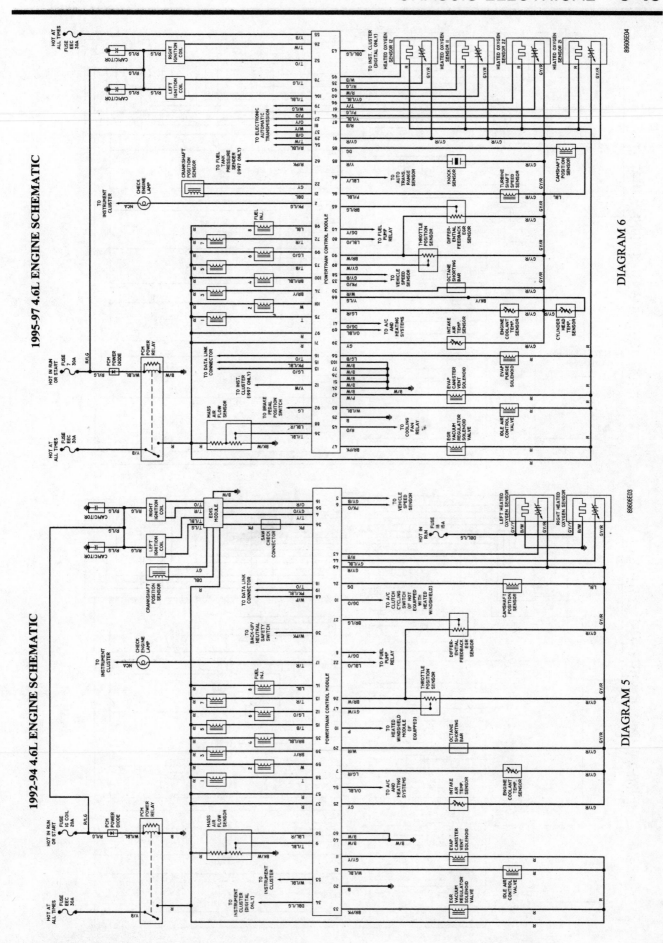

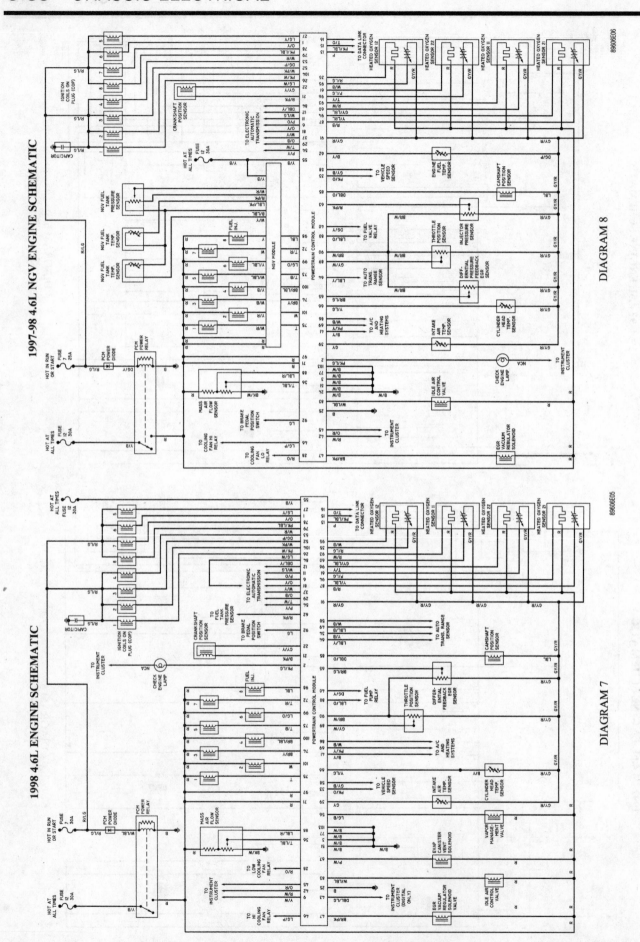

1997-98 4.6L NGV ENGINE SCHEMATIC

DIAGRAM 8

1998 4.6L ENGINE SCHEMATIC

DIAGRAM 7

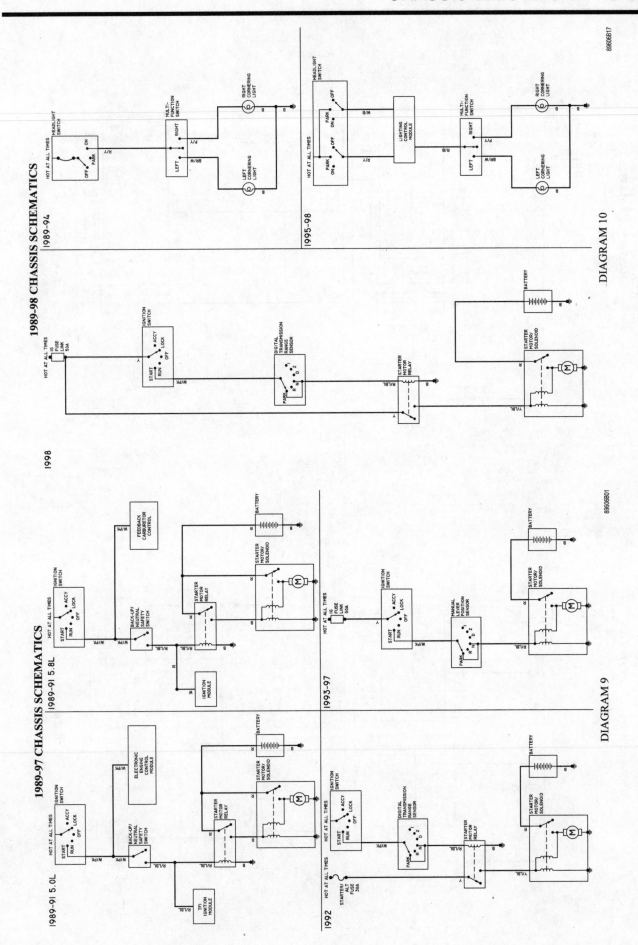

DIAGRAM 10

DIAGRAM 9

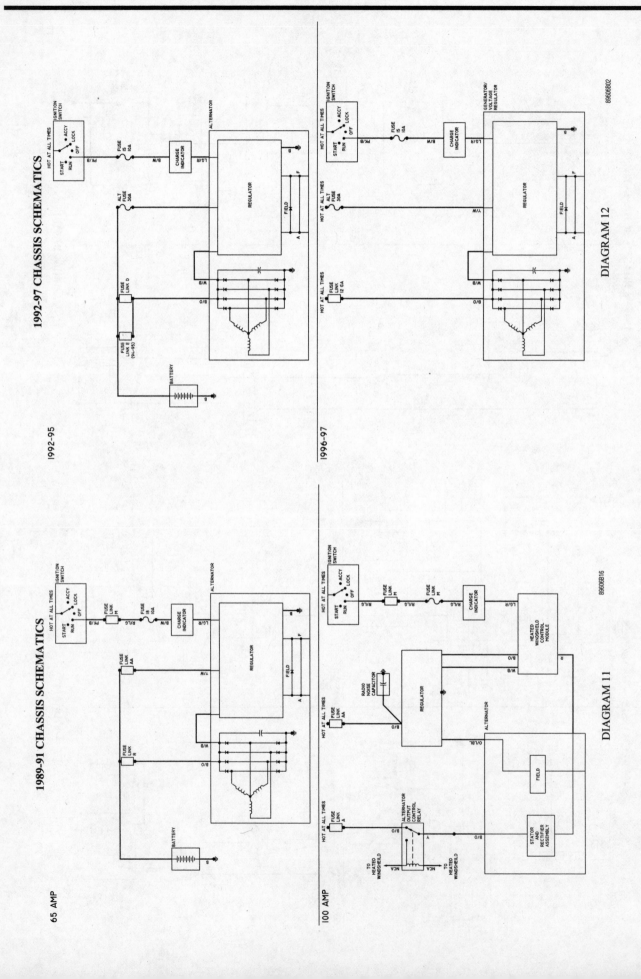

1992-97 CHASSIS SCHEMATICS

1992-95

65 AMP

1989-91 CHASSIS SCHEMATICS

100 AMP

1996-97

DIAGRAM 12

DIAGRAM 11

89606B02

89606B16

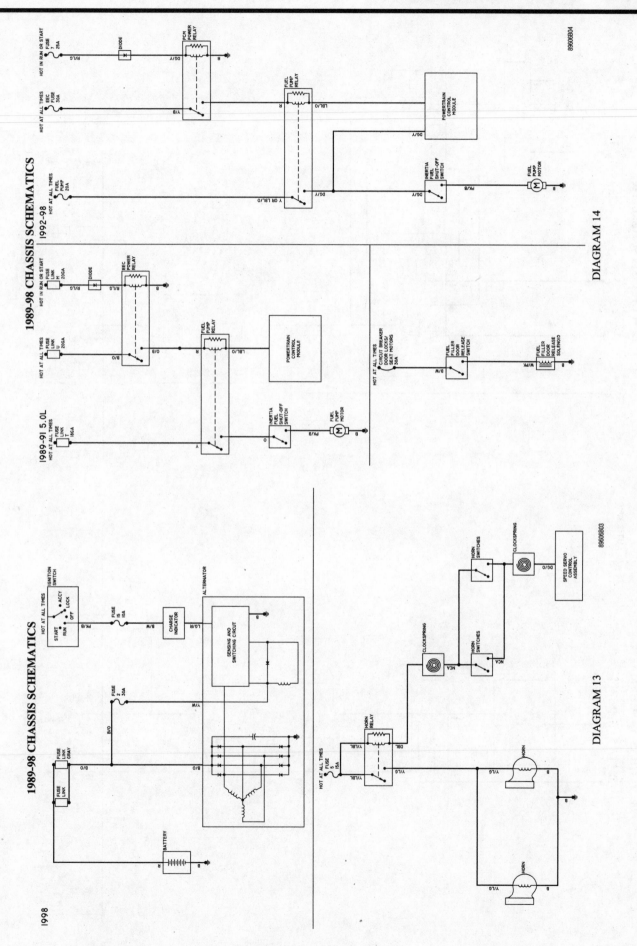

1989-98 CHASSIS SCHEMATICS

1992-98

DIAGRAM 14

1989-91 5.0L

1989-98 CHASSIS SCHEMATICS

1998

DIAGRAM 13

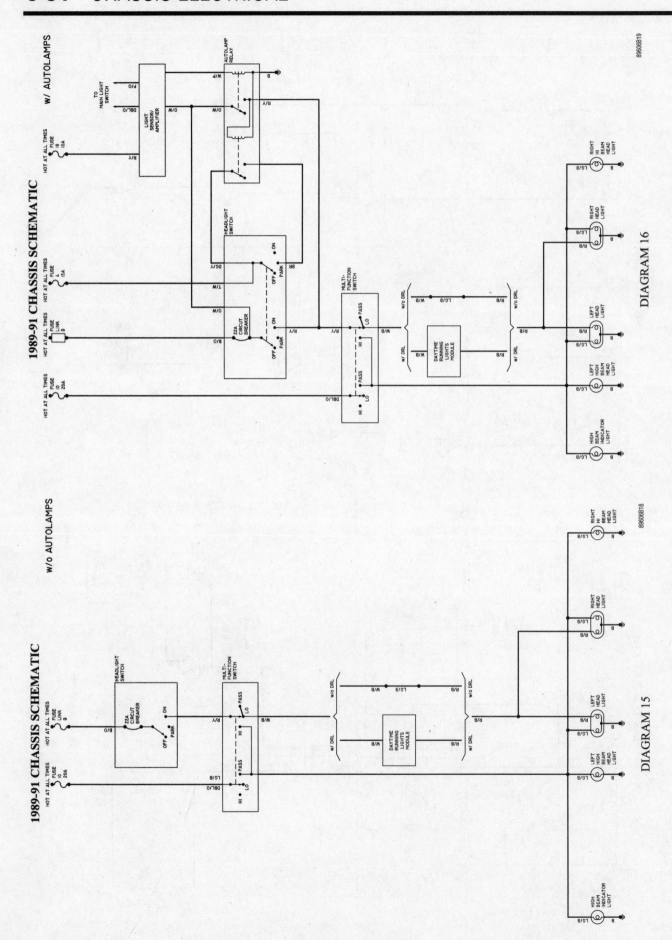

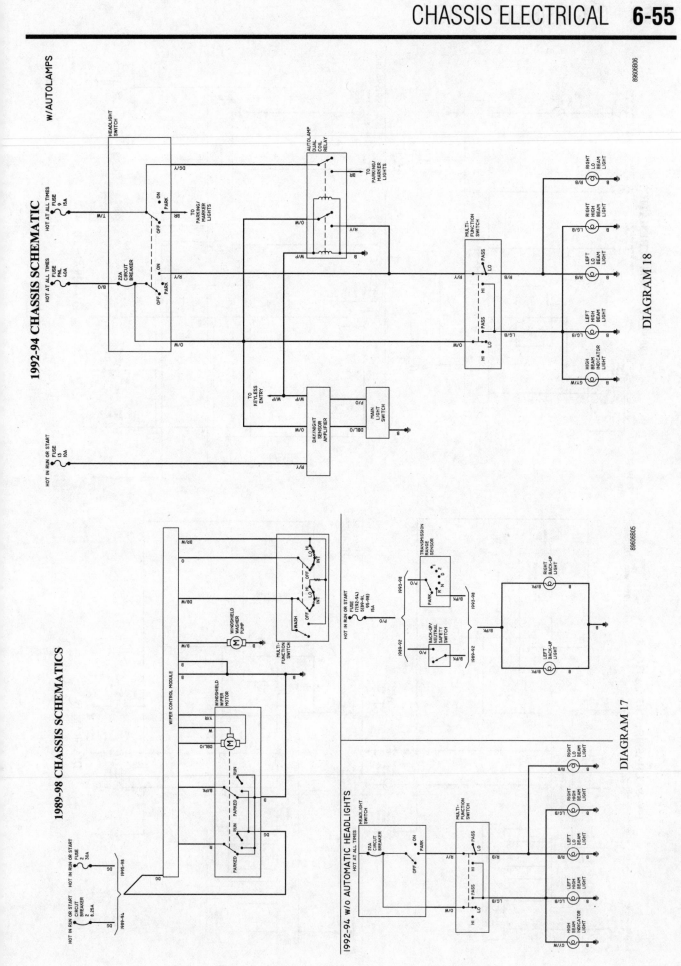

w/AUTOLAMPS

1992-94 CHASSIS SCHEMATIC

DIAGRAM 18

89606B06

1989-98 CHASSIS SCHEMATICS

DIAGRAM 17

89606B05

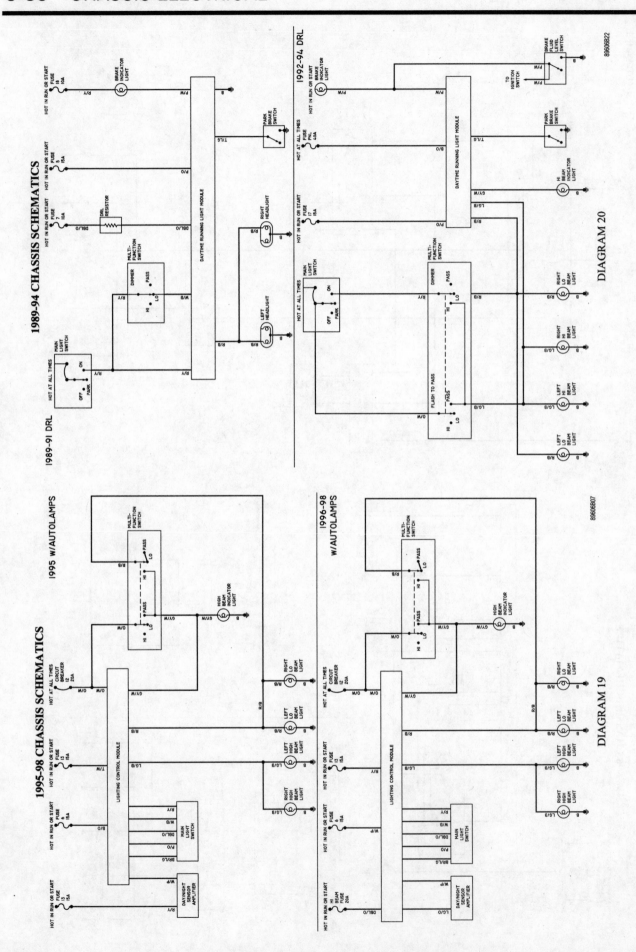

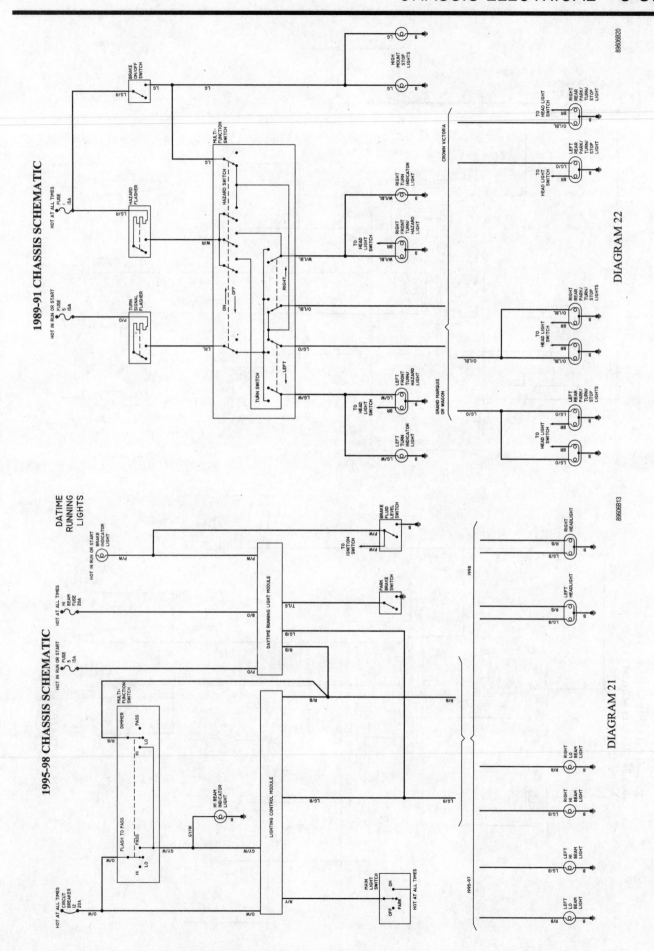

1989-91 CHASSIS SCHEMATIC

DIAGRAM 22

1995-98 CHASSIS SCHEMATIC

DATIME RUNNING LIGHTS

DIAGRAM 21

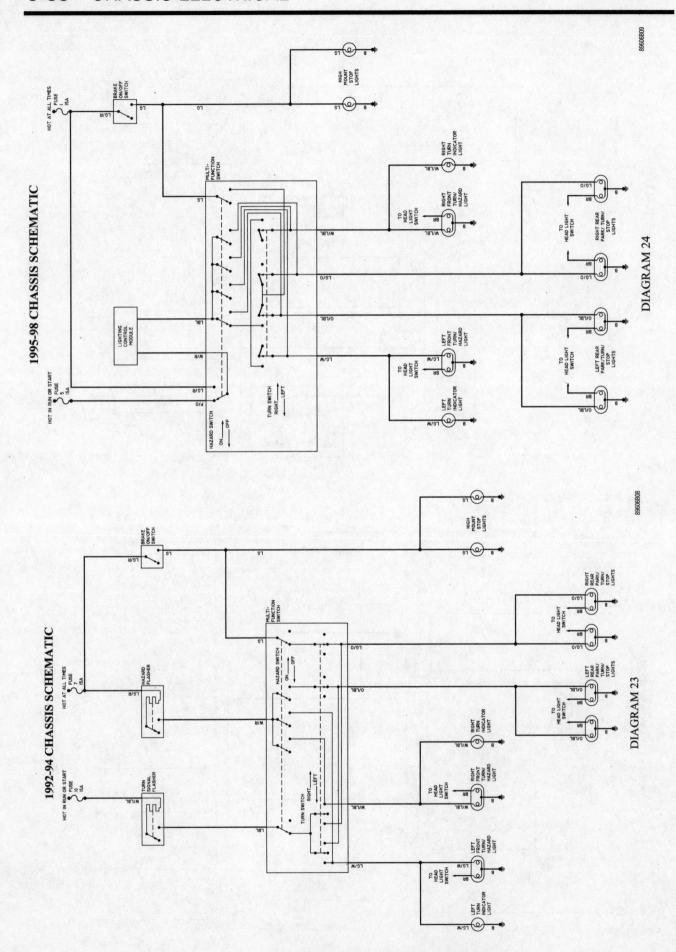

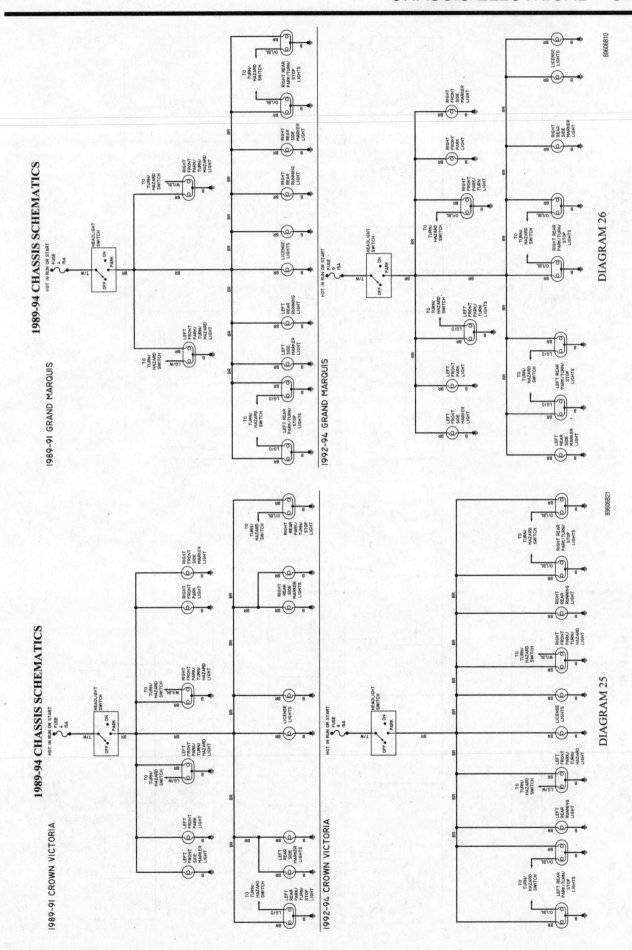

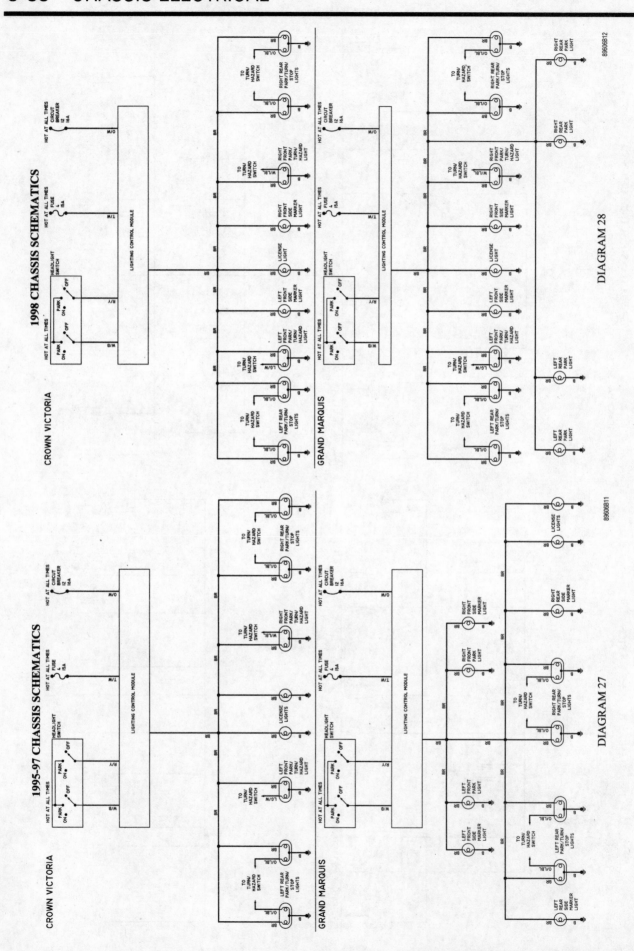

1998 CHASSIS SCHEMATICS

CROWN VICTORIA

GRAND MARQUIS

DIAGRAM 28

1995-97 CHASSIS SCHEMATICS

CROWN VICTORIA

GRAND MARQUIS

DIAGRAM 27

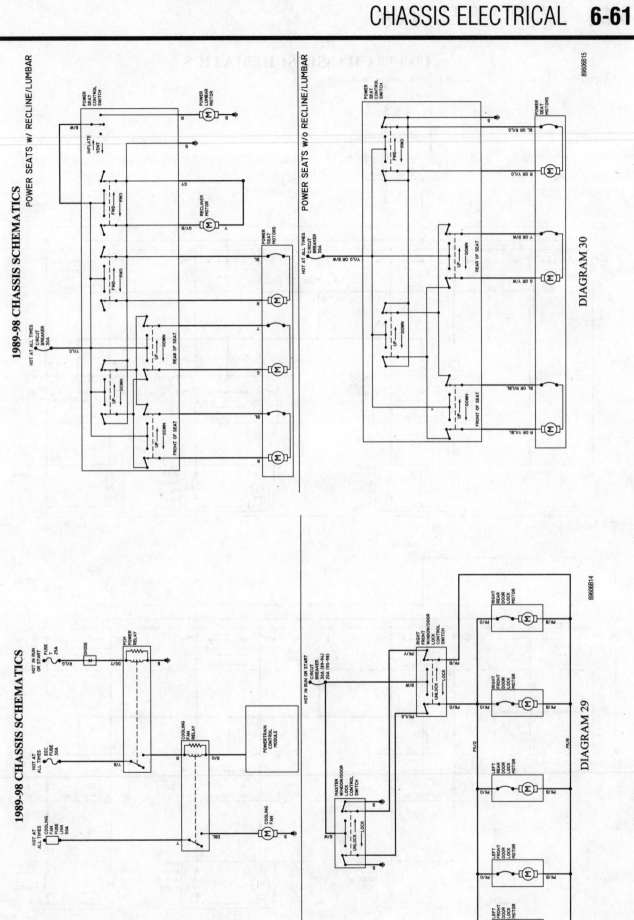

1989-98 CHASSIS SCHEMATICS

POWER SEATS w/ RECLINE/LUMBAR

POWER SEATS w/o RECLINE/LUMBAR

DIAGRAM 30

1989-98 CHASSIS SCHEMATICS

DIAGRAM 29

1989-98 CHASSIS SCHEMATICS

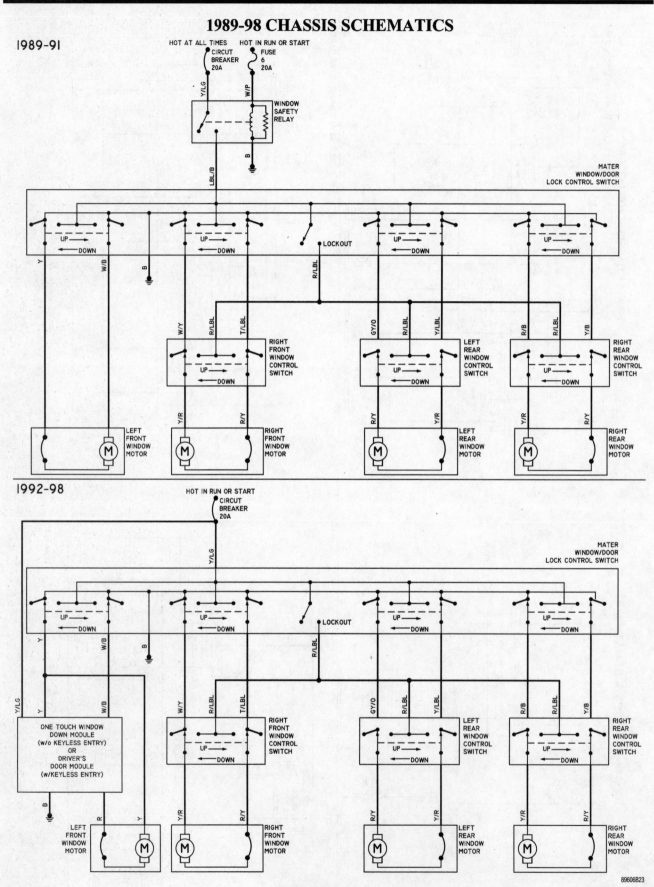

DIAGRAM 31

89606B23

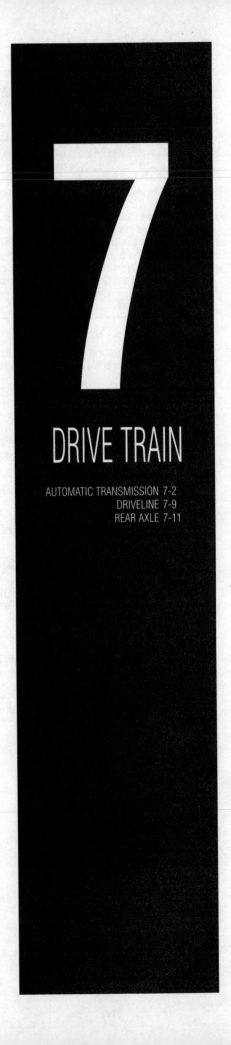

7

DRIVE TRAIN

AUTOMATIC TRANSMISSION

Understanding the Automatic Transmission

The automatic transmission allows engine torque and power to be transmitted to the rear wheels within a narrow range of engine operating speeds. It will allow the engine to turn fast enough to produce plenty of power and torque at very low speeds, while keeping it at a sensible rpm at high vehicle speeds (and it does this job without driver assistance). The transmission uses a light fluid as the medium for the transmission of power. This fluid also works in the operation of various hydraulic control circuits and as a lubricant. Because the transmission fluid performs all of these functions, trouble within the unit can easily travel from one part to another. For this reason, and because of the complexity and unusual operating principles of the transmission, a very sound understanding of the basic principles of operation will simplify troubleshooting.

TORQUE CONVERTER

▶ See Figure 1

The torque converter replaces the conventional clutch. It has three functions:
1. It allows the engine to idle with the vehicle at a standstill, even with the transmission in gear.
2. It allows the transmission to shift from range-to-range smoothly, without requiring that the driver close the throttle during the shift.
3. It multiplies engine torque to an increasing extent as vehicle speed drops and throttle opening is increased. This has the effect of making the transmission more responsive and reduces the amount of shifting required.

The torque converter is a metal case which is shaped like a sphere that has

been flattened on opposite sides. It is bolted to the rear end of the engine's crankshaft. Generally, the entire metal case rotates at engine speed and serves as the engine's flywheel. The case contains three sets of blades. One set is attached directly to the case. This set forms the torus or pump. Another set is directly connected to the output shaft, and forms the turbine. The third set is mounted on a hub which, in turn, is mounted on a stationary shaft through a one-way clutch. This third set is known as the stator. A pump, which is driven by the converter hub at engine speed, keeps the torque converter full of transmission fluid at all times. Fluid flows continuously through the unit to provide cooling. Under low speed acceleration, the torque converter functions as follows:

The torus is turning faster than the turbine. It picks up fluid at the center of the converter and, through centrifugal force, slings it outward. Since the outer edge of the converter moves faster than the portions at the center, the fluid picks up speed. The fluid then enters the outer edge of the turbine blades. It then travels back toward the center of the converter case along the turbine blades. In impinging upon the turbine blades, the fluid loses the energy picked up in the torus. If the fluid was now returned directly into the torus, both halves of the converter would have to turn at approximately the same speed at all times, and torque input and output would both be the same. In flowing through the torus and turbine, the fluid picks up two types of flow, or flow in two separate directions. It flows through the turbine blades, and it spins with the engine. The stator, whose blades are stationary when the vehicle is being accelerated at low speeds, converts one type of flow into another. Instead of allowing the fluid to flow straight back into the torus, the stator's curved blades turn the fluid almost 90° toward the direction of rotation of the engine. Thus the fluid does not flow as fast toward the torus, but is already spinning when the torus picks it up. This has the effect of allowing the torus to turn much faster than the turbine. This difference in speed may be compared to the difference in speed between the smaller and larger gears in any gear train. The result is that engine power output is higher, and engine torque is multiplied. As the speed of the turbine increases, the fluid spins faster and faster in the direction of engine rotation. As a result, the ability of the stator to redirect the fluid flow is reduced. Under cruising conditions, the stator is eventually forced to rotate on its one-way clutch in the direction of engine rotation. Under these conditions, the torque converter begins to behave almost like a solid shaft, with the torus and turbine speeds being almost equal.

PLANETARY GEARBOX

▶ See Figures 2, 3 and 4

The ability of the torque converter to multiply engine torque is limited. Also, the unit tends to be more efficient when the turbine is rotating at relatively high speeds. Therefore, a planetary gearbox is used to carry the power output of the turbine to the driveshaft.

Planetary gears function very similarly to conventional transmission gears. However, their construction is different in that three elements make up one gear

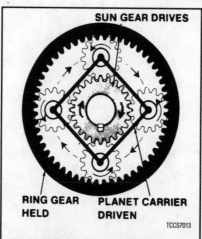

Fig. 1 The torque converter housing is rotated by the engine's crankshaft, and turns the impeller—The impeller then spins the turbine, which gives motion to the turbine shaft, driving the gears

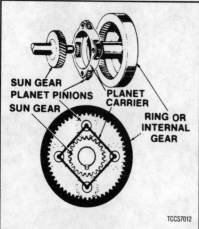

Fig. 2 Planetary gears work in a similar fashion to manual transmission gears, but are composed of three parts

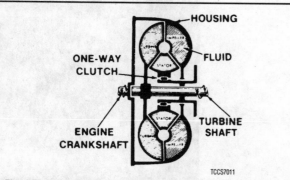

Fig. 3 Planetary gears in the maximum reduction (low) range. The ring gear is held and a lower gear ratio is obtained

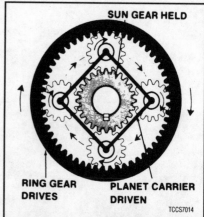

Fig. 4 Planetary gears in the minimum reduction (drive) range. The ring gear is allowed to revolve, providing a higher gear ratio

system, and, in that all three elements are different from one another. The three elements are: an outer gear that is shaped like a hoop, with teeth cut into the inner surface; a sun gear, mounted on a shaft and located at the very center of the outer gear; and a set of three planet gears, held by pins in a ring-like planet carrier, meshing with both the sun gear and the outer gear. Either the outer gear or the sun gear may be held stationary, providing more than one possible torque multiplication factor for each set of gears. Also, if all three gears are forced to rotate at the same speed, the gearset forms, in effect, a solid shaft.

Most automatics use the planetary gears to provide various reductions ratios. Bands and clutches are used to hold various portions of the gearsets to the transmission case or to the shaft on which they are mounted. Shifting is accomplished, then, by changing the portion of each planetary gearset which is held to the transmission case or to the shaft.

SERVOS AND ACCUMULATORS

♦ See Figure 5

The servos are hydraulic pistons and cylinders. They resemble the hydraulic actuators used on many other machines, such as bulldozers. Hydraulic fluid enters the cylinder, under pressure, and forces the piston to move to engage the band or clutches.

The accumulators are used to cushion the engagement of the servos. The transmission fluid must pass through the accumulator on the way to the servo. The accumulator housing contains a thin piston which is sprung away from the discharge passage of the accumulator. When fluid passes through the accumulator on the way to the servo, it must move the piston against spring pressure, and this action smoothes out the action of the servo.

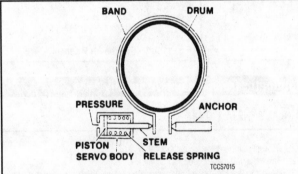

Fig. 5 Servos, operated by pressure, are used to apply or release the bands, to either hold the ring gear or allow it to rotate

HYDRAULIC CONTROL SYSTEM

The hydraulic pressure used to operate the servos comes from the main transmission oil pump. This fluid is channeled to the various servos through the shift valves. There is generally a manual shift valve which is operated by the transmission selector lever and an automatic shift valve for each automatic upshift the transmission provides.

➡**Many new transmissions are electronically controlled. On these models, electrical solenoids are used to better control the hydraulic fluid. Usually, the solenoids are regulated by an electronic control module.**

There are two pressures which affect the operation of these valves. One is the governor pressure which is effected by vehicle speed. The other is the modulator pressure which is effected by intake manifold vacuum or throttle position. Governor pressure rises with an increase in vehicle speed, and modulator pressure rises as the throttle is opened wider. By responding to these two pressures, the shift valves cause the upshift points to be delayed with increased throttle opening to make the best use of the engine's power output.Most transmissions also make use of an auxiliary circuit for downshifting. This circuit may be actuated by the throttle linkage the vacuum line which actuates the modulator, by a cable or by a solenoid. It applies pressure to a special downshift surface on the shift valve or valves.The transmission modulator also governs the line pressure, used to actuate the servos. In this way, the clutches and bands will be actuated with a force matching the torque output of the engine.

Fluid Pan And Filter Service

REMOVAL & INSTALLATION

Refer to Section 1 for transmission pan removal and filter service.

Neutral Safety Switch

REMOVAL & INSTALLATION

1989–91 Models Only

➡**On 1992 and later models, the neutral safety switch is incorporated into the Manual Lever Position or Transmission Range MLP/TR sensor. Refer to the MLP/TR sensor procedure in this section.**

The neutral safety switch is located on the transmission case above the manual lever.
1. Set the parking brake.
2. Place the selector lever in the manual **L** position.
3. Remove the air cleaner assembly.
4. Disconnect the negative battery cable.
5. Disconnect the neutral safety switch electrical harness from the switch by lifting the harness straight up off the switch without side-to-side motion.
6. Reach in the area of the left hand dash panel, using a 24 inch extension, universal adapter and socket tool T74P–77247–A or equivalent, and remove the neutral safety switch and O-ring.

➡**Use of different tools could crush or puncture the walls of the switch.**

To install:
7. Install the neutral safety switch and new O-ring using socket tool T74P–77247–A or equivalent.
8. Tighten the switch to 8–11 ft. lbs. (11–15 Nm).
9. Connect the neutral safety switch to the wiring harness.
10. Connect the negative battery cable.
11. Check that the vehicle starts in the **N** or **P** position.

ADJUSTMENT

No adjustment is possible on the neutral safety switch.

Manual Lever Position (MLP) Sensor/Transmission Range (TR) Sensor

REMOVAL & INSTALLATION

♦ See Figures 6, 7, 8, 9 and 10

1. Disconnect the negative battery cable.
2. Raise and support the vehicle safely on jackstands.
3. Place the transmission in Neutral.
4. Remove and discard the manual control lever nut, then remove the lever from the transmission.
5. Detach the TR sensor electrical harness connector, remove the TR sensor retaining bolts, then pull the TR sensor off of the transmission case.
To install:
6. Position the TR sensor against the transmission case and loosely install the 2 retaining screws.
7. Attach the TR sensor electrical harness connector.
8. Use an alignment tool, such as the TR Sensor Alignment Tool T93P–70010–A, to align the TR sensor slots.
9. Tighten the TR sensor bolts to 80–100 inch lbs. (9–11 Nm).
10. Position the manual control lever onto the TR sensor, then install the new lever nut to 22–26 ft. lbs. (30–35 Nm).
11. Lower the vehicle.
12. Connect the negative battery cable.

Fig. 6 Unfasten the nut for the manual control lever and . . .

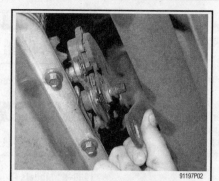

Fig. 7 . . . remove the lever from the sensor

Fig. 8 Detach the connector from the TR sensor

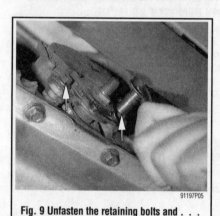

Fig. 9 Unfasten the retaining bolts and . . .

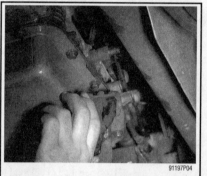

Fig. 10 . . . remove the sensor from the transmission

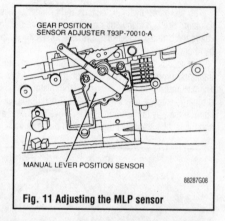

Fig. 11 Adjusting the MLP sensor

ADJUSTMENT

♦ **See Figure 11**

➥**Park is the last detent when the manual control lever is full forward. Return 2 detents toward the output shaft for Neutral.**

1. Position the manual control lever in **Neutral**.
2. Raise the and safely support the vehicle.
3. Loosen the sensor retaining bolts.
4. Insert Gear Position Sensor Adjuster tool T93P-700 10-A or equivalent, into the slots.
5. Align all 3 slots on the MLP sensor with 3 tabs on the tool.
6. Tighten the attaching screws to 80–100 inch lbs. (9–11 Nm).
7. Lower the vehicle.

Extension Housing Seal

REMOVAL & INSTALLATION

1. Raise and safely support the vehicle.
2. Remove the driveshaft according to the procedure in this section.
3. Carefully remove the seal, using a suitable seal removal tool.
4. Inspect the sealing surface of the driveshaft yoke for scoring or damage. If scored or damaged, the yoke must be replaced.
5. Inspect the seal bore in the extension housing for burrs or damage. Burrs can be removed with crocus cloth.
   To install:
6. Install the seal in the housing using a suitable seal installer; the seal should be firmly seated in the bore.
7. Coat the inside diameter of the rubber portion of the seal with grease.
8. Install the driveshaft as described in this Section.
9. Lower the vehicle. Operate the vehicle and check for leaks.

Automatic Transmission Assembly

REMOVAL & INSTALLATION

1. Disconnect the negative battery cable.
2. Raise the vehicle and support safely.
3. Drain the fluid from the transmission by removing all the transmission pan bolts except for one on each corner. Loosen the 4 bolts on the corner and drop the oil pan to allow the fluid to drain into a container. When drained, reinstall a few of the bolts to hold the pan in place.
4. Remove the converter bottom cover and remove the converter drain plug, to allow the converter to drain. After the converter has drained, reinstall the drain plug and tighten.
5. Remove the converter to flywheel nuts by turning the converter to expose the nuts.

➥**Crank the engine over with a wrench on the crankshaft pulley attaching bolt.**

6. Mark the position of the driveshaft on the rear axle flange and remove the driveshaft. Install a suitable plug in the transmission extension housing to prevent fluid leakage.
7. Disconnect the starter cable and remove the starter.
8. Disconnect the wiring from the neutral safety switch.
9. Remove the mount-to-crossmember and crossmember-to-frame bolts.
10. Remove the mount-to-transmission bolts.
11. On 1989 vehicles, disconnect the manual rod from the transmission manual lever using grommet removal tool T84P–7341–A or equivalent. On 1990–92 vehicles, disconnect the shift cable from the transmission. If equipped, disconnect the throttle valve cable from the transmission throttle valve lever.
12. On 1993–98 vehicles, detach the wiring connectors.
13. Remove the bellcrank bracket from the converter housing.
14. Position a suitable jack and raise the transmission.
15. Remove the transmission mount and crossmember.

➡️**It may be necessary to disconnect or remove interfering exhaust system components.**

16. Lower the transmission to gain access to the oil cooler lines.
17. Disconnect the oil cooler lines from the transmission.
18. If equipped, disconnect the speedometer cable from the extension housing.
19. Remove the transmission dipstick tube-to-engine block retaining bolt and remove the tube and dipstick from the transmission.
20. Secure the transmission to the jack with a chain and remove the transmission-to-engine bolts.
21. Carefully pull the transmission and converter assembly rearward and lower them from the vehicle.

To install:

22. Tighten the converter drain plug to 21–23 ft. lbs. (28–30 Nm).
23. If removed, position the converter on the transmission and rotate into position to make sure the drive flats are fully engaged in the pump gear.

➡️**Lubricate the pilot with chassis grease.**

24. Raise the converter and transmission assembly.
25. Rotate the converter until the studs and drain plug are in alignment with the holes in the flywheel. Align the orange balancing marks on the converter stud and flywheel bolt hole if balancing marks are present.
26. Move the converter and transmission assembly forward into position, being careful not to damage the flywheel and converter pilot.

➡️**The converter face must rest squarely against the flywheel. This indicates that the converter pilot is not binding in the engine crankshaft. To ensure the converter is properly seated, grasp a converter stud. It should move freely back and forth in the flywheel hole. If the converter will not move, the transmission must be removed and the converter repositioned so the impeller hub is properly engaged in the pump gear.**

27. Install the transmission-to-engine attaching bolts. Tighten the bolts to 40–50 ft. lbs. (55–68 Nm).
28. Remove the safety chain from around the transmission.
29. Install a new O-ring on the lower end of the transmission dipstick tube and install the tube to the transmission case.
30. If equipped, connect the speedometer cable to the transmission case.
31. Connect the oil cooler lines to the right side of the transmission case.
32. Position the crossmember on the side supports.

33. Position the rear mount on the crossmember and install the attaching bolt/nut.
34. Secure the engine rear support to the transmission extension housing.
35. Install any exhaust system components, if removed.
36. Lower the transmission and remove the jack.
37. Secure the crossmember to the side supports with the attaching bolts.
38. If equipped, connect the throttle valve linkage to the throttle valve lever. On 1993–98 vehicles, attach the wiring harness connectors.
39. On 1989 vehicles, connect the manual linkage rod to the transmission manual lever using grommet installation tool T84P–7341–B or equivalent. On 1990–92 vehicles, connect the shift cable.
40. Install the converter to flywheel attaching nuts and tighten to 20–34 ft. lbs. (27–46 Nm).
41. Install the converter housing cover.
42. Secure the starter motor in place and attach all electrical connections.
43. Install the driveshaft, aligning the marks that were made during removal.
44. Install the transmission fluid pan bolts and tighten, evenly, to 107–119 inch lbs. (12–13.5 Nm).
45. Lower the vehicle.
46. Fill the transmission with the proper type and quantity of fluid, start the engine and check the transmission for leakage.
47. Adjust the linkage as required.

ADJUSTMENTS

Shift Linkage

1989 VEHICLES

▶ See Figure 12

1. Place the selector lever in the **OVERDRIVE** position, tight against the overdrive stop.
2. An 8 lb. weight should be hung on the selector lever to ensure the lever remains against the overdrive stop during the linkage adjustment.
3. Loosen the shift rod adjusting bolt.
4. Shift the transmission into **OVERDRIVE** by pushing the column shift rod downward to the lowest position and pulling up 3 detents.

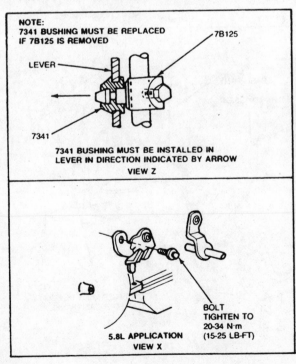

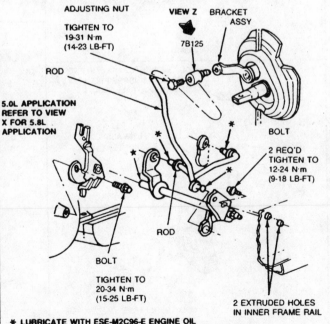

Fig. 12 Automatic transmission shift linkage—1989 vehicles

5. Make sure the selector lever has not moved from the overdrive stop. Tighten the bolt to 14–23 ft. lbs. (19–31 Nm).

6. Check the transmission operation for all selector lever detent positions.

1990–92 VEHICLES

▶ **See Figure 13**

1. Loosen the adjusting stud nut at the transmission shift lever.

2. From the passenger compartment, place the steering column selector lever in **OVERDRIVE** and hold the selector lever in position by placing a 3 lb. weight (8 lb. weight on 1990 vehicles) on the lever.

3. Rotate the transmission manual lever clockwise to low and return it 2 detent positions counterclockwise to the **OVERDRIVE** position.

4. Align the flats of the adjusting stud with the flats of the cable slot and install the cable on the stud.

➡**Do not push or pull on the rod while assembling the rod to the stud.**

5. Tighten the adjusting stud nut and washer assembly to 10–18 ft. lbs. (13–25 Nm).

6. Check the shift lever for proper operation.

1993–98 VEHICLES

▶ **See Figures 14 and 15**

1. Place the shift lever in the **OVERDRIVE** position. Hang a 3 lb. weight on the shift lever to make sure it is firmly located on the OVERDRIVE detent.

2. Use a small prybar in the slot of the slide adjuster to open the adjuster.

3. Move the transmission manual shift lever to the **OVERDRIVE** position, second detent from the most rearward position.

4. Push the slide adjuster closed.

5. Check the operation of the transmission in each selector lever position. Make sure the neutral safety switch is functioning properly.

Shift Indicator Cable

▶ **See Figure 16**

1. Remove the instrument panel lower trim panel.

2. Place the steering column selector lever in the **OVERDRIVE** position and hold the lever in position by placing a 3 lb. weight (8 lb. weight on 1989–1990 vehicles) on the lever.

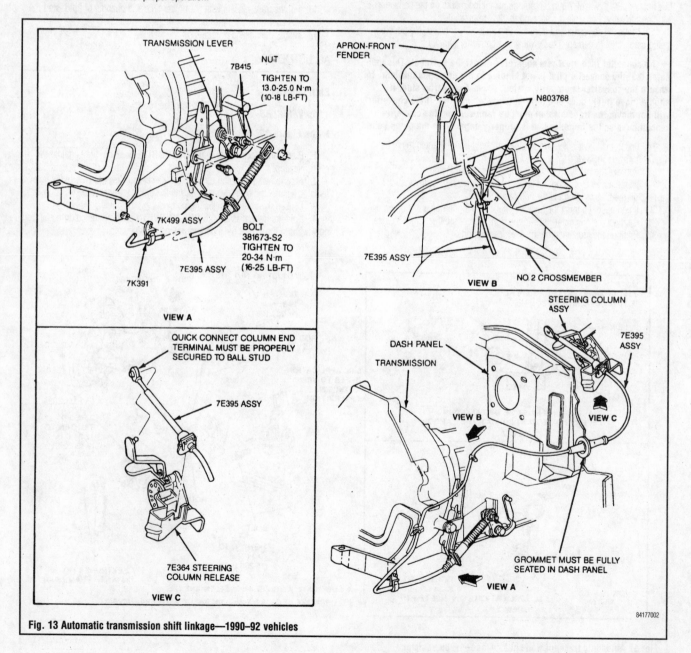

Fig. 13 Automatic transmission shift linkage—1990–92 vehicles

84177002

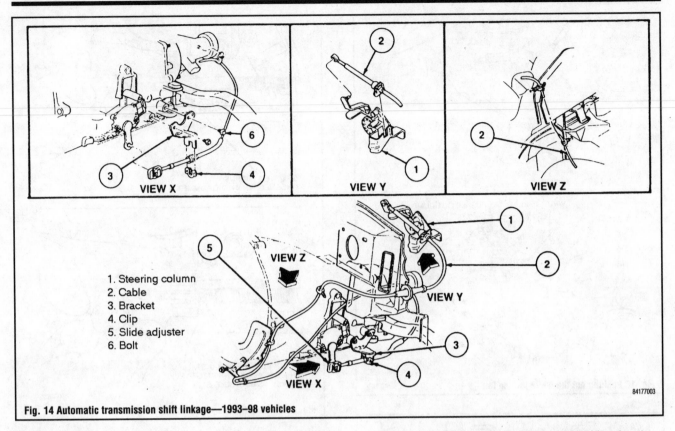

Fig. 14 Automatic transmission shift linkage—1993–98 vehicles

1. Steering column
2. Cable
3. Bracket
4. Clip
5. Slide adjuster
6. Bolt

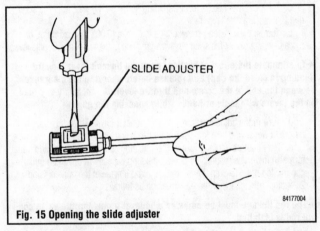

Fig. 15 Opening the slide adjuster

3. Rotate the adjustment screw located on the right side of the column to align the indicator within the letter "O" on the standard cluster adjustment.

4. If equipped with the electronic cluster, align the indicator so that both calibration dots are white when parallel to the steering column centerline.

5. Cycle the shift lever through all of the positions and check that the transmission range indicator covers the proper letter or number in each position.

6. Install the instrument panel lower trim panel.

Throttle Valve Linkage

4.6L AND 5.0L ENGINES

▶ See Figures 17, 18, 19 and 20

1. Set the parking brake and place the shift selector in **N**.

2. Remove the air cleaner cover and inlet tube from the throttle body inlet to access the throttle lever and cable.

3. Using a small prybar, pry the grooved pin on the cable assembly out of the grommet on the throttle body lever. Push out the white locking tab.

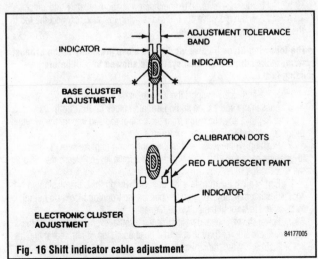

Fig. 16 Shift indicator cable adjustment

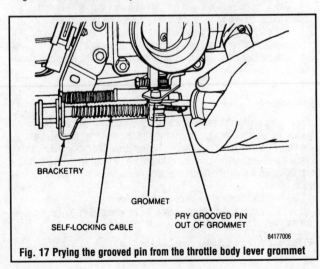

Fig. 17 Prying the grooved pin from the throttle body lever grommet

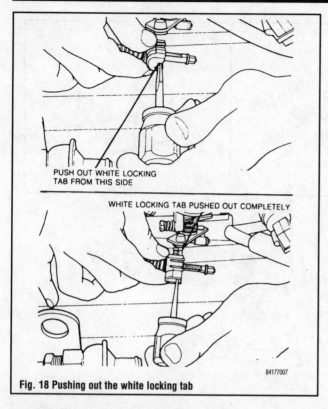

Fig. 18 Pushing out the white locking tab

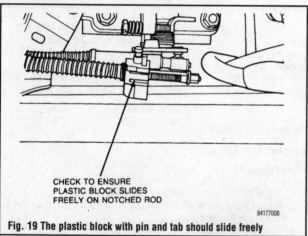

Fig. 19 The plastic block with pin and tab should slide freely

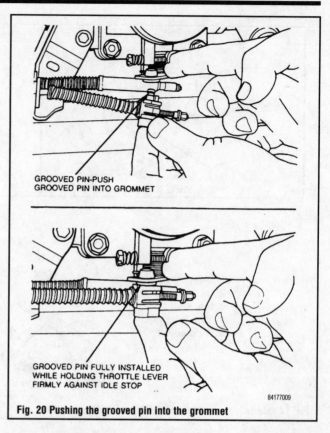

Fig. 20 Pushing the grooved pin into the grommet

4. Check the plastic block with pin and tab; it should slide freely on the notched rod. If not, the white tab may not be pushed out far enough.

5. While holding the throttle lever firmly against the idle stop, push the grooved pin into the grommet on the throttle lever as far as it will go.

6. Make sure the throttle lever does not move while pushing the pin into the grommet.

7. Install the air cleaner cover and inlet tube.

5.8L ENGINE

Before any engine throttle valve linkage adjustments can be made, the throttle lever at the carburetor must be positioned at its minimum idle stop. Make sure the engine idle speed is set to specification, then shut the engine off and remove the air cleaner. De-cam the fast idle cam on the carburetor so the throttle lever is against the idle stop or throttle solenoid positioner stop. Adjust the linkage as follows:

1. Adjust the linkage at the carburetor as follows:
   a. Make sure the carburetor is set at the minimum idle stop. Set the parking brake and place the transmission in **N**.

➡**The transmission selector lever must be in N.**

b. Back out the linkage lever adjusting screw all the way, until the screw end is flush with the lever face.

c. Turn in the adjusting screw until a thin shim (0.005 in. maximum), or piece of writing paper fits snugly between the end of the screw and throttle lever.

➡**To eliminate the effect of friction, push the linkage lever forward (tending to close the gap) and release before checking the clearance between the end of the screw and throttle lever. Do not apply any load on the levers with tools or hands while checking the gap.**

d. Turn in the adjusting screw an additional 3 turns. Three turns are preferred, however one turn is permissible if screw travel is limited.

e. If it is not possible to turn in the adjusting screw at least one additional turn or if there was insufficient screw adjusting capacity to obtain an initial gap in Step b, go to Step 2 and adjust the rod linkage at the transmission.

2. Adjust the linkage at the transmission as follows:

➡**The rod linkage must be adjusted whenever a new throttle valve control rod is installed.**

a. Set the linkage lever adjustment screw at approximately mid-range.

b. If a new throttle valve control rod is being installed, connect the rod to the linkage lever at the carburetor.

➡**The following Steps involve working in close proximity to the exhaust system. Make sure the exhaust system is allowed to cool before proceeding further.**

c. Raise and safely support the vehicle.

d. Loosen the bolt on the sliding trunnion block on the throttle valve control rod. Remove any corrosion from the control rod and free up the trunnion block so it slides freely on the control rod.

e. Push up on the lower end of the control rod to make sure the linkage lever at the carburetor is firmly against the throttle lever. Release the force on the rod; the rod must stay up.

f. Firmly push the throttle valve control lever on the transmission up against its internal stop. Tighten the bolt on the trunnion block. Do not relax force on the lever until the bolt is tightened.

g. Lower the vehicle and verify that the throttle lever is still against the minimum idle stop or throttle solenoid positioner stop. If not, repeat the linkage adjustment at the transmission.

DRIVELINE

Driveshaft and U-Joints

REMOVAL & INSTALLATION

▶ See Figures 21, 22, 23, 24 and 25

1. Raise and safely support the vehicle.
2. Mark the position of the driveshaft yoke on the axle companion flange so they can be reassembled in the same way to maintain balance.
3. Remove the flange bolts and disconnect the driveshaft from the axle companion flange.
4. Allow the rear of the driveshaft to drop down slightly.
5. Pull the driveshaft and slip yoke rearward until the yoke just clears the transmission extension housing seal. Mark the position of the slip yoke in relation to the transmission output shaft, then remove the driveshaft.
6. Plug the transmission to prevent fluid leakage.

To install:

7. Lubricate the yoke splines with suitable grease.
8. Remove the plug from the transmission and inspect the extension housing seal; replace if necessary.
9. Align the slip yoke and output shaft with the marks made at removal and install the yoke into the transmission extension housing. Be careful not to bottom the slip yoke hard against the transmission seal.
10. Rotate the axle flange, as necessary, to align the marks made during removal.
11. Install the driveshaft yoke to the axle flange. Install the bolts and tighten to 71–95 ft. lbs. (95–130 Nm).
12. Lower the vehicle.

U-JOINT REPLACEMENT

▶ See Figures 26, 27, 28, 29 and 30

1. Remove the driveshaft from the vehicle and place it in a vise, being careful not to damage it.
2. Mark the position of the yokes in relation to the driveshaft tube, so they can be reinstalled the same way.
3. Remove the snap-rings which retain the bearing cups in the yokes and in both ends of the driveshaft.
4. Remove the driveshaft tube from the vise and position the U-joint in the vise with a socket smaller than the bearing cup on one side and a socket larger than the bearing cup on the other side.
5. Slowly tighten the jaws of the vise so that the smaller socket forces the U-joint spider and the opposite bearing cup out of the driveshaft and into the larger socket.
6. Remove the U-joint from the vise and remove the socket from over the bearing cup. The bearing cup should be forced out of the driveshaft enough to grip and remove with pliers.
7. Drive the spider in the opposite direction in the same manner as in Step 4 in order to make the opposite bearing cup accessible, and pull it free with pliers. Use this procedure to remove all bearing cups from both U-joints.
8. After removing the bearing cups, remove the spiders from the driveshaft and yokes.
9. Thoroughly clean all dirt and foreign material from the yoke areas of the driveshaft and yokes.
10. Start a new bearing cup into the yoke of the driveshaft. Install the new spider in the driveshaft yoke and bearing. Position the yoke in the vise. Slowly close the vise, pressing the bearing cup into the yoke. Use the smaller

Fig. 21 The bolts retaining the rear driveshaft yoke-to-differential flange require a 12mm, 12 point wrench or socket to loosen them

Fig. 22 Remove the bolts retaining the rear driveshaft yoke-to-differential flange

Fig. 23 Separate the driveshaft from the axle flange and . . .

Fig. 24 . . . disengage the driveshaft from the transmission output shaft

Fig. 25 Insert a plug onto the splines of the transmission output shaft to prevent fluid from leaking out

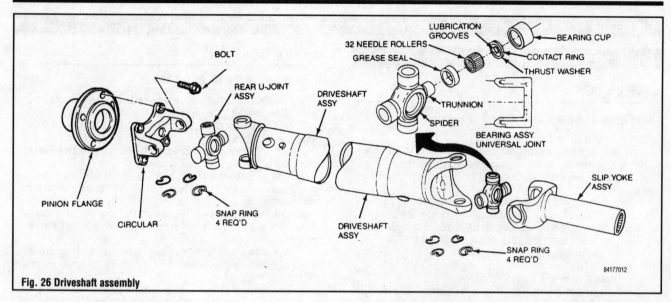

Fig. 26 Driveshaft assembly

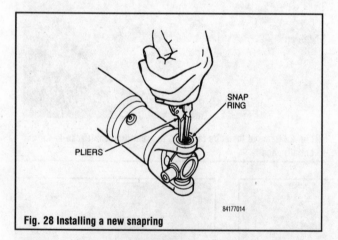

Fig. 27 Removing the bearing cup

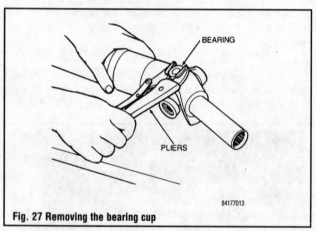

Fig. 28 Installing a new snapring

socket to press the cup in far enough so that the retaining snapring can be installed.

11. Open the vise and start a new bearing cup in the opposite hole. Press the bearing cup into the yoke in the same manner as in Step 9. Make sure the spider assembly is in line with the bearing cup as it is pressed in.

✴✴ WARNING

It is very easy to damage or misalign the needle rollers in the bearing cup if the spider assembly is not kept in line with the bearing cup during assembly. If the U-joint binds easily and/or the bearing cup cannot be pressed in far enough to install the snapring, one or more needle rollers has probably been knocked to the bottom of the cup. Remove the bearing cup, reposition the needle rollers and reinstall.

12. Install all remaining U-joint cups in the same manner. When installing the slip yoke and rear yoke, make sure the marks align that were made during removal. Make sure all snap-rings are properly installed.

13. Check the U-joints for freedom of movement. If binding has resulted from misalignment during assembly, a sharp rap on the yoked with a brass or plastic hammer will seat the bearing cups. Take care to support the shaft end and do not strike the bearing cups during this procedure. Make sure the U-joints are free to rotate easily without binding before installing the driveshaft.

14. If supplied, install the grease fittings in the U-joints.

15. Install the driveshaft.

16. Grease the new U-joints if they are equipped with grease fittings.

DRIVESHAFT BALANCING

▶ **See Figures 31, 32, 33 and 34**

Driveline vibration or shudder, felt mainly on acceleration, coasting or under engine braking, can be caused, among other things, by improper driveshaft installation or imbalance. If driveshaft vibration is suspected, proceed as follows:

1. Raise and safely support the vehicle.

2. Remove the rear wheel and tire assemblies and the rear drum or rotor assemblies.

3. Mark the position of the driveshaft to the rear axle companion flange.

4. Mark one hole position on the driveshaft yoke at the rear of the driveshaft with the letter A and the 8 circular axle flange holes (starting with the mating hole with driveshaft position A) from one through eight. Position A1 is considered the original index position.

5. Disconnect the driveshaft from the rear axle flange and re-index 180 degrees at axle position A5. Check for vibration at road test speed. If vibration is still present, evaluate positions A3 and A7.

6. If further improvement is desired, evaluate the remaining positions that are located between the best of the 2 previous positions, A3 and A7. If the vehicle tests okay at any point during this procedure, do not proceed further.

7. If re-indexing at the axle is unsuccessful, disconnect the driveshaft and re-index 180 degrees at the transmission output shaft only.

8. Reconnect the driveshaft and check for vibration at road test speed. If the vehicle tests okay, do not proceed further.

➡ **While the driveshaft is removed from the vehicle, manipulate the U-joints in each direction of rotation. If the U-joint feels stiff or has a notchy, gritty feel in any direction, replace the U-joints.**

9. If re-indexing at both the axle and transmission is unsuccessful, mark the rear of the driveshaft in 4 equal parts and number than 1, 2, 3 and 4. Install a screw-type hose clamp with the screw at position 1.

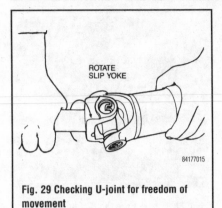

Fig. 29 Checking U-joint for freedom of movement

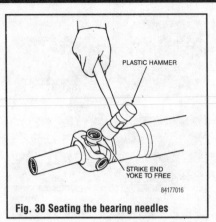

Fig. 30 Seating the bearing needles

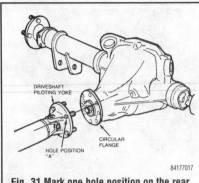

Fig. 31 Mark one hole position on the rear driveshaft yoke with the letter A

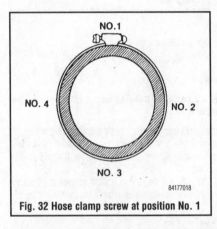

Fig. 32 Hose clamp screw at position No. 1

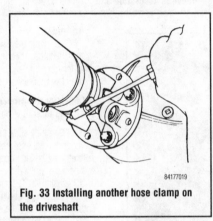

Fig. 33 Installing another hose clamp on the driveshaft

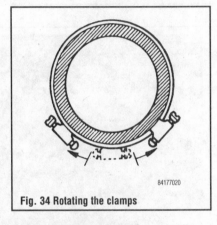

Fig. 34 Rotating the clamps

10. Check for vibration at road test speed. Rotate the clamp to each of the other 3 positions and check for vibration.

11. If the vibration is worse in all positions, go to Step 15. If the vibration is better in any one position, go to Step 11. If the vibration is better in any two positions, rotate the clamp screw to a mid-point between the two positions.

12. Install another clamp, with the screw In the same position as the first clamp. Check for vibration at road test speed.

13. If the vibration is acceptable, do not proceed further, the problem is corrected. If the vibration is the same, or worse, go to Step 13.

14. Rotate the screws of the clamps equally away from each other about ½ in. Check for vibration at road test speed.

15. If the vibration is acceptable, do not proceed further, the problem is corrected. If the vibration is not acceptable, go to Step 15.

16. Install the drum or rotor assemblies and wheel and tire assemblies. Road test the vehicle; vibration felt when the car is raised may be acceptable during a road test.

17. If the vibration is acceptable, the problem is corrected. If the vibration is not acceptable, investigate other driveline components: wheels, tires, axle bearings, etc.

➡**If the vibration was corrected with the addition of clamps, the clamps will be left on the driveshaft permanently. Check the clamp clearance after installation to prevent any contact with the floorpan or other parts.**

REAR AXLE

Axle Shaft, Bearing and Seal

REMOVAL & INSTALLATION

◢ **See Figures 35 thru 46**

1. Raise and safely support the vehicle.
2. Remove the wheel and tire assembly and remove the brake drum or brake rotor.
3. Clean all dirt from the area of the carrier cover.
4. Drain the axle lubricant by removing the housing cover.
5. Remove the differential pinion shaft lock bolt and differential pinion shaft.
6. Push the flanged end of axle shafts toward the center of the vehicle and remove the C-lock from the button end of the axle shaft.
7. Remove the axle shaft from the housing, being careful not to damage the anti-lock brake sensor ring, if equipped.
8. Insert wheel bearing and seal replacer tool T85L–1225–AH or equivalent, in the bore and position it behind the bearing so the tangs on the tool engage the bearing outer race. Remove the bearing and seal as a unit using an impact slide hammer.

Fig. 35 Remove the side gear pinion shaft lockbolt and . . .

Fig. 36 . . . the side gear pinion shaft

Fig. 37 Push the axles in so that the C-clip groove is accessible and . . .

Fig. 38 . . . remove the C-clips from the axle shafts

Fig. 39 Grasp the axle and slide it out of the tube

To install:

9. Lubricate the new bearing with rear axle lubricant.

10. Install the bearing into the housing bore using a suitable bearing installer.

11. Install a new axle seal using a seal installer.

➡**Check for the presence of an axle shaft O-ring on the spline end of the shaft and install, if not present.**

12. Carefully slide the axle shaft into the axle housing, without damaging the bearing/seal assembly or anti-lock brake sensor ring, if equipped. Start the splines into the side gear and push firmly until the button end of the axle shaft can be seen in the differential case.

13. Install the C-lock on the button end of the axle shaft splines, then push the shaft outboard until the shaft splines engage and the C-lock seats in the counterbore of the differential side gear.

14. Insert the differential pinion shaft through the case and pinion gears, aligning the hole in the shaft with the lock bolt hole. Apply locking compound to the lock bolt and install in the case and pinion shaft. Tighten to 15–30 ft. lbs. (20–41 Nm).

15. Cover the inside of the differential case with a shop rag and clean the machined surface of the carrier and cover. Remove the shop rag.

16. Apply a ⅛–³⁄₁₆ in. wide bead of silicone sealer to the cover and install on the carrier. Tighten the bolts in a crisscross pattern. Final torque the cover retaining bolts to 28–35 ft. lbs. (38–47 Nm).

17. Add rear axle lubricant to the carrier to a level ¼–⁹⁄₁₆ in. below the bot-

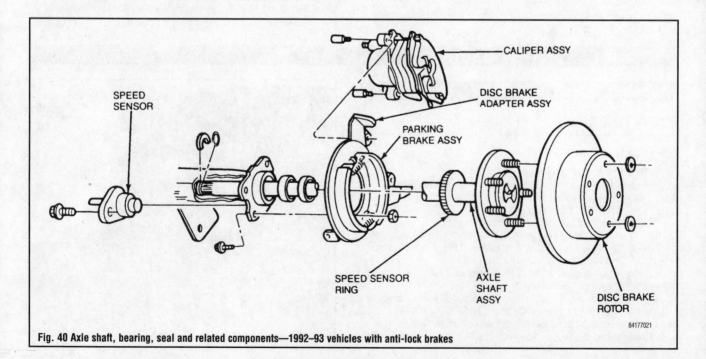

Fig. 40 Axle shaft, bearing, seal and related components—1992–93 vehicles with anti-lock brakes

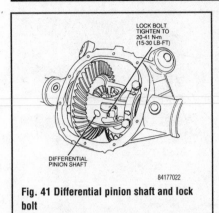

Fig. 41 Differential pinion shaft and lock bolt

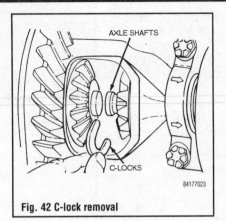

Fig. 42 C-lock removal

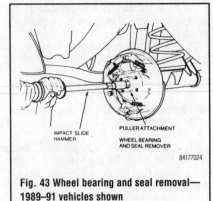

Fig. 43 Wheel bearing and seal removal— 1989–91 vehicles shown

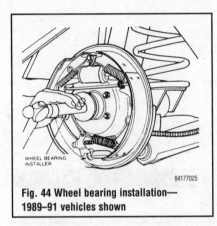

Fig. 44 Wheel bearing installation— 1989–91 vehicles shown

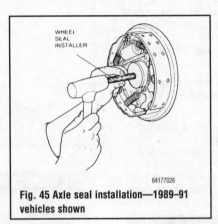

Fig. 45 Axle seal installation—1989–91 vehicles shown

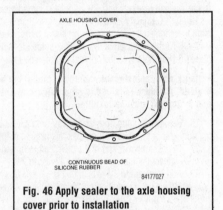

Fig. 46 Apply sealer to the axle housing cover prior to installation

tom of the fill hole. If equipped with limited slip differential, add friction modifier C8AZ–19B564–A or equivalent. Install the filler plug and tighten to 15–30 ft. lbs. (20–41 Nm).

18. Install the brake calipers and rotors or the brake drums, as required. Install the wheel and tire assembly and lower the vehicle.

Pinion Seal

REMOVAL & INSTALLATION

▶ **See Figures 47, 48, 49, 50 and 51**

1. Raise and safely support the vehicle.
2. Remove the wheel and tire assemblies and remove the brake drums or brake rotors.
3. Mark the position of the driveshaft yoke on the axle companion flange so they may be reassembled in the same way to maintain balance.

4. Disconnect the driveshaft from the rear axle companion flange, remove the driveshaft and remove the driveshaft from the extension housing.
5. Plug the extension housing to prevent leakage.
6. Install an inch pound torque wrench on the pinion nut and record the torque required to maintain rotation of the pinion through several revolutions.
7. While holding the companion flange with holder tool T78P–4851–A or equivalent, remove the pinion nut.
8. Clean the area around the oil seal and place a drain pan under the seal.
9. Mark the companion flange in relation to the pinion shaft so the flange can be installed in the same position.
10. Remove the rear axle companion flange using tool T65L–4851–B or equivalent.

✳✳ WARNING

Never strike the companion flange with a hammer.

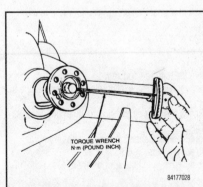

Fig. 47 Prior to disassembly, record the torque required to maintain pinion rotation through several revolutions

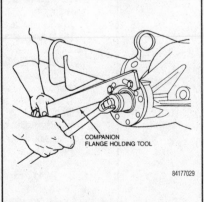

Fig. 48 Removing the pinion nut

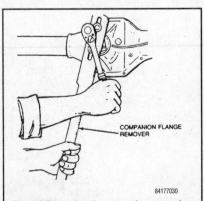

Fig. 49 Removing the rear axle companion flange

11. Position a small prybar under the flange of the pinion seal and carefully strike with a hammer to wedge the prybar between the seal flange and differential housing.

12. Pry up on the metal flange of the pinion seal. Install gripping pliers and strike with a hammer until the pinion seal is removed.

To install:

13. Apply grease to the lips of the seal.

14. Clean the oil seal seat surface and install the seal in the carrier using seal replacer tool T79P–4676–A or equivalent.

15. Check the companion flange and pinion shaft splines for burrs. If burrs are evident, remove them using crocus cloth.

16. Apply a small amount of lubricant to the companion flange splines, align the marks on the flange and the pinion shaft and install the flange.

17. Install a new nut on the pinion shaft and apply lubricant on the washer side of the nut.

18. Hold the flange with the holder tool while tightening the nut. Rotate the pinion occasionally to ensure proper seating. Take frequent pinion bearing torque preload readings until the original recorded preload reading is obtained.

19. If the original recorded preload is less than 8–14 inch lbs. (0.9–1.6 Nm), then tighten the nut until the rotational torque of to 8–14 inch lbs. (0.9–1.6 Nm) is obtained. If the original preload is higher than 8–14 inch lbs. (0.9–1.6 Nm), tighten to the original recorded preload.

➡ **Under no circumstances should the pinion nut be backed off to reduce preload. If reduced preload is required, a new collapsible pinion spacer and pinion nut must be installed.**

20. Remove the plug from the transmission extension housing and install the front end of the driveshaft on the transmission output shaft.

21. Connect the rear end of the driveshaft to the axle companion flange, aligning the scribe marks. Tighten the 4 bolts to 71–95 ft. lbs. (95–130 Nm).

22. Add lubricant to the axle until it is ¼–⁹⁄₁₆ in. below the bottom of the fill hole with the axle in operating position. If equipped with limited slip differential, add friction modifier C8AZ19B564A or equivalent.

❋❋ WARNING

Make sure the axle vent is not plugged with debris.

23. Install the brake drums or rotors.

24. Install the wheel and tire assemblies and lower the vehicle.

25. Operate the vehicle and check for leaks.

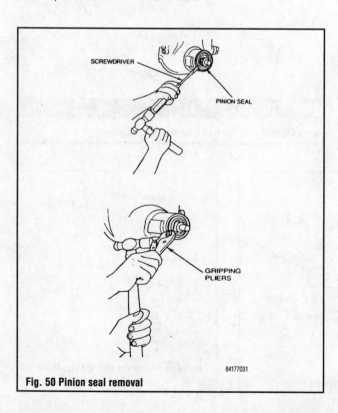

Fig. 50 Pinion seal removal

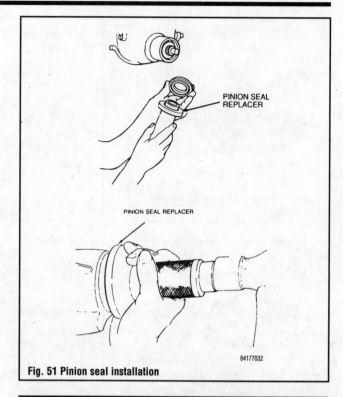

Fig. 51 Pinion seal installation

Axle Housing Assembly

REMOVAL & INSTALLATION

▸ **See Figure 52**

1. Raise and safely support the vehicle.

2. Position safety stands under the rear frame crossmember.

3. Remove the cover and drain the axle lubricant.

4. Remove the wheel and tire assemblies.

5. Remove the brake drums or brake rotors.

6. If equipped, remove the anti-lock brake speed sensors.

7. Remove the lock bolt from the differential pinion shaft and remove the shaft.

8. Push the axle shafts inward to remove the C-locks and remove the axle shafts.

9. If equipped with drum brakes, remove the 4 retaining nuts from each backing plate and wire the backing plate to the underbody.

10. If equipped with disc brakes, remove the disc brake adapter bracket, bolts and J-nuts. Remove the 4 retaining nuts from each adapter and wire the adapters to the underbody.

11. Mark the position of the driveshaft yoke on the axle companion flange.

12. Disconnect the driveshaft at the companion flange and wire it to the underbody.

13. Support the axle housing with jackstands.

14. Disengage the brake line from the clips that retain the line to the axle housing.

15. Disconnect the vent from the rear axle housing.

16. If equipped with air springs, remove them according to the procedure in Section 8.

17. Disconnect the lower shock absorber studs from the mounting brackets on the axle housing.

18. Remove the nuts and bolts and disconnect the upper arms from the mountings on the axle housing ear brackets.

19. Lower the axle housing assembly until the springs are released and lift out the springs.

20. Remove the nuts and bolts and disconnect the suspension lower arms at the axle housing.

21. Lower the axle housing and remove it from the vehicle.

To install:

22. Position the axle housing under the vehicle and raise the axle with a hoist or jack.

23. Connect the lower suspension arms to their mounting brackets on the axle housing. Do not tighten the bolts and nuts at this time.

24. Reposition the rear springs.

25. Raise the housing into position.

26. Connect the upper arms to the mounting ears on the housing. Tighten the nuts and bolts to 103–133 ft. lbs. (140180 Nm). Tighten the lower arm bolts and nuts to 103–133 ft. lbs. (140–180 Nm).

27. Install the axle vent and install the brake line to the clips that retain the line to the axle housing.

28. Secure the brake junction block to the housing cast boss.

29. Connect the air spring lines as described in Section 8.

30. If equipped with drum brakes, install the brake backing plates on the axle housing flanges.

31. If equipped with disc brakes, install the disc brake adapters and tighten the nuts to 20–29 ft. lbs. (27–40 Nm). Install the disc brake adapter brackets, bolts and J-nuts. Tighten to 20–39 ft. lbs. (27–54 Nm).

32. Connect the lower shock absorber studs to the mounting bracket on the axle housing.

33. Connect the driveshaft to the companion flange and tighten the bolts and nuts to 70–95 ft. lbs. (95–130 Nm).

34. Slide the rear axle shafts into the housing until the splines enter the side gear. Push the axle shafts inward and install the C-lock at the end of each shaft spline. Pull the shafts outboard until the C-lock enters the recess in the side gears.

35. Install the pinion shaft. Apply locking compound to the pinion shaft lock bolt. Install and tighten to 15–30 ft. lbs. (20–41 Nm).

36. Install the rear brake drums or disc brake rotors and calipers.

37. Install the anti-lock brake speed sensor, if equipped.

38. Install the rear carrier cover using new silicone sealer. Tighten to 28–35 ft. lbs. (38–47 Nm).

39. Add rear axle lubricant to the carrier to a level ¼–⁹⁄₁₆ in. below the bottom of the fill hole. If equipped with limited slip, add friction modifier C8AZ–19B564–A or equivalent. Install the filler plug and tighten to 15–30 ft. lbs. (20–41 Nm).

40. Install the wheel and tire assemblies.

41. Lower the vehicle.

42. Road test the vehicle.

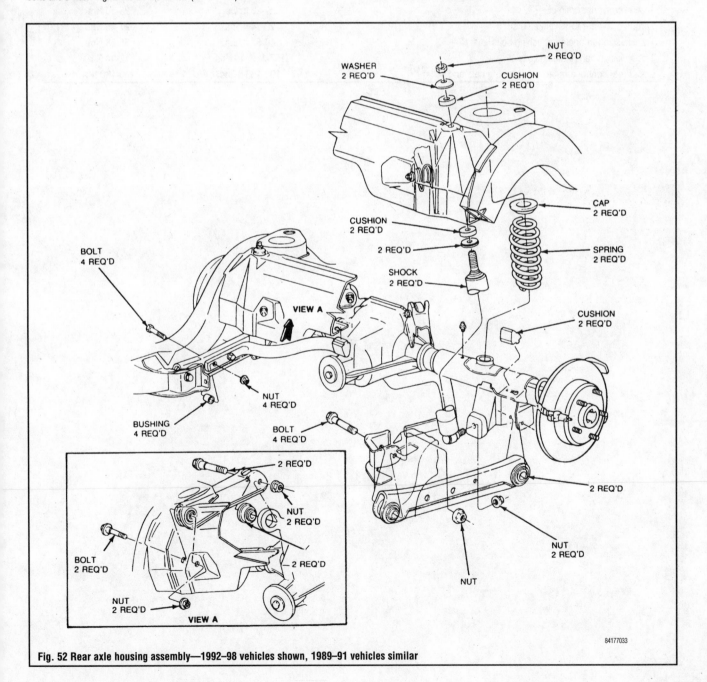

Fig. 52 Rear axle housing assembly—1992–98 vehicles shown, 1989–91 vehicles similar

84177033

TORQUE SPECIFICATIONS

Components	English	Metric
Anti-lock wheel speed sensor	40-60 inch lbs.	5-7 Nm
Axle housing cover bolts	28-35 ft. lbs.	38-47 Nm
Axle housing drain plug	15-30 ft. lbs.	20-41 Nm
Driveshaft retaining bolts	71-95 ft. lbs.	90-130 Nm
Lower rear control arms-to-axle housing nuts and bolts	103-133 ft. lbs.	140-180 Nm
Manual control lever-to-TR/MLP sensor	22-26 ft. lbs.	30-35 Nm
Manual lever positioning switch/TR sensor retaining bolts	80-100 inch lbs.	9-11 Nm
Neutral safety switch	8-11 ft. lbs.	11-15 Nm
Pinion nut	160 ft. lbs.	217 Nm
Pinion shaft lockbolt	15-30 ft. lbs.	20-41 Nm
Shift lever adjusting bolt		
1989 models	14-23 ft. lbs.	19-31 Nm
1990-92 models	10-18 ft. lbs.	13-25 Nm
Torque converter drain plug	21-23 ft. lbs.	28-30 Nm
Torque converter-to-flexplate nuts	20-34 ft. lbs.	27-46 Nm
Transmission-to-engine attaching bolts	40-50 ft. lbs.	55-68 Nm
Transmission pan retaining bolts	107-119 inch lbs.	12-14 Nm
Upper rear control arms-to-axle housing nuts and bolts	103-133 ft. lbs.	140-180 Nm

89607C01

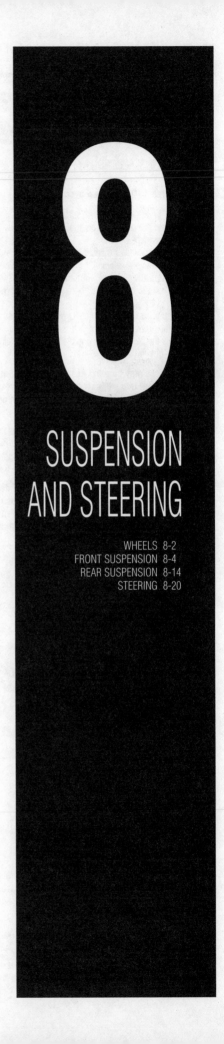

8

SUSPENSION AND STEERING

WHEELS

Wheels

REMOVAL & INSTALLATION

▶ **See Figures 1, 2, 3, 4 and 5**

1. Park the vehicle on a level surface.
2. Remove the jack, tire iron and, if necessary, the spare tire from their storage compartments.
3. Check the owner's manual or refer to Section 1 of this manual for the jacking points on your vehicle. Then, place the jack in the proper position.
4. If equipped with lug nut trim caps, remove them by either unscrewing or pulling them off the lug nuts, as appropriate. Consult the owner's manual, if necessary.
5. If equipped with a wheel cover or hub cap, insert the tapered end of the tire iron in the groove and pry off the cover.
6. Apply the parking brake and block the diagonally opposite wheel with a wheel chock or two.

➡**Wheel chocks may be purchased at your local auto parts store, or a block of wood cut into wedges may be used. If possible, keep one or two of the chocks in your tire storage compartment, in case any of the tires has to be removed on the side of the road.**

7. If equipped with an automatic transmission, place the selector lever in **P** or Park; with a manual transmission, place the shifter in Reverse.
8. With the tires still on the ground, use the tire iron/wrench to break the lug nuts loose.

➡**If a nut is stuck, never use heat to loosen it or damage to the wheel and bearings may occur. If the nuts are seized, one or two heavy hammer blows directly on the end of the bolt usually loosens the rust. Be careful, as continued pounding will likely damage the brake drum or rotor.**

9. Using the jack, raise the vehicle until the tire is clear of the ground. Support the vehicle safely using jackstands.
10. Remove the lug nuts, then remove the tire and wheel assembly.
To install:
11. Make sure the wheel and hub mating surfaces, as well as the wheel lug studs, are clean and free of all foreign material. Always remove rust from the wheel mounting surface and the brake rotor or drum. Failure to do so may cause the lug nuts to loosen in service.
12. Install the tire and wheel assembly and hand-tighten the lug nuts.
13. Using the tire wrench, tighten all the lug nuts, in a crisscross pattern, until they are snug.
14. Raise the vehicle and withdraw the jackstand, then lower the vehicle.
15. Using a torque wrench, tighten the lug nuts in a crisscross pattern to 85–105 ft. lbs. (115–142 Nm). Check your owner's manual or refer to Section 1 of this manual for the proper tightening sequence.

✳✳ WARNING

Do not overtighten the lug nuts, as this may cause the wheel studs to stretch or the brake disc (rotor) to warp.

16. If so equipped, install the wheel cover or hub cap. Make sure the valve stem protrudes through the proper opening before tapping the wheel cover into position.
17. If equipped, install the lug nut trim caps by pushing them or screwing them on, as applicable.
18. Remove the jack from under the vehicle, and place the jack and tire iron/wrench in their storage compartments. Remove the wheel chock(s).
19. If you have removed a flat or damaged tire, place it in the storage compartment of the vehicle and take it to your local repair station to have it fixed or replaced as soon as possible.

INSPECTION

Inspect the tires for lacerations, puncture marks, nails and other sharp objects. Repair or replace as necessary. Also check the tires for treadwear and air pressure as outlined in Section 1 of this manual.
Check the wheel assemblies for dents, cracks, rust and metal fatigue. Repair or replace as necessary.

Wheel Lug Studs

REMOVAL & INSTALLATION

With Disc Brakes

▶ **See Figures 6, 7 and 8**

1. Raise and support the appropriate end of the vehicle safely using jackstands, then remove the wheel.

TCCA8P02

Fig. 1 With the vehicle still on the ground, break the lug nuts loose using the wrench end of the tire iron

TCCA8P03

Fig. 2 After the lug nuts have been loosened, raise the vehicle using the jack until the tire is clear of the ground

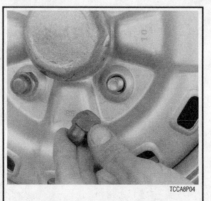

TCCA8P04

Fig. 3 Remove the lug nuts from the studs

TCCA8P05

Fig. 4 Remove the wheel and tire assembly from the vehicle

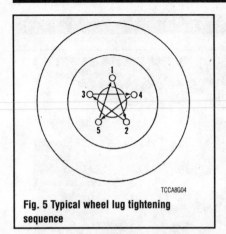

Fig. 5 Typical wheel lug tightening sequence

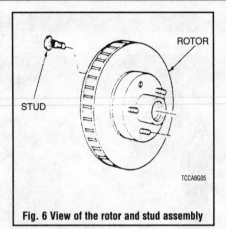

Fig. 6 View of the rotor and stud assembly

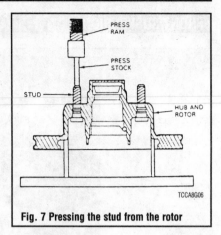

Fig. 7 Pressing the stud from the rotor

2. Remove the brake pads and caliper. Support the caliper aside using wire or a coat hanger. For details, please refer to Section 9 of this manual.

3. Remove the outer wheel bearing and lift off the rotor. For details on wheel bearing removal, installation and adjustment, please refer to Section 1 of this manual.

4. Properly support the rotor using press bars, then drive the stud out using an arbor press.

➡If a press is not available, CAREFULLY drive the old stud out using a blunt drift. MAKE SURE the rotor is properly and evenly supported or it may be damaged.

To install:

5. Clean the stud hole with a wire brush and start the new stud with a hammer and drift pin. Do not use any lubricant or thread sealer.

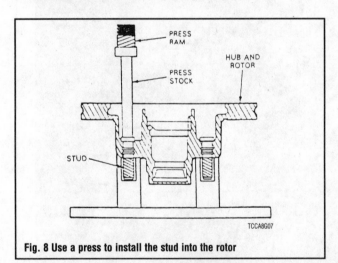

Fig. 8 Use a press to install the stud into the rotor

6. Finish installing the stud with the press.

➡If a press is not available, start the lug stud through the bore in the hub, then position about 4 flat washers over the stud and thread the lug nut. Hold the hub/rotor while tightening the lug nut, and the stud should be drawn into position. MAKE SURE THE STUD IS FULLY SEATED, then remove the lug nut and washers.

7. Install the rotor and adjust the wheel bearings.

8. Install the brake caliper and pads.

9. Install the wheel, then remove the jackstands and carefully lower the vehicle.

10. Tighten the lug nuts to the proper torque.

With Drum Brakes

♦ See Figures 9, 10 and 11

1. Raise the vehicle and safely support it with jackstands, then remove the wheel.

2. Remove the brake drum.

3. If necessary to provide clearance, remove the brake shoes, as outlined in Section 9 of this manual.

4. Using a large C-clamp and socket, press the stud from the axle flange.

5. Coat the serrated part of the stud with liquid soap and place it into the hole.

To install:

6. Position about 4 flat washers over the stud and thread the lug nut. Hold the flange while tightening the lug nut, and the stud should be drawn into position. MAKE SURE THE STUD IS FULLY SEATED, then remove the lug nut and washers.

7. If applicable, install the brake shoes.

8. Install the brake drum.

9. Install the wheel, then remove the jackstands and carefully lower the vehicle.

10. Tighten the lug nuts to the proper torque.

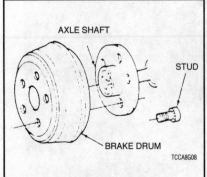

Fig. 9 Exploded view of the drum, axle flange and stud

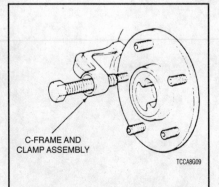

Fig. 10 Use a C-clamp and socket to press out the stud

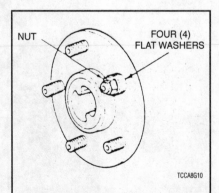

Fig. 11 Force the stud onto the axle flange using washers and a lug nut

FRONT SUSPENSION

FRONT SUSPENSION COMPONENT LOCATIONS

1. Lower control arm assembly
2. Shock absorber
3. Steering knuckle and spindle assembly
4. Stabilizer bar link (located on the end of the bar)
5. Stabilizer bar bushing and bracket
6. Drag link assembly
7. Steering gear and sector shaft
8. Stabilizer bar assembly
9. Pitman arm
10. Inner tie rod end
11. Upper control arm and ball joint assembly
12. Tie rod adjusting sleeve
13. Outer tie rod end
14. Lower ball joint assembly
15. Coil spring

89608P52

Coil Springs

REMOVAL & INSTALLATION

♦ **See Figures 12, 13 and 14**

1. Raise and safely support the vehicle.
2. Remove the wheel and tire assembly.

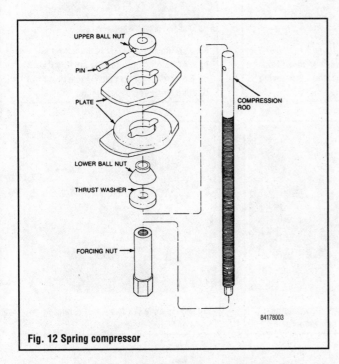

Fig. 12 Spring compressor

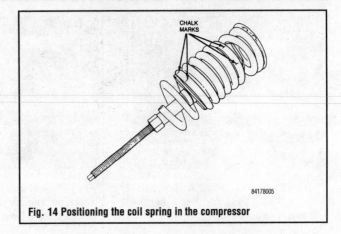

Fig. 14 Positioning the coil spring in the compressor

3. On 1989–91 vehicles, disconnect the stabilizer bar link from the lower arm.

4. Remove the shock absorber. Remove the steering link from the pitman arm.

5. Using a suitable spring compressor tool, install 1 plate with the pivot ball seat facing downward into the coils of the spring. Rotate the plate, so it is flush with the upper surface of the lower arm.

6. Install the other plate with the pivot ball seat facing upward into the coils of the spring. Insert the upper ball nut through the coils of the spring, so the nut rests in the upper plate.

7. Insert the compression rod into the opening in the lower arm, through the upper and lower plate and upper ball nut. Insert the securing pin through the upper ball nut and compression rod.

➥**This pin can only be inserted 1 way into the upper ball nut because of a stepped hole design.**

8. With the upper ball nut secured, turn the upper plate so it walks up the coil until it contacts the upper spring seat. Then back off ½ turn.

9. Install the lower ball nut and thrust washer on the compression rod and screw on the forcing nut. Tighten the forcing nut until the spring is compressed enough so it is free in its seat.

10. Remove the 2 lower arm pivot bolts, disengage the lower arm from the frame crossmember and remove the spring.

11. If a new spring is to be installed, perform the following:

a. Mark the position of the upper and lower plates on the spring with chalk.

b. With an assistant, compress a new spring for installation and measure the compressed length and the amount of curvature of the old spring.

12. Loosen the forcing nut to relieve the spring tension and remove the tools from the spring.

To install:

13. Assemble the spring compressor and locate in the same position as indicated in Step 11a.

14. Before compressing the coil spring, make sure the upper ball nut securing the pin is inserted properly.

15. Compress the coil spring until the spring height reaches the dimension obtained in Step 11b.

16. Position the coil spring assembly into the lower arm and reverse the removal procedure.

Shock Absorbers

REMOVAL & INSTALLATION

♦ **See Figures 15 thru 21**

❋❋ CAUTION

All vehicles except police applications are equipped with gas-pressurized shock absorbers which will extend unassisted. Do not apply heat or flame to the shock absorber tube.

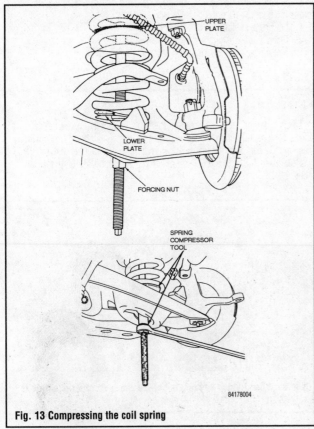

Fig. 13 Compressing the coil spring

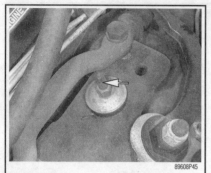

Fig. 15 The shock top mount retaining nut and washer are accessible through the engine compartment

Fig. 16 Special tools, such as these from Lisle®, are extremely helpful in removing the upper mounting nut

Fig. 17 The large socket is placed on the upper retaining nut, and the small socket on the shock absorber shaft to keep it from rotating while removing the nut

Fig. 18 Hold the small socket and turn the large socket counterclockwise to loosen the upper mounting nut

Fig. 19 Remove the upper mounting nut and washer from the shock absorber

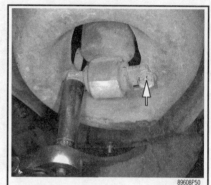

Fig. 20 Remove the two lower retaining bolts and . . .

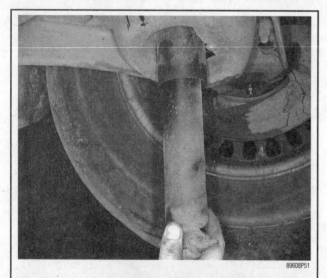

Fig. 21 . . . remove the shock by lowering it out of the vehicle

1. Remove the nut, washer and bushing from the upper end of the shock absorber.

2. Raise and safely support the vehicle by the frame rails allowing the front wheels to hang.

3. Remove the 2 bolts securing the shock absorber to the lower control arm and remove the shock absorber.

To install:

4. Prior to installation, purge a new shock of air by repeatedly extending it in its normal position and compressing it while inverted.

5. Install a new bushing and washer on the top of the shock absorber and position the unit inside the front spring. Install the 2 lower attaching bolts and torque them to 13–16 ft. lbs. (17–23 Nm).

6. Lower the vehicle.

7. Place a new bushing and washer on the shock absorber top stud and install a new attaching nut. Tighten to 26 ft. lbs. (41 Nm).

TESTING

▶ See Figure 22

The purpose of the shock absorber is simply to limit the motion of the spring during compression and rebound cycles. If the vehicle is not equipped with these motion dampers, the up and down motion would multiply until the vehicle was alternately trying to leap off the ground and to pound itself into the pavement.

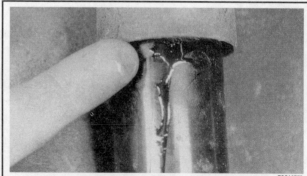

Fig. 22 When fluid is seeping out of the shock absorber, it's time to replace it

Contrary to popular rumor, the shocks do not affect the ride height of the vehicle. This is controlled by other suspension components such as springs and tires. Worn shock absorbers can affect handling; if the front of the vehicle is rising or falling excessively, the "footprint" of the tires changes on the pavement and steering is affected.

The simplest test of the shock absorber is simply push down on one corner of the unladen vehicle and release it. Observe the motion of the body as it is released. In most cases, it will come up beyond it original rest position, dip back below it and settle quickly to rest. This shows that the damper is controlling the spring action. Any tendency to excessive pitch (up-and-down) motion or failure to return to rest within 2-3 cycles is a sign of poor function within the shock absorber. Oil-filled shocks may have a light film of oil around the seal, resulting from normal breathing and air exchange. This should NOT be taken as a sign of failure, but any sign of thick or running oil definitely indicates failure. Gas filled shocks may also show some film at the shaft; if the gas has leaked out, the shock will have almost no resistance to motion.

While each shock absorber can be replaced individually, it is recommended that they are changed as a pair (both front or both rear) to maintain equal response on both sides of the vehicle. Chances are quite good that if one has failed, its mate is weak also.

Upper Ball Joint

INSPECTION

▶ **See Figure 23**

1. Raise the vehicle and place floor jacks beneath the lower control arms.
2. Make sure the front wheel bearings are properly adjusted.
3. Inspect the lower ball joint and replace the lower control arm assembly, if required.
4. Have an assistant grasp the bottom of the tire and move the wheel in and out.
5. As the wheel is being moved, observe the upper control arm where the spindle attaches to it. Any movement between the upper part of the spindle and the upper control arm indicates a bad ball joint which must be replaced.

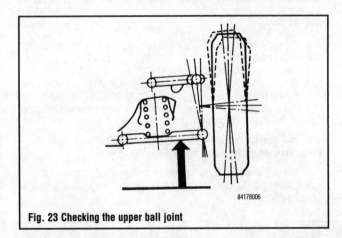

Fig. 23 Checking the upper ball joint

REMOVAL & INSTALLATION

1989–91 Vehicles

➡**Ford Motor Company recommends replacement of the upper control arm and ball joint as an assembly. However, aftermarket replacement parts are available, which can be installed using the following procedure.**

1. Raise the vehicle and support on frame points so the front wheels fall to their full down position.
2. Remove the wheel and tire assembly.
3. Drill a ⅛ in. (3mm) hole completely through each ball joint attaching rivet.
4. Using a large chisel, cut off the head of each rivet and drive them from the arm.

5. Place a jack under the lower arm and raise to compress the coil spring.
6. Remove the cotter pin and attaching nut from the ball joint stud.
7. Using a ball joint removal tool, loosen the ball joint stud from the spindle and remove the ball joint from the arm.

To install:

8. Clean all metal burrs from the arm and install the new ball joint, using the service part nuts and bolts to attach the ball joint. Do not attempt to rivet the ball joint once it has been removed.
9. Install the ball joint stud into the spindle. Tighten the ball joint-to-upper spindle nut to 60–90 ft. lbs. (81–122 Nm). Continue to tighten until the slot for the cotter pin is aligned. Install a new cotter pin.
10. Install the wheel and tire assembly.
11. Lower the vehicle.
12. Check front end alignment.

1992–98 Vehicles

▶ **See Figures 24 and 25**

1. Raise and safely support the vehicle with safety stands under the frame behind the lower arm. Remove the wheel and tire assembly.
2. Position a floor jack under the lower arm at the lower ball joint area. The floor jack will support the spring load on the lower arm.
3. Remove the retaining nut and pinch bolt from the upper ball joint stud.
4. Mark the position of the alignment cams. When replacing the ball joint, this will approximate the current alignment.
5. Remove the 2 nuts retaining the ball joint to the upper arm. Remove the ball joint and spread the slot with a suitable prybar to separate the ball joint stud from the spindle.

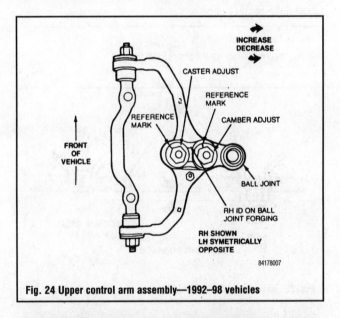

Fig. 24 Upper control arm assembly—1992–98 vehicles

Fig. 25 Upper ball joint-to-knuckle junction

To install:

➡️**The upper ball joints differ from side to side. Be sure to use the proper ball joint on each side.**

6. Position the ball joint on the upper arm and insert the ball stud into the spindle.

7. Install the pinch bolt and retaining nut. Tighten to 67 ft. lbs. (92 Nm).

8. Install the alignment cams to the approximate position at removal. If not marked, install in neutral position.

9. Install the 2 nuts attaching the ball joint to the arm. Hold the cams and tighten the nuts to 90–109 ft. lbs. (122–149 Nm) on 1992 vehicles or 107–129 ft. lbs. (145–175 Nm) on 1993–98 vehicles.

10. Remove the floor jack from the lower arm and install the wheel and tire assembly. Remove the safety stands and lower the vehicle.

11. Check and adjust the front end alignment.

Lower Ball Joint

INSPECTION

▶ **See Figure 26**

1. Support the vehicle in normal driving position with ball joints loaded.

2. Wipe the grease fitting and ball joint cover checking surface clean. The checking surface is the round boss into which the grease fitting is threaded.

3. The checking surface should project outside the cover. If the checking surface is inside the cover, replace the lower control arm assembly.

REMOVAL & INSTALLATION

The ball joint is an integral part of the lower control arm. If the ball joint is defective, the entire lower control arm must be replaced.

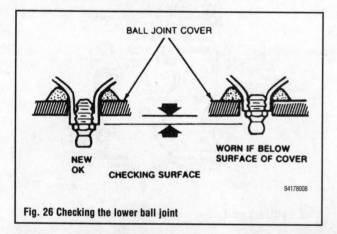

Fig. 26 Checking the lower ball joint

Stabilizer Bar

REMOVAL & INSTALLATION

▶ **See Figures 27, 28 and 29**

1. Raise the front of the vehicle and place jackstands under the lower control arms.

2. On 1989–91 vehicles, remove the link nuts and disconnect the stabilizer bar from the links.

3. On 1992–98 vehicles, remove the retaining nuts from the pinch bolts at the spindles. Spread the slots in the spindles with a prybar to free the ball studs. Be careful not to damage the ball joint stud seal.

4. Remove the stabilizer bar brackets from the frame and remove the stabilizer bar. If worn, cut the insulators from the stabilizer bar.

5. On 1992–98 vehicles, remove the retaining nuts from the ball joint studs at the end of the bar. Use a suitable separator tool (puller) to separate the links from the ends of the stabilizer bar.

To install:

6. Coat the necessary parts of the stabilizer bar with rubber lubricant. Slide new insulators onto the stabilizer bar.

7. On 1992–98 vehicles, install the ball joint links into the ends of the bar with the retaining nuts. Tighten to 30–40 ft. lbs. (40–55 Nm).

8. On 1989–91 vehicles, attach the ends of the stabilizer bar to the lower control arm with new nuts and links. Tighten the nuts to 9–15 ft. lbs. (12–20 Nm). Install the insulator brackets and tighten the bolts to 14–26 ft. lbs. (19–35 Nm).

9. On 1992–98 vehicles, position the bar under the vehicle and engage the upper ball joint links to the spindles. Install the insulator brackets with the retaining nuts. Tighten the pinch bolts and nuts at the spindles to 30–40 ft. lbs. (40–55 Nm) Tighten the bracket-to-frame nuts to 44–59 ft. lbs. (59–81 Nm).

Upper Control Arm

REMOVAL & INSTALLATION

1989–91 Vehicles

1. Raise and safely support the vehicle on safety stands positioned on the frame just behind the lower arm.

2. Remove the wheel and tire assembly.

3. Remove the cotter pin from the upper ball joint stud nut. Loosen the nut a few turns but do not remove.

4. Install a suitable ball joint press, between the upper and lower ball joint studs with the adapter screw on top.

➡️**This tool should be seated firmly against the ends of both studs, not against the nuts or lower stud cotter pin.**

5. With a wrench, turn the adapter screw until the tool places the stud under compression. Tap the spindle near the upper stud with a hammer to loosen the stud in the spindle.

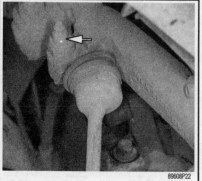

Fig. 27 Stabilizer bar link-to-knuckle junction

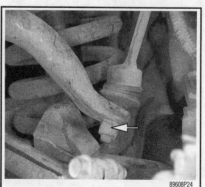

Fig. 28 Remove the stabilizer bar link-to-stabilizer bar retaining nut

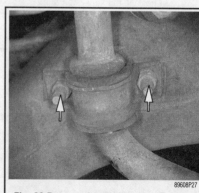

Fig. 29 Remove the stabilizer bar bushing bracket retaining bolts

➡️**Do not loosen the stud from the spindle with tool pressure only. Do not contact the boot seal with the hammer.**

6. Remove the tool from between the ball joint studs and place a floor jack under the lower arm.

7. Remove the upper arm attaching bolts and the upper arm.

To install:

8. Transfer the rebound bumper from the old arm to the new arm, or replace the bumper if worn or damaged.

9. Position the upper arm shaft to the frame bracket. Install the 2 attaching bolts and washers. Tighten to 100–140 ft. lbs. (136–190 Nm).

10. Connect the upper ball joint stud to the spindle and install the attaching nut. Tighten the nut to 60–90 ft. lbs. (81–122 Nm). Continue to tighten the nut until the slot for the cotter pin is aligned. Install a new cotter pin.

11. Install the wheel and tire assembly and lower the vehicle. Check the front end alignment.

1992–98 Vehicles

1. Raise and safely support the vehicle on safety stands positioned on the frame just behind the lower arm.

2. Remove the wheel and tire assembly and position a floor jack under the lower arm.

3. Remove the retaining nut from the upper ball joint stud to spindle pinch bolt. Tap the pinch bolt to remove from the spindle.

4. Using a suitable prybar, spread the slot to allow the ball joint stud to release out of the spindle.

5. Remove the upper arm retaining bolts and the upper arm.

To install:

6. Transfer the rebound bumper from the old arm to the new arm, or replace the bumper if worn or damaged.

7. Use reference marks from the camber and caster cams as initial settings.

8. Position the upper arm shaft to the frame bracket. Install the 2 retaining bolts and washers. Position the arm in the center of the slot adjustment range and tighten to 100–140 ft. lbs.

9. Connect the upper ball joint stud to the spindle and install the retaining pinch bolt and nut. Tighten the nut to 67 ft. lbs. (92 Nm).

10. Install the wheel and tire assembly and lower the vehicle. Check the front end alignment.

CONTROL ARM BUSHING REPLACEMENT

▶ **See Figures 30, 31, 32, 33 and 34**

1. Remove the upper control arm from the vehicle, as outlined in this section.

2. Remove the nuts and washers from both ends of the control arm shaft. Discard the nuts.

3. Press the bushings from the control arm and shaft using a suitable C-clamp tool (shown in the accompanying figure), and its adapters.

4. Position the shaft and new bushings to the upper control arm. Use the C-clamp tool and adapters to press the new bushings into place.

5. Make sure the control arm shaft is positioned so the serrated side contacts the frame.

6. Install an inner washer, rear bushing only, and 2 outer washers with new nuts on each end of the shaft. Tighten the nuts to 85–100 ft. lbs. (115–136 Nm).

Lower Control Arm

REMOVAL & INSTALLATION

▶ **See Figure 35**

1. Raise the front of the vehicle and position safety stands on the frame behind the lower control arms.

2. Remove the wheel and tire assembly.

3. Remove the brake caliper and suspend with a length of wire; do not let the caliper hang by the brake hose.

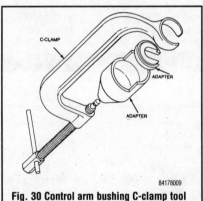

Fig. 30 Control arm bushing C-clamp tool and adapters

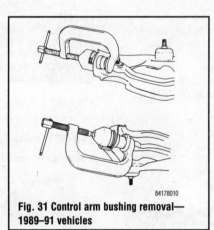

Fig. 31 Control arm bushing removal— 1989–91 vehicles

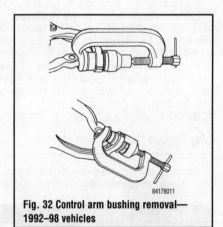

Fig. 32 Control arm bushing removal— 1992–98 vehicles

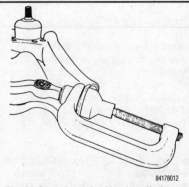

Fig. 33 Control arm bushing installation— 1989–91 vehicles

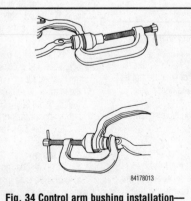

Fig. 34 Control arm bushing installation— 1992–98 vehicles

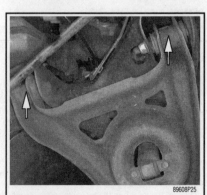

Fig. 35 Lower control arm-to-frame mounting

4. Remove the brake rotor and dust shield.

5. Remove the anti-lock brake sensor, if equipped.

6. Remove the jounce bumper; inspect and save for installation if in good condition. Remove the shock absorber.

7. On 1989–91 vehicles, disconnect the stabilizer link from the lower arm.

8. Disconnect the steering center link from the pitman arm.

9. Remove the cotter pin and loosen the lower ball joint stud nut 1–2 turns.

➡**Do not remove the nut at this time.**

10. On 1989–91 vehicles, install a suitable ball joint press tool to place the ball joint stud under compression. With the stud under compression, tap the spindle sharply with a hammer to loosen the stud in the spindle. Remove the ball joint press tool.

11. On 1992–98 vehicles, tap the spindle boss sharply to relieve the stud pressure. Tap the spindle sharply, near the lower stud, with a hammer to loosen the stud in the spindle.

12. Place a floor jack under the lower arm.

13. Remove the coil spring as described in this section.

14. Remove the ball joint nut and remove the lower control arm.

To install:

15. Position the arm assembly ball joint stud into the spindle and install the nut. Tighten to 80–120 ft. lbs. (108–163 Nm). Continue to tighten until the slot for the cotter pin is aligned. Install a new cotter pin.

16. Position the coil spring into the upper spring pocket and raise the lower arm, aligning the holes in the arm with the holes in the crossmember. Install the bolts and nuts with the washer installed on the front bushing. Do not tighten at this time.

➡**Make sure the pigtail of the lower coil of the spring is in the proper location of the seat on the lower arm, between the 2 holes.**

17. Remove the spring compressor tool.

18. Connect the steering center link at the pitman arm and install the nut. Tighten to 44–46 ft. lbs. (59–63 Nm). Continue to tighten until the slot for the cotter pin is aligned. Install a new cotter pin.

19. Install the shock absorber and the jounce bumper.

20. Install the dust shield, rotor and caliper.

21. Install the anti-lock brake sensor, if equipped.

22. On 1989–91 vehicles, position the stabilizer link to the lower control arm and install the link, bushing and retaining nut. Tighten to 9–15 ft. lbs. (12–20 Nm).

23. Install the wheel and tire assembly and lower the vehicle.

24. With the vehicle supported on the wheels and tires at normal curb height, tighten the lower control arm-to-crossmember bolts to 109–140 ft. lbs. (148–190 Nm).

25. Check the front end alignment.

CONTROL ARM BUSHING REPLACEMENT

The control arm bushings are integral with the lower control arm. If the bushings are defective, the entire lower control arm must be replaced.

Knuckle and Spindle

REMOVAL & INSTALLATION

1. Raise the front of the vehicle and position safety stands on the frame behind the lower control arms.

2. Remove the wheel and tire assembly.

3. Remove the brake caliper and suspend with a length of wire; do not let the caliper hang by the brake hose. Remove the brake rotor and dust shield.

4. Remove the anti-lock brake sensor, if equipped.

5. Disconnect the tie rod end from the spindle using a suitable separator tool (puller).

6. On 1989–91 vehicles, proceed as follows:

a. Remove and discard the cotter pins from both ball joint studs and loosen the stud nuts 1–2 turns. Do not remove the nuts at this time.

b. Position a suitable ball joint press tool between the upper and lower ball joint studs. Turn the tool with a wrench until the tool places the studs under compression.

c. Using a hammer, sharply hit the spindle near the studs to loosen the studs from the spindle.

7. On 1992–98 vehicles, proceed as follows:

a. Remove and discard the cotter pin from the lower ball joint stud and loosen the stud nut 1–2 turns. Do not remove the nut at this time.

b. Using a hammer, sharply hit the spindle near the stud to loosen the stud from the spindle.

c. Remove the pinch bolts from the upper ball joint and stabilizer link ball joint at the spindle.

8. Position a floor jack under the lower control arm at the lower ball joint area, and raise the jack to support the lower arm.

➡**The jack will support the spring load on the lower control arm.**

9. On 1989–91 vehicles, remove the upper and lower ball joint stud nuts and remove the spindle.

10. On 1992–98 vehicles, remove the lower ball joint stud nut. Pry the slots with a suitable prybar at the upper ball joint and link ball joint to separate from the spindle.

11. Remove the spindle.

To install:

12. On 1992–98 vehicles, position the spindle on the stabilizer bar upper ball joint stud. Install the pinch bolt and loosely install the nut.

13. Position the spindle on the lower ball joint stud and install the stud nut. Tighten the nut to 80–119 ft. lbs. (108–162 Nm). Continue to tighten the nut until a slot for the cotter pin is aligned. Install a new cotter pin.

14. Raise the lower arm and guide the upper ball joint stud into the spindle.

15. On 1989–91 vehicles, install the upper ball joint stud nut and tighten to 60–90 ft. lbs. (81–122 Nm). Continue to tighten the nut until a slot for the cotter pin is aligned. Install a new cotter pin.

16. On 1992–98 vehicles, install the upper ball joint stud pinch bolt and nut. Tighten the nut to 67 ft. lbs. (92 Nm). Tighten the stabilizer link to spindle pinch bolt nut to 30–50 ft. lbs. (40–55 Nm).

17. Connect the tie rod end to the spindle. Install the nut and tighten to 43–46 ft. lbs. (59–63 Nm). Continue to tighten the nut until the slot for the cotter pin is aligned and install a new cotter pin.

18. Install the brake dust shield, caliper, rotor and anti-lock brake sensor, if equipped.

19. Install the wheel and tire assembly and lower the vehicle.

20. Check the front end alignment.

Front Wheel Bearings

REMOVAL & INSTALLATION

1989–91 Vehicles

▶ **See Figures 36, 37, 38, 39 and 40**

1. Raise and support the vehicle safely.

2. Remove the wheel and tire assembly and the disc brake caliper. Suspend the caliper with a length of wire; do not let it hang from the brake hose.

3. Pry off the dust cap. Tap out and discard the cotter pin. Remove the nut retainer.

4. Being careful not to drop the outer bearing, pull off the brake disc and wheel hub assembly.

5. Remove the inner grease seal using a prybar. Remove the inner wheel bearing.

6. Clean the wheel bearings with solvent and inspect them for pits, scratches and excessive wear. Wipe all the old grease from the hub and inspect the bearing races (cups). If either bearings or races are damaged, the bearing races must be removed and the bearings and races replaced as an assembly.

7. If the bearings are to be replaced, drive out the races (cups) from the hub using a brass drift, or pull them from the hub using a puller.

8. Make sure the spindle, hub and bearing assemblies are clean prior to installation.

To install:

9. If the bearing races (cups) were removed, install new ones using a suitable bearing race installer. Pack the bearings with high-temperature wheel bearing grease using a bearing packer. If a packer is not available, work as much grease as possible between the rollers and cages using your hands.

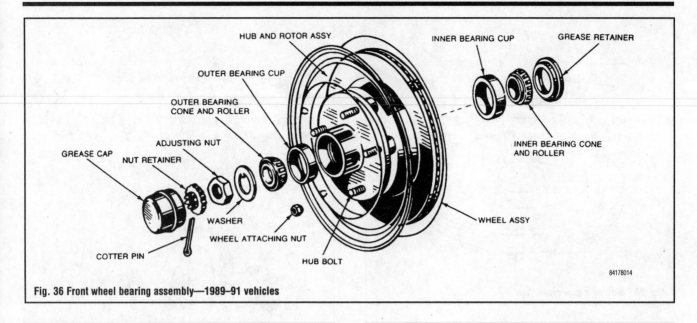

Fig. 36 Front wheel bearing assembly—1989–91 vehicles

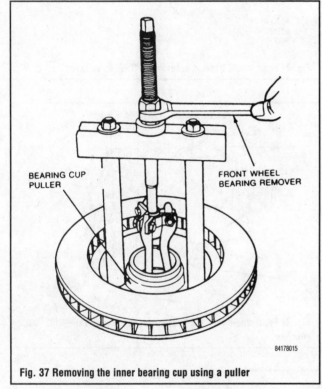

Fig. 37 Removing the inner bearing cup using a puller

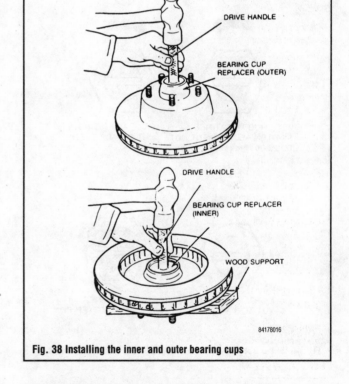

Fig. 38 Installing the inner and outer bearing cups

10. Coat the inner surface of the hub and bearing races (cups) with grease.

11. Install the inner bearing in the hub. Using a seal installer, install a new grease seal into the hub. Lubricate the lip of the seal with grease.

12. Install the hub/disc assembly on the spindle, being careful not to damage the oil seal.

13. Install the outer bearing, washer and spindle nut. Install the caliper and the wheel and tire assembly. Adjust the bearings as follows:

   a. Loosen the adjusting nut 3 turns and rock the wheel in and out a few times to release the brake pads from the rotor.

   b. While rotating the wheel and hub assembly in a counterclockwise direction, tighten the adjusting nut to 17–25 ft. lbs. (23–34 Nm).

   c. Back off the adjusting nut ½ turn, then retighten to 10–28 inch lbs. (1.1–3.2 Nm).

   d. Install the nut retainer and a new cotter pin. Replace the grease cap.

14. Lower the vehicle.

15. Before driving the vehicle, pump the brake pedal several times to restore normal brake pedal travel.

Front Hub and Bearing

REMOVAL & INSTALLATION

1992–98 Vehicles

▶ See Figures 41, 42 and 43

1. Raise and safely support the vehicle.
2. Remove the wheel and tire assembly.
3. Remove and discard the grease cap from the hub.

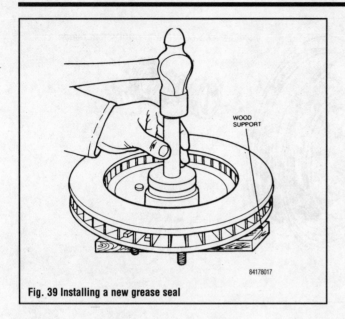

Fig. 39 Installing a new grease seal

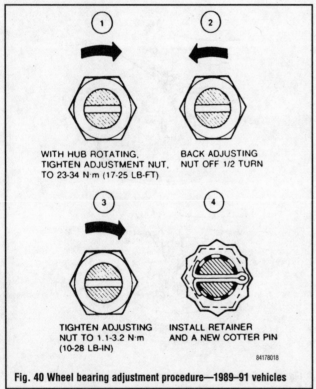

① WITH HUB ROTATING, TIGHTEN ADJUSTMENT NUT, TO 23-34 N·m (17-25 LB-FT)

② BACK ADJUSTING NUT OFF 1/2 TURN

③ TIGHTEN ADJUSTING NUT TO 1.1-3.2 N·m (10-28 LB-IN)

④ INSTALL RETAINER AND A NEW COTTER PIN

Fig. 40 Wheel bearing adjustment procedure—1989–91 vehicles

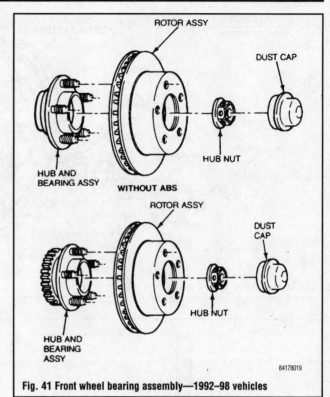

Fig. 41 Front wheel bearing assembly—1992–98 vehicles

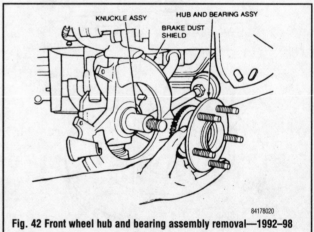

Fig. 42 Front wheel hub and bearing assembly removal—1992–98 vehicles

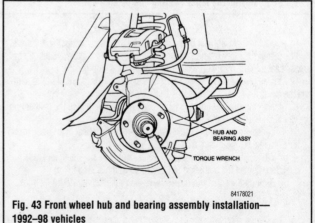

Fig. 43 Front wheel hub and bearing assembly installation—1992–98 vehicles

4. Remove the brake caliper. Suspend the caliper with a length of wire; do not let it hang from the brake hose.

5. Remove the rotor. If the factory installed push on nuts are installed, remove them first.

6. Remove and discard the wheel hub nut.

7. Remove the hub and bearing assembly.

To install:

8. Install the hub and bearing assembly. Install a new wheel hub nut and tighten to 189–254 ft. lbs. (255–345 Nm).

9. Install the rotor and push on nuts, if equipped. Install a new grease cap.

10. Install the brake caliper.

11. Install the wheel and tire assembly.

12. Lower the vehicle.

Wheel Alignment

If the tires are worn unevenly, if the vehicle is not stable on the highway or if the handling seems uneven in spirited driving, the wheel alignment should be checked. If an alignment problem is suspected, first check for improper tire inflation and other possible causes. These can be worn suspension or steering components, accident damage or even unmatched tires. If any worn or damaged components are found, they must be replaced before the wheels can be properly aligned. Wheel alignment requires very expensive equipment and involves minute adjustments which must be accurate; it should only be performed by a trained technician. Take your vehicle to a properly equipped shop.

Following is a description of the alignment angles which are adjustable on most vehicles and how they affect vehicle handling. Although these angles can apply to both the front and rear wheels, usually only the front suspension is adjustable.

CASTER

♦ See Figure 44

Looking at a vehicle from the side, caster angle describes the steering axis rather than a wheel angle. The steering knuckle is attached to a control arm or strut at the top and a control arm at the bottom. The wheel pivots around the line between these points to steer the vehicle. When the upper point is tilted back, this is described as positive caster. Having a positive caster tends to make the wheels self-centering, increasing directional stability. Excessive positive caster makes the wheels hard to steer, while an uneven caster will cause a pull to one side. Overloading the vehicle or sagging rear springs will affect caster, as will raising the rear of the vehicle. If the rear of the vehicle is lower than normal, the caster becomes more positive.

CAMBER

♦ See Figure 45

Looking from the front of the vehicle, camber is the inward or outward tilt of the top of wheels. When the tops of the wheels are tilted in, this is negative camber; if they are tilted out, it is positive. In a turn, a slight amount of negative camber helps maximize contact of the tire with the road. However, too much negative camber compromises straight-line stability, increases bump steer and torque steer.

TOE

♦ See Figure 46

Looking down at the wheels from above the vehicle, toe angle is the distance between the front of the wheels, relative to the distance between the back of the wheels. If the wheels are closer at the front, they are said to be toed-in or to have negative toe. A small amount of negative toe enhances directional stability and provides a smoother ride on the highway.

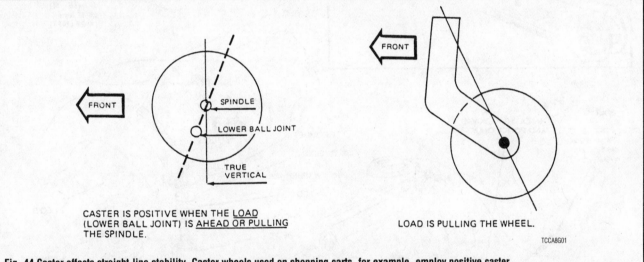

SPINDLE

LOWER BALL JOINT

TRUE VERTICAL

CASTER IS POSITIVE WHEN THE <u>LOAD</u> (LOWER BALL JOINT) IS <u>AHEAD OR PULLING</u> THE SPINDLE.

FRONT

LOAD IS PULLING THE WHEEL.

TCCA8G01

Fig. 44 Caster affects straight-line stability. Caster wheels used on shopping carts, for example, employ positive caster

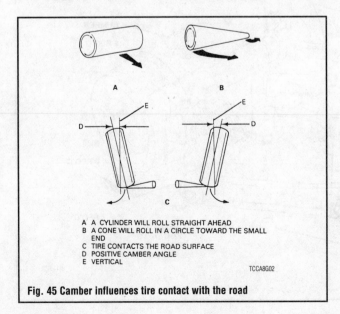

A   A CYLINDER WILL ROLL STRAIGHT AHEAD
B   A CONE WILL ROLL IN A CIRCLE TOWARD THE SMALL END
C   TIRE CONTACTS THE ROAD SURFACE
D   POSITIVE CAMBER ANGLE
E   VERTICAL

TCCA8G02

Fig. 45 Camber influences tire contact with the road

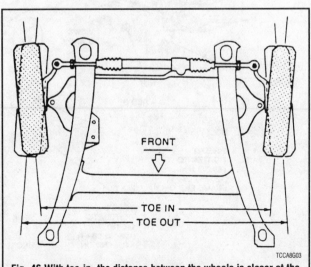

FRONT

TOE IN
TOE OUT

TCCA8G03

Fig. 46 With toe-in, the distance between the wheels is closer at the front than at the rear

REAR SUSPENSION

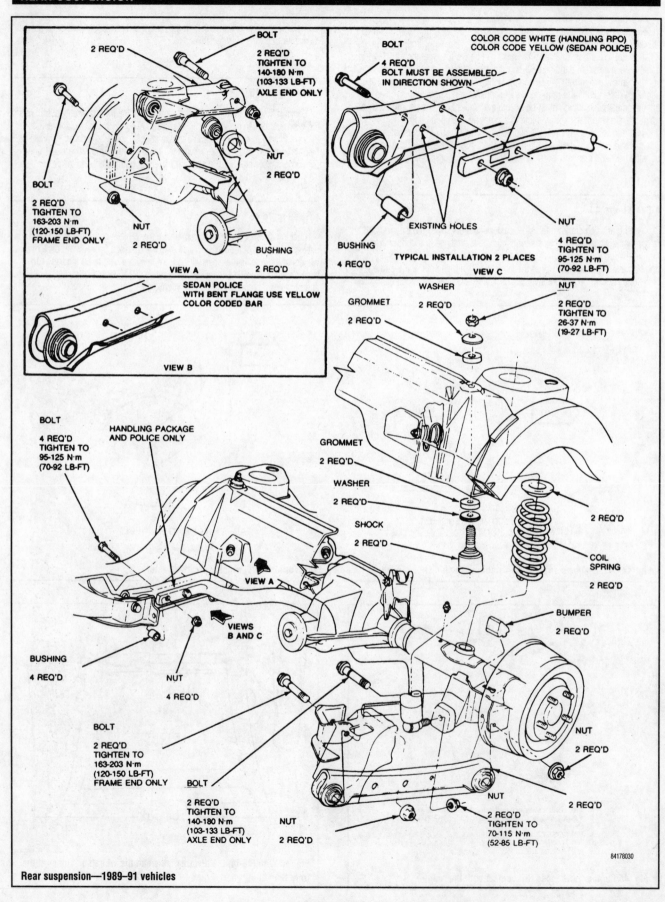

Rear suspension—1989–91 vehicles

84178030

REAR SUSPENSION COMPONENT LOCATIONS (EXCEPT AIR SPRING SUSPENSION)

1. Stabilizer bar link
2. Coil spring assembly
3. Upper control arm assembly
4. Lower control arm assembly
5. Shock absorber
6. Stabilizer bar bushing and bracket
7. Stabilizer bar assembly

89608P53

Coil Springs

REMOVAL & INSTALLATION

1. Raise and safely support the vehicle.
2. Place jackstands under the frame side rails.
3. Support the rear axle housing.
4. Remove the rear stabilizer bar, if equipped.
5. Disconnect the lower studs of both rear shock absorbers from the mounting brackets on the axle tube.
6. Unsnap the right parking brake cable from the right upper arm retainer before lowering the axle.
7. Lower the axle housing until the coil springs are released.
8. Remove the springs and insulators.

To install:

9. Position the spring in the upper and lower seats with an insulator between the upper end of the spring and frame seat.
10. Raise the axle and connect the shock absorbers to the mounting brackets. Install new retaining nuts and tighten to 56–76 ft. lbs. (77–103 Nm).
11. Snap the right parking cable into the upper arm retainer. Install the stabilizer bar, if equipped.
12. Remove the support from the rear axle housing.
13. Carefully lower the vehicle.

Air Springs

REMOVAL & INSTALLATION

▸ See Figures 47 thru 57

✳✳ CAUTION

Before servicing any air suspension component, disconnect power to the system by turning the air suspension switch OFF or by disconnecting the negative battery cable. Do not remove an air spring under any circumstances when there is pressure in the air spring. Do not remove any components supporting an air spring without either exhausting the air or providing support for the air spring.

1. Turn the air suspension switch OFF.
2. Raise and safely support the vehicle on the frame. The suspension must be fully down with no load.
3. Remove the heat shield, as required.
4. Remove the spring retainer clip.
5. Remove the air spring solenoid as follows:
   a. Detach the electrical connector and then disconnect the air line.
   b. Remove the solenoid clip.
   c. Rotate the solenoid counterclockwise to the first stop.
   d. Pull the solenoid straight out slowly to the second stop to bleed air from the system.

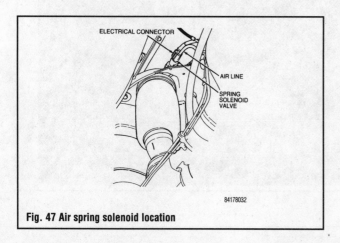

Fig. 47 Air spring solenoid location

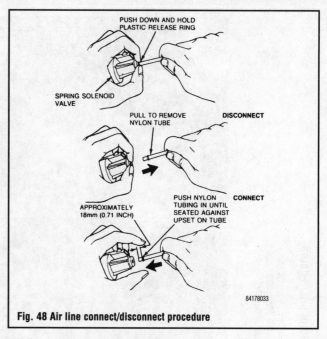

Fig. 48 Air line connect/disconnect procedure

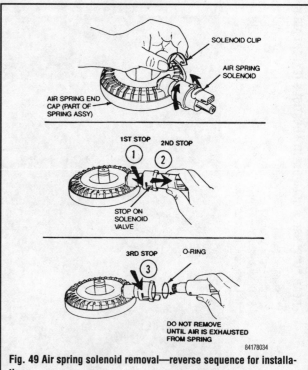

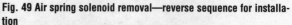

Fig. 49 Air spring solenoid removal—reverse sequence for installation

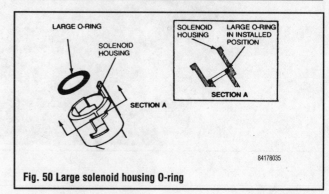

Fig. 50 Large solenoid housing O-ring

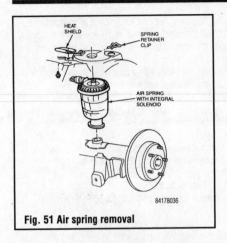

Fig. 51 Air spring removal

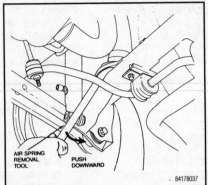

Fig. 52 Removing the spring piston-to-axle spring seat

Fig. 53 New air spring appearance prior to installation

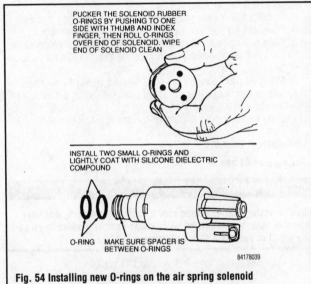

Fig. 54 Installing new O-rings on the air spring solenoid

Code	Description
23	Vent Rear
26	Compress Rear
31	Cycle Compressor On and Off Repeatedly
32	Cycle Vent Solenoid Valve Open and Closed Repeatedly
33	Cycle Spring Solenoid Valves Open and Closed Repeatedly

Fig. 56 Air suspension codes

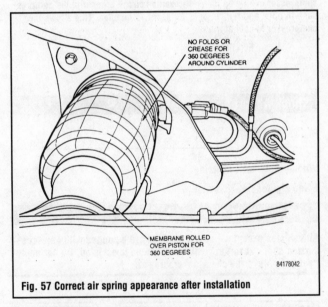

Fig. 57 Correct air spring appearance after installation

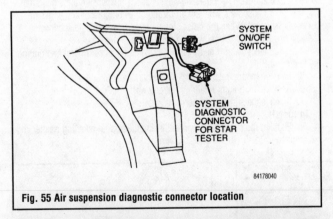

Fig. 55 Air suspension diagnostic connector location

✳✳ CAUTION

Do not fully release the solenoid until the air is completely bled from the air spring or personal injury may result.

e. After the air is fully bled from the system, rotate counterclockwise to the third stop and remove the solenoid from the solenoid housing. Remove the large O-ring from the solenoid housing.

6. Remove the spring piston-to-axle spring seat as follows:

a. Insert a suitable air spring removal tool, between the axle tube and the spring seat on the forward side of the axle.

b. Position the tool so its flat end rests on the piston knob. Push downward, forcing the piston and retainer clip off the axle spring seat.

7. Remove the air spring.

To install:

8. Install the air spring solenoid as follows:

a. Check the solenoid O-rings for cuts or abrasion. Replace the O-rings as required. Lightly grease the O-ring area of the solenoid and the larger solenoid housing O-ring with silicone dielectric compound.

b. Insert the solenoid into the air spring end cap and rotate clockwise to the third stop, push in to the second stop, then rotate clockwise to the first stop.

c. Install the solenoid clip. Inspect the wire harness connector and ensure the rubber gasket is in place at the bottom of the connector cavity.

9. Install the air spring into the frame spring seat, taking care to keep the solenoid air and electrical connections clean and free of damage.

10. Connect the push on spring retainer clip to the knob of the spring cap from the top side of the frame spring seat.

11. Attach the air line and electrical connector to the solenoid. Install the heat shield to frame spring seat, if required.

12. Align the air spring piston to axle seats. Squeeze to increase pressure and push downward on the piston, snapping the piston to axle seat at rebound and supported by the shock absorber.

➡**The air springs may be damaged if the suspension is allowed to compress before the spring is inflated.**

13. Refill the air spring as follows:

a. Turn the air suspension switch ON. The ignition switch must be **ON** and the engine running or a battery charger must be connected to the battery to reduce battery drain.

b. Fold back or remove the right luggage compartment trim panel and attach SUPER STAR II tester 007–0041–A or equivalent to the air suspension diagnostic connector, which is located near the air suspension switch.

c. Set the tester to EEC-IV/MCU mode. Also set the tester to FAST mode. Release the tester button to the HOLD (up) position and turn the tester ON.

d. Depress the tester button to TEST (down) position. A Code 10 will be displayed. Within 2 minutes a Code 13 will be displayed. After Code 13 is displayed, release the tester button to HOLD (up) position, wait 5 seconds and depress the tester button to TEST (down) position. Ignore any codes displayed.

e. Release the tester button to the HOLD (up) position. Wait at least 20 seconds, then depress the tester button to TEST (down) position. Within 10 seconds, the codes will be displayed in the order shown.

f. Within 4 seconds after Code 26 is displayed, release the tester button to the HOLD (up) position. Waiting longer than 4 seconds may result in Functional Test 31 being entered. The compressor will fill the air springs with air as long as the tester button is in the HOLD (up) position. To stop filling the air springs, depress the tester button to the TEST (down) position.

➡**It is possible to overheat the compressor during this operation. If the compressor overheats, the self-resetting circuit breaker in the compressor will open and remain open for about 15 minutes. This allows the compressor to cool down.**

g. To exit Functional Test 26, disconnect the tester and turn the ignition switch OFF.

14. Lower the vehicle.

Shock Absorbers

REMOVAL & INSTALLATION

Without Automatic Leveling

▶ **See Figures 58, 59 and 60**

✳✳ CAUTION

All vehicles except police applications are equipped with gas-pressurized shock absorbers which will extend unassisted. Do not apply heat or flame to the shock absorber tube.

1. If equipped with air suspension, turn the air suspension switch OFF.
2. Raise and safely support the vehicle. Make sure the rear axle is supported.
3. To assist in removing the upper attachment on shock absorbers using a plastic dust tube, place an open-end wrench on the hex stamped into the dust tube's metal cap. For shock absorbers with a steel dust tube, simply grasp the tube to prevent stud rotation when loosening the retaining nut.
4. Remove the shock absorber retaining nut, washer and insulator from the stud on the upper side of the frame. Discard the nut. Compress the shock to clear the hole in the frame and remove the inner insulator and washer from the upper retaining stud.
5. Remove the self-locking retaining nut and disconnect the shock absorber lower stud from the mounting bracket on the rear axle.

To install:

6. Prime the new shock absorber as follows:

a. With the shock absorber right side up (as installed in the vehicle), extend it fully.

b. Turn the shock upside down and fully compress it.

c. Repeat the previous two steps at least 3 times to make sure any trapped air has been expelled.

7. Place the inner washer and insulator on the upper retaining stud and position the shock absorber with the stud through the hole in the frame.

8. While holding the shock absorber in position, install the outer insulator, washer and a new stud nut on the upper side of the frame. Tighten the nut to 25 ft. lbs. (34 Nm).

9. Extend the shock absorber and place the lower stud in the mounting bracket hole on the rear axle housing. Install a new self-locking nut and tighten to 56–76 ft. lbs. (77–103 Nm).

10. Lower the vehicle and, if equipped, turn the air suspension switch ON.

With Automatic Leveling

▶ **See Figures 61 and 62**

✳✳ WARNING

When removing and installing rear air shock absorbers, it is very important that this procedure be followed exactly. Failure to do so may result in damaged shock absorbers.

1. Make sure the ignition switch is in the **OFF** position.
2. Detach the height sensor connector link before allowing the rear axle to hang free.
3. Raise and safely support the vehicle so the suspension arms hang free. The rear shock absorbers will vent air through the compressor and a hissing noise will be heard. When the noise stops, the air lines can be disconnected. A residual pressure of 8–24 psi will remain in the air lines.
4. Disconnect the air line by pushing in on the retainer ring(s) and pulling the line(s) out.
5. Remove the top retaining nut, washer and bushing.
6. Remove the bottom retaining nut and washer.
7. Remove the shock absorber.

To install:

8. Position the shock absorber and install the bottom retaining washer and nut. Tighten to 52–85 ft. lbs. (70–115 Nm).

Fig. 58 Support the rear axle assembly before attempting to remove the shock absorber

Fig. 59 Remove the lower shock absorber mount

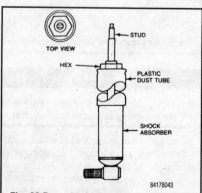

Fig. 60 Rear shock absorber—except with automatic leveling suspension

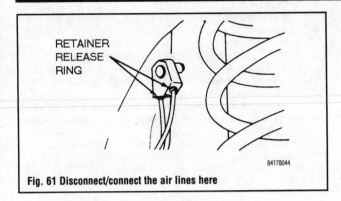

Fig. 61 Disconnect/connect the air lines here

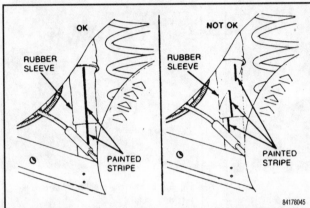

Fig. 62 Make sure the rubber sleeve on the air shock absorber is not wrapped up

9. Install the top bushing, washer and retaining nut. Tighten to 14–26 ft. lbs. (19–35 Nm).

➡Check the rubber sleeve on the shock absorber to be sure it is not wrapped up. To assist in identifying wrap-up during installation, a white stripe is on the rubber sleeve and on the shock absorber body. The stripes should align. To correct a wrap-up condition, loosen the upper shock retaining nut and turn the shock to align the stripes. Retighten the retaining nut.

10. Connect the air line to the shock absorber by pushing in on the retainer ring and installing the air line.
11. Attach the height sensor connecting link and lower the vehicle.

TESTING

To test the shock absorbers, refer to the shock testing procedure under front suspension.

Control Arms

REMOVAL & INSTALLATION

Upper Control Arm

♦ See Figure 63

➡If one upper control arm requires replacement, also replace the upper control arm on the other side of the vehicle. If both upper arms are to be replaced, remove and install one at a time to prevent the axle from rolling or slipping sideways. If both upper control arms and both lower control arms are to be removed at the same time, remove both coil or air springs, as detailed in this section.

Fig. 63 Upper control arm-to-axle mounting

1. If equipped, turn the air suspension switch OFF.
2. Raise the vehicle and support the frame side rails with jackstands.
3. Support the rear axle under the differential pinion nose as wheel as under the axle.
4. Unsnap the parking brake cable from the upper arm retainer. If equipped, disconnect the height sensor from the ball stud on the left upper control arm.
5. Remove and discard the nut and bolt retaining the upper arm to the axle housing. Disconnect the arm from the housing.
6. Remove and discard the nut and bolt retaining the upper arm to the frame bracket and remove the arm.
   To install:
7. Hold the upper arm in place on the front arm bracket and install a new retaining bolt and self-locking nut. Do not tighten at this time.
8. Secure the upper arm to the axle housing with new retaining bolts and nuts. The bolts must be pointed toward the front of the vehicle.
9. Raise the suspension with a jack until the upper arm rear pivot hole is in position with the hole in the axle bushing. Install a new pivot bolt and nut with the nut facing inboard.
10. Tighten the upper arm-to-axle pivot bolts to 103–132 ft. lbs. (140–180 Nm) and upper arm-to-frame pivot bolts to 119–149 ft. lbs. (162–203 Nm).
11. Snap the parking brake cable into the upper arm retainer. Connect the height sensor to the ball stud on the left upper arm, if equipped.
12. Remove the supports from the frame and axle and lower the vehicle. If equipped, turn the air suspension switch ON.

Lower Control Arm

➡If one lower control arm requires replacement, also replace the lower control arm on the other side of the vehicle. If both upper control arms and both lower control arms are to be removed at the same time, remove both coil or air springs, as detailed in this Section.

1. If equipped, turn the air suspension switch OFF.
2. Mark the rear shock absorber tube relative to the protective sleeve with the vehicle in the normal ride height position.
3. Raise the vehicle and support the frame side rails with jackstands. Allow the axle housing to hang with the shock absorbers fully extended to relieve spring pressure.
4. Remove the stabilizer bar, if equipped.
5. Support the axle with jackstands under the differential pinion nose as well as under the axle.
6. Remove and discard the lower arm pivot bolts and nuts and remove the lower arm.
   To install:
7. Position the lower arm to the frame bracket and axle. Install new bolts and nuts with the nuts facing outboard.
8. Raise the axle to the normal ride height position, compressing the shock absorbers to the marks made during the removal procedure. Tighten the lower arm-to-axle pivot bolt to 103–132 ft. lbs. (140–180 Nm) and lower arm-to-frame pivot bolt to 119–149 ft. lbs. (162–203 Nm).
9. Install the stabilizer bar, if equipped.
10. Remove the jackstands and lower the vehicle.
11. If equipped, turn the air suspension switch ON.

Stabilizer Bar

REMOVAL & INSTALLATION

◆ See Figures 64, 65 and 66

1. If equipped, turn the air suspension switch OFF.
2. Raise the vehicle and support the frame side rails with jackstands. Allow the axle housing to hang with the shock absorbers fully extended.
3. On 1989–91 vehicles, remove the bolts, nuts and spacers retaining the stabilizer bar to the lower control arms and remove the stabilizer bar. Discard the bolts and nuts.
4. On 1992–98 vehicles, disconnect the stabilizer bar arms from the links.

Remove the bolts and brackets retaining the stabilizer bar to the rear axle and remove the stabilizer bar.

To install:

5. On 1989–91 vehicles, align the 4 holes in the stabilizer bar with the holes in the lower control arms. Install the color coded end of the bar on the right side of the vehicle. Install 4 new bolts and nuts and the existing spacers. Tighten to 70–92 ft. lbs. (95–125 Nm).
6. On 1992–98 vehicles, install 2 brackets onto the stabilizer bar insulators and hook both brackets into the T-slot of the rear axle bracket. Install the retaining bolts and tighten to 16–21 ft. lbs. (21–29 Nm). Connect the stabilizer bar eyes to the links using insulators, nuts and washers. Tighten to 13–17 ft. lbs. (17–23 Nm).
7. Remove the jackstands and lower the vehicle.
8. If equipped, turn the air suspension switch ON.

Fig. 64 Remove the bolts and brackets retaining the stabilizer bar to the rear axle

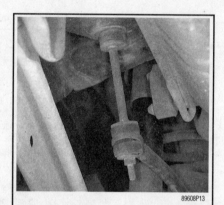

Fig. 65 The stabilizer bar link assembly

Fig. 66 Remove the stabilizer bar-to-link retaining nuts

STEERING

Steering Wheel

REMOVAL & INSTALLATION

1989 Vehicles

1. Disconnect the negative battery cable.
2. Remove the horn pad and cover assembly.
3. Detach the horn electrical connector.
4. If equipped, detach the cruise control switch electrical connector.
5. Remove and discard the steering wheel bolt.
6. Remove the steering wheel using a suitable puller.

➡Do not use a knock-off type steering wheel puller or strike the retaining bolt with a hammer. This could cause damage to the steering shaft bearing.

To install:

7. Align the index marks on the steering wheel and shaft and install the steering wheel.
8. Install a new steering wheel retaining bolt and tighten to 30–35 ft. lbs. (41–47 Nm).
9. Attach the cruise control electrical connector, if equipped.
10. Attach the horn electrical connector and install the horn pad and cover.
11. Connect the negative battery cable.

1990–98 Vehicles

◆ See Figures 67 thru 75

> ❊❊ **CAUTION**
>
> **The air bag system must be disarmed, before working on the system. Failure to do so may result in deployment of the air bag and possible personal injury.**

1. Center the front wheels in the straight-ahead position.
2. Properly disarm the air bag system; see the procedure in Section 6.
3. Remove the 4 air bag module retaining bolts and lift the module off the steering wheel.
4. Disconnect the air bag wire harness from the air bag module and remove the module from the steering wheel.

> ❊❊ **CAUTION**
>
> **When carrying a live air bag, make sure the bag and trim cover are pointed away from the body. In the unlikely event of an accidental deployment, the bag will then deploy with minimal chance of injury. When placing a live air bag on a bench or other surface, always face the bag and trim cover up, away from the surface. This will reduce the motion of the module if it is accidentally deployed.**

5. Disconnect the cruise control wire harness from the steering wheel, if equipped.
6. Remove and discard the steering wheel bolt.
7. Remove the steering wheel using a suitable puller. Route the contact assembly wire harness through the steering wheel as the wheel is lifted off the shaft.

➡Do not use a knock-off type steering wheel puller or strike the retaining bolt with a hammer. This could cause damage to the steering shaft bearing.

To install:

8. Make sure the front wheels are in the straight-ahead position.
9. Route the contact assembly wire harness through the steering wheel opening at the 3 o'clock position and install the steering wheel on the steering shaft. The steering wheel and shaft alignment marks should be aligned. Make sure the air bag contact wire is not pinched.
10. Install a new steering wheel retaining bolt and tighten to 23–33 ft. lbs. (31–45 Nm).
11. If equipped, connect the cruise control wire harness to the wheel and

Fig. 67 Remove the air bag module retaining bolts

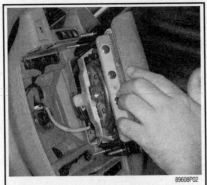

Fig. 68 Lift the air bag module from the steering wheel . . .

Fig. 69 . . . then detach the connectors on the air bag module and remove the module

Fig. 70 Always carry a live air bag module with the bag and trim cover facing away from your body

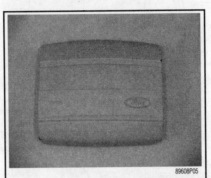

Fig. 71 Always place an air bag module on a table or other flat surface with the bag and trim cover pointing up

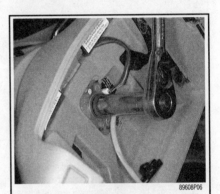

Fig. 72 Remove the steering wheel retaining bolt . . .

Fig. 73 . . . then install a suitable puller onto the steering wheel

Fig. 74 Tighten the forcing screw of the puller to loosen the steering wheel and . . .

Fig. 75 . . . remove the wheel from the steering column

snap the connector assembly into the steering wheel clip. Make sure the wiring does not get trapped between the steering wheel and contact assembly.

12. Connect the air bag wire harness to the air bag module and install the module to the steering wheel. Tighten the module retaining nuts to 24–32 inch lbs. (2.7–3.7 Nm).

13. Enable the air bag system according to the procedure in Section 6.

Multi-Function Switch

The multi-function switch incorporates the turn signal, dimmer and windshield wiper switch functions on 1990–98 vehicles. The multi-function switch incorporates only the turn signal and dimmer function on 1989 vehicles. For windshield wiper switch removal and installation on 1989 vehicles, refer to the procedure located later in this section.

REMOVAL & INSTALLATION

1989 Vehicles

▶ See Figure 76

1. Disconnect the negative battery cable.
2. Remove the switch lever by grasping and pulling straight out.
3. Remove the steering column cover retaining screws and remove the cover.
4. Remove the shroud retaining screws and remove the shroud.
5. With the wiring connectors exposed, carefully lift the connector retainer tabs and detach the connectors.
6. Remove the switch retaining screws and lift up the switch assembly.
7. Installation is the reverse of the removal procedure.

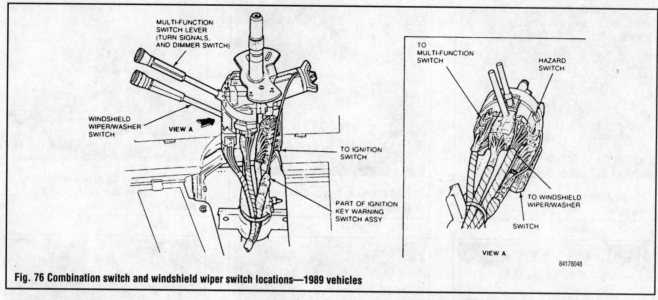

Fig. 76 Combination switch and windshield wiper switch locations—1989 vehicles

1990–98 Vehicles

▶ **See Figure 77**

1. Disconnect the negative battery cable.
2. If equipped with tilt column, move the column to the lowest position, then remove the tilt lever.
3. Remove the ignition lock cylinder; refer to the procedure in this Section.
4. Remove the shroud screws and remove the upper and lower shrouds.
5. Remove the 2 self-tapping screws attaching the combination switch to the steering column casting and remove the switch.
6. Remove the wiring harness retainer and detach the 2 electrical connectors.
7. Installation is the reverse of the removal procedure.

Windshield Wiper Switch

REMOVAL & INSTALLATION

1989 Vehicles

1. Disconnect the negative battery cable.
2. Remove the split steering column cover retaining screws.

3. Separate the halves and remove the wiper switch retaining screws.
4. Detach the electrical connector and remove the wiper switch.
5. Installation is the reverse of the removal procedure.

Ignition Switch

REMOVAL & INSTALLATION

1. Disconnect the negative battery cable.
2. On 1989 vehicles with tilt column, remove the upper extension shroud by unsnapping the shroud from the retaining clip at the 9 o'clock position.
3. Remove the steering column shroud by removing the attaching screws. On 1990–98 vehicles, remove the tilt lever, if equipped.
4. On 1990–98 vehicles, remove the instrument panel lower steering column cover.
5. Detach the electrical connector from the ignition switch.
6. Rotate the ignition key lock cylinder to the **RUN** position.
7. Remove the 2 screws attaching the ignition switch.
8. Disengage the ignition switch from the actuator pin and remove the switch.
   To install:
9. Adjust the new ignition switch by sliding the carrier to the **RUN** position.

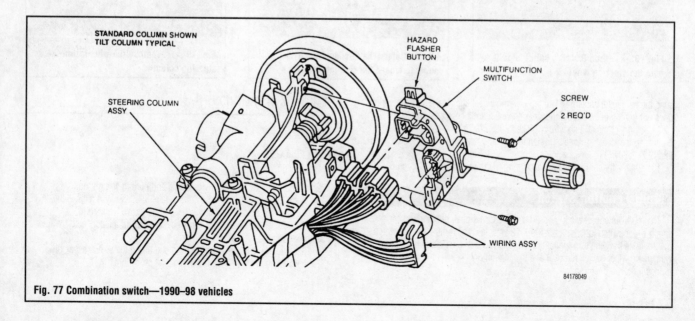

Fig. 77 Combination switch—1990–98 vehicles

10. Check to ensure that the ignition key lock cylinder is in the **RUN** position. The **RUN** position is achieved by rotating the key lock cylinder approximately 90 degrees from the **LOCK** position.

11. Install the ignition switch onto the actuator pin.

12. Align the switch mounting holes and install the attaching screws. Tighten the screws to 50–69 inch lbs. (5.6–7.9 Nm).

13. Attach the electrical connector to the ignition switch.

14. Connect the negative battery cable.

15. Check the ignition switch for proper function in **START** and **ACC** positions. Make sure the column is locked in the **LOCK** position.

16. Install the remaining components in the reverse order of removal.

Ignition Lock Cylinder

REMOVAL & INSTALLATION

Functional Lock

▶ See Figures 78 and 79

The following procedure is for vehicles with functioning lock cylinders. Ignition keys are available for these vehicles or the ignition key numbers are known and the proper key can be made.

1. Disconnect the negative battery cable. If equipped, properly disarm the air bag system; refer to Section 6.

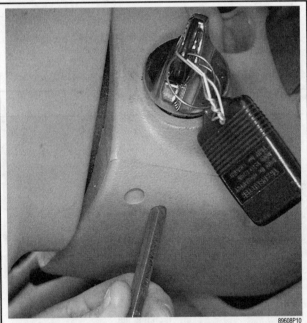

Fig. 78 Turn the ignition switch to the RUN position and push the lock cylinder release pin with a suitable punch . . .

Fig. 79 . . . then pull the lock cylinder from the steering column housing

2. On 1989 vehicles, remove the trim shroud halves by removing the attaching screws. Remove the electrical connector from the key warning switch.

3. Turn the ignition to the **RUN** position.

4. Place a ⅛ in. diameter wire pin or small drift punch in the hole in the casting surrounding the lock cylinder and depress the retaining pin while pulling out on the lock cylinder to remove it from the column housing.

To install:

5. To install the lock cylinder, turn it to the **RUN** position and depress the retaining pin. Insert the lock cylinder into its housing in the lock cylinder casting.

6. Make sure the cylinder is fully seated and aligned in the interlocking washer before turning the key to the **OFF** position. This action will permit the cylinder retaining pin to extend into the hole in the lock cylinder housing.

7. Using the ignition key, rotate the cylinder to ensure the correct mechanical operation in all positions.

8. Check for proper start in **P** or **N**. Also make sure the start circuit cannot be actuated in **D** or **R** positions and that the column is locked in the **LOCK** position.

9. Attach the key warning buzzer electrical connector and install the trim shrouds, if required.

Non-Functional Lock

The following procedure is for vehicles with non-functioning locks. On these vehicles, the lock cylinder cannot be rotated due to a lost or broken key, the key number is not known, or the lock cylinder cap is damaged and/or broken, preventing the lock cylinder from rotating.

1. Disconnect the negative battery cable.

2. If equipped, properly disarm the air bag system; refer to Section 6.

3. Remove the steering wheel; refer to the procedure in this section.

4. On 1989 vehicles, remove the trim shroud halves by removing the attaching screws.

5. Remove the electrical connector from the key warning switch.

6. On 1989–90 vehicles, drill out the retaining pin using a ⅛ in. diameter drill, being careful not to drill deeper than ½ in. Position a chisel at the base of the ignition lock cylinder. Strike the chisel with sharp blows, using a hammer, to break the cap away from the lock cylinder.

7. On 1991–98 vehicles, use channel lock or vise grip type pliers to twist the lock cylinder cap until it separates from the lock cylinder.

8. Drill approximately 1¾ in. down the middle of the ignition key slot, using a ⅜ in. diameter drill bit, until the lock cylinder breaks loose from the breakaway base of the lock cylinder. Remove the lock cylinder and drill shavings from the lock cylinder housing.

9. Remove the snapring or retainer, washer and steering column lock gear. Thoroughly clean all drill shavings and other foreign materials from the casting.

10. Inspect the lock cylinder housing for damage and replace, as necessary.

To install:

11. Install the ignition lock cylinder and check for smooth operation.

12. Attach the electrical connector to the key warning switch and install the trim shrouds, if necessary.

13. Install the steering wheel and connect the negative battery cable.

Steering Linkage

▶ See Figure 80

REMOVAL & INSTALLATION

Pitman Arm

▶ See Figures 81 thru 87

1. Position the front wheels in the straight-ahead position.

2. Raise and safely support the vehicle.

3. Remove and discard the cotter pin from the castellated nut that attaches the center link to the pitman arm. Remove the castellated nut.

4. Disconnect the center link from the pitman arm using a suitable separator tool (puller).

5. Remove the pitman arm retaining nut and lockwasher.

6. Make sure the front wheel are in the straight-ahead position. Remove the pitman arm from the steering gear sector shaft using a suitable pitman arm puller.

To install:

7. With the front wheels in the straight-ahead position, place the pitman

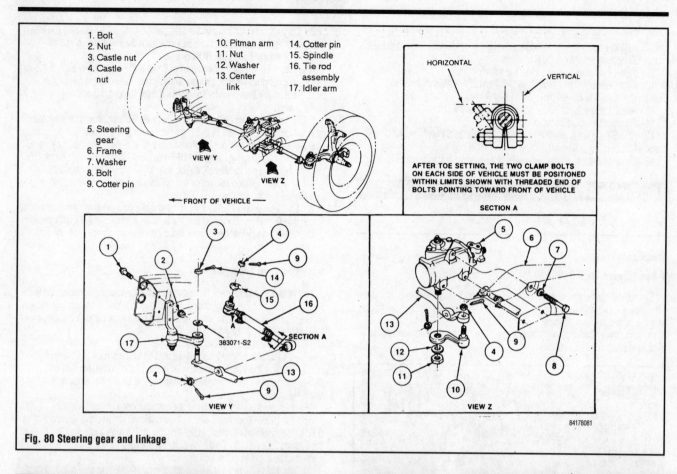

1. Bolt
2. Nut
3. Castle nut
4. Castle nut
5. Steering gear
6. Frame
7. Washer
8. Bolt
9. Cotter pin
10. Pitman arm
11. Nut
12. Washer
13. Center link
14. Cotter pin
15. Spindle
16. Tie rod assembly
17. Idler arm

HORIZONTAL   VERTICAL

AFTER TOE SETTING, THE TWO CLAMP BOLTS ON EACH SIDE OF VEHICLE MUST BE POSITIONED WITHIN LIMITS SHOWN WITH THREADED END OF BOLTS POINTING TOWARD FRONT OF VEHICLE

SECTION A

← FRONT OF VEHICLE →

VIEW Y

VIEW Z

SECTION A

383071-S2

84178081

Fig. 80 Steering gear and linkage

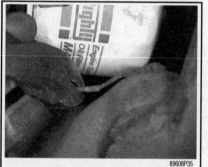

Fig. 81 Remove and discard the cotter pin from the castellated nut that attaches the center link to the pitman arm

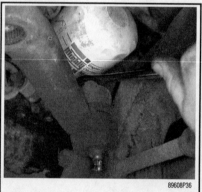

Fig. 82 Remove the castellated nut

Fig. 83 A large deepwell socket, typically 1 5/16 in., is needed to remove the pitman arm retaining nut

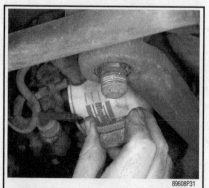

Fig. 84 Remove the pitman arm retaining nut and lockwasher

Fig. 85 Install a suitable pitman arm puller onto the pitman arm

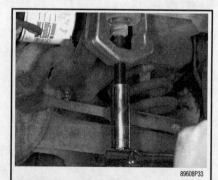

Fig. 86 Carefully tighten the puller's forcing screw until the pitman arm breaks loose

Fig. 87 Remove the pitman arm from the steering gear sector shaft

arm, pointing it rearward, on the sector shaft. Align the blind tooth on the pitman arm with the blind tooth on the steering gear sector shaft.

8. Install the nut and lockwasher and tighten to 233–250 ft. lbs. (316–338 Nm).

9. Install the center link on the pitman arm and install the castellated nut. Tighten the nut to 43–47 ft. lbs. (59–63 Nm) and install a new cotter pin.

➡️**If, after the nut has been torqued, the nut castellations and stud hole do not align for cotter pin installation, tighten the nut further until the cotter pin can be installed. Never loosen the nut to align the holes.**

10. Lower the vehicle.

Idler Arm

▶ **See Figure 88**

1. Raise and safely support the vehicle.
2. Remove the cotter pin, nut and washer retaining the center link to the idler arm. Discard the cotter pin.
3. Remove the center link from the idler arm.

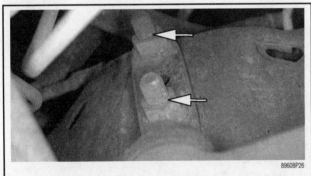

Fig. 88 Remove the bolts and nuts holding the idler arm to the frame

4. Remove the bolts and nuts holding the idler arm to the frame and remove the idler arm.

To install:

5. Install the idler arm to the frame with the bolts and nuts. Tighten to 85–97 ft. lbs. (115–132 Nm).

6. Place the idler arm and front wheels in the straight-ahead position to maintain steering wheel alignment and prevent bushing damage.

7. Install the center link nut and washer and tighten to 43–47 ft. lbs. (59–63 Nm). Install a new cotter pin.

➡️**If, after the nut has been torqued, the nut castellations and stud hole do not align for cotter pin installation, tighten the nut further until the cotter pin can be installed. Never back off the nut.**

8. Lower the vehicle.

Center Link

▶ **See Figure 89**

1. Raise and safely support the vehicle.
2. Remove the cotter pins and nuts that attach the inner tie rod ends to the center link. Discard the cotter pins.
3. Disconnect the inner tie rod ends from the center link using a suitable separator tool (puller).
4. Remove the cotter pin and nut that retains the pitman arm to the center link. Disconnect the pitman arm from the center link using a suitable separator tool (puller).
5. Remove the cotter pin and nut retaining the idler arm to the center link and remove the center link. Discard the cotter pin.

To install:

6. Position the center link to the pitman arm and idler arm and loosely install the nuts. Place the idler arm and front wheels in the straight-ahead position to maintain steering wheel alignment and prevent bushing damage. Tighten the nuts to 43–47 ft. lbs. (59–63 Nm) and install new cotter pins.

➡️**If, after the nut has been torqued, the nut castellations and stud hole do not align for cotter pin installation, tighten the nut further until the cotter pin can be installed. Never back off the nut.**

7. Install the tie rode ends on the center link and tighten the nuts to 43–47 ft. lbs. (59–63 Nm). Install new cotter pins.

8. Lower the vehicle.

9. Check the toe and adjust, if necessary.

Tie Rod Ends

▶ **See Figures 90 thru 96**

1. Raise and support the vehicle safely.
2. Remove the cotter pin and nut from the tie rod end ball stud.
3. Loosen the tie rod adjusting sleeve clamp bolts and remove the rod end from the spindle arm or center link, using a suitable puller, as shown in the accompanying figure.
4. Remove the tie rod end from the sleeve, counting the exact number of turns required to do so. Discard all parts removed from the sleeve.

Fig. 89 Remove the cotter pins and nuts that attach the inner tie rod ends to center link

Fig. 90 Remove the tie rod end-to-steering knuckle retaining nut

Fig. 91 A special removal tool like this one from Lisle® can be used to remove the tie rod end from the knuckle. Just install the tool on the tie rod end and tighten the forcing screw to . . .

Fig. 92 Remove the tie rod end from the knuckle

Fig. 93 Spraying a quality rust penetrant onto the tie rod adjusting sleeve is a good idea before attempting to remove it

Fig. 94 Loosen the adjusting sleeve bolt

Fig. 95 Mark the tie rod end before removal to ensure to reinstall it as close as possible to the previous alignment position

Fig. 96 Grasp the tie rod end with a pair of pliers or other suitable tool and slowly turn it out of the adjusting sleeve to remove it

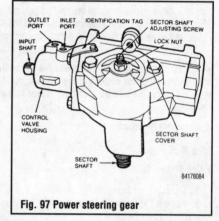
Fig. 97 Power steering gear

To install:

5. Install the new tie rod end into the sleeve, using the exact number of turns it took to remove the old one. Install the tie rod end ball stud into the spindle arm or center link.

6. Install the stud nut. Tighten to 43–47 ft. lbs. (59–63 Nm) and install a new cotter pin.

➡**If, after the nut has been torqued, the nut castellations and stud hole do not align for cotter pin installation, tighten the nut further until the cotter pin can be installed. Never back off the nut.**

7. Check the toe and adjust if necessary. Loosen the clamps from the sleeve and oil the sleeve, clamps, bolts and nuts. Position the adjusting sleeve clamps as shown in the figure, then tighten the clamp nuts to 20–22 ft. lbs. (27–29 Nm).

Power Steering Gear

ADJUSTMENTS

Meshload

♦ **See Figure 97**

Should excessive steering lash be encountered, a meshload adjustment may be required. Adjust the total-over-center position load to eliminate excessive lash between the sector and rack teeth as follows:

1. Disconnect the pitman arm from the sector shaft.
2. Disconnect the fluid return line at the reservoir. Cap the reservoir return line pipe.
3. Place the end of the return line in a clean container and turn the steering wheel from left stop to right stop several times to discharge the fluid from the gear.
4. Turn the steering wheel to 45 degrees from the left stop.
5. Using an inch pound torque wrench on the steering wheel nut, determine the torque required to rotate the shaft slowly approximately ¼ turn from the 45

degree position. If equipped with tilt column, place the steering wheel in the center tilt position.

6. Turn the steering wheel back to center and determine the torque required to rotate the shaft back and forth across the center position. If the reading is not to specification, loosen the nut and turn the adjuster screw until the reading is to specification. Tighten the wheel nut while holding the screw in place.

7. Check the readings and replace the pitman arm and steering wheel hub cover.

8. Connect the fluid return line to the reservoir and fill the reservoir. Check the belt tension and adjust, if necessary.

REMOVAL & INSTALLATION

♦ **See Figure 98**

1. Disconnect the negative battery cable.
2. Remove the stone shield.
3. Tag the pressure and return lines so they may be reassembled in their original positions.
4. Disconnect the pressure and return lines from the steering gear. Plug the lines and ports in the gear to prevent the entry of dirt.

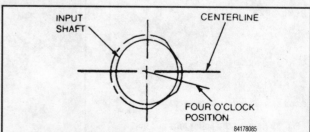
Fig. 98 During installation, position the steering gear input shaft as shown on 1992–98 vehicles

5. Remove the clamp bolts retaining the flexible coupling to the steering gear.
6. Raise and safely support the vehicle.
7. Remove the nut from the sector shaft.
8. Remove the pitman arm from the sector shaft with a suitable pitman arm removal tool. Remove the tool from the pitman arm.

✳✳ WARNING

Do not damage the seals and/or gear housing. Do not use a non-approved tool such as a pickle fork.

9. Support the steering gear and remove the steering gear retaining bolts.
10. Work the gear free of the flex coupling and remove the gear.
11. If the flex coupling did not come off with the gear, lift it off the shaft.

To install:

12. Turn the steering wheel to the straight-ahead position.
13. Center the steering gear input shaft with the indexing flat facing downward on 1989–91 vehicles. On 1992–98 vehicles, center the steering gear input shaft with the centerline of the 2 indexing flats at 4 o'clock.
14. Slide the steering gear input shaft into the flex coupling and into place on the frame side rail. Install the retaining bolts and tighten to 50–65 ft. lbs. (68–88 Nm).
15. Make sure the wheels are in the straight-ahead position. Install the pitman arm on the sector shaft and install the lockwasher and nut. Tighten the nut to 233–250 ft. lbs. (316–338 Nm).
16. Move the flex coupling into place on the steering gear input shaft. Install the retaining bolt and tighten to 20–30 ft. lbs. (27–41 Nm).
17. Connect the pressure and return lines to the steering gear and tighten the lines. Fill the reservoir and turn the steering wheel from stop-to-stop to distribute the fluid. Check the fluid level and add fluid, if necessary.
18. Start the engine and turn the steering wheel from left to right.
19. Check for leaks.
20. Install the stone shield.

Power Steering Pump

REMOVAL & INSTALLATION

▶ **See Figures 99 and 100**

1. Disconnect the negative battery cable.
2. Disconnect the fluid return hose at the pump and drain the fluid into a container.
3. Remove the pressure hose from the pump and, if necessary, drain the fluid into a container. Do not remove the fitting from the pump.
4. Disconnect the belt from the pulley. On 5.0L and 5.8L engines, use a suitable pulley removal tool, to remove the pulley.
5. Remove the mounting bolts and remove the pump.

To install:

6. On 5.0L and 5.8L engines, place the pump on the mounting bracket and install the bolts at the front of the pump. Tighten to 30–45 ft. lbs. (40–62 Nm).

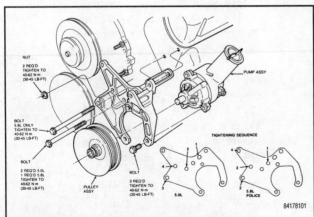

Fig. 99 Power steering pump—5.0L and 5.8L engines

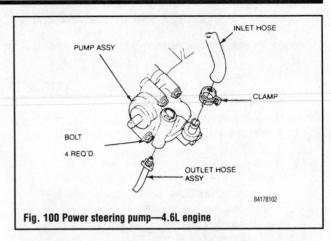

Fig. 100 Power steering pump—4.6L engine

7. On 4.6L engine, place the pump on the mounting bosses of the engine block and install the bolts at the side of the pump. Tighten to 15–22 ft. lbs. (20–30 Nm).
8. On 5.0L and 5.8L engines, install the pump pulley using a suitable pulley replacer tool.
9. Place the belt on the pump pulley and adjust the tension, if necessary.
10. Install the pressure hose to the pump fitting. Tighten the tube nut with a tube nut wrench rather than with an open-end wrench. Tighten to 20–25 ft. lbs. (27–34 Nm) on 1989–91 vehicles or 35–45 ft. lbs. (47–60 Nm) on 1992–98 vehicles.

➡**Do not overtighten this fitting. Swivel and/or end play of the fitting is normal and does not indicate a loose fitting. Over-tightening the tube nut can collapse the tube nut wall, resulting in a leak and requiring replacement of the entire pressure hose assembly. Use of an open-end wrench to tighten the nut can deform the tube nut hex which may result in improper torque and may make further servicing of the system difficult.**

11. Connect the return hose to the pump and tighten the clamp.
12. Fill the reservoir with the proper type and quantity of fluid.
13. Bleed the air from the power steering system, as outlined in this section.

BLEEDING

1. Disconnect the ignition coil.
2. Raise and safely support the vehicle so the front wheels are off the floor.
3. Fill the power steering fluid reservoir.
4. Crank the engine with the starter and add fluid until the level remains constant.
5. While cranking the engine, rotate the steering wheel from lock-to-lock.

➡**The front wheels must be off the floor during lock-to-lock rotation of the steering wheel.**

6. Check the fluid level and add fluid, if necessary.
7. Connect the ignition coil wire. Start the engine and allow it to run for several minutes.
8. Rotate the steering wheel from lock-to-lock.
9. Shut off the engine and check the fluid level. Add fluid, if necessary.
10. If air is still present in the system, purge the system of air using power steering pump air evacuator tool 021–00014 or equivalent, as follows:
   a. Make sure the power steering pump reservoir is full to the COLD FULL mark on the dipstick or to just above the minimum indication on the reservoir.
   b. Tightly insert the rubber stopper of the air evacuator assembly into the pump reservoir fill neck.
   c. Apply 15 in. Hg maximum vacuum on the pump reservoir for a minimum of 3 minutes with the engine idling. As air purges from the system, vacuum will fall off. Maintain adequate vacuum with the vacuum source.
   d. Release the vacuum and remove the vacuum source. Fill the reservoir to the COLD FULL mark or to just above the minimum indication on the reservoir.
   e. With the engine idling, apply 15 in. Hg vacuum to the pump reservoir. Slowly cycle the steering wheel from lock-to-lock every 30 seconds for approximately 5 minutes. Do not hold the steering wheel on the stops while cycling. Maintain adequate vacuum with the vacuum source as the air purges.

f. Release the vacuum and remove the vacuum source. Add fluid, if necessary.

g. Start the engine and cycle the steering wheel.

h. Check for oil leaks at all connections.

11. In severe cases of aeration, it may be necessary to repeat Steps 10b–10f.

TORQUE SPECIFICATIONS

Components	English	Metric
Air bag retaining screws		
1990 models	35-53 inch lbs.	4-6 Nm
1991-98 models	24-32 inch lbs.	3-4 Nm
Front Suspension		
Lower ball joint-to-spindle	80-120 ft. lbs.	108-163 Nm
Lower control arm-to-crossmember bolts	109-140 ft. lbs.	148-190 Nm
Shock absorbers		
Lower mount bolts	13-16 ft. lbs.	17-23 Nm
Upper mount nut	26 ft. lbs.	41 Nm
Stabilizer bar bracket bolts/nuts		
1989-91 models	14-26 ft. lbs.	19-35 Nm
1992-98 models	44-59 ft. lbs.	59-81 Nm
Stabilizer bar link nuts		
1989-91 models	9-15 ft. lbs.	12-20 Nm
1992-98 models	30-40 ft. lbs.	40-55 Nm
Upper ball joint pinch bolt (1992-98 modelsonly)	67 ft. lbs.	92 Nm
Upper ball joint-to-control arm nuts		
1992 models	90-109 ft. lbs.	122-149 Nm
1993-98 models	107-129 ft. lbs.	145-175 Nm
Upper ball joint-to-spindle nuts (1989-91 models only)	60-90 ft. lbs.	81-122 Nm
Upper control arm shaft nuts	85-100 ft. lbs.	115-136 Nm
Upper control arm-to-frame bolts	100-140 ft. lbs.	136-190 Nm
Wheel hub retaining nut		
1992-98 models	189-254 ft. lbs.	255-345 Nm
Power steering pressure hose unions		
1989-91 models	20-25 ft. lbs.	27-34 Nm
1992-98 models	35-45 ft. lbs.	47-60 Nm
Power steering pump retaining bolts		
4.6L engine	15-22 ft. lbs.	20-30 Nm
5.0/5.8L engine	30-45 ft. lbs.	40-62 Nm
Rear suspension		
Lower control arm-to-axle bolt	103-132 ft. lbs.	140-180 Nm
Lower control arm-to-frame bolt	119-149 ft. lbs.	162-203 Nm
Shock absorber		
Air shock lower retaining nuts	52-85 ft. lbs.	70-115 Nm
Except air shock retaining nuts	56-76 ft. lbs.	77-103 Nm
Upper shock mount nut	25 ft. lbs.	34 Nm
Stabilzer bar-to-arm bolts (1989-91 models only)	70-92 ft. lbs.	95-125 Nm
Stabilzer bar-to-axle nuts (1992-98 models only)	16-21 ft. lbs.	21-29 Nm
Stabilzer bar link retaining nuts (1992-98 models only)	13-17 ft. lbs.	17-23 Nm
Upper control arm-to-axle bolt	103-132 ft. lbs.	140-180 Nm
Upper control arm-to-frame bolt	119-149 ft. lbs.	162-203 Nm
Steering linkage		
Center link-to-idler arm nut	43-47 ft. lbs.	59-63 Nm
Center link-to-pitman arm nut	43-47 ft. lbs.	59-63 Nm
Idler arm-to-frame nuts	85-97 ft. lbs.	115-132 Nm
Pitman arm nut	233-250 ft. lbs.	316-338 Nm
Tie rod end nut	43-47 ft. lbs.	59-63 Nm
Tie rod sleeve clamp nut	20-22 ft. lbs.	27-29 Nm
Steering wheel retaining bolt		
1989 models	30-35 ft. lbs.	41-47 Nm
1990-98 models	23-33 ft. lbs.	31-45 Nm
Wheel lug nuts	85-105 ft. lbs.	115-142 Nm

89608C01

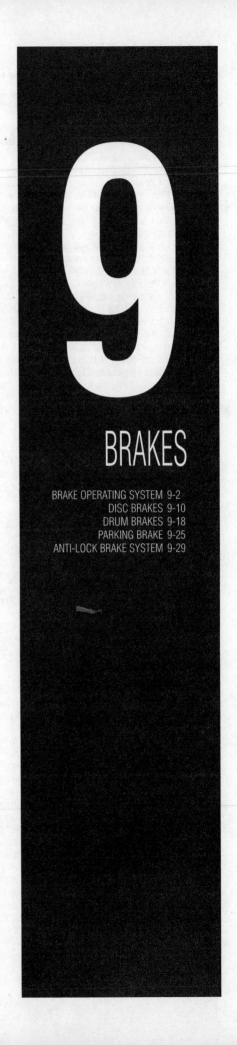

9

BRAKES

BRAKE OPERATING SYSTEM

Basic Operating Principles

Hydraulic systems are used to actuate the brakes of all modern automobiles. The system transports the power required to force the frictional surfaces of the braking system together from the pedal to the individual brake units at each wheel. A hydraulic system is used for two reasons.

First, fluid under pressure can be carried to all parts of an automobile by small pipes and flexible hoses without taking up a significant amount of room or posing routing problems.

Second, a great mechanical advantage can be given to the brake pedal end of the system, and the foot pressure required to actuate the brakes can be reduced by making the surface area of the master cylinder pistons smaller than that of any of the pistons in the wheel cylinders or calipers.

The master cylinder consists of a fluid reservoir along with a double cylinder and piston assembly. Double type master cylinders are designed to separate the front and rear braking systems hydraulically in case of a leak. The master cylinder coverts mechanical motion from the pedal into hydraulic pressure within the lines. This pressure is translated back into mechanical motion at the wheels by either the wheel cylinder (drum brakes) or the caliper (disc brakes).

Steel lines carry the brake fluid to a point on the vehicle's frame near each of the vehicle's wheels. The fluid is then carried to the calipers and wheel cylinders by flexible tubes in order to allow for suspension and steering movements.

In drum brake systems, each wheel cylinder contains two pistons, one at either end, which push outward in opposite directions and force the brake shoe into contact with the drum.

In disc brake systems, the cylinders are part of the calipers. At least one cylinder in each caliper is used to force the brake pads against the disc.

All pistons employ some type of seal, usually made of rubber, to minimize fluid leakage. A rubber dust boot seals the outer end of the cylinder against dust and dirt. The boot fits around the outer end of the piston on disc brake calipers, and around the brake actuating rod on wheel cylinders.

The hydraulic system operates as follows: When at rest, the entire system, from the piston(s) in the master cylinder to those in the wheel cylinders or calipers, is full of brake fluid. Upon application of the brake pedal, fluid trapped in front of the master cylinder piston(s) is forced through the lines to the wheel cylinders. Here, it forces the pistons outward, in the case of drum brakes, and inward toward the disc, in the case of disc brakes. The motion of the pistons is opposed by return springs mounted outside the cylinders in drum brakes, and by spring seals, in disc brakes.

Upon release of the brake pedal, a spring located inside the master cylinder immediately returns the master cylinder pistons to the normal position. The pistons contain check valves and the master cylinder has compensating ports drilled in it. These are uncovered as the pistons reach their normal position. The piston check valves allow fluid to flow toward the wheel cylinders or calipers as the pistons withdraw. Then, as the return springs force the brake pads or shoes into the released position, the excess fluid reservoir through the compensating ports. It is during the time the pedal is in the released position that any fluid that has leaked out of the system will be replaced through the compensating ports.

Dual circuit master cylinders employ two pistons, located one behind the other, in the same cylinder. The primary piston is actuated directly by mechanical linkage from the brake pedal through the power booster. The secondary piston is actuated by fluid trapped between the two pistons. If a leak develops in front of the secondary piston, it moves forward until it bottoms against the front of the master cylinder, and the fluid trapped between the pistons will operate the rear brakes. If the rear brakes develop a leak, the primary piston will move forward until direct contact with the secondary piston takes place, and it will force the secondary piston to actuate the front brakes. In either case, the brake pedal moves farther when the brakes are applied, and less braking power is available.

All dual circuit systems use a switch to warn the driver when only half of the brake system is operational. This switch is usually located in a valve body which is mounted on the firewall or the frame below the master cylinder. A hydraulic piston receives pressure from both circuits, each circuit's pressure being applied to one end of the piston. When the pressures are in balance, the piston remains stationary. When one circuit has a leak, however, the greater pressure in that circuit during application of the brakes will push the piston to one side, closing the switch and activating the brake warning light.

In disc brake systems, this valve body also contains a metering valve and, in some cases, a proportioning valve. The metering valve keeps pressure from traveling to the disc brakes on the front wheels until the brake shoes on the rear wheels have contacted the drums, ensuring that the front brakes will never be used alone. The proportioning valve controls the pressure to the rear brakes to lessen the chance of rear wheel lock-up during very hard braking.

Warning lights may be tested by depressing the brake pedal and holding it while opening one of the wheel cylinder bleeder screws. If this does not cause the light to go on, substitute a new lamp, make continuity checks, and, finally, replace the switch as necessary.

The hydraulic system may be checked for leaks by applying pressure to the pedal gradually and steadily. If the pedal sinks very slowly to the floor, the system has a leak. This is not to be confused with a springy or spongy feel due to the compression of air within the lines. If the system leaks, there will be a gradual change in the position of the pedal with a constant pressure.

Check for leaks along all lines and at wheel cylinders. If no external leaks are apparent, the problem is inside the master cylinder.

DISC BRAKES

Instead of the traditional expanding brakes that press outward against a circular drum, disc brake systems utilize a disc (rotor) with brake pads positioned on either side of it. An easily-seen analogy is the hand brake arrangement on a bicycle. The pads squeeze onto the rim of the bike wheel, slowing its motion. Automobile disc brakes use the identical principle but apply the braking effort to a separate disc instead of the wheel.

The disc (rotor) is a casting, usually equipped with cooling fins between the two braking surfaces. This enables air to circulate between the braking surfaces making them less sensitive to heat buildup and more resistant to fade. Dirt and water do not drastically affect braking action since contaminants are thrown off by the centrifugal action of the rotor or scraped off the by the pads. Also, the equal clamping action of the two brake pads tends to ensure uniform, straight line stops. Disc brakes are inherently self-adjusting. There are three general types of disc brake:

- A fixed caliper.
- A floating caliper.
- A sliding caliper.

The fixed caliper design uses two pistons mounted on either side of the rotor (in each side of the caliper). The caliper is mounted rigidly and does not move.

The sliding and floating designs are quite similar. In fact, these two types are often lumped together. In both designs, the pad on the inside of the rotor is moved into contact with the rotor by hydraulic force. The caliper, which is not held in a fixed position, moves slightly, bringing the outside pad into contact with the rotor. There are various methods of attaching floating calipers. Some pivot at the bottom or top, and some slide on mounting bolts. In any event, the end result is the same.

DRUM BRAKES

Drum brakes employ two brake shoes mounted on a stationary backing plate. These shoes are positioned inside a circular drum which rotates with the wheel assembly. The shoes are held in place by springs. This allows them to slide toward the drums (when they are applied) while keeping the linings and drums in alignment. The shoes are actuated by a wheel cylinder which is mounted at the top of the backing plate. When the brakes are applied, hydraulic pressure forces the wheel cylinder's actuating links outward. Since these links bear directly against the top of the brake shoes, the tops of the shoes are then forced against the inner side of the drum. This action forces the bottoms of the two shoes to contact the brake drum by rotating the entire assembly slightly (known as servo action). When pressure within the wheel cylinder is relaxed, return springs pull the shoes back away from the drum.

Most modern drum brakes are designed to self-adjust themselves during application when the vehicle is moving in reverse. This motion causes both shoes to rotate very slightly with the drum, rocking an adjusting lever, thereby causing rotation of the adjusting screw. Some drum brake systems are designed to self-adjust during application whenever the brakes are applied. This on-board adjustment system reduces the need for maintenance adjustments and keeps both the brake function and pedal feel satisfactory.

POWER BOOSTERS

Virtually all modern vehicles use a vacuum assisted power brake system to multiply the braking force and reduce pedal effort. Since vacuum is always available when the engine is operating, the system is simple and efficient. A vacuum diaphragm is located on the front of the master cylinder and assists the driver in applying the brakes, reducing both the effort and travel he must put into moving the brake pedal.

The vacuum diaphragm housing is normally connected to the intake manifold by a vacuum hose. A check valve is placed at the point where the hose enters the diaphragm housing, so that during periods of low manifold vacuum brakes assist will not be lost.

Depressing the brake pedal closes off the vacuum source and allows atmospheric pressure to enter on one side of the diaphragm. This causes the master cylinder pistons to move and apply the brakes. When the brake pedal is released, vacuum is applied to both sides of the diaphragm and springs return the diaphragm and master cylinder pistons to the released position.

If the vacuum supply fails, the brake pedal rod will contact the end of the master cylinder actuator rod and the system will apply the brakes without any power assistance. The driver will notice that much higher pedal effort is needed to stop the car and that the pedal feels harder than usual.

Vacuum Leak Test

1. Operate the engine at idle without touching the brake pedal for at least one minute.
2. Turn off the engine and wait one minute.
3. Test for the presence of assist vacuum by depressing the brake pedal and releasing it several times. If vacuum is present in the system, light application will produce less and less pedal travel. If there is no vacuum, air is leaking into the system.

System Operation Test

1. With the engine **OFF**, pump the brake pedal until the supply vacuum is entirely gone.
2. Put light, steady pressure on the brake pedal.
3. Start the engine and let it idle. If the system is operating correctly, the brake pedal should fall toward the floor if the constant pressure is maintained.

Power brake systems may be tested for hydraulic leaks just as ordinary systems are tested.

Troubleshooting the Brake System

Problem	Cause	Solution
Low brake pedal (excessive pedal travel required for braking action.)	• Excessive clearance between rear linings and drums caused by inoperative automatic adjusters	• Make 10 to 15 alternate forward and reverse brake stops to adjust brakes. If brake pedal does not come up, repair or replace adjuster parts as necessary.
	• Worn rear brakelining	• Inspect and replace lining if worn beyond minimum thickness specification
	• Bent, distorted brakeshoes, front or rear	• Replace brakeshoes in axle sets
	• Air in hydraulic system	• Remove air from system. Refer to Brake Bleeding.
Low brake pedal (pedal may go to floor with steady pressure applied.)	• Fluid leak in hydraulic system	• Fill master cylinder to fill line; have helper apply brakes and check calipers, wheel cylinders, differential valve tubes, hoses and fittings for leaks. Repair or replace as necessary.
	• Air in hydraulic system	• Remove air from system. Refer to Brake Bleeding.
	• Incorrect or non-recommended brake fluid (fluid evaporates at below normal temp).	• Flush hydraulic system with clean brake fluid. Refill with correct-type fluid.
	• Master cylinder piston seals worn, or master cylinder bore is scored, worn or corroded	• Repair or replace master cylinder
Low brake pedal (pedal goes to floor on first application—o.k. on subsequent applications.)	• Disc brake pads sticking on abutment surfaces of anchor plate. Caused by a build-up of dirt, rust, or corrosion on abutment surfaces	• Clean abutment surfaces
Fading brake pedal (pedal height decreases with steady pressure applied.)	• Fluid leak in hydraulic system	• Fill master cylinder reservoirs to fill mark, have helper apply brakes, check calipers, wheel cylinders, differential valve, tubes, hoses, and fittings for fluid leaks. Repair or replace parts as necessary.
	• Master cylinder piston seals worn, or master cylinder bore is scored, worn or corroded	• Repair or replace master cylinder
Decreasing brake pedal travel (pedal travel required for braking action decreases and may be accompanied by a hard pedal.)	• Caliper or wheel cylinder pistons sticking or seized	• Repair or replace the calipers, or wheel cylinders
	• Master cylinder compensator ports blocked (preventing fluid return to reservoirs) or pistons sticking or seized in master cylinder bore	• Repair or replace the master cylinder
	• Power brake unit binding internally	• Test unit according to the following procedure: (a) Shift transmission into neutral and start engine (b) Increase engine speed to 1500 rpm, close throttle and fully depress brake pedal (c) Slow release brake pedal and stop engine (d) Have helper remove vacuum check valve and hose from power unit. Observe for backward movement of brake pedal. (e) If the pedal moves backward, the power unit has an internal bind—replace power unit

TCCA9C01

Troubleshooting the Brake System (cont.)

Problem	Cause	Solution
Spongy brake pedal (pedal has abnormally soft, springy, spongy feel when depressed.)	Air in hydraulic system	Remove air from system. Refer to Brake Bleeding.
	Brakeshoes bent or distorted	Replace brakeshoes
	Brakelining not yet seated with drums and rotors	Burnish brakes
	Rear drum brakes not properly adjusted	Adjust brakes
Hard brake pedal (excessive pedal pressure required to stop vehicle. May be accompanied by brake fade.)	Loose or leaking power brake unit vacuum hose	Tighten connections or replace leaking hose
	Incorrect or poor quality brakelining	Replace with lining in axle sets
	Bent, broken, distorted brakeshoes	Replace brakeshoes
	Calipers binding or dragging on mounting pins. Rear brakeshoes dragging on support plate.	Replace brake mounting pins and bushings. Clean rust or burrs from rear brake support plate ledges and lubricate ledges with molydisulfide grease. NOTE: If ledges are deeply grooved or scored, do not attempt to sand or grind them smooth—replace support plate.
	Caliper, wheel cylinder, or master cylinder pistons sticking or seized	Repair or replace parts as necessary
	Power brake unit vacuum check valve malfunction	Test valve according to the following procedure: (a) Start engine, increase engine speed to 1500 rpm, close throttle and immediately stop engine (b) Wait at least 90 seconds then depress brake pedal (c) If brakes are not vacuum assisted for 2 or more applications, check valve is faulty
	Power brake unit has internal bind	Test unit according to the following procedure: (a) With engine stopped, apply brakes several times to exhaust all vacuum in system (b) Shift transmission into neutral, depress brake pedal and start engine (c) If pedal height decreases with foot pressure and less pressure is required to hold pedal in applied position, power unit vacuum system is operating normally. Test power unit. If power unit exhibits a bind condition, replace the power unit.
	Master cylinder compensator ports (at bottom of reservoirs) blocked by dirt, scale, rust, or have small burrs (blocked ports prevent fluid return to reservoirs).	Repair or replace master cylinder CAUTION: Do not attempt to clean blocked ports with wire, pencils, or similar implements. Use compressed air only.
	Brake hoses, tubes, fittings clogged or restricted	Use compressed air to check or unclog parts. Replace any damaged parts.
	Brake fluid contaminated with improper fluids (motor oil, transmission fluid, causing rubber components to swell and stick in bores	Replace all rubber components, combination valve and hoses. Flush entire brake system with DOT 3 brake fluid or equivalent.
	Low engine vacuum	Adjust or repair engine

TCCA9002

Troubleshooting the Brake System (cont.)

Problem	Cause	Solution
Grabbing brakes (severe reaction to brake pedal pressure.)	Brakelining(s) contaminated by grease or brake fluid	Determine and correct cause of contamination and replace brakeshoes in axle sets
	Parking brake cables incorrectly adjusted or seized	Adjust cables. Replace seized cables.
	Incorrect brakelining or lining loose on brakeshoes	Replace brakeshoes in axle sets
	Caliper anchor plate bolts loose	Tighten bolts
	Rear brakeshoes binding on support plate ledges	Clean and lubricate ledges. Replace support plate(s) if ledges are deeply grooved. Do not attempt to smooth ledges by grinding.
	Incorrect or missing power brake reaction disc	Install correct disc
	Rear brake support plates loose	Tighten mounting bolts
Dragging brakes (slow or incomplete release of brakes)	Brake pedal binding at pivot	Loosen and lubricate
	Power brake unit has internal bind	Inspect for internal bind. Replace unit if internal bind exists.
	Parking brake cables incorrectly adjusted or seized	Adjust cables. Replace seized cables.
	Rear brakeshoe return springs weak or broken	Replace return springs. Replace brakeshoe if necessary in axle sets.
	Automatic adjusters malfunctioning	Repair or replace adjuster parts as required
	Caliper, wheel cylinder or master cylinder pistons sticking or seized	Repair or replace parts as necessary
	Master cylinder compensating ports blocked (fluid does not return to reservoirs).	Use compressed air to clear ports. Do not use wire, pencils, or similar objects to open blocked ports.
Vehicle moves to one side when brakes are applied	Incorrect front tire pressure	Inflate to recommended cold (reduced load) inflation pressure
	Worn or damaged wheel bearings	Replace worn or damaged bearings
	Brakelining on one side contaminated	Determine and correct cause of contamination and replace brakelining in axle sets
	Brakeshoes on one side bent, distorted, or lining loose on shoe	Replace brakeshoes in axle sets
	Support plate bent or loose on one side	Tighten or replace support plate
	Brakelining not yet seated with drums or rotors	Burnish brakelining
	Caliper anchor plate loose on one side	Tighten anchor plate bolts
	Caliper piston sticking or seized	Repair or replace caliper
	Brakelinings water soaked	Drive vehicle with brakes lightly applied to dry linings
	Loose suspension component attaching or mounting bolts	Tighten suspension bolts. Replace worn suspension components.
	Brake combination valve failure	Replace combination valve
Chatter or shudder when brakes are applied (pedal pulsation and roughness may also occur.)	Brakeshoes distorted, bent, contaminated, or worn	Replace brakeshoes in axle sets
	Caliper anchor plate or support plate loose	Tighten mounting bolts
	Excessive thickness variation of rotor(s)	Refinish or replace rotors in axle sets

TCCA9003

❈❈ WARNING

Clean, high quality brake fluid is essential to the safe and proper operation of the brake system. You should always buy the highest quality brake fluid that is available. If the brake fluid becomes contaminated, drain and flush the system, then refill the master cylinder with new fluid. Never reuse any brake fluid. Any brake fluid that is removed from the system should be discarded.

Brake Light Switch

REMOVAL & INSTALLATION

1. Disconnect the negative battery cable.
2. Detach the electrical connector at the switch. The locking tab on the connector must be lifted before the connector can be removed.
3. Remove the hairpin retainer, slide the brake light switch, the pushrod and the nylon washers and bushings away from the pedal and remove the switch.

➡Since the switch side plate nearest the brake pedal is slotted, it is not necessary to remove the brake master cylinder pushrod and washer from the brake pedal pin.

To install:
4. Position the switch so the U-shaped side is nearest the pedal and directly over/under the pin. Then slide the switch down/up trapping the master cylinder pushrod and black bushing between the switch side plates.
5. Push the switch and pushrod assembly firmly toward the brake pedal arm.
6. Assemble the outside white plastic washer to the pin and install the hairpin retainer to trap the whole assembly.
7. Attach the wire harness connector to the switch.
8. Check the switch for proper operation.

➡The brake light switch wire harness must be long enough to travel with the switch during full pedal stroke. If wire length is insufficient, reroute the harness or service, as required.

Master Cylinder

REMOVAL & INSTALLATION

1989–94 Vehicles

▶ See Figures 1 thru 8

1. Disconnect the negative battery cable.
2. If equipped with anti-lock brakes, depress the brake pedal several times to exhaust all vacuum in the system.
3. Use a flare nut wrench to remove the brake lines from the primary and secondary outlet ports of the master cylinder.
4. On vehicles without anti-lock brakes, detach the brake warning indicator switch connector.
5. On vehicles with anti-lock brakes, remove the electrical connector bracket retaining nut and detach the fluid level indicator electrical connector.
6. If equipped with anti-lock brakes, disconnect the Hydraulic Control Unit (HCU) supply hose at the master cylinder and secure in a position to prevent loss of brake fluid.
7. Remove the nuts attaching master cylinder to the brake booster assembly.
8. Slide the master cylinder forward and upward to remove it from the vehicle.

To install:
9. Bench bleed the master cylinder as described in this section.
10. If equipped with anti-lock brakes, install a new seal in the groove in the master cylinder mounting face.
11. Install the master cylinder on the booster studs and install the mounting nuts. Tighten the nuts to 21 ft. lbs. (21–29 Nm).
12. Fill the reservoir with brake fluid and cover the reservoir with a shop towel.

Fig. 1 Remove the master cylinder reservoir cap and fluid level sensor

Fig. 2 Use a pair of pliers to slide the clamp off the HCU supply hose . . .

Fig. 3 . . . then remove the hose from the master cylinder

Fig. 4 Use a suitable flare nut wrench to loosen the brake line fittings

Fig. 5 Place a rag under the lines, then remove the lines from the master cylinder

Fig. 6 Remove the two master cylinder-to-booster retaining nuts and . . .

Fig. 7 . . . remove the master cylinder from the booster and remove it from the vehicle

89609P13

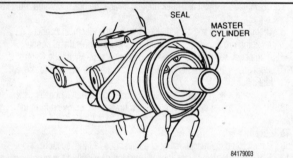

Fig. 8 If equipped with ABS, install a new seal in the groove in the master cylinder mounting face

84179003

※ WARNING

Clean, high quality brake fluid is essential to the safe and proper operation of the brake system. You should always buy the highest quality brake fluid that is available. If the brake fluid becomes contaminated, drain and flush the system, then refill the master cylinder with new fluid. Never reuse any brake fluid. Any brake fluid that is removed from the system should be discarded. Also, do not allow any brake fluid to come in contact with a painted surface; it will damage the paint.

13. Connect the vehicle brake lines to the master cylinder.
14. Bleed each brake line at the master cylinder using the following procedure:
  a. Have an assistant pump the brake pedal 10 times and then hold firm pressure on the pedal.
  b. Position a shop towel under the rear most brake line fitting. Loosen the fitting with a tube wrench until a stream of brake fluid comes out. Have the assistant maintain pressure on the brake pedal until the brake line fitting is tightened again.
  c. Repeat this operation until clear, bubble free fluid comes out from around the brake line fitting.
  d. Repeat this bleeding operation at the front brake line fitting.
15. If equipped, attach the HCU supply hose to the master cylinder.
16. Attach the brake warning indicator switch connector or the fluid level indicator electrical connector, as required.
17. Install the electrical connector bracket and retaining nut, if equipped.
18. Bleed the brake system.
19. Fill the master cylinder reservoir to the proper level.
20. Operate the brakes several times, then check for external hydraulic leaks.

1995–98 Vehicles

1. Disconnect the negative battery cable.
2. Depress the brake pedal several times to exhaust all vacuum in the power brake booster.
3. Remove and plug the brake lines from the primary and secondary outlet ports of the master cylinder.
4. Detach the brake warning indicator switch connector.

5. If equipped with ABS and traction assist, remove 2 bolts retaining the proportioning valve bracket to the master cylinder. Secure the proportioning valve and brake lines in a position to prevent damage or loss of brake fluid.
6. Remove 2 nuts retaining the brake master cylinder to the power brake booster assembly.
7. Slide the master cylinder forward and upward to remove it from the vehicle.
To install:
8. If replacing the brake master cylinder, bench bleed the master cylinder before installation.
9. Install the brake master cylinder to the power brake booster mounting studs and install 2 retaining nuts. Torque the nuts to 16–21 ft. lbs. (21–29 Nm).
10. If equipped with ABS and traction assist, place the proportioning valve bracket in position and install 2 retaining bolts. Torque the bolts to 14–19 ft. lbs. (19–26 Nm).
11. Unplug and install the primary and secondary brake lines to the brake master cylinder outlet ports. Torque the brake line fittings to 10–15 ft. lbs. (14–20 Nm).
12. Reconnect the brake warning indicator switch connector.
13. Properly bleed the brake system using clean DOT 3 or equivalent, brake fluid from a closed container.

※ CAUTION

If raising the vehicle for brake bleeding and the vehicle is equipped with air suspension, the air suspension switch, located on the right-hand side of the luggage compartment, must be turned to the OFF position before raising the vehicle.

14. Fill the master cylinder reservoir to the proper level.
15. Operate the brakes several times, then check for external hydraulic leaks.
16. Reconnect the negative battery cable.
17. If equipped with air suspension, turn the air suspension switch to the ON position, if disabled.
18. Road test the vehicle and check the brake system for proper operation.

BENCH BLEEDING

※ WARNING

All new master cylinders should be bench bled prior to installation. Bleeding a new master cylinder on the vehicle is not a good idea. With air trapped inside, the master cylinder piston may bottom in the bore and possibly cause internal damage.

1. Secure the master cylinder in a bench vise using soft jaws.
2. Remove the master cylinder reservoir cap.
3. Manufacture or purchase bleeding tubes and install them on the master cylinder as illustrated.
4. Fill the master cylinder reservoir with clean, fresh brake fluid until the level is within 0.25 in. (6.35mm) of the reservoir top.

➡**Ensure the bleeding tubes are below the level of the brake fluid, otherwise air may get into the system making your bleeding efforts ineffective.**

5. Use a blunt tipped rod (a long socket extension works well) to slowly depress the master cylinder piston. Make sure the piston travels full its full stroke.
6. As the piston is depressed, bubbles will come out of the bleeding tubes. Continue depressing and releasing the piston until all bubbles cease.
7. Refill the master cylinder with fluid.
8. Remove the bleeding tubes.
9. Install the master cylinder reservoir cap.
10. Install the master cylinder on the vehicle.

Power Brake Booster

REMOVAL & INSTALLATION

Vehicles Without ABS

♦ See Figure 9

1. Disconnect the negative battery cable.

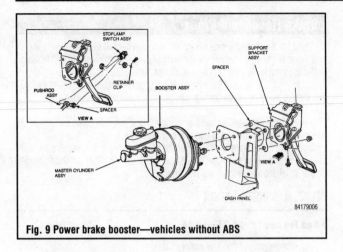

Fig. 9 Power brake booster—vehicles without ABS

2. Remove the master cylinder from the booster and move it aside without disconnecting the brake lines. Be careful not to kink the brake lines.
3. Disconnect the manifold vacuum hose from the booster check valve.
4. Working inside the vehicle below the instrument panel, remove the brake light switch connector.
5. Remove the switch retaining pin and slide the switch off the brake pedal pin just far enough for the outer arm to clear the pin, then remove the switch. Be careful not to damage the switch.
6. Remove the booster-to-dash panel attaching nuts.
7. Slide the booster pushrod, nylon washers, if equipped, and bushing off the brake pedal pin.
8. Slide the pushrod out from the engine side of the dash panel (firewall) and remove the booster.

To install:
9. Place the booster in position on the dash panel.
10. Working inside the vehicle, install the inner nylon washer, if equipped, booster pushrod and bushing on the brake pedal pin.
11. Install the booster-to-dash panel attaching nuts and tighten to 21 ft. lbs. (29 Nm).
12. Position the brake light switch so it straddles the booster pushrod with the switch slot toward the pedal blade and the hole just clearing the pin. Be careful not to bend or deform the switch.
13. Install the nylon washer on the pin, and secure all parts to the pin with the hairpin retainer. Make sure the retainer is fully installed and locked over the pedal pin.
14. Attach the brake light switch electrical connector.
15. Connect the manifold vacuum hose to the booster check valve using a hose clamp.
16. Install the master cylinder and tighten the nuts to 21 ft. lbs. (29 Nm).
17. Connect the negative battery cable.
18. Start the engine and check power brake operation.

Vehicles With ABS

▶ **See Figure 10**

1. Disconnect the negative battery cable.
2. Pump the brake pedal until all vacuum is removed from the booster. This will prevent the O-ring from being sucked into the booster during disassembly.
3. Remove the electrical connector bracket retaining nut from the master cylinder stud and detach the connector.
4. Working in the engine compartment, remove the cruise control actuator cable and cruise control servo; refer to Section 6.
5. Disconnect the manifold vacuum hose from the booster check valve.
6. Detach the fluid level indicator electrical connector from the master cylinder reservoir cap.
7. Use a flare nut wrench to disconnect the brake lines from the master cylinder outlet ports and remove the Hydraulic Control Unit (HCU) supply hose. Plug the ports and reservoir feed to prevent brake fluid from leaking onto paint and wiring.
8. Working inside the passenger compartment, detach the brake light switch electrical connector from the switch.
9. Disengage the pedal position switch from the stud.
10. Remove the hairpin retainer and outer nylon washer from the pedal pin. Slide the brake light switch off the pedal pin just far enough for the arm to clear the pin.
11. Remove the switch, being careful not to damage it during removal.
12. Remove the booster-to-dash panel attaching nuts. Slide the bushing and booster pushrod off the brake pedal pin.
13. From inside the engine compartment, move the booster forward until the booster studs clear the dash panel.
14. Remove the booster/master cylinder assembly and place it on a clean bench.
15. Remove the master cylinder-to-booster nuts and slide the master cylinder away from the booster.

To install:
16. Make sure the O-ring is in place in the groove on the master cylinder, then slide the master cylinder onto the booster studs. Install the nuts and tighten to 21 ft. lbs. (29 Nm).
17. Position the booster/master cylinder assembly on the dash.
18. Working inside the passenger compartment, install the booster pushrod and bushing on the brake pedal pin.
19. Install the booster-to-dash panel nuts and tighten to 21 ft. lbs. (29 Nm).
20. Position the brake light switch so it straddles the booster pushrod with the switch slot toward the pedal blade and the hole just clearing the pin. Slide the switch completely onto the pin. Be careful not to bend or deform the switch.
21. Install the nylon washer on the pin, and secure all parts to the pin with the hairpin retainer. Make sure the retainer is fully installed and locked over the pedal pin.
22. Attach the brake light switch electrical connector.
23. If equipped, install and adjust the pedal travel switch as explained under the ABS portion of this section.
24. Install the cruise control servo and cruise control actuator cable; refer to Section 6.
25. Connect the brake lines to the master cylinder and attach the low pressure hose to the reservoir.
26. Attach the manifold vacuum hose to the booster check valve and the electrical connector to the master cylinder reservoir cap.

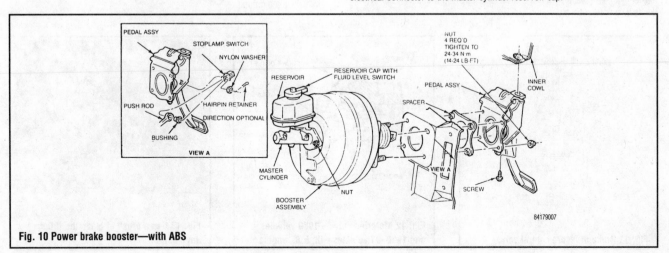

Fig. 10 Power brake booster—with ABS

27. Attach the electrical connector and install the retaining bracket and nut.
28. Connect the negative battery cable.
29. Bleed the brake system.

Brake Pressure Control Valve

REMOVAL & INSTALLATION

▶ **See Figure 11**

1. Disconnect the brake inlet lines and the rear lines from the brake control valve assembly.
2. Remove the screw retaining the control valve assembly to the frame and remove the brake control valve.

To install:

3. Position the control valve on the frame and secure with the retaining screw.
4. Connect the rear brake outlet lines to the control valve assembly and tighten the line nuts to 10–18 ft. lbs. (14–24 Nm).
5. Connect the inlet lines to the control valve assembly and tighten the line nuts to 10–18 ft. lbs. (14–24 Nm).
6. Bleed the brake system.

Metering Valve

REMOVAL & INSTALLATION

▶ **See Figure 12**

1. Disconnect the front brake system inlet line and the left and right front brake outlet lines from the metering valve.
2. Remove the screw retaining the metering valve to the frame and remove the metering valve from the vehicle.

To install:

3. Position the metering valve on the frame and secure with the retaining screw. Tighten the screw to 7–11 ft. lbs. (10–14 Nm).
4. Connect the front brake outlet lines to the metering valve assembly and tighten the line nuts to 10–18 ft. lbs. (14–24 Nm).
5. Connect the front brake inlet line to the metering valve assembly and tighten the line nut to 10–18 ft. lbs. (14–24 Nm).
6. Bleed the brake system.

➡**If the brake system is pressure bled, the metering valve bleeder rod must be pushed in.**

Proportioning Valve

REMOVAL & INSTALLATION

The proportioning valve, equipped on 1998 models only, is located on the master cylinder outlet port. It can only be replaced along with the master cylinder as a complete assembly.

Brake Hoses and Pipes

Metal lines and rubber brake hoses should be checked frequently for leaks and external damage. Metal lines are particularly prone to crushing and kinking under the vehicle. Any such deformation can restrict the proper flow of fluid and therefore impair braking at the wheels. Rubber hoses should be checked for cracking or scraping; such damage can create a weak spot in the hose and it could fail under pressure.

Any time the lines are removed or disconnected, extreme cleanliness must be observed. Clean all joints and connections before disassembly (use a stiff bristle brush and clean brake fluid); be sure to plug the lines and ports as soon as they are opened. New lines and hoses should be flushed clean with brake fluid before installation to remove any contamination.

REMOVAL & INSTALLATION

▶ **See Figures 13, 14, 15 and 16**

1. Disconnect the negative battery cable.
2. Raise and safely support the vehicle on jackstands.
3. Remove any wheel and tire assemblies necessary for access to the particular line you are removing.
4. Thoroughly clean the surrounding area at the joints to be disconnected.
5. Place a suitable catch pan under the joint to be disconnected.
6. Using two wrenches (one to hold the joint and one to turn the fitting), disconnect the hose or line to be replaced.
7. Disconnect the other end of the line or hose, moving the drain pan if necessary. Always use a back-up wrench to avoid damaging the fitting.
8. Disconnect any retaining clips or brackets holding the line and remove the line from the vehicle.

➡**If the brake system is to remain open for more time than it takes to swap lines, tape or plug each remaining clip and port to keep contaminants out and fluid in.**

To install:

9. Install the new line or hose, starting with the end farthest from the master cylinder. Connect the other end, then confirm that both fittings are correctly threaded and turn smoothly using finger pressure. Make sure the new line will not rub against any other part. Brake lines must be at least 1/2 in. (13mm) from the steering column and other moving parts. Any protective shielding or insulators must be reinstalled in the original location.

✳✳ WARNING

Make sure the hose is NOT kinked or touching any part of the frame or suspension after installation. These conditions may cause the hose to fail prematurely.

10. Using two wrenches as before, tighten each fitting.
11. Install any retaining clips or brackets on the lines.
12. If removed, install the wheel and tire assemblies, then carefully lower the vehicle to the ground.

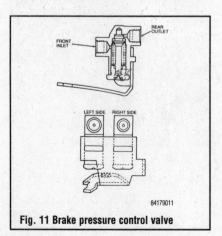

84179011

Fig. 11 Brake pressure control valve

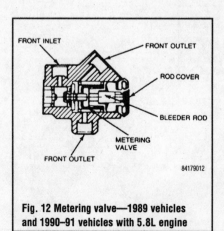

84179012

Fig. 12 Metering valve—1989 vehicles and 1990–91 vehicles with 5.8L engine

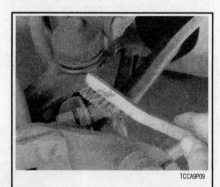

TCCA9P09

Fig. 13 Use a brush to clean the fittings of any debris

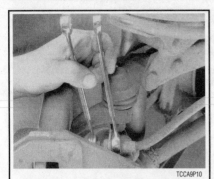

Fig. 14 Use two wrenches to loosen the fitting. If available, use flare nut type wrenches

Fig. 15 Any gaskets/crush washers should be replaced with new ones during installation

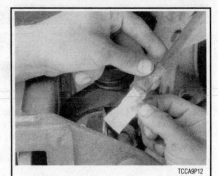

Fig. 16 Tape or plug the line to prevent contamination

13. Refill the brake master cylinder reservoir with clean, fresh brake fluid, meeting DOT 3 specifications. Properly bleed the brake system.

14. Connect the negative battery cable.

Bleeding Brake System

▶ See Figures 17, 18, 19 and 20

When any part of the hydraulic system has been disconnected for repair or replacement, air may get into the lines and cause spongy pedal action

Fig. 17 Remove the bleeder screw rubber dust cover—front caliper

(because air can be compressed and brake fluid cannot). To correct this condition, it is necessary to bleed the hydraulic system so to be sure all air is purged.

When bleeding the brake system, bleed one brake cylinder at a time, beginning at the cylinder with the longest hydraulic line (farthest from the master cylinder) first. ALWAYS Keep the master cylinder reservoir filled with brake fluid during the bleeding operation. Never use brake fluid that has been drained from the hydraulic system, no matter how clean it is.

The primary and secondary hydraulic brake systems are separate and are bled independently. During the bleeding operation, do not allow the reservoir to run dry. Keep the master cylinder reservoir filled with brake fluid.

1. Clean all dirt from around the master cylinder fill cap, remove the cap and fill the master cylinder with brake fluid until the level is within ¼ in. (6mm) of the top edge of the reservoir.

2. Clean the bleeder screws at all 4 wheels. The bleeder screws are located on the back of the brake backing plate (drum brakes) and on the top of the brake calipers (disc brakes).

3. Attach a length of rubber hose over the bleeder screw and place the other end of the hose in a glass jar, submerged in brake fluid.

4. Open the bleeder screw ½–¾ turn. Have an assistant slowly depress the brake pedal.

5. Close the bleeder screw and tell your assistant to allow the brake pedal to return slowly. Continue this process to purge all air from the system.

6. When bubbles cease to appear at the end of the bleeder hose, close the bleeder screw and remove the hose. Tighten the bleeder securely.

7. Check the master cylinder fluid level and add fluid accordingly. Do this after bleeding each wheel.

8. Repeat the bleeding operation at the remaining 3 wheels, ending with the one closet to the master cylinder.

9. Fill the master cylinder reservoir to the proper level.

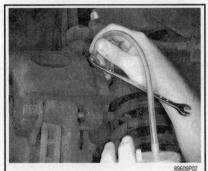

Fig. 18 Attach a length of rubber hose over the bleeder screw and place the other end of the hose in a glass jar

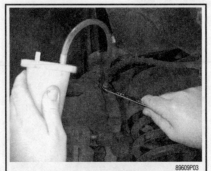

Fig. 19 Open the bleeder valve using a suitable size wrench while an assistant depresses the brake pedal

Fig. 20 Bleeder screw location—rear caliper

DISC BRAKES

Brake Pads

REMOVAL & INSTALLATION

Front

▶ **See Figures 21 thru 28**

1. Remove and discard half the brake fluid from the master cylinder. Properly dispose of the used brake fluid.
2. Raise and safely support vehicle.
3. Remove the front wheel and tire assemblies.
4. Remove the caliper locating pins and remove the caliper from the anchor plate and rotor, but do not disconnect the brake hose.
5. Remove the outer brake pad from the caliper assembly and remove the inner brake pad from the caliper piston.
6. Inspect the disc brake rotor for scoring and wear. Replace or machine, as necessary.
7. Suspend the caliper inside the fender housing with a length of wire. Do not let the caliper hang by the brake hose.

To install:

8. Use a large C-clamp and wood block to push the caliper piston back into its bore.

9. Install new locating pin insulators in the caliper housing, using a fabricated tool as shown in the accompanying figure. Check to see if both insulator flanges straddle the housing holes.

➡**Do not attempt to install the rubber insulators with a sharp edged tool.**

10. Install the inner brake pad in the caliper piston. Be careful not to bend the pad clips in the piston, or distortion and rattles can result.
11. Install the outer brake pad, making sure the clips are properly seated. The outer pads are marked left-hand (LH) and right-hand (RH) and must be installed in the proper caliper.

➡**Make sure that the large diameter of the pins are through the outer pad hole to prevent possible binding or bending.**

12. Install the caliper over the rotor with the outer brake pad against the rotor's braking surface. This prevents pinching the piston boot between the inner brake pad and the piston.
13. Lubricate the caliper locating pins and the inside of the locating pin insulators with silicone dielectric grease.
14. Install the caliper locating pins and thread them into the spindle/anchor plate assembly by hand.
15. Tighten the caliper locating pins to 45–65 ft. lbs. (61–88 Nm).
16. Install the wheel and tire assembly.
17. Lower the vehicle.
18. Pump the brake pedal prior to moving the vehicle to seat the brake pads.
19. Refill the master cylinder.
20. Road test the vehicle.

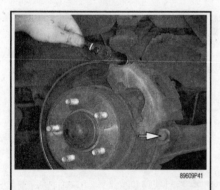

Fig. 21 Removing the caliper locating pins

Fig. 22 Remove the front brake caliper from the rotor

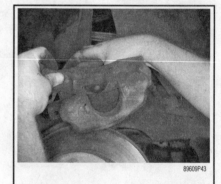

Fig. 23 Removing the outer brake pad

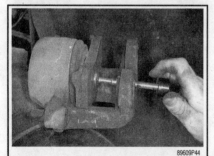

Fig. 24 There are several ways to compress the piston into the caliper. One way is to use a special tool like this one from Lisle®

Fig. 25 Another way to compress the piston is to use a large pair of pliers

Fig. 26 And probably the most popular way is to use a large C-clamp. Just remember to keep the old inner pad in the caliper to keep the piston from being damaged

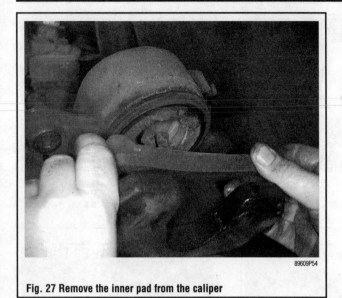

Fig. 27 Remove the inner pad from the caliper

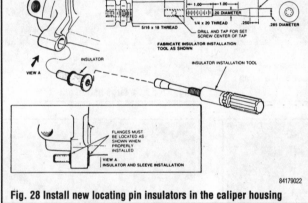

Fig. 28 Install new locating pin insulators in the caliper housing

Rear

▶ See Figures 29 thru 40

1. Remove and discard half the brake fluid from the master cylinder. Properly dispose of the used brake fluid.
2. Raise and safely support vehicle.
3. Remove the rear wheel and tire assemblies.
4. Remove the caliper locating pins.
5. Lift the caliper off the rotor and anchor plate using a rotating motion. Do not disconnect the brake hose.

✳ WARNING

Do not pry directly against the plastic piston or damage to the piston will occur.

6. Remove the inner and outer brake pads.
7. Inspect the disc brake rotor for scoring and wear. Replace or machine, as necessary.
8. Suspend the caliper inside the fender housing with a length of wire. Do not let the caliper hang by the brake hose.

To install:

9. Use a large C-clamp and wood block to push the caliper piston back into its bore.

Fig. 29 Installed view of the rear disc brake assembly

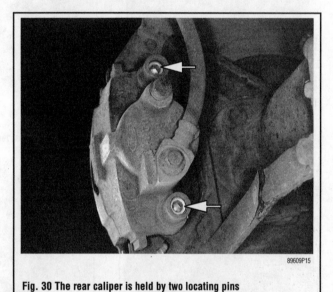

Fig. 30 The rear caliper is held by two locating pins

Fig. 31 The rear caliper pins typically require a 6mm hex bit

Fig. 32 Remove the caliper locating pins and . . .

Fig. 33 . . . remove the caliper from the rotor

Fig. 34 Place the caliper in a secure place and remove the outer pad

Fig. 35 Safely support the caliper using mechanic's wire or another suitable device

Fig. 36 Compress the caliper piston using a suitable special tool or . . .

Fig. 37 . . . a large pair of pliers

Fig. 38 The safest method is to use a large C-clamp

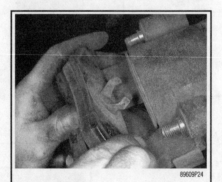

Fig. 39 After the piston is compressed, remove the inner brake pad

Fig. 40 Thoroughly clean the caliper mounting bracket and caliper of any rust or dirt

✳ WARNING

Never apply the C-clamp directly to the plastic caliper piston; damage to the piston may result.

10. Remove all rust buildup from the inside of the caliper legs (outer pad contact area).

11. Install the inner brake pad, then the outer brake pad, making sure the clips are properly seated.

12. Position the caliper above the rotor with the anti-rattle spring located on the lower adapter support arm. Install the caliper over the rotor with a rotating motion. Make sure the inner pad is properly positioned.

13. Insert the caliper locating pins and thread them in by hand. Tighten them to 19–26 ft. lbs. (26–35 Nm).

14. Install the wheel and tire assembly and lower the vehicle.

15. Pump the brake pedal prior to moving the vehicle to seat the brake pads.

16. Refill the master cylinder.

17. Road test the vehicle.

INSPECTION

♦ **See Figures 41 and 42**

✳ CAUTION

Older brake pads or shoes may contain asbestos, which has been determined to be cancer causing agent. Never clean the brake surfaces with compressed air! Avoid inhaling any dust from any brake surface! When cleaning brake surfaces, use a commercially available brake cleaning fluid.

Inspect the brake pads for wear using a ruler, Vernier caliper or other suitable device. Compare measurements to the brake specifications chart. If the lining is

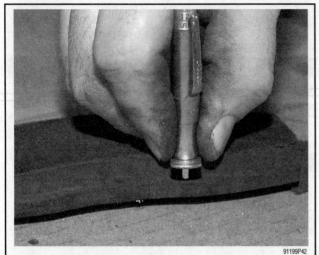

Fig. 41 A gauge that measures in 1/32's of an inch is available to measure brake pad thickness

Fig. 42 A ruler can also be used. Make sure to measure the pads in several places, since pads can wear unevenly

thinner than specification or there is evidence of the lining being contaminated by brake fluid or oil, make the necessary repairs and replace all brake pad assemblies (a complete axle set).

Brake Caliper

REMOVAL & INSTALLATION

✳✳ CAUTION

Older brake pads or shoes may contain asbestos, which has been determined to be cancer causing agent. Never clean the brake surfaces with compressed air! Avoid inhaling any dust from any brake surface! When cleaning brake surfaces, use a commercially available brake cleaning fluid.

Front

▸ See Figures 43, 44 and 45

1. Raise and safely support the vehicle.
2. Remove the front wheel and tire assembly.

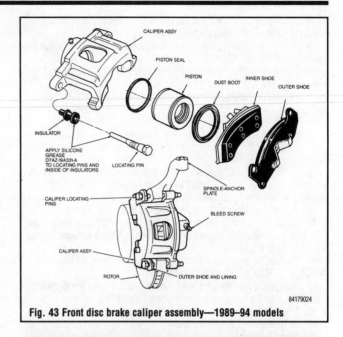

Fig. 43 Front disc brake caliper assembly—1989–94 models

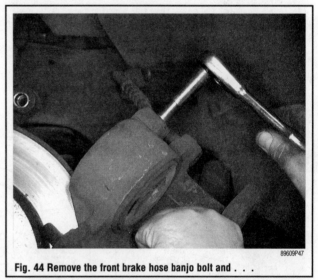

Fig. 44 Remove the front brake hose banjo bolt and . . .

Fig. 45 . . . remove the hose from the caliper. Be careful, as the brake fluid can be messy

3. Loosen the brake line fitting that connects the brake hose to the brake line at the frame bracket. Plug the brake line.

4. Remove the retaining clip from the hose and bracket and disengage the hose from the bracket.

5. Remove the hollow bolt attaching the brake hose to the caliper and remove the brake hose. Discard the sealing washers.

6. Remove the caliper locating pins and remove the caliper. If removing both calipers, mark the right and left sides so they may be reinstalled correctly.

To install:

7. Install the caliper over the rotor with the outer brake pad against the rotor's braking surface. This prevents pinching the piston boot between the inner brake pad and the piston.

8. Lubricate the locating pins and the inside of the locating pin insulators with silicone dielectric grease. Install the caliper locating pins and thread them into the spindle/anchor plate assembly by hand.

9. Tighten the caliper locating pins to 45–65 ft. lbs. (61–88 Nm).

10. Install new sealing washers on each side of the brake hose fitting outlet and install the hollow bolt, through the hose fitting and into the caliper. Tighten the bolt to 30 ft. lbs. (41 Nm).

11. Position the other end of the brake hose in the bracket and install the retaining clip. Make sure the hose is not twisted.

12. Remove the plug from the brake line, connect the brake line to the brake hose and tighten the fitting nut to 10–18 ft. lbs. (13–24 Nm).

13. Bleed the brake system.

14. Install the wheel and tire assembly.

15. Lower the vehicle.

16. Apply the brake pedal several times before moving the vehicle, to position the brake pads.

17. Road test the vehicle.

Rear

▶ **See Figures 46 and 47**

1. Raise and safely support the vehicle.
2. Remove the rear wheel and tire assembly.

3. Remove the brake fitting retaining bolt from the caliper and disconnect the flexible brake hose from the caliper. Plug the hose and the caliper fitting.

4. Remove the caliper locating pins. Lift the caliper off the rotor and anchor plate using a rotating motion.

✳✳ WARNING

Do not pry directly against the plastic piston or damage to the piston will occur.

To install:

5. Position the caliper assembly above the rotor with the anti-rattle spring located on the lower adapter support arm. Install the caliper over the rotor with a rotating motion. Make sure the inner pad is properly positioned.

6. Install the caliper locating pins and start them in the threads by hand. Tighten them to 19–26 ft. lbs. (26–35 Nm).

7. Install the brake hose on the caliper with a new gasket on each side of the fitting outlet. Insert the retaining bolt and tighten to 30–40 ft. lbs. (40–54 Nm).

8. Bleed the brake system, install the wheel and tire assembly and lower the vehicle.

9. Pump the brake pedal prior to moving the vehicle to position the linings.

10. Road test the vehicle.

OVERHAUL

▶ **See Figures 48 thru 55**

✳✳ CAUTION

Older brake pads or shoes may contain asbestos, which has been determined to be cancer causing agent. Never clean the brake surfaces with compressed air! Avoid inhaling any dust from any brake surface! When cleaning brake surfaces, use a commercially available brake cleaning fluid.

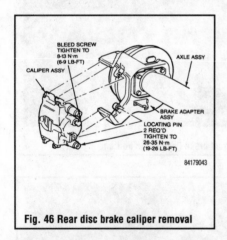

Fig. 46 Rear disc brake caliper removal

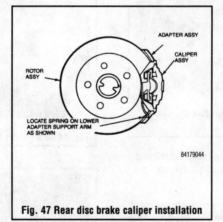

Fig. 47 Rear disc brake caliper installation

Fig. 48 For some types of calipers, use compressed air to drive the piston out of the caliper, but make sure to keep your fingers clear

Fig. 49 Withdraw the piston from the caliper bore

Fig. 50 On some vehicles, you must remove the anti-rattle clip

Fig. 51 Use a prytool to carefully pry around the edge of the boot . . .

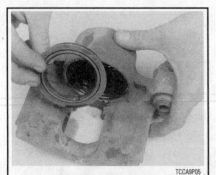

Fig. 52 . . . then remove the boot from the caliper housing, taking care not to score or damage the bore

Fig. 53 Use extreme caution when removing the piston seal; DO NOT scratch the caliper bore

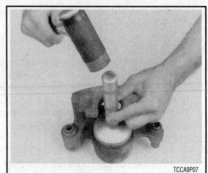

Fig. 54 Use the proper size driving tool and a mallet to properly seal the boots in the caliper housing

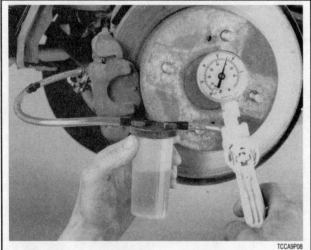

Fig. 55 There are tools, such as this Mighty-Vac, available to assist in proper brake system bleeding

➡Some vehicles may be equipped dual piston calipers. The procedure to overhaul the caliper is essentially the same with the exception of multiple pistons, O-rings and dust boots.

1. Remove the caliper from the vehicle and place on a clean workbench.

❊❊ CAUTION

NEVER place your fingers in front of the pistons in an attempt to catch or protect the pistons when applying compressed air. This could result in personal injury!

➡Depending upon the vehicle, there are two different ways to remove the piston from the caliper. Refer to the brake pad replacement procedure to make sure you have the correct procedure for your vehicle.

2. The first method is as follows:
    a. Stuff a shop towel or a block of wood into the caliper to catch the piston.
    b. Remove the caliper piston using compressed air applied into the caliper inlet hole. Inspect the piston for scoring, nicks, corrosion and/or worn or damaged chrome plating. The piston must be replaced if any of these conditions are found.
3. For the second method, you must rotate the piston to retract it from the caliper.
4. If equipped, remove the anti-rattle clip.
5. Use a prytool to remove the caliper boot, being careful not to scratch the housing bore.
6. Remove the piston seals from the groove in the caliper bore.
7. Carefully loosen the brake bleeder valve cap and valve from the caliper housing.

8. Inspect the caliper bores, pistons and mounting threads for scoring or excessive wear.
9. Use crocus cloth to polish out light corrosion from the piston and bore.
10. Clean all parts with denatured alcohol and dry with compressed air.

To assemble:
11. Lubricate and install the bleeder valve and cap.
12. Install the new seals into the caliper bore grooves, making sure they are not twisted.
13. Lubricate the piston bore.
14. Install the pistons and boots into the bores of the calipers and push to the bottom of the bores.
15. Use a suitable driving tool to seat the boots in the housing.
16. Install the caliper in the vehicle.
17. Install the wheel and tire assembly, then carefully lower the vehicle.
18. Properly bleed the brake system.

Brake Disc (Rotor)

REMOVAL & INSTALLATION

Front

1989–91 VEHICLES

◆ See Figure 56

1. Raise and safely support the vehicle.
2. Remove the wheel and tire assembly.
3. Remove the caliper from the spindle and rotor, but do not disconnect the

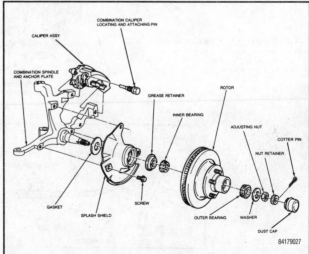

Fig. 56 Front disc brake rotor and related components—1989–91 vehicles

brake hose. Suspend the caliper inside the fender housing with a length of wire. Do not let the caliper hang by the brake hose.

4. Remove the grease cap from the hub and remove the cotter pin, nut retainer and adjusting nut.

5. Grasp the hub/rotor assembly and pull it out far enough to loosen the washer and outer wheel bearing. Push the hub/rotor assembly back onto the spindle and remove the washer and outer wheel bearing.

6. Remove the hub/rotor assembly from the spindle.

7. Inspect the rotor for scoring and wear. Replace or machine as necessary. If machining, observe the minimum thickness specification.

To install:

8. If the rotor is being replaced, remove the protective coating from the new rotor with brake cleaner. Pack a new set of bearings with high-temperature wheel bearing grease and install the inner roller bearing in the inner cup. Pack grease lightly between the lips of a new seal and install the seal, using a seal installer.

9. If the original rotor is being installed, make sure the grease in the hub is clean and adequate, the inner bearing and grease seal are lubricated and in good condition, and the rotor braking surfaces are clean.

10. Install the hub/rotor assembly on the spindle. Keep the assembly centered on the spindle to prevent damage to the grease seal or spindle threads.

11. Install the outer wheel bearing, washer and adjusting nut. Adjust the wheel bearings according to the procedure in Section 8, then install the nut retainer, cotter pin and grease cap.

12. Install the caliper and the wheel and tire assembly.

13. Lower the vehicle.

14. Apply the brake pedal several times before moving the vehicle, to position the brake pads.

1992–98 VEHICLES

▶ **See Figures 57 and 58**

1. Raise and safely support the vehicle.
2. Remove the wheel and tire assembly.
3. Remove the caliper from the spindle and rotor, but do not disconnect the brake hose.

Fig. 58 Remove the rotor from the wheel hub by carefully pulling it straight off

4. Suspend the caliper inside the fender housing with a length of wire. Do not let the caliper hang by the brake hose.

5. Remove the rotor retaining push nuts, if equipped, and remove the rotor from the hub.

6. Inspect the rotor for scoring and wear. Replace or machine as necessary. If machining, observe the minimum thickness specification.

To install:

7. If the rotor is being replaced, remove the protective coating from the new rotor with brake cleaner. If the original rotor is being installed, make sure the braking surfaces are clean.

8. Install the rotor on the hub.

9. Install the caliper and the wheel and tire assembly. Lower the vehicle.

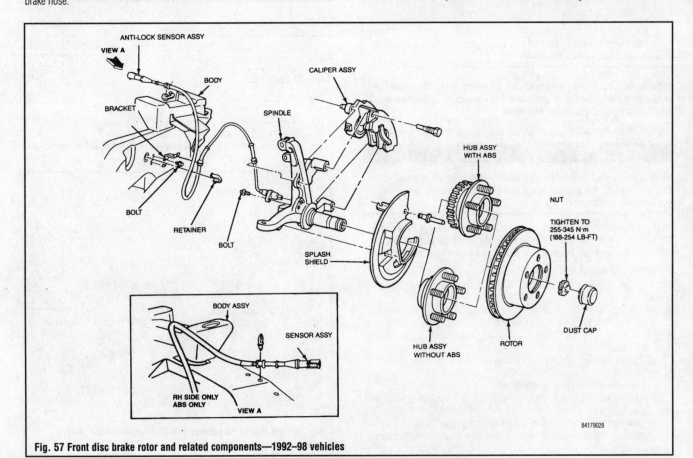

Fig. 57 Front disc brake rotor and related components—1992–98 vehicles

10. Apply the brake pedal several times before moving the vehicle, to position the brake pads.

Rear

▶ See Figure 59

1. Raise and safely support the vehicle.
2. Remove the wheel and tire assembly.
3. Remove the caliper, but do not disconnect the brake hose.
4. Suspend the caliper inside the fender housing with a length of wire. Do not let the caliper hang by the brake hose.
5. Remove the rotor retaining push nuts and remove the rotor from the hub.

➡ If additional force is required to remove the rotor, apply penetrating oil to the rotor/flange mating surface. Install a suitable 3-jaw puller and remove the rotor. If excessive force must be used during rotor removal, the rotor should be checked for lateral run-out before reinstallation.

6. Inspect the rotor for scoring and wear. Replace or machine as necessary. If machining, observe the minimum thickness specification.

To install:

7. If the rotor is being replaced, remove the protective coating from the new rotor with brake cleaner. If the original rotor is being installed, make sure the rotor braking and mounting surfaces are clean.
8. Install the rotor. The pushnuts do not have to be reinstalled.
9. Install the caliper and the wheel and tire assembly.
10. Lower the vehicle.
11. Pump the brake pedal to position the brake pads, before moving the vehicle.
12. Road test the vehicle.

Fig. 59 To remove to rear disc brake rotor, simply pull it straight off the hub after the caliper is removed

INSPECTION

▶ See Figures 60, 61 and 62

Rotor thickness should be measured any time a brake inspection is done. Rotor thickness can be measured using a brake rotor micrometer or Vernier caliper. Measure the rotor thickness in several places around the rotor. Compare the thickness to the specifications chart found at the end of this section.

The run-out of the brake rotor should be checked any time a vibration during braking occurs. Excessive run-out can be caused by a build-up of rust scale or other particles on the rotor or hub surfaces. Remove the rotor and thoroughly clean the hub and rotor-to-hub mounting surface on the back of the rotor. Mount a dial indicator to a suspension member and zero the indicator stylus on the face of the rotor. Rotate the rotor 360 degrees by hand and record the run-out.

Compare measurements to the brake specifications chart. If the thickness and run-out do not meet specifications, replace the rotor.

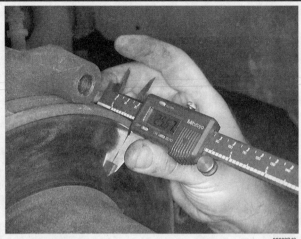

Fig. 60 Check brake rotor thickness in several places around the rotor using a Vernier caliper

Fig. 61 On the front rotor, the minimum thickness specification is usually stamped on the inside edge

Fig. 62 The minimum thickness is typically stamped on the rear rotor in the location shown here

DRUM BRAKES

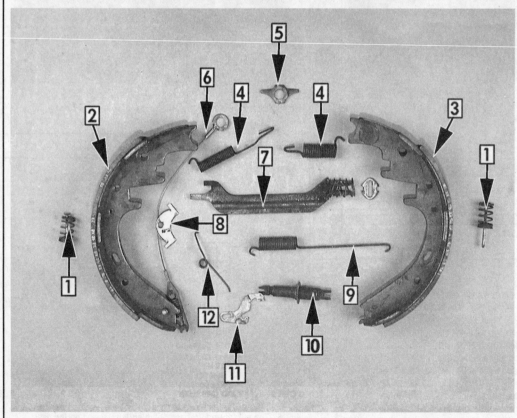

REAR DRUM BRAKE COMPONENTS

1. Shoe hold-down spring and retainer
2. Primary brake shoe
3. Secondary brake shoe
4. Brake shoe retracting springs
5. Anchor pin guide plate
6. Shoe adjusting lever cable
7. Parking brake strut
8. Shoe adjusting lever cable guide
9. Brake shoe adjusting screw spring
10. Brake adjuster screw
11. Brake shoe adjusting lever
12. Adjusting lever return spring
13. Wheel cylinder
14. Parking brake lever retaining clip
15. Parking brake lever

91199P75

Brake Drums

REMOVAL & INSTALLATION

▶ See Figure 63

✖ CAUTION

Older brake pads or shoes may contain asbestos, which has been determined to be cancer causing agent. Never clean the brake surfaces with compressed air! Avoid inhaling any dust from any brake surface! When cleaning brake surfaces, use a commercially available brake cleaning fluid.

1. Raise and safely support the vehicle securely on jackstands.
2. Remove the tire and wheel assembly.
3. Remove the three retaining clips (if equipped), then remove the brake drum.

➡ **It may be necessary to back off the brake shoe adjustment in order to remove the brake drum. This is because the drum might be grooved or worn from being in service for an extended period of time.**

➡ **Before installing a new brake drum, be sure to remove any protective coating with brake cleaner or a suitable fast-drying degreaser.**

4. Install the brake drum in the reverse order of removal, then adjust the brakes as outlined later in this section.

91199P01

Fig. 63 Lift the brake drum from the shoes and backing plate

INSPECTION

▶ See Figures 64 and 65

Check that there are no cracks or chips in the braking surface. Excessive bluing indicates overheating and a replacement drum is needed. The drum can be machined to remove minor damage and to establish a rounded braking surface on a warped drum. Never exceed the maximum oversize of the drum when machining the braking surface.

✖ CAUTION

Older brake pads or shoes may contain asbestos, which has been determined to be cancer causing agent. Never clean the brake surfaces with compressed air! Avoid inhaling any dust from any brake surface! When cleaning brake surfaces, use a commercially available brake cleaning fluid.

The brake drum inside diameter and run-out can be measured using a brake drum micrometer. The drum should be measured every time a brake inspection is performed. Take the inside diameter readings at points 90° apart from each other on the drum to measure the run-out. The maximum inside diameter is stamped on the rim of the drum or on the inside above the lug nut stud holes and is also contained in the brake specifications chart at the end of this section.

Brake Shoes

INSPECTION

▶ See Figure 66

✖ CAUTION

Older brake pads or shoes may contain asbestos, which has been determined to be cancer causing agent. Never clean the brake surfaces with compressed air! Avoid inhaling any dust from any brake surface! When cleaning brake surfaces, use a commercially available brake cleaning fluid.

Inspect the brake shoes for wear using a ruler or Vernier caliper. Compare measurements to the brake specifications chart. If the lining is thinner than specification or there is evidence of the lining being contaminated by brake fluid or oil, repair the leak and replace all brake shoe assemblies (a complete axle set). In addition to the shoes inspect all springs and brake shoe hardware for wear and replace as necessary.

REMOVAL & INSTALLATION

▶ See Figures 67 thru 85

1. Raise and safely support the vehicle securely on jackstands.
2. Remove the wheel and tire assembly, then remove the brake drum.

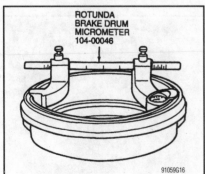

ROTUNDA
BRAKE DRUM
MICROMETER
104-00046

91059G16

Fig. 64 Measure the drum using a micrometer made especially for brake drums

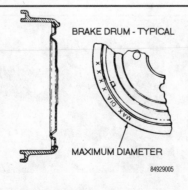

BRAKE DRUM - TYPICAL

MAXIMUM DIAMETER

84929005

Fig. 65 Brake drum maximum diameter location

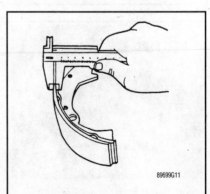

89699G11

Fig. 66 Measure brake shoe thickness in several places around the shoe

Fig. 67 Remove the brake shoe retracting springs . . .

Fig. 68 . . . from both sides

Fig. 69 Rotate the hold down spring retainer and . . .

Fig. 70 . . . remove the hold down spring from the primary brake shoe

Fig. 71 Remove the primary shoe and unhook the adjusting spring from the shoe

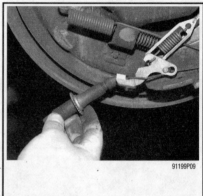

Fig. 72 Remove the adjusting screw

Fig. 73 Remove the brake shoe adjusting lever cable

Fig. 74 Remove the adjusting spring

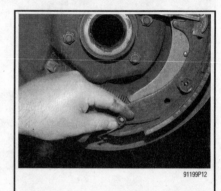

Fig. 75 Remove the adjusting lever return spring

Fig. 76 Remove the anchor pin guide plate

Fig. 77 Remove the parking brake strut

Fig. 78 Remove the secondary shoe hold down spring and . . .

Fig. 79 . . . lift the secondary shoe from the backing plate

Fig. 80 Remove the parking brake lever horseshoe clip apart and . . .

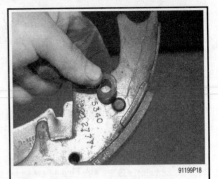

Fig. 81 . . . remove the washer from under the horseshoe clip

Fig. 82 Remove the secondary brake shoe from the parking brake lever

Fig. 83 Thoroughly clean and . . .

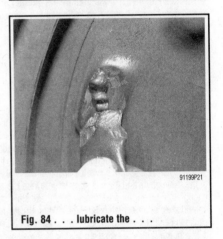

Fig. 84 . . . lubricate the . . .

Fig. 85 . . . shoe contact points on the backing plate

➡When servicing drum brakes, only dissemble and assemble one side at a time, leaving the remaining side intact for reference.

❋❋ **CAUTION**

Older brake pads or shoes may contain asbestos, which has been determined to be cancer causing agent. Never clean the brake surfaces with compressed air! Avoid inhaling any dust from any brake surface! When cleaning brake surfaces, use a commercially available brake cleaning fluid.

3. Contract the brake shoes by pulling the self-adjusting lever away from the starwheel adjustment screw and turn the starwheel up and back until the pivot nut is drawn onto the starwheel as far as it will come.

4. Pull the adjusting lever, cable and automatic adjuster spring down and toward the rear to unhook the pivot hook from the large hole in the secondary shoe web. Do not attempt to pry the pivot hook from the hole.

5. Remove the automatic adjuster spring and the adjusting lever.

6. Remove the secondary shoe-to-anchor spring. Remove the primary shoe-to-anchor spring and unhook the cable anchor. Remove the anchor pin plate.

7. Remove the cable guide from the secondary shoe.

8. Remove the shoe hold-down springs, shoes, adjusting screw, pivot nut, and socket. Note the color of each hold-down spring for assembly. To remove the hold-down springs, reach behind the brake backing plate and place one finger on the end of one of the brake hold-down spring mounting pins. Using a pair of pliers, grasp the washer type retainer on top of the hold-down spring that corresponds to the pin which you are holding. Push down on the pliers and turn them 90° to align the slot in the washer with the head on the spring mounting pin. Remove the spring and washer retainer and repeat this operation on the hold down spring on the other shoe.

9. Remove the parking brake link and spring. Disconnect the parking brake cable from the parking brake lever.

10. After removing the rear brake secondary shoe, disassemble the parking brake lever from the shoe by removing the retaining clip and spring washer.

To install:

11. Assemble the parking brake lever to the secondary shoe and secure it with the spring washer and retaining clip.

12. Apply a light coating of Lubriplate®, or equivalent, at the points where the brake shoes contact the backing plate.

13. Position the brake shoes on the backing plate, and install the hold-down spring pins, springs, and spring washer type retainers. On the rear brake, install the parking brake link, spring and washer. Connect the parking brake cable to the parking brake lever.

14. Install the anchor pin plate, and place the cable anchor over the anchor pin with the crimped side toward the backing plate.

15. Install the primary shoe-to-anchor spring with the brake tool.

16. Install the cable guide on the secondary shoe web with the flanged holes fitted into the hole in the secondary shoe web. Thread the cable around the cable guide groove.

17. Install the secondary shoe-to-anchor (long) spring. Be sure that the cable end is not cocked or binding on the anchor pin when installed. All of the parts should be flat on the anchor pin. Remove the wheel cylinder piston clamp.

18. Apply Lubriplate®, or equivalent, to the threads and the socket end of the adjusting starwheel screw. Turn the adjusting screw into the adjusting pivot nut to the limit of the threads and then back off ½ turn.

➡**Interchanging the brake shoe adjusting screw assemblies from one side of the vehicle to the other would cause the brake shoes to retract rather than expand each time the automatic adjusting mechanism is operated. To prevent this, the socket end of the adjusting screw is stamped with an "R" or an "L" for "RIGHT" or "LEFT". The adjusting pivot nuts can be distinguished by the number of lines machined around the body of the nut; one line indicates left hand nut and two lines indicate a right hand nut.**

19. Place the adjusting socket on the screw and install this assembly between the shoe ends with the adjusting screw nearest to the secondary shoe.

20. Place the cable hook into the hole in the adjusting lever from the backing plate side. The adjusting levers are stamped with an **R** (right) or a **L** (left) to indicate their installation on the right or left hand brake assembly.

21. Position the hooked end of the adjuster spring in the primary shoe web and connect the loop end of the spring to the adjuster lever hole.

22. Pull the adjuster lever, cable and automatic adjuster spring down toward the rear to engage the pivot hook in the large hole in the secondary shoe web.

23. After installation, check the action of the adjuster by pulling the section of the cable guide and the adjusting lever toward the secondary shoe web far enough to lift the lever past a tooth on the adjusting screw starwheel. The lever should snap into position behind the next tooth, and release of the cable should cause the adjuster spring to return the lever to its original position. This return action of the lever will turn the adjusting screw starwheel one tooth. The lever should contact the adjusting screw starwheel one tooth above the centerline of the adjusting screw.

If the automatic adjusting mechanism does not perform properly, check the following:

24. Check the cable and fittings. The cable ends should fill or extend slightly beyond the crimped section of the fittings. If this is not the case, replace the cable.

25. Check the cable guide for damage. The cable groove should be parallel to the shoe web, and the body of the guide should lie flat against the web. Replace the cable guide if this is not so.

26. Check the pivot hook on the lever. The hook surfaces should be square with the body on the lever for proper pivoting. Repair or replace the hook as necessary.

27. Make sure that the adjusting screw starwheel is properly seated in the notch in the shoe web.

28. Install the brake drum and the wheel and tire assembly

29. Carefully lower the vehicle.

ADJUSTMENTS

The drum brakes are self-adjusting and require a manual adjustment only after the brake shoes have been replaced, or when the length of the adjusting screw has been changed while performing some other service operation, as, for example, when taking off brake drums.

To adjust the brakes, perform the procedures that follow:

Drum Installed

▶ **See Figure 86**

1. Raise and support the rear of the vehicle on jackstands.
2. Remove the rubber plug from the adjusting slot on the backing plate.

✳✳ CAUTION

Brake shoes may contain asbestos, which has been determined to be a cancer causing agent. Never clean the brake surfaces with compressed air! Avoid inhaling any dust from any brake surface! When cleaning brake surfaces, use a commercially available brake cleaning fluid.

3. Insert a brake adjusting spoon into the slot and engage the lowest possible tooth on the starwheel. Move the end of the brake spoon downward to move the starwheel upward and expand the adjusting screw. Repeat this operation until the brakes lock the wheels.

4. Insert a small screwdriver or piece of firm wire (coat hanger wire) into the adjusting slot and push the automatic adjusting lever out and free of the starwheel on the adjusting screw and hold it there.

5. Engage the topmost tooth possible on the starwheel with the brake adjusting spoon. Move the end of the adjusting spoon upward to move the adjusting screw starwheel downward and contact the adjusting screw. Back off the adjusting screw starwheel until the wheel spins freely with a minimum of drag. Keep track of the number of turns that the starwheel is backed off, or the number of strokes taken with the brake adjusting spoon.

6. Repeat this operation for the other side. When backing off the brakes on the other side, the starwheel adjuster must be backed off the same number of turns to prevent side-to-side brake pull.

7. Remove the jackstands and lower the vehicle.

8. After the brakes are adjusted make several stops while backing the vehicle up, to equalize the brakes at both of the wheels. Road test the vehicle.

Drum Removed

▶ **See Figures 87 and 88**

✳✳ CAUTION

Brake shoes may contain asbestos, which has been determined to be a cancer causing agent. Never clean the brake surfaces with compressed air! Avoid inhaling any dust from any brake surface! When cleaning brake surfaces, use a commercially available brake cleaning fluid.

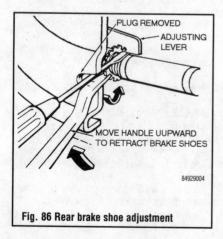

Fig. 86 Rear brake shoe adjustment

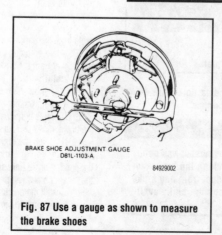

Fig. 87 Use a gauge as shown to measure the brake shoes

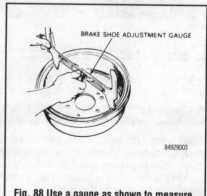

Fig. 88 Use a gauge as shown to measure the drum

1. Make sure that the shoe-to-contact pad areas are clean and properly lubricated.
2. Using an inside caliper check the inside diameter of the drum. Measure across the diameter of the assembled brake shoes, at their widest point.
3. Turn the adjusting screw so that the diameter of the shoes is 0.030 in. (0.76mm) less than the brake drum inner diameter.
4. Install the drum.

Wheel Cylinders

REMOVAL & INSTALLATION

▶ See Figures 89, 90, 91 and 92

1. Raise and safely support the vehicle.
2. Remove the rear wheel and tire assembly.
3. Remove the brake drum retainers, if equipped.
4. Grasp the brake drum and remove.
5. If the drum will not slide off with light force, then the brake shoes need to be backed off.

❄❄ CAUTION

Brake shoes may contain asbestos, which has been determined to be a cancer causing agent. Never clean the brake surfaces with compressed air! Avoid inhaling any dust from any brake surface! When cleaning brake surfaces, use a commercially available brake cleaning fluid.

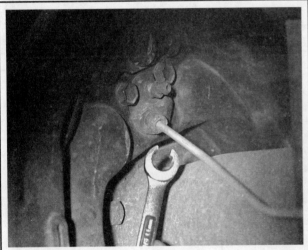

Fig. 89 Use a suitable size flare nut wrench to . . .

6. Remove the brake drum and the brake shoes, as outlined in this section.

❄❄ CAUTION

Brake fluid contains polyglycol ethers and polyglycols. Avoid contact with the eyes and wash your hands thoroughly after handling brake fluid. If you do get brake fluid in your eyes, flush your eyes with clean, running water for 15 minutes. If eye irritation persists, or if you have taken brake fluid internally, IMMEDIATELY seek medical assistance.

7. Use a flare nut wrench to disconnect the brake line at the wheel cylinder.
8. Remove the 2 bolts securing the wheel cylinder to the backing plate and remove the wheel cylinder.
To install:
9. Reinstall the wheel cylinder to the brake backing plate and install the 2 retaining bolts. Torque the retaining bolts to 84–108 inch. lbs. (10–13 Nm).
10. Reconnect the brake line to the wheel cylinder and torque the fitting, with a flare nut wrench, to 10–18 ft. lbs. (14–24 Nm).
11. Lubricate the rear brake shoe contact points on the backing plate with an appropriate grease.
12. Install the brake shoes.
13. Make sure that the brake drum and brake shoes are clean of any oils or protective coatings.
14. Reinstall the brake drum.
15. Bleed the brake system of air until a firm pedal is achieved. Top off the brake fluid in the master cylinder.

❄❄ WARNING

Clean, high quality brake fluid is essential to the safe and proper operation of the brake system. You should always buy the highest quality brake fluid that is available. If the brake fluid becomes contaminated, drain and flush the system, then refill the master cylinder with new fluid. Never reuse any brake fluid. Any brake fluid that is removed from the system should be discarded. Also, do not allow any brake fluid to come in contact with a painted surface; it will damage the paint.

16. Reinstall the wheel and tire assembly.
17. Lower the vehicle.
18. Pump the brake pedal several times to assure good, firm pedal feel.
19. Road test the vehicle and check the brake system for proper operation.

OVERHAUL

▶ See Figures 93 thru 102

Wheel cylinder overhaul kits may be available, but often at little or no savings over a reconditioned wheel cylinder. It often makes sense with these components to substitute a new or reconditioned part instead of attempting an overhaul.

If no replacement is available, or you would prefer to overhaul your wheel cylinders, the following procedure may be used. When rebuilding and

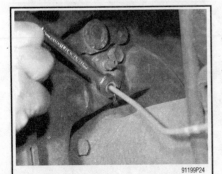

Fig. 90 . . . loosen the brake line fitting on the wheel cylinder

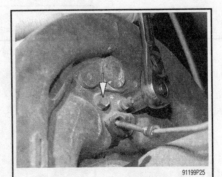

Fig. 91 Remove the wheel cylinder retaining bolts and . . .

Fig. 92 . . . remove the wheel cylinder from the backing plate

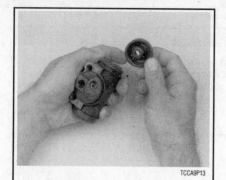

Fig. 93 Remove the outer boots from the wheel cylinder

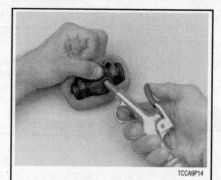

Fig. 94 Compressed air can be used to remove the pistons and seals

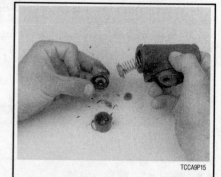

Fig. 95 Remove the pistons, cup seals and spring from the cylinder

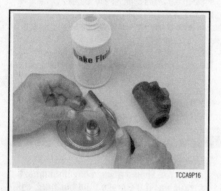

Fig. 96 Use brake fluid and a soft brush to clean the pistons . . .

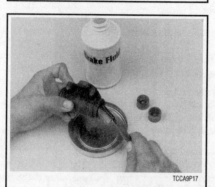

Fig. 97 . . . and the bore of the wheel cylinder

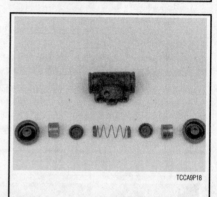

Fig. 98 Once cleaned and inspected, the wheel cylinder is ready for assembly

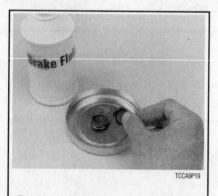

Fig. 99 Lubricate the cup seals with brake fluid

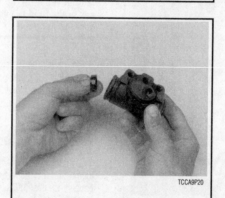

Fig. 100 Install the spring, then the cup seals in the bore

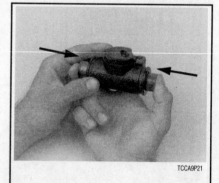

Fig. 101 Lightly lubricate the pistons, then install them

installing wheel cylinders, avoid getting any contaminants into the system. Always use clean, new, high quality brake fluid. If dirty or improper fluid has been used, it will be necessary to drain the entire system, flush the system with proper brake fluid, replace all rubber components, then refill and bleed the system.

1. Remove the wheel cylinder from the vehicle and place on a clean workbench.

2. First remove and discard the old rubber boots, then withdraw the pistons. Piston cylinders are equipped with seals and a spring assembly, all located behind the pistons in the cylinder bore.

3. Remove the remaining inner components, seals and spring assembly. Compressed air may be useful in removing these components. If no compressed air is available, be VERY careful not to score the wheel cylinder bore when removing parts from it. Discard all components for which replacements were supplied in the rebuild kit.

4. Wash the cylinder and metal parts in denatured alcohol or clean brake fluid.

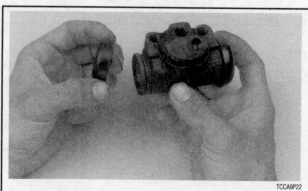

Fig. 102 The boots can now be installed over the wheel cylinder ends

5. Allow the parts to air dry or use compressed air. Do not use rags for cleaning, since lint will remain in the cylinder bore.

PARKING BRAKE

Cable(s)

REMOVAL AND INSTALLATION

Front Cable

1989–91 VEHICLES

▶ **See Figures 103, 104 and 105**

1. Raise and safely support the vehicle.
2. On 1989 vehicles, loosen the adjusting nut at the adjuster.
3. Disconnect the cable from the intermediate for 1989 or rear for 1990–91 cable connector located along the left side frame rail.
4. Use a 13mm box end wrench to depress the retaining tabs and remove the conduit retainer from the frame. Remove screw holding the plastic inner fender apron to the frame, at the rear of the fender panel.
5. Pull back the fender apron.
6. If equipped, remove the spring clip retainer that holds the parking brake cable to the frame.
7. Pull the cable through the frame and let it hang in the wheel housing. Lower the vehicle.
8. Inside the passenger compartment, remove the sound deadener cover from the cable at the dash panel.
9. On 1989 vehicles, remove the spring retainer and cable end from the clevis at the parking brake control.
10. On 1990–91 vehicles, pull the cable until the parking brake control take up spring tang is at full clockwise position. Fabricate a tool from metal of the dimensions shown in the illustration, then use it to retain the reel spring and disconnect the cable from the take up reel.

11. Using a 13mm box end wrench, depress the retaining tabs and remove the conduit from the control assembly. Push the cable down through the dash panel and remove cable from inside the wheel housing.

To install:
12. Start the cable through the opening in the dash panel inside the passenger compartment.

6. Inspect the piston and replace it if it shows scratches.
7. Lubricate the cylinder bore and seals using clean brake fluid.
8. Position the spring assembly.
9. Install the inner seals, then the pistons.
10. Insert the new boots into the counterbores by hand. Do not lubricate the boots.
11. Install the wheel cylinder.

13. On 1989 vehicles, connect the end of the cable to the parking brake control clevis and secure it with a spring clip.
14. On 1990–91 vehicles, connect the end of the cable to the parking brake control take up reel.
15. Press the tabbed conduit retainer into the parking brake control and install the sound deadener cover patch at the dash panel.
16. Raise and safely support the vehicle.
17. Insert the cable through the frame member toward the rear of the vehicle. Press the tabbed conduit retainer into the frame hole.
18. On 1989 vehicles, install the cable-to-frame spring clip retainer behind the fender apron and connect the front cable to the intermediate cable connector on the left side frame rail.
19. On 1990–91 vehicles, attach the control cable to the rear cable connector on the left side frame rail and use pliers to remove the fabricated tool used to retain the take up reel.
20. Lower the vehicle.
21. On 1989 vehicles, adjust the parking brake.
22. On 1990–91 vehicles, check parking brake operation.

1992–94 VEHICLES

1. If equipped with air suspension, the air suspension switch, located on the right-hand side of the luggage compartment, must be turned to the OFF position before raising the vehicle.
2. Raise and safely support the vehicle.
3. Detach the cable from the rear cable connector located along the left side frame rail.
4. Use a 13mm box end wrench or equivalent, to depress the retaining tabs and remove the conduit retainer from the frame. Remove the screw holding the plastic inner fender apron to the frame.
5. Pull back the fender apron to expose the front brake cable and conduit.
6. Pull the cable through the frame and let it hang in the wheel housing.
7. Lower the vehicle.
8. Inside the passenger compartment, remove the sound deadener cover from the cable at the dash panel.

➡**If a shipping clip from a new cable is available, it can be used to secure the reel spring. If no clip is available, a tool must be fabricated. Do not attempt this job without the tool.**

9. If a shipping clip is not available, fabricate a tool to the correct dimensions.

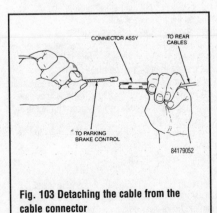

Fig. 103 Detaching the cable from the cable connector

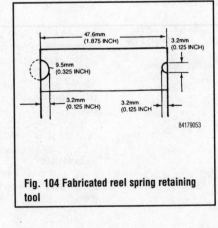

Fig. 104 Fabricated reel spring retaining tool

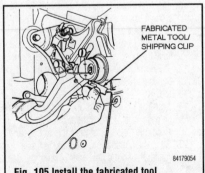

Fig. 105 Install the fabricated tool between the control assembly take up spring tang and mounting bracket

10. Pull the front parking brake cable until the parking brake control take-up spring tang is at the full clockwise position. Use the shipping clip or fabricated tool to retain the reel spring.

11. Disconnect the cable from the take-up reel.

❊❊ CAUTION

Keep fingers away from the reel mechanism while the clip or fabricated tool is in place.

12. Using a 13mm box end wrench or equivalent, depress the retaining tabs and remove the conduit from the control assembly. Push the cable down through the dash panel and remove cable from inside the wheel housing.

To install:

13. Start the cable through the opening in the dash panel inside the passenger compartment.

14. Reconnect the end of the cable to the parking brake control take-up reel.

15. Press the tabbed conduit retainer into the parking brake control and install the sound deadener cover patch at the dash panel.

16. Raise and safely support the vehicle.

17. Insert the front parking brake cable through the frame member toward the rear of the vehicle. Press the tabbed conduit retainer into the frame hole.

18. Reattach the control cable to the rear cable connector on the left side frame rail and use pliers to remove the shipping clip or fabricated tool used to retain the take-up reel.

19. Lower the vehicle.

20. If equipped with air suspension, turn the air suspension switch to the ON position.

21. Check the parking brake system for proper operation.

1995–98 VEHICLES

1. If equipped with air suspension, the air suspension switch, located on the right-hand side of the luggage compartment, must be turned to the OFF position before raising the vehicle.

2. Fully release the parking brake.

3. Raise and safely support the vehicle.

4. Release the cable tension as follows:

a. Remove the rear cable from the black plastic cable retainer under the floorpan by unsnapping and pulling out the rear cable and conduit.

b. Removal of cable tension requires 2 people to disengage and reload the tensioner. One person is to unlock the tensioner by pulling downward on the clip. When the clip is disengaged, the second person is to apply the parking brake control fully to the last notch. The tensioner spring will compress allowing the cable slack to return.

c. Lock the tensioner by pushing up on the clip. Make sure the locking lever is secure by rotating it toward the threaded rod. Wrap tape or wire around the locking lever and threaded rod to prevent accidental release.

5. Detach the front parking brake cable from the left-hand rear cable at the cable connector located along the left side frame rail.

6. Use a 13mm box-end wrench or equivalent, to depress the retaining tabs and remove the conduit retainer from the frame. Remove the screw holding the plastic inner fender apron to the frame.

7. Pull back the fender apron to expose the front brake cable and conduit.

8. Pull the cable through the frame and let it hang in the wheel housing.

9. Lower the vehicle.

10. Inside the passenger compartment, remove the sound deadener cover from the cable at the dash panel.

11. Disconnect the brake cable from the parking brake control at the clevis.

12. Using a 13mm box-end wrench or equivalent, depress the retaining tabs and remove the conduit from the control assembly.

13. Push the cable down through the dash panel and remove cable from inside the wheel housing.

To install:

14. Start the front parking brake cable through the opening in the dash panel inside the passenger compartment.

15. Reconnect the end of the cable to the parking brake control clevis.

16. Snap the conduit into the parking brake control.

17. Install the sound deadener cover at the dash panel.

18. Raise and safely support the vehicle.

19. Insert the cable through the frame member toward the rear of the vehicle. Press the tabbed conduit retainer into the frame hole.

20. Reattach the front cable to the rear cable connector.

21. Set the initial tensioner adjustment as follows:

a. Remove the tape or wire wrapped around the locking lever during the tensioner release procedure.

b. Grasp the tensioner around the housing, then using a hook-type tool, unlock the tensioner clip by pulling downward with the tool. The tensioner spring will take up the slack in the front parking brake cable and preload the parking brake cable assembly.

c. While holding the tensioner, lock the clip by pushing up on the bottom of the clip. If the clip does not slide up, move the assembly slightly to align the closest groove on adjuster rod to the clip.

d. Apply 125 lbs. (170N) of force to the parking brake control. Release the parking brake control. Repeat application and release twice.

e. Repeat the initial tensioner adjustment procedure again to take up any additional slack.

f. Snap the retainer shut.

22. Lower the vehicle.

23. If equipped with air suspension, turn the air suspension switch to the ON position.

24. Check for proper parking brake operation.

25. Adjust the parking brake cable as necessary.

Intermediate Cable

1989 VEHICLES

1. Raise and safely support the vehicle. Loosen the cable adjusting nut.

2. Disconnect the parking brake release spring at the frame.

3. Detach the cable from the cable connectors and remove it from the vehicle.

To install:

4. Attach the intermediate cable to the front and rear cable connectors. Make sure the rearward end of the cable goes through the release spring before attaching the cable to the connector.

5. Attach the release spring to the frame.

6. Adjust the parking brake and lower the vehicle.

Rear Cables

1989–91 VEHICLES

1. Raise and safely support the vehicle.

2. On 1990–91 vehicles, detach the control cable from the rear cable at the connector.

3. On 1989 vehicles, disconnect the parking brake release spring at the frame.

4. On 1990–91 vehicles with dual exhaust, disconnect the parking brake cable retainer spring at the frame.

5. On 1989 vehicles, detach the left cable from the intermediate cable connector.

6. On 1990–91 vehicles, disconnect the left cable from the right cable at the adjuster bracket.

7. On 1989 vehicles, use a 13mm box end wrench to depress the tabs and remove the left conduit retainer from the rod adjuster. Remove the cable retainer from the left lower arm.

8. Release the right cable tabbed conduit retainer from the frame, using a 13mm box end wrench.

9. On 1989 vehicles, remove the clip retaining the right cable to the frame crossmember. Remove the cable retainer from the right lower arm and disconnect the cable from the retainer on the right upper arm.

10. On 1990–91 vehicles, remove the cable retainer from the left shock bracket and disconnect the cable from the retainer on the crossmember and upper control arm clip.

11. Remove the wheel and tire assemblies and the brake drums.

12. Working on the wheel side of the rear brake, remove the brake automatic adjuster spring. Compress the prongs on the parking brake cable so they can pass through the hole in the backing plate. Pull the cable retainer through the hole.

13. With the tension off the cable spring at the parking brake lever, lift the cable end out of the slot in the lever.

14. Remove the cable through the backing plate hole.

To install:

15. Position the cables approximately in their installed position. Insert enough of the parking brake cable through the backing plate hole, so the cable end can be attached to the parking brake lever on the rear brake shoe.

16. Pull the excess slack from the cable wire inside the brake, and push the cable conduit through the backing plate hole until the retainer prongs expand. The prongs must be securely locked in place. Install the automatic brake adjuster spring.

17. Install the brake drums and wheel and tire assemblies.

18. On 1989 vehicles, attach the right cable to the right upper and lower arms, frame crossmember and through the frame bracket using the existing retaining clips. Press the tabbed retainer into the crossmember hole until it is securely locked into place.

19. On 1990–91 vehicles, attach the right cable to the crossmember retainer hook and through the upper control arm clip. Press the tabbed retainer into the crossmember hole until it is securely locked into place.

20. On 1989 vehicles, attach the left cable to the left lower arm with the retainer, and route the cable toward the front of the vehicle. Be sure to route the cable over the right cable. Install the left cable through the flanged hole in the adjuster and press the tabbed retainer into place.

21. On 1990–91 vehicles, attach the left cable to the drum backing plate and route the cable toward the front of the vehicle under the right cable between the stabilizer bar stud and shock. Connect the right cable end to the equalizer bracket (part of the left cable).

22. On 1989 vehicles, attach the left cable end to the connector at the intermediate cable. Insert the threaded rod of the right cable through the 2 holes in the adjuster. Loosely attach the adjuster nut.

23. On 1989 vehicles, install the cable release springs to the frame attaching hole and adjust the parking brake. On 1990–91 vehicles, attach the rear cable connector to the control cable.

24. Lower the vehicle. On 1990–91 vehicles, check the operation of the parking brake control.

1992–94 VEHICLES

1. Raise and safely support the vehicle.
2. Detach the control cable from the rear cable at the connector.
3. Disconnect the parking brake cable retainer spring at the frame, if equipped with dual exhaust.
4. Disconnect the left cable from the right cable at the adjuster bracket.
5. Release the right cable tabbed conduit retainer from the frame, using a 13mm box end wrench.
6. Remove the cable retainer from the left shock bracket, the wire retainer on the left axle bracket and disconnect the cable from the retainer on the right axle tube by removing the bolt and retainer.
7. Remove the cable retaining E-clip and cable eyelet from the brake lever. Pull the cable out of the disc brake adapter boss.
8. Remove the cables.

To install:

9. Insert the brake cable through the mounting boss and connect it to the lever.
10. Push the cable conduit through the mounting boss and install the retaining clip.
11. Attach the right cable to the axle retaining clip, through the wire retainer and left shock absorber plastic loop.
12. Press the tabbed retainer into the crossmember hole until locked into place.
13. Route the left cable under the right cable between the stabilizer bar stud and shock absorber. Connect the right cable end to the equalizer bracket (part of the left cable).
14. Connect the rear cable connector to the control cable. Lower the vehicle and check parking brake operation.

1995–98 VEHICLES

1. If equipped with air suspension, the air suspension switch, located on the right-hand side of the luggage compartment, must be turned to the OFF position before raising the vehicle.
2. Fully release the parking brake.
3. Raise and safely support the vehicle.
4. Release the parking brake cable tension as follows:
    a. Remove the rear cable from the black plastic cable retainer under the floorpan by unsnapping and pulling out the rear cable and conduit.
    b. Removal of cable tension requires 2 people to disengage and reload the tensioner. One person is to unlock the tensioner by pulling downward on the clip. When the clip is disengaged, the second person is to apply the parking brake control fully to the last notch. The tensioner spring will compress allowing the cable slack to return.
    c. Lock the tensioner by pushing up on the clip. Make sure the locking lever is secure by rotating it toward the threaded rod. Wrap tape or wire around the locking lever and threaded rod to prevent accidental release.
5. Detach the front parking brake cable from the rear parking brake cable at the connector.
6. Disconnect the parking brake cable retainer at the frame.
7. Detach the left-hand cable from the right-hand cable at the connector.
8. Release the rear parking brake cable right-hand tabbed conduit retainer from the frame, using a 13mm box-end wrench, or equivalent.
9. Remove the right-hand cable tie-strap from the stabilizer bar, wire retainer on the left-hand axle bracket and disconnect the rear cable from the retainer on the right-hand axle housing by removing the bolt and retainer.
10. Remove the cable retaining E-clip and cable eyelet from the rear parking brake cable. Pull the rear parking brake cable and conduit out of the rear disc brake caliper adapter mounting boss.
11. Remove the rear parking brake cables and their conduits from the vehicle.

To install:

12. Insert the cable and conduit through the mounting boss on the rear disc brake caliper and connect it to the parking brake lever.
13. Pull the rear parking brake cable through the mounting boss and install the retaining clip.
14. Attach the right-hand rear parking brake cable to the retaining clip. Press the tabbed retainer into the crossmember hole until it is locked into position.
15. Route the left-hand parking brake cable to go under the right-hand cable between the stabilizer bar stud and shock absorber. Reconnect the right-hand cable end to the connector assembly (part of the left-hand parking brake rear cable and conduit).
16. Attach a new tie-down strap on the right-hand cable to the rear stabilizer bar.
17. Reconnect the rear parking brake cable and conduit connector to the front parking brake cable.
18. Set the initial tensioner adjustment as follows:
    a. Remove the tape or wire wrapped around the locking lever during the tensioner release procedure.
    b. Grasp the tensioner around the housing, then using a hook-type tool, unlock the tensioner clip by pulling downward with the tool. The tensioner spring will take up the slack in the front parking brake cable and preload the parking brake cable assembly.
    c. While holding the tensioner, lock the clip by pushing up on the bottom of the clip. If the clip does not slide up, move the assembly slightly to align the closest groove on adjuster rod to the clip.
    d. Apply 125 lbs. (170N) of force to the parking brake control. Release the parking brake control. Repeat application and release twice.
    e. Repeat the initial tensioner adjustment procedure again to take up any additional slack.
    f. Snap the retainer shut.
19. Lower the vehicle.
20. If equipped with air suspension, turn the air suspension switch to the ON position.
21. Check for proper parking brake operation.
22. Adjust the parking brake cable as necessary.

ADJUSTMENT

1989 Vehicles

1. Make sure the parking brake is fully released.
2. Place the transmission in **N**.
3. Raise and safely support the vehicle.
4. Tighten the adjusting nut against the cable equalizer, causing a rear wheel brake drag. Loosen the adjusting nut until the rear brakes are fully released. There should be no brake drag.
5. Lower the vehicle and check the operation of the parking brake.

1990–94 Vehicles

➡The following procedure is to be used only if a new parking brake control assembly is installed. All components of the parking brake system must be installed prior to the adjustment procedure. The parking brake control with automatic tensioning is preset by means of a shipping clip. The following procedure must be followed in sequence and must be done with the vehicle weight on the axle.

1. Verify removal of the shipping clip. The take-up reel will apply tension to the system.
2. Depress the parking brake control to the 8th notch.
3. Push the parking brake control pedal to release.
4. Check the parking brake function as follows:
    a. Apply the parking brake with a full stroke, to the 9th or 10th notch.
    b. Release the parking brake by shifting the vehicle into a forward gear with the engine running. The control must release.
    c. Apply the parking brake with a full stroke, to the 9th or 10th notch.
    d. Manually release the parking brake with the push-to-release feature.
5. With the control in the OFF position, the rear brakes must not drag. Check for movement of the rear cables from their conduits when the intermediate cable is deflected with a force of 10–15 lbs.

1995–98 Vehicles

1. If equipped with air suspension, the air suspension switch, located on the right-hand side of the luggage compartment, must be turned to the OFF position before raising the vehicle.
2. Make sure the parking brake is fully released.
3. Raise and safely support the vehicle.
4. Hold the tensioner at the housing, then install the hooked end of a suitable tool into the rounded end of the clip between the clip and the housing. Unlock the clip by pulling downward with the tool and support the tensioner. The tensioner spring will take up cable slack and preload the cables. While holding the tensioner, lock the clip by pushing up on the bottom of the clip. If the clip does not slide up, move the assembly slightly to align the closest groove on the adjuster rod to the clip.
5. Apply 125 lbs. (170N) of foot pedal effort and then release the parking brake control. Repeat application and release procedure at least twice.
6. Repeat the entire procedure starting with unlocking the clip to allow the tensioner spring to take up any slack.
7. After repeating the procedure, snap the retainer shut.
8. Lower the vehicle.
9. If equipped with air suspension, turn the air suspension switch to the ON position.
10. Check the parking brake system for proper operation.

Brake Shoes

REMOVAL & INSTALLATION

1992–93 Vehicles

▶ See Figures 106, 107 and 108

1. Raise and safely support the vehicle.
2. Remove the rear axle shaft; refer to Section 7.
3. Disconnect the brake cable from the lever.
4. Remove the brake shoe retaining springs and pins.
5. Set the adjuster assembly to the shortest length. Pull the shoes away from the backing plate slightly and spread them enough to remove the adjuster assembly.
6. Remove the upper return (adjuster) spring.
7. Lift the shoes over the support and remove the shoes and actuating lever as an assembly. Make sure the lever does not damage the boot or pull the boot out of position.
8. Disassemble the shoes, lever and springs.

To install:

9. Install the lower return springs and actuating lever to the brake shoes.
10. Make sure the boot is properly positioned in the backing plate. Install the shoes by first inserting the lever through the boot, then lowering the shoes into position.
11. Install the upper return (adjuster) spring and install the adjuster assembly.

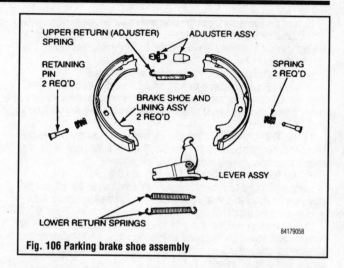

Fig. 106 Parking brake shoe assembly

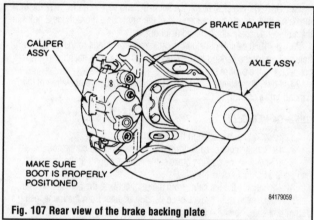

Fig. 107 Rear view of the brake backing plate

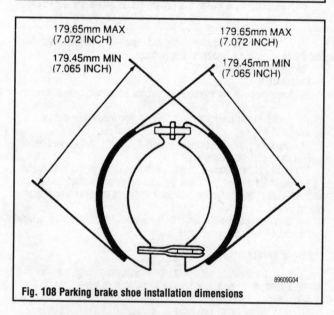

Fig. 108 Parking brake shoe installation dimensions

12. Install the brake shoe retaining springs and pins.
13. Connect the brake cable to the lever.
14. Install the rear axle shaft.
15. Center the brake shoes on the backing plate. Using an 8 in. micrometer or calipers, gauge the brake shoes to the dimensions shown in the accompanying figure.

ANTI-LOCK BRAKE SYSTEM

General Information

The 4-Wheel Anti-lock Brake System (ABS) is an electronically operated, all wheel brake control system. Major components include the power brake booster, master cylinder, the wheel speed sensors, and the Hydraulic Control Unit (HCU) which contains the control module, a relay, and the pressure control valves.

The system is designed to retard wheel lockup during periods of high wheel slip when braking. Retarding wheel lockup is accomplished by modulating fluid pressure to the wheel brake units. When the control module detects a variation in voltage across the wheel speed sensors, the ABS is activated. The control module opens and closes various valves located inside the HCU. These valves, called dump and isolation valves, modulate the hydraulic pressure to the wheels by applying and venting the pressure to the brake fluid circuits.

Some models are equipped with a Traction Assist (TA) system. The TA system senses wheel spin upon acceleration, turns on the Hydraulic Control Unit (HCU) pump and applies fluid pressure to the appropriate rear wheel. Two additional isolation valves in the HCU will also close to permit fluid to flow only to the rear wheels.

The TA system will only function up to 25 mph. The system also monitors TA usage to avoid overheating the rear brakes. If the system does sense brake overheating, the ABS module will inhibit TA operation until the rear brakes are permitted to cool down.

Diagnosis

▶ See Figures 109, 110, 111 and 112

The diagnosis of the ABS system is rather complex and requires quite a few special tools including scan tools, special test harnesses and other special and expensive tools. Alternative methods and common sense can be substituted, however, We at Chilton feel that it is beyond the scope of the average do-it-yourselfer. If you experience the amber ABS light on in the instrument cluster of your vehicle, check the fluid level in the master cylinder first. Low fluid level will usually illuminate the amber ABS light as well as, but not always, the red BRAKE lamp in the instrument cluster. The low fluid level could indicate a leak, but sometimes just indicates low, worn brake linings that have caused the caliper pistons and wheel cylinders to extend further, and thus using more fluid to exert force on them. Inspect the brake system for hydraulic fluid leaks and also inspect the brake linings for excessive wear.

The ABS module performs system tests and self-tests during startup and normal operation. The valves, wheel sensors and fluid level circuits are monitored for proper operation. If a fault is found, the ABS will be deactivated and the amber ANTI LOCK light will be lit until the ignition is turned OFF. When the light is lit, the Diagnostic Trouble Code (DTC) may be obtained. Under normal

4-WHEEL ABS DIAGNOSTIC TROUBLE CODES

Code	Description
B1342	Anit-lock brake control module failure
B1317	Battery voltage high
C1095	Pump motor
C1145	Right front anti-lock brake sensor (electrical/static)
C1148	Right front anti-lock brake sensor (dynamic)
C1155	Left front anti-lock brake sensor (electrical/static)
C1158	Left front anti-lock brake sensor (dynamic)
C1165	Right rear anti-lock brake sensor (electrical/static)
C1168	Right rear anti-lock brake sensor (dynamic)
C1175	Left rear anti-lock brake sensor (electrical/static)
C1178	Left rear anti-lock brake sensor (dynamic)
C1194	Left front outlet valve circuit failure
C1198	Left front inlet valve circuit failure
C1214	Right front isolation valve
C1233	Left front speed sensor signal missing
C1234	Right front speed sensor signal missing
C1235	Right rear speed sensor signal missing
C1236	Left rear speed sensor signal missing
C1242	Left rear outlet valve circuit failure
C1246	Right rear outlet valve circuit failure
C1250	Left rear inlet valve circuit failure
C1254	Right rear inlet valve circuit failure
C1258	Left front speed sensor signal comparison failure
C1259	Right front speed sensor signal comparison failure
C1260	Right rear speed sensor signal comparison failure
C1261	Left rear speed sensor signal comparison failure
C1267	ABS function temporarily disabled
C1400	Traction assist valve failure

89609G01

Fig. 110 1995 ABS DIAGNOSTIC TROUBLE CODE INDEX

DTC	Source
B1342	ECU Internal Failure
B1676	Battery Voltage Out of Range
C1095	Hydraulic Pump Motor Circuit Failure
C1145	RF Wheel Speed Input Circuit Failure
C1155	LF Wheel Speed Input Circuit Failure
C1165	RR Wheel Speed Input Circuit Failure
C1175	LR Wheel Speed Input Circuit Failure
C1233	LF Wheel Speed Signal Missing
C1234	RF Wheel Speed Signal Missing
C1235	RR Wheel Speed Signal Missing
C1236	LR Wheel Speed Comparison Failure Signal Missing

89609G02

Fig. 111 1996 ABS DIAGNOSTIC TROUBLE CODE INDEX

SERVICE CODE (COMPONENT)	PINPOINT TEST STEP
11 (ABS Module)	AA1
17 (Reference Voltage)	BB1
18 (Isolation Valve No. 1)	BB18
19 (Isolation Valve No. 2)	BB20
22 (LH Front Inlet Valve) or reference voltage (ABS only)	BB1
23 (LH Front Outlet Valve)	BB4
24 (RH Front Inlet Valve)	BB6
25 (RH Front Outlet Valve)	BB8
26 (RH Rear Inlet Valve)	BB10
27 (RH Rear Outlet Valve)	BB12
28 (LH Rear Inlet Valve)	BB14
29 (LH Rear Outlet Valve)	BB16
31 (LH Front Sensor)	CC1
32 (RH Front Sensor)	CC8
33 (RH Rear Sensor)	CC15
34 (LH Rear Sensor)	CC22
35 (LH Front Sensor)	CC1
36 (RH Front Sensor)	CC8
37 (RH Rear Sensor)	CC15

SERVICE CODE (COMPONENT)	PINPOINT TEST STEP
38 (LH Rear Sensor)	CC22
41 (LH Front Sensor)	CC1
42 (RH Front Sensor)	CC8
43 (RH Rear Sensor)	CC15
44 (LH Rear Sensor)	CC22
51 (LH Front Outlet Valve)	DD1
52 (RH Front Outlet Valve)	DD5
53 (RH Rear Outlet Valve)	DD9
54 (LH Rear Outlet Valve)	DD13
55 (LH Front Sensor)	CC1
56 (RH Front Sensor)	CC8
57 (RH Rear Sensor)	CC15
58 (LH Rear Sensor)	CC22
61 (FLS Circuits)	EE1
62 (Travel Switch)	EE1
63 (Pump Motor Speed Sensor)	EE11
64 (Pump Motor Pressure)	EE32
66 (Pressure Switch)	EE1
67 (Pump Motor Relay)	E1
71 (LH Front Sensor)	CC1
72 (RH Front Sensor)	CC8
73 (RH Rear Sensor)	CC15
74 (LH Rear Sensor)	CC22
75 (LH Front Sensor)	CC1
76 (RH Front Sensor)	CC8
77 (RH Rear Sensor)	CC15
78 (LH Rear Sensor)	CC22

84179084

Fig. 109 1992–94 DIAGNOSTIC TROUBLE CODE INDEX

DTC	Description
C1095	Hydraulic Pump Motor Failure
C1145	RF Speed Sensor—Input Circuit Failure
C1155	LF Speed Sensor—Input Circuit Failure
C1165	RR Speed Sensor—Input Circuit Failure
C1175	LR Speed Sensor—Input Circuit Failure
C1233	LF Wheel Speed—Input Signal Missing
C1234	RF Wheel Speed—Input Signal Missing
C1235	RR Wheel Speed—Input Signal Missing
C1236	LR Wheel Speed—Input Signal Missing
B1342	ECU Defective
B1485	Brake Pedal Position Switch Failure
B1676	Battery Voltage Out of Range

89609G03

Fig. 112 1997–98 ABS DIAGNOSTIC TROUBLE CODE INDEX

operation, the light will stay on for about 2 seconds while the ignition switch is in the ON position and will go out shortly after.

The Diagnostic Trouble Codes (DTC) are an alphanumeric code and a scan tool, such as Rotunda NGS Tester 007-00500 or its equivalent, is required to retrieve the codes. Refer to the manufacturer's instructions for operating the tool and retrieving the codes.

The Data Link Connector (DLC) for the ABS is located under the hood on models prior to 1995. On 1995–98 models, the OBDII connector located under the driver's side of the instrument panel, underneath the steering column, is used to retrieve the DTC's..

Control Module

REMOVAL & INSTALLATION

1992–94 Vehicles

▶ See Figure 113

1. Disconnect the negative battery cable.
2. Locate the ABS module at the left front side of the radiator support.
3. Detach the 55-pin connector from the ABS module. Unlock the connector by pulling up the lever completely. Move the end of the connector away from the ABS module until all terminals are clear, then pull the connector up and out of the slots in the ABS module.
4. Remove the 3 screws attaching the ABS module to the mounting bracket and remove the ABS module.

To install:

5. Align the ABS module with the bracket so that the lever is facing the drivers side of the vehicle. If all 3 mounting holes in the ABS module do not line up with the holes in the mounting bracket, the ABS module is incorrectly aligned with the bracket. Install the 3 attaching screws and tighten to 40–60 inch lbs. (4.5–6.8 Nm).
6. Attach the 55-pin connector by installing the bottom part of the connector into the slots in the ABS module and pushing the top portion of the connector into the ABS module. Then, pull the locking lever completely down to ensure proper installation.
7. Connect the negative battery cable.

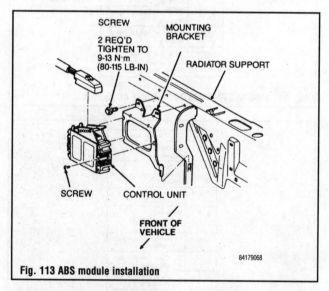

Fig. 113 ABS module installation

1995–98 Vehicles

➡The control module is located on the HCU. To facilitate the removal of the module, the HCU must be removed. If the proper tools for bleeding the ABS system are not available, you will need to have a professional technician perform this repair.

✳✳ WARNING

Electronic modules are sensitive to static electrical charges. If exposed to these charges, damage may result.

1. Disconnect the negative battery cable.
2. Remove the HCU as described in this section.
3. Remove the module retaining screws, then remove the anti-lock brake control module.
4. Installation is the reverse of the removal procedure.

Hydraulic Control Unit (HCU)

REMOVAL & INSTALLATION

1992–94 Vehicles

▶ See Figure 114

1. Disconnect the negative battery cable and remove the air cleaner and air outlet tube.
2. Detach the 19-pin connector from the HCU to the wire harness and detach the 4-pin connector from the HCU to the pump motor relay.
3. Remove the 2 lines from the inlet ports and the 4 lines from the outlet ports of the HCU. Plug each port to prevent brake fluid from spilling onto the paint and wiring.

✳✳ CAUTION

Brake fluid contains polyglycol ethers and polyglycols. Avoid contact with the eyes and wash your hands thoroughly after handling brake fluid. If you do get brake fluid in your eyes, flush your eyes with clean, running water for 15 minutes. If eye irritation persists, or if you have taken brake fluid internally, IMMEDIATELY seek medical assistance.

4. Remove the 3 nuts retaining the HCU assembly to the mounting bracket and remove the assembly from the vehicle.

➡The nut on the front of the HCU also retains the relay mounting bracket.

To install:

5. Position the HCU assembly into the mounting bracket. Install the 3 retaining nuts and tighten to 12–18 ft. lbs. (16–24 Nm). Make sure the ABS pump motor relay bracket is retained by the front bracket nut.

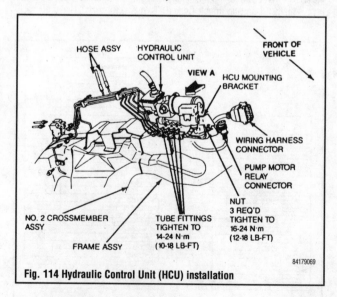

Fig. 114 Hydraulic Control Unit (HCU) installation

6. Connect the 4 lines to the outlet ports on the side of the HCU and the 2 lines to the inlet ports on the rear of the HCU. Tighten the line fittings to 10–18 ft. lbs. (14–24 Nm).

7. Attach the 19-pin connector to the harness and the 4-pin connector to the pump motor relay.

8. Install the air cleaner and air outlet tube.

9. Connect the battery cables, properly bleed the brake system and check for fluid leaks.

1995–98 Vehicles

1. Disconnect the negative battery cable.
2. Detach the anti-lock brake control module electrical connectors.

✳✳ CAUTION

Brake fluid contains polyglycol ethers and polyglycols. Avoid contact with the eyes and wash your hands thoroughly after handling brake fluid. If you do get brake fluid in your eyes, flush your eyes with clean, running water for 15 minutes. If eye irritation persists, or if you have taken brake fluid internally, IMMEDIATELY seek medical assistance.

3. Disconnect and plug the hydraulic brake lines.
4. Remove the HCU retaining bolts and remove the HCU.
5. If necessary, remove the HCU bracket.

To install:

6. If removed, install the HCU bracket.
7. Position the HCU.
8. Install and tighten the retaining bolts.
9. Connect the hydraulic brake lines.
10. Attach the anti-lock brake control module electrical connectors.
11. Connect the negative battery cable.
12. Bleed the 4-wheel ABS, as outlined in this section.

Pedal Travel Switch

REMOVAL & INSTALLATION

▶ **See Figure 115**

➡**The pedal travel switch is only equipped on 1992–94 models with ABS.**

1. Disconnect the negative battery cable.
2. Detach the wire harness lead from the switch connector.
3. Using a suitable tool, pry the connector locator out of the holes in the brake pedal support.
4. Unsnap the switch hook from the pin on the ABS adapter bracket.
5. Holding the brake pedal down to gain access, squeeze the tabs on the switch mounting clip with a suitable tool and push the clip through the hole in the dump valve adapter bracket.
6. Remove the rearmost screw on the ABS adapter bracket and loosen the second screw. Rotate the bracket and remove the switch and wire assembly.

To install:

7. Route the switch wire harness through the lower triangular hole in the brake pedal support.

8. Align the ABS adapter bracket with the mounting hole in the sidewall of the brake pedal support and install the rearmost screw. Then, tighten both bracket mounting screws.

9. Install the electrical connector and locator to the right side of the brake pedal support.

10. Holding the brake pedal down, insert the switch mounting clip into the hole in the dump valve adapter bracket and push firmly until a click is heard.

11. Rotate the switch and check that the mounting clip ears are fully engaged.

12. Adjust the switch and connect the negative battery cable.

ADJUSTMENT

Any time the switch is unhooked from the pin for any reason, the following adjustment procedure should be performed to ensure correct switch adjustment.

1. Push the switch plunger fully into the switch housing. This zeroes out the switch adjustment so that it can be automatically reset to the correct dimension.

2. Slowly pull the arm back out of the switch housing past the detent point.

➡**At this point it should be impossible to reattach the arm to the pin unless the brake pedal is forced down.**

3. To complete the adjustment, depress the brake pedal until the switch hook can be snapped onto the pin. Snap the hook onto the pin and pull the brake pedal back up to its normal at rest position. This automatically sets the switch to the proper adjustment.

Speed Sensors

REMOVAL & INSTALLATION

Front

▶ **See Figures 116, 117, 118 and 119**

1. Disconnect the negative battery cable.
2. From inside engine compartment, detach sensor assembly 2-pin connector from the wiring harness.
3. Remove the steel routing clip attaching the sensor wire to the tube bundle on the left sensor or remove the plastic routing clip attaching the sensor wire to the frame on the right sensor.
4. Remove the rubber coated spring steel clip holding the sensor wire to the frame.
5. Remove the sensor wire from the steel routing clip on the frame and from the dust shield.
6. Remove the sensor attaching bolt from the front spindle and slide the sensor out of the mounting hole.

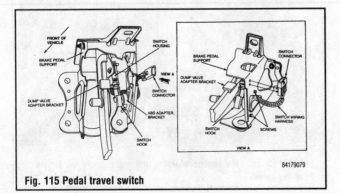

Fig. 115 Pedal travel switch

Fig. 116 The speed sensor sits directly over the exciter ring in the front knuckle

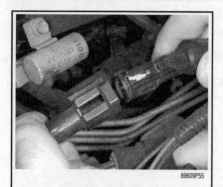

Fig. 117 Detach the speed sensor connector in the engine compartment

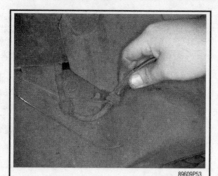

Fig. 118 Remove the speed sensor harness from the routing clips

Fig. 119 A special E6 Torx® socket is required to remove the speed sensor retaining bolt

To install:

7. Install the sensor into the mounting hole in the front spindle and attach with the mounting bolt. Tighten to 40–60 inch lbs. (4.5–6.8 Nm).

8. Insert the sensor routing grommets into the dust shield and steel bracket on the frame. Route the wire into the engine compartment.

9. Install the rubber coated steel clip that holds the sensor wire to the frame into the hole in the frame.

10. Install the steel clip that holds sensor wire to tube bundle on left side or plastic clip that holds sensor to frame on right side.

11. Reconnect the 2-pin connector to wire harness. Connect the negative battery cable.

Rear

▶ **See Figures 120, 121, 122, 123 and 124**

1. Disconnect the negative battery cable.

2. From inside luggage compartment, detach 2-pin sensor connector from wiring harness and push sensor wire through hole in floor.

3. From below vehicle, remove sensor wire from routing bracket located on top of rear axle carrier housing and remove steel clip holding sensor wire and brake tube against axle housing.

4. Remove screw from clip holding sensor wire and brake tube to bracket on axle.

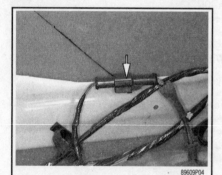

Fig. 120 Detach the speed sensor connector in the luggage compartment

Fig. 121 Grasp the harness and . . .

Fig. 122 . . . remove it from the routing brackets

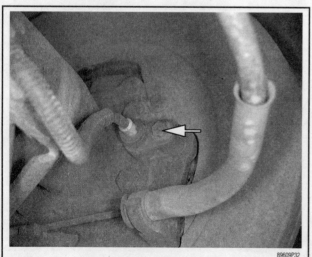

Fig. 123 The rear speed sensor is mounted on the back of the hub assembly

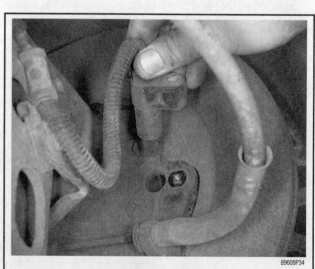

Fig. 124 Remove the sensor retaining bolt and remove the sensor from the hub

5. Remove sensor to rear adapter retaining bolt and remove sensor.

To install:

6. Insert sensor adapter and install retaining bolt. Tighten to 40–60 inch lbs. (4.5–6.8 Nm).

7. Attach the clip holding the sensor and brake tube to the bracket on the axle housing and secure with the retaining screw. Tighten the screw to 40–60 inch lbs. (4.5–6.8 Nm).

8. Install steel clip around axle tube that holds sensor wire and brake tube against axle tube and push spool-shaped grommet into clip located on top of axle carrier housing.

9. Push sensor wire connector up through hole in floor and seat large round grommet into hole.

10. Reconnect sensor 2-pin connector to wiring harness inside luggage compartment.

Tone (Exciter) Ring

REMOVAL & INSTALLATION

Front

▶ **See Figure 125**

1. Raise and safely support the vehicle.
2. Remove the wheel and tire assembly.
3. Remove the caliper, rotor and hub assemblies.
4. Remove the indicator ring from the hub using a suitable 3-jaw puller.

To install:

5. Support the center of the hub so that the wheel studs do not rest on the work surface.

6. Position the new ring on the hub making sure the ring is not cocked. Place a flat plate on top of the ring and press until it is flush with the top of the hub.

7. Install the hub, rotor and caliper assemblies.

8. Install the wheel and tire assembly and lower the vehicle.

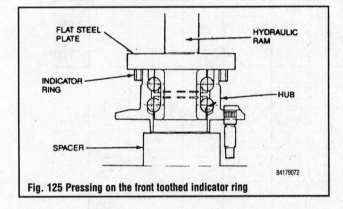

Fig. 125 Pressing on the front toothed indicator ring

Rear

▶ **See Figure 126**

1. Raise and safely support the vehicle.
2. Remove the wheel and tire assembly.
3. Remove the rear axle shaft; refer to Section 7.
4. Using a thin blade cold chisel between the indicator ring and axle flange, strike the chisel evenly around the flange forcing the indicator ring off its journal.

✳✳ WARNING

Be extremely careful not to scratch or nick the wheel bearing and seal journal.

To install:

5. Remove any burrs or nicks from the sensor ring journal.

6. Position a suitable sensor ring installation tool on a press with the pilot ring facing down.

7. Place the new sensor ring over the installation tool.

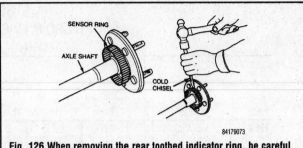

Fig. 126 When removing the rear toothed indicator ring, be careful not to damage the wheel bearing and seal journal

8. Insert the axle shaft through the tool and place a suitable pinion bearing cup replacement tool over the end of the axle shaft.

9. Press the axle shaft until the axle shaft bottoms out on the axle flange.

10. Install the axle shaft into the rear axle.

11. Install the wheel and tire assembly and lower the vehicle.

Bleeding the ABS System

1992–94 Vehicles

➡The ABS brake system must be bled using Anti-lock Test Adapter T90P-50-ALA, or equivalent. If the procedure is not followed correctly, air will stay trapped in the Hydraulic Control Unit (HCU) which will lead to a spongy brake pedal.

1. To bleed the master cylinder and the HCU, connect the anti-lock tester wiring harness to the 55-pin harness connector of the ABS module.

2. Place the bleed/harness switch in the bleed position.

3. Turn the ignition switch to the **ON** position.

4. Push the motor button on the tester down, starting the pump motor. The pump motor will run for 60 seconds.

5. After 20 seconds of pump motor operation, push and hold the valve button down. Hold the valve button down for 20 seconds.

6. The pump motor will continue to run for an additional 20 seconds.

7. The master cylinder and HCU should be free of air and the brake lines must now be bleed using the conventional method for non-ABS brake systems by bleeding the wheels in the following sequence: right-hand rear, left-hand front, left-hand rear and right-hand front.

8. Road test the vehicle and check for proper brake system operation.

1995–98 Vehicles

Whenever service is performed on the ABS valve block or pump and motor assembly, the following procedure must be performed to make sure no air is trapped in the ABS control and modulator assembly. If this procedure is not done, the vehicle operator could experience a spongy pedal after the ABS is actuated. This procedure requires the use of the Ford New Generation STAR (NGS) Tester, or equivalent.

1. First bleed the entire brake system conventionally as outlined earlier in this section.

2. Reattach the NGS Tester to the data link connector as though retrieving codes.

3. Make sure the ignition is in the **RUN** position.

4. Follow the instructions on the NGS screen. Choose the correct vehicle and model year, go to DIAGNOSTIC DATA LINK menu item, choose ABS MODULE, choose FUNCTION TESTS and choose SERVICE BLEED.

5. The NGS will prompt you to depress the brake pedal. Make sure you press hard on the brake pedal, and hold it down for approximately 5 seconds while the NGS opens the outlet valves in the brake pressure control valve block. When the outlet valves are opened, you should immediately feel the pedal drop. It is very important that you continue pushing the pedal all the way to the floor. The NGS will then instruct you to release the brake pedal. After you release the brake pedal, the NGS will run the ABS hydraulic pump motor for approximately 15 seconds.

6. Repeat the previous step to ensure that all air is bleed from the ABS unit. Upon completion, the NGS will display SERVICE BLEED PROCEDURE COMPLETED.

7. Repeat the conventional bleeding procedure.

8. Once complete, road test the vehicle and check for proper brake system operation.

BRAKE SPECIFICATIONS
FORD CROWN VICTORIA AND MERCURY GRAND MARQUIS
All measurements in inches unless noted

Year	Model		Master Cylinder Bore	Brake Disc Original Thickness	Brake Disc Minimum Thickness	Brake Disc Maximum Runout	Brake Drum Diameter Original Inside Diameter	Brake Drum Diameter Max. Wear Limit	Brake Drum Diameter Maximum Machine Diameter	Minimum Lining Thickness Front	Minimum Lining Thickness Rear
1989	Crown Victoria	F	1.000	1.030	0.972	0.003	—	—	—	0.125	—
		R	—	—	—	—	①	NA	②	—	0.031
	Grand Marquis	F	1.000	1.030	0.972	0.003	—	—	—	0.125	—
		R	—	—	—	—	①	NA	②	—	0.031
1990	Crown Victoria	F	1.000	1.030	0.972	0.003	—	—	—	0.125	—
		R	—	—	—	—	①	NA	②	—	0.031
	Grand Marquis	F	1.000	1.030	0.972	0.003	—	—	—	0.125	—
		R	—	—	—	—	①	NA	②	—	0.031
1991	Crown Victoria	F	1.000	1.030	0.972	0.003	—	—	—	0.125	—
		R	—	—	—	—	①	NA	②	—	0.031
	Grand Marquis	F	1.000	1.030	0.972	0.003	—	—	—	0.125	—
		R	—	—	—	—	①	NA	②	—	0.031
1992	Crown Victoria	F	1.000	1.024	0.974	0.003	—	—	—	0.125	—
		R	—	0.500	0.440	0.003	—	—	—	—	0.125
	Grand Marquis	F	1.000	1.024	0.974	0.003	—	—	—	0.125	—
		R	—	0.500	0.440	0.003	—	—	—	—	0.125
1993	Crown Victoria	F	1.000	1.024	0.974	0.003	—	—	—	0.125	—
		R	—	0.500	0.440	0.003	—	—	—	—	0.125
	Grand Marquis	F	1.000	1.024	0.974	0.003	—	—	—	0.125	—
		R	—	0.500	0.440	0.003	—	—	—	—	0.125
1994	Crown Victoria	F	1.000	1.024	0.974	0.003	—	—	—	0.125	—
		R	—	0.500	0.440	0.003	—	—	—	—	0.125
	Grand Marquis	F	1.000	1.024	0.974	0.003	—	—	—	0.125	—
		R	—	0.500	0.440	0.003	—	—	—	—	0.125
1995	Crown Victoria	F	1.000	1.024	0.974	0.003	—	—	—	0.125	—
		R	—	0.500	0.440	0.003	—	—	—	—	0.125
	Grand Marquis	F	1.000	1.024	0.974	0.003	—	—	—	0.125	—
		R	—	0.500	0.440	0.003	—	—	—	—	0.125
1996	Crown Victoria	F	1.000	1.024	0.974	0.003	—	—	—	0.125	—
		R	—	0.500	0.440	0.003	—	—	—	—	0.125
	Grand Marquis	F	1.000	1.024	0.974	0.003	—	—	—	0.125	—
		R	—	0.500	0.440	0.003	—	—	—	—	0.125
1997	Crown Victoria	F	1.000	1.024	0.974	0.003	—	—	—	0.125	—
		R	—	0.500	0.440	0.003	—	—	—	—	0.125
	Grand Marquis	F	1.000	1.024	0.974	0.003	—	—	—	0.125	—
		R	—	0.500	0.440	0.003	—	—	—	—	0.125
1998	Crown Victoria	F	1.000	1.100	1.010	0.002	—	—	—	0.125	—
		R	—	0.500	0.440	0.003	—	—	—	—	0.125
	Grand Marquis	F	1.000	1.100	1.010	0.002	—	—	—	0.125	—
		R	—	0.500	0.440	0.003	—	—	—	—	0.125

NOTE: Follow specifications stamped on rotor or drum if figures differ from those in this chart.

NA - Not Available

F - Front

R - Rear

① Sedan 10.000
  Police, taxi, and trailer tow 11.030

② Sedan 10.060
  Police, taxi, and trailer tow 11.090

89609C01

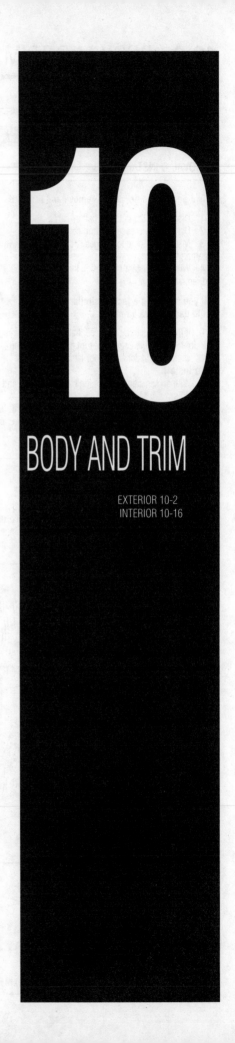

10

BODY AND TRIM

EXTERIOR

Doors

REMOVAL & INSTALLATION

➡**Two people are needed to remove and install the doors.**

1. Disconnect the negative battery cable.
2. Detach the necessary wiring connectors.
3. Matchmark the door hinges to the body. This will aid in alignment when installing the door.
4. With an assistant supporting the door, remove the hinge retaining bolts and remove the door.

➡**If you are using a jack or similar tool to support the door, be careful not to damage the paint.**

5. If the door is to be replaced, transfer the following components to the new door if in usable condition: trim panel, watershield, outside mouldings, clips, window regulators and door latch components.

To install:

6. With an assistant positioning the door, install and partially tighten the hinge bolts.
7. Align the door and tighten the bolts to 19–25 ft. lbs. (25–35 Nm).
8. Attach the necessary wiring connectors and connect the negative battery cable.

ADJUSTMENT

Door Hinges

▶ **See Figures 1, 2 and 3**

The door hinges provide sufficient adjustment to correct most door misalignment conditions. The holes of the hinge and/or the hinge attaching points are enlarged or elongated to provide for hinge and door alignment.

➡**Do not cover up a poor door alignment with a latch striker adjustment.**

1. Refer to the figures to determine which hinge bolts must be loosened to move the door in the desired direction.
2. Loosen the hinge bolts just enough to permit movement of the door with a padded prybar.
3. Move the door the estimated necessary distance, then tighten the hinge bolts to 19–25 ft. lbs. (25–35 Nm).

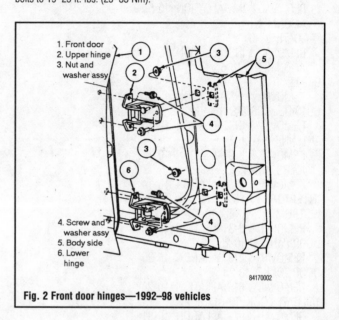

1. Front door
2. Upper hinge
3. Nut and washer assy
4. Screw and washer assy
5. Body side
6. Lower hinge

84170002

Fig. 2 Front door hinges—1992–98 vehicles

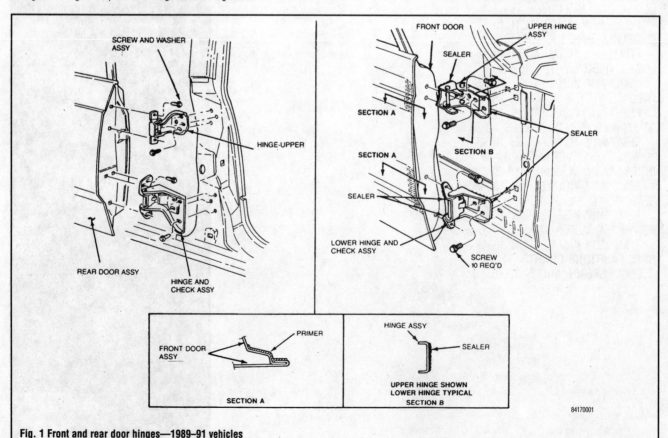

Fig. 1 Front and rear door hinges—1989–91 vehicles

84170001

4. Check the door fit to make sure there is no bind or interference with the adjacent panel.
5. Repeat the operation until the desired fit is obtained.
6. Check the striker plate alignment for proper door closing.

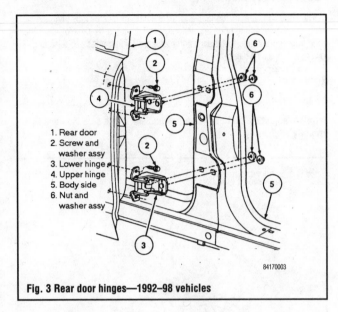

Fig. 3 Rear door hinges—1992–98 vehicles

1. Rear door
2. Screw and washer assy
3. Lower hinge
4. Upper hinge
5. Body side
6. Nut and washer assy

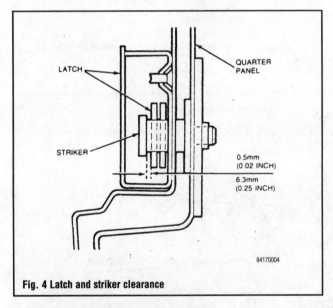

Fig. 4 Latch and striker clearance

LATCH
STRIKER
QUARTER PANEL
0.5mm (0.02 INCH)
6.3mm (0.25 INCH)

Door Latch Striker

▶ See Figures 4 and 5

The latch striker should be shimmed to get the clearance between the striker and the latch. To check this clearance, clean the latch jaws and the striker area. Apply a thin layer of dark grease to the striker. As the door is opened and closed, a measurable pattern will result on the latch striker. Use a maximum of 2 shims on 1989–90 vehicles or one shim on 1991–98 vehicles, under the striker. Use Torx® drive bit set D79P–2100–T or equivalent, to loosen and tighten the latch striker to 25–32 ft. lbs. (35–45 Nm).

Hood

REMOVAL & INSTALLATION

▶ See Figures 6, 7, 8, 9 and 10

1. Open and support the hood.
2. Mark the position of the hood hinges on the hood.
3. Protect the body with covers to prevent damage to the paint.
4. With the help of an assistant, remove the 2 bolts attaching each hinge to the hood, being careful not to let the hood slip when the bolts are removed.
5. Remove the hood from the vehicle.

To install:

6. With the help of an assistant, position the hood on its hinges and install the attaching bolts.
7. Remove the body covers.
8. Adjust the hood for an even fit between the fenders and a flush fit with the front of the fenders.
9. Adjust the hood latch, if necessary.

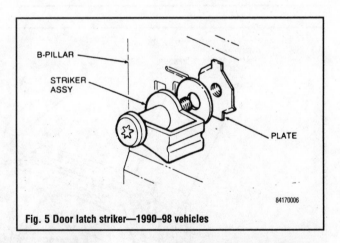

B-PILLAR
STRIKER ASSY
PLATE

Fig. 5 Door latch striker—1990–98 vehicles

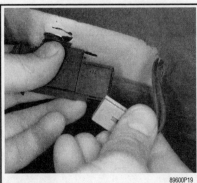

Fig. 6 Detach the connector for the underhood lamp

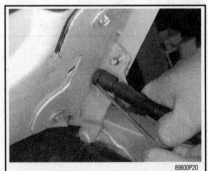

Fig. 7 Release the hood lift-to-body retaining clips and remove the hood lifts from the pivot ball

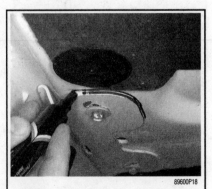

Fig. 8 Matchmark the hood-to-hinge position

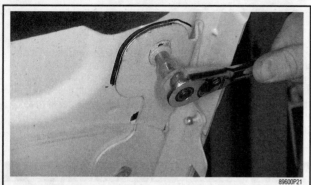

Fig. 9 While an assistant supports the hood, remove the hinge bolts from one side of the hood

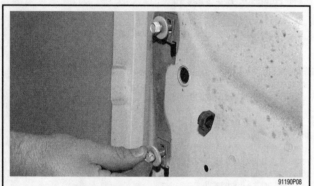

Fig. 10 A good way to keep track of the hood hinge-to-hood bolts is to install the bolts into the hood while storing the hood

ALIGNMENT

Hood Alignment

◆ **See Figures 11 and 12**

The hood can be adjusted fore-and-aft and side-to-side by loosening the hood-to-hinge retaining bolts and repositioning the hood. To raise or lower the hood, loosen the hinge-to-fender reinforcement retaining bolts and raise or lower the hinge as necessary.

Hood Latch

◆ **See Figure 13**

➡Before adjusting the hood latch mechanism, make sure the hood is properly aligned.

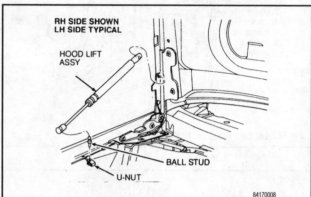

Fig. 12 Hood hinge (shown with gas cylinder removed)—1992–98 vehicles

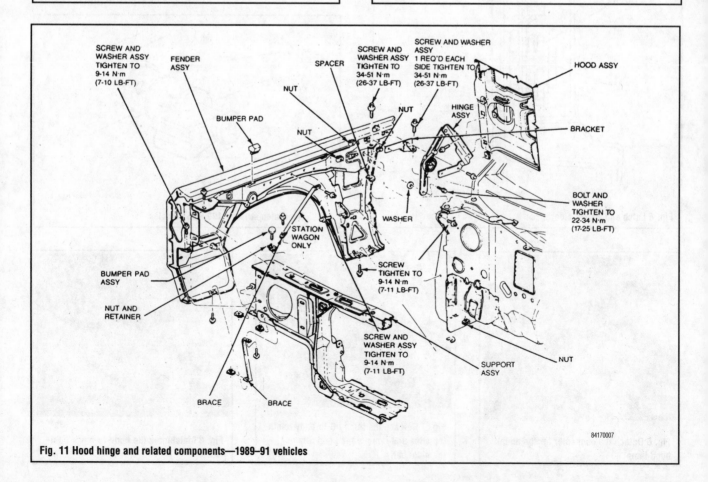

Fig. 11 Hood hinge and related components—1989–91 vehicles

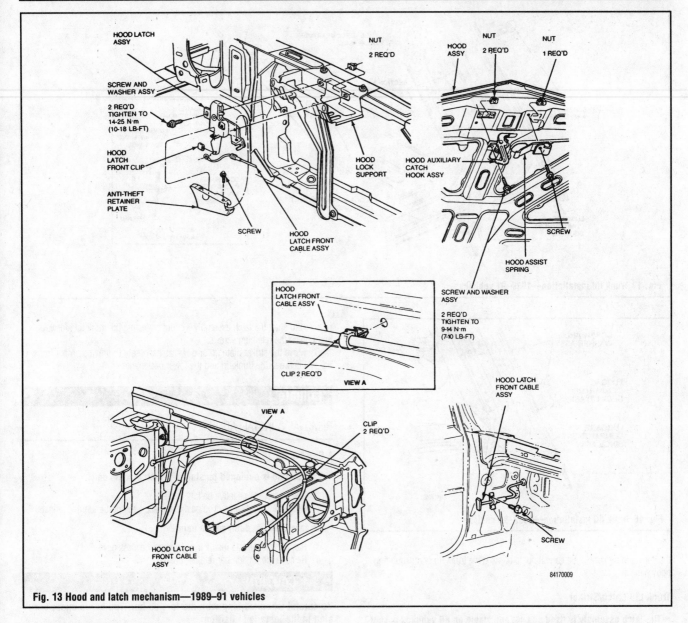

Fig. 13 Hood and latch mechanism—1989–91 vehicles

1. Loosen the hood latch attaching bolts until they are just loose enough to move the latch.

2. Move the latch side-to-side to align it with the opening in the hood inner panel.

3. Loosen the locknuts on the 2 hood bumpers and lower the bumpers.

4. Move the hood latch up or down as required to obtain a flush fit between the top of the hood and fenders when an upward pressure is applied to the front of the hood.

5. Tighten the hood latch attaching screws to 7–10 ft. lbs. (9–14 Nm).

6. Raise the 2 hood bumpers to eliminate any looseness at the front of the hood when closed.

7. Tighten the hood bumper locknuts.

8. Open and close the hood several times, to check operation.

Trunk Lid

REMOVAL & INSTALLATION

▶ **See Figures 14 and 15**

1. Open the trunk lid.

2. Mark the position of the trunk lid relative to the trunk lid hinges.

3. Protect the body with covers to prevent damage to the paint.

4. With the help of an assistant, remove the 2 bolts attaching each hinge to the trunk lid, being careful not to let the trunk lid slip when the bolts are removed.

5. Remove the trunk lid from the vehicle.

To install:

6. With the help of an assistant, position the trunk lid on its hinges and install the attaching bolts.

7. Remove the body covers.

8. Adjust the trunk lid's position in the trunk lid opening.

9. Adjust the trunk lid latch and/or striker, if necessary.

ALIGNMENT

Trunk Lid Alignment

The trunk lid can be shifted fore-and-aft by loosening the hinge-to-trunk lid retaining screws. The up and down adjustment is made by loosening the hinge-to-trunk lid retaining screws and raising or lowering the trunk lid.

The trunk lid should be adjusted for an even and parallel fit with the trunk lid opening. The trunk lid should also be adjusted up and down for a flush fit with

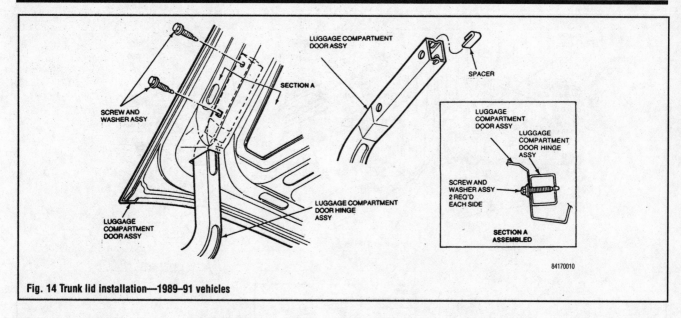

Fig. 14 Trunk lid installation—1989–91 vehicles

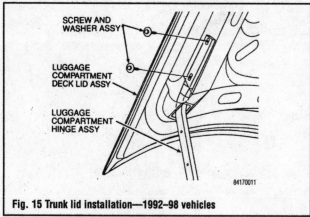

Fig. 15 Trunk lid installation—1992–98 vehicles

the surrounding panels. Be careful not to damage the trunk lid or surrounding body panels.

Trunk Lid Latch/Striker

➡The latch assembly is fixed and not adjustable on all vehicles except 1989–91 Grand Marquis. Any latch adjustment must be made at the striker.

EXCEPT 1989–91 GRAND MARQUIS

➡Before adjusting the striker, open and close the trunk lid to double-check the striker alignment.

1. On 1992–98 Crown Victoria, remove the scuff plate striker covering before attempting any striker adjustment.
2. Loosen the 2 screw and washer assemblies and adjust the striker by moving up and down or from side-to-side as necessary.
3. Tighten the screw and washer assemblies to 7–10 ft. lbs. (9–14 Nm).

➡Do not try to correct a poor trunk lid alignment with a latch striker adjustment.

1989–91 GRAND MARQUIS

The striker can be adjusted up and down and the latch can be adjusted side-to-side.

1. Before adjusting the trunk lid make sure the trunk lid is properly aligned.
2. To adjust the striker, loosen the retaining screws, move the striker as

required to enter the latch assembly without deflecting the trunk lid sideways, and tighten the retaining screws.

3. Move the striker plate up or down as necessary to provide proper trunk lid seal between the trunk lid and the lower back panel.

Tailgate

REMOVAL & INSTALLATION

▶ **See Figure 16**

➡The tailgate is equipped on station wagon models only.

1. Disconnect the negative battery cable.
2. Open the tailgate as a drop gate and place a support under the tailgate.

➡Be careful not to damage the paint.

3. Remove the tailgate inside trim panel and access cover.
4. Remove the torsion bar retainer bracket.

✳ CAUTION

Be careful when working with the torsion bar. The bar is under tension in the installed position.

5. Raise the tailgate glass and latch the upper tailgate latch by hand. Make sure the glass is supported.
6. Remove the wiring harness from the tailgate.
7. Mark the location of the hinge to the tailgate and remove the nuts attaching the hinge to the tailgate.
8. Actuate the outside handle to disengage the lower latch and remove the tailgate.
9. Installation is the reverse of the removal procedure.

ALIGNMENT

Upper Latch-To-Lower Latch Link

▶ **See Figure 17**

1. Place the tailgate latches in the closed (latched) position.
2. Disconnect the upper latch-to-lower latch link from the lower latch.
3. Adjust the upper latch-to-lower latch link to engage with the lower latch (no load on the link).
4. To check the adjustment, the upper latch must not close when the lower latch is in the open position. The upper and lower latches must open at approximately the same time when the outside handle is operated.

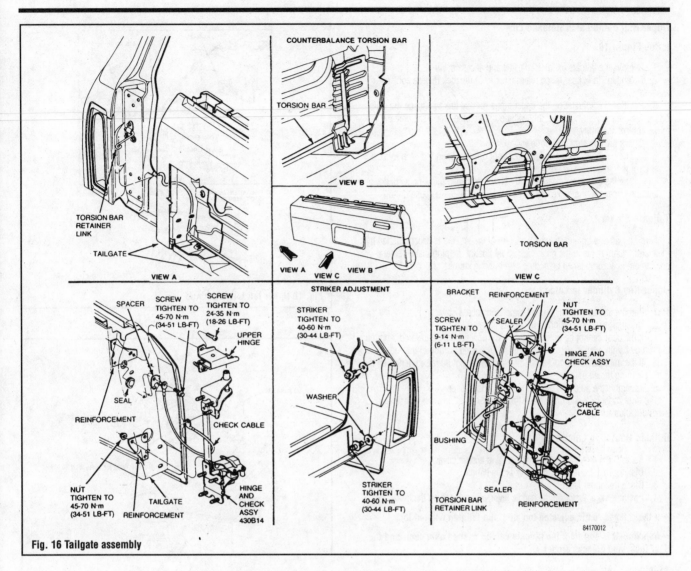

Fig. 16 Tailgate assembly

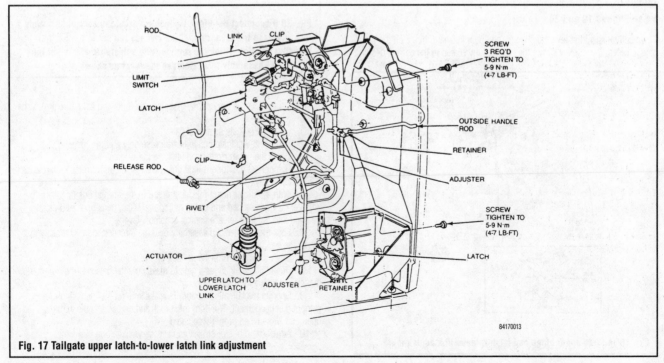

Fig. 17 Tailgate upper latch-to-lower latch link adjustment

Upper Hinge And Latch Release Link

▶ **See Figure 18**

1. Remove the tailgate inside trim panel and access cover.
2. Disengage the upper hinge release link from the lock release control assembly.
3. Position the adjuster on the upper hinge release link to engage the lever on the lock release control assembly with no load on the link. Assemble the link to the control assembly.
4. Check the adjustment as follows:
   a. The power window regulator must not operate when the latch release control is in the released position.
   b. The inside release handle must not operate when the window is down and the upper latch is locked by either the key or the inside push button.

Tailgate Striker

Fore-and-aft and up and down adjustment of the strikers is accomplished by means of square holes in the pillar, backed by floating tapping plates. Lateral adjustment is accomplished by adding or removing shims.

Upper Key Cylinder to Latch Link

1. Remove the tailgate inside trim panel and access cover.
2. Disengage the key cylinder link from the key cylinder.
3. If the door cannot be unlocked or the window cannot be lowered, shorten the rod by turning the adjuster deeper into the threaded portion of the rod.
4. If the door cannot be locked or the window cannot be raised, lengthen the rod by turning the adjuster.
5. Assemble the adjusted link to the key cylinder lever.

The door must lock and unlock and the window must open and close when properly adjusted.

Outside Handle to Latch Link

1. Remove the tailgate inside trim panel and access cover.
2. Disengage the outside handle link at the handle.
3. Close the upper latch.
4. Position the adjuster on the handle lever with no load on the link.

➡**If the release rod is adjusted too long, the tailgate will not lock.**

➡**Adjustment is correct if the tailgate can be opened as a door, and the door locks and unlocks properly.**

Tailgate

▶ **See Figures 19 and 20**

Visually inspect the lever position to the upper left-hand hinge on the tailgate to determine whether or not the lever is fully seated in the correct design

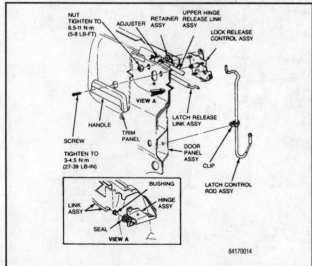

Fig. 18 Tailgate upper hinge and latch release link adjustment

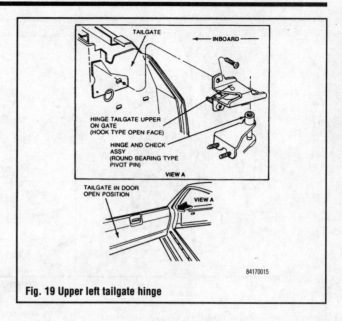

Fig. 19 Upper left tailgate hinge

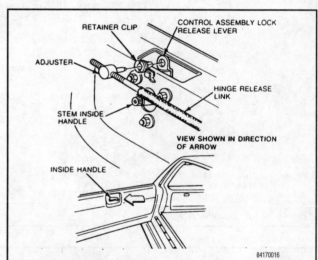

Fig. 20 Disconnect the hinge release rod from the control assembly lock. Release the lever and let the release rod set in the normal standing position. Align the retainer and adjuster to easily set into the control assembly lock. Release the lever as shown

position. If the lever is only partially seated, the following adjustment must be made:

1. Open the tailgate as a drop gate.
2. Remove the tailgate inside handle assembly and trim panel.
3. Close the upper right-hand latch on the tailgate.
4. Disconnect the upper hinge link rod retainer clip from the lock release control assembly.
5. With the upper hinge release link rod in the normal position, turn the adjuster on the threaded end of the rod so that it can be aligned and easily inserted into the lock release control assembly lever.
6. Lock the retainer clip assembly over the threaded rod and loosely install the inside handle.
7. Open the upper right-hand latch on the tailgate.
8. Operate the tailgate as a gate to make sure the gate is not binding and the latches lock and unlock properly.
9. Operate the tailgate as a door to make sure that it opens and closes without disengagement. The door must lock and unlock and the window must open and close when properly adjusted.
10. Adjust the hinge or striker, as necessary. Install the trim panel.

Grille

REMOVAL & INSTALLATION

Crown Victoria

1989–91 MODELS

▶ See Figure 21

1. Remove the headlight doors.
2. Remove the 4 screws from the front of the grille.
3. Remove the locking tabs from the grille opening panel and remove the grille.

To install:

4. Insert the locking tabs into the grille opening panel.
5. Install the 4 screws in the front of the grille.
6. Install the headlight doors.

➡There is no grille removal and installation procedure for 1992 vehicles, as this model year did not feature a grille.

1993–98 MODELS

▶ See Figure 22

1. Open the hood.
2. Working behind the grille opening panel, use a small flat blade prybar to depress the barbs on the 7 retainers across the top of the grille.
3. Release the 2 retainers at the bottom of the grille and remove the grille from the vehicle.

To install:

4. Line up the 7 retainers across the top of the grille to the holes in the grille opening panel.
5. Carefully insert the retainers and push in until fully seated.
6. Push in the bottom of the grille to snap in the bottom 2 retainers.

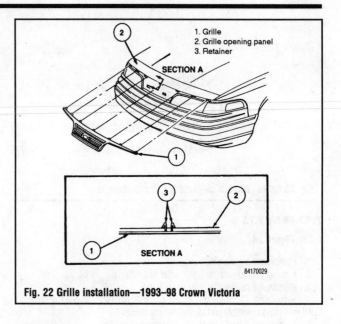

Fig. 22 Grille installation—1993–98 Crown Victoria

Grand Marquis

1989–91 MODELS

▶ See Figure 23

1. Depress the grille's 6 snap-in tabs with a flat blade tool.
2. Pull the tabs out of the grille opening panel and remove the grille.

To install:

3. Align the snap-in tabs with the slots in the grille opening panel.
4. Firmly press the tabs into the slots in the grille opening panel.

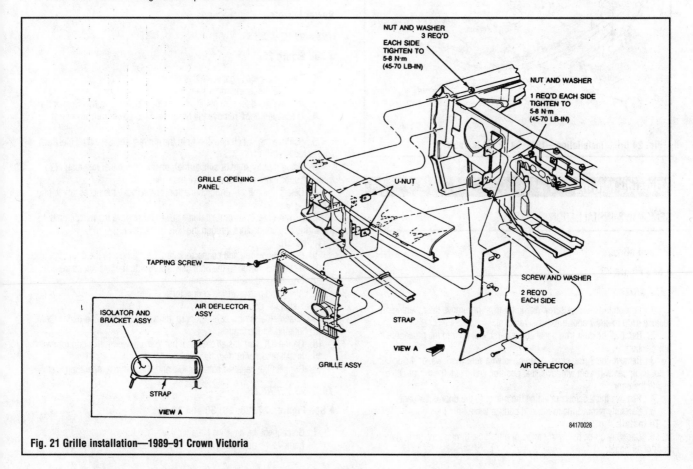

Fig. 21 Grille installation—1989–91 Crown Victoria

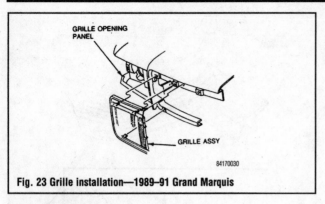

Fig. 23 Grille installation—1989–91 Grand Marquis

1992–98 MODELS

▶ See Figure 24

1. Remove the sight shield.
2. Remove the side marker lights; refer to Section 6.
3. Remove the headlights; refer to Section 6.
4. Remove the 11 retaining nuts and 4 screws retaining the grille opening panel moulding assembly and remove as one piece.
5. Remove the 4 retaining bolts and remove the grille.

To install:

6. Install the grille and secure with the 4 retaining bolts.
7. Install the grille opening panel moulding assembly and secure with the nuts and screws.
8. Install the headlights and the side marker lights.
9. Install the sight shield.

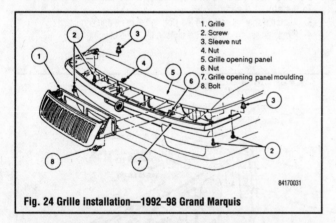

1. Grille
2. Screw
3. Sleeve nut
4. Nut
5. Grille opening panel
6. Nut
7. Grille opening panel moulding
8. Bolt

Fig. 24 Grille installation—1992–98 Grand Marquis

Outside Mirrors

REMOVAL & INSTALLATION

Manual Mirrors

▶ See Figure 25

LEFT SIDE

1. Loosen the bezel setscrew (standard trim) or remove the retaining nut (deluxe trim) to allow door trim panel removal.
2. Remove the door trim panel and watershield; refer to the procedure in this Section.
3. Remove the 2 ring clips, if equipped with vent windows, or 4 ring clips, if not equipped with vent windows, that position and retain the mirror cable inside the door.
4. Remove the 2 screws retaining the mirror to the door outer panel.
5. Carefully remove the mirror and control cable from the door.

To install:

6. Carefully guide the mirror actuator and cable through the hole in the door outer panel.

7. Install the 2 screws that hold the mirror assembly on the door outer panel and tighten securely.
8. Properly position the control cable and retain with the ring clips.
9. After inserting the control lever through the holes in the watershield and trim panel armrest, install the door trim panel and watershield.
10. Secure the control lever in the bezel (standard trim) with its setscrew or in the trim panel armrest (deluxe trim) with the large nut.
11. Check mirror operation.

RIGHT SIDE

1. Remove the large nut retaining the control lever in the instrument panel.
2. Push the control lever through the hole and disengage the 3 plastic cable guides located along the lower backside of the instrument panel.
3. Push out the A-pillar plug and pull the cable through the hole.
4. Remove the door trim panel and watershield; refer to the procedure in this Section.
5. From inside the door, remove the door grommet. Carefully pull the cable and rubber plug(s) through the hole in the face of the door inner panel and through the support strap.
6. Remove the 2 screws that retain the mirror to the door outer panel.
7. Carefully remove the mirror and control cable from the door.

To install:

8. Carefully guide the control lever and cable through the hole in the door outer panel. Install the 2 screws that hold the mirror assembly on the door outer panel and tighten securely.
9. Position the cable inside the door and through the support strap.
10. Insert the control lever and cable through the hole in the door inner panel and carefully seat the rubber plug.
11. Insert the control lever and cable through the hole in the door hinge and carefully seat the rubber plug.
12. Position the cable along the lower backside of the instrument panel and engage the 3 plastic cable guides.
13. Push the control lever through the hole in the instrument panel and secure with the large nut.
14. Check mirror operation.

Power Mirrors

1989–91 VEHICLES

▶ See Figure 26

1. Disconnect the negative battery cable.
2. Remove the interior door handle.
3. Remove the door trim panel; refer to the procedure in this Section.
4. On the left door, remove the bezel from the power mirror control switch.
5. Remove the switch housing from the armrest and detach all electrical connectors.
6. Using a putty knife or similar tool, pry the trim panel retaining clips from the door inner panel and remove the panel.
7. Detach the mirror wiring connectors and remove the necessary wiring guides.
8. Remove the 2 mirror retaining screws and remove the mirror, guiding the wiring and connectors through the hole in the door.

To install:

9. Guide the wiring and connectors through the hole in the door.
10. Install the mirror on the door and secure with the retaining screws.
11. Position and install the wiring guides.
12. Attach the mirror wiring connectors.
13. Install the door trim panel.
14. Attach all electrical connectors to the switch housing and install the switch housing on the armrest.
15. On the left door, install the bezel nut to the power mirror control switch.
16. Install the interior door handle.
17. Connect the negative battery cable and check mirror operation.

1992–98 VEHICLES

▶ See Figures 27, 28, 29, 30 and 31

1. Disconnect the negative battery cable.
2. Remove the door trim panel; refer to the procedure in this Section.

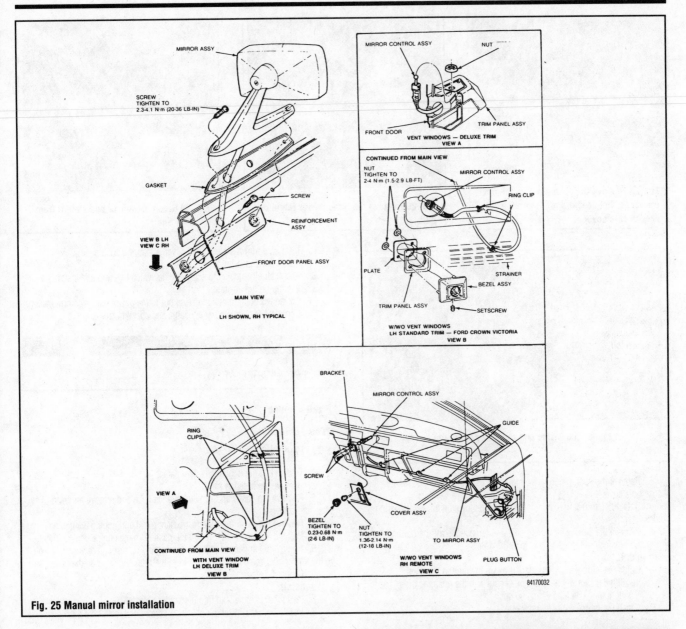

Fig. 25 Manual mirror installation

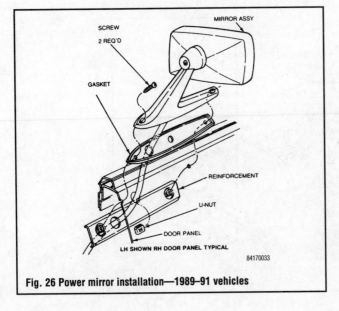

Fig. 26 Power mirror installation—1989–91 vehicles

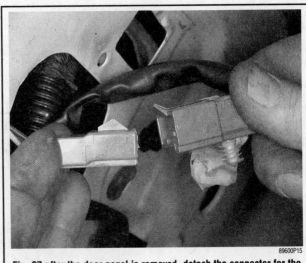

Fig. 27 after the door panel is removed, detach the connector for the power mirror

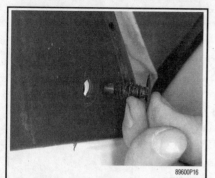

Fig. 28 Remove the push pin from the mirror access hole cover and remove the access hole cover

Fig. 29 Remove the three mirror retaining nuts

Fig. 30 Grasp the mirror and slide it from the door and . . .

Fig. 31 . . . guide the wiring and connector out of the access hole in the door

3. Remove the push pin from the mirror access hole cover and remove the access hole cover.

4. Detach the mirror wiring connectors and remove the necessary wiring guides.

5. Remove the 3 mirror retaining nuts and remove the mirror, guiding the wiring and connectors through the hole in the door.

To install:

6. Guide the wiring and connectors through the hole in the door.

7. Install the mirror on the door and secure with the retaining nuts.

8. Position and install the wiring guides.

9. Attach the mirror wiring connectors.

10. Install the mirror access hole cover. Install the push pin.

11. Install the door trim panel.

12. Attach all electrical connectors to the switch housing and install the switch housing on the armrest.

13. On the left door, install the bezel nut to the power mirror control switch.

14. Connect the negative battery cable and check mirror operation.

Antenna

REMOVAL & INSTALLATION

Fixed Antenna

1989 VEHICLES

▶ See Figure 32

1. Disconnect the negative battery cable.

2. Remove the antenna mast.

3. Remove the base cap from the antenna base and remove the base attaching screws.

4. Remove the radio from the instrument panel and unplug the antenna lead.

5. Pull the antenna lead through the dash from the engine compartment.

6. Pull the antenna base and cable assembly up through the antenna hole in the fender after removing the cable from the retaining clips on the heater and air conditioner hoses.

To install:

7. Insert the antenna lead into the fender hole.

8. Install the base-to-fender attaching screws and install the base cap.

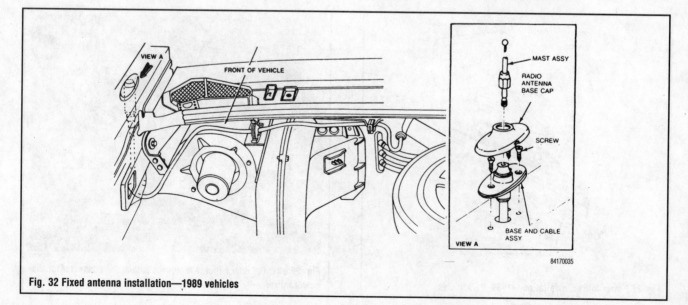

Fig. 32 Fixed antenna installation—1989 vehicles

9. Install the antenna mast into the base.

10. Pass the cable through the locator clips on the heater and air conditioner hoses.

11. Route the antenna cable through the dash panel from the engine compartment. Seat the grommet by pulling the cable from inside the passenger compartment.

12. Connect the antenna lead to the radio and install the radio in the instrument panel.

13. Connect the negative battery cable.

1990–91 VEHICLES

▶ See Figure 33

1. Disconnect the negative battery cable.
2. Remove the antenna mast.
3. Remove the base cap from the antenna base and remove the base attaching screws.
4. Unplug the antenna lead from the antenna cable extension at the right end of the instrument panel under the glove compartment door.
5. Pull the antenna lead through the "A" pillar from the underside of the fender.
6. Pull the antenna base and cable assembly up through the antenna hole in the fender.

To install:

7. Insert the antenna lead into the fender hole.
8. Install the base-to-fender attaching screws and install the base cap.
9. Install the antenna mast into the base.
10. Route the antenna cable through the hole in the "A" pillar from the underside of the fender. Seat the grommet by pulling the cable from inside the passenger compartment.
11. Connect the antenna lead to the cable extension located at the right end of the instrument panel.
12. Connect the negative battery cable.

1992–98 VEHICLES

▶ See Figure 34

1. Disconnect the negative battery cable.
2. Remove the antenna mast.
3. Remove the antenna nut and stanchion from the top of the fender.
4. Unplug the antenna lead from the antenna cable extension at the right end of the instrument panel under the glove compartment door.
5. Pull the antenna lead through the "A" pillar from the underside of the fender.
6. Remove the screw retaining the bottom of the antenna bracket to the fender.
7. Lower the antenna base, bracket and cable assembly from the underside of the fender.

To install:

8. Install the antenna assembly through the bottom of the fender.
9. Install the stanchion and nut and tighten the nut to 50–70 inch lbs. (6–8 Nm).
10. Install the screw retaining the bottom of the antenna bracket to the fender.
11. Install the antenna mast into the base.
12. Route the antenna cable through the hole in the "A" pillar from the underside of the fender. Seat the grommet by pulling the cable from inside the passenger compartment.
13. Connect the antenna lead to the cable extension located at the right end of the instrument panel.
14. Connect the negative battery cable.

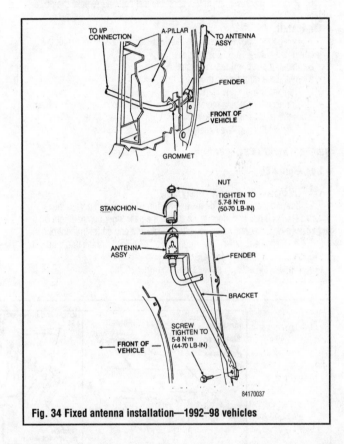

Fig. 34 Fixed antenna installation—1992–98 vehicles

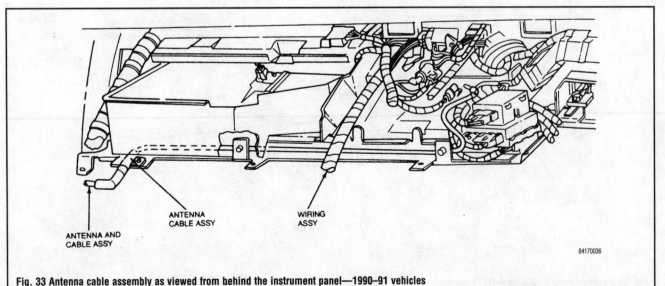

Fig. 33 Antenna cable assembly as viewed from behind the instrument panel—1990–91 vehicles

Power Antenna

1989 VEHICLES

▶ **See Figure 35**

1. Disconnect the negative battery cable.
2. Lower the antenna inside the engine compartment and disconnect the antenna lead from the power antenna near the right-hand plastic fender apron.
3. Disconnect the antenna motor wires from the antenna overlay wire assembly connector.
4. Remove the antenna nut and chrome trim stanchion.
5. Remove the fender attaching bolts from the right fender to partially loosen the fender from the vehicle and to gain access to the antenna.
6. Remove the power antenna support bracket bolt and remove the power antenna.

To install:

7. Position the power antenna to the right-hand fender hole. Install the stanchion and nut.
8. Install the support bracket mounting nut.
9. Install the right fender mounting bolts.
10. Connect the antenna lead..
11. Connect the antenna motor wires from the antenna overlay wire assembly connector in the engine compartment.
12. Connect the negative battery cable.

1990–98 VEHICLES

▶ **See Figure 36**

1. Disconnect the negative battery cable.
2. Lower the antenna inside the engine compartment and detach the antenna lead and power connector located in the passenger compartment on the right cowl side (antenna connection attached at right end on instrument panel).
3. Pull the antenna and power lead through the "A" pillar from the underside of the fender.
4. Remove the antenna nut and chrome trim stanchion.

5. Remove the power antenna support bracket screw and remove the power antenna.

To install:

6. Position the power antenna to the right-hand fender hole.
7. Install the stanchion and nut.
8. Install the support bracket retaining screw and tighten.
9. Route the antenna cable and power lead through the hole in the "A" pillar from the underside of the fender.
10. Seat the grommet by pulling the cable from inside the passenger compartment.
11. Connect the antenna lead and power lead at the right cowl side inside the passenger compartment.
12. Connect the negative battery cable.

Fenders

REMOVAL & INSTALLATION

▶ **See Figures 37 and 38**

1. Remove the front panel assembly and bumper; refer to the procedure in this Section.
2. Remove the battery if removing the right fender.
3. Remove the one cowl seal assembly-to-fender retaining screw.
4. Remove the hood; refer to the procedure in this Section.
5. Remove the 2 fender-to-radiator support panel upper brace retaining screws and remove the brace.
6. Remove the one fender apron-to-frame retaining screw (inside the wheel opening).
7. Remove the access cover retained by one push pin inside the rear of the fender apron and remove the center fender-to-cowl retaining screw (inside the access opening). If equipped, remove the one push pin retaining the apron to the fender (next to the access opening).
8. Remove the fender-to-radiator support panel retaining screws.

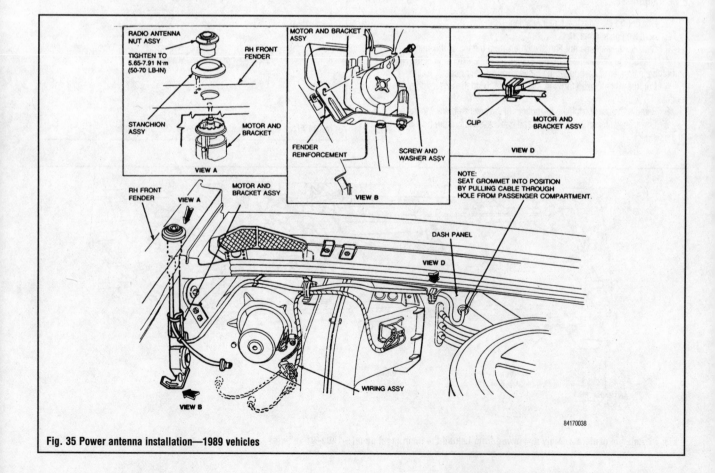

Fig. 35 Power antenna installation—1989 vehicles

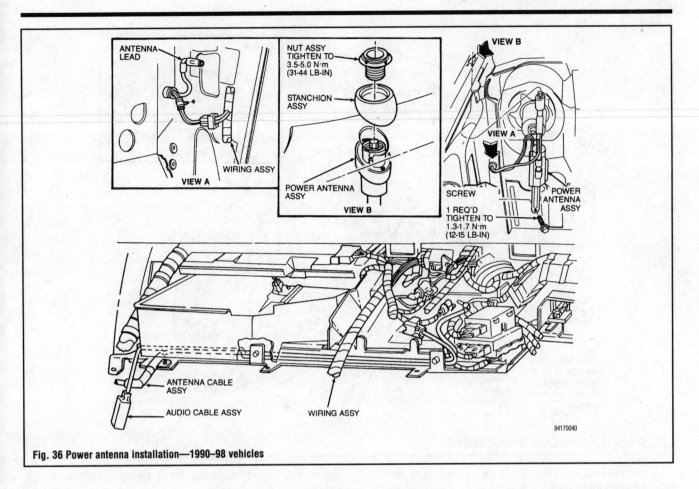

Fig. 36 Power antenna installation—1990–98 vehicles

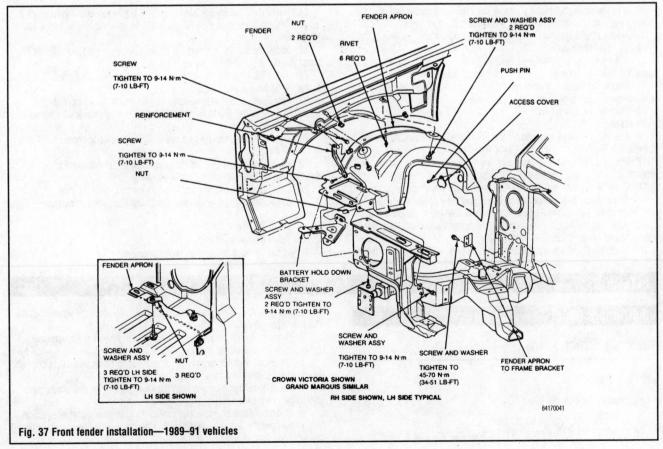

Fig. 37 Front fender installation—1989–91 vehicles

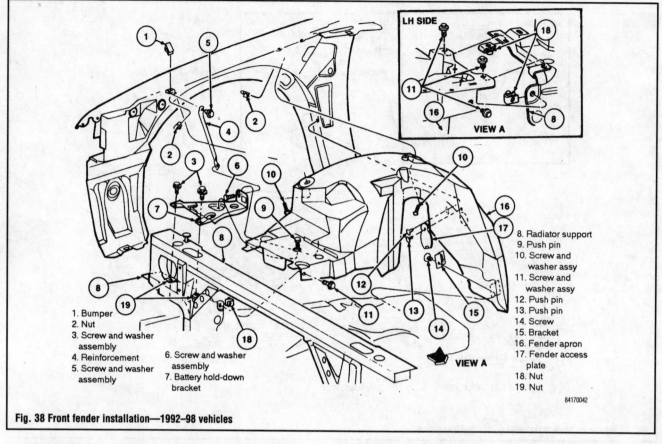

1. Bumper
2. Nut
3. Screw and washer assembly
4. Reinforcement
5. Screw and washer assembly
6. Screw and washer assembly
7. Battery hold-down bracket
8. Radiator support
9. Push pin
10. Screw and washer assy
11. Screw and washer assy
12. Push pin
13. Push pin
14. Screw
15. Bracket
16. Fender apron
17. Fender access plate
18. Nut
19. Nut

Fig. 38 Front fender installation—1992–98 vehicles

84170042

9. Remove the screws (3 left side or one right side) retaining the fender apron to the radiator support panel.

10. If removing the right fender, remove the 2 nuts and screws retaining the battery hold-down bracket to the fender and radiator support panel.

11. Remove the 3 upper and 2 lower fender-to-cowl retaining screws.

12. Remove the fender.

13. If the apron is to be removed, remove the 2 screws inside the top of the apron. On 1989–91 vehicles, drill out the 6 rivets at the wheel opening.

14. On the right fender, remove the 2 fender-to-battery hold-down bracket reinforcement brace screws and remove the brace.

15. Remove the apron.

To install:

16. Position the apron in the fender and install the 2 screws inside the top of the apron. Tighten to 7–10 ft. lbs. (9–14 Nm).

17. Position the fender-to-battery hold-down bracket reinforcement brace and install the 2 screws. Tighten to 7–10 ft. lbs. (9–14 Nm).

18. On 1989–91 vehicles, install 6 new rivets at the wheel opening.

19. Position the fender to the vehicle and install the 3 upper fender-to-cowl retaining screws. Tighten the 2 screws entering the cowl top to 25–38 ft. lbs. (34–51 Nm). Tighten the one screw entering the fender through the front of the hood hinge to 17–25 ft. lbs. (22–34 Nm).

20. Install the 2 lower fender-to-cowl retaining screws. Tighten to 7–10 ft.

lbs. (9–14 Nm) on 1989–91 vehicles or 17–25 ft. lbs. (22–34 Nm) on 1992–98 vehicles.

21. Install the 2 battery support/hold-down bracket-to-fender apron nuts and screws. Tighten the screws to 7–10 ft. lbs. (9–14 Nm) and nuts to 5–8 ft. lbs. (7–11 Nm).

22. Install the screws retaining the fender apron to the radiator support panel and tighten to 7–10 ft. lbs. (9–14 Nm).

23. Install the fender-to-radiator support panel screws and tighten to 7–10 ft. lbs. (9–14 Nm).

24. Install the center fender-to-cowl screw through the access hole and tighten to 7–10 ft. lbs. (9–14 Nm). Install the access hole cover with the push pin retainer.

25. Install the fender apron-to-frame retaining screw and tighten to 7–10 ft. lbs. (9–14 Nm).

26. Position the fender-to-radiator support panel upper brace and tighten the retaining screws to 7–10 ft. lbs. (9–14 Nm).

27. Install the one cowl seal assembly-to-fender retaining screw.

28. Check the fit of the fender to the door and hood and position as required.

29. Install the hood.

30. Install the battery, if removed.

31. Install the front panel assembly and bumper.

INTERIOR

Instrument Panel

REMOVAL & INSTALLATION

1989 Vehicles

▶ See Figures 39 and 40

1. Disconnect the negative battery cable.

2. Remove the 2 screws attaching the instrument panel pad to the instru-

ment panel at each defroster opening. Be careful not to drop the screws into the defroster openings.

3. Remove the one screw attaching each outboard end of the instrument panel pad to the instrument panel.

4. On Crown Victoria, remove one pad attaching screw near the upper right corner of the glove compartment door.

5. Remove the 5 screws attaching the lower edge of the instrument panel pad to the instrument panel.

6. Pull the instrument panel pad rearward and remove it from the vehicle.

7. Remove the 2 screws attaching the steering column opening cover to the instrument panel and remove the cover.

8. Loosen the right and left front door sill plate screws, then remove the right and left cowl side trim panels.

9. Detach the wiring harnesses from the steering column at the multiple connectors.

10. Disconnect the transmission selector indicator from the steering column.

11. Remove the nuts and washers attaching the steering column to the instrument panel brace and lay the steering column down on the seat.

12. Remove the one screw attaching the lower flange brace to the lower flange of the instrument panel just to the right of the steering column opening.

13. Remove the one screw attaching the instrument panel support to the lower edge of the instrument panel below the A/C-heater control assembly.

14. Disconnect the speedometer cable from the speedometer by pushing the cable retainer sideways and pulling the cable from the speedometer.

15. Remove the glove compartment from the instrument panel.

16. Detach the temperature control cable from the plenum and detach the vacuum jumper harness at the vacuum multiple connector located above the floor air distribution duct.

17. Disconnect the antenna cable from the radio, if equipped.

18. Remove the 5 screws attaching the top of the instrument panel to the cowl at the windshield opening.

19. Remove the one bolt attaching each lower end of the instrument panel to the cowl side (A-pillar).

20. Cover the steering column and seat with a protective cover and lay the instrument panel on the seat, detaching any wiring or other connections as necessary to allow the instrument panel to lay on the seat.

To install:

21. Position the instrument panel near the cowl and attach any wiring or other connections that were detached in Step 19.

22. Install one bolt attaching each lower end of the instrument panel to the cowl side (A-pillar).

23. Install 5 screws to attach the top of the instrument panel to the cowl panel at the windshield opening.

24. Connect the antenna cable to the radio, if equipped.

25. Attach the vacuum jumper harness (from the control assembly) to the plenum vacuum harness at the vacuum multiple connector located above the floor air distribution duct.

26. Connect and adjust the temperature control cable to the temperature blend door. See Section 6.

27. Connect the speedometer cable to the speedometer.

28. Install one screw to attach the instrument panel support to the lower edge of the instrument panel below the A/C-heater control assembly.

29. Install one screw to attach the lower flange brace to the lower flange of the instrument panel just to the right of the steering column opening.

30. Install the glove compartment and check the arms.

31. Install the right and left cowl side trim panels and tighten the door sill plate attaching screws.

32. Position the steering column to the instrument panel brace and install the retaining nuts and washers.

33. Connect the transmission indicator to the steering column.

34. Attach the wire harnesses to the steering column at the multiple connectors.

35. Install the steering column opening cover.

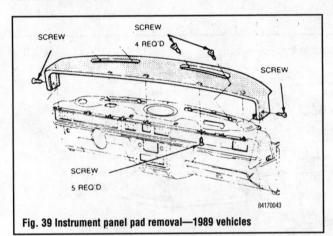

Fig. 39 Instrument panel pad removal—1989 vehicles

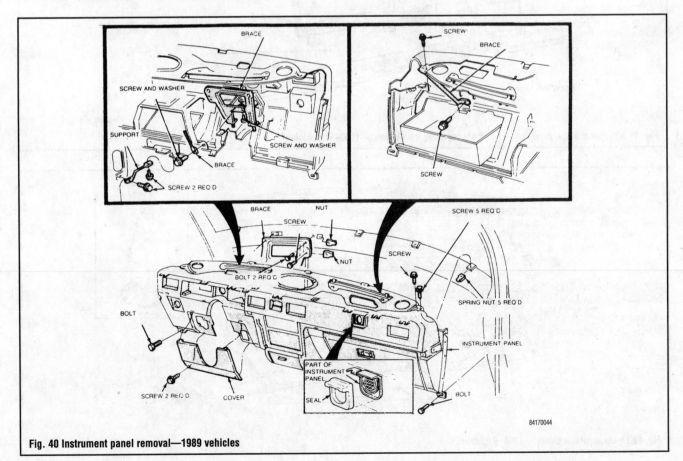

Fig. 40 Instrument panel removal—1989 vehicles

36. Position the instrument panel pad to the instrument panel and install the 5 screws along the lower edge of the pad.

37. Install one screw to attach each outboard end of the pad to the instrument panel.

38. On Crown Victoria, install one pad attaching screw near the upper right corner of the glove compartment door.

39. Install 2 instrument panel pad attaching screws at each defroster opening. Be careful not to drop the screws into the defroster opening.

40. Connect the negative battery cable.

41. Check operation of all instruments, lights, controls and the A/C-heater system.

1990–91 Vehicles

▶ **See Figures 41 thru 53**

1. Position the front wheels in the straight-ahead position.

2. Disconnect the negative battery cable. Properly disarm the air bag system; refer Section 6.

3. Remove the right and left mouldings from the instrument panel by pulling up and snapping out of the retainers.

4. Remove the right and left lower insulator panels from the instrument panel.

5. Remove the 5 bolts retaining the lower instrument panel steering column cover and remove the cover.

6. Remove the 2 bolts and reinforcement from under the steering column.

7. Remove the ignition lock cylinder; refer to Section 8.

8. Remove the tilt lever and the upper and lower steering column shrouds.

9. Disconnect the wiring from the steering column switches and the transmission range selector cable from the column.

➡ **Do not rotate the steering column shaft.**

10. Place a cover on the front seat to protect it from damage.

11. Remove the 4 nuts retaining the steering column to the instrument panel and lower the column on the front seat.

12. Install the lock cylinder to make sure the steering column shaft does not turn.

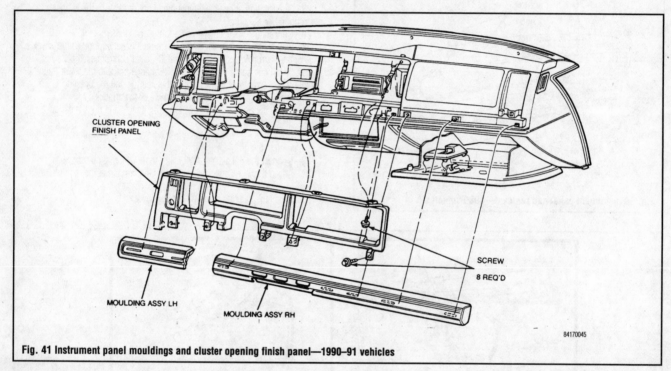

84170045

Fig. 41 Instrument panel mouldings and cluster opening finish panel—1990–91 vehicles

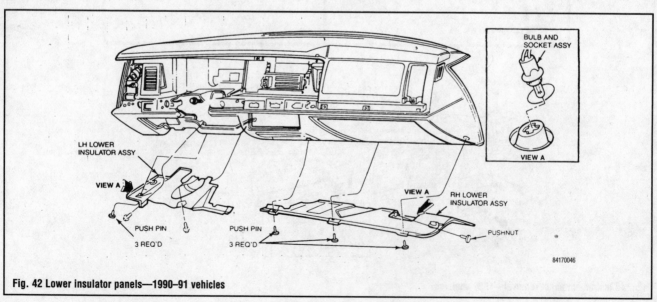

84170046

Fig. 42 Lower insulator panels—1990–91 vehicles

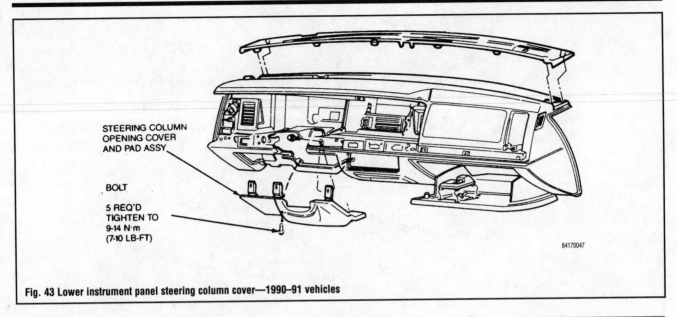

STEERING COLUMN
OPENING COVER
AND PAD ASSY

BOLT

5 REQ'D
TIGHTEN TO
9-14 N·m
(7-10 LB-FT)

84170047

Fig. 43 Lower instrument panel steering column cover—1990–91 vehicles

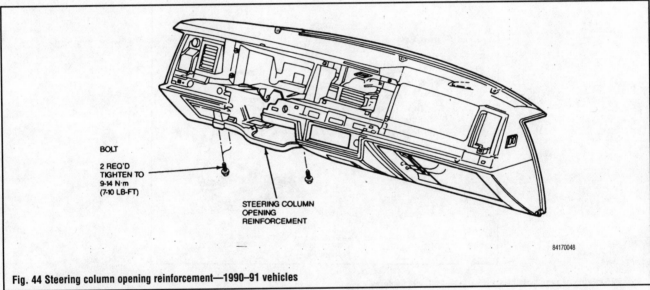

BOLT

2 REQ'D
TIGHTEN TO
9-14 N·m
(7-10 LB-FT)

STEERING COLUMN
OPENING
REINFORCEMENT

84170048

Fig. 44 Steering column opening reinforcement—1990–91 vehicles

13. Open the glove compartment door and depress the sides inward to lower the glove compartment assembly toward the floor.

14. Through the left side of the glove compartment opening, remove the 2 bolts retaining the instrument panel to the dash panel brace.

15. Through the top of the glove compartment opening, remove the one bolt retaining the brace to the instrument panel.

16. Remove the right and left cowl trim panels.

17. Disconnect the wires of the main wire loom from the engine compartment on both the right and left sides.

18. Disengage the rubber grommets from the dash panel, then feed the wire loom through the hole in the dash panel into the passenger compartment.

19. Disconnect the wires from the instrument panel at the right and left cowl sides.

20. Remove the one bolt and nut retaining the instrument panel to the left side and the one bolt retaining the instrument panel to the right side.

21. Pull up to unsnap the upper finish panel and remove the upper finish panel.

22. Using the steering column and glove compartment openings, and by reaching under the instrument panel, detach all electrical connections, vacuum hoses, demister hose, heater-A/C vacuum lines and radio antenna.

23. Close the glove compartment door and support the instrument panel.

24. Remove the 3 screws retaining the top of the instrument panel to the cowl top and disconnect any remaining wires.

25. Remove the instrument panel from the vehicle.

26. If the instrument panel is being replaced, transfer all parts to the new panel.

To install:

27. Carefully position the instrument panel in the vehicle and install the 3 screws retaining the top of the instrument panel to the cowl top.

28. Open the glove compartment door and depress the sides inward to lower the glove compartment assembly toward the floor.

29. Attach the radio antenna and all electrical connections and vacuum lines.

30. Install the upper finish panel.

31. Install the bolt retaining the instrument panel to the right side and tighten to 16–25 ft. lbs. (22–34 Nm).

32. Install the bolt and nut retaining the instrument panel on the left side and tighten to 33–51 ft. lbs. (45–70 Nm).

33. Connect the instrument panel wires at the right and left cowl sides.

34. Feed the main wire loom through the hole in the dash panel into the engine compartment. Secure the rubber grommets in the dash panel.

35. Connect the main wire loom wires on the right and left sides.

36. Install the right and left cowl trim panels.

37. Install the bolts retaining the instrument panel to the dash panel brace.

38. Close the glove compartment door.

39. Remove the lock cylinder from the steering column.

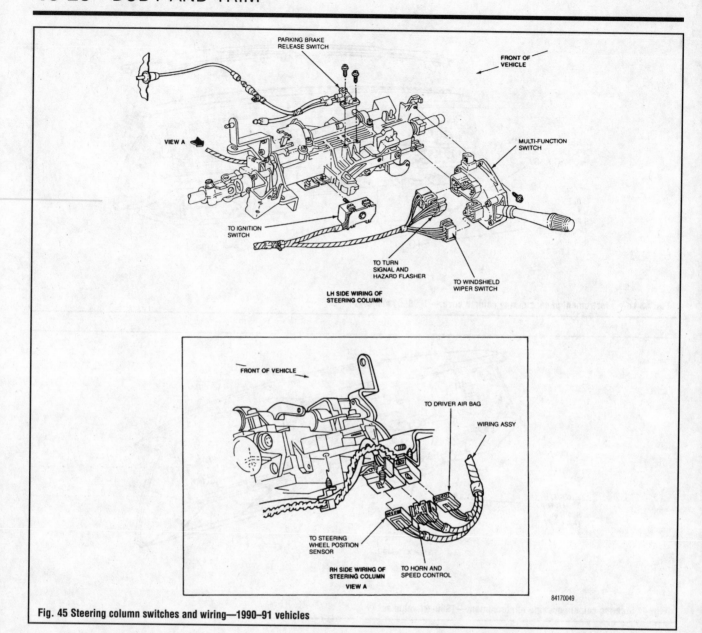

Fig. 45 Steering column switches and wiring—1990–91 vehicles

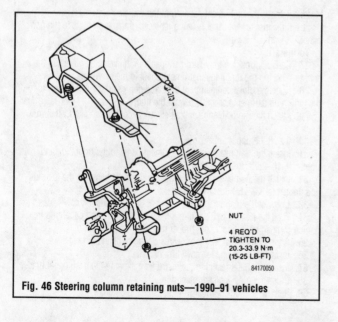

Fig. 46 Steering column retaining nuts—1990–91 vehicles

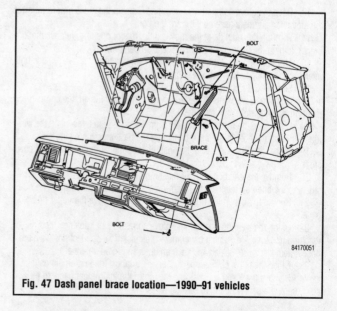

Fig. 47 Dash panel brace location—1990–91 vehicles

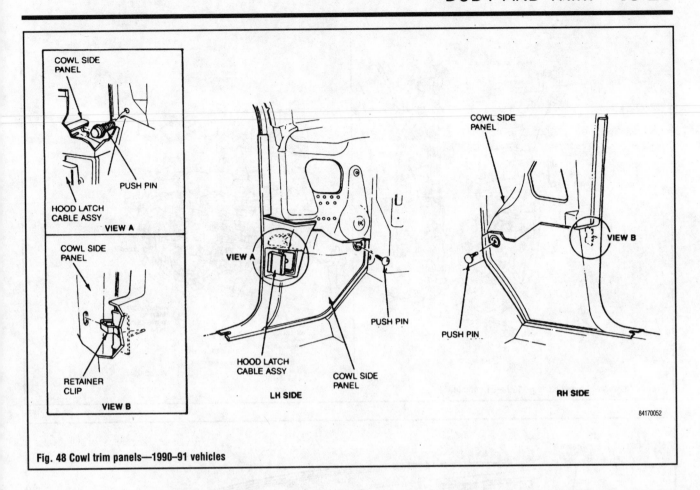

Fig. 48 Cowl trim panels—1990–91 vehicles

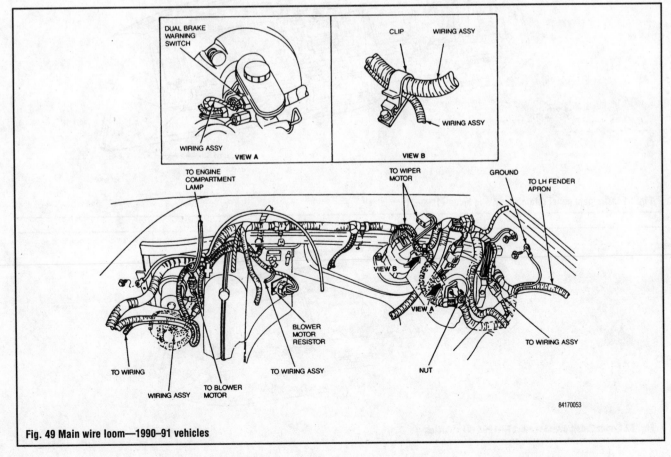

Fig. 49 Main wire loom—1990–91 vehicles

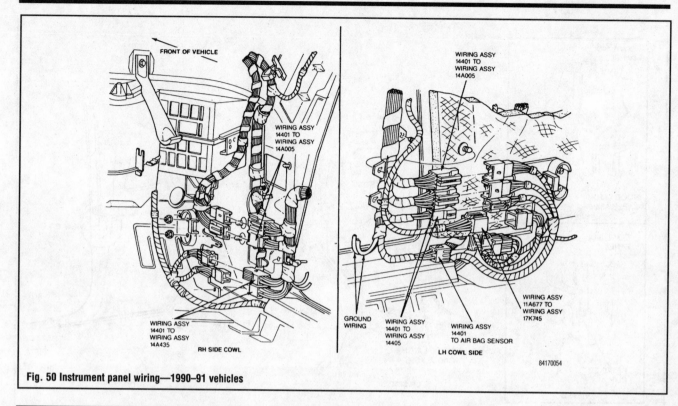

Fig. 50 Instrument panel wiring—1990–91 vehicles

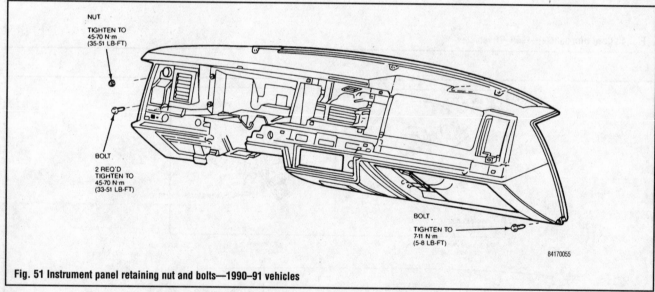

Fig. 51 Instrument panel retaining nut and bolts—1990–91 vehicles

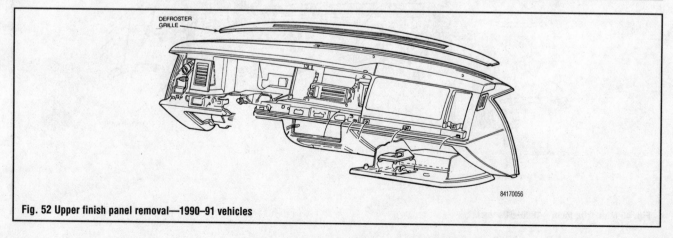

Fig. 52 Upper finish panel removal—1990–91 vehicles

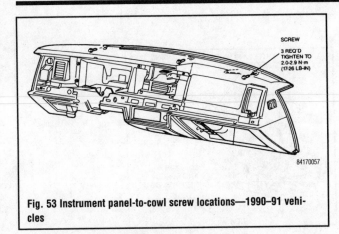

SCREW
3 REQ'D
TIGHTEN TO
2.0-2.9 N·m
(17-26 LB-IN)

84170057

Fig. 53 Instrument panel-to-cowl screw locations—1990–91 vehicles

40. Raise the column into position and install the 4 retaining nuts. Tighten to 15–25 ft. lbs. (21–34 Nm).
41. Connect the transmission range selector cable to the steering column and the wiring to the steering column switches.
42. Install the steering column shrouds and the tilt lever.
43. Install the ignition lock cylinder.
44. Install the reinforcement under the steering column and tighten the bolts to 7–10 ft. lbs. (9–14 Nm).
45. Install the lower instrument panel steering column cover and tighten the bolts to 7–10 ft. lbs. (9–14 Nm).
46. Install the lower insulator panels and the instrument panel mouldings.
47. Connect the negative battery cable.
48. Enable the air bag system.
49. Check operation of all instruments, lights, controls and the A/C-heater system. Check the air bag indicator operation.

1992–98 Vehicles

▶ **See Figures 54 thru 59**

1. Position the front wheels in the straight-ahead position.
2. Disconnect the negative battery cable.
3. Properly disarm the air bag system; see Section 6.
4. Remove the right and left mouldings from the instrument panel by pulling up and snapping out of the retainers.
5. Remove the right and left lower insulator panels from the instrument panel.
6. Remove the 5 bolts retaining the lower instrument panel steering column cover and remove the cover.
7. Remove the 2 bolts and reinforcement from under the steering column.
8. Pull up to unsnap the upper finish panel and remove the upper finish panel.
9. Remove the ignition lock cylinder; refer to Section 8.
10. Remove the tilt lever and the upper and lower steering column shrouds.
11. Disconnect the wiring from the steering column switches and the transmission range selector cable from the column.

➡ **Do not rotate the steering column shaft.**

12. Place a cover on the front seat to protect it from damage.
13. Remove the 4 nuts retaining the steering column to the instrument panel and lower the column on the front seat.
14. Install the lock cylinder to make sure the steering column shaft does not turn.
15. Open the glove compartment door and depress the sides inward.
16. Lower the glove compartment assembly toward the floor.
17. Through the left side of the glove compartment opening, remove the 2 bolts retaining the instrument panel to the dash panel brace.
18. Remove the right and left cowl trim panels.
19. Disconnect the wires of the main wire loom from the engine compartment on both the right and left sides.
20. Disengage the rubber grommets from the dash panel, then feed the wire loom through the hole in the dash panel into the passenger compartment.
21. Disconnect the wires from the instrument panel at the right and left cowl sides.

22. Remove the 2 lower bolts retaining the instrument panel to the A-pillar.
23. Using the steering column and glove compartment openings, and by reaching under the instrument panel, detach all electrical connections, vacuum hoses, demister hose, heater-A/C vacuum lines and radio antenna.
24. Close the glove compartment door and support the instrument panel.
25. Remove the 5 screws retaining the top of the instrument panel to the cowl top and disconnect any remaining wires.
26. Remove the instrument panel from the vehicle.
27. If the instrument panel is being replaced, transfer all parts to the new panel.

To install:
28. Carefully position the instrument panel in the vehicle and install the 5 screws retaining the top of the instrument panel to the cowl top.
29. Open the glove compartment door and depress the sides inward to lower the glove compartment assembly toward the floor.
30. Attach the radio antenna and all electrical connections and vacuum lines.
31. Install the 2 lower bolts retaining the instrument panel to the A-pillar and tighten to 17–25 ft. lbs. (22–34 Nm).
32. Connect the instrument panel wires at the right and left cowl sides.
33. Feed the main wire loom through the hole in the dash panel into the engine compartment.
34. Secure the rubber grommets in the dash panel.

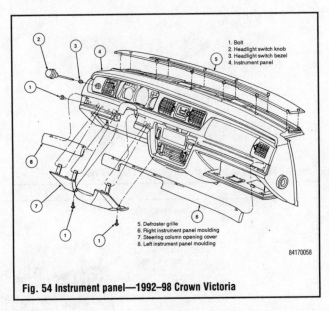

1. Bolt
2. Headlight switch knob
3. Headlight switch bezel
4. Instrument panel

5. Defroster grille
6. Right instrument panel moulding
7. Steering column opening cover
8. Left instrument panel moulding

84170058

Fig. 54 Instrument panel—1992–98 Crown Victoria

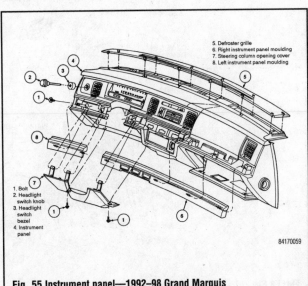

5. Defroster grille
6. Right instrument panel moulding
7. Steering column opening cover
8. Left instrument panel moulding

1. Bolt
2. Headlight switch knob
3. Headlight switch bezel
4. Instrument panel

84170059

Fig. 55 Instrument panel—1992–98 Grand Marquis

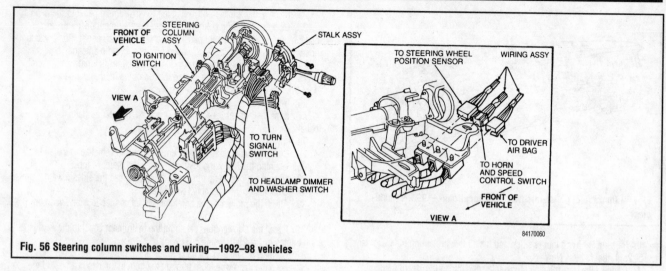

Fig. 56 Steering column switches and wiring—1992–98 vehicles

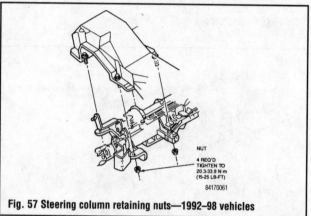

Fig. 57 Steering column retaining nuts—1992–98 vehicles

35. Connect the main wire loom wires on the right and left sides.
36. Install the right and left cowl trim panels.
37. Install the bolts retaining the instrument panel to the dash panel brace.
38. Close the glove compartment door.
39. Remove the lock cylinder from the steering column.
40. Raise the column into position and install the 4 retaining nuts. Tighten to 15–25 ft. lbs. (21–34 Nm).
41. Connect the transmission range selector cable to the steering column and the wiring to the steering column switches.
42. Install the steering column shrouds and the tilt lever.
43. Install the ignition lock cylinder.
44. Install the upper finish panel.
45. Install the reinforcement under the steering column and tighten the bolts to 7–10 ft. lbs. (9–14 Nm).
46. Install the lower instrument panel steering column cover and tighten the bolts to 7–10 ft. lbs. (9–14 Nm).
47. Install the lower insulator panels and the instrument panel mouldings.

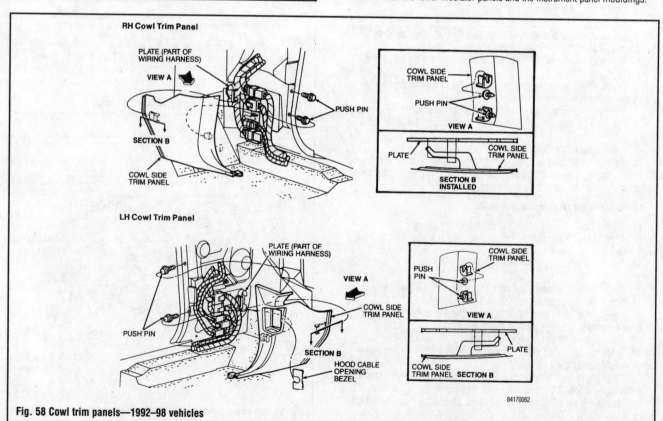

Fig. 58 Cowl trim panels—1992–98 vehicles

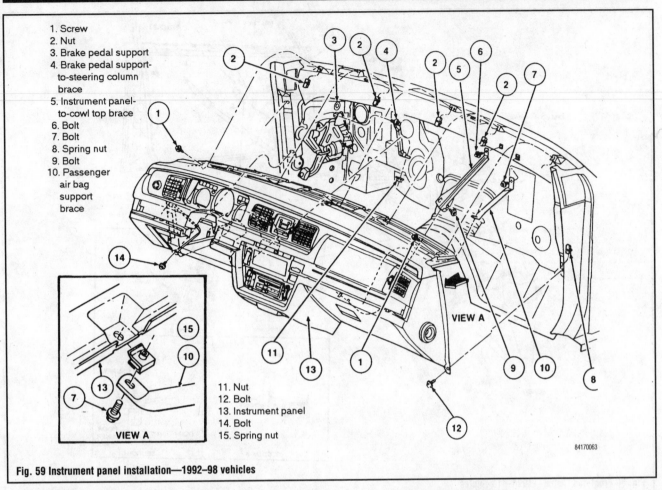

1. Screw
2. Nut
3. Brake pedal support
4. Brake pedal support-to-steering column brace
5. Instrument panel-to-cowl top brace
6. Bolt
7. Bolt
8. Spring nut
9. Bolt
10. Passenger air bag support brace

11. Nut
12. Bolt
13. Instrument panel
14. Bolt
15. Spring nut

VIEW A

84170063

Fig. 59 Instrument panel installation—1992–98 vehicles

48. Connect the negative battery cable.
49. Enable the air bag system.
50. Check operation of all instruments, lights, controls and the A/C-heater system.
51. Check the air bag indicator operation.

Door Panels

REMOVAL & INSTALLATION

1989–91 Vehicles

♦ See Figures 60 and 61

1. Disconnect the negative battery cable.
2. On 1990–91 vehicles, remove the speaker grille.
3. Remove the retaining screws from the door inside handle cup.
4. If equipped with armrest courtesy lamps, remove the lens, detach the bulb and wiring assembly from the pull cup and remove the pull cup.
5. Working through the pull cup opening, disconnect the remote lock rod from the lock knob.
6. Remove the retaining screw and the remote mirror bezel nut from the power window regulator housing switch plate, if equipped.
7. Raise the plate to expose the window switch and power door lock switch and disconnect the switches.
8. Remove the retaining screws from the armrest finish panel.
9. Remove the retaining screws from the armrest and remove the armrest.
10. Using a suitable trim pad removal tool, carefully pry the trim panel plastic push pin retainers from the door inner panel.

➡**Do not use the trim panel to pry the clips from the door inner panel. Replace any bent, damaged or missing push pins.**

11. Disconnect the radio speaker wiring, if equipped.
12. Remove the trim panel and watershield.
To install:
13. If the door panel is to be replaced, transfer the plastic push pins to the new panel. Make sure that the watershield is positioned correctly to the door sheet metal. Remove the door pull handle from the old panel and transfer to the new one.
14. Position the door panel loosely to the door belt opening and route the wiring harness through the appropriate access holes in the panel.
15. Connect the radio speaker, if equipped.
16. Align the plastic push pins on the door panel to the holes in the door sheet metal and press the pins into place.
17. Install the armrest and route the window regulator, remote mirror cable and power lock harness through the access hole.
18. Install the armrest finish panel.
19. Install the power window regulator switch plate housing to the armrest connecting the power window switch, power door lock switch and remote mirror bezel nut, if equipped, prior to securing the retainer screw.
20. Connect the lock remote rod to the lock knob retainer boss.

➡**Make sure that the remote rod is fully seated into the retainer boss, then function manually or with the power switch to ensure smooth operation of the lock knob.**

21. Install the bulb and wiring assembly.
22. Install the lamp lens, if equipped, and the pull cup.
23. On 1990–91 vehicles, install the speaker grille.
24. Connect the negative battery cable.

1992–98 Vehicles

♦ See Figures 62 thru 73

1. Disconnect the negative battery cable.
2. If removing the driver's door panel, remove the nut from the outside rearview mirror control switch.

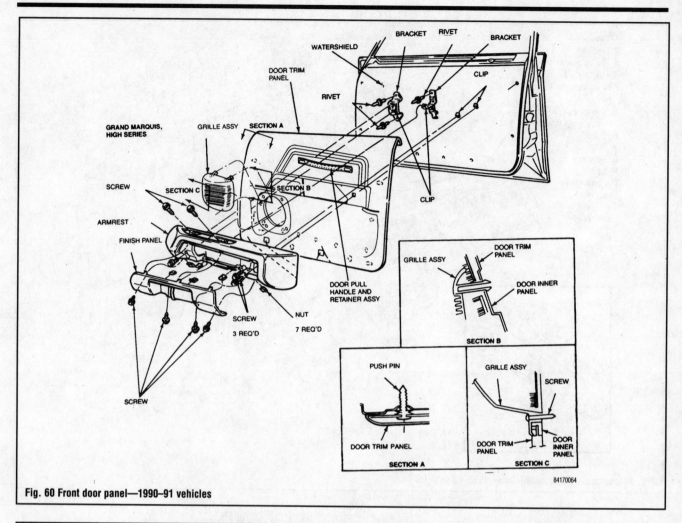

Fig. 60 Front door panel—1990–91 vehicles

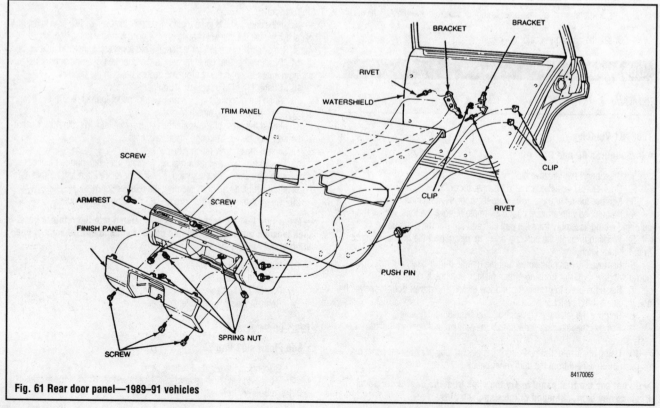

Fig. 61 Rear door panel—1989–91 vehicles

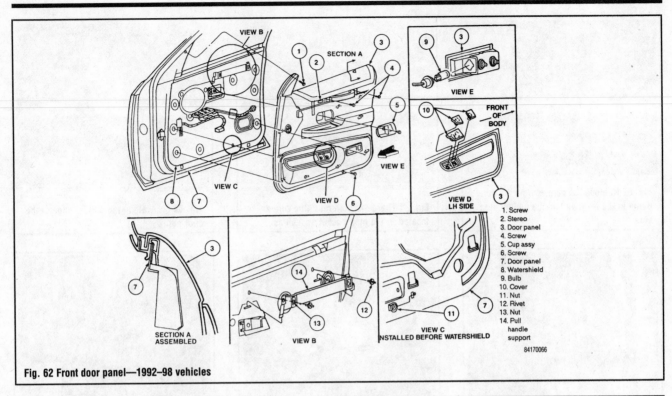

1. Screw
2. Stereo
3. Door panel
4. Screw
5. Cup assy
6. Screw
7. Door panel
8. Watershield
9. Bulb
10. Cover
11. Nut
12. Rivet
13. Nut
14. Pull handle support

84170066

Fig. 62 Front door panel—1992–98 vehicles

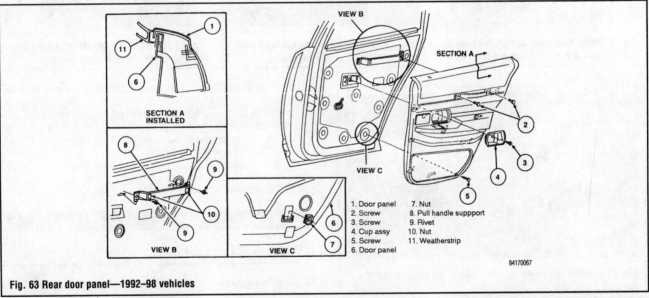

1. Door panel
2. Screw
3. Screw
4. Cup assy
5. Screw
6. Door panel
7. Nut
8. Pull handle suppport
9. Rivet
10. Nut
11. Weatherstrip

84170067

Fig. 63 Rear door panel—1992–98 vehicles

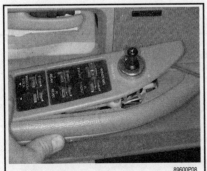

89600P08

Fig. 64 Remove the window regulator switch housing by gently prying up, starting at the front

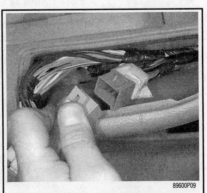

89600P09

Fig. 65 Detach the switch housing electrical connector and remove the housing

89600P01

Fig. 66 Remove the door inside handle cup

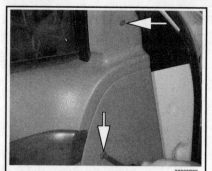

Fig. 67 Remove the screws from the door panel in the front and on the upper extension

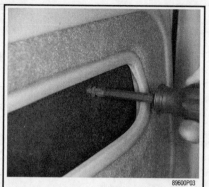

Fig. 68 There are also retaining screws located in the map pocket as well as . . .

Fig. 69 . . . along the bottom edge of the door panel

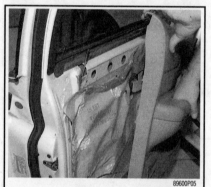

Fig. 70 Lift the door panel upward and snap out the panel to remove it from the door

Fig. 71 Rotate the door marker lamp bulb and remove it from the door panel

Fig. 72 Detach the connectors for the trunklid and fuel door release switches

Fig. 73 Slide the relay connector off of the door panel and remove the door panel from the vehicle

3. Remove the window regulator switch housing by gently prying up, starting at the front.

4. Detach all connectors from the switch housing.

5. Remove the door inside handle cup.

6. Remove the push pin from the door trim panel upper front extension and remove the screw.

7. Remove the lower self-tapping screw retaining the door trim panel to the door inner panel.

8. On Grand Marquis, pry up the screw covers from the door pull handle and remove the screws and handle.

9. Lift the door panel upward and snap out the panel.

10. Disconnect the necessary wire harnesses and remove the panel.

To install:

11. Connect the wire harnesses to the door panel, as necessary.

12. Install the door panel by pushing in and down until it snaps into place.

13. Install all self-tapping screws retaining the door trim panel to the door inner panel.

14. On Grand Marquis, install the door pull handle, tighten the screws and install the screw covers.

15. Install the push pin covering screw on the panel upper front extension.

16. Install the inside door handle cup.

17. Install the window regulator switch housing and install the nut on the outside rearview mirror control switch, if removed.

18. Connect the negative battery cable.

Door Locks

REMOVAL & INSTALLATION

Front Door Latch

♦ **See Figures 74 and 75**

1. Remove the door trim panel and the watershield.

2. Mark the location of the rear run lower retaining bolt and remove the bolt.

3. Disconnect the outside release rod.

4. Check all rod connections. Correct any misconnected or loose connections and check operation before replacing parts.

5. Disconnect the rods from the latch.

✳✳ WARNING

The remote link and the latch-to-lock cylinder rod cannot be removed because of the rod's end configuration.

6. Remove the lock cylinder rod from the lock cylinder lever.

7. Remove the power actuator, power rod and clip, if equipped.

8. Remove the door latch remote control.

9. Remove the latch assembly retaining screws.

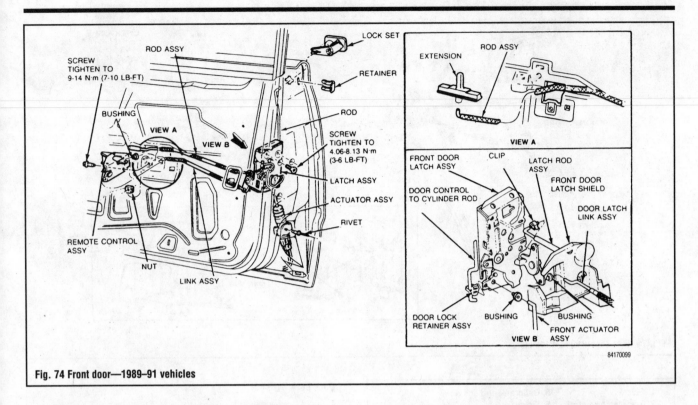

Fig. 74 Front door—1989–91 vehicles

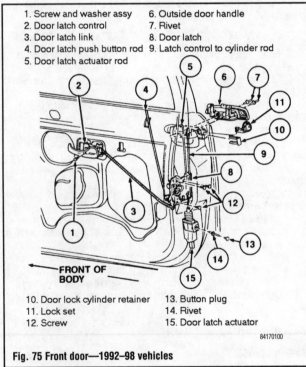

1. Screw and washer assy
2. Door latch control
3. Door latch link
4. Door latch push button rod
5. Door latch actuator rod
6. Outside door handle
7. Rivet
8. Door latch
9. Latch control to cylinder rod

FRONT OF BODY

10. Door lock cylinder retainer
11. Lock set
12. Screw
13. Button plug
14. Rivet
15. Door latch actuator

84170100

Fig. 75 Front door—1992–98 vehicles

10. Disconnect the door indicator switch wire, if equipped, and remove the latch from the door.

11. Remove the anti-theft shield from the latch.

12. Remove the remote link, the latch-to-lock cylinder rods, and the door indicator switch from the latch where applicable.

To install:

13. Install new rod retaining clips and grommets in the new latch assembly, using the removed latch as a guide.

14. Position the door indicator switch to the latch and install the attaching screw.

15. Install the anti-theft shield to the latch.

16. Install the remote link and the latch-to-lock cylinder rod.

17. Position the latch in the door and connect the wire to the door indicator switch.

18. Install the latch and retaining screws with the anti-theft shield.

19. Install the door latch remote control.

20. Connect the latch-to-lock cylinder rod to the lock cylinder lever, manual lock rod and power lock rod, if equipped.

21. Connect the outside release rod to the latch and check latch operation.

22. Install the rear run lower attaching bolt in the original position.

23. Install the door trim panel and watershield.

Rear Door Latch

▶ **See Figures 76 and 77**

1. Remove the door trim panel and watershield.

2. Disconnect the door latch-actuating rod from the latch assembly.

3. Remove the rear door latch bellcrank.

4. Remove the door latch remote control.

5. Disconnect the power lock rod, if equipped.

6. Remove the three latch assembly retaining screws.

7. Disconnect the wire from the door indicator switch, if equipped, and remove the latch assembly from the door.

8. Remove the door indicator switch from the latch assembly and remove the 2 link assemblies from the latch.

To install:

9. Install new clips and grommets in the new latch assembly, using the removed latch as a guide.

10. Install the door indicator switch on the latch assembly.

11. Install the 2 link assemblies into the lower lever grommets.

12. Connect the power lock rod, if equipped.

13. Position the latch assembly on the door and connect the wire to the door indicator switch, if equipped.

14. Install the 3 retaining screws.

15. Connect the door latch-actuating rod to the latch assembly.

16. Install the door latch bellcrank and remote control.

17. Check latch operation, then install the door panel and watershield.

Door Latch Remote Control

1. Remove the door trim panel and watershield.

2. Remove the retaining screw and disengage the attaching tab.

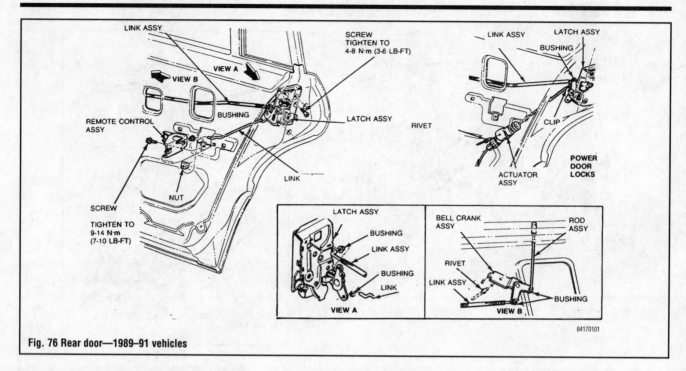

Fig. 76 Rear door—1989–91 vehicles

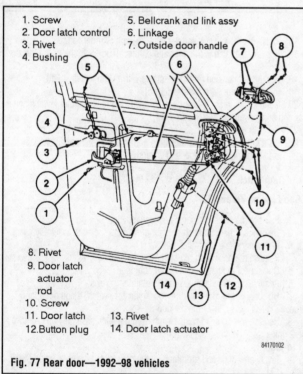

1. Screw
2. Door latch control
3. Rivet
4. Bushing
5. Bellcrank and link assy
6. Linkage
7. Outside door handle
8. Rivet
9. Door latch actuator rod
10. Screw
11. Door latch
12. Button plug
13. Rivet
14. Door latch actuator

Fig. 77 Rear door—1992–98 vehicles

3. Rotate the remote control clockwise on the right door or counterclockwise on the left door while moving it forward to disconnect the remote control from the remote control rod and the door.

To install:

4. Install a new rod end bushing to the remote control if the remote control is being replaced.

5. Position the remote control to the door inner panel with the remote control rod started into the remote control bushing. Rotate the remote control ¼ turn onto the remote rod (counterclockwise on the right door or clockwise on the left door).

6. Engage the tab on the remote control into the slot on the inner panel and install the retaining screw.

7. Check remote control and latch operation.

8. Install the trim panel and watershield.

Door Lock Cylinder

1. Remove the trim panel and position the watershield away from the access holes.

2. On 1992–98 vehicles, disconnect the door latch actuator rod from the latch.

3. Remove the 2 rivets retaining the outside door handle to the door and remove the handle and rod from the door.

4. Disconnect the lock control-to-door lock cylinder rod at the lock cylinder arm.

5. Remove the door lock cylinder retainer and remove the lock cylinder from the door.

To install:

6. Transfer the lock cylinder arm to the new lock cylinder. Replace the rod retainer if it shows any signs of wear or warpage.

7. Position the lock cylinder in the door and install the lock cylinder retainer.

8. Connect the lock control-to-door lock cylinder rod at the lock cylinder and secure the retainer.

9. On 1992–98 vehicles, proceed as follows:

  a. Transfer the actuator rod to a new outside door handle plastic bushing slot, if the handle is to replaced.

  b. Insert the handle and rod into the door and install 2 rivets.

  c. Connect the door latch actuator rod to the door latch.

  d. Check the operation of the outside door handle and the door latch.

10. Carefully position the watershield to the inner panel and install the door panel.

Power Door Lock Actuator Motor

1989–91 VEHICLES

1. Disconnect the negative battery cable.
2. Remove the door trim panel and watershield.
3. Disconnect the actuator motor link from the door latch.
4. Remove the pop-rivet attaching the motor to the door.
5. Detach the wiring connector and remove the actuator motor.

To install:

6. Attach the wiring connector to the actuator motor.
7. Position the motor in the door and secure with a pop-rivet.
8. Connect the actuator motor link to the door latch.

➡ **Be careful that the actuator's boot does not twist during installation. The pop-rivet must be installed so the bracket base is tight to the inner panel.**

9. Install the watershield and door panel.
10. Connect the negative battery cable.

1992–98 VEHICLES

1. Disconnect the negative battery cable.
2. Remove the door trim panel and watershield.
3. Remove the pop-rivet attaching the motor to the door.
4. Detach the wiring connector and remove the actuator motor.
5. Remove the door latch and disconnect the actuator motor link from the door latch.
6. Remove the actuator motor.

To install:

7. Connect the actuator motor link to the door latch.
8. Position the motor in the door and secure with a pop-rivet.

➡**The pop-rivet must be installed so the bracket base is tight to the inner panel.**

9. Attach the wiring connector to the actuator motor.
10. Install the watershield and door panel.
11. Connect the negative battery cable.

Power Door Lock Switch

1989–91 VEHICLES

1. Disconnect the negative battery cable.
2. Remove the inside handle cup and press down on the lock rod to disengage the rod from the snapring and knob.
3. Remove the attaching screw and switch housing from the armrest.
4. Remove the 2 screws attaching the connector to the switch housing.
5. Carefully pry the switch from the connector using a suitable tool. Be careful not to damage the electrical contact pins.
6. Installation is the reverse of the removal procedure.

1992–98 VEHICLES

♦ See Figure 78

1. Disconnect the negative battery cable.
2. If removing the driver's door switch, remove the nut from the outside rearview mirror control switch.
3. Gently pry up the front portion of the switch housing.
4. Gently pry up the sides and rear of the switch housing from the armrest cavity.
5. Remove the 2 screws retaining the connector to the switch housing.
6. Carefully pry the switch from the connector using a suitable tool. Be careful not to damage the electrical contact pins.
7. Installation is the reverse of the removal procedure.

Tailgate Lock

REMOVAL & INSTALLATION

♦ See Figure 79

Tailgate Upper Latch

1. Remove the tailgate trim panel and access cover.
2. Disconnect the power lock actuator link from the latch, if equipped.
3. Disconnect the 3 links with double 90 degree ends from the clips on the other end of the link.
4. Disconnect the center control to upper latch link at the latch end.
5. Rotate the push-button rod out of the bushing in the latch lever.
6. Detach the wire connector from the power window switch and limit switch.
7. Remove the 3 latch retaining screws and remove the latch.

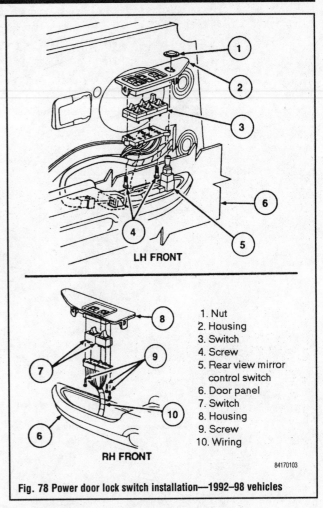

LH FRONT

RH FRONT

1. Nut
2. Housing
3. Switch
4. Screw
5. Rear view mirror control switch
6. Door panel
7. Switch
8. Housing
9. Screw
10. Wiring

84170103

Fig. 78 Power door lock switch installation—1992–98 vehicles

To install:

8. Transfer the rods and clips to the new latch. Make sure the rods and clips are inserted into the same side of the lever.
9. Position the latch in the tailgate and install the 3 retaining screws, taking care to position all rods.
10. Attach the rods to the connecting components.
11. Connect the center control to the upper latch link.
12. Attach the wiring connectors to the power window switch and limit switch.
13. Connect the power lock actuator, if equipped.
14. Install the access cover and trim panel on the tailgate

Tailgate Lower Latch

1. Remove the interior trim panel and access cover from the tailgate.
2. Disconnect the latch actuator link from the lower latch.
3. Remove the 3 lower latch retaining screws and remove the lower latch from the tailgate.

To install:

4. Install a new retainer clip in the lower latch.
5. Position the lower latch to the tailgate and install the 3 retaining screws.
6. Adjust and connect the latch actuator link to the lower latch.
7. Adjust the lower latch striker, if necessary.
8. Install the access panel and trim panel on the tailgate.

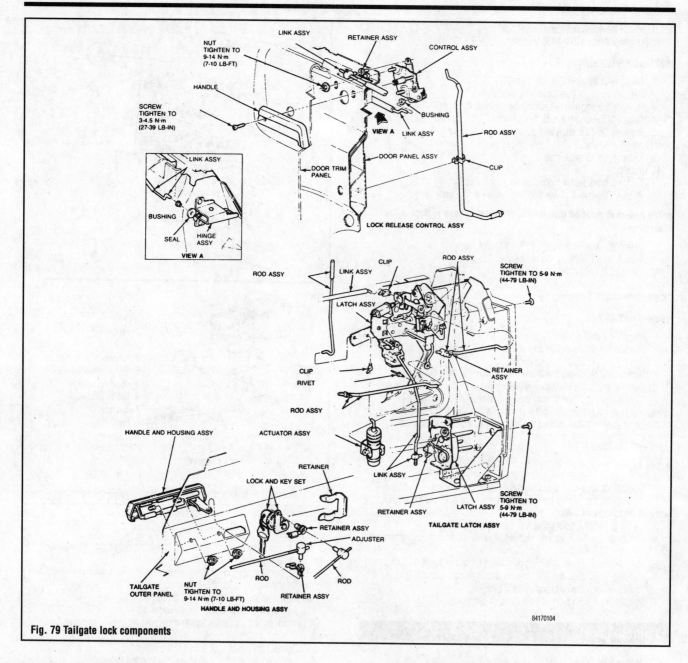

Fig. 79 Tailgate lock components

Tailgate Lock Release Control

1. Remove the inside handle.
2. Remove the interior trim panel and access cover from the tailgate.
3. Raise the tailgate glass.
4. Disconnect the upper hinge release link and latch control rod from the lock release control.
5. Remove the 3 release control retaining nuts and rotate the control assembly off the latch release link assembly.

To install:

6. Install new clips and bushings onto the new control assembly.
7. Rotate the release control onto the upper latch link.
8. Position the tailgate and install the 3 retaining nuts.
9. Connect the other 2 rods to the lock release control and adjust.
10. Install the trim panel and the inside handle.

Tailgate Lock Cylinder

1. Remove the tailgate inside trim panel and the access hole cover.
2. Disconnect the latch release link and remove the latch rod assembly from the lock cylinder.

3. Remove the lock cylinder.

To install:

4. Transfer the retainer to the new lock cylinder and insert the lock cylinder into the tailgate.
5. Install the lock cylinder retainer and the latch release link into the clip.
6. Install the tailgate access hole cover and the trim panel.

Tailgate Lock Actuator

1. Disconnect the negative battery cable.
2. Remove the tailgate trim panel and watershield.
3. Remove the rivet retaining the lock actuator rod from the latch.
4. Detach the wiring connector and remove the actuator.

To install:

5. Attach the wiring connector to the actuator.
6. Connect the lock actuator rod to the latch and assemble to the tailgate inner panel. Install the watershield and trim panel.

➡ **Be careful that the actuator boot does not twist during installation. The pop-rivet must be installed so the bracket base is tight to the inner panel.**

Door Glass

REMOVAL & INSTALLATION

1989–91 Vehicles

FRONT DOOR

▶ **See Figure 80**

1. Remove the door trim panel and watershield.
2. Raise the glass to gain access to the 3 glass bracket retaining rivets.
3. Position a suitable block support between the door outer panel and the glass bracket to stabilize the glass during rivet removal.
4. Remove the center pin of each rivet with a drift punch. Drill out the remainder of the rivet with a ¼ in. diameter drill, being careful not to enlarge the rivet attachment.

> ❋❋ **WARNING**
>
> **Do not attempt to pry the rivets out as damage to the glass bracket and glass spacer retainer could result.**

5. Remove the glass.
   To install:
6. Install the spacer and retainer assemblies into the glass retention holes. Make sure each assembly is securely fastened.
7. Insert the glass into the door between the door belt weatherstrips.
8. Position the regulator arm slide assembly into the C-channel of the glass bracket.
9. Position the glass to the glass bracket and install three ¼ in. blind rivets. Three ¼ in.-20 bolt, washer and nut assemblies can also be used to attach the glass to the glass bracket.
10. If necessary, loosen the upper and lower retaining screws on the run and bracket assembly to position the glass in the door frame.
11. Install the door trim panel and watershield.

REAR DOOR

▶ **See Figures 81 and 82**

1. Remove the door trim panel and watershield.
2. Remove the glass-to-glass bracket retaining rivets. Remove the center pin from the rivets with a drift punch and drill the head from each rivet with a ¼ in. diameter drill. Lower the glass approximately 6 in. and let it rest in the door well.
3. Remove the door window glass inner stabilizer retaining screw and remove the stabilizer assembly.
4. Remove the retainer and division bar glass run attaching screw and washer assembly at the bottom.
5. Remove the screw and washer assembly at the top of the division bar at the door frame. Tilt the division bar and main glass forward and remove the weather-strip from the top of the door frame.
6. Remove the stationary vent glass and weather-strip from the door frame.
7. Position the retainer, division bar and main glass in the upright position. Pull the main glass and division bar above and outside the door frame. Swing the glass and division bar assembly's 90 degrees from the door frame and work the glass and division bar upward and out of the door channel between the belt mouldings.
   To install:

➡ **The rear door glass, rear door window glass channel, division bar glass run, and retainer and division bar assembly are preassembled prior to installation.**

8. Install the glass channel to the glass using glass Everseal tape or equivalent, 0.065 in. (1.65mm) thick **x** 1¾ in. (44.45mm) wide **x** 17 ¾ in. (450.85mm) long. Be sure to align the notches in the glass to the cutouts within the glass channel. Clear tape from channel for installing glass guides.
9. Install 2 nylon guides into the glass channel slots and snap the Mylar flocked glass run over the glass channel.
10. Lubricate the inside section of the retainer and division bar assembly with silicone lubricant. Place the retainer and division bar assembly over the nylon guides and slide over the glass channel.

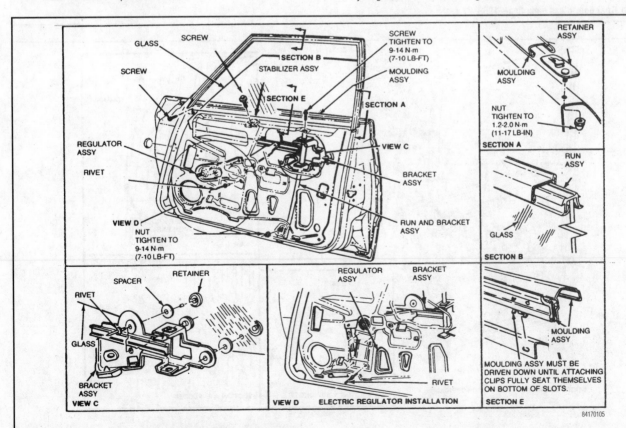

Fig. 80 Front door glass and related components—1989–91 vehicles

84170105

11. Install the run assembly into the door frame (front and top of door). Leave the last 6 in. (152mm) of run assembly next to the division bar hanging loose out of the door frame.

12. While holding the rear door glass, retainer and division bar 90 degrees from the door, insert the retainer and division bar between the door belt weather-strip. Swing the glass inboard to the belt and install loosely in the door channel. The upper front corner of the glass should touch the beltline in this position.

➡ **Lubricate the belt and vent weatherstrips with silicone lubricant or soapy solution for easier installation.**

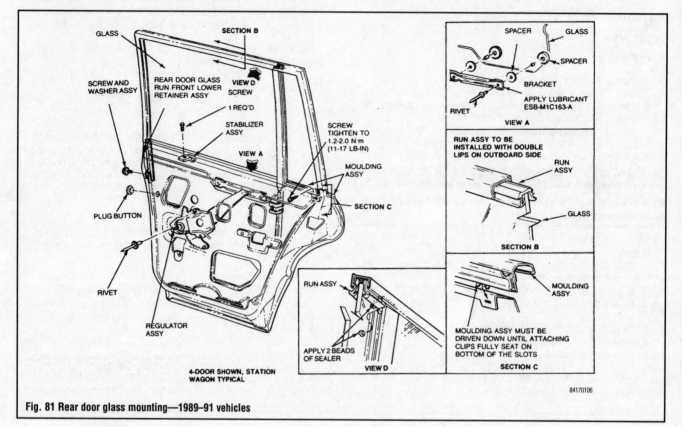

Fig. 81 Rear door glass mounting—1989–91 vehicles

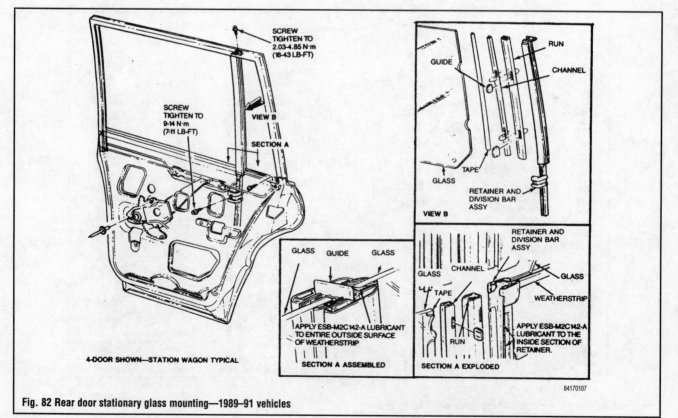

Fig. 82 Rear door stationary glass mounting—1989–91 vehicles

13. Preassemble fixed rear window glass and weather-strip and install firmly into the rear of the door frame.

14. Set the main glass and retainer and division bar into position and install the top screw and washer assembly. Make sure that the sealer at the screw head covers the hole for a tight seal.

15. Install the loose 6 in. of run assembly into the door frame and division bar. Install the remaining flocked run into the frame.

16. Install the retainer and division bar retaining screw.

17. Install the window glass inner stabilizer assembly with the retaining screw.

18. Install 2 glass-to-glass bracket rivets or use ¼ in.-20 **x** 1 bolts and nuts.

19. Install the retainer assembly rear door glass. Run the front lower (front guide) with the upper bracket locked into the frame and loosely attach the bottom bracket to the front face of the door (hinge face) with the screw and washer assembly. Install the flocked run into the front guide. Lower the glass to make sure there is no binding. Tighten the screw and washer assembly.

20. Install the door watershield and trim panel.

1992–98 Vehicles

♦ **See Figures 83 and 84**

1. Remove the door trim panel and watershield.

2. Loosen the glass run retainer retaining screw and position the retainer forward.

3. Lower the glass to gain access to the 2 glass bracket rivets.

4. Position a suitable block support between the door outer panel and the glass bracket to stabilize the glass during rivet removal.

5. Remove the center pins from the rivets using a drift punch. Drill out the remainder of the rivets using a ¼ in. diameter drill.

✳✳ WARNING

Do not attempt to pry out the rivets as damage to the glass could result.

6. Remove the glass.

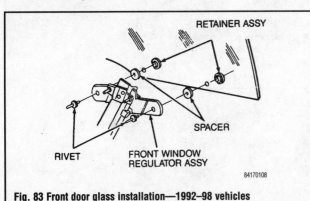

Fig. 83 Front door glass installation—1992–98 vehicles

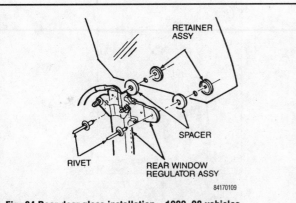

Fig. 84 Rear door glass installation—1992–98 vehicles

To install:

7. Insert the glass into the door between the outer belt weather-strip and inner panel.

8. Position the glass into the door frame and lower the window to align with the regulator bracket.

9. Install two ¼ in. blind rivets. Two ¼-20 **x** 1 in. screw, washer and nut assemblies can also be used. Tighten the screws to no more than 7–10 ft. lbs. (9–14 Nm).

10. Adjust the door glass as follows:

   a. Loosen, but do not remove, the upper regulator retaining nuts.

   b. Raise the glass to the full-up position and tighten the nuts to 7–10 ft. lbs. (9–14 Nm).

   c. Loosen, but do not remove, the front glass run retainer bolt.

   d. Lower the glass to the full down position and tighten the run retainer bolt to 7–10 ft. lbs. (9–14 Nm).

11. Install the door trim panel and watershield.

Door Window Regulator

REMOVAL & INSTALLATION

1989–91 Vehicles

FRONT DOOR

1. Remove the door trim panel and watershield.

2. Support the glass in the full-up position.

3. Detach the power window motor wiring connector, if equipped.

4. Remove the center pin from the regulator retaining rivets (3 rivets on manual window, 4 rivets on power window) with a drift punch. Using a ¼ in. diameter drill, drill out the remainder of the rivet, being careful not to enlarge the sheet metal retaining holes.

✳✳ CAUTION

If the regulator counterbalance spring must be removed or replaced for any reason, make sure that the regulator arms are in a fixed position prior to removal to prevent possible injury during C-spring unwind.

5. Disengage the regulator arm slide from the glass bracket C-channel and remove the regulator from the door.

To install:

6. Position the regulator in the door and insert the square slide into the glass bracket C-channel.

7. Position the regulator to the retaining holes in the door inner panel. Install 3 (manual window) or 4 (power window) ¼ in. blind rivets. Three (manual window) or 4 (power window) ¼ in.-20 **x** ½ in. screw and washer assemblies and ¼ in.-20 nut and washer assemblies can also be used.

8. Attach the power window wiring connector, if equipped.

9. Cycle the regulator to check for proper operation.

10. Install the door trim panel and watershield.

REAR DOOR

1. Remove the door trim panel and watershield.

2. Remove the 3 retaining rivets (manual) or 4 rivets (power). Remove the center pin from the rivets with a drift punch. Drill out the head of the rivet using a ¼ in. diameter drill. Be careful not to enlarge the sheet metal holes during drilling.

3. Remove the regulator arm roller from the glass bracket channel and remove the regulator from the door.

To install:

4. Lubricate the window regulator rollers, shafts and the entire length of the roller guides with multi-purpose grease.

5. Install the regulator into the access hole in the inner panel.

6. Position the regulator arm roller into the glass bracket channel.

7. Install the rivets attaching the regulator to the door inner panel. Three (manual window) or 4 (power window) ¼ in.-20 **x** ½ in. screw and washer assemblies and ¼ in.-20 nut and washer assemblies can also be used.

8. Install the watershield and door trim panel.

1992–98 Vehicles

▶ **See Figure 85**

OPERATIONAL WINDOW

1. Remove the door trim panel and watershield.
2. Remove the door glass.
3. Detach the power window motor wiring connector.
4. Remove the two ¼ in. rivets attaching the lower bracket of the regulator to the inner panel. Use a drift punch to knock out the center pins, then drill out the remainder of the rivet with a ¼ in. diameter drill. Be careful not to enlarge the sheet metal holes in the door inner panel.
5. Remove the 3 motor retaining screws from inside the door to remove the motor from the bracket assembly.
6. Remove the 2 upper regulator retaining nuts and remove the regulator from the door.

To install:

7. Apply an even coating of multi-purpose grease to the window regulator rollers, shafts and the entire length of the roller guides.
8. Install the regulator into the access hole in the inner panel.
9. Position the regulator using the upper regulator studs and tabs on the motor mounting bracket.

10. Install the rivets attaching the regulator to the door inner panel. Two ¼ in.-20 x ½ in. screw and washer assemblies and ¼ in.-20 nut and washer assemblies can also be used.
11. Install the 2 upper regulator retaining nuts. Install the motor, being careful not to overtighten the screws.
12. Install and adjust the door glass.
13. Install the watershield and door trim panel.

DOWN AND INOPERABLE WINDOW

1. Disconnect the negative battery cable.
2. Remove the door trim panel and watershield.
3. Remove the motor retaining screws through the holes.

❋❋ WARNING

Be careful not to strike or scratch the glass, as it could break.

4. Remove the motor assembly from the drum housing.
5. Raise the glass to the full-up position by hand and secure with a clamp.
6. Remove the regulator as outlined in the previous procedure.

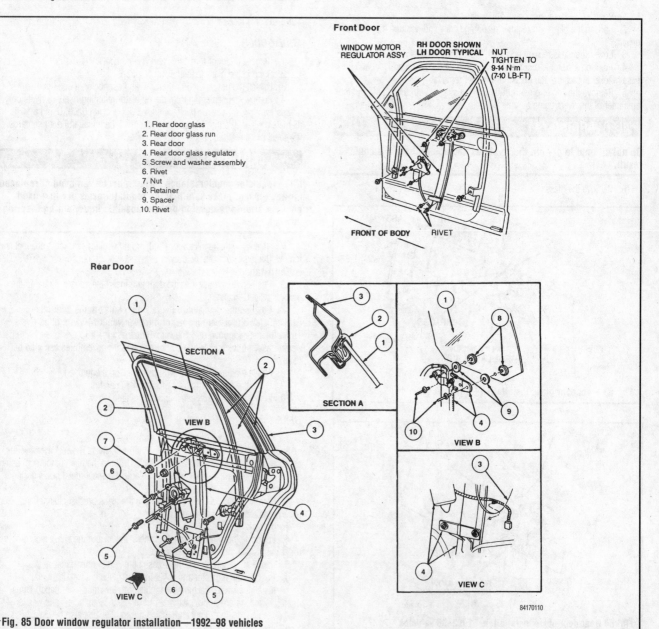

1. Rear door glass
2. Rear door glass run
3. Rear door
4. Rear door glass regulator
5. Screw and washer assembly
6. Rivet
7. Nut
8. Retainer
9. Spacer
10. Rivet

Front Door

WINDOW MOTOR REGULATOR ASSY
RH DOOR SHOWN LH DOOR TYPICAL
NUT TIGHTEN TO 9-14 N·m (7-10 LB-FT)

FRONT OF BODY   RIVET

Rear Door

SECTION A
VIEW B
VIEW C

SECTION A

VIEW B

VIEW C

84170110

Fig. 85 Door window regulator installation—1992–98 vehicles

To install:

7. Install the regulator as described in the previous procedure.

8. Assemble the motor drive assembly to the drum housing. Align the mounting holes in the motor with the holes in the drum housing.

9. Align the motor drive assembly to the mounting bracket.

10. Install the 3 retaining screws to the mounting bracket.

11. Connect the motor wire to the harness.

12. Connect the negative battery cable.

13. Remove the clamp and check window operation.

14. Install the watershield and door trim panel.

Power Window Motor

REMOVAL & INSTALLATION

1989–91 Vehicles

▶ **See Figures 86 and 87**

1. Open the door and raise the window to the full-up position, if possible.

2. Disconnect the negative battery cable.

3. Remove the door trim panel and watershield.

4. Disconnect the power window motor wiring.

5. Check inside the door to make sure that electrical wires are not in-line of the holes to be drilled. Using a ½ in. drill bit, drill three ½ in. diameter holes in the door inner panel. Use the drill dimples in the door panel to locate the holes.

✴ CAUTION

Prior to motor assembly removal, make sure that the regulator arm is in a fixed position to prevent counterbalance spring unwind.

6. Remove the 3 window motor mounting bolts.

7. Push the motor toward the outside sheet metal to disengage the motor assembly from the regulator gear. If the window is down, push against the motor with a suitable tool through the drilled access holes. After the motor is disengaged, pull the window up.

8. Remove the motor from inside the door.

To install:

9. Position the motor and drive to the regulator and install the 3 screws snug—not tight.

10. Install the plug button in the lower access hole drilled into the door and paint body color. This hole will not be covered up by the door trim panel. Install 2 pieces of pressure sensitive waterproof tape approximately 1 in. square to seal the upper access holes covered by the door trim panel.

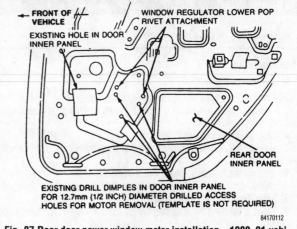

Fig. 87 Rear door power window motor installation—1989–91 vehicles

11. Attach the motor wires at the connector and cycle the glass to ensure gear engagement. After the gears are engaged, tighten the 3 motor and drive retaining screws.

12. Install the watershield and door trim panel.

13. Connect the negative battery cable.

14. Check the window for proper operation.

➡ **Make sure that all drain holes at the bottom of the doors are open to prevent water accumulation over the motors.**

1992–98 Vehicles

1. Disconnect the negative battery cable.

2. Remove the door trim panel and watershield.

3. Detach the motor wires at the multiple connector.

4. Remove the motor retaining screws using Torx® drive bit set D79P–2100–T or equivalent, and separate the motor from the bracket and cable drum housing.

5. Remove the motor from inside the door.

To install:

6. Position the motor and drive to the cable drum housing and motor mounting bracket. Install the 3 motor screws and tighten.

7. Connect the power window motor wiring.

8. Connect the negative battery cable.

9. Check window operation.

10. Install the watershield and door trim panel.

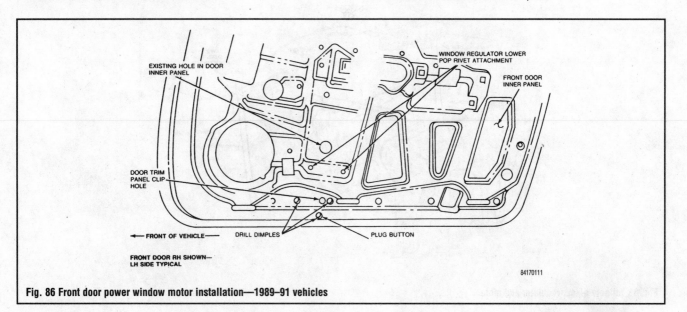

Fig. 86 Front door power window motor installation—1989–91 vehicles

Tailgate Window Motor

REMOVAL & INSTALLATION

▶ **See Figure 88**

1. Remove the tailgate trim panel and watershield.
2. Remove the tailgate inner panel lower access cover.
3. Lower the tailgate to the DOWN position and raise the glass until the glass brackets are accessible.
4. Disconnect the negative battery cable.
5. Remove the center pin from the glass-to-glass bracket rivets with a drift punch.
6. Drill the heads from the rivets with a ¼ in. drill and remove the rivets.
7. Disconnect the wires from the rear window defroster terminals, if equipped.
8. Slide the glass from the tailgate.
9. Remove the glass brackets from the regulator arm rollers and equalizer bracket.
10. Detach the motor wires at the connector.
11. Remove both run assemblies.
12. Remove the 4 regulator attaching rivets and remove the regulator from the tailgate.
13. Drill a ⁵⁄₁₆ in. hole through the regulator sector gear and regulator plate.
14. Install a ¼ in. bolt and nut through the hole to prevent the sector gear from moving when the motor and drive assembly is removed from the regulator.
15. Remove the motor and drive from the regulator.

To install:

16. Install the motor and drive to the regulator.
17. Position the regulator in the tailgate and install ¼ in. blind rivets or ¼ in.-20 **x** 1 in. bolts and ¼ in.-20 nuts.
18. Install both run assemblies to the tailgate.
19. Attach the motor wires at the connector.
20. Install the glass brackets on the regulator arm rollers and equalizer bracket.
21. Position the glass into the tailgate and glass brackets. Make sure the spacers are placed between the glass and the glass bracket.

22. Install ¼ in.-20 **x** 1 in. bolts and ¼ in.-20 nuts or blind rivets to attach the glass bracket to the glass.
23. Adjust the glass as follows:
   a. Full-up position: The glass should be properly positioned within the glass opening to ensure a good seal with the weather-strip. The top edge of the glass should be parallel to the top of the glass opening when the glass is closed. To adjust, loosen each upper stop bracket attaching nut and check the glass fit. If the glass does not fit properly, loosen the equalizer bracket nuts and move the glass until the top edge of the glass is parallel to the glass opening. Tighten the equalizer bracket nuts. After the glass has been positioned in the opening, move the upper stop brackets down firmly against the stops and tighten the attaching nuts.
   b. Side-to-side position: Loosen the 2 lower left-hand guide-to-bracket attaching screws. Move the glass from side-to-side as necessary to obtain a good glass overlap with the weather-strip on each side of the glass. Tighten the guide attaching screws after adjustment.
   c. In and out tilt: The top edge of the glass can be tilted in or out to obtain a good seal against the weather-strip. To adjust, loosen the guide-to-bracket and lower run attaching screws. Move the run in or out as necessary to move the glass top edge against the weather-strip to obtain a good seal. Tighten the attaching screws after a good seal is obtained.
24. Connect the negative battery cable.
25. Connect the wires to the rear window defroster terminals, if equipped.
26. Install the tailgate inner panel lower access cover and the watershield and tailgate trim panel.

Windshield and Fixed Glass

REMOVAL & INSTALLATION

If your windshield, or other fixed window, is cracked or chipped, you may decide to replace it with a new one yourself. However, there are two main reasons why replacement windshields and other window glass should be installed only by a professional automotive glass technician: safety and cost.

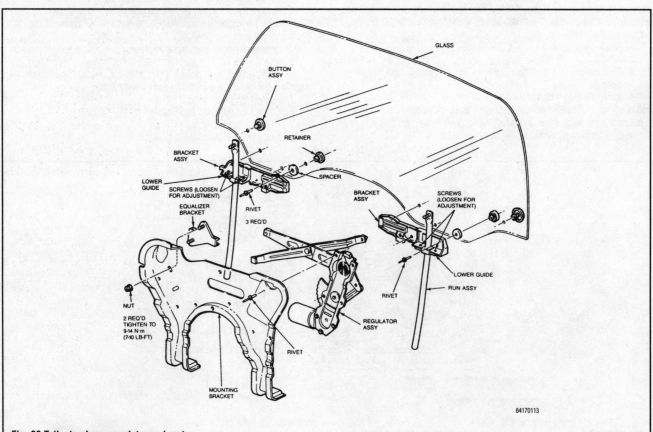

Fig. 88 Tailgate glass, regulator and motor

The most important reason a professional should install automotive glass is for safety. The glass in the vehicle, especially the windshield, is designed with safety in mind in case of a collision. The windshield is specially manufactured from two panes of specially-tempered glass with a thin layer of transparent plastic between them. This construction allows the glass to "give" in the event that a part of your body hits the windshield during the collision, and prevents the glass from shattering, which could cause lacerations, blinding and other harm to passengers of the vehicle. The other fixed windows are designed to be tempered so that if they break during a collision, they shatter in such a way that there are no large pointed glass pieces. The professional automotive glass technician knows how to install the glass in a vehicle so that it will function optimally during a collision. Without the proper experience, knowledge and tools, installing a piece of automotive glass yourself could lead to additional harm if an accident should ever occur.

Cost is also a factor when deciding to install automotive glass yourself. Performing this could cost you much more than a professional may charge for the same job. Since the windshield is designed to break under stress, an often life saving characteristic, windshields tend to break VERY easily when an inexperienced person attempts to install one. Do-it-yourselfers buying two, three or even four windshields from a salvage yard because they have broken them during installation are common stories. Also, since the automotive glass is designed to prevent the outside elements from entering your vehicle, improper installation can lead to water and air leaks. Annoying whining noises at highway speeds from air leaks or inside body panel rusting from water leaks can add to your stress level and subtract from your wallet. After buying two or three windshields, installing them and ending up with a leak that produces a noise while driving and water damage during rainstorms, the cost of having a professional do it correctly the first time may be much more alluring. We here at Chilton, therefore, advise that you have a professional automotive glass technician service any broken glass on your vehicle.

WINDSHIELD CHIP REPAIR

▶ **See Figures 89 thru 103**

➡**Check with your state and local authorities on the laws for state safety inspection. Some states or municipalities may not allow chip repair as a viable option for correcting stone damage to your windshield.**

Fig. 89 Small chips on your windshield can be fixed with an aftermarket repair kit, such as the one from Loctite

Fig. 90 To repair a chip, clean the windshield with glass cleaner and dry it completely

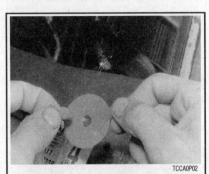
Fig. 91 Remove the center from the adhesive disc and peel off the backing from one side of the disc . . .

Fig. 92 . . . then press it on the windshield so that the chip is centered in the hole

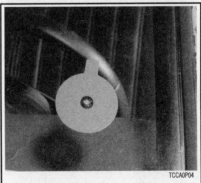
Fig. 93 Be sure that the tab points upward on the windshield

Fig. 94 Peel the backing off the exposed side of the adhesive disc . . .

Fig. 95 . . . then position the plastic pedestal on the adhesive disc, ensuring that the tabs are aligned

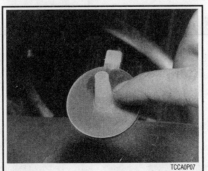
Fig. 96 Press the pedestal firmly on the adhesive disc to create an adequate seal . . .

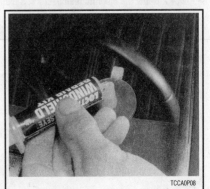
Fig. 97 . . . then install the applicator syringe nipple in the pedestal's hole

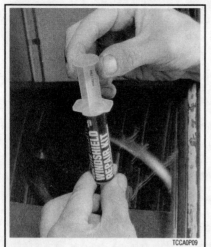

Fig. 98 Hold the syringe with one hand while pulling the plunger back with the other hand

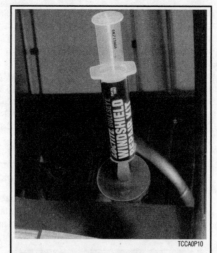

Fig. 99 After applying the solution, allow the entire assembly to sit until it has set completely

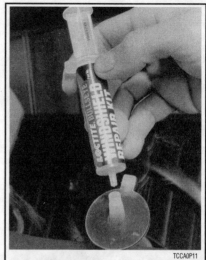

Fig. 100 After the solution has set, remove the syringe from the pedestal . . .

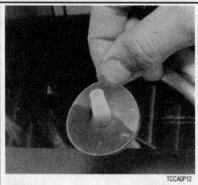

Fig. 101 . . . then peel the pedestal off of the adhesive disc . . .

Fig. 102 . . . and peel the adhesive disc off of the windshield

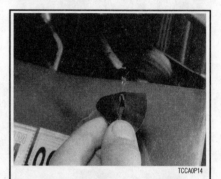

Fig. 103 The chip will still be slightly visible, but it should be filled with the hardened solution

Although severely cracked or damaged windshields must be replaced, there is something that you can do to prolong or even prevent the need for replacement of a chipped windshield. There are many companies which offer windshield chip repair products, such as Loctite's® Bullseye¬ windshield repair kit. These kits usually consist of a syringe, pedestal and a sealing adhesive. The syringe is mounted on the pedestal and is used to create a vacuum which pulls the plastic layer against the glass. This helps make the chip transparent. The adhesive is then injected which seals the chip and helps to prevent further stress cracks from developing. Refer to the sequence of photos to get a general idea of what windshield chip repair involves.

➡Always follow the specific manufacturer's instructions.

Inside Rear View Mirror

REMOVAL & INSTALLATION

Mirror

1989–91 VEHICLES

▸ See Figure 104

1. Loosen the mirror-to-mounting bracket setscrew.
2. Remove the mirror by sliding upward and away from the mounting bracket.
3. Installation is the reverse of the removal procedure.

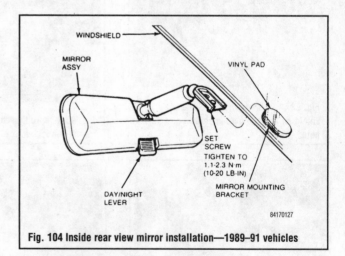

Fig. 104 Inside rear view mirror installation—1989–91 vehicles

1992 VEHICLES

1. Insert a small, flat screwdriver into the slot until the spring is contacted.
2. Remove the mirror by pushing on the spring with the screwdriver while sliding the mirror upward and away from the mounting bracket.
3. Installation is the reverse of the removal procedure.

1993–98 VEHICLES

♦ See Figure 105

1. While firmly holding the mirror, insert inside mirror removal tool T91T–17700–A or equivalent, into the slot until the button is contacted.

2. Remove the mirror by pushing the mirror upward and away from the mounting bracket.

3. Installation is the reverse of the removal procedure.

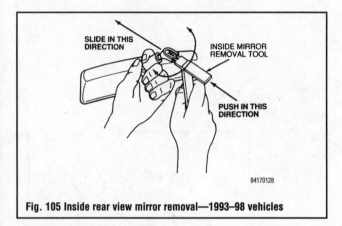

Fig. 105 Inside rear view mirror removal—1993–98 vehicles

Mirror Mounting Bracket

➡ **It will be necessary to obtain rear view mirror adhesive kit D9AZ–19554–CA or equivalent, for the following procedure.**

1. If the bracket vinyl pad remains on the windshield, apply low heat from a suitable heat gun until the vinyl softens. Peel the vinyl off the windshield and discard.

To install:

2. Make sure the glass, bracket and rear view mirror adhesive kit are at least at room temperature, 65–75°F (18.3–23.9°C).

3. Locate and mark the mirror mounting bracket location on the outside surface of the windshield.

4. Thoroughly clean the bonding surfaces of the glass and bracket to remove old adhesive. Use mild abrasive cleaner on the glass and fine sandpaper on the bracket to lightly roughen the surface. Wipe clean with an alcohol moistened cloth.

5. Crush the accelerator vial (part of the rear view mirror adhesive kit) and apply the accelerator to the bonding surface of the bracket and windshield. Let dry for 3 minutes.

6. Apply 2 drops of rear view mirror adhesive to the mounting surface of the bracket. Using a clean toothpick or wooden match, quickly spread the adhesive evenly over the mounting surface of the bracket.

7. Quickly position the mounting bracket on the windshield. The ⅜ in. (9.5mm) circular depression in the bracket must be toward the bottom edge and toward the inside of the passenger compartment. Press the bracket firmly against the windshield for one minute.

8. Allow the bond to set for 5 minutes.

9. Remove any excess bonding material from the windshield with an alcohol dampened cloth.

Seats

REMOVAL & INSTALLATION

Front

MANUAL SEAT

♦ See Figures 106, 107 and 108

1. Remove the insulator retaining rivets, if equipped, and the insulators from the front and rear of the seat tracks.

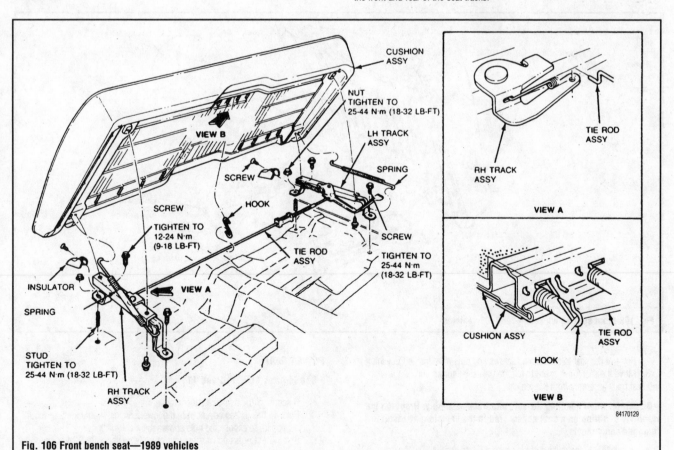

Fig. 106 Front bench seat—1989 vehicles

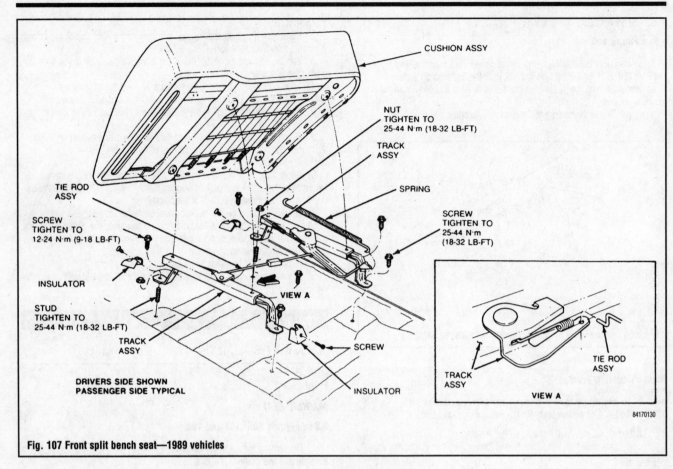

Fig. 107 Front split bench seat—1989 vehicles

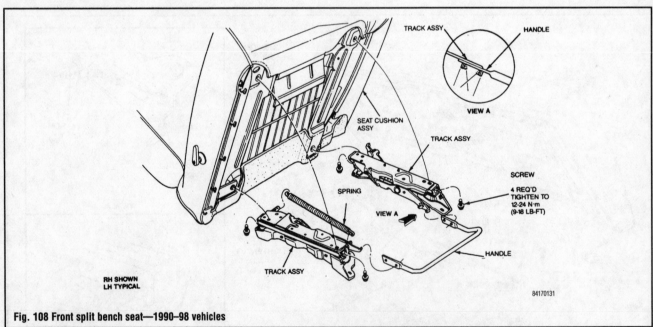

Fig. 108 Front split bench seat—1990–98 vehicles

2. Remove the seat track retaining screws and nuts from inside the vehicle.

3. Move the seat full-forward to release the assist spring and lift the seat and seat track assembly from the vehicle.

➠**Be careful when handling the seat and track assembly. Dropping the assembly or sitting on a seat not secured in the vehicle may result in damaged components.**

4. Installation is the reverse of the removal procedure.

POWER SEAT

▶ **See Figures 109, 110 and 111**

1. Disconnect the negative battery cable.

2. Remove the access covers from the lower shields, if equipped, or insulators, if equipped, to expose the nuts and washers and/or bolts.

3. Remove the nuts and washers and/or bolts retaining the seat track to the floorpan.

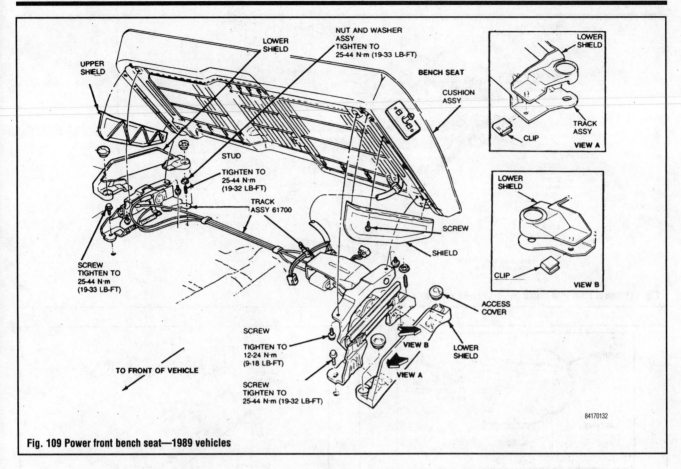

Fig. 109 Power front bench seat—1989 vehicles

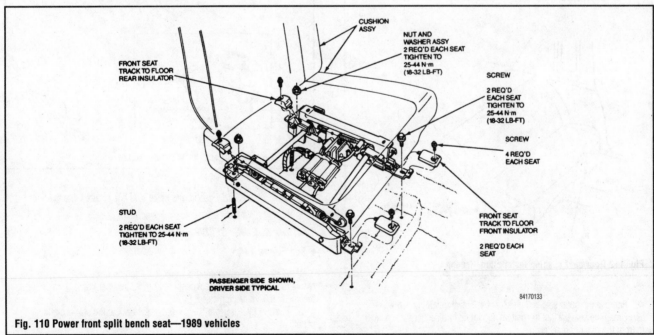

Fig. 110 Power front split bench seat—1989 vehicles

4. Lift the seat up enough to access the seat harness connector and detach the connector.

5. On 1989 vehicles, remove the bolt(s) attaching the seat belts to the floor.

6. Remove the seat and track assembly from the vehicle.

7. Installation is the reverse of the removal procedure.

Rear

SEDAN

♦ See Figures 112 and 113

1. Apply knee pressure to the lower front portion of the rear seat cushion. Push rearward to disengage the seat cushion from the retainer brackets.

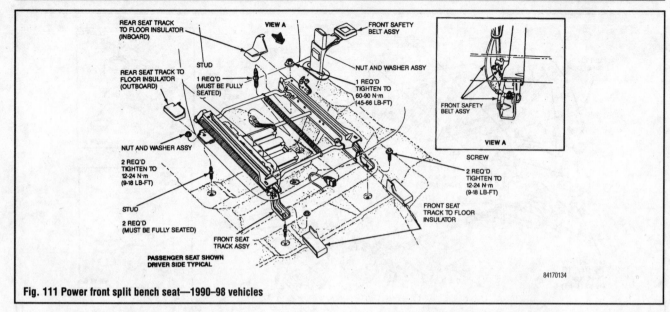

Fig. 111 Power front split bench seat—1990–98 vehicles

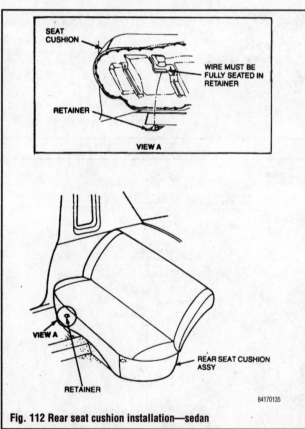

Fig. 112 Rear seat cushion installation—sedan

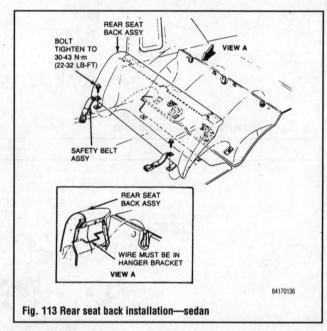

Fig. 113 Rear seat back installation—sedan

9. Check the rear seat cushion to make sure it is secured into the floor retainer.

STATION WAGON—SECOND SEAT

▶ See Figure 114

1. Apply knee pressure to the lower front portion of the seat cushion. Push rearward to disengage the seat cushion from the retainer brackets and remove the cushion from the vehicle.
2. Remove the 3 screws attaching the seat back to the seat back floor panel.
3. Pull the bottom of the seat back forward and lift the seat back off the seat back floor panel.

To install:

4. Position the seat back to the seat back floor panel and secure with the attaching screws.
5. Position the seat cushion into the vehicle.
6. Apply knee pressure to the lower portion of the seat cushion, pushing rearward and down to lock the cushion into position.
7. Check the seat cushion to make sure it is secured into the floor retainer.

2. Remove the outer seat belt and seat back lower retaining screws.
3. Grasp the seat back at the bottom and lift up to disengage the hanger wire from the retainer brackets.
4. Remove the seat back from the vehicle.

To install:

5. Position the seat back into the vehicle so that the hanger wire is engaged with the retaining brackets.
6. Install the outer seat belt and seat back lower retainer screws. Tighten to 22–32 ft. lbs. (30–43 Nm).
7. Position the seat cushion into the vehicle.
8. Apply knee pressure to the lower portion of the seat cushion, pushing rearward and down to lock the cushion into position.

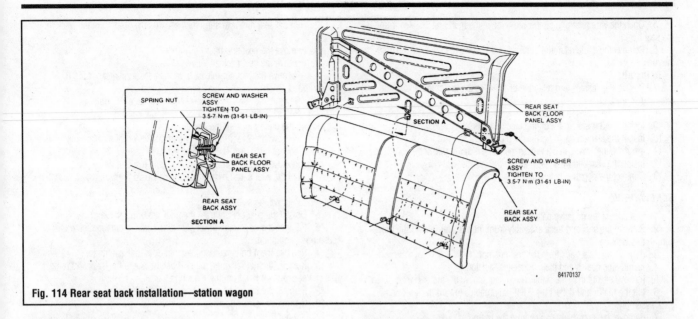

Fig. 114 Rear seat back installation—station wagon

STATION WAGON—AUXILIARY SEAT

▶ See Figure 115

1. Remove the 2 lower retaining screws securing the rear seat back to the folding floor.
2. Lift up and disengage the upper clips of the rear seat back from the top of the folding floor.
3. Disengage the seat cushion latch and remove the seat cushion from the vehicle.

To install:

4. Position the rear seat cushion into the vehicle and engage the seat cushion pin and latch.
5. Center the seat back on the folding floor and push down, engaging the upper clips of the back to the top of the folding floor.
6. Install 2 screws at the lower edge of the auxiliary load floor panel and tighten to 7–10 ft. lbs. (9–14 Nm).

Power Seat Motor

REMOVAL & INSTALLATION

1989 Vehicles

➡ **1989 vehicles can be equipped with one of 2 types of power seat systems. One uses a rack and pinion drive, the other a screw-type drive.**

RACK AND PINION DRIVE

1. Disconnect the negative battery cable.
2. Remove the seat and track assembly from the vehicle; refer to the procedure in this Section.
3. Remove the 3 motor-to-mounting bracket attaching bolts.
4. Remove the clamps retaining the drive cables to the seat tracks.

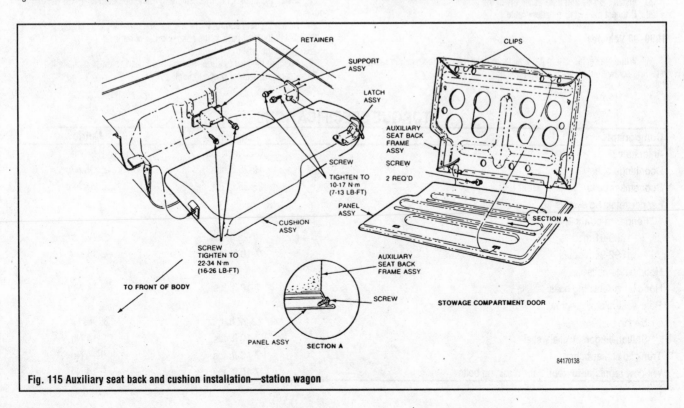

Fig. 115 Auxiliary seat back and cushion installation—station wagon

5. Open the wire retaining straps and remove the motor and cables from the seat track.

6. Remove the cable retaining brackets and remove the drive cables from the motor.

To install:

7. Position the cables and retaining brackets to the motor and install the retaining screws.

8. Position the cables to the seat tracks and the motor to the mounting bracket.

9. Install the 3 motor-to-mounting bracket bolts.

10. Install the clamps retaining the drive cables to the seat tracks.

11. Insert the motor wire in the wire straps and attach the wire at the connector.

12. Install the seat and track assembly in the vehicle.

13. Connect the negative battery cable.

SCREW DRIVE

1. Disconnect the negative battery cable.

2. Remove the seat and track assembly from the vehicle; refer to the procedure in this Section.

3. Remove the seat track from the seat cushion.

4. Identify the cables and their respective locations.

5. Remove the nut from the stabilizer rod and remove the motor bracket screw.

6. Lift the motor and deflect the 3 left-hand cables toward the left-hand track assembly.

7. Remove the 3 left-hand cables from the motor.

8. Move the motor along the stabilizer rod to the right, disengaging the right-hand cables.

9. Lift and slide the motor off of the stabilizer rod.

10. Remove the 2 locknuts retaining the motor to the mounting bracket.

To install:

11. Secure the motor to the mounting bracket using the 2 locknuts.

12. Insert the stabilizer rod through the motor and lower the motor into place.

13. Position the 3 left-hand drive cables to the motor.

14. Fully engage the square ends of the cables into the motor armature.

15. Align the right-hand drive cable ends with the motor armature.

16. With the 3 left-hand cables engaged in the motor, lift the motor and insert the right-hand cable into the motor, being sure to fully engage the square end of the cable into the motor armature.

17. Lower the motor into place.

18. Install the screw retaining the motor bracket to the seat track and tighten.

19. Install the nut retaining the motor to the stabilizer rod.

20. Install the seat and track assembly in the vehicle.

21. Connect the negative battery cable.

1990–98 Vehicles

1. While the seat is still in the vehicle, remove the rear Torx® head motor retaining screw from the track assembly.

2. Run the seat motor to align the gear with the notches in the track assembly.

3. Remove the seat and track assembly.

4. Remove the seat back as follows:

a. Remove the recliner release lever handle, bezel and spacer, if equipped.

b. Remove the seat back release knob and bezel, if equipped.

c. Pull back the rear outboard cushion trim cover at the carpet and remove the push pin from the frame.

d. Remove the 2 rear (one upper and one lower) hog rings to expose the lower recliner latch or 4-door recliner lock out plate.

e. Remove the 2 retaining bolts and cable retainer, if equipped.

f. Lift the seat back upward and pull outboard to disengage the center hinge.

g. Remove the seat back.

5. Detach the seat control from the track assembly at the connectors.

6. Remove the upper and lower shield(s) from the outboard side of the seat cushion, if equipped.

7. Remove the 4 bolts retaining each track to the seat frame.

8. Remove the nut retaining the seat belt buckle to the track and remove the center occupant belt from the mounting slot.

9. Remove the track and motor assembly from the seat.

10. Remove the assist springs.

11. Tap out the roll pins retaining the inner track assembly to the motor and outer track assembly.

12. Remove the 2 motor retaining nuts and remaining Torx® head screw.

13. Carefully separate the motor from the seat track assembly.

14. Remove the drive cross shaft.

To install:

15. Position the motor to the seat track assembly. Make sure the guide is in place around the gear.

16. Install the motor retaining nuts and front Torx® head screw.

17. Assemble the inner track assembly and drive cross shaft to the outer track and motor assembly.

18. Install the roll pins. Make sure the tracks are aligned in proper position.

19. Install the assist springs.

20. Position the track and motor assembly to the seat cushion.

21. Install the 4 track-to-cushion retaining bolts.

22. Install the center occupant belt through the mounting slot and install the seat belt buckle and retaining nut to the track.

23. Install the upper and lower shield(s) to the outboard seat cushion, if equipped.

24. Attach the seat control to the track assembly at the connectors.

25. Install the seat back in the reverse order of removal.

26. Install the seat in the vehicle.

27. Position the seat to allow the rear Torx® head screw to be installed.

28. Check the seat for proper operation.

TORQUE SPECIFICATIONS

Components	English	Metric
Antenna nut	50-70 inch lbs.	6-8 Nm
Door hinge bolts	19-25 ft. lbs.	25-35 Nm
Door striker bolts	25-32 ft. lbs.	35-45 Nm
Fender retaining screws		
Fender-to-cowl panel		
1989-91 models	17-25 ft. lbs.	22-34 Nm
1992-98 models	7-10 ft. lbs.	9-14 Nm
Hood hinge bolts	18 ft. lbs.	24 Nm
Hood latch retaining bolts	7-10 ft. lbs.	9-14 Nm
Rear seat retaining screws		
Sedan	22-32 ft. lbs.	30-43 Nm
Station wagon auxiliary seat	7-10 ft. lbs.	9-14 Nm
Trunk lid striker bolts	7-10 ft. lbs.	9-14 Nm
Window regulator-to-door glass retaining bolts	7-10 ft. lbs.	9-14 Nm

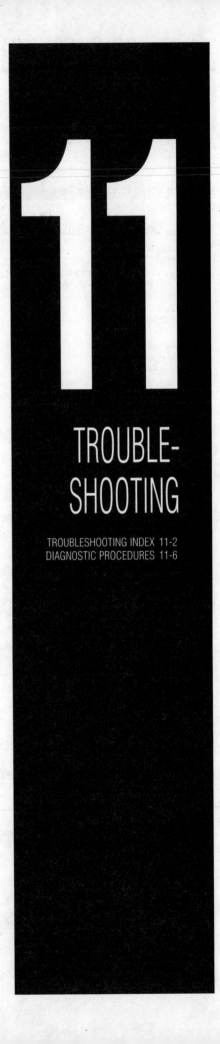

11

TROUBLE-SHOOTING

Condition   **Section/Item Number**

The following troubleshooting charts are divided into 7 sections covering engine, drive train, brakes, wheels/tires/steering/suspension, electrical accessories, instruments and gauges, and climate control. The first portion (or index) consists of a list of symptoms, along with section and item numbers. After selecting the appropriate condition, refer to the corresponding diagnostic procedure in the second portion's specified location.

INDEX

SECTION 1. ENGINE

A. Engine Starting Problems

Gasoline Engines

Engine turns over, but will not start	1-A, 1
Engine does not turn over when attempting to start	1-A, 2
Engine stalls immediately when started	1-A, 3
Starter motor spins, but does not engage	1-A, 4
Engine is difficult to start when cold	1-A, 5
Engine is difficult to start when hot	1-A, 6

Diesel Engines

Engine turns over but won't start	1-A, 1
Engine does not turn over when attempting to start	1-A, 2
Engine stalls after starting	1-A, 3
Starter motor spins, but does not engage	1-A, 4
Engine is difficult to start	1-A, 5

B. Engine Running Conditions

Gasoline Engines

Engine runs poorly, hesitates	1-B, 1
Engine lacks power	1-B, 2
Engine has poor fuel economy	1-B, 3
Engine runs on (diesels) when turned off	1-B, 4
Engine knocks and pings during heavy acceleration, and on steep hills	1-B, 5
Engine accelerates but vehicle does not gain speed	1-B, 6

Diesel Engines

Engine runs poorly	1-B, 1
Engine lacks power	1-B, 2

C. Engine Noises, Odors and Vibrations

Engine makes a knocking or pinging noise when accelerating	1-C, 1
Starter motor grinds when used	1-C, 2
Engine makes a screeching noise	1-C, 3
Engine makes a growling noise	1-C, 4
Engine makes a ticking or tapping noise	1-C, 5
Engine makes a heavy knocking noise	1-C, 6
Vehicle has a fuel odor when driven	1-C, 7
Vehicle has a rotten egg odor when driven	1-C, 8
Vehicle has a sweet odor when driven	1-C, 9
Engine vibrates when idling	1-C, 10
Engine vibrates during acceleration	1-C, 11

D. Engine Electrical System

Battery goes dead while driving	1-D, 1
Battery goes dead overnight	1-D, 2

E. Engine Cooling System

Engine overheats	1-E, 1
Engine loses coolant	1-E, 2
Engine temperature remains cold when driving	1-E, 3
Engine runs hot	1-E, 4

F. Engine Exhaust System

Exhaust rattles at idle speed	1-F, 1
Exhaust system vibrates when driving	1-F, 2
Exhaust system seems too low	1-F, 3
Exhaust seems loud	1-F, 4

Condition	Section/Item Number

SECTION 2. DRIVE TRAIN

A. Automatic Transmission

Transmission shifts erratically	2-A, 1
Transmission will not engage	2-A, 2
Transmission will not downshift during heavy acceleration	2-A, 3

B. Manual Transmission

Transmission grinds going into forward gears while driving	2-B, 1; 2-C, 2
Transmission jumps out of gear	2-B, 2
Transmission difficult to shift	2-B, 3; 2-C, 2
Transmission leaks fluid	2-B, 4

C. Clutch

Clutch slips on hills or during sudden acceleration	2-C, 1
Clutch will not disengage, difficult to shift	2-C, 2
Clutch is noisy when the clutch pedal is pressed	2-C, 3
Clutch pedal extremely difficult to press	2-C, 4
Clutch pedal remains down when pressed	2-C, 5
Clutch chatters when engaging	2-C, 6

D. Differential and Final Drive

Differential makes a low pitched rumbling noise	2-D, 1
Differential makes a howling noise	2-D, 2

E. Transfer Assembly

All Wheel and Four Wheel Drive Vehicles

Leaks fluid from seals or vent after being driven	2-E, 1
Makes excessive noise while driving	2-E, 2
Jumps out of gear	2-E, 3

F. Driveshaft

Rear Wheel, All Wheel and Four Wheel Drive Vehicles

Clunking noise from center of vehicle shifting from forward to reverse	2-F, 1
Excessive vibration from center of vehicle when accelerating	2-F, 2

G. Axles

All Wheel and Four Wheel Drive Vehicles

Front or rear wheel makes a clicking noise	2-G, 1
Front or Rear wheel vibrates with increased speed	2-G, 2

Front Wheel Drive Vehicles

Front wheel makes a clicking noise	2-G, 3
Rear wheel makes a clicking noise	2-G, 4

Rear Wheel Drive Vehicles

Front or rear wheel makes a clicking noise	2-G, 5
Rear wheel shudders or vibrates	2-G, 6

H. Other Drive Train Conditions

Burning odor from center of vehicle when accelerating	2-H, 1; 2-C, 1; 3-A, 9
Engine accelerates, but vehicle does not gain speed	2-H, 2; 2-C, 1; 3-A, 9

SECTION 3. BRAKE SYSTEM

Brakes pedal pulsates or shimmies when pressed	3-A, 1
Brakes make a squealing noise	3-A, 2
Brakes make a grinding noise	3-A, 3
Vehicle pulls to one side during braking	3-A, 4
Brake pedal feels spongy or has excessive brake pedal travel	3-A, 5
Brake pedal feel is firm, but brakes lack sufficient stopping power or fade	3-A, 6

Condition	Section/Item Number
Vehicle has excessive front end dive or locks rear brakes too easily	3-A, 7
Brake pedal goes to floor when pressed and will not pump up	3-A, 8
Brakes make a burning odor	3-A, 9

SECTION 4. WHEELS, TIRES, STEERING AND SUSPENSION

A. Wheels and Wheel Bearings

All Wheel and Four Wheel Drive Vehicles
Front wheel or wheel bearing loose — 4-A, 1
Rear wheel or wheel bearing loose — 4-A, 2

Front Wheel Drive Vehicles
Front wheel or wheel bearing loose — 4-A, 1
Rear wheel or wheel bearing loose — 4-A, 2

Rear Wheel Drive Vehicles
Front wheel or wheel bearing loose — 4-A, 1
Rear wheel or wheel bearing loose — 4-A, 2

B. Tires

Tires worn on inside tread — 4-B, 1
Tires worn on outside tread — 4-B, 2
Tires worn unevenly — 4-B, 3

C. Steering

Excessive play in steering wheel — 4-C, 1
Steering wheel shakes at cruising speeds — 4-C, 2
Steering wheel shakes when braking — 3-A, 1
Steering wheel becomes stiff when turned — 4-C, 4

D. Suspension

Vehicle pulls to one side — 4-D, 1
Vehicle is very bouncy over bumps — 4-D, 2
Vehicle seems to lean excessively in turns — 4-D, 3
Vehicle ride quality seems excessively harsh — 4-D, 4
Vehicle seems low or leans to one side — 4-D, 5

E. Driving Noises and Vibrations

Noises
Vehicle makes a clicking noise when driven — 4-E, 1
Vehicle makes a clunking or knocking noise over bumps — 4-E, 2
Vehicle makes a low pitched rumbling noise when driven — 4-E, 3
Vehicle makes a squeaking noise over bumps — 4-E, 4

Vibrations
Vehicle vibrates when driven — 4-E, 5

SECTION 5. ELECTRICAL ACCESSORIES

A. Headlights

One headlight only works on high or low beam — 5-A, 1
Headlight does not work on high or low beam — 5-A, 2
Headlight(s) very dim — 5-A, 3

B. Tail, Running and Side Marker Lights

Tail light, running light or side marker light inoperative — 5-B, 1
Tail light, running light or side marker light works intermittently — 5-B, 2
Tail light, running light or side marker light very dim — 5-B, 3

C. Interior Lights

Interior light inoperative — 5-C, 1
Interior light works intermittently — 5-C, 2
Interior light very dim — 5-C, 3

Condition	Section/Item Number

D. Brake Lights

One brake light inoperative	5-D, 1
Both brake lights inoperative	5-D, 2
One or both brake lights very dim	5-D, 3

E. Warning Lights

Ignition, Battery and Alternator Warning Lights, Check Engine Light, Anti-Lock Braking System (ABS) Light, Brake Warning Light, Oil Pressure Warning Light, and Parking Brake Warning Light

Warning light(s) remains on after the engine is started	5-E, 1
Warning light(s) flickers on and off when driving	5-E, 2
Warning light(s) inoperative with ignition on, and engine not started	5-E, 3

F. Turn Signal and 4-Way Hazard Lights

Turn signals or hazard lights come on, but do not flash	5-F, 1
Turn signals or hazard lights do not function on either side	5-F, 2
Turn signals or hazard lights only work on one side	5-F, 3
One signal light does not work	5-F, 4
Turn signals flash too slowly	5-F, 5
Turn signals flash too fast	5-F, 6
Four-way hazard flasher indicator light inoperative	5-F, 7
Turn signal indicator light(s) do not work in either direction	5-F, 8
One turn signal indicator light does not work	5-F, 9

G. Horn

Horn does not operate	5-G, 1
Horn has an unusual tone	5-G, 2

H. Windshield Wipers

Windshield wipers do not operate	5-H, 1
Windshield wiper motor makes a humming noise, gets hot or blows fuses	5-H, 2
Windshield wiper motor operates but one or both wipers fail to move	5-H, 3
Windshield wipers will not park	5-H, 4

SECTION 6. INSTRUMENTS AND GAUGES

A. Speedometer (Cable Operated)

Speedometer does not work	6-A, 1
Speedometer needle fluctuates when driving at steady speeds	6-A, 2
Speedometer works intermittently	6-A, 3

B. Speedometer (Electronically Operated)

Speedometer does not work	6-B, 1
Speedometer works intermittently	6-B, 2

C. Fuel, Temperature and Oil Pressure Gauges

Gauge does not register	6-C, 1
Gauge operates erratically	6-C, 2
Gauge operates fully pegged	6-C, 3

SECTION 7. CLIMATE CONTROL

A. Air Conditioner

No air coming from air conditioner vents	7-A, 1
Air conditioner blows warm air	7-A, 2
Water collects on the interior floor when the air conditioner is used	7-A, 3
Air conditioner has a moldy odor when used	7-A, 4

B. Heater

Blower motor does not operate	7-B, 1
Heater blows cool air	7-B, 2
Heater steams the windshield when used	7-B, 3

1. ENGINE

1-A. Engine Starting Problems

Gasoline Engines

1. Engine turns over, but will not start
a. Check fuel level in fuel tank, add fuel if empty.
b. Check battery condition and state of charge. If voltage and load test below specification, charge or replace battery.
c. Check battery terminal and cable condition and tightness. Clean terminals and replace damaged, worn or corroded cables.
d. Check fuel delivery system. If fuel is not reaching the fuel injectors; check for a loose electrical connector or defective fuse, relay or fuel pump and replace as necessary.
e. Engine may have excessive wear or mechanical damage such as low cylinder cranking pressure, a broken camshaft drive system, insufficient valve clearance or bent valves.
f. Check for fuel contamination such as water in the fuel. During winter months, the water may freeze and cause a fuel restriction. Adding a fuel additive may help, however the fuel system may require draining and purging with fresh fuel.
g. Check for ignition system failure. Check for loose or shorted wires or damaged ignition system components. Check the spark plugs for excessive wear or incorrect electrode gap. If the problem is worse in wet weather, check for shorts between the spark plugs and the ignition coils.
h. Check the engine management system for a failed sensor or control module.

2. Engine does not turn over when attempting to start
a. Check the battery state of charge and condition. If the dash lights are not visible or very dim when turning the ignition key on, the battery has either failed internally or discharged, the battery cables are loose, excessively corroded or damaged, or the alternator has failed or internally shorted, discharging the battery. Charge or replace the battery, clean or replace the battery cables, and check the alternator output.
b. Check the operation of the neutral safety switch. On automatic transmission vehicles, try starting the vehicle in both Park and Neutral. On manual transmission vehicles, depress the clutch pedal and attempt to start. On some vehicles, these switches can be adjusted. Make sure the switches or wire connectors are not loose or damaged. Replace or adjust the switches as necessary.
c. Check the starter motor, starter solenoid or relay, and starter motor cables and wires. Check the ground from the engine to the chassis. Make sure the wires are not loose, damaged, or corroded. If battery voltage is present at the starter relay, try using a remote starter to start the vehicle for test purposes only. Replace any damaged or corroded cables, in addition to replacing any failed components.
d. Check the engine for seizure. If the engine has not been started for a long period of time, internal parts such as the rings may have rusted to the cylinder walls. The engine may have suffered internal damage, or could be hydro-locked from ingesting water. Remove the spark plugs and carefully attempt to rotate the engine using a suitable breaker bar and socket on the crankshaft pulley. If the engine is resistant to moving, or moves slightly and then binds, do not force the engine any further before determining the problem.

3. Engine stalls immediately when started
a. Check the ignition switch condition and operation. The electrical contacts in the run position may be worn or damaged. Try restarting the engine with all electrical accessories in the off position. Sometimes turning the key on an off will help in emergency situations, however once the switch has shown signs of failure, it should be replaced as soon as possible.
b. Check for loose, corroded, damaged or shorted wires for the ignition system and repair or replace.
c. Check for manifold vacuum leaks or vacuum hose leakage and repair or replace parts as necessary.
d. Measure the fuel pump delivery volume and pressure. Low fuel pump pressure can also be noticed as a lack of power when accelerating. Make sure the fuel pump lines are not restricted. The fuel pump output is not adjustable and requires fuel pump replacement to repair.
e. Check the engine fuel and ignition management system. Inspect the sensor wiring and electrical connectors. A dirty, loose or damaged sensor or control module wire can simulate a failed component.
f. Check the exhaust system for internal restrictions.

4. Starter motor spins, but does not engage
a. Check the starter motor for a seized or binding pinion gear.
b. Remove the flywheel inspection plate and check for a damaged ring gear.

5. Engine is difficult to start when cold
a. Check the battery condition, battery state of charge and starter motor current draw.

Replace the battery if marginal and the starter motor if the current draw is beyond specification.
b. Check the battery cable condition. Clean the battery terminals and replace corroded or damaged cables.
c. Check the fuel system for proper operation. A fuel pump with insufficient fuel pressure or clogged injectors should be replaced.
d. Check the engine's tune-up status. Note the tune-up specifications and check for items such as severely worn spark plugs; adjust or replace as needed. On vehicles with manually adjusted valve clearances, check for tight valves and adjust to specification.
e. Check for a failed coolant temperature sensor, and replace if out of specification.
f. Check the operation of the engine management systems for fuel and ignition; repair or replace failed components as necessary.

6. Engine is difficult to start when hot
a. Check the air filter and air intake system. Replace the air filter if it is dirty or contaminated. Check the fresh air intake system for restrictions or blockage.
b. Check for loose or deteriorated engine grounds and clean, tighten or replace as needed.
c. Check for needed maintenance. Inspect tune-up and service related items such as spark plugs and engine oil condition, and check the operation of the engine fuel and ignition management system.

Diesel Engines

1. Engine turns over but won't start
a. Check engine starting procedure and restart engine.
b. Check the glow plug operation and repair or replace as necessary.
c. Check for air in the fuel system or fuel filter and bleed the air as necessary.
d. Check the fuel delivery system and repair or replace as necessary.
e. Check fuel level and add fuel as needed.
f. Check fuel quality. If the fuel is contaminated, drain and flush the fuel tank.
g. Check engine compression. If compression is below specification, the engine may need to be renewed or replaced.
h. Check the injection pump timing and set to specification.
i. Check the injection pump condition and replace as necessary.
j. Check the fuel nozzle operation and condition or replace as necessary.

2. Engine does not turn over when attempting to start
a. Check the battery state of charge and condition. If the dash lights are not visible or very dim when turning the ignition key on, the battery has either failed internally or discharged, the battery cables are loose, excessively corroded or damaged, or the alternator has failed or internally shorted, discharging the battery. Charge or replace the battery, clean or replace the battery cables, and check the alternator output.
b. Check the operation of the neutral safety switch. On automatic transmission vehicles, try starting the vehicle in both Park and Neutral. On manual transmission vehicles, depress the clutch pedal and attempt to start. On some vehicles, these switches can be adjusted. Make sure the switches or wire connectors are not loose or damaged. Replace or adjust the switches as necessary.
c. Check the starter motor, starter solenoid or relay, and starter motor cables and wires. Check the ground from the engine to the chassis. Make sure the wires are not loose, damaged, or corroded. If battery voltage is present at the starter relay, try using a remote starter to start the vehicle for test purposes only. Replace any damaged or corroded cables, in addition to replacing any failed components.
d. Check the engine for seizure. If the engine has not been started for a long period of time, internal parts such as the rings may have rusted to the cylinder walls. The engine may have suffered internal damage, or could be hydro-locked from ingesting water. Remove the injectors and carefully attempt to rotate the engine using a suitable breaker bar and socket on the crankshaft pulley. If the engine is resistant to moving, or moves slightly and then binds, do not force the engine any further before determining the cause of the problem.

3. Engine stalls after starting
a. Check for a restriction in the fuel return line or the return line check valve and repair as necessary.
b. Check the glow plug operation for turning the glow plugs off too soon and repair as necessary.
c. Check for incorrect injection pump timing and reset to specification.
d. Test the engine fuel pump and replace if the output is below specification.
e. Check for contaminated or incorrect fuel. Completely flush the fuel system and replace with fresh fuel.
f. Test the engine's compression for low compression. If below specification, mechanical repairs are necessary to repair.
g. Check for air in the fuel. Check fuel tank fuel and fill as needed.

h. Check for a failed injection pump. Replace the pump, making sure to properly set the pump timing.

4. Starter motor spins, but does not engage
a. Check the starter motor for a seized or binding pinion gear.
b. Remove the flywheel inspection plate and check for a damaged ring gear.

1-B. Engine Running Conditions

Gasoline Engines

1. Engine runs poorly, hesitates
a. Check the engine ignition system operation and adjust if possible, or replace defective parts.
b. Check for restricted fuel injectors and replace as necessary.
c. Check the fuel pump output and delivery. Inspect fuel lines for restrictions. If the fuel pump pressure is below specification, replace the fuel pump.
d. Check the operation of the engine management system and repair as necessary.

2. Engine lacks power
a. Check the engine's tune-up status. Note the tune-up specifications and check for items such as severely worn spark plugs; adjust or replace as needed. On vehicles with manually adjusted valve clearances, check for tight valves and adjust to specification.
b. Check the air filter and air intake system. Replace the air filter if it is dirty or contaminated. Check the fresh air intake system for restrictions or blockage.
c. Check the operation of the engine fuel and ignition management systems. Check the sensor operation and wiring. Check for low fuel pump pressure and repair or replace components as necessary.
d. Check the throttle linkage adjustments. Check to make sure the linkage is fully opening the throttle. Replace any worn or defective bushings or linkages.
e. Check for a restricted exhaust system. Check for bent or crimped exhaust pipes, or internally restricted mufflers or catalytic converters. Compare inlet and outlet temperatures for the converter or muffler. If the inlet is hot, but outlet cold, the component is restricted.
f. Check for a loose or defective knock sensor. A loose, improperly torqued or defective knock sensor will decrease spark advance and reduce power. Replace defective knock sensors and install using the recommended torque specification.
g. Check for engine mechanical conditions such as low compression, worn piston rings, worn valves, worn camshafts and related parts. An engine which has severe mechanical wear, or has suffered internal mechanical damage must be rebuilt or replaced to restore lost power.
h. Check the engine oil level for being overfilled. Adjust the engine's oil level, or change the engine oil and filter, and top off to the correct level.
i. Check for an intake manifold or vacuum hose leak. Replace leaking gaskets or worn vacuum hoses.
j. Check for dragging brakes and replace or repair as necessary.
k. Check tire air pressure and tire wear. Adjust the pressure to the recommended settings. Check the tire wear for possible alignment problems causing increased rolling resistance, decreased acceleration and increased fuel usage.
l. Check the octane rating of the fuel used during refilling, and use a higher octane rated fuel.

3. Poor fuel economy
a. Inspect the air filter and check for any air restrictions going into the air filter housing. Replace the air filter if it is dirty or contaminated.
b. Check the engine for tune-up and related adjustments. Replace worn ignition parts, check the engine ignition timing and fuel mixture, and set to specifications if possible.
c. Check the tire size, tire wear, alignment and tire pressure. Large tires create more rolling resistance, smaller tires require more engine speed to maintain a vehicle's road speed. Excessive tire wear can be caused by incorrect tire pressure, incorrect wheel alignment or a suspension problem. All of these conditions create increased rolling resistance, causing the engine to work harder to accelerate and maintain a vehicle's speed.
d. Inspect the brakes for binding or excessive drag. A sticking brake caliper, overly adjusted brake shoe, broken brake shoe return spring, or binding parking brake cable or linkage can create a significant drag, brake wear and loss of fuel economy. Check the brake system operation and repair as necessary.

4. Engine runs on (diesels) when turned off
a. Check for idle speed set too high and readjust to specification.
b. Check the operation of the idle control valve, and replace if defective.
c. Check the ignition timing and adjust to recommended settings. Check for defective sensors or related components and replace if defective.
d. Check for a vacuum leak at the intake manifold or vacuum hose and replace defective gaskets or hoses.
e. Check the engine for excessive carbon build-up in the combustion chamber. Use a recommended decarbonizing fuel additive or disassemble the cylinder head to remove the carbon.

f. Check the operation of the engine fuel management system and replace defective sensors or control units.
g. Check the engine operating temperature for overheating and repair as necessary.

5. Engine knocks and pings during heavy acceleration, and on steep hills
a. Check the octane rating of the fuel used during refilling, and use a higher octane rated fuel.
b. Check the ignition timing and adjust to recommended settings. Check for defective sensors or related components and replace if defective.
c. Check the engine for excessive carbon build-up in the combustion chamber. Use a recommended decarbonizing fuel additive or disassemble the cylinder head to remove the carbon.
d. Check the spark plugs for the correct type, electrode gap and heat range. Replace worn or damaged spark plugs. For severe or continuous high speed use, install a spark plug that is one heat range colder.
e. Check the operation of the engine fuel management system and replace defective sensors or control units.
f. Check for a restricted exhaust system. Check for bent or crimped exhaust pipes, or internally restricted mufflers or catalytic converters. Compare inlet and outlet temperatures for the converter or muffler. If the inlet is hot, but outlet cold, the component is restricted.

6. Engine accelerates, but vehicle does not gain speed
a. On manual transmission vehicles, check for causes of a slipping clutch. Refer to the clutch troubleshooting section for additional information.
b. On automatic transmission vehicles, check for a slipping transmission. Check the transmission fluid level and condition. If the fluid level is too high, adjust to the correct level. If the fluid level is low, top off using the recommended fluid type. If the fluid exhibits a burning odor, the transmission has been slipping internally. Changing the fluid and filter may help temporarily, however in this situation a transmission may require overhauling to ensure long-term reliability.

Diesel Engines

1. Engine runs poorly
a. Check the injection pump timing and adjust to specification.
b. Check for air in the fuel lines or leaks, and bleed the air from the fuel system.
c. Check the fuel filter, fuel feed and return lines for a restriction and repair as necessary.
d. Check the fuel for contamination, drain and flush the fuel tank and replenish with fresh fuel.

2. Engine lacks power
a. Inspect the air intake system and air filter for restrictions and, if necessary, replace the air filter.
b. Verify the injection pump timing and reset if out of specification.
c. Check the exhaust for an internal restriction and replace failed parts.
d. Check for a restricted fuel filter and, if restricted, replace the filter.
e. Inspect the fuel filler cap vent . When removing the filler cap, listen for excessive hissing noises indicating a blockage in the fuel filler cap vents. If the filler cap vents are blocked, replace the cap.
f. Check the fuel system for restrictions and repair as necessary.
g. Check for low engine compression and inspect for external leakage at the glow plugs or nozzles. If no external leakage is noted, repair or replace the engine.

ENGINE PERFORMANCE TROUBLESHOOTING HINTS

When troubleshooting an engine running or performance condition, the mechanical condition of the engine should be determined *before* lengthy troubleshooting procedures are performed.

The engine fuel management systems in fuel injected vehicles rely on electronic sensors to provide information to the engine control unit for precise fuel metering. Unlike carburetors, which use the incoming air speed to draw fuel through the fuel metering jets in order to provide a proper fuel-to-air ratio, a fuel injection system provides a specific amount of fuel which is introduced by the fuel injectors into the intake manifold or intake port, based on the information provided by electronic sensors.

The sensors monitor the engine's operating temperature, ambient temperature and the amount of air entering the engine, engine speed and throttle position to provide information to the engine control unit, which, in turn, operates the fuel injectors by electrical pulses. The sensors provide information to the engine control unit using low voltage electrical signals. As a result, an unplugged sensor or a poor electrical contact could cause a poor running condition similar to a failed sensor.

When troubleshooting a fuel related engine condition on fuel injected vehicles, carefully inspect the wiring and electrical connectors to the related components. Make sure the electrical connectors are fully connected, clean and not physically damaged. If necessary, clean the electrical contacts using electrical contact cleaner. The use of cleaning agents not specifically designed for electrical contacts should not be used, as they could leave a surface film or damage the insulation of the wiring.

The engine electrical system provides the necessary electrical power to operate the vehicle's electrical accessories, electronic control units and sensors. Because engine management systems are sensitive to voltage changes, an alternator which over or undercharges could cause engine running problems or component failure. Most alternators utilize internal voltage regulators which cannot be adjusted and must be replaced individually or as a unit with the alternator.

Ignition systems may be controlled by, or linked to, the engine fuel management system. Similar to the fuel injection system, these ignition systems rely on electronic sensors for information to determine the optimum ignition timing for a given engine speed and load. Some ignition systems no longer allow the ignition timing to be adjusted. Feedback from low voltage electrical sensors provide information to the control unit to determine the amount of ignition advance. On these systems, if a failure occurs the failed component must be replaced. Before replacing suspected failed electrical components, carefully inspect the wiring and electrical connectors to the related components. Make sure the electrical connectors are fully connected, clean and not physically damaged. If necessary, clean the electrical contacts using electrical contact cleaner. The use of cleaning agents not specifically designed for electrical contacts should be avoided, as they could leave a surface film or damage the insulation of the wiring.

1-C. Engine Noises, Odors and Vibrations

1. Engine makes a knocking or pinging noise when accelerating
a. Check the octane rating of the fuel being used. Depending on the type of driving or driving conditions, it may be necessary to use a higher octane fuel.
b. Verify the ignition system settings and operation. Improperly adjusted ignition timing or a failed component, such as a knock sensor, may cause the ignition timing to advance excessively or prematurely. Check the ignition system operation and adjust, or replace components as needed.
c. Check the spark plug gap, heat range and condition. If the vehicle is operated in severe operating conditions or at continuous high speeds, use a colder heat range spark plug. Adjust the spark plug gap to the manufacturer's recommended specification and replace worn or damaged spark plugs.

2. Starter motor grinds when used
a. Examine the starter pinion gear and the engine ring gear for damage, and replace damaged parts.
b. Check the starter mounting bolts and housing. If the housing is cracked or damaged replace the starter motor and check the mounting bolts for tightness.

3. Engine makes a screeching noise
a. Check the accessory drive belts for looseness and adjust as necessary.
b. Check the accessory drive belt tensioners for seizing or excessive bearing noises and replace if loose, binding, or excessively noisy.
c. Check for a seizing water pump. The pump may not be leaking; however, the bearing may be faulty or the impeller loose and jammed. Replace the water pump.

4. Engine makes a growling noise
a. Check for a loose or failing water pump. Replace the pump and engine coolant.
b. Check the accessory drive belt tensioners for excessive bearing noises and replace if loose or excessively noisy.

5. Engine makes a ticking or tapping noise
a. On vehicles with hydraulic lash adjusters, check for low or dirty engine oil and top off or replace the engine oil and filter.
b. On vehicles with hydraulic lash adjusters, check for collapsed lifters and replace failed components.
c. On vehicles with hydraulic lash adjusters, check for low oil pressure caused by a restricted oil filter, worn engine oil pump, or oil pressure relief valve.
d. On vehicles with manually adjusted valves, check for excessive valve clearance or worn valve train parts. Adjust the valves to specification or replace worn and defective parts.
e. Check for a loose or improperly tensioned timing belt or timing chain and adjust or replace parts as necessary.
f. Check for a bent or sticking exhaust or intake valve. Remove the engine cylinder head to access and replace.

6. Engine makes a heavy knocking noise
a. Check for a loose crankshaft pulley or flywheel; replace and torque the mounting bolt(s) to specification.
b. Check for a bent connecting rod caused by a hydro-lock condition. Engine disassembly is necessary to inspect for damaged and needed replacement parts.
c. Check for excessive engine rod bearing wear or damage. This condition is also associated with low engine oil pressure and will require engine disassembly to inspect for damaged and needed replacement parts.

7. Vehicle has a fuel odor when driven
a. Check the fuel gauge level. If the fuel gauge registers full, it is possible that the odor is caused by being filled beyond capacity, or some spillage occurred during

refueling. The odor should clear after driving an hour, or twenty miles, allowing the vapor canister to purge.
b. Check the fuel filler cap for looseness or seepage. Check the cap tightness and, if loose, properly secure. If seepage is noted, replace the filler cap.
c. Check for loose hose clamps, cracked or damaged fuel delivery and return lines, or leaking components or seals, and replace or repair as necessary.
d. Check the vehicle's fuel economy. If fuel consumption has increased due to a failed component, or if the fuel is not properly ignited due to an ignition related failure, the catalytic converter may become contaminated. This condition may also trigger the check engine warning light. Check the spark plugs for a dark, rich condition or verify the condition by testing the vehicle's emissions. Replace fuel fouled spark plugs, and test and replace failed components as necessary.

8. Vehicle has a rotten egg odor when driven
a. Check for a leaking intake gasket or vacuum leak causing a lean running condition. A lean mixture may result in increased exhaust temperatures, causing the catalytic converter to run hotter than normal. This condition may also trigger the check engine warning light. Check and repair the vacuum leaks as necessary.
b. Check the vehicle's alternator and battery condition. If the alternator is overcharging, the battery electrolyte can be boiled from the battery, and the battery casing may begin to crack, swell or bulge, damaging or shorting the battery internally. If this has occurred, neutralize the battery mounting area with a suitable baking soda and water mixture or equivalent, and replace the alternator or voltage regulator. Inspect, service, and load test the battery, and replace if necessary.

9. Vehicle has a sweet odor when driven
a. Check for an engine coolant leak caused by a seeping radiator cap, loose hose clamp, weeping cooling system seal, gasket or cooling system hose and replace or repair as needed.
b. Check for a coolant leak from the radiator, coolant reservoir, heater control valve or under the dashboard from the heater core, and replace the failed part as necessary.
c. Check the engine's exhaust for white smoke in addition to a sweet odor. The presence of white, steamy smoke with a sweet odor indicates coolant leaking into the combustion chamber. Possible causes include a failed head gasket, cracked engine block or cylinder head. Other symptoms of this condition include a white paste build-up on the inside of the oil filler cap, and softened, deformed or bulging radiator hoses.

10. Engine vibrates when idling
a. Check for loose, collapsed, or damaged engine or transmission mounts and repair or replace as necessary.
b. Check for loose or damaged engine covers or shields and secure or replace as necessary.

11. Engine vibrates during acceleration
a. Check for missing, loose or damaged exhaust system hangers and mounts; replace or repair as necessary.
b. Check the exhaust system routing and fit for adequate clearance or potential rubbing; repair or adjust as necessary.

1-D. Engine Electrical System

1. Battery goes dead while driving
a. Check the battery condition. Replace the battery if the battery will not hold a charge or fails a battery load test. If the battery loses fluid while driving, check for an overcharging condition. If the alternator is overcharging, replace the alternator or voltage regulator. (A voltage regulator is typically built into the alternator, necessitating alternator replacement or overhaul.)
b. Check the battery cable condition. Clean or replace corroded cables and clean the battery terminals.
c. Check the alternator and voltage regulator operation. If the charging system is over or undercharging, replace the alternator or voltage regulator, or both.
d. Inspect the wiring and wire connectors at the alternator for looseness, a missing ground or defective terminal, and repair as necessary.
e. Inspect the alternator drive belt tension, tensioners and condition. Properly tension the drive belt, replace weak or broken tensioners, and replace the drive belt if worn or cracked.

2. Battery goes dead overnight
a. Check the battery condition. Replace the battery if the battery will not hold a charge or fails a battery load test.
b. Check for a voltage draw, such as a trunk light, interior light or glove box light staying on. Check light switch position and operation, and replace if defective.
c. Check the alternator for an internally failed diode, and replace the alternator if defective.

1-E. Engine Cooling System

1. Engine overheats

a. Check the coolant level. Set the heater temperature to full hot and check for internal air pockets, bleed the cooling system and inspect for leakage. Top off the cooling system with the correct coolant mixture.

b. Pressure test the cooling system and radiator cap for leaks. Check for seepage caused by loose hose clamps, failed coolant hoses, and cooling system components such as the heater control valve, heater core, radiator, radiator cap, and water pump. Replace defective parts and fill the cooling system with the recommended coolant mixture.

c. On vehicles with electrically controlled cooling fans, check the cooling fan operation. Check for blown fuses or defective fan motors, temperature sensors and relays, and replace failed components.

d. Check for a coolant leak caused by a failed head gasket, or a porous water jacket casting in the cylinder head or engine block. Replace defective parts as necessary.

e. Check for an internally restricted radiator. Flush the radiator or replace if the blockage is too severe for flushing.

f. Check for a damaged water pump. If coolant circulation is poor, check for a loose water pump impeller. If the impeller is loose, replace the water pump.

2. Engine loses coolant

a. Pressure test the cooling system and radiator cap for leaks. Check for seepage caused by loose hose clamps, failed coolant hoses, and cooling system components such as the heater control valve, heater core, radiator, radiator cap, and water pump. Replace defective parts and fill the cooling system with the recommended coolant mixture.

b. Check for a coolant leak caused by a failed head gasket, or a porous water jacket casting in the cylinder head or engine block. Replace defective parts as necessary.

3. Engine temperature remains cold when driving

a. Check the thermostat operation. Replace the thermostat if it sticks in the open position.

b. On vehicles with electrically controlled cooling fans, check the cooling fan operation. Check for defective temperature sensors and stuck relays, and replace failed components.

c. Check temperature gauge operation if equipped to verify proper operation of the gauge. Check the sensors and wiring for defects, and repair or replace defective components.

4. Engine runs hot

a. Check for an internally restricted radiator. Flush the radiator or replace if the blockage is too severe for flushing.

b. Check for a loose or slipping water pump drive belt. Inspect the drive belt condition. Replace the belt if brittle, cracked or damaged. Check the pulley condition and properly tension the belt.

c. Check the cooling fan operation. Replace defective fan motors, sensors or relays as necessary.

d. Check temperature gauge operation if equipped to verify proper operation of the gauge. Check the sensors and wiring for defects, and repair or replace defective components.

e. Check the coolant level. Set the heater temperature to full hot, check for internal air pockets, bleed the cooling system and inspect for leakage. Top off the cooling system with the correct coolant mixture. Once the engine is cool, recheck the fluid level and top off as needed.

NOTE: The engine cooling system can also be affected by an engine's mechanical condition. A failed head gasket or a porous casting in the engine block or cylinder head could cause a loss of coolant and result in engine overheating.

Some cooling systems rely on electrically driven cooling fans to cool the radiator and use electrical temperature sensors and relays to operate the cooling fan. When diagnosing these systems, check for blown fuses, damaged wires and verify that the electrical connections are fully connected, clean and not physically damaged. If necessary, clean the electrical contacts using electrical contact cleaner. The use of cleaning agents not specifically designed for electrical contacts could leave a film or damage the insulation of the wiring.

1-F. Engine Exhaust System

1. Exhaust rattles at idle speed

a. Check the engine and transmission mounts and replace mounts showing signs of damage or wear.

b. Check the exhaust hangers, brackets and mounts. Replace broken, missing or damaged mounts.

c. Check for internal damage to mufflers and catalytic converters. The broken pieces from the defective component may travel in the direction of the exhaust flow and collect and/or create a blockage in a component other than the one which failed, causing engine running and stalling problems. Another symptom of a restricted exhaust is low engine manifold vacuum. Remove the exhaust system and carefully remove any loose or broken pieces, then replace any failed or damaged parts as necessary.

d. Check the exhaust system clearance, routing and alignment. If the exhaust is making contact with the vehicle in any manner, loosen and reposition the exhaust system.

2. Exhaust system vibrates when driving

a. Check the exhaust hangers, brackets and mounts. Replace broken, missing or damaged mounts.

b. Check the exhaust system clearance, routing and alignment. If the exhaust is making contact with the vehicle in any manner, check for bent or damaged components and replace, then loosen and reposition the exhaust system.

c. Check for internal damage to mufflers and catalytic converters. The broken pieces from the defective component may travel in the direction of the exhaust flow and collect and/or create a blockage in a component other than the one which failed, causing engine running and stalling problems. Another symptom of a restricted exhaust is low engine manifold vacuum. Remove the exhaust system and carefully remove any loose or broken pieces, then replace any failed or damaged parts as necessary.

3. Exhaust system hangs too low

a. Check the exhaust hangers, brackets and mounts. Replace broken, missing or damaged mounts.

b. Check the exhaust routing and alignment. Check and replace bent or damaged components. If the exhaust is not routed properly, loosen and reposition the exhaust system.

4. Exhaust sounds loud

a. Check the system for looseness and leaks. Check the exhaust pipes, clamps, flange bolts and manifold fasteners for tightness. Check and replace any failed gaskets.

b. Check and replace exhaust silencers that have a loss of efficiency due to internally broken baffles or worn packing material.

c. Check for missing mufflers and silencers that have been replaced with straight pipes or with non-original equipment silencers.

NOTE: Exhaust system rattles, vibration and proper alignment should not be overlooked. Excessive vibration caused by collapsed engine mounts, damaged or missing exhaust hangers and misalignment may cause surface cracks and broken welds, creating exhaust leaks or internal damage to exhaust components such as the catalytic converter, creating a restriction to exhaust flow and loss of power.

2. DRIVE TRAIN

2-A. Automatic Transmission

1. Transmission shifts erratically

a. Check and if not within the recommended range, add or remove transmission fluid to obtain the correct fluid level. Always use the recommended fluid type when adding transmission fluid.

b. Check the fluid level condition. If the fluid has become contaminated, fatigued from excessive heat or exhibits a burning odor, change the transmission fluid and filter using the recommended type and amount of fluid. A fluid which exhibits a burning odor indicates that the transmission has been slipping internally and may require future repairs.

c. Check for an improperly installed transmission filter, or missing filter gasket, and repair as necessary.

d. Check for loose or leaking gaskets, pressure lines and fittings, and repair or replace as necessary.

e. Check for loose or disconnected shift and throttle linkages or vacuum hoses, and repair as necessary.

2. Transmission will not engage

a. Check the shift linkage for looseness, wear and proper adjustment, and repair as necessary.

b. Check for a loss of transmission fluid and top off as needed with the recommended fluid.

c. If the transmission does not engage with the shift linkage correctly installed and the proper fluid level, internal damage has likely occurred, requiring transmission removal and disassembly.

3. Transmission will not downshift during heavy acceleration

a. On computer controlled transmissions, check for failed sensors or control units and repair or replace defective components.

b. On vehicles with kickdown linkages or vacuum servos, check for proper linkage adjustment or leaking vacuum hoses or servo units.

NOTE: Many automatic transmissions use an electronic control module, electrical sensors and solenoids to control transmission shifting. When troubleshooting a vehicle with this type of system, be sure the electrical connectors are fully connected, clean and not physically damaged. If necessary, clean the electrical contacts using electrical contact cleaner. The use of cleaning agents not specifically designed for electrical contacts could leave a film or damage the insulation of the wiring.

2-B. Manual Transmission

1. Transmission grinds going into forward gears while driving
a. Check the clutch release system. On clutches with a mechanical or cable linkage, check the adjustment. Adjust the clutch pedal to have 1 inch (25mm) of free-play at the pedal.
b. If the clutch release system is hydraulically operated, check the fluid level and, if low, top off using the recommended type and amount of fluid.
c. Synchronizers worn. Remove transmission and replace synchronizers.
d. Synchronizer sliding sleeve worn. Remove transmission and replace sliding sleeve.
e. Gear engagement dogs worn or damaged. Remove transmission and replace gear.

2. Transmission jumps out of gear
a. Shift shaft detent springs worn. Replace shift detent springs.
b. Synchronizer sliding sleeve worn. Remove transmission and replace sliding sleeve.
c. Gear engagement dogs worn or damaged. Remove transmission and replace gear.
d. Crankshaft thrust bearings worn. Remove engine and crankshaft, and repair as necessary.

3. Transmission difficult to shift
a. Verify the clutch adjustment and, if not properly adjusted, adjust to specification.
b. Synchronizers worn. Remove transmission and replace synchronizers.
c. Pilot bearing seized. Remove transmission and replace pilot bearing.
d. Shift linkage or bushing seized. Disassemble the shift linkage, replace worn or damaged bushings, lubricate and reinstall.

4. Transmission leaks fluid
a. Check the fluid level for an overfilled condition. Adjust the fluid level to specification.
b. Check for a restricted transmission vent or breather tube. Clear the blockage as necessary and check the fluid level. If necessary, top off with the recommended lubricant.
c. Check for a porous casting, leaking seal or gasket. Replace defective parts and top off the fluid level with the recommended lubricant.

2-C. Clutch

1. Clutch slips on hills or during sudden acceleration
a. Check for insufficient clutch pedal free-play. Adjust clutch linkage or cable to allow about 1 inch (25mm) of pedal free-play.
b. Clutch disc worn or severely damaged. Remove engine or transmission and replace clutch disc.
c. Clutch pressure plate is weak. Remove engine or transmission and replace the clutch pressure plate and clutch disc.
d. Clutch pressure plate and/or flywheel incorrectly machined. If the clutch system has been recently replaced and rebuilt, or refurbished parts have been used, it is possible that the machined surfaces decreased the clutch clamping force. Replace defective parts with new replacement parts.

2. Clutch will not disengage, difficult to shift
a. Check the clutch release mechanism. Check for stretched cables, worn linkages or failed clutch hydraulics and replace defective parts. On hydraulically operated clutch release mechanisms, check for air in the hydraulic system and bleed as necessary.
b. Check for a broken, cracked or fatigued clutch release arm or release arm pivot. Replace defective parts and properly lubricate upon assembly.
c. Check for a damaged clutch hub damper or damper spring. The broken parts tend to become lodged between the clutch disc and the pressure plate. Disassemble clutch system and replace failed parts.
d. Check for a seized clutch pilot bearing. Disassemble the clutch assembly and replace the defective parts.
e. Check for a defective clutch disc. Check for warpage or lining thicknesses larger than original equipment.

3. Clutch is noisy when the clutch pedal is pressed
a. Check the clutch pedal stop and pedal free-play adjustment for excessive movement and adjust as necessary.
b. Check for a worn or damaged release bearing. If the noise ceases when the pedal is released, the release bearing should be replaced.

c. Check the engine crankshaft axial play. If the crankshaft thrust bearings are worn or damaged, the crankshaft will move when pressing the clutch pedal. The engine must be disassembled to replace the crankshaft thrust bearings.

4. Clutch pedal extremely difficult to press
a. Check the clutch pedal pivots and linkages for binding. Clean and lubricate linkages.
b. On cable actuated clutch systems, check the cable routing and condition. Replace kinked, frayed, damaged or corroded cables and check cable routing to avoid sharp bends. Check the engine ground strap for poor conductivity. If the ground strap is marginal, the engine could try to ground itself via the clutch cable, causing premature failure.
c. On mechanical linkage clutches, check the linkage for binding or misalignment. Lubricate pivots or linkages and repair as necessary.
d. Check the release bearing guide tube and release fork for a lack of lubrication. Install a smooth coating of high temperature grease to allow smooth movement of the release bearing over the guide tube.

5. Clutch pedal remains down when pressed
a. On mechanical linkage or cable actuated clutches, check for a loose or disconnected link.
b. On hydraulically actuated clutches, check the fluid level and check for a hydraulic leak at the clutch slave or master cylinder, or hydraulic line. Replace failed parts and bleed clutch hydraulic system. If no leakage is noted, the clutch master cylinder may have failed internally. Replace the clutch master cylinder and bleed the clutch hydraulic system.

6. Clutch chatters when engaging
a. Check the engine flywheel for warpage or surface variations and replace or repair as necessary.
b. Check for a warped clutch disc or damaged clutch damper hub. Remove the clutch disc and replace.
c. Check for a loose or damaged clutch pressure plate and replace defective components.

NOTE: The clutch is actuated either by a mechanical linkage, cable or a clutch hydraulic system. The mechanical linkage and cable systems may require the clutch pedal free-play to be adjusted as the clutch disc wears. A hydraulic clutch system automatically adjusts as the clutch wears and, with the exception of the clutch pedal height, no adjustment is possible.

2-D. Differential and Final Drive

1. Differential makes a low pitched rumbling noise
a. Check fluid level type and amount. Replace the fluid with the recommended type and amount of lubricant.
b. Check the differential bearings for wear or damage. Remove the bearings, inspect the drive and driven gears for wear or damage, and replace components as necessary.

2. Differential makes a howling noise
a. Check fluid level type and amount. Replace the fluid with the recommended type and amount of lubricant.
b. Check the differential drive and driven gears for wear or damage, and replace components as necessary.

2-E. Transfer Assembly

All Wheel and Four Wheel Drive Vehicles

1. Leaks fluid from seals or vent after being driven
a. Fluid level overfilled. Check and adjust transfer case fluid level.
b. Check for a restricted breather or breather tube, clear and check the fluid level and top off as needed.
c. Check seal condition and replace worn, damaged, or defective seals. Check the fluid level and top off as necessary.

2. Makes excessive noise while driving
a. Check the fluid for the correct type of lubricant. Drain and refill using the recommended type and amount of lubricant.
b. Check the fluid level. Top off the fluid using the recommended type and amount of lubricant.
c. If the fluid level and type of lubricant meet specifications, check for internal wear or damage. Remove assembly and disassemble to inspect for worn, damaged, or defective components.

3. Jumps out of gear
a. Stop vehicle and make sure the unit is fully engaged.
b. Check for worn, loose or an improperly adjusted linkage. Replace and/or adjust linkage as necessary.
c. Check for internal wear or damage. Remove assembly and disassemble to inspect for worn, damaged, or defective components.

2-F. Driveshaft

Rear Wheel, All Wheel and Four Wheel Drive Vehicles

1. Clunking noise from center of vehicle shifting from forward to reverse
a. Worn universal joint. Remove driveshaft and replace universal joint.

2. Excessive vibration from center of vehicle when accelerating
a. Worn universal joint. Remove driveshaft and replace universal joint.
b. Driveshaft misaligned. Check for collapsed or damaged engine and transmission mounts, and replace as necessary.
c. Driveshaft bent or out of balance. Replace damaged components and reinstall.
d. Driveshaft out of balance. Remove the driveshaft and have it balanced by a competent professional, or replace the driveshaft assembly.

NOTE: Most driveshafts are linked together by universal joints; however, some manufacturers use Constant Velocity (CV) joints or rubber flex couplers.

2-G. Axles

All Wheel and Four Wheel Drive Vehicles

1. Front or rear wheel makes a clicking noise
a. Check for debris such as a pebble, nail or glass in the tire or tire tread. Carefully remove the debris. Small rocks and pebbles rarely cause a puncture; however, a sharp object should be removed carefully at a facility capable of performing tire repairs.
b. Check for a loose, damaged or worn Constant Velocity (CV) joint and replace if defective.

2. Front or rear wheel vibrates with increased speed
a. Check for a bent rim and replace, if damaged.
b. Check the tires for balance or internal damage and replace if defective.
c. Check for a loose, worn or damaged wheel bearing and replace if defective.
d. Check for a loose, damaged or worn Constant Velocity (CV) joint and replace if defective.

Front Wheel Drive Vehicles

3. Front wheel makes a clicking noise
a. Check for debris such as a pebble, nail or glass in the tire or tire tread. Carefully remove the debris. Small rocks and pebbles rarely cause a puncture; however, a sharp object should be removed carefully at a facility capable of performing tire repairs.

b. Check for a loose, damaged or worn Constant Velocity (CV) joint and replace if defective.

4. Rear wheel makes a clicking noise
a. Check for debris such as a pebble, nail or glass in the tire or tire tread. Carefully remove the debris. Small rocks and pebbles rarely cause a puncture; however, a sharp object should be removed carefully at a facility capable of performing tire repairs.

Rear Wheel Drive Vehicles

5. Front or rear wheel makes a clicking noise
a. Check for debris such as a pebble, nail or glass in the tire or tire tread. Carefully remove the debris. Small rocks and pebbles rarely cause a puncture; however, a sharp object should be removed carefully at a facility capable of performing tire repairs.

6. Rear wheel shudders or vibrates
a. Check for a bent rear wheel or axle assembly and replace defective components.
b. Check for a loose, damaged or worn rear wheel bearing and replace as necessary.

2-H. Other Drive Train Conditions

1. Burning odor from center of vehicle when accelerating
a. Check for a seizing brake hydraulic component such as a brake caliper. Check the caliper piston for surface damage such as rust, and measure for out-of-round wear and caliper-to-piston clearance. For additional information on brake related odors, refer to section 3-A, condition number 9.
b. On vehicles with a manual transmission, check for a slipping clutch. For possible causes and additional information, refer to section 2-C, condition number 1.
c. On vehicles with an automatic transmission, check the fluid level and condition. Top off or change the fluid and filter using the recommended replacement parts, lubricant type and amount. If the odor persists, transmission removal and disassembly will be necessary.

2. Engine accelerates, but vehicle does not gain speed
a. On vehicles with a manual transmission, check for a slipping or damaged clutch. For possible causes and additional information refer to section 2-C, condition number 1.
b. On vehicles with an automatic transmission, check the fluid level and condition. Top off or change the fluid and filter using the recommended replacement parts, lubricant type and amount. If the slipping continues, transmission removal and disassembly will be necessary.

3. BRAKE SYSTEM

3-A. Brake System Troubleshooting

1. Brake pedal pulsates or shimmies when pressed
a. Check wheel lug nut torque and tighten evenly to specification.
b. Check the brake rotor for trueness and thickness variations. Replace the rotor if it is too thin, warped, or if the thickness varies beyond specification. Some rotors can be machined; consult the manufacturer's specifications and recommendations before using a machined brake rotor.
c. Check the brake caliper or caliper bracket mounting bolt torque and inspect for looseness. Torque the mounting bolts and inspect for wear or any looseness, including worn mounting brackets, bushings and sliding pins.
d. Check the wheel bearing for looseness. If the bearing is loose, adjust if possible, otherwise replace the bearing.

2. Brakes make a squealing noise
a. Check the brake rotor for the presence of a ridge on the outer edge; if present, remove the ridge or replace the brake rotor and brake pads.
b. Check for debris in the brake lining material, clean and reinstall.
c. Check the brake linings for wear and replace the brake linings if wear is approaching the lining wear limit.
d. Check the brake linings for glazing. Inspect the brake drum or rotor surface and replace, along with the brake linings, if the surface is not smooth or even.
e. Check the brake pad or shoe mounting areas for a lack of lubricant or the presence of surface rust. Clean and lubricate with a recommended high temperature brake grease.

3. Brakes make a grinding noise
a. Check the brake linings and brake surface areas for severe wear or damage. Replace worn or damaged parts.
b. Check for a seized or partially seized brake causing premature or uneven brake wear, excessive heat and brake rotor or drum damage. Replace defective parts and inspect the wheel bearing condition, which could have been damaged due to excessive heat.

4. Vehicle pulls to one side during braking
a. Check for air in the brake hydraulic system. Inspect the brake hydraulic seals, fluid lines and related components for fluid leaks. Remove the air from the brake system by bleeding the brakes. Be sure to use fresh brake fluid that meets the manufacturer's recommended standards.
b. Check for an internally restricted flexible brake hydraulic hose. Replace the hose and flush the brake system.
c. Check for a seizing brake hydraulic component such as a brake caliper. Check the caliper piston for surface damage such as rust, and measure for out-of-round wear and caliper-to-piston clearance. Overhaul or replace failed parts and flush the brake system.
d. Check the vehicle's alignment and inspect for suspension wear. Replace worn bushings, ball joints and set alignment to the manufacturer's specifications.
e. If the brake system uses drum brakes front or rear, check the brake adjustment. Inspect for seized adjusters and clean or replace, then properly adjust.

5. Brake pedal feels spongy or has excessive travel
a. Check the brake fluid level and condition. If the fluid is contaminated or has not been flushed every two years, clean the master cylinder reservoir, and bleed and flush the brakes using fresh brake fluid that meets the manufacturer's recommended standards.
b. Check for a weak or damaged flexible brake hydraulic hose. Replace the hose and flush the brake system.
c. If the brake system uses drum brakes front or rear, check the brake adjustment. Inspect for seized adjusters and clean or replace, then properly adjust.

6. Brake pedal feel is firm, but brakes lack sufficient stopping power or fade
a. Check the operation of the brake booster and brake booster check valve. Replace worn or failed parts.
b. Check brake linings and brake surface areas for glazing and replace worn or damaged parts.
c. Check for seized hydraulic parts and linkages, and clean or replace as needed.

7. Vehicle has excessive front end dive or locks rear brakes too easily
a. Check for worn, failed or seized brake proportioning valve and replace the valve.
b. Check for a seized, disconnected or missing spring or linkage for the brake proportioning valve. Replace missing parts or repair as necessary.

8. Brake pedal goes to floor when pressed and will not pump up
a. Check the brake hydraulic fluid level and inspect the fluid lines and seals for leakage. Repair or replace leaking components, then bleed and flush the brake system using fresh brake fluid that meets the manufacturer's recommended standards.
b. Check the brake fluid level. Inspect the brake fluid level and brake hydraulic seals. If the fluid level is ok, and the brake hydraulic system is free of hydraulic leaks, replace the brake master cylinder, then bleed and flush the brake system using fresh brake fluid that meets the manufacturer's recommended standards.

9. Brakes produce a burning odor
a. Check for a seizing brake hydraulic component such as a brake caliper. Check the caliper piston for surface damage such as rust, and measure for out-of-round wear and caliper-to-piston clearance. Overhaul or replace failed parts and flush the brake system.
b. Check for an internally restricted flexible brake hydraulic hose. Replace the hose and flush the brake system.
c. Check the parking brake release mechanism, seized linkage or cable, and repair as necessary.

BRAKE PERFORMANCE TROUBLESHOOTING HINTS

Brake vibrations or pulsation can often be diagnosed on a safe and careful test drive. A brake vibration which is felt through the brake pedal while braking, but not felt in the steering wheel, is most likely caused by brake surface variations in the rear brakes. If both the brake pedal and steering wheel vibrate during braking, a surface variation in the front brakes, or both front and rear brakes, is very likely.

A brake pedal that pumps up with repeated use can be caused by air in the brake hydraulic system or, if the vehicle is equipped with rear drum brakes, the brake adjusters may be seized or out of adjustment. A quick test for brake adjustment on vehicles with rear drum brakes is to pump the brake pedal several times with the vehicle's engine not running and the parking brake released. Pump the brake pedal several times and continue to apply pressure to the brake pedal. With pressure being applied to the brake pedal, engage the parking brake. Release the brake pedal and quickly press the brake pedal again. If the brake pedal pumped up, the rear brakes are in need of adjustment. Do not compensate for the rear brake adjustment by adjusting the parking brake, this will cause premature brake lining wear.

To test a vacuum brake booster, pump the brake pedal several times with the vehicle's engine off. Apply pressure to the brake pedal and then start the engine. The brake pedal should move downward about one inch (25mm).

4. WHEELS, TIRES, STEERING AND SUSPENSION

4-A. Wheels and Wheel Bearings

1. Front wheel or wheel bearing loose

All Wheel and Four Wheel Drive Vehicles
a. Torque lug nuts and axle nuts to specification and recheck for looseness.
b. Wheel bearing worn or damaged. Replace wheel bearing.

Front Wheel Drive Vehicles
a. Torque lug nuts and axle nuts to specification and recheck for looseness.
b. Wheel bearing worn or damaged. Replace wheel bearing.
c. Wheel bearing out of adjustment. Adjust wheel bearing to specification; if still loose, replace.

Rear Wheel Drive Vehicles
a. Wheel bearing out of adjustment. Adjust wheel bearing to specification; if still loose, replace.
b. Torque lug nuts to specification and recheck for looseness.
c. Wheel bearing worn or damaged. Replace wheel bearing.

2. Rear wheel or wheel bearing loose

All Wheel and Four Wheel Drive Vehicles
a. Torque lug nuts and axle nuts to specification and recheck for looseness.
b. Wheel bearing worn or damaged. Replace wheel bearing.

Front Wheel Drive Vehicles
a. Wheel bearing out of adjustment. Adjust wheel bearing to specification; if still loose, replace.
b. Torque lug nuts to specification and recheck for looseness.
c. Wheel bearing worn or damaged. Replace wheel bearing.

Rear Wheel Drive Vehicles
a. Torque lug nuts to specification and recheck for looseness.
c. Wheel bearing worn or damaged. Replace wheel bearing.

4-B. Tires

1. Tires worn on inside tread
a. Check alignment for a toed-out condition. Check and set tire pressures and properly adjust the toe.
b. Check for worn, damaged or defective suspension components. Replace defective parts and adjust the alignment.

2. Tires worn on outside tread
a. Check alignment for a toed-in condition. Check and set tire pressures and properly adjust the toe.
b. Check for worn, damaged or defective suspension components. Replace defective parts and adjust the alignment.

3. Tires worn unevenly
a. Check the tire pressure and tire balance. Replace worn or defective tires and check the alignment; adjust if necessary.

b. Check for worn shock absorbers. Replaced failed components, worn or defective tires and check the alignment; adjust if necessary.
c. Check the alignment settings. Check and set tire pressures and properly adjust the alignment to specification.
d. Check for worn, damaged or defective suspension components. Replace defective parts and adjust the alignment to specification.

4-C. Steering

1. Excessive play in steering wheel
a. Check the steering gear free-play adjustment and properly adjust to remove excessive play.
b. Check the steering linkage for worn, damaged or defective parts. Replace failed components and perform a front end alignment.
c. Check for a worn, damaged, or defective steering box, replace the steering gear and check the front end alignment.

2. Steering wheel shakes at cruising speeds
a. Check for a bent front wheel. Replace a damaged wheel and check the tire for possible internal damage.
b. Check for an unevenly worn front tire. Replace the tire, adjust tire pressure and balance.
c. Check the front tires for hidden internal damage. Tires which have encountered large pot holes or suffered other hard blows may have sustained internal damage and should be replaced immediately.
d. Check the front tires for an out-of-balance condition. Remove, spin balance and reinstall. Torque all the wheel bolts or lug nuts to the recommended specification.
e. Check for a loose wheel bearing. If possible, adjust the bearing, or replace the bearing if it is a non-adjustable bearing.

3. Steering wheel shakes when braking
a. Refer to section 3-A, condition number 1.

4. Steering wheel becomes stiff when turned
a. Check the steering wheel free-play adjustment and reset as needed.
b. Check for a damaged steering gear assembly. Replace the steering gear and perform a front end alignment.
c. Check for damaged or seized suspension components. Replace defective components and perform a front end alignment.

4-D. Suspension

1. Vehicle pulls to one side
a. Tire pressure uneven. Adjust tire pressure to recommended settings.
b. Tires worn unevenly. Replace tires and check alignment settings.
c. Alignment out of specification. Align front end and check thrust angle.
d. Check for a dragging brake and repair or replace as necessary.

2. Vehicle is very bouncy over bumps
a. Check for worn or leaking shock absorbers or strut assemblies and replace as necessary.
b. Check for seized shock absorbers or strut assemblies and replace as necessary.

NOTE: When one shock fails, it is recommended to replace front or rear units as pairs.

3. Vehicle leans excessively in turns

a. Check for worn or leaking shock absorbers or strut assemblies and replace as necessary.

b. Check for missing, damaged, or worn stabilizer links or bushings, and replace or install as necessary.

4. Vehicle ride quality seems excessively harsh

a. Check for seized shock absorbers or strut assemblies and replace as necessary.

b. Check for excessively high tire pressures and adjust pressures to vehicle recommendations.

5. Vehicle seems low or leans to one side

a. Check for a damaged, broken or weak spring. Replace defective parts and check for a needed alignment.

b. Check for seized shock absorbers or strut assemblies and replace as necessary.

c. Check for worn or leaking shock absorbers or strut assemblies and replace as necessary.

4-E. Driving Noises and Vibrations

Noises

1. Vehicle makes a clicking noises when driven

a. Check the noise to see if it varies with road speed. Verify if the noise is present when coasting or with steering or throttle input. If the clicking noise frequency changes with road speed and is not affected by steering or throttle input, check the tire treads for a stone, piece of glass, nail or another hard object imbedded into the tire or tire tread. Stones rarely cause a tire puncture and are easily removed. Other objects may create an air leak when removed. Consider having these objects removed immediately at a facility equipped to repair tire punctures.

b. If the clicking noise varies with throttle input and steering, check for a worn Constant Velocity (CV-joint) joint, universal (U- joint) or flex joint.

2. Vehicle makes a clunking or knocking noise over bumps

a. A clunking noise over bumps is most often caused by excessive movement or clearance in a suspension component. Check the suspension for soft, cracked, damaged or worn bushings. Replace the bushings and check the vehicle's alignment.

b. Check for loose suspension mounting bolts. Check the tightness on subframe bolts, pivot bolts and suspension mounting bolts, and torque to specification.

c. Check the vehicle for a loose wheel bearing. Some wheel bearings can be adjusted for looseness, while others must be replaced if loose. Adjust or replace the bearings as recommended by the manufacturer.

d. Check the door latch adjustment. If the door is slightly loose, or the latch adjustment is not centered, the door assembly may create noises over bumps and rough surfaces. Properly adjust the door latches to secure the door.

3. Vehicle makes a low pitched rumbling noise when driven

a. A low pitched rumbling noise is usually caused by a drive train related bearing and is most often associated with a wheel bearing which has been damaged or worn. The damage can be caused by excessive brake temperatures or physical contact with a pot hole or curb. Sometimes the noise will vary when turning. Left hand turns increase the load on the vehicle's right side, and right turns load the left side. A failed front wheel bearing may also cause a slight steering wheel vibration when turning. A bearing which exhibits noise must be replaced.

b. Check the tire condition and balance. An internally damaged tire may cause failure symptoms similar to failed suspension parts. For diagnostic purposes, try a known good set of tires and replace defective tires.

4. Vehicle makes a squeaking noise over bumps

a. Check the vehicle's ball joints for wear, damaged or leaking boots. Replace a ball joint if it is loose, the boot is damaged and leaking, or the ball joint is binding. When replacing suspension parts, check the vehicle for alignment.

b. Check for seized or deteriorated bushings. Replace bushings that are worn or damaged and check the vehicle for alignment.

c. Check for the presence of sway bar or stabilizer bar bushings which wrap around the bar. Inspect the condition of the bushings and replace if worn or damaged. Remove the bushing bracket and apply a thin layer of suspension grease to the area where the bushings wrap around the bar and reinstall the bushing brackets.

Vibrations

5. Vehicle vibrates when driven

a. Check the road surface. Roads which have rough or uneven surfaces may cause unusual vibrations.

b. Check the tire condition and balance. An internally damaged tire may cause failure symptoms similar to failed suspension parts. For diagnostic purposes, try a known good set of tires and replace defective tires immediately.

c. Check for a worn Constant Velocity (CV-joint) joint, universal (U- joint) or flex joint and replace if loose, damaged or binding.

d. Check for a loose, bent, or out-of-balance axle or drive shaft. Replace damaged or failed components.

NOTE: Diagnosing failures related to wheels, tires, steering and the suspension system can often times be accomplished with a careful and thorough test drive. Bearing noises are isolated by noting whether the noises or symptoms vary when turning left or right, or occur while driving a straight line. During a left hand turn, the vehicle's weight shifts to the right, placing more force on the right side bearings, such that if a right side wheel bearing is worn or damaged, the noise or vibration should increase during light-to-heavy acceleration. Conversely, on right hand turns, the vehicle tends to lean to the left, loading the left side bearings.

Knocking noises in the suspension when the vehicle is driven over rough roads, railroad tracks and speed bumps indicate worn suspension components such as bushings, ball joints or tie rod ends, or a worn steering system.

5. ELECTRICAL ACCESSORIES

5-A. Headlights

1. One headlight only works on high or low beam

a. Check for battery voltage at headlight electrical connector. If battery voltage is present, replace the headlight assembly or bulb if available separately. If battery voltage is not present, refer to the headlight wiring diagram to troubleshoot.

2. Headlight does not work on high or low beam

a. Check for battery voltage and ground at headlight electrical connector. If battery voltage is present, check the headlight connector ground terminal for a proper ground. If battery voltage and ground are present at the headlight connector, replace the headlight assembly or bulb if available separately. If battery voltage or ground is not present, refer to the headlight wiring diagram to troubleshoot.

b. Check the headlight switch operation. Replace the switch if the switch is defective or operates intermittently.

3. Headlight(s) very dim

a. Check for battery voltage and ground at headlight electrical connector. If battery voltage is present, trace the ground circuit for the headlamp electrical connector, then clean and repair as necessary. If the voltage at the headlight electrical connector is significantly less than the voltage at the battery, refer to the headlight wiring diagram to troubleshoot and locate the voltage drop.

5-B. Tail, Running and Side Marker Lights

1. Tail light, running light or side marker light inoperative

a. Check for battery voltage and ground at light's electrical connector. If battery voltage is present, check the bulb socket and electrical connector ground terminal for a proper ground. If battery voltage and ground are present at the light connector, but not in the socket, clean the socket and the ground terminal connector. If battery voltage and ground are present in the bulb socket, replace the bulb. If battery voltage or ground is not present, refer to the wiring diagram to troubleshoot for an open circuit.

b. Check the light switch operation and replace if necessary.

2. Tail light, running light or side marker light works intermittently

a. Check the bulb for a damaged filament, and replace if damaged.

b Check the bulb and bulb socket for corrosion, and clean or replace the bulb and socket.

c. Check for loose, damaged or corroded wires and electrical terminals, and repair as necessary.

d. Check the light switch operation and replace if necessary.

3. Tail light, running light or side marker light very dim

a. Check the bulb and bulb socket for corrosion and clean or replace the bulb and socket.

b. Check for low voltage at the bulb socket positive terminal or a poor ground. If voltage is low, or the ground marginal, trace the wiring to, and check for loose, damaged or corroded wires and electrical terminals; repair as necessary.

c. Check the light switch operation and replace if necessary.

5-C. Interior Lights

1. Interior light inoperative

a. Verify the interior light switch location and position(s), and set the switch in the correct position.

b. Check for battery voltage and ground at the interior light bulb socket. If battery voltage and ground are present, replace the bulb. If voltage is not present, check the interior light fuse for battery voltage. If the fuse is missing, replace the fuse. If the fuse has blown, or if battery voltage is present, refer to the wiring diagram to troubleshoot the cause for an open or shorted circuit. If ground is not present, check the door switch contacts and clean or repair as necessary.

2. Interior light works intermittently

a. Check the bulb for a damaged filament, and replace if damaged.

b. Check the bulb and bulb socket for corrosion, and clean or replace the bulb and socket.

c. Check for loose, damaged or corroded wires and electrical terminals; repair as necessary.

d. Check the door and light switch operation, and replace if necessary.

3. Interior light very dim

a. Check the bulb and bulb socket for corrosion, and clean or replace the bulb and socket.

b. Check for low voltage at the bulb socket positive terminal or a poor ground. If voltage is low, or the ground marginal, trace the wiring to, and check for loose, damaged or corroded wires and electrical terminals; repair as necessary.

c. Check the door and light switch operation, and replace if necessary.

5-D. Brake Lights

1. One brake light inoperative

a. Press the brake pedal and check for battery voltage and ground at the brake light bulb socket. If present, replace the bulb. If either battery voltage or ground is not present, refer to the wiring diagram to troubleshoot.

2. Both brake lights inoperative

a. Press the brake pedal and check for battery voltage and ground at the brake light bulb socket. If present, replace both bulbs. If battery voltage is not present, check the brake light switch adjustment and adjust as necessary. If the brake light switch is properly adjusted, and battery voltage or the ground is not present at the bulb sockets, or at the bulb electrical connector with the brake pedal pressed, refer to the wiring diagram to troubleshoot the cause of an open circuit.

3. One or both brake lights very dim

a. Press the brake pedal and measure the voltage at the brake light bulb socket. If the measured voltage is close to the battery voltage, check for a poor ground caused by a loose, damaged, or corroded wire, terminal, bulb or bulb socket. If the ground is bolted to a painted surface, it may be necessary to remove the electrical connector and clean the mounting surface, so the connector mounts on bare metal. If battery voltage is low, check for a poor connection caused by either a faulty brake light switch, a loose, damaged, or corroded wire, terminal or electrical connector. Refer to the wiring diagram to troubleshoot the cause of a voltage drop.

5-E. Warning Lights

1. Warning light(s) stay on when the engine is started

Ignition, Battery or Alternator Warning Light

a. Check the alternator output and voltage regulator operation, and replace as necessary.

b. Check the warning light wiring for a shorted wire.

Check Engine Light

a. Check the engine for routine maintenance and tune-up status. Note the engine tune-up specifications and verify the spark plug, air filter and engine oil condition; replace and/or adjust items as necessary.

b. Check the fuel tank for low fuel level, causing an intermittent lean fuel mixture. Top off fuel tank and reset check engine light.

c. Check for a failed or disconnected engine fuel or ignition component, sensor or control unit and repair or replace as necessary.

d. Check the intake manifold and vacuum hoses for air leaks and repair as necessary.

e. Check the engine's mechanical condition for excessive oil consumption.

Anti-Lock Braking System (ABS) Light

a. Check the wheel sensors and sensor rings for debris, and clean as necessary.

b. Check the brake master cylinder for fluid leakage or seal failure and replace as necessary.

c. Check the ABS control unit, pump and proportioning valves for proper operation; replace as necessary.

d. Check the sensor wiring at the wheel sensors and the ABS control unit for a loose or shorted wire, and repair as necessary.

Brake Warning Light

a. Check the brake fluid level and check for possible leakage from the hydraulic lines and seals. Top off brake fluid and repair leakage as necessary.

b. Check the brake linings for wear and replace as necessary.

c. Check for a loose or shorted brake warning light sensor or wire, and replace or repair as necessary.

Oil Pressure Warning Light

a. Stop the engine immediately. Check the engine oil level and oil filter condition, and top off or change the oil as necessary.

b. Check the oil pressure sensor wire for being shorted to ground. Disconnect the wire from the oil pressure sensor and with the ignition in the ON position, but not running, the oil pressure light should not be working. If the light works with the wire disconnected, check the sensor wire for being shorted to ground. Check the wire routing to make sure the wire is not pinched and check for insulation damage. Repair or replace the wire as necessary and recheck before starting the engine.

c. Remove the oil pan and check for a clogged oil pick-up tube screen.

d. Check the oil pressure sensor operation by substituting a known good sensor.

e. Check the oil filter for internal restrictions or leaks, and replace as necessary.

WARNING: If the engine is operated with oil pressure below the manufacturer's specification, severe (and costly) engine damage could occur. Low oil pressure can be caused by excessive internal wear or damage to the engine bearings, oil pressure relief valve, oil pump or oil pump drive mechanism.

Before starting the engine, check for possible causes of rapid oil loss, such as leaking oil lines or a loose, damaged, restricted, or leaking oil filter or oil pressure sensor. If the engine oil level and condition are acceptable, measure the engine's oil pressure using a pressure gauge, or determine the cause for the oil pressure warning light to function when the engine is running, before operating the engine for an extended period of time. Another symptom of operating an engine with low oil pressure is the presence of severe knocking and tapping noises.

Parking Brake Warning Light

a. Check the brake release mechanism and verify the parking brake has been fully released.

b. Check the parking brake light switch for looseness or misalignment.

c. Check for a damaged switch or a loose or shorted brake light switch wire, and replace or repair as necessary.

2. Warning light(s) flickers on and off when driving

Ignition, Battery or Alternator Warning Light

a. Check the alternator output and voltage regulator operation. An intermittent condition may indicate worn brushes, an internal short, or a defective voltage regulator. Replace the alternator or failed component.

b. Check the warning light wiring for a shorted, pinched or damaged wire and repair as necessary.

Check Engine Light

a. Check the engine for required maintenance and tune-up status. Verify engine tune-up specifications, as well as spark plug, air filter and engine oil condition; replace and/or adjust items as necessary.

b. Check the fuel tank for low fuel level causing an intermittent lean fuel mixture. Top off fuel tank and reset check engine light.

c. Check for an intermittent failure or partially disconnected engine fuel and ignition component, sensor or control unit; repair or replace as necessary.

d. Check the intake manifold and vacuum hoses for air leaks, and repair as necessary.

e. Check the warning light wiring for a shorted, pinched or damaged wire and repair as necessary.

Anti-Lock Braking System (ABS) Light

a. Check the wheel sensors and sensor rings for debris, and clean as necessary.

b. Check the brake master cylinder for fluid leakage or seal failure and replace as necessary.

c. Check the ABS control unit, pump and proportioning valves for proper operation, and replace as necessary.

d. Check the sensor wiring at the wheel sensors and the ABS control unit for a loose or shorted wire and repair as necessary.

Brake Warning Light

a. Check the brake fluid level and check for possible leakage from the hydraulic lines and seals. Top off brake fluid and repair leakage as necessary.
b. Check the brake linings for wear and replace as necessary.
c. Check for a loose or shorted brake warning light sensor or wire, and replace or repair as necessary.

Oil Pressure Warning Light

a. Stop the engine immediately. Check the engine oil level and check for a sudden and rapid oil loss, such as a leaking oil line or oil pressure sensor, and repair or replace as necessary.
b. Check the oil pressure sensor operation by substituting a known good sensor.
c. Check the oil pressure sensor wire for being shorted to ground. Disconnect the wire from the oil pressure sensor and with the ignition in the ON position, but not running, the oil pressure light should not be working. If the light works with the wire disconnected, check the sensor wire for being shorted to ground. Check the wire routing to make sure the wire is not pinched and check for insulation damage. Repair or replace the wire as necessary and recheck before starting the engine.
d. Remove the oil pan and check for a clogged oil pick-up tube screen.

Parking Brake Warning Light

a. Check the brake release mechanism and verify the parking brake has been fully released.
b. Check the parking brake light switch for looseness or misalignment.
c. Check for a damaged switch or a loose or shorted brake light switch wire, and replace or repair as necessary.

3. Warning light(s) inoperative with ignition on, and engine not started

a. Check for a defective bulb by installing a known good bulb.
b. Check for a defective wire using the appropriate wiring diagram(s).
c. Check for a defective sending unit by removing and then grounding the wire at the sending unit. If the light comes on with the ignition on when grounding the wire, replace the sending unit.

5-F. Turn Signal and 4-Way Hazard Lights

1. Turn signals or hazard lights come on, but do not flash

a. Check for a defective flasher unit and replace as necessary.

2. Turn signals or hazard lights do not function on either side

a. Check the fuse and replace, if defective.
b. Check the flasher unit by substituting a known good flasher unit.
c. Check the turn signal electrical system for a defective component, open circuit, short circuit or poor ground.

3. Turn signals or hazard lights only work on one side

a. Check for failed bulbs and replace as necessary.
b. Check for poor grounds in both housings and repair as necessary.

4. One signal light does not work

a. Check for a failed bulb and replace as necessary.
b. Check for corrosion in the bulb socket, and clean and repair as necessary.
c. Check for a poor ground at the bulb socket, and clean and repair as necessary.

5. Turn signals flash too slowly

a. Check signal bulb(s) wattage and replace with lower wattage bulb(s).

6. Turn signals flash too fast

a. Check signal bulb(s) wattage and replace with higher wattage bulb(s).
b. Check for installation of the correct flasher unit and replace if incorrect.

7. Four-way hazard flasher indicator light inoperative

a. Verify that the exterior lights are functioning and, if so, replace indicator bulb.
b. Check the operation of the warning flasher switch and replace if defective.

8. Turn signal indicator light(s) do not work in either direction

a. Verify that the exterior lights are functioning and, if so, replace indicator bulb(s).
b. Check for a defective flasher unit by substituting a known good unit.

9. One turn signal indicator light does not work

a. Check for a defective bulb and replace as necessary.
b. Check for a defective flasher unit by substituting a known good unit.

5-G. Horn

1. Horn does not operate

a. Check for a defective fuse and replace as necessary.
b. Check for battery voltage and ground at horn electrical connections when pressing the horn switch. If voltage is present, replace the horn assembly. If voltage or ground is not present, refer to Chassis Electrical coverage for additional troubleshooting techniques and circuit information.

2. Horn has an unusual tone

a. On single horn systems, replace the horn.
b. On dual horn systems, check the operation of the second horn. Dual horn systems have a high and low pitched horn. Unplug one horn at a time and recheck operation. Replace the horn which does not function.
c. Check for debris or condensation build-up in horn and verify the horn positioning. If the horn has a single opening, adjust the opening downward to allow for adequate drainage and to prevent debris build-up.

5-H. Windshield Wipers

1. Windshield wipers do not operate

a. Check fuse and replace as necessary.
b. Check switch operation and repair or replace as necessary.
c. Check for corroded, loose, disconnected or broken wires and clean or repair as necessary.
d. Check the ground circuit for the wiper switch or motor and repair as necessary.

2. Windshield wiper motor makes a humming noise, gets hot or blows fuses

a. Wiper motor damaged internally; replace the wiper motor.
b. Wiper linkage bent, damaged or seized. Repair or replace wiper linkage as necessary.

3. Windshield wiper motor operates, but one or both wipers fail to move

a. Windshield wiper motor linkage loose or disconnected. Repair or replace linkage as necessary.
b. Windshield wiper arms loose on wiper pivots. Secure wiper arm to pivot or replace both the wiper arm and pivot assembly.

4. Windshield wipers will not park

a. Check the wiper switch operation and verify that the switch properly interrupts the power supplied to the wiper motor.
b. If the wiper switch is functioning properly, the wiper motor parking circuit has failed. Replace the wiper motor assembly. Operate the wiper motor at least one time before installing the arms and blades to ensure correct positioning, then recheck using the highest wiper speed on a wet windshield to make sure the arms and blades do not contact the windshield trim.

6. INSTRUMENTS AND GAUGES

6-A. Speedometer (Cable Operated)

1. Speedometer does not work

a. Check and verify that the speedometer cable is properly seated into the speedometer assembly and the speedometer drive gear.
b. Check the speedometer cable for breakage or rounded-off cable ends where the cable seats into the speedometer drive gear and into the speedometer assembly. If damaged, broken or the cable ends are rounded off, replace the cable.
c. Check speedometer drive gear condition and replace as necessary.
d. Install a known good speedometer to test for proper operation. If the substituted speedometer functions properly, replace the speedometer assembly.

2. Speedometer needle fluctuates when driving at steady speeds.

a. Check speedometer cable routing or sheathing for sharp bends or kinks. Route cable to minimize sharp bends or kinks. If the sheathing has been damaged, replace the cable assembly.
b. Check the speedometer cable for adequate lubrication. Remove the cable, inspect for damage, clean, lubricate and reinstall. If the cable has been damaged, replace the cable.

3. Speedometer works intermittently

a. Check the cable and verify that the cable is fully installed and the fasteners are secure.
b. Check the cable ends for wear and rounding, and replace as necessary.

6-B. Speedometer (Electronically Operated)

1. Speedometer does not work
a. Check the speed sensor pickup and replace as necessary.
b. Check the wiring between the speed sensor and the speedometer for corroded terminals, loose connections or broken wires and clean or repair as necessary.
c. Install a known good speedometer to test for proper operation. If the substituted speedometer functions properly, replace the speedometer assembly.

2. Speedometer works intermittently
a. Check the wiring between the speed sensor and the speedometer for corroded terminals, loose connections or broken wires and clean or repair as necessary.
b. Check the speed sensor pickup and replace as necessary.

6-C. Fuel, Temperature and Oil Pressure Gauges

1. Gauge does not register
a. Check for a missing or blown fuse and replace as necessary.
b. Check for an open circuit in the gauge wiring. Repair wiring as necessary.

c. Gauge sending unit defective. Replace gauge sending unit.
d. Gauge or sending unit improperly installed. Verify installation and wiring, and repair as necessary.

2. Gauge operates erratically
a. Check for loose, shorted, damaged or corroded electrical connections or wiring and repair as necessary.
b. Check gauge sending units and replace as necessary.

3. Gauge operates fully pegged
a. Sending unit-to-gauge wire shorted to ground.
b. Sending unit defective; replace sending unit.
c. Gauge or sending unit not properly grounded.
d. Gauge or sending unit improperly installed. Verify installation and wiring, and repair as necessary.

7. CLIMATE CONTROL

7-A. Air Conditioner

1. No air coming from air conditioner vents
a. Check the air conditioner fuse and replace as necessary.
b. Air conditioner system discharged. Have the system evacuated, charged and leak tested by an MVAC certified technician, utilizing approved recovery/recycling equipment. Repair as necessary.
c. Air conditioner low pressure switch defective. Replace switch.
d. Air conditioner fan resistor pack defective. Replace resistor pack.
e. Loose connection, broken wiring or defective air conditioner relay in air conditioning electrical circuit. Repair wiring or replace relay as necessary.

2. Air conditioner blows warm air
a. Air conditioner system is discharged. Have the system evacuated, charged and leak tested by an MVAC certified technician, utilizing approved recovery/recycling equipment. Repair as necessary.
b. Air conditioner compressor clutch not engaging. Check compressor clutch wiring, electrical connections and compressor clutch, and repair or replace as necessary.

3. Water collects on the interior floor when the air conditioner is used
a. Air conditioner evaporator drain hose is blocked. Clear the drain hose where it exits the passenger compartment.
b. Air conditioner evaporator drain hose is disconnected. Secure the drain hose to the evaporator drainage tray under the dashboard.

4. Air conditioner has a moldy odor when used
a. The air conditioner evaporator drain hose is blocked or partially re-stricted, allowing condensation to build up around the evaporator and drainage tray. Clear the drain hose where it exits the passenger compartment.

7-B. Heater

1. Blower motor does not operate
a. Check blower motor fuse and replace as necessary.
b. Check blower motor wiring for loose, damaged or corroded contacts and repair as necessary.
c. Check blower motor switch and resistor pack for open circuits, and repair or replace as necessary.
d. Check blower motor for internal damage and repair or replace as necessary.

2. Heater blows cool air
a. Check the engine coolant level. If the coolant level is low, top off and bleed the air from the cooling system as necessary and check for coolant leaks.
b. Check engine coolant operating temperature. If coolant temperature is below specification, check for a damaged or stuck thermostat.
c. Check the heater control valve operation. Check the heater control valve cable or vacuum hose for proper installation. Move the heater temperature control from hot to cold several times and verify the operation of the heater control valve. With the engine at normal operating temperature and the heater temperature control in the full hot position, carefully feel the heater hose going into and exiting the control valve. If one heater hose is hot and the other is much cooler, replace the control valve.

3. Heater steams the windshield when used
a. Check for a loose cooling system hose clamp or leaking coolant hose near the engine firewall or under the dash area, and repair as necessary.
b. Check for the existence of a sweet odor and fluid dripping from the heater floor vents, indicating a failed or damaged heater core. Pressure test the cooling system with the heater set to the fully warm position and check for fluid leakage from the floor vents. If leakage is verified, remove and replace the heater core assembly.

NOTE: On some vehicles, the dashboard must be disassembled and removed to access the heater core.

GLOSSARY

AIR/FUEL RATIO: The ratio of air-to-gasoline by weight in the fuel mixture drawn into the engine.

AIR INJECTION: One method of reducing harmful exhaust emissions by injecting air into each of the exhaust ports of an engine. The fresh air entering the hot exhaust manifold causes any remaining fuel to be burned before it can exit the tailpipe.

ALTERNATOR: A device used for converting mechanical energy into electrical energy.

AMMETER: An instrument, calibrated in amperes, used to measure the flow of an electrical current in a circuit. Ammeters are always connected in series with the circuit being tested.

AMPERE: The rate of flow of electrical current present when one volt of electrical pressure is applied against one ohm of electrical resistance.

ANALOG COMPUTER: Any microprocessor that uses similar (analogous) electrical signals to make its calculations.

ARMATURE: A laminated, soft iron core wrapped by a wire that converts electrical energy to mechanical energy as in a motor or relay. When rotated in a magnetic field, it changes mechanical energy into electrical energy as in a generator.

ATMOSPHERIC PRESSURE: The pressure on the Earth's surface caused by the weight of the air in the atmosphere. At sea level, this pressure is 14.7 psi at 32°F (101 kPa at 0°C).

ATOMIZATION: The breaking down of a liquid into a fine mist that can be suspended in air.

AXIAL PLAY: Movement parallel to a shaft or bearing bore.

BACKFIRE: The sudden combustion of gases in the intake or exhaust system that results in a loud explosion.

BACKLASH: The clearance or play between two parts, such as meshed gears.

BACKPRESSURE: Restrictions in the exhaust system that slow the exit of exhaust gases from the combustion chamber.

BAKELITE: A heat resistant, plastic insulator material commonly used in printed circuit boards and transistorized components.

BALL BEARING: A bearing made up of hardened inner and outer races between which hardened steel balls roll.

BALLAST RESISTOR: A resistor in the primary ignition circuit that lowers voltage after the engine is started to reduce wear on ignition components.

BEARING: A friction reducing, supportive device usually located between a stationary part and a moving part.

BIMETAL TEMPERATURE SENSOR: Any sensor or switch made of two dissimilar types of metal that bend when heated or cooled due to the different expansion rates of the alloys. These types of sensors usually function as an on/off switch.

BLOWBY: Combustion gases, composed of water vapor and unburned fuel, that leak past the piston rings into the crankcase during normal engine operation. These gases are removed by the PCV system to prevent the buildup of harmful acids in the crankcase.

BRAKE PAD: A brake shoe and lining assembly used with disc brakes.

BRAKE SHOE: The backing for the brake lining. The term is, however, usually applied to the assembly of the brake backing and lining.

BUSHING: A liner, usually removable, for a bearing; an anti-friction liner used in place of a bearing.

CALIPER: A hydraulically activated device in a disc brake system, which is mounted straddling the brake rotor (disc). The caliper contains at least one piston and two brake pads. Hydraulic pressure on the piston(s) forces the pads against the rotor.

CAMSHAFT: A shaft in the engine on which are the lobes (cams) which operate the valves. The camshaft is driven by the crankshaft, via a belt, chain or gears, at one half the crankshaft speed.

CAPACITOR: A device which stores an electrical charge.

CARBON MONOXIDE (CO): A colorless, odorless gas given off as a normal byproduct of combustion. It is poisonous and extremely dangerous in confined areas, building up slowly to toxic levels without warning if adequate ventilation is not available.

CARBURETOR: A device, usually mounted on the intake manifold of an engine, which mixes the air and fuel in the proper proportion to allow even combustion.

CATALYTIC CONVERTER: A device installed in the exhaust system, like a muffler, that converts harmful byproducts of combustion into carbon dioxide and water vapor by means of a heat-producing chemical reaction.

CENTRIFUGAL ADVANCE: A mechanical method of advancing the spark timing by using flyweights in the distributor that react to centrifugal force generated by the distributor shaft rotation.

CHECK VALVE: Any one-way valve installed to permit the flow of air, fuel or vacuum in one direction only.

CHOKE: A device, usually a moveable valve, placed in the intake path of a carburetor to restrict the flow of air.

CIRCUIT: Any unbroken path through which an electrical current can flow. Also used to describe fuel flow in some instances.

CIRCUIT BREAKER: A switch which protects an electrical circuit from overload by opening the circuit when the current flow exceeds a predetermined level. Some circuit breakers must be reset manually, while most reset automatically.

COIL (IGNITION): A transformer in the ignition circuit which steps up the voltage provided to the spark plugs.

COMBINATION MANIFOLD: An assembly which includes both the intake and exhaust manifolds in one casting.

COMBINATION VALVE: A device used in some fuel systems that routes fuel vapors to a charcoal storage canister instead of venting them into the atmosphere. The valve relieves fuel tank pressure and allows fresh air into the tank as the fuel level drops to prevent a vapor lock situation.

COMPRESSION RATIO: The comparison of the total volume of the cylinder and combustion chamber with the piston at BDC and the piston at TDC.

CONDENSER: 1. An electrical device which acts to store an electrical charge, preventing voltage surges. 2. A radiator-like device in the air conditioning system in which refrigerant gas condenses into a liquid, giving off heat.

CONDUCTOR: Any material through which an electrical current can be transmitted easily.

CONTINUITY: Continuous or complete circuit. Can be checked with an ohmmeter.

COUNTERSHAFT: An intermediate shaft which is rotated by a mainshaft and transmits, in turn, that rotation to a working part.

CRANKCASE: The lower part of an engine in which the crankshaft and related parts operate.

CRANKSHAFT: The main driving shaft of an engine which receives reciprocating motion from the pistons and converts it to rotary motion.

CYLINDER: In an engine, the round hole in the engine block in which the piston(s) ride.

CYLINDER BLOCK: The main structural member of an engine in which is found the cylinders, crankshaft and other principal parts.

CYLINDER HEAD: The detachable portion of the engine, usually fastened to the top of the cylinder block and containing all or most of the combustion chambers. On overhead valve engines, it contains the valves and their operating parts. On overhead cam engines, it contains the camshaft as well.

DEAD CENTER: The extreme top or bottom of the piston stroke.

DETONATION: An unwanted explosion of the air/fuel mixture in the combustion chamber caused by excess heat and compression, advanced timing, or an overly lean mixture. Also referred to as "ping".

DIAPHRAGM: A thin, flexible wall separating two cavities, such as in a vacuum advance unit.

DIESELING: A condition in which hot spots in the combustion chamber cause the engine to run on after the key is turned off.

DIFFERENTIAL: A geared assembly which allows the transmission of motion between drive axles, giving one axle the ability to turn faster than the other.

DIODE: An electrical device that will allow current to flow in one direction only.

DISC BRAKE: A hydraulic braking assembly consisting of a brake disc, or rotor, mounted on an axle, and a caliper assembly containing, usually two brake pads which are activated by hydraulic pressure. The pads are forced against the sides of the disc, creating friction which slows the vehicle.

DISTRIBUTOR: A mechanically driven device on an engine which is responsible for electrically firing the spark plug at a predetermined point of the piston stroke.

DOWEL PIN: A pin, inserted in mating holes in two different parts allowing those parts to maintain a fixed relationship.

DRUM BRAKE: A braking system which consists of two brake shoes and one or two wheel cylinders, mounted on a fixed backing plate, and a brake drum, mounted on an axle, which revolves around the assembly.

DWELL: The rate, measured in degrees of shaft rotation, at which an electrical circuit cycles on and off.

ELECTRONIC CONTROL UNIT (ECU): Ignition module, module, amplifier or igniter. See Module for definition.

ELECTRONIC IGNITION: A system in which the timing and firing of the spark plugs is controlled by an electronic control unit, usually called a module. These systems have no points or condenser.

END-PLAY: The measured amount of axial movement in a shaft.

ENGINE: A device that converts heat into mechanical energy.

EXHAUST MANIFOLD: A set of cast passages or pipes which conduct exhaust gases from the engine.

FEELER GAUGE: A blade, usually metal, or precisely predetermined thickness, used to measure the clearance between two parts.

FIRING ORDER: The order in which combustion occurs in the cylinders of an engine. Also the order in which spark is distributed to the plugs by the distributor.

FLOODING: The presence of too much fuel in the intake manifold and combustion chamber which prevents the air/fuel mixture from firing, thereby causing a no-start situation.

FLYWHEEL: A disc shaped part bolted to the rear end of the crankshaft. Around the outer perimeter is affixed the ring gear. The starter drive engages the ring gear, turning the flywheel, which rotates the crankshaft, imparting the initial starting motion to the engine.

FOOT POUND (ft. lbs. or sometimes, ft.lb.): The amount of energy or work needed to raise an item weighing one pound, a distance of one foot.

FUSE: A protective device in a circuit which prevents circuit overload by breaking the circuit when a specific amperage is present. The device is constructed around a strip or wire of a lower amperage rating than the circuit it is designed to protect. When an amperage higher than that stamped on the fuse is present in the circuit, the strip or wire melts, opening the circuit.

GEAR RATIO: The ratio between the number of teeth on meshing gears.

GENERATOR: A device which converts mechanical energy into electrical energy.

HEAT RANGE: The measure of a spark plug's ability to dissipate heat from its firing end. The higher the heat range, the hotter the plug fires.

HUB: The center part of a wheel or gear.

HYDROCARBON (HC): Any chemical compound made up of hydrogen and carbon. A major pollutant formed by the engine as a byproduct of combustion.

HYDROMETER: An instrument used to measure the specific gravity of a solution.

INCH POUND (inch lbs.; sometimes in.lb. or in. lbs.): One twelfth of a foot pound.

INDUCTION: A means of transferring electrical energy in the form of a magnetic field. Principle used in the ignition coil to increase voltage.

INJECTOR: A device which receives metered fuel under relatively low pressure and is activated to inject the fuel into the engine under relatively high pressure at a predetermined time.

INPUT SHAFT: The shaft to which torque is applied, usually carrying the driving gear or gears.

INTAKE MANIFOLD: A casting of passages or pipes used to conduct air or a fuel/air mixture to the cylinders.

JOURNAL: The bearing surface within which a shaft operates.

KEY: A small block usually fitted in a notch between a shaft and a hub to prevent slippage of the two parts.

MANIFOLD: A casting of passages or set of pipes which connect the cylinders to an inlet or outlet source.

MANIFOLD VACUUM: Low pressure in an engine intake manifold formed just below the throttle plates. Manifold vacuum is highest at idle and drops under acceleration.

MASTER CYLINDER: The primary fluid pressurizing device in a hydraulic system. In automotive use, it is found in brake and hydraulic clutch systems and is pedal activated, either directly or, in a power brake system, through the power booster.

MODULE: Electronic control unit, amplifier or igniter of solid state or integrated design which controls the current flow in the ignition primary circuit based on input from the pick-up coil. When the module opens the primary circuit, high secondary voltage is induced in the coil.

NEEDLE BEARING: A bearing which consists of a number (usually a large number) of long, thin rollers.

OHM: (Ω) The unit used to measure the resistance of conductor-to-electrical flow. One ohm is the amount of resistance that limits current flow to one ampere in a circuit with one volt of pressure.

OHMMETER: An instrument used for measuring the resistance, in ohms, in an electrical circuit.

OUTPUT SHAFT: The shaft which transmits torque from a device, such as a transmission.

OVERDRIVE: A gear assembly which produces more shaft revolutions than that transmitted to it.

OVERHEAD CAMSHAFT (OHC): An engine configuration in which the camshaft is mounted on top of the cylinder head and operates the valve either directly or by means of rocker arms.

OVERHEAD VALVE (OHV): An engine configuration in which all of the valves are located in the cylinder head and the camshaft is located in the cylinder block. The camshaft operates the valves via lifters and pushrods.

OXIDES OF NITROGEN (NOx): Chemical compounds of nitrogen produced as a byproduct of combustion. They combine with hydrocarbons to produce smog.

OXYGEN SENSOR: Use with the feedback system to sense the presence of oxygen in the exhaust gas and signal the computer which can reference the voltage signal to an air/fuel ratio.

PINION: The smaller of two meshing gears.

PISTON RING: An open-ended ring with fits into a groove on the outer diameter of the piston. Its chief function is to form a seal between the piston and cylinder wall. Most automotive pistons have three rings: two for compression sealing; one for oil sealing.

PRELOAD: A predetermined load placed on a bearing during assembly or by adjustment.

PRIMARY CIRCUIT: the low voltage side of the ignition system which consists of the ignition switch, ballast resistor or resistance wire, bypass, coil, electronic control unit and pick-up coil as well as the connecting wires and harnesses.

PRESS FIT: The mating of two parts under pressure, due to the inner diameter of one being smaller than the outer diameter of the other, or vice versa; an interference fit.

RACE: The surface on the inner or outer ring of a bearing on which the balls, needles or rollers move.

REGULATOR: A device which maintains the amperage and/or voltage levels of a circuit at predetermined values.

RELAY: A switch which automatically opens and/or closes a circuit.

RESISTANCE: The opposition to the flow of current through a circuit or electrical device, and is measured in ohms. Resistance is equal to the voltage divided by the amperage.

RESISTOR: A device, usually made of wire, which offers a preset amount of resistance in an electrical circuit.

RING GEAR: The name given to a ring-shaped gear attached to a differential case, or affixed to a flywheel or as part of a planetary gear set.

ROLLER BEARING: A bearing made up of hardened inner and outer races between which hardened steel rollers move.

ROTOR: 1. The disc-shaped part of a disc brake assembly, upon which the brake pads bear; also called, brake disc. 2. The device mounted atop the distributor shaft, which passes current to the distributor cap tower contacts.

SECONDARY CIRCUIT: The high voltage side of the ignition system, usually above 20,000 volts. The secondary includes the ignition coil, coil wire, distributor cap and rotor, spark plug wires and spark plugs.

SENDING UNIT: A mechanical, electrical, hydraulic or electro-magnetic device which transmits information to a gauge.

SENSOR: Any device designed to measure engine operating conditions or ambient pressures and temperatures. Usually electronic in nature and designed to send a voltage signal to an on-board computer, some sensors may operate as a simple on/off switch or they may provide a variable voltage signal (like a potentiometer) as conditions or measured parameters change.

SHIM: Spacers of precise, predetermined thickness used between parts to establish a proper working relationship.

SLAVE CYLINDER: In automotive use, a device in the hydraulic clutch system which is activated by hydraulic force, disengaging the clutch.

SOLENOID: A coil used to produce a magnetic field, the effect of which is to produce work.

SPARK PLUG: A device screwed into the combustion chamber of a spark ignition engine. The basic construction is a conductive core inside of a ceramic insulator, mounted in an outer conductive base. An electrical charge from the spark plug wire travels along the conductive core and jumps a preset air gap to a grounding point or points at the end of the conductive base. The resultant spark ignites the fuel/air mixture in the combustion chamber.

SPLINES: Ridges machined or cast onto the outer diameter of a shaft or inner diameter of a bore to enable parts to mate without rotation.

TACHOMETER: A device used to measure the rotary speed of an engine, shaft, gear, etc., usually in rotations per minute.

THERMOSTAT: A valve, located in the cooling system of an engine, which is closed when cold and opens gradually in response to engine heating, controlling the temperature of the coolant and rate of coolant flow.

TOP DEAD CENTER (TDC): The point at which the piston reaches the top of its travel on the compression stroke.

TORQUE: The twisting force applied to an object.

TORQUE CONVERTER: A turbine used to transmit power from a driving member to a driven member via hydraulic action, providing changes in drive ratio and torque. In automotive use, it links the driveplate at the rear of the engine to the automatic transmission.

TRANSDUCER: A device used to change a force into an electrical signal.

TRANSISTOR: A semi-conductor component which can be actuated by a small voltage to perform an electrical switching function.

TUNE-UP: A regular maintenance function, usually associated with the replacement and adjustment of parts and components in the electrical and fuel systems of a vehicle for the purpose of attaining optimum performance.

TURBOCHARGER: An exhaust driven pump which compresses intake air and forces it into the combustion chambers at higher than atmospheric pressures. The increased air pressure allows more fuel to be burned and results in increased horsepower being produced.

VACUUM ADVANCE: A device which advances the ignition timing in response to increased engine vacuum.

VACUUM GAUGE: An instrument used to measure the presence of vacuum in a chamber.

VALVE: A device which control the pressure, direction of flow or rate of flow of a liquid or gas.

VALVE CLEARANCE: The measured gap between the end of the valve stem and the rocker arm, cam lobe or follower that activates the valve.

VISCOSITY: The rating of a liquid's internal resistance to flow.

VOLTMETER: An instrument used for measuring electrical force in units called volts. Voltmeters are always connected parallel with the circuit being tested.

WHEEL CYLINDER: Found in the automotive drum brake assembly, it is a device, actuated by hydraulic pressure, which, through internal pistons, pushes the brake shoes outward against the drums.

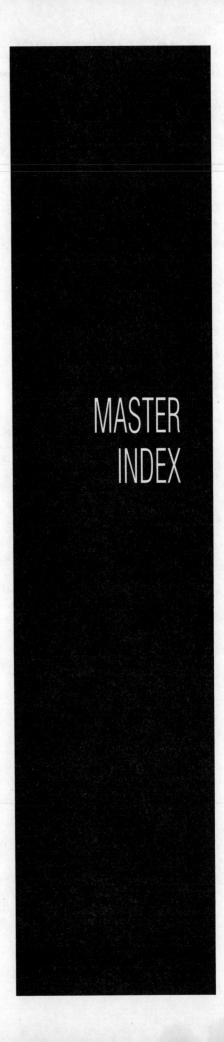

MASTER

INDEX

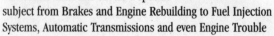